The Developing Child

Understanding Children and Parenting

The Developing Child

Understanding Children and Parenting

Sixth Edition

Holly E. Brisbane

Macmillan/McGraw-Hill

New York, New York Columbus, Ohio Mission Hills, California Peoria, Illinois

CONTRIBUTORS

Carol Alford
Teacher and Department Chairperson
Consumer and Family Studies
Fort Collins High School
Fort Collins, Colorado

Arlene Fulton
Child Development Specialist
Oklahoma Cooperative Extension Service
Stillwater, Oklahoma

REVIEWERS

Dr. Ethan Bergman
Nutrition Consultant/Professor
Central Washington University
Ellensburg, Washington

Marcia Britton-Wheeler
Department Chairperson, Home Economics
Julian High School
Chicago, Illinois

Pat Brodeen
Teen Parent Coordinator
San Antonio, Texas

Laurie Kanyer
Family Life Specialist
Yakima Valley Memorial Hospital
Yakima, Washington

Judy Lee
Director
Yakima Valley Community College Childcare Center
Yakima, Washington

Darlene Montz
Early Childhood Consultant
Yakima, Washington

Linda Murray
Family Life Instructor
Yakima Valley Community College
Yakima, Washington

Nancy Horn
Home Economics Teacher
Fresno High School
Fresno, California

Gail Park Fast
Certified Childbirth Educator
Yakima, Washington

Mary Patrick
Coordinator of Home Economics and Family Life
Yakima Valley Community College
Yakima, Washington

Mary Richmond
Home Economics Teacher
San Luis Obispo High School
San Luis Obispo, California

Judy Solomon-Marks
Child Development Instructor
North Valley Occupational Center
Los Angeles Unified School District
Mission Hills, California

Dr. Allen G. South
Gynecologist/Obstetrician
Yakima, Washington

Nancy South
Site Coordinator for Early Childhood Center
Yakima, Washington

Printed in the United States of America.

Send all inquires to:
Glencoe/McGraw-Hill
3008 W. Willow Knolls Drive
Peoria, IL 61614-1083

ISBN 0-02-642671-4 (Student Edition)
ISBN 0-02-642672-2 (Teacher's Wraparound Edition)

3 4 5 6 7 8 9 10 VHJ 99 98 97 96 95

CONTENTS

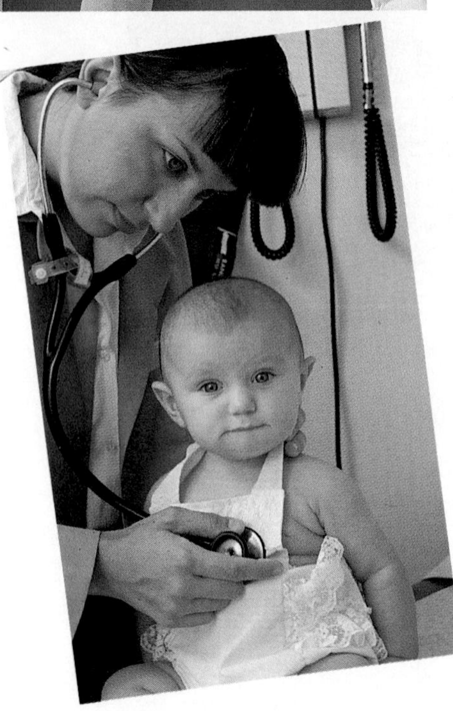

UNIT 5 THE CHILD FROM FOUR TO SIX 410

UNIT 6 SPECIAL AREAS OF STUDY 482

FEATURES

Ask the Experts

Building Self-Esteem

Charts

Cultural Exchange

Parenting in Action

Positive Parenting Skills

MEET THE EXPERTS

Asa Hilliard
UNIVERSITY PROFESSOR OF URBAN STUDIES

Asa Hilliard is a Fuller E. Callaway Professor of Urban Education at Georgia State University and was instrumental in setting program requirements and standards of professional training for the Head Start Program.

He earned an Ed.D in Educational Psychology from the University of Denver where he also taught in the College of Education and in the Philosophy Colloquium for the Centennial Scholars Honors Program.

Dr. Hilliard feels that students will learn ways of professional thinking by first having as much experience as possible with children, and he urges students to "have faith in your ability to think and learn." He challenges professional educators to seek a greater balance between unstructured play and programmed instruction.

Jackie Mault
DIRECTOR OF SPECIAL SERVICES

Jackie Mault brings to her profession a background rich in diverse experiences. She has worked in childhood education administration, with a State Department of Education, the public school at the community level, and as a consultant.

In her position as Director of Special Services, she develops and manages programs for children from birth through high school. Currently, the rural community of Toppenish, Washington, challenges her talents. Dr. Mault urges people to "continue to meet the demands of the changing families and work within the communities for quality, comprehensive care." She feels that students should keep all options open and pursue career paths that are fulfilling and reality-based.

She received her doctorate from the University of Oregon, and in her spare time, teaches college-level classes at Heritage College in Toppenish.

Pat Brodeen
TEEN PARENT COORDINATOR

Pat Brodeen has been a teacher at Theodore Roosevelt High School in San Antonio, Texas for the past 22 years. She received both her bachelor and master of science degrees in Home Economics from Texas Tech University, specializing in Child Development and Family Studies.

Six years ago, Ms. Brodeen became one of the first teachers of the School Age Parenting class for teen parents at Roosevelt High School. She finds her greatest reward in watching a teen develop into a responsible parent. Her concern is for the teenage parent caught in the dilemma of being both a child and a parent. She advises teen parents to "stay in school if you want to avoid a lifetime of dependency."

When not involved with school, Ms. Brodeen finds time for her husband, four adult daughters, and an adolescent son.

MEET THE EXPERTS

Dr. Van D Stone
PEDIATRICIAN

Dr. Stone is a practicing pediatrician in Tupelo, Mississippi, and Chief of Pediatrics at Baptist Medical Center in Little Rock, Arkansas. He received his medical degree at Mississippi Medical School in Jackson, Mississippi, and his pediatric training at Arkansas Children's Hospital.

Over the last twenty years he has seen a substantial change in the area of children's nutrition and is pleased that "parents of all ages are open to new ideas and methods of quality care." Many of his patients' mothers are teens whose mothers participate in raising their grandchildren. He finds that these younger grandmothers are familiar with current trends in child care, and he values the wisdom of their experience.

In spite of his many obligations, including his own four children, Dr. Stone enjoys taking time to play with his young patients.

Jean Illsley Clarke
AUTHOR AND PARENTING WORKSHOP FACILITATOR

Jean Illsley Clarke is the director of J.I. Consultants in Minneapolis, where she designs and directs workshops in self-esteem, parenting, and group dynamics. Her emphasis is on observation and group activities, which she believes are vital to self-improvement. International studies have convinced her that people have much to learn from observing the customs and habits of other cultures. She stresses that "all human needs are the same; how we meet those needs will vary from one group to another."

Jean Clarke received an Honorary Doctorate of Human Service from Sierra University in Costa Mesa, California. Much of her background in child-rearing came from teaching and on-site research abroad.

Her publication credits include several books, magazine and journal articles, as well as videotapes and a local television show. Currently, she is co-author of a new book called *Help! For Parents of School-Age Children and Teenagers.*

Linda Espinosa
DIRECTOR OF PRIMARY EDUCATION

Linda Espinosa is Director of Primary Education for the Redwood City School District, and Treasurer of the National Association of Education for Young Children. She received her doctorate in Educational Design and Implementation from the University of Chicago where she studied multiple influences on child education, such as early experiences, geography, and culture.

While an undergraduate in college, Dr. Espinosa ignored warnings that a career in child education was pointless. She urges students to "follow your passion in whatever field you choose. Talented people are too often discouraged from professions where their energy is needed."

In a recent contribution to *Developmentally Appropriate Curriculum and Assessment Guidelines*, Dr. Espinosa examines the process of the changing school system and suggests ways to develop programs that can serve as models for other schools.

NOPQRSTUVWXYZ
ABC
2
+2
4

UNIT 1

Children, Parenting, and You

CHILDREN LEARN WHAT THEY LIVE

If children live with criticism, They learn to condemn.
If children live with hostility, They learn to fight.
If children live with ridicule,They learn to be shy.
If children live with shame, They learn to feel guilty.
If children live with tolerance, They learn to be patient.
If children live with encouragement, They learn confidence.
If children live with praise, They learn to appreciate.
If children live with firmness, They learn justice.
If children live with security, They learn to like themselves.
If children live with acceptance and friendship,
They learn to find love in the world.

Dorothy Law Nolte

CHAPTER 1

Growing with Children

Trisha sat brushing Emily's long, dark hair after the little girl's bath. Emily stood before her, swaddled in a huge towel.

"You have really pretty hair, Emily."

The little girl smiled and said, "Thanks, Trisha."

Trisha felt really lucky that she had this afternoon job. She was taking care of Emily, while Emily's mom worked as a bookkeeper a few days a week. Trisha was getting lots of experience in how to relate to young children and how to provide for their needs.

Trisha liked Emily a lot. Sometimes they had Emily's little friends in to play, other times they walked to the park, and yet other times Trisha and Emily played quietly with building blocks and other toys. Sometimes Emily snuggled close to Trisha as the older girl read stories to her. As Trisha read, she traced under the words with her finger. Emily was starting to learn some of the words. Before long Emily would be able to read by herself and that made Trisha feel good.

SECTION 1

Children and You

OBJECTIVES

- Evaluate your attitude toward children.
- Identify benefits of studying children.

TERMS TO LEARN

behavior
child development

Understanding how children fit into your life—both now and in the future—can help you understand yourself. You can begin by exploring your attitudes towards children. By doing so, you will discover that parenting skills are needed by almost everyone who comes in contact with children, whether they are parents or not. This understanding can also help you make meaningful plans for your future.

Children in Your Life

How would you describe your relationships with the children in your life today? Do you like children? Do you talk with and enjoy children of all ages? Do you know what to do when you are caring for children of different ages? Just as important—do children like you?

Think about these questions seriously. Your honest answers tell a great deal about you—the person you are today, the child you once were, and the adult you will become. After you have studied child development, you will have a better understanding of these questions and the meaning of your answers.

Perhaps children seem just naturally to enjoy being with you. In that case, you probably enjoy children and feel comfortable with them. On the other hand, perhaps children seem a little uncomfortable around you—and you feel uncomfortable with them. People vary a great deal in the way they feel and act toward children.

Your relationship with young children—brothers, sisters, friends, or babysitting charges—depends on your interest in children. It also depends on your knowledge of their changing stages and needs, and on your skill in applying that knowledge.

As a young child, do you remember how much fun it was when older children and teens spent time with you? Now you are on the other side of that relationship. The more you understand children, the more you will enjoy being with them.

Why Study Children?

Learning about children is important in more ways than you may realize. Learning about children and their development can improve your understanding both of children and of yourself. It can also help you think about your future in relation to parenthood and career choices.

Understanding Children

As you study children, you will read about them, observe them, talk with them, play with them, and help them. In the process, your understanding of children will grow in many ways.

- **You will more fully appreciate all characteristics of human development.** **Child development** is *the study of how children grow in different ways—physically, mentally, emotionally, and socially*. As you discover the variety and complexity of growth, you will begin to understand why children remain dependent on their parents for such a long time. You will learn why they need affection in order to grow emotionally. You will also understand why they need the guidance and support of older people.
- **Your powers of observation will improve.** Books cannot teach everything you need to learn about children. Children are all around you, perhaps even in your own home. With some background and interest, you can increase your knowledge of children every day.

PARENTING IN ACTION

Caring for Children

Jim, who is 16, babysits three afternoons a week for his sister's two children, a kindergarten-age son named Kyle and an infant daughter named Kelly. One day, Jim mentioned his job to his friends Chris and Sue.

"Babysitting? How boring!" Chris responded. "My kid brother is a pest. How can you stand two little kids?"

Sue had a different reaction. "You take care of two children on your own? That's a lot of responsibility. Aren't you nervous—especially with a tiny baby?"

"It's not so bad," Jim told them. "My nephew reminds me of myself when I was his age. We have a lot of fun playing with his toy cars. As for Kelly—my sister leaves me plenty of instructions. If I didn't help out, my sister wouldn't be able to keep her part-time job. It's a way for me to earn extra money, too. Besides, I may decide to be a father someday—and I'm thinking about being a teacher or a doctor. This is a pretty good way to see if I'm cut out for working with children."

THINK AND DISCUSS

1. How does Jim benefit from his babysitting job? Which benefits do you think are most important to him? Which would be most important to you?
2. Do you assume that Jim has a natural ability for working with children? Why or why not? What has Jim done to learn about children?
3. What disadvantages do Jim's friends see in his babysitting job? What other disadvantages might there be?

- **You will begin to see why children act, feel, and think as they do.** Have you ever misinterpreted or been confused by something that a child said or did? That's normal. It can be difficult to understand children, especially before they learn to talk. Yet there is predictable, appropriate **behavior**—*a way of acting or responding*—for every stage of life. For example, when a two-year-old tries and fails to pull a tricycle up a flight of stairs, an angry outburst is predictable behavior. That same behavior from a frustrated ten-year-old, however, would not be considered appropriate.
- **You will be able to apply your learning to everyday life.** Simply studying child development is not enough; you need to apply your knowledge to real situations. For example, you may have a four-year-old sister who grabs your softball

glove at every opportunity. Your response to her actions may change when you understand her motivation: Younger children naturally admire those who are older, and they like to imitate the people they admire. With this understanding in mind, you may be able to accept your sister's actions as complimentary, rather than simply annoying.

- **You will learn practical techniques of caring for children.** Children respond favorably to people who care for them with confidence. Knowing how to bathe a baby, how to select and prepare a nutritious meal for a toddler, and how to encourage a three-year-old to settle down for a nap will give you that confidence. It will also bring you considerable satisfaction.
- **You will discover that children are fun.** The more time you spend with children, the more you can appreciate how delightful they are. In their innocence, humor, and generous affection, you will find much that is fascinating and rewarding.

Understanding Yourself

As you learn to understand children better, you will also come to know yourself better. You will learn more about what makes you the person you are.

You may think of yourself as a different person from the child you were a decade ago. It's true that you have grown and changed in many ways. However, no one changes entirely. The young man or woman you are right now has developed from the child you once were and will continue to develop into your adult self. Experience, education, and life's situations help you mature. Still, the self you have already developed will always be a part of you.

You may want to ask family members or older friends what you were like as a young child. Maybe they will recall that you were "a typical kid"—close to average development. Perhaps, though, they will describe you as "a quiet child" or "amazingly independent" or "constantly active." How closely do those descriptions of your young self correspond to the personality you have today? The similarities may surprise you!

As you study child development, you will discover that all children are similar in some ways. You will also find that every child has characteristics that are unique. In addition, you will see that development continues throughout life. All these insights can help you understand yourself.

Your own childhood has influenced your life today. What do you remember about your childhood? What do others recall about you?

ASK THE EXPERTS

Making a Difference in a Child's Life

Dr. Asa Hilliard is a Fuller E. Callaway Professor of Urban Education at Georgia State University.

I enjoy young children, and I'm interested in spending time with them. However, I'm still not sure that when I take care of children, I have a truly positive influence on them. What can I do to make a difference in a child's life?

You're off to a good start in making a positive difference to children—you are interested, and you are concerned about learning how to help children. Your attitude in itself is a contribution to a child with whom you spend time.

I think what you need now is a chance to watch others work with children; you also need comfortable experiences that will help you develop your own abilities and confidence.

Probably the best way to learn about interacting with children is to watch parents and teachers who work successfully with young children. As part of your child development class, you will probably have opportunities to watch teachers in preschools and schools, child care workers in homes or centers, and parents as they care for their children.

Take time to observe these experienced people carefully. How do they talk to children? How do they listen? How do they use words, facial expressions, and physical contact to encourage and support children? How do they use positive reinforcement to guide children's behavior?

After your observation, think about how each teacher or parent approached the children. What did the adult do to guide the children? How did he or she nurture each child? Which of these approaches will you feel comfortable using when you interact with children?

Remember, when you observe successful parents and teachers, you are looking at models. These are people who can guide your behavior in interacting with children, but they are not patterns for you to copy exactly. As you learn more and more about children and about successful approaches and attitudes, you will develop your own personal style of interacting successfully with young children.

It's also important to remember that, just as teachers and parents serve as your models, you serve as a model for young children. When you are confident and comfortable, children will feel confident and comfortable with you. In addition, young children will observe—and try out for themselves—the attitudes, words, and actions that you demonstrate.

Dr. Asa Hilliard

Thinking About Your Future

Your increased understanding of children will be valuable not only now, but throughout your lifetime. Today, it may simply help you understand your family or the children in your neighborhood. You may also want to use your knowledge and skills, working as a babysitter, a teacher's aide, or a playground supervisor. In the future, your understanding of children may help you become successful as a parent or as a worker in a career related to child care.

Studying children at this point in your life can help you make decisions about your future career. For example, a high school student was planning to be a nurse at the beginning of a child study course, but by the end of the course had decided to go into teaching. The reason? "Now that I understand them better, I like kids more than I used to. I want to work with a group of children."

A classmate expressed a different reaction: "I thought I wanted to be a teacher, but now I'm not so sure. I didn't have any idea how much responsibility was involved!"

Learning about child development can also help you think about parenthood and prepare for its responsibilities. "It's made me more aware that having a child is really a lifetime commitment," one student commented. Another said, "I have the feeling I could handle anything now. I'm going to adopt about six children."

One instructor of a child study class stated, "Parenthood is the most important occupation most of us are ever engaged in. Whatever this course may or may not accomplish in helping these students make a choice of occupation, I know it will help them be better parents."

SECTION 1 REVIEW

CHECK YOUR UNDERSTANDING

1. List the three main benefits of studying children.
2. What is child development?
3. What is behavior?
4. List two benefits of learning practical techniques of caring for children.
5. During which stages of life does development continue?
6. How can studying child development help students plan their future?

DISCUSS AND DISCOVER

1. Do you agree that parenthood is one of the most important occupations anyone may have? Why or why not? What particular aspects of parenting make it difficult? What do you think makes it rewarding?
2. Identify at least two magazines designed to help people understand and deal with young children. Browse through several issues of both magazines. What questions do the articles raise? What kinds of answers or suggestions do they provide? How helpful do you think these magazines might be for first-time parents? For experienced parents? For people who are not parents but are interested in children?

SECTION 2

Childhood: A Time for Development

OBJECTIVES

- Compare childhood in the past and in the present.
- Give examples of progress in understanding how and why children develop as they do.
- Describe five characteristics of development.
- Explain influences on development.

TERMS TO LEARN

environment
formula
heredity
nutrition
sequence

What does *childhood* mean to you? Do you picture a baby taking a few stumbling steps? A four-year-old playing on a swing? A classroom of fifth-graders? What makes children different from adults?

What Is Childhood?

However you respond to the questions above, you probably think of childhood as a period of life separate from adulthood. During this separate period, development occurs very rapidly. Human beings begin childhood almost completely dependent on adults for every need. By the time childhood ends, most people have become mature and ready for independence.

You would probably also agree that children have special needs as they grow and learn. Imagine you were preparing to spend a day with a five-year-old. You would not plan the same activities you would plan for spending the day with someone your own age, and you wouldn't expect to talk about the same things you discuss with people your own age. You wouldn't expect the five-year-old to think, feel, or behave exactly as you do.

We now consider childhood a distinct period of life, and many people have made a special study of this period. They have devoted time and effort to finding out more about how children develop, what their special needs are, and how those needs can best be met. Many important concepts have emerged from this kind of study; perhaps the most important is that childhood has a significant influence on later life. Those who study children and human development believe that every child has a right to a happy, healthy, loving childhood.

However, childhood has not always been considered a separate, important stage of life. In fact, childhood—as we know it—is a fairly recent "discovery."

Childhood: Past and Present

What adjectives do you think of when you see the children in this picture? Is that how you would describe childhood?

Before the beginning of the twentieth century, few people in Western civilization believed that there was anything unusual or important about the early years of life. During the Middle Ages and the centuries that followed, European adults were almost totally unaware of the special needs of children. They did not recognize the importance of providing children with sunshine, wholesome food, protection, loving care, and a variety of learning experiences.

Artworks created in these earlier centuries reflect society's attitude toward children. In paintings and statues, children appeared as miniature adults. They had the proportions, expressions, and clothing of grown-ups.

During the colonial period in America, people still believed that children differed from adults only in size, experience, and abilities. Children were dressed, fed, and doctored just as adults were.

These ideas persisted into the nineteenth century. An example is Louisa May Alcott's famous novel, *Little Women*. The book's central character, Jo, is constantly in trouble because she acts like the exuberant child she is rather than the little lady that girls of her time were expected to be.

Some of the differences between childhood in the past and childhood in the present are the result of changing attitudes toward children. Others are the result of advances in technology.

Work

In the past, children were expected to work hard at an early age. In American pioneer families, children were expected to take care of many farming and household tasks. During the Industrial Revolution, many children worked as laborers in factories.

Today, most children in our society are not thrown into the world of adult work so abruptly. The "job" of young children is simply to grow, learn, and play. Children assume responsibility gradually by helping with household tasks and, later, by taking part-time jobs.

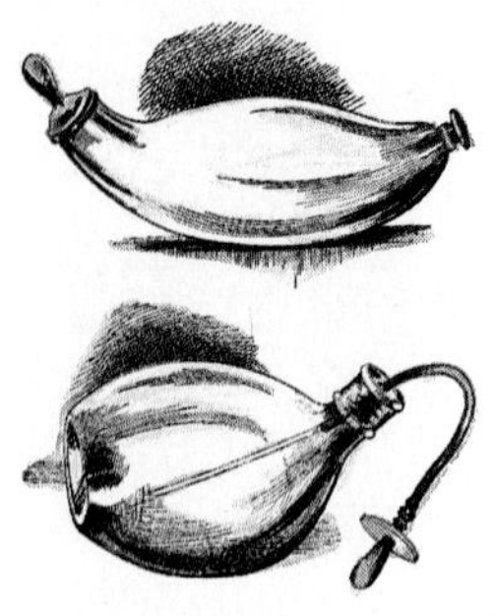

Would you recognize these objects as early baby bottles? They date back to around the turn of the century. Why do you think they are shaped so unusually?

Health and Nutrition

Before the beginning of the twentieth century, parents could not hope to raise every child born to them. Diseases such as diphtheria, typhoid fever, and smallpox caused the deaths of children in almost every family. Today, in the United States and other developed countries, these and many other diseases have been controlled by medical advances, personal cleanliness, and strict public health regulations.

In the past, babies either thrived on breast-feeding, or they died. Today, of course, breast-feeding still provides an infant with complete **nutrition**—*a balance of all the food substances needed for health and growth*. Parents also have the option of bottle-feeding a baby with commercially prepared **formula**, which is *a mixture of milk or milk substitutes and added nutrients*. Infant formulas are safe and scientifically balanced for nutrition. Special formulas are available for infants with digestive problems or other special health needs. Older babies now usually eat strained, unseasoned foods, made either commercially or at home, rather than the adult table food served to babies in the past.

WHY PINK AND BLUE?

The custom of dressing boys in blue and girls in pink has its origin in the idea of protecting newborns from evil spirits. Blue, as the color of the heavens, was especially potent in frightening away demons, hence it was allotted to the most important child, the boy. Girls were thought so little of in early centuries that there was no point in giving them a particular color; pink was probably a later attempt to balance the color scheme. A European legend is much prettier. Baby boys were found under cabbages, which were somewhat blue in color. A baby girl was born in the heart of a pink rose.

Dress

Until the seventeenth century, children were dressed as small adults. Around that time, special clothing styles began to develop for children, though these styles did not encourage activity and play. Even early in the twentieth century, all children wore dresses for the first years of life.

Preschool boys and girls were dressed alike until the early part of the twentieth century. Then styles began to change, and sex differences were reinforced by the style and color of clothes worn from infancy on.

Today, young children now usually wear clothing that is suitable in both style and color for either boys or girls. Modern children wear practical, washable, lightweight garments designed to provide freedom of movement and maximum comfort.

Parental Love

Although childhood in the past was different in many ways from what we know today, one thing has not changed—the love of parents for their children. History is filled with stories that include striking examples of parental love.

Despite their genuine affection, parents in the past had little awareness of the special needs of children. They did not know how to encourage the best physical, emotional, social, or intellectual development. This kind of knowledge is fairly recent.

The Growth of Child Study

Attitudes toward children have changed. Our society now attaches great importance to understanding and guiding children. The fact that you are studying and learning about children is one indication of this change in attitude.

Over the past several generations, interest in studying children and their behavior has grown remarkably. For the first time, researchers and scholars have been able to study child growth and development scientifically. Several pioneering scholars have made basic contributions to our understanding and appreciation of children and childhood.

- Alfred Binet, a French psychologist, developed a series of tests to measure intellectual processes.
- Jean Piaget, a Swiss psychologist, theorized that intelligence develops in stages that are related to age. According to Piaget's theories, the new mental abilities at each stage determine the limits of what a child can learn during that period.
- Sigmund Freud, an Austrian physician, developed the theory that the emotional experiences of childhood have a lasting effect on the personality of an adult.
- In the United States, theorists including Arnold Gesell and Erik Erikson have explored child development in terms of social and emotional growth.

Much remains to be learned about children. However, with the help of scientific research, the superstitions and misunderstandings of the past are being replaced by sound knowledge.

Today there are many resources available to help parents in the study of children.

Information about children and their needs has become not only more complete but also more readily available. In the past, older family members were almost the only source of information and advice about child care and development. Today, people without the help of nearby relatives can find books, articles, and radio and television programs on the subject of child development.

All these resources can give you valuable knowledge about children. Still, the best way to understand human development is to study and observe it for yourself.

Characteristics of Development

The study of childhood has led to an understanding of some basic facts about human development. You may be able to recognize examples of these characteristics of development in your own life and in the lives of other people you know.

- **Development is similar for everyone.** Children all over the world go through the same stages of development in approximately the same order. For example, all babies lift their head before they can lift their body, and all stand before they can walk.
- **Development builds on earlier learning.** The skills a child learns at age two build directly on those he or she mastered at age one. After learning to walk, a child will soon be able to run. Before learning to speak in sentences, a child must learn to say single words. Thus, development follows an orderly **sequence**, *a step-by-step pattern.*
- **Development proceeds at an individual rate.** Although all children follow a similar pattern of development, each child is an individual. The style and rate of growth differ from one child to another.
- **The different areas of development are interrelated.** In studying children, it is convenient to focus on one area of development at a time. However, it is important to remember that, as a child grows, many kinds of changes are taking place at once. A child does not, for example, develop physically one week and emotionally the next week. All areas of development—physical, intellectual, social, and emotional—interact continually.
- **Development is continuous throughout life.** It does not stop at a certain age. Sometimes development is rapid; at other times, it is much slower. We all continue to develop in many ways throughout our lives.

All children follow a similar step-by-step pattern of development, yet each child is unique in many ways. Can you see how physical, intellectual, emotional, and social development influence one another?

The Importance of Play

One of the most effective ways to learn about children and their development is to observe them and interact with them in their most natural setting—the world of play. Play makes an essential contribution to a child's development. Consider all the ways that play benefits children:

- **Physically.** Activities such as running, climbing, jumping rope, and riding a tricycle help the large muscles of the back, arms, and legs develop. Strength and balance improve as a result. Activities such as putting puzzles together, finger painting, and stringing beads help develop control of the small muscles.
- **Intellectually.** A toy or game does not have to be "educational" to promote intellectual development. Simple play activities, such as singing nursery rhymes, stacking blocks, and sorting through a box of buttons, provide experiences in gathering, organizing, and using information about the world.

- **Emotionally.** Play can help children work through life's challenges and problems. For example, acting out the role of a parent, a fire fighter, or a jungle explorer can diminish the frustrations of being a small person in a big world.
- **Socially.** As children grow, they progress from playing alone to playing beside one another. Gradually, they learn to play together and to get along with others—sharing and taking turns. Leadership, friendly competition, and cooperation are some of the valuable social skills that children learn through play.

Guidelines for Observing Children at Play

Direct experiences with young children will enhance your understanding of child growth and development. Here are some guidelines to help you observe young children.

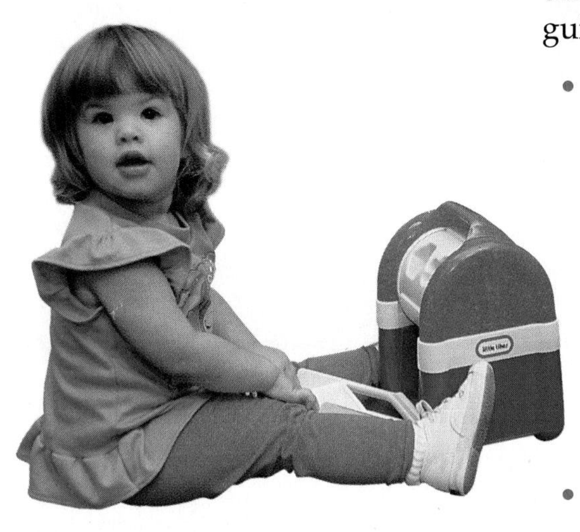

- **Choose a time and a place.** The setting in which you observe children may vary. Some of your observations may be made informally; for example, you might watch children playing at a park. Other observations will be more formal; you might observe in a preschool classroom, in a family child care home, or in a private home, for example. For a formal observation, phone ahead and set up a scheduled time for your observation. Once you arrive, observe from a position that will not interfere with children's routine or play activities.
- **Record what you observe.** Writing down what you observe helps you recognize patterns of behavior, rates of growth, and stages of development. It also helps you identify individual differences in children. When you record your observations, the effects of environment and of other people on each child also become more apparent.

  In recording your observation, use action words to identify children's behavior and development. Here's an example: *Curtis took off the fire fighter's hat and handed it to Jane, saying, "You can have the dumb old hat." He turned and walked away from the housekeeping area toward the blocks.*

  During observations, look at children objectively—seeing them as they are—rather than subjectively. In other words, try to avoid being influenced by who you think the child is or what you think the child should be doing.

  On each set of observation records, include the following basic information: the title of the observation, your name, the date and time of the observation, the names and ages of the children observed, the number of children present, the number of adults working with the children, and the type of situation you are observing (such as a private preschool or a kindergarten in a public school, for example). Also include notes about any other relevant information, such as *during a field trip* or *on the outdoor play yard.*

- **Watch how children interact with other children and with adults.** As you observe, ask yourself questions such as these: With which other children does this child interact? How does the child communicate with other children? Under what circumstances does the child approach an adult? How does the child ask an adult for help? Does the child use words or gestures?
- **Keep observation information confidential.** Any information you gather about a child—whether from your own observations or from discussions you have overheard or participated in—should be shared only with your child development teacher or with the child's parents. Talking about a child's behavior, attitudes, or abilities with anyone else is inappropriate.

Each of these four children has a different personality. What might you record on an observation sheet about each?

Influences on Development

As you observe children in play, you will see that each child is a unique individual. Why and how does each child develop as a unique individual? Aspects of the child's development are influenced by various factors, beginning even before birth and continuing throughout his or her life.

Being encouraged to appreciate music is an example of an environmental influence.

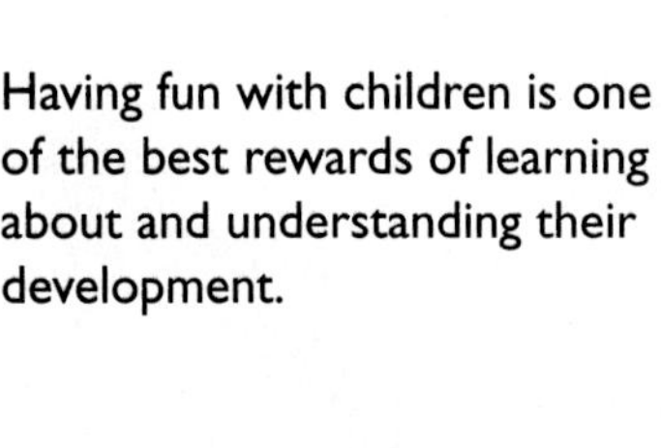

Having fun with children is one of the best rewards of learning about and understanding their development.

One important influence on development is **heredity**, *the passing on of characteristics that are physically inherited from previous generations.* Another important influence on development is **environment**, *the people, places, and things that surround and influence an individual.* Scientists and philosophers have debated for centuries whether heredity or environment has the stronger influence. Today, most agree that the two work together.

Consider how heredity and environment have helped shape your development. From your parents and past generations, you inherited your own physical characteristics out of millions of possibilities. When you were born, you became part of a family whose relationships are unique. Directly or indirectly, your family passed on certain attitudes and certain ways of doing things. These behaviors reflect your family's personal and religious or moral values; they also reflect the customs of the society in which you live.

Eventually, every individual chooses to join many groups outside the family. These groups may include friends, classmates, coworkers, neighbors, social clubs, religious and personal organizations, and many others. Each group exerts some influence on its members' thoughts and actions. You are also influenced by the type of community you live in, what you read, what you see on television, your personal experiences, and countless other forces.

This is not to say that you copy the attitudes and actions of everyone you come in contact with. In fact, sometimes you may try to do just the opposite! Because you are an individual, you always react to outside influences in your own unique way. Still, you are constantly being shaped by people and experiences.

The same is true for every child. During infancy and early childhood, outside forces have an especially strong influence on development. That is why caring for children is such an important responsibility—and such a challenging opportunity.

Children and You

You are in an excellent position to study children—close to adulthood, yet not so removed from childhood that you cannot remember it clearly. Bring your resources—all your resources—to enrich your study. Become involved personally, and you will find the study of children enjoyable and rewarding.

As you learn, you will find some of your opinions challenged, others reinforced. You will discover answers to questions that have puzzled you. You will also raise questions to which there are no answers yet. Perhaps someday you will help find the answers to some of those questions.

SECTION 2 REVIEW

CHECK YOUR UNDERSTANDING

1. How were children regarded during the colonial period in America?
2. What is nutrition?
3. What is formula?
4. List three factors that have resulted in the control of many dangerous diseases.
5. What theory did Jean Piaget contribute to child development studies?
6. List five characteristics of development.
7. Explain the difference between heredity and environment.

DISCUSS AND DISCOVER

1. Discuss your ideas about this statement from the chapter: "The job of young children is simply to grow, learn, and play." In what sense are these activities a job for young children? What do children contribute by performing this job? What do they get in return? Should adults help children in this job? If so, how? If not, why not?
2. Read about diphtheria, typhoid fever, or smallpox: What are the symptoms of the disease? What results can it have? How is it spread? How is it treated? How can it be prevented? Has the disease been completely eliminated, or does it still pose some dangers? Share and discuss your findings with classmates.

SUMMARY

- Your relationship with young children depends on your interest and your knowledge.
- Study, observation, and practical experience help you understand children.
- Understanding children will help you better understand yourself.
- Your knowledge about children and your experiences with them can help you think about parenthood and about career choices.
- Childhood today is different from childhood in the past. The differences result largely from changes in attitude and advances in health care and nutrition.
- The study of child growth and development is a recent science.
- Development always follows an orderly sequence, but it proceeds at individual rates.
- All aspects of development are interrelated, and development is continuous.
- A variety of hereditary and environmental influences affect development.

REVIEWING THE FACTS

1. What can students learn from thinking seriously about their relationships with young children?
2. List four ways in which your understanding of children will grow as you study child development.
3. List two questions about your own future that studying child development can help you consider.
4. About how long ago did most people in Western civilization begin to regard childhood as a separate, important stage of life?
5. What responsibilities did children in American pioneer families have?
6. What are epidemics? How common are they in the United States now?
7. Who was Alfred Binet? What did he contribute to our understanding of children?
8. What theory did Sigmund Freud develop?
9. What is a sequence?
10. List four benefits of play for children.
11. What is the difference between an objective and a subjective observation?
12. Define these terms: *heredity, environment*.

EXPLORING FURTHER

1. Every day for one week, check a local newspaper for articles about children and parenting. Read and save all the articles you find. At the end of a week, bring to class the two articles you consider most interesting; share and discuss them with your classmates. (Section 1)
2. Think about your own concept of childhood. Using magazines, photographs, and your own artwork as sources, collect pictures and use them to create a collage that communicates your concept. Share and discuss your collage with a group of classmates. (Section 2)
3. Bring to class an article of clothing that you wore as a baby or a photograph of yourself as a baby. Discuss the particular outfit you wore, comparing it with the outfits worn by others, both boys and girls. For whom was your outfit suitable? What kinds of activities did it encourage? Would you expect a baby today to wear a similar outfit? (Section 2)

THINKING CRITICALLY

1. **Synthesize.** Discuss your response to the following statement: "Only students who already are parents, who plan to become parents, or who want careers in child-related fields should study child development." Do you agree or disagree? Why?
2. **Compare and contrast.** Why do you think parents allowed their children to work long hours as factory laborers during the Industrial Revolution? How do you think those parents felt about their children? About their children's work? Why don't American parents send their children to work in factories today? Do you think the fact that children no longer work in factories means that parents are better today than they were 200 years ago? Why or why not?
3. **Analyze.** How do you think your heredity has affected your development? How do you think your environment has affected your development? What examples can you cite—in yourself, your family, or your friends—of the interacting influences of heredity and environment? Which do you consider more influential on the development of young children, heredity or environment? Why?

CROSS-CURRICULUM CONNECTIONS

1. **Art.** Examine one or more art books, and select a painting or sculpture that depicts at least one child. When was the artwork created? What attitudes toward children does it portray? Share and discuss your findings with the rest of your class.
2. **Reading.** Read *Little Women* by Louisa May Alcott. As you read, identify specific incidents that reflect nineteenth-century attitudes toward children, parents, and families. With a group of classmates, compare and discuss your ideas.

OBSERVING AND PARTICIPATING

Making Child Observations Meaningful

As part of your child development class, you may have an opportunity to observe young children in action and to participate in their care and education. Direct experiences with young children will enhance your understanding of child growth and development. Writing down exactly what you see enables you to review the facts later and form a clear idea of what the children are like.

Choose one of the following activities. Spend time observing or participating with young children, and record your observations and reactions in your journal. Then share and discuss your journal entry with a group of classmates.

- **Observing.** Spend time in a child care center or in a public place, such as a playground, observing three or more children of the same age. How are the children alike? How are they different?
- **Observing.** Spend about half an hour observing an infant under six months of age; spend another half hour observing a six-year-old. How many specific differences in development can you notice? Do you think you would find as many differences if you observed a ten-year-old and a sixteen-year-old? A thirty-year-old and a thirty-six-year old? What conclusions can you draw about development during childhood?
- **Participating.** Take care of one or two young children for half a day. Notice how you feel about the children. How confident are you at the beginning of your time with the children? As the time together passes, do you feel more comfortable and confident—or less? Also, notice how the children respond to you. How do their responses affect your feelings about your abilities?

CHAPTER 2

Living in Families

SECTION 1 Understanding Families

SECTION 2 Considerations of Parenthood

Uncle Cleon turned his attention to the hand puppet and said, "Mr. Rabbit, tell Tyeisha about the family picnic and all the relatives she's going to meet."

"Sure," replied the rabbit. "There'll be some people you've already met—Aunt Alice, Uncle Webb, and Uncle Sam. Do you remember them?"

"Yes, I think so. Will there be anyone else I know?" asked Tyeisha.

"Well," said the rabbit flopping his ears, "you remember your cousin Brad? He'll be there with his new baby sister Amy. I think Chrissie and Derrick are coming too, and they'll probably bring Ashley—that's Derrick's daughter from his first marriage."

"Wait, what about Grandma and Grandpa?" demanded Tyeisha. "Are they going to be there too?"

"Of course, silly" the rabbit nodded. "It's a family reunion! There'll be all of your cousins, aunts, uncles, and grandparents. There will even be some people, well—they're not really related—they just act like family. You are going to have so much fun!"

"But how am I going to remember all of their names?" wondered Tyeisha.

"Don't worry, Tyeisha, you'll have me at the picnic. Rabbits have a knack for remembering names."

SECTION 1 Understanding Families

OBJECTIVES

- Explain the importance of the family.
- Identify various types of families
- Identify stages in the family life cycle.
- Explain how social trends affect the family.
- Explain ways to strengthen the family.

TERMS TO LEARN

adoption
blended family
commitment
coping skills
extended family
family
family life cycle
foster child
nuclear family
single-parent family

When you think about the word, *family,* what comes to mind—your own family at home? A friend's family? A family you see on a favorite TV program? There are many different groups of people that function as families.

The Importance of Families

A **family** is *a group of two or more people who care about each other and are committed to each other.* Usually, the members of a family live together, and in most families, the members are related by marriage, by birth, or by adoption.

People seem to have a need for families. Perhaps you've heard someone say—or have even said yourself—something like this: "We've known him for years—he's like family." "You know I care about you—you're like family to me." "I know I can always count on her—she's like part of my family."

Why does family seem to matter so much? A family is every child's first connection to the world. As a child gets older, family provides a safe environment from which to explore—and to which he or she can return.

All the members benefit from a family. The family provides an important sense of belonging for every member. Within a family, each individual has the opportunity to love and to be loved, to care and to be cared for, to help others and to receive help.

A strong family foundation is one of the best gifts for a child. The family is the child's first connection to the world and it provides each individual with the opportunity to love and to be loved.

Types of Families

Family groups take many different forms. As you probably know from experience, family groups may vary widely in size and structure. A family may include a single parent and several children, or two parents and one child, or two married or committed adults with no children. Some people form their own unique family groups. For example, two or more single adults may live together as a family, helping each other meet the individual and group needs of all the family members.

In spite of these many variations, there are four main kinds of family groups: the nuclear family, the extended family, the single-parent family, and the blended family.

The Nuclear Family

A **nuclear family** is *a family group with two generations—a father and mother and at least one child—sharing the same household.* There are, of course, many variations among nuclear families, depending at least in part on the occupation of the parents and on the number and ages of the children. In some nuclear fami-

BUILDING SELF-ESTEEM

Telling the Truth about Adoption

An adopted child can be expected to ask why his or her biological parents "gave me away." Parents should avoid saying that the biological parents did not want the child. A simple "I don't know, honey, but I'm glad it worked out this way," accompanied by a hug, is much better. This helps avoid the feeling of rejection that some adopted children have. Showing adopted children that they are loved and wanted helps them realize that they truly belong in the family—and that they will not be given up again. Children need to understand that it is often difficult, but necessary and unselfish, for birth parents to give up a child.

lies, one parent works outside the home to provide family income. The other parent stays home to care for the children and to keep the household functioning. In other nuclear families, both parents work outside the home. The number of dual-earner nuclear families has grown rapidly in recent decades and has contributed to an ever-increasing need for quality child care.

Although the majority of nuclear families include only the parents' biological children, some nuclear families include adopted children and/or foster children.

Attitudes toward **adoption**, *the legal process in which people obtain the permanent right to raise a child who is not biologically their own*, have undergone some important changes in recent decades. In the past, children were always matched as closely as possible to their adoptive parents, with special consideration given to their race, ethnic and religious background, and physical characteristics.

Now, the emphasis of adoption is on finding good homes for children who need them. Matching the characteristics of parents and adoptive children is no longer considered especially important. Older children, disabled children, children from other countries, and children of mixed races are adopted much more frequently than in the past.

Some families choose to care for a **foster child**, *a child whose parents or other close family members are unable to care for him or her*. In these cases, foster parents assume temporary legal responsibility for the child.

Although family groups may vary widely in size and structure, healthy families show appreciation and commitment to one another and share quality time together.

The important consideration in any family is not how its members are related, but whether they are able to provide each other with love, care, and support.

The Extended Family

An **extended family** is *a family group that includes relatives other than parents and children within a single household.* A woman raises her two grandsons. An elderly man lives with his daughter, his son-in-law, and his granddaughter.

The term *extended family* sometimes also refers to additional relatives outside the household—the cousins, aunts, uncles, grandparents, and great-grandparents who don't live with a young person but who can be important sources of emotional support and guidance.

The Single-Parent Family

A **single-parent family** is *a family group that consists of one parent and one or more children sharing a household.* The parent in this type of family may be either a mother or a father. That parent may be raising children alone because he or she has never married or because he or she has been left alone after a divorce or death.

Single parenting puts many demands on the parent. He or she has a great deal of responsibility, little free time, and no spouse with whom to share problems. Many single parents find support in a network of friends and relatives who feel involved both with the parent and with the child or children in the family. Some communities have organizations for single parents, which provide emotional support and social opportunities.

BUILDING SELF-ESTEEM

Positive Role Models

One special concern that faces single parents is every child's need to develop positive relationships with adults of both genders. A child needs a close and meaningful relationship with a caring adult who is the opposite gender of the single parent. The parent's adult friends and relatives can often provide a positive example of male or female behavior and relationships. In addition, some single parents, especially those in big cities, can turn to programs such as Big Brothers, Big Sisters, or scouts for help.

The Blended Family

A **blended family** is *a family group that consists of a married couple and at least one child from a parent's previous relationship.* Like other types of families, blended families can involve many variations.

In the first few months or years, the members of a blended family may experience problems in establishing a new family unit. Everyone has to learn about a new person while living with him or her. Accommodations and compromises may be necessary on many different levels.

Stepparenting brings many challenges. However, when all family members work together to overcome problems, the results can be rewarding for everyone. Both stepchildren and stepparents can benefit from the new perspectives and resources that are brought to the family.

The Family Life Cycle

There are many differences between families, but there are similarities, too. Each family group goes through the **family life cycle**—*a series of stages in a predictable order*—though, of course, the timing and duration of these stages may vary widely from family to family. The chart on page 43 gives an overview of the stages through which families develop.

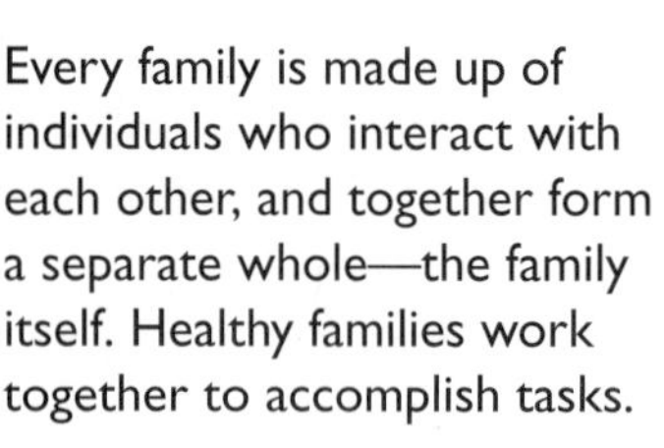

Every family is made up of individuals who interact with each other, and together form a separate whole—the family itself. Healthy families work together to accomplish tasks.

THE FAMILY LIFE CYCLE

As you study the chart, think about the special challenges and rewards that may be associated with each stage in the family life cycle. Also consider how adults who never marry, who marry but do not have children, who divorce, or who divorce and remarry may experience their own special versions of the family life cycle.

BEGINNING STAGE

A couple works to establish a home and a marriage relationship.

CHILDBEARING STAGE

The couple prepares and adjusts to parenthood.

CHILD-REARING STAGE

As children grow, the parents work to meet their children's changing needs and help them develop independence.

LAUNCHING STAGE

Children gradually leave home to support themselves. Parents help their children adapt to life on their own.

EMPTY-NEST STAGE

After the last child has left home, the couple renews their relationship and adjusts to the change in their parenting role.

RETIREMENT STAGE

The couple adjusts to the aging process. They may develop new interests or renew old ones.

VARIATIONS IN THE FAMILY LIFE CYCLE

Any of the following situations may change the pattern of the family life cycle or the characteristics of each stage:

- Single adulthood
- Single parenthood
- Divorce
- Remarriage
- Couples without children

Trends Affecting Family Systems

Families of every type and in every stage of the family life cycle are affected by social trends. As the number of individuals in various societal groups change, the entire society experiences shifts that affect the family system. For example, as more women become active in the work force, society faces a growing need for facilities and individuals that provide quality child care. Another current trend is the rising population of older citizens. Some current trends create additional stresses on family systems; other trends may encourage family unity. Other examples of trends in society are: changing family roles, mobility, and awareness of family values.

Cultural Exchange

FAMILIES—PRESERVING CULTURAL HERITAGE

All families, whether consciously or not, pass down to successive generations the essence of their culture in the form of values, behavior, foods, language, customs, and traditions. Immigrant families are often faced with the challenge to preserve their values and belief systems while assimilating into mainstream society. As cultures adapt and modify, so does the concept of a traditional family pattern. This process is call *enculturation.*

The best way to influence children is to recognize the inherent strengths within all families. Sharing stories of past experiences, discussing feelings, and exploring traditions are the first steps to preserving your cultural heritage. Think about what your culture has to offer, and what you have learned from others. What unique qualities will you pass on to your descendants?

Changing Family Roles

Not long ago, each member of a family group had a clearly defined role to play. Traditionally, a husband cared for the family by earning money; a wife cared for the family by raising children and running the household. Children attended school and anticipated assuming the same family roles they saw their parents filling. Each family member knew what was expected.

In recent decades, family roles have become much less clearly defined. Increasing numbers of families are headed by single parents or by two employed parents. Adults in these families may face particular stresses in arranging quality care for their children, in setting aside time to spend with their children, and in scheduling time for their own needs and activities.

Mobile Society

A hundred years ago, it was not unusual for an adult to die in the same home where he or she had been born. Today, most adults no longer live in the same community—much less the same home—they were born in. Our society has become very mobile; individuals and families move often.

Because of these frequent moves, families often lack close, supportive connections with friends and relatives. Family groups need to rely more on their own members and on long-distance relationships with members of their extended families and their familylike friends.

Awareness of Family Values

In recent years, the importance of the family unit has gained increasing recognition. The term *family values* is heard around the country. Many people feel strongly that government institutions should offer encouragement and support to families. They believe that laws and programs should help ensure that all children, elderly, disabled, and sick individuals are able to experience the best quality of life possible. They also believe in providing affordable and accessible health care for all families.

ASK THE EXPERTS

Employers and Families

Linda Espinosa is the Director of Primary Education for the Redwood City School District in California and is Treasurer of the National Association of Education for Young Children.

I'm curious about the relationship between businesses and families. How are the needs of American families changing? What are employers doing to meet those changing needs?

Your question focuses on an interesting issue: the effects that companies have on their employees' lives, and the effects of employees' lives—including their family needs—on companies.

You're right to notice that the needs of American families are changing. For a number of different reasons, more and more parents are working outside the home. More than 80 percent of mothers with children under age 18 are employed. In addition, the number of single-parent families is on the rise. It is estimated that 60 percent of today's children will live in a single-parent family before they reach 18. These changes have caused gradual revisions in work policies, making many businesses more "family friendly."

"Family friendly" policies are still in the developing stages. It is estimated that from 10 to 25 percent of all companies in the United States provide some kind of support for employees' families. In most cases, this support involves flexible working hours or cafeteria-type health benefits. It may also involve before-tax support for child care costs.

A few progressive companies go beyond these basic family-support policies. For example, some employers provide on-site child care centers or educational scholarship opportunities. The numbers are still small, but there is a growing trend for companies to support the needs of families.

Businesses and other employers— like society as a whole—seem increasingly aware of the importance of educating and caring for all children. As employees ask for—and make use of—new policies, employers respond by providing increasing support for all family members.

Linda Espinosa

Linda Espinosa

The Need for Healthy Families

Every healthy family system fulfills certain functions. A family provides each member with protection, economic support, emotional support, a sense of identity and acceptance, and opportunities for personal development. By functioning in these ways, the family benefits not only its own family members but also other individuals and families, as well as the larger community in which the family lives.

Each family serves another vitally important function: It assumes responsibility for the socialization of children. Within the family setting, young children begin to learn about acceptable behavior: What kind of language is appropriate? How should a young child speak to adults? To other children? How should anger and frustration be expressed? What are the appropriate ways to express affection? These and many similar questions are first answered by a child's family—usually not through words and explanations, but through daily examples and modeling desirable behavior.

As children grow and come into contact with influences outside the family, their families continue to guide their behavior and direct their learning. Parents and other responsible family members explain guidelines and discuss the reasons for particular kinds of behavior. They also reinforce each child's appropriate behavior and correct inappropriate behavior.

Children of all ages make important contributions to the family.

How Can Families Be Strengthened?

Because families serve such important functions in society, they should be supported and encouraged. Family members themselves can assume major responsibility for strengthening their own family.

Recognizing the characteristics of strong, fully functioning families can help people in all situations understand how to help strengthen their own families. The first step in strengthening one's own family is knowing what to look for in a healthy family. Next, the family members can identify the strengths of their own family. Finally, they can strive to improve the areas that need strengthening.

Members of strong families show commitment to the family, make a point of spending time together, communicate openly with one another, show appreciation for one another, share beliefs and traditions, and use coping skills effectively.

Commitment

A **commitment** is *a pledge or promise of loyalty*. In a healthy family, each member of the family group feels a commitment to the family as a unit and to the other family members. A commitment to family is reflected in polite and respectful behavior toward one another, in friendly support, and in consideration.

For busy adults and teenagers, commitment to family is reflected in decisions to spend time with other family members. A parent who consistently thinks, "Oh well, the kids are old enough to get their own dinner tonight—I'll just stay at the office and keep working," does not display a commitment to family. On the other hand, a high school student who says, "Thanks—I'd love to go along, but my family's expecting me. We always have dinner together and watch a video on Thursday," is showing a strong commitment to family.

Time Together

Healthy families plan time to spend together. As the family members grow and change, the activities they do together change. A family with young children might set aside a weekend afternoon to spend in the park. A family with teenagers might decide to spend one Saturday each month on a sports outing—skiing in the winter and biking in the summer, for example.

Time spent together should not be limited to recreation and entertainment. Family members can spend time together shopping for groceries, reading aloud, taking a walk, refinishing furniture—or doing almost anything that interests and involves everyone. For many families, eating meals together provides an important opportunity for sharing time and discussing interests, problems, successes, and concerns.

Communication

Open communication is essential in any strong family system. Family members of all ages should show their interest and involvement by talking and listening to each other.

When family members talk openly, they can't possibly agree all the time. Learning to express and work through differences of opinion can help family members feel close and secure. Family members can be encouraged to recognize, express, and react to a full range of emotions—anger, fear, joy, anxiety, love, elation—in a strong family with active communication skills.

Appreciation

Individuals in strong, healthy families like each other—and say so. They affirm each other, and they speak and act affectionately to each other. Each family member is appreciated for who he or she is, not for what he or she looks like, has, or does. Individuals do not make the mistake of remaining silent when there is an opportunity to praise another family member.

Shared Beliefs

Strong families usually share a clear set of beliefs and traditions. These beliefs may—or may not—be based on the teachings and practice of organized religion. Whatever their basis, shared beliefs provide a sense of commitment and an essential frame of reference for making decisions.

Often, shared beliefs involve rituals and traditions that further unite family members. Family members may attend weekly services together, for example, or they may participate together in volunteer activities on a regular basis. They may also have special holiday celebrations or family gatherings. Each of these enhances the family's sense of kinship and roots.

Coping Skills

Every family has to deal with stresses and problems; strong families confront those difficulties openly and use **coping skills**, *techniques that help people solve a problem or adapt to a situation.*

Members of a healthy family begin by recognizing that having problems or difficulties is not a sign of weakness. Instead of ignoring problems, they develop skills in identifying potentially serious problems and attacking them early. Members of a healthy family do not become unduly concerned or stressed by unpleasant events. When family members try to solve problems, they consider several options, and they make sure that everyone involved has a chance to contribute. They further recognize that not all problems can be solved within the family, so they seek and accept help from support systems and from professional sources. As these families find solutions, they experience satisfaction and become healthier, ready to face and solve the next problem that may arise.

SECTION 1 REVIEW

CHECK YOUR UNDERSTANDING

1. Name three ways that the family benefits its members.
2. What is the difference between a foster child and an adopted child?
3. What are the stages in the family life cycle?
4. How has the trend toward a mobile society affected families?
5. What five things does a healthy family system provide for each family member?
6. How does a family assume responsibility for the socialization of children?
7. How do shared rituals and traditions help family members feel united?
8. What are coping skills?

DISCUSS AND DISCOVER

1. In your opinion, what makes members of the extended family important to children who live in nuclear families, single-parent families, or blended families? How can extended family members help parents? How can they help children? What role should grandparents and other extended family members assume in the lives of young children? What problems might they face in trying to assume that role?
2. With a group of classmates, compile a list of traditions and rituals that families might share. Then discuss your list: Which of the traditions and rituals does your family take part in? Which would you like to have your family practice? Why? How could each of the traditions and rituals enhance a family's sense of unity?

Considerations of Parenthood

SECTION 2

OBJECTIVES

- Discuss the changes that parenthood brings.
- List questions couples should consider before deciding on parenthood.

TERMS TO LEARN

parenthood

Family groups take many different forms and come in many different sizes. Many adults choose to expand their family group by having children. However, the decision to become a parent should not be taken lightly. Parenthood brings many changes, and there are several important questions to consider before one decides whether or not to become a parent.

Parenthood Brings Changes

Any person who becomes a mother or father of a biological or an adopted child enters into **parenthood**, *the state of being a parent*. Having a child brings dramatic and long-lasting changes to every parent's life. Some of these changes involve joy and deep satisfaction. Other changes can be difficult to deal with, especially when parents are unprepared for them.

New Responsibilities

Raising a child is more than just a day-to-day assignment. It is a lifelong commitment. A child's needs for physical care, financial support, love, and guidance continue until adulthood. Being a parent means having a constant concern for the present and future welfare of another human being. Once they become parents, people are no longer able to consider only their own wants and needs when making choices and planning for the future.

For first-time parents, these new responsibilities can seem overwhelming. Good management is the key to fulfilling these responsibilities. New parents need to manage their time, money, energy, knowledge, and skills in meeting their responsibilities. They also may call on family, friends, and community resources for help and support.

A big part of being a parent is accepting responsibility for the child's welfare– not just a few days or weeks, but for many years.

Changes in Lifestyle

New parents face important adjustments in their day-to-day living. Caring for a child—especially a newborn baby—takes a surprising amount of time and energy. A newborn must be fed every few hours around the clock, in addition to being diapered, bathed, played with, and comforted. When you add laundry and other household chores, it's not hard to see why new parents feel they have no time for themselves.

With a child of any age, parents are faced with limits on their personal freedom. This is an especially difficult adjustment for new parents. Suddenly, it's not so easy to go anywhere on the spur of the moment.

Emotional Adjustments

Parenthood, with its changes in lifestyle and new responsibilities, requires a number of emotional adjustments. Going through so many changes at once is stressful in itself. It takes time for new parents to sort through their conflicting feelings and grow accustomed to their new role.

Most new parents are happy, proud, and excited. However, most also experience a variety of more difficult and confusing feelings. Common reactions include the following:

- Anxiety about the baby and how to care for him or her.
- Fear of not being a good parent.

- Frustration at the loss of personal freedom and the addition of new responsibilities.
- Loneliness and isolation from spending most of the time at home with the baby.
- Doubts about the decision to become a parent.
- Worry over financial matters.
- Jealousy of the baby and the attention he or she gets.
- Depression related to exhaustion or to the physical changes of pregnancy and birth.

Each new parent's attitude and individual situation affect his or her ability to handle these emotional adjustments. The adjustments, of course, are easier for parents who are prepared for these reactions and who understand that they are normal. With the patience and support of family members and friends, most new parents eventually resolve their conflicting feelings. They are able to get over the rough spots and enjoy the positive aspects of parenthood.

It's natural for a new parent to feel a bit left out if the baby gets all the attention. What could this couple do to solve the problem?

Changes in Relationships

When a child is born or adopted, the parents have the unique experience of getting to know a new family member. At the same time, the parents are likely to experience changes in the way they interact with each other, with other family members, and with friends. This is especially true for first-time parents.

There's no doubt that the birth of a baby can be a wonderful time for new parents. However, it can also cause problems between them. New parents are likely to be physically exhausted and under emotional stress. Suddenly, they are faced with new roles, new worries, and a baby who demands a great deal of time and energy. All these can put a strain on the parents' relationship.

Parents who are anxious or frustrated sometimes take out their feelings on their spouse. Without patience and understanding on both sides of the relationship, tempers may flare. A marriage may also suffer when one or both partners are so involved with child care that they neglect each other. Money problems are another source of conflict. Many new parents need more living space at a time when expenses for doctors, baby items, and child care are already adding up.

The couples who adjust most easily during the early, difficult time are those who plan carefully. They read books and articles on parenting and child care. They talk to family members or friends who have been through the experience. Many take parenting or child care classes before or after the baby's arrival.

Like the relationship between new parents, the parents' relationships with family and friends also undergo changes. New parents usually find they have little time or freedom for the social life they once enjoyed. They may also feel they have less in common with some of their friends than before. New friendships may develop with other parents who can understand and share their experiences.

A new child brings new roles to extended family members—grandparent, aunt, uncle, cousin, perhaps sister or brother. Like the child's parents, these other family members may have to adjust to their new roles. For example, a couple may feel that the well-meaning advice offered by the baby's grandparents is a criticism of their own ability to care for the child. They may resent what they see as interference in their decisions. Meanwhile, the grandparents may feel hurt that their offers of advice are rejected. Sometimes the situation is the opposite. Grandparents may feel overburdened if a child's parents expect them to provide more help than they can manage.

On the positive side, many new parents feel that having a child brings them closer to their own parents. For the first time, they truly understand what being a parent is like. Grandparents and other relatives can share their experiences with the new parents and give help, advice, and support.

When there are already children in the family, the arrival of a new baby can bring on jealousy and misbehavior. Parents and other close family members need to be understanding and provide special attention and love.

The birth of a new brother or sister can bring happiness, love, and fun. At the same time, it alters the relationships within the family.

The Rewards of Parenthood

In spite of all the adjustments and problems involved, parenthood can bring many joys. Nothing is quite like a baby's first smile or a hug from a three-year-old. Parents discover special feelings of happiness, pride, and love that are different from anything they have felt before.

Raising children can give parents a great sense of accomplishment. They may also find that having children can enrich an already strong marriage. By helping their children discover the world, they can see it with new eyes themselves.

Making Decisions About Parenthood

Deciding whether or not to become a parent is one of the most important decisions most people ever make. Those who are thinking about parenthood should get as clear a picture of it as possible before they make a decision. They should also take a realistic look at themselves. The decision of whether to have children—and when to have them—may depend on these five considerations: emotional maturity, desire for parenthood, health, management skills, and finances.

Parenthood is a major step. When a couple fully understands the responsibilities involved as well as their own feelings and motivations, they will be better able to make a wise decision.

Emotional Maturity

Being a parent, like being an adult, involves more than physical maturity. It requires emotional maturity as well. That means being responsible enough to put someone else's needs before your own. It means being secure enough to devote your full attention to an infant without expecting to receive attention in return. It also means being able to hold your temper when you find that a toddler has dumped all the dirt out of the plants on the window sill.

Age is no guarantee of emotional maturity. However, most people do become better able to handle situations like these as they grow older. Prospective parents should take an honest look at their emotional maturity. Are their expectations of parenthood realistic? Are they equipped to handle the pressures and responsibilities involved? If they have any doubts, they should decide to postpone parenthood.

Desire for Parenthood

"Do I really want to be a parent?" This question can be difficult to answer. Just as important, and often just as difficult, is this question: "Why do I want a child now?"

Not all reasons for wanting children indicate real preparation for parenthood. Think about the reasons shown in the chart on page 54.

WHY PARENTHOOD?

UNSOUND REASONS	SOUND REASONS
• Our marriage is in trouble. Maybe this will solve our problems.	• Having children will add depth to our relationship, which is already strong.
• A baby is someone who will love me and belong to me.	• I want to give a baby my care and love.
• I feel like I'm nobody. Being a parent will make me somebody.	• I feel good about myself. I believe that parenthood will be a meaningful and rewarding experience.
• I want someone who will take care of me when I'm old.	• I want to experience the special bond between parent and child that lasts for a lifetime.
• Our parents want grandchildren.	• I love children, and I want to be a parent.

Prospective parents should try to understand their own desires and doubts as clearly as possible. Only in this way can they be sure of their decision.

Health Considerations

The health of prospective parents is an important consideration, particularly before pregnancy. It is best for both prospective parents to go to the doctor for a checkup. If either has a medical problem, it could affect the health of the baby or their ability to care for the child.

The age of the prospective mother should also be considered. If she is under seventeen or over thirty-five, pregnancy is riskier for both the mother and the baby.

Parents must be willing to do without things they might enjoy in order to devote time, energy, and other resources to the child's needs.

Management Skills

Because parenting is such a complex task, it requires good management skills. Parents must evaluate their family's needs and wants and then decide on the family's goals. Parents are also responsible for finding resources they can use to reach the family's goals. Successful parents consider their options and make sound decisions. Finally, they evaluate this management process by deciding whether their decisions have helped the family progress toward its goals.

Financial Considerations

The expenses that raising a child add to a family budget can be surprisingly large. Before deciding on parenthood, couples should take a careful look at the costs involved over the years ahead. They may need to make some changes in their way of life and set aside some savings.

New parents need skill in money management. Expenses increase, and if one parent stays home with the baby, income drops. A personal checking account can help parents control and keep track of their expenses. If they find they need a loan, parents must know how to shop for the loan, apply for it, and plan for and manage its repayment. These are all skills that parents should acquire before they have children.

SECTION 2 REVIEW

CHECK YOUR UNDERSTANDING

1. List three responsibilities that parents must face.
2. How does parenthood typically change a couple's lifestyle?
3. List four emotional reactions common among new parents.
4. What are the five factors a couple should consider as they decide whether to have children?
5. List two unsound reasons for choosing to become a parent.
6. What money management skills are parents likely to need?

DISCUSS AND DISCOVER

1. With a group of classmates, take turns acting out various situations in which parents express their feelings about having a new child. Identify the specific emotions being expressed, and discuss the probable reasons for those emotions.
2. Discuss parenthood with parents from two families. Which aspects of parenting do they find most difficult? Most rewarding? How does parenthood differ from their expectations? How does it change as the family grows and/or as children grow older? Summarize what you have learned, either in a brief oral report to your classmates or in a short written report.

SUMMARY

- All members of a family benefit from the family and have responsibilities to the family.
- There are many kinds of family groups; the most common are the nuclear family, the extended family, the single-parent family, and the blended family.
- Families are affected by societal trends, including changing family roles, greater mobility, and an awareness of family values.
- In healthy families, family members show commitment to the family, spend time together, use good communication skills, show appreciation for each other, share traditions, and have good coping skills.
- Parenthood brings new responsibilities, changes in lifestyle, emotional adjustments, changes in relationships, and special rewards.
- Before deciding to have children, prospective parents should evaluate their own emotional maturity, desire for parenthood, health, management skills, and financial readiness.

REVIEWING THE FACTS

1. What is a family?
2. What is an extended family?
3. What is a blended family?
4. How should parents respond to an adopted child's interest in his or her biological parents?
5. How have family roles changed in recent decades?
6. Briefly describe a situation in which family members demonstrate their commitment to the family.
7. What can families do to spend time together?
8. In a healthy family, which emotions can be acceptably expressed?
9. What effect does parenthood often have on a couple's relationships with friends?
10. Why do parents need management skills?

EXPLORING FURTHER

1. Collect newspaper and magazine articles about family members who show their support and consideration for one another. Discuss these articles with your classmates, noting the variety of family groups represented. Then use your articles as part of a bulletin board display about healthy families. (Section 1)
2. Make a list of local sites, events, and outings appropriate for families that include teenagers. Work with classmates to plan, make, and display posters advertising two or three of your choices. Include in your posters some information about the importance of spending time together with family members. (Section 1)
3. With a group of classmates, develop a list of specific questions prospective parents can use in deciding whether they are ready to have children. Organize your questions into the five categories of consideration: emotional maturity, desire for parenthood, health, management skills, and finances. Then design and prepare an attractive handout entitled "Am I Ready for Parenthood?" Share your handout with interested students and, if appropriate, with others in your community. (Section 2)
4. Survey five parents to find out how old they were when their first child was born. Looking back, do they think they were too young, too old, or about the right age. Combine and discuss the survey results in class. (Section 2)

THINKING CRITICALLY

1. **Analyze.** Why is it important to understand the characteristics of a healthy family? How do you think you and other students should use those characteristics to evaluate the families in which you were raised? What should be the purpose of your evaluation? Why do you consider that an appropriate purpose?
2. **Analyze.** The adoption of older children can present special challenges for parents and other family members. What potential problems do you think may be associated with the adoption of older children? What might cause those problems? How do you think adoptive parents should deal with those problems? Why?
3. **Synthesize.** Why is it important to make decisions about parenthood before pregnancy begins? What effects do you think an unplanned pregnancy can have on a married couple? On an unmarried couple? Do you think there is one best way for couples to respond to an unplanned pregnancy? If so, what is it? If not, why not?

CROSS-CURRICULUM CONNECTIONS

1. **Math.** With a group of classmates, survey a selected portion of your school population. Collect information about the kind of family group in which students are living in now and the kind of family group they hope to live in as adults. Then plan and draw a graph or chart that summarizes the information you have gathered.
2. **Writing.** Plan and write a skit or a short story about parents' adjusting to life with a new baby.

OBSERVING AND PARTICIPATING

Observing Family Relationships

Choose one of the following activities, and spend time observing or participating with families. Record your observations in your journal. Then, with a group of classmates, discuss what you have learned from your chosen activity.

- **Observing.** Spend time observing family groups in a public place, such as a mall, a park, or a fast-food restaurant. Notice how the members of each family interact. How are they spending time together? How do they show appreciation for each other? What signs of family commitment can you identify? What other indications of a strong family group do you observe?
- **Participating.** Introduce your own family group to an activity that could be established as a family ritual or tradition. Discuss your own interest in the activity, and encourage other family members to respond openly with their own opinions and ideas. Why are you interested in establishing that activity as a family ritual or tradition? How interested do the other members of your family appear to be? How do you account for their interest—or lack of interest?
- **Observing.** Observe a first-time parent caring for a young baby during a period of two hours or more. What demands does the baby make? How does the parent respond to those demands? What else does the parent attempt to accomplish during this period? With what success? What emotional responses does the parent seem to have to the infant? To the responsibilities involved in caring for the infant?

STORY
MAKER

CHAPTER 3

Effective Parenting Skills

Alex's mother called him and said "I'm ready to read now" as she settled into a big easy chair. "You choose some books from the shelf and bring them to me."

"Okay, Mom," Alex called. He grabbed a book and hurried over to her.

"Let's see," she said, taking the book from Alex. "Oh, this is the book about steam shovels. We read it this morning—and last night. Don't you want a different book?"

"No," answered Alex. "This is my best book. I want to hear this book."

"Okay, Alex, if this is the book you like best, we'll read it," his mother said.

Alex nestled into his mother's lap and looked happily at the cover of his favorite book. "See, Mom," he explained, pointing, "this is the great big steam shovel. And this is where they have to dig the holes."

Alex paused for a moment. Then he asked, "Mom, what are you waiting for? Let's start reading."

SECTION 1

What Is Parenting?

OBJECTIVES

- Describe how parents and other caregivers can encourage a child's development.
- Explain the importance of giving children love and support.
- List techniques for communicating positively with children.

TERMS TO LEARN

deprivation
parenting

Many people spend large parts of their lives caring for children. They become parents of their own children, or they care for other parents' children—as teachers, child care workers, doctors, psychologists, or workers in other fields. All these people need parenting skills. These are skills that, unfortunately, no one is born with—but that, fortunately, everyone can learn.

Parenting: A Learning Process

Unlike parenthood, which is simply a state or condition, **parenting** is a process—*the process of caring for children and helping them grow and learn.*

Parenting is a complicated task. It requires an understanding of a child's needs in all areas, and it requires the family leadership to meet those needs. It involves providing physical care, encouragement, love, support, and guidance. All these should be provided with the goal of helping each child develop to his or her fullest capacity.

How do people qualify to undertake all these tasks? No one has to pass a test to become a parent. There isn't even one right method of parenting. To care for children well, however, a person needs many different parenting skills.

It takes time and practice to develop parenting skills. In addition, the skills a parent or caregiver needs change as children grow up. Infants' needs are different from those of preschoolers or teens. Parents continue to need to adapt their parenting skills at each stage of a child's development. For these reasons, effective caregivers continue to develop parenting skills all their

Parenting begins with physical care, but it does not end there. Love, encouragement, and positive guidance are just as important.

lives. These are some of the steps they take to expand and improve their parenting skills:

- They ask the advice of friends and family members.
- They read books and magazine articles about parenting.
- They observe other parents and children.
- They attend parenting classes.
- They gain experience with children.

Today there is a trend toward more formal training in parenting for those with children of all ages. Parents can take courses in hospitals, at schools, through community organizations, or from private instructors. Many communities have a variety of options for parents who want to learn more about children.

Most of the groups that offer parenting courses do so because they are interested in the healthy growth and development of children. They work to ensure that parents respect the rights of children and know how to nurture, discipline, and guide children in ways that respect these rights.

An important aspect of developing parenting skills is learning to nurture children. A parent or other caregiver nurtures a child by providing encouragement and enriching experiences. Nurturing also involves showing love, support, concern, and understanding.

Parenting courses, offered through hospitals, schools, and community organizations, enable people to learn more about child development and parenting skills.

ASK THE EXPERTS

Learning About Parenting Skills

Jean Illsley Clarke is the director of J.I. Consultants in Minneapolis, Minnesota where she designs and conducts workshops on self-esteem, parenting, and group dynamics.

I'm just beginning to understand what a big job parenting is. I want to start learning and practicing parenting skills now, before I have children of my own. Where can I go to learn more about effective parenting?

You're right about parenting—it is a big job, probably the most important job anyone can undertake. You'll be glad to know that there are many different resources for learning effective parenting skills.

You can learn a lot about effective parenting by watching the parents of young children whom you consider healthy and contented, alert and responsive. When you have the opportunity to observe such a family, notice how the parent responds to the child's words and actions, avoids put-downs, respects the child as an individual, and shows the child love and care. Notice how the parent comforts a sad child and offers protection and information to a frightened child. Notice, too, how the parent accepts a child's anger, insists that no one gets hurt, and helps the angry child express and deal with his or her emotions. Notice how family members have fun together, and watch as the parent helps a child celebrate being happy. As you observe a family, ask yourself, "If I were this child, would this parent's actions, words, and attitudes help me feel secure?" If your answer is yes, consider how you can apply those actions, words, and attitudes in your own relationships with children.

Another good way to learn about effective parenting is to discuss the topic with the parent of a child you admire. Ask that parent to tell you about his or her approach to parenting. You might also ask grandparents—yours or someone else's—to explain how parenting is different today from the parenting practices they remember.

If you enjoy reading, you can get ideas about parenting from books, pamphlets, and magazines. Audiotapes and videotapes can also be good resources. Libraries and schools often loan tapes, as well as books and pamphlets, on many aspects of parenting.

You can also learn a lot about parenting by examining your own childhood. List the things adults did that were helpful for you as a child. Think about how you can do those things to help your own child, in your own way. Then list the things adults did that were not helpful. Consider how you can do things differently, without going too far in the opposite direction.

Gather all the information and ideas about parenting you can find; consider them all and think about what will work for you. Learning about parenting is exciting, and it is an undertaking that can last a lifetime. I believe it is the most important single thing each of us can do.

Jean Illsley Clarke

Jean Illsley Clarke

Understanding Children

Have you ever heard an adult tell a child, "Act your age"? Children usually *do* act their age. The trouble is, parents and other caregivers often do not understand what to expect from children. Learning about children's capabilities, interests, and needs at various ages is an essential first step in helping children develop.

Parents and other caregivers need to have realistic expectations. Giving a preschooler a puzzle that is too difficult will frustrate and discourage the child. An understanding parent or caregiver can help guide the child toward a more suitable activity.

Parents and caregivers who have learned about the various stages all children go through are better able to handle the difficult or unsettling stages when they occur. For example, Liz was bewildered at first because her nine-month-old daughter suddenly began crying whenever a stranger approached. As the crying episodes continued, Liz became more and more impatient with the baby. Then she learned from her own mother that all babies go through a stage of stranger anxiety—a development that indicates babies can distinguish new, strange people from their familiar caregivers. From then on, Liz looked on her daughter's outbursts as a sign of healthy development rather than as a problem.

In addition to recognizing normal patterns of development, parents and other caregivers should learn to understand and respect the differences between children. Some learn to walk earlier than others. Some children need more encouragement to make friends. The more time parents spend interacting with and observing their children, the better they will be able to meet each child's individual needs.

Providing Enrichment and Encouragement

Part of a parent's job is to teach children. Parents are children's first teachers. Children naturally learn by exploring their world, trying new things, and imitating others. Nurturing parents give children the freedom they need in order to learn. They provide positive examples, encouragement, and enriching experiences.

As much as possible, caregivers should eliminate barriers that might prevent children from discovering things on their own. For an infant or a toddler, this means putting away breakable objects, covering up electrical outlets, locking up poisons, and so on. For a preschooler, it might mean letting the child dig for worms without worrying about dirty hands and clothes.

Give children plenty of opportunity for exploratory play. That may mean letting a child get her hands and clothes dirty. The activities that provide the most learning, creativity, and fun are often the messiest.

Enrichment can be provided through everyday objects and experiences. Parents and others who hold and talk to an infant, play with the baby, and give him or her safe objects to look at and handle are stimulating the infant's growth and development. Caregivers can turn daily routines into learning experiences for a child of any age. In a supermarket, for example, a parent can help a three-year-old name objects and colors, smell a ripe pineapple, and learn about how onions grow. A parent might let an older child steer the cart, find certain products, and count change.

Parents should not push children to try activities they are not yet ready for. On the other hand, parents should not hold children back just because they are afraid a child might fail. Trying and failing are part of learning about life. A child's efforts should be acknowledged and praised. Mistakes should be met with understanding and patience. These responses encourage children to try again, no matter what the outcome.

When Children Are Deprived

Unfortunately, some children grow up with parents who have not learned parenting skills and who do not encourage learning. By the time they are four years old, these children are measurably behind others in development. They suffer from **deprivation**, *the lack of a healthy, nurturing environment.*

The words *deprivation* and *poverty* are sometimes mistakenly used to mean the same thing. Children who are deprived may come from families who are wealthy or poor—or anywhere between. To avoid depriving their children, parents need not money, but the know-how, the concern, and the willingness to make time for teaching.

Fortunately, the effects of deprivation are not irreversible. Development that has been delayed by deprivation can be improved once a child's environment is enriched.

Providing Love and Support

In many ways, nurturing is the same as loving. Love is the sum of the caring and positive things we do for the benefit of others. Children need love just as much as they need food to eat and a place to sleep.

Parents can show children their love in many different ways. Hugs, kisses, and smiles are clear indicators of a parent's love. Listening patiently and attentively is another effective way to show love. This lets children know that parents respect their feelings and are concerned about their ideas and interests. Parents can also show love and support by giving time and attention—helping a child fix a broken toy or discussing ways to get along better with a playmate, for example.

Some parents have difficulty showing affection for their children. They may be embarrassed or feel that displays of affection will make their children "too soft." Without a loving parent's recognition of their accomplishments, however, children feel insecure and worthless. They may resort to inappropriate behavior just to get attention. It is difficult for such children to form healthy relationships because they have never learned how to give and receive love.

Overparenting

Some parents become overprotective and overattentive. They tend to shower the child with too much attention, too many toys, and too many treats. Such a parent makes excuses for the child's inappropriate behavior and tries to shield the child from difficult or unpleasant experiences.

An overprotective parent forgets that children learn from trial and error and that mistakes are an essential part of the growth process. A child who has been overparented continues to seek out adult help. He or she lacks the initiative to try out new things independently. Because parents have always made choices for them, such children may have difficulty making decisions on their own.

BUILDING SELF-ESTEEM

Parental Love: The Greatest Gift of all

Think back to your childhood. What do you remember best about your parents and family life? For many people, "it's the little things" that mean the most. Going on camping trips, baking holiday cookies, riding bikes, watching a favorite television program, and participating in other daily rituals. These people feel that spending time together and sharing in the little things in life have been some of the most memorable and enriching family experiences.

Some parents worry, however, that they don't have enough money to give their children the "finer" things in life, a special trip, money for clothes, or a new car. Instead, all parents need to remember that the greatest gift for children can't be wrapped in a package or tied with a bow. It's the love that comes from a warm, nurturing, and caring parent—truly the greatest gift anyone can give to his or her child.

Communicating Positively

Good communication is an important part of the relationship between children and caregivers. Being a good listener is one way to show children that you respect them. The way you talk to children is equally important. Children are most responsive when you speak in kind, respectful tones and use simple language.

Techniques for good communication depend somewhat on a child's age, but include:

- Get on the child's level. Sit or kneel so that you are eye-to-eye with the child.
- Be simple. Use words the child can understand.
- Be clear. Think in terms of the child's point of view.
- Be positive and polite. Hearing a constant series of "don'ts" is discouraging. Try saying, "Please shut the door quietly."
- Give praise and love. Everyone needs to hear good things about themselves, but especially impressionable young children. Remember, too, that a smile or hug can often say more than words.

Using good communication skills has many benefits. It can help you avoid conflict and misunderstanding. When communication is based on mutual respect and love, children learn to value their own thoughts and ideas. They also learn to respect other people's opinions. Open, trusting communication is the foundation for a good lifelong relationship between parent and child.

SECTION 1 REVIEW

CHECK YOUR UNDERSTANDING

1. What is the difference between parenting and parenthood?
2. List four steps caregivers can take to expand and improve their parenting skills.
3. How does a parent or other caregiver nurture a child?
4. What is deprivation?
5. Why is it important for parents to show affection for their children?
6. What is overparenting? What negative effects can overparenting have on children?
7. List five guidelines to follow when communicating with young children.

DISCUSS AND DISCOVER

1. Do you know anyone who seems to be a "natural parent"? If so, what makes you consider that person such a good parent? Where do you think he or she learned parenting skills? What do you consider the most important influence on an individual's parenting skills? Why?
2. With a group of classmates, brainstorm a list of resources parents and prospective parents can use in gathering relevant information about child development. Then organize your list of resources from most accessible to least accessible.

Guiding Children's Behavior

SECTION 2

OBJECTIVES

- Discuss effective techniques for encouraging appropriate behavior.
- Explain how and why to set limits.
- Discuss effective ways of dealing with misbehavior.

TERMS TO LEARN

conscience
discipline
negative reinforcement
positive reinforcement
self-discipline
time-out

One of the most challenging aspects of a parent's job is **discipline**, *the task of helping children learn to behave in acceptable ways*. The term *discipline*, when understood in this way, means the same as the term *guidance*—both refer to directing children toward acceptable forms of behavior.

Understanding Discipline

Some people think of discipline only in terms of punishment. Actually, punishment is just a small part of effective guidance. It should be used only when necessary and only in specific ways, as you will learn. Furthermore, discipline does not mean "making children behave." Children cannot be forced to act according to adult standards. However, when caregivers combine firmness with understanding, children can learn to control their actions.

This learning process is a very important part of a child's development. It relates to the child's emotional and social development. Effective guidance helps children learn to get along with others and to deal with their own feelings in acceptable ways. It promotes security and a positive feeling about self.

Guidance is also part of moral development. Very young children understand right and wrong only in terms of being praised or scolded. Gradually, children begin to understand *why* certain actions are right or wrong. They develop a **conscience**, *an inner sense of what is right*.

The ultimate goal of discipline is to help children achieve **self-discipline**, *the ability to control one's own behavior*. Effective guidance helps children learn, to direct their own behavior in a responsible way. In the process, children learn how to make decisions, and take responsibility for their actions. Discipline is important to the child's task of gaining independence.

Self-discipline develops gradually. It shows whenever a child behaves appropriately without having to be told how by a caregiver.

These are three keys to effective discipline:

- Encouraging appropriate behavior.
- Setting and enforcing limits.
- Dealing with inappropriate behavior in effective ways.

Encouraging Appropriate Behavior

Put yourself in the place of a young child. Suppose no one ever explains what kind of behavior is expected or praises you for doing the right thing. Every so often, you are punished for something. Perhaps it is for talking too loudly in a movie theater one day and for pulling someone's hair the next day. How are you likely to respond? A child cannot learn anything constructive from that kind of situation. A child would have no way of understanding what kinds of behavior are considered wrong and what kinds of behavior are expected instead.

Discipline that is practiced only after a child has done something wrong has little chance of success. To be effective, discipline should begin with encouraging appropriate behavior through examples, explanations, praise, and choices.

Setting a Good Example

Children are great imitators. Children learn best by being shown what to do rather than by just being told. For instance, parents who want their child to talk politely to others should set a good example by talking politely themselves to all the people they have contact with.

The desire to imitate applies to all the examples set for children—not just the good examples. For example, five-year-old Mark notices that his parents and his older sister all tell occasional lies to their friends. Is it any wonder that Mark rebels when his parents remind him, "Always tell the truth"?

Matthew needs to be shown—not just told—that a real dog should be handled more gently than a stuffed toy.

Telling What Is Expected

Children need to be told what is expected of them in ways they can understand. At first, it is not necessary to explain the reasons for expected behavior. For a one-year-old, the instruction "Pat the doggy," combined with a demonstration of gentle handling, is enough.

Around the age of three, children begin to understand simple reasoning. Then this might be a more helpful direction: "It hurts the dog when you pull his tail. If you want to play with him, you will have to be gentle." Understanding why the behavior is necessary makes it easier for children this age and older to follow the rules.

Praising Appropriate Behavior

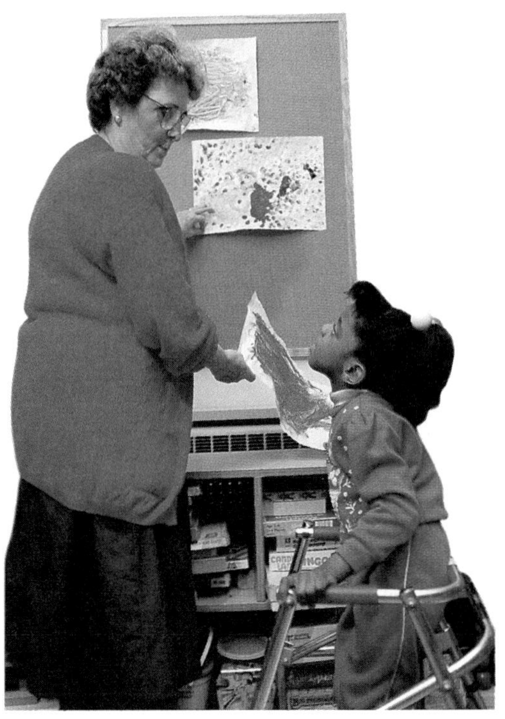

Giving praise is an excellent way to provide encouragement. Praise helps children feel good about themselves. It also makes them want to continue the desired behavior. Praise is an example of what researchers call **positive reinforcement**, *a response that encourages a particular behavior*. When children associate their actions with a reward, such as attention and praise, they are likely to repeat those actions.

These guidelines can help you offer children effective, encouraging praise:

- **Be specific.** Focus on what the child is doing appropriately. For example, you might say, "You remembered to brush your teeth, didn't you? I'm proud of you!"
- **Be sincere and positive.** Children are quick to sense when praise is false or halfhearted. A mumbled "That's nice" or "You didn't mess up too much this time" can't be genuinely encouraging.
- **Give the praise as soon as possible.** A compliment given for something done the previous day has little meaning for a child. When praise is given soon after the desired behavior, the child is able to associate the two.
- **Tailor the praise to the needs of the child.** For example, many children need encouraging praise when they manage to sit quietly and listen to stories. However, a child who also remains silent during a sing-along doesn't need praise for being quiet during the story time. Observing children can help caregivers know which behaviors need to be encouraged.

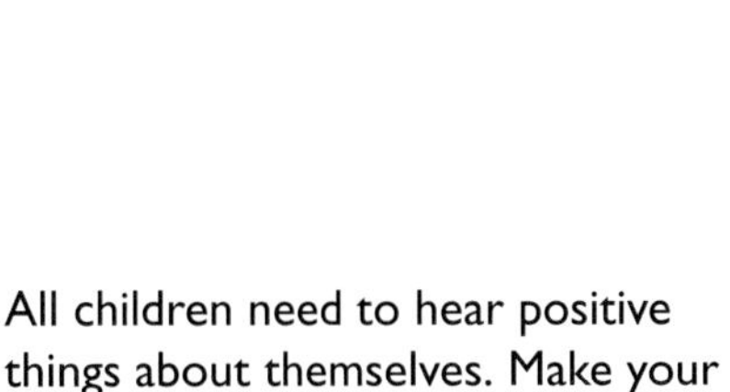

All children need to hear positive things about themselves. Make your praise specific and sincere.

Offering Choices

As children become more mature, they should be allowed to make some decisions about their behavior. This helps them learn that they are responsible for their own actions. It also minimizes feelings of frustration. A parent or other caregiver, rather than making demands, can offer the child a choice and respect the child's decision.

For example, three-year-old Gavin sometimes hits his younger sister. To encourage appropriate behavior, his parent might say, "You seem to be angry with Sonya. I know sometimes she wants to play with the same toy you do, and that makes you angry. I cannot allow you to hurt her. Would you like to choose one of your toys she can play with, or would you like me to sit down and build a house with both of you?"

A caregiver should offer only alternatives that are readily available and should make sure the child's choice is carried out. Whatever choice the child makes, it must be honored. If it is not, the child will lose trust in the parent.

When examples, simple instructions, praise, and choices are combined, efforts to improve the child's behavior are likely to succeed.

Being told that you can't do somethng isn't quite so bad if you can choose what to do instead.

PARENTING IN ACTION

Encouraging Appropriate Behavior

Becky was frustrated because her four-year-old son Jamal never put his toys away. Sometimes Becky put them away herself. Most of the time, however, she was too busy to worry about the toys, and they were simply left out. When friends or relatives came by, Becky was embarrassed by the mess. Her scoldings upset Jamal but did little to solve the problem.

Finally, Becky tried a new approach. One evening before bathtime, she sat down with Jamal as he played. She explained, "Jamal, if you pick up your toys after you've finished playing with them, they won't become lost or broken. I'll help you put the toys away and show you where they go. Should we start with the blocks or the train set?"

Though he was reluctant at first, Jamal soon became interested in this new game. When they were finished, Becky said, "Thank you for putting your toys away. You did a good job."

This scene was repeated on the following evenings. Jamal was more than willing to please his mother once he had been shown how. After a few weeks, he was able to put the toys away all by himself. Occasional reminders were all he needed.

Becky also found that handling the situation this way reduced her own frustration. Although the house was indeed much neater now, she no longer got upset if things were not perfectly orderly at all times. Both she and Jamal were happier.

THINK AND DISCUSS

1. What did Jamal learn from Becky's earlier approach to the problem of his toys? What new techniques did she use to encourage him to put his toys away?
2. What might have happened if Becky had started putting Jamal's toys away on her own? What might have happened if she had insisted that Jamal put his toys away without her help?
3. How did this solution benefit Jamal? How did it benefit Becky?

Setting Limits

Setting limits is another way to guide children toward appropriate, safe behavior. The term *limits* may refer to physical restrictions, such as preventing a child from crossing the street. Another kind of limit is a rule of behavior: "We don't hit other people."

As children grow older they need fewer restrictions, especially when they show they will follow rules.

"Yes, you may ride the bike, but you must wear this helmet." Setting limits for activities helps create conditions that are right and safe for the child.

What Should the Limits Be?

In deciding on specific limits, parents and other caregivers often follow this general guideline: Limits should keep children from hurting themselves, other people, or property. The specific limits that a parent or other caregiver sets will depend on the individual child. Children will respect and follow limits if they are few and reasonable. When setting limits, parents and other caregivers should keep these questions in mind:

- Does the limit allow the child to learn, explore, and grow? Too much restriction hinders development.
- Is the limit fair and appropriate for the child's age? A toddler might be restricted to a fenced-in yard. By school age, the same child may be permitted to walk to school alone and to visit a friend who lives down the street.
- Does the limit benefit the child, or is it merely for adults' convenience? Restrictions should not be placed on behavior simply because that kind of behavior interferes with an adult's orderly routine.

Making Limits Clear

Limits should be simple and briefly stated—for example, "We walk inside the house. Running is done outside." Be prepared to repeat the limits or rules several times. Young children do not realize that the same rule applies to different situations.

The most useful limits are those that a child can succeed in following. For example, restricting three-year-old Julie to splashing her sister "just a little" during pool playtime is not a useful limit. A three-year-old doesn't yet have the experience to know what "just a little" splashing is. More than likely, "a little" will soon become what an adult considers "a lot" without Julie's ever recognizing any difference. A better limit in this case would be "no splashing." A three-year-old can understand what that means and can succeed in complying with that limit.

Limits should be presented to the child in a calm, direct tone of voice that indicates the limit is real and to be respected. When introducing a limit, it is best to follow these steps:

- **Be understanding of the child's desires.** "I know you think it's fun to draw on the wall."
- **Set the limit, and explain it.** "You may not draw on the wall. We use paper to draw on."
- **Acknowledge the child's feelings.** "I know you may not be happy with this, but sometimes I must make rules."
- **Give alternatives.** "You may draw on this piece of paper, or you may play with your blocks. Which would you like to do?"

Once established and explained, limits should be firmly and consistently enforced. Children respect their parents more if they know their parents stick to the rules. Parents who give in teach their children that they do not mean what they say.

When you explain limits to a child, use language that is simple and clear. Although you should be firm, avoid scolding or belittling the child.

Dealing with Inappropriate Behavior

No matter how much adults do to encourage appropriate behavior, all children misbehave sometimes. Parents and other caregivers must deal with this misbehavior appropriately and effectively.

One thing that determines how a caregiver should respond to misbehavior is the child's age. A one-year-old who bites another child can be told, "No! Don't bite," but the child should not be expected to understand the meaning of his or her action. Behavior at this age can best be controlled by distraction. On the other hand, a four-year-old is capable of understanding that biting is unacceptable behavior and can be expected to control any urges to bite another person.

These are the questions a caregiver should ask when responding to a child's misbehavior:

- Does the child understand that the behavior is wrong?
- Was the behavior intentional (done on purpose), or was it simply beyond the child's control?

To this child, a cat's tail looks like a convenient handle to grab. Would this be intentional or unintentional misbehavior?

Unintentional Misbehavior

With children of any age, misbehavior is sometimes unintentional. For example, a three-year-old may cry or whine if forced to wait a long time for food at a restaurant. This is a natural reaction to being hungry, not deliberate misbehavior. A young child simply does not have the patience of an adult in that situation. Similarly, a child may drop a glass of milk that is too heavy, or accidentally break a vase that should have been put out of reach. These examples of misbehavior, because they are unintentional, should not be punished.

Misbehavior is also unintentional if the child had no way of knowing it was wrong. For example, while playing in the park, Tyler picked a flower and brought it to his father. Tyler's father did not get angry with him or scold him. Instead, Tyler's father explained that the flowers in the park were for everyone to look at and enjoy, not to pick. Since this limit had never been presented to him before, Tyler was not deliberately misbehaving.

Using Punishment Effectively

When children deliberately do something that they know is wrong, some form of punishment may be necessary. Punishment is **negative reinforcement**, *a response that tends to discourage a particular behavior from being repeated*. Punishing should never take the place of encouraging appropriate behavior and setting clear limits. When used with good judgment, however, punishment can be a part of positive and effective discipline.

Being careless near traffic is an example of misbehavior that can be dangerous. In this situation, letting the child suffer the natural consequences is not an appropriate means of discipline.

The first time a child breaks a rule, the parent or caregiver may choose to give a warning rather than punishment. Even a child who usually has good self-control occasionally makes mistakes. Mistakes are especially likely under unusual circumstances, such as the excitement of a birthday party.

Punishment should be in proportion to the seriousness of the misbehavior. A relatively minor offense, such as forgetting to put away a bicycle one time, does not deserve a severe punishment. In this case, it might be fair for the child to have to give up using the bicycle for a day—but not for a whole week.

Reasonable punishment will not cause a child to resent his or her parents—as long as the parent has established a positive, mutual relationship of love and respect with the child. The parent should also be careful to make clear that he or she disapproves of the child's behavior but continues to approve of the child as a person. Children must be assured that their parents love them and want to help them learn how to behave properly.

Following are some useful techniques for dealing with inappropriate behavior. These techniques can be used in many situations.

- **Natural consequences.** Sometimes it is punishment enough for a child to suffer the consequences, or natural results, of his or her own misbehavior. For example, although her grandmother has called her twice to come to dinner, Sandra does not respond. Sandra's grandmother does not ask the other family members to wait any longer, nor does she save seconds of mashed potatoes for the child. Instead, her grandmother lets Sandra eat by herself when she does finally come to the table. Next time, Sandra will be more likely to come when called.

- **Loss of privileges.** In some cases, the natural consequences of a child's actions are not appropriate to use as punishment. For example, suppose a five-year-old keeps running into the street while playing. The natural consequences of that behavior are likely to be serious injuries. A good way to deal with this situation might be to give a warning that if the child runs into the street again, there will be no more outdoor play that day. This type of punishment is most effective for children five or older. The privilege that is taken away should always be related to the misbehavior so that the child associates the two.

For older children, "time out" might mean going to a quiet place to think about what happened and why what they did was wrong.

- **Ignoring misbehavior.** Sometimes a child misbehaves simply to get attention. As long as the behavior is not harmful, the best "punishment" is to ignore the child. Any other reaction will give the child the desired attention and make it likely that the behavior will be repeated.
- **Time-out.** Another way to respond to misbehavior is to use a **time-out,** *a short period of time spent sitting away from the presence of others or from the center of activity.* Some families have a "time-out chair." This is a place where the child must sit for a short time until he or she can settle down enough to return to playing. It is important to explain the purpose of this isolation. For example, the caregiver can say, "You are angry and you're not acting appropriately. You need time to calm down. You may return to playing with the others when you can do so without hitting." A time-out is an effective method of discipline because it reinforces the idea that the child must learn to control his or her own behavior.

Poor Disciplinary Measures

Some methods of punishment should be avoided. These methods are not effective in helping children learn self-discipline:

- **Don't rely on spanking or other forms of physical punishment.** Most child care experts recommend that parents and other caregivers avoid spanking children. While spanking may stop misbehavior for the moment, it doesn't help the child learn proper behavior. It is also demeaning, both for the parent and for the child. Parents sometimes use spanking as a way to vent their own anger and frustration. This sets a poor example. The child simply learns that it's all right to use hitting and fighting instead of learning how to control strong emotions.
- **Don't threaten to withhold love.** When a parent says, "I won't love you anymore if you don't stop hitting your brother," the child is left with a fear of being rejected and abandoned. Withholding love doesn't show the child how to correct misbehavior. It merely fills the child with needless anxiety.
- **Don't offer bribes.** Bribing a child with a special treat if he or she stops misbehaving is not an effective method of discipline. Instead of learning self-control, the child learns to look for an external reward for good behavior.
- **Don't make the child promise to behave.** In the process of learning to control their behavior, children will naturally

make mistakes. When a promise has been made, the child may feel forced to lie about misbehavior rather than disappoint someone he or she loves.

- **Don't try to control the child through shame or guilt.** When a child misbehaves, it is natural for the parent to feel anger and disappointment. These feelings should be expressed, but calmly and reasonably. Parents should be careful to avoid ridiculing the child's mistakes. They should not use responses such as these: "How could you do a thing like that?" or "If this keeps up, you'll never amount to anything." Instead, a parent might say, "I know you're feeling bad about what happened. Let's see how we can make things better."
- **Don't shout or yell in an attempt to control the child's behavior.** Like spanking, yelling only reinforces a child's sense of powerlessness. A loud, harsh voice often frightens a child into compliance. It cannot, however, help the child develop an understanding of appropriate behavior.

Handling Conflict

Discipline can create conflict between parents and children. Children may feel angry when they can't get their way. Parents must be prepared to deal with this anger. They should not make the child feel guilty about his or her anger; everyone in a family must remember that anger is a normal emotion.

Parent-child chats about acceptable behavior can be a time to reinforce both consistent discipline and loving reassurance.

Instead of encouraging guilt, parents should give children an opportunity to discuss the conflict and to express their anger. It may help to discuss the misbehavior and the punishment some time after the incident. In this discussion, the parent can help the child understand why he or she misbehaved. The parent can also explain what the child should have done instead and can offer reassurance and encouragement.

Parents should allow the child to express his or her feelings about a situation. They should then agree on any discipline needed.

Consistency

Being consistent is the key to guiding children's behavior. Consistency helps children learn the limits of behavior. It helps them know what is expected of them and what responses to expect from their parents. This knowledge helps children feel secure.

Children lose trust and confidence in a parent or caregiver who constantly changes limits or fails to enforce limits in a consistent manner. If a parent or caregiver laughs at a child's behavior one day and punishes the same behavior the next day, the child will feel confused and insecure. When more than one person cares for a child, they should agree in advance on limits and on methods of enforcing those limits. If caregivers do not agree, children quickly learn to use the inconsistency to their own advantage.

SECTION 2 REVIEW

CHECK YOUR UNDERSTANDING

1. What is discipline?
2. What is the ultimate goal of discipline? What does that involve?
3. List three keys to effective discipline.
4. List four guidelines for praising a child's good behavior.
5. List three questions parents should ask themselves as they choose specific limits for children.
6. List two questions parents should ask themselves before responding to a child's misbehavior.
7. What does a child learn from being spanked?

DISCUSS AND DISCOVER

1. Do you think it is possible to raise a child without using any form of punishment? Why or why not? If you think punishment is necessary, which form do you consider most effective? Why? How and when do you think that kind of punishment should be used?
2. How does the discipline of parents and caregivers help a child develop self-discipline? What effect do you think punishment has on the development of self-discipline? Why?

SECTION 3

Providing Substitute Care

OBJECTIVES

- Explain the need for substitute care.
- Describe the types of substitute care available.

TERMS TO LEARN

child care aide
child care center
family child care
Head Start
latchkey children
Montessori preschool
nanny
parent cooperative
play group
preschool

One of the responsibilities of parents is providing quality substitute care when they must be away from their children. In some families, substitute care is needed only occasionally. However, an increasing number of parents depend on others to care for their children on a regular basis.

The Need for Substitute Care

There are several reasons for the trend toward placing children in substitute care:

- Many children live in one-parent homes, and the single parent typically has a full-time job. In this situation, the parent usually needs full-time or at least part-time substitute child care.
- In many two-parent families, both parents work away from home. Unless the parents have different work schedules, the children usually need substitute care.
- Some parents who do provide full-time care for their own children at home feel that their children can benefit from the social aspects of a preschool. In such situations, the young child usually attends a child care facility two or three times a week.

Types of Substitute Care

Parents who are faced with finding substitute care must choose wisely from the many types of child care services available. All provide the child with physical care and a place to play. Some also include planned activities to encourage the child's physical, emotional, social, and intellectual development. A few also provide health and social services for the child and, in some cases, for the family as well.

Child care services are provided in two general settings. Some services are offered in a home. Others are provided in a child care center. Within these two basic categories, each type of care has its own advantages and disadvantages. Finding the best type of care for the individual child is extremely important for the child's future and for the parents' peace of mind.

Home-Based Care

Many young children receive substitute care in their own home or in another family's home. Care in a home setting may be easier for a child to get used to because the surroundings are familiar. Home-based care may also be more readily available and convenient for parents. Usually, it involves a smaller group of children than center-based care. This makes it an especially good choice for infants and other children who need a great deal of individual attention. There are three main types of home-based care:

The growing need for quality substitute child care has revived the nineteenth-century tradition of the nanny. The nanny lives with the family and is trained in all aspects of child development and child care.

- **Care in the child's own home.** Many parents prefer to have their child cared for by someone who comes to their own home. Almost all parents make use of this type of care at least occasionally, as for an evening out. Many parents also use it on a regular basis. In-home care is especially convenient. However, it can be costly, and it does not usually provide an opportunity for playing with other children outside the family.

  The caregiver may be a member of the child's extended family, a friend, or a babysitter. A less common alternative is to employ a live-in child care provider. Although a live-in arrangement is relatively expensive, it has the advantage of making reliable care available at almost any time of day or night.

  The need for quality substitute care has revived the nineteenth-century tradition of the **nanny**, *a specially trained person employed to provide live-in child care services.* Many modern nannies have completed a course of academic study in all areas of child development and care. They may have also completed a period of supervised on-the-job training. Among those who can afford their services, nannies are in high demand.

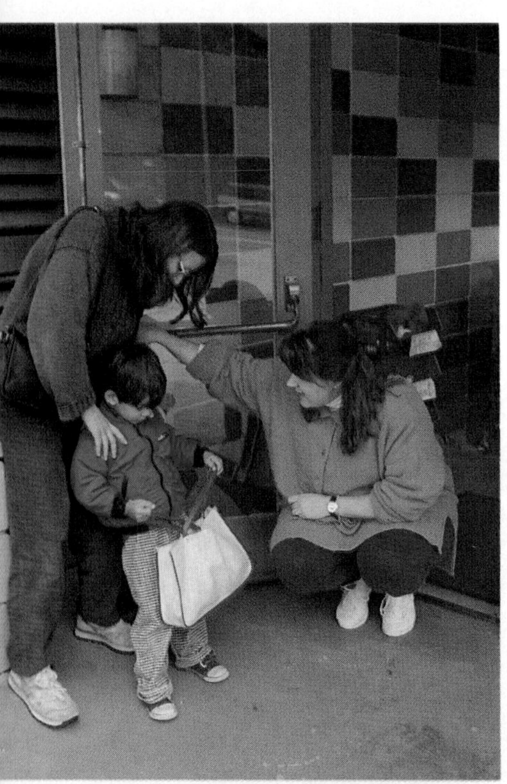

Quality family child care programs are licensed. They must meet minimum health and safety requirements and are limited to the number of children they can accept.

- **Family child care.** For some young children, parents choose **family child care**, *a child care arrangement in which a small number of children are cared for in the caregiver's home.* Family child care combines the familiarity of a home setting with opportunities for social play and learning. Since the group size is small, all the children can be given individual attention. The cost of family child care is usually less than for care in the child's own home.

- **Play groups.** A **play group** is *a child care arrangement in which a group of parents take turns caring for each other's children in their own homes.* A play group is similar to family child care, but it involves a number of different homes and caregivers. The children are usually brought to the home of the parent who is providing care. Most play groups involve no fees. This type of substitute care is often a good choice for parents who do not work full-time.

Quality home-based care includes a daily routine of quiet and active times. Both planned activities and informal play are included. Caregivers should participate with the children in some of their activities. At other times, the caregivers should supervise as the children play by themselves. In no care setting should the children simply be placed in front of a television set or left without supervision.

Center-Based Care

Many communities have facilities in which a staff of several adults care for one or more groups of children. These child care centers vary widely in their hours of operation; in the size, training, and experience of the staff; in the ages of children accepted; in the activities, equipment, and play areas provided; and in fees charged.

Some child care centers are businesses run for profit. Others charge fees to cover expenses but do not try to make a profit. Still others are funded by the city, state, or federal government. Care at government-funded centers may be offered free or at a reduced cost to those who qualify.

Child care centers must meet minimum health and safety requirements in order to be licensed. The license also limits the number of children a center may accept, depending on space, facilities, and the size of the staff.

These are the most common types of center-based child care:

- **Child care centers.** A **child care center** is *a facility designed primarily to provide care for children of working parents.* A variety of activities is typically offered at a child care center. Some centers may emphasize specific learning activities, while others may allow more time for informal play. Usually, there is a daily routine with time set aside for indoor and outdoor play, meals, and naps. Most child care centers are designed for children aged two years and older. Some centers provide care for infants.

Center-based care allows children to have social interaction and learning experiences under the guidance of a trained adult.

- **Preschools.** A **preschool** is *a child care center that provides educational programs, usually for children aged three to five.* A preschool typically offers activities designed to enrich the child's development in all areas. For example, there may be games to help children improve motor skills, language skills, and social skills. Art, music, and science activities may be a regular part of the program. The staff usually includes one or more teachers and a number of aides. (A **child care aide** is *an assistant to the person in charge of a child care program.*)

  Usually, a preschool operates half-day sessions two or more days a week. Some centers combine nursery school and a child care program as a convenience for working parents.

- **Parent cooperatives.** A **parent cooperative** is *a child care facility in which part of the supervision is provided by the parents of enrolled children, who take turns donating their services.* While they are helping supervise the children, the parents are guided by a preschool teacher or other qualified caregiver who organizes the program. A parent cooperative offers several important advantages. Working at the center helps

The federal government began the Head Start program in the 1960s. It continues in operation today, offering lower-income families a program to enhance the development of their children.

Montessori preschools provide an exploratory child care program that is less structured.

parents understand their child's development. In addition, a parent cooperative provides relatively inexpensive care. However, this type of care is rarely suitable for a parent who works full-time.

- **Head Start centers.** In the 1960s, the federal government began **Head Start**, *a program of locally operated child care facilities designed to help lower-income and disadvantaged children function effectively at home, in school, and in the community.* Most Head Start centers serve three- to five-year-olds.

  Head Start offers a variety of activities that enhance development. In addition, it offers meals that provide one-third to one-half of a child's daily nutritional needs. Head Start also provides health care and social services, such as counseling, for both parents and children. Parents are expected to become actively involved in the Head Start program.

- **Montessori preschools.** Some child care centers provide a specialized program that is different from the traditional preschool. An example is the **Montessori preschool**, *an educational facility for three- to six-year-olds that provides special learning materials which children are free to explore on their own.* This type of program is named for Dr. Maria Montessori, the founder of the methods used. In a Montessori classroom, the children are encouraged to explore the materials and to move from one activity to another as they wish.

Care for Older Children

Infants, toddlers, and preschoolers are not the only children who need substitute care. Many school-aged children also need care. They may have a gap of several hours between the time school lets out and the time parents arrive home from work.

Some children do not receive substitute care during these after-school hours. Often this is because affordable care is not available. It is estimated that our country now has at least two million **latchkey children**, *children who are unsupervised from the time they come home from school until their parents return from work.* If their parents leave for work early, these children may also be alone before school.

Child care experts advise against leaving children without adult supervision before the teen years. An increasing number of school, community groups, and nonprofit agencies are arranging activities to fill the parenting gap for latchkey children. These programs include supervised recreation, such as games, films, and art projects. Children may also do homework, read, or rest. Some programs provide before-school supervision, including breakfast.

Choosing Substitute Care

Which type of child care is best for an individual child? There are no easy answers. Parents must consider many factors. The types of care available locally, the costs, the convenience, and the particular needs of the child will all influence the decision.

It is essential that the parents visit each home or child care center they are considering. The child should be taken along on these visits, because the child's happiness and well-being are among the most important considerations. As they evaluate each care facility, parents might use the checklist on page 87 as a guide.

Once the parents have chosen a child care facility, they should drop by unexpectedly from time to time. These visits can help make the parent confident that the care is and remains as it was promised. After the child has attended the program for two or three weeks, the parent can ask the child how he or she feels about it. The child's happiness is the most dependable indicator of quality in child care.

Most children enjoy a quality preschool environment that promotes healthy social interaction. In what other ways do these children benefit from this outdoor environment?

CHECKLIST FOR EVALUATING QUALITY CARE

THE CAREGIVER

- How many children are there for each caregiver?
- Do the caregivers seem to have time for each child?
- What type of training or experience has the caregiver had?
- Is the caregiver warm and loving toward the children? Calm and patient?
- Does the caregiver provide and direct activities well?
- Does the caregiver participate with the children frequently and respond to their questions?
- Do you agree with the caregiver's child-rearing attitudes and with the methods of discipline used?
- Does the caregiver seem to understand and respond to children's individual needs?
- Does the caregiver regularly take time to talk with parents about their children?

THE PROGRAM AND FACILITIES

- Where do the children eat, sleep, and play? Are the areas safe, comfortable, and sanitary?
- What kinds of social and learning opportunities are provided?
- Are books, toys, and large-play equipment available?
- Are children encouraged to participate in a variety of activities?
- Is there enough indoor and outdoor space for the children to play without crowding?
- If meals or snacks are provided, are they nutritious?
- Are the rules and routines reasonable? Are they easy for children to understand?
- What arrangements will be made if the caregiver is away or ill? What arrangements are made for children who are ill?

OVERALL IMPRESSIONS

- Do the children seem to be involved and happy?
- If you were a child, would you like to spend time there?

The Effects of Substitute Child Care

Professionals in all areas of child care and development agree that emotional and intellectual development are directly influenced by a child's environment and experiences, beginning at birth. These professionals consider parents a child's best source of love and learning.

Many child development specialists advise that a parent should stay home to provide child care for as long as possible. For many parents, however, the longest possible options for staying home may not extend more than a few weeks beyond the child's birth. Extended maternity or paternity leave is not an option for many working parents. Does this mean that parents must choose between having an income to pay household bills and giving their child a good start in life?

Fortunately, parents do not usually have to make this kind of choice. Long-term studies find that good substitute care has no adverse effects on children's intellectual and emotional development. The key, of course, is finding good substitute care. Parents must spend time, care, and effort selecting a substitute caregiver for their child. The best caregiver is someone who enjoys the child and spends time playing with him or her. In a group facility, there should be a warm, caring atmosphere and enough staff to provide each child with individual attention.

A COMMUNITY OF FAMILIES

Many parents worry about how the emotional and social development of their children will be affected by having multiple caregivers. Reassurance comes from research that suggests the number of caregivers is not as important as the stability and responsiveness of those caregivers. A study of children raised in an Israeli kibbutz, for example, supports this idea. In the kibbutz, young children are raised communally by several caregivers. The children stay in residential nurseries and see their parents only a few hours a day or even just on the weekends. These children show normal, healthy development, both emotionally and socially, as long as the caregivers are sensitive and responsive.

Whether a child is cared for in a private home or in a child care center, parents may choose to drop in periodically to check the facility and its care.

Quality child care programs recognize the need they are filling and the influence they have on the physical and emotional development of children. Parents can improve the quality of child care by making their particular needs and wants known. Active involvement helps parents and other concerned individuals ensure that their expectations for quality child care are being met.

Child care centers often provide children with opportunities they might not otherwise have. Children can take part in a variety of planned learning activities. Some child care centers encourage parent participation.

SECTION 3 REVIEW

CHECK YOUR UNDERSTANDING

1. List three reasons for the trend toward placing children in substitute care.
2. What is a nanny?
3. How is family child care different from a play group? How are the the two kinds of care similar?
4. List one advantage and one disadvantage of a parent cooperative.
5. Who are latchkey children? What special needs do they have?
6. List four factors that influence a parent's decision about child care.
7. List four questions parents should try to answer during a visit to a child care facility they are considering.

DISCUSS AND DISCOVER

1. Working with a group of other students, gather information about child care facilities in your community. Organize your information into listings of home-based care facilities and center-based care facilities. Include the address and phone number of each facility, as well as basic information about ages of children they accept and hours of operation. Make your listings available to interested parents.
2. What makes the selection of substitute care for children an especially difficult decision for parents? What factors do you think influence the choices parents make? Why do different families make different decisions about substitute care?

SUMMARY

- Acquiring parenting skills is a lifelong learning process.
- Caregivers who understand children and their individual differences are better able to promote healthy development.
- Children need encouragement, enriching experiences, love, and support.
- Good behavior should be encouraged through examples, simple explanations, praise, and reasonable choices.
- Children want and need reasonable limits on their behavior.
- A child's misbehavior should be handled calmly in a manner appropriate to the situation.
- Many different types of substitute child care, both home-based and center-based, are available.

REVIEWING THE FACTS

1. List four places where formal training in parenting is often offered.
2. Why should parents and other caregivers learn about the various stages all children go through?
3. How should parents and other caregivers respond to a child's mistakes? Why?
4. How are discipline and punishment related? What are the differences between the two?
5. What is a conscience?
6. Why is it so important for parents and other caregivers to set a good example for children?
7. What is positive reinforcement? What is negative reinforcement? Give an example of each.
8. List two reasons for allowing children to make decisions about their own behavior.
9. List four methods of punishment that parents and other caregivers should avoid using.
10. What is the difference between a play group and a parent cooperative?
11. What do long-term studies show about the effects of substitute care on the development of children?

EXPLORING FURTHER

1. Find out about parenting classes offered in your community. Note when and where the classes are offered. Also find out who is welcome in the classes and what fee, if any, is charged. Then make fliers or posters to share the information you have gathered. (Section 1)
2. Read a magazine article that deals with disciplining children. What definition of discipline is stated or implied in the article? What approaches are recommended? Why? What do you think of the attitudes expressed in the article.? Discuss your ideas with classmates. (Section 2)
3. Working with a group of classmates, prepare and administer a questionnaire to gather data about the use of substitute child care in your community. Decide what kinds of information you want, and plan questions to elicit that kind of information. Finally, summarize the information in a graph or chart, and post that summary in your classroom. (Section 3)
4. Gather information about a Head Start program in your area. When was it established? Whom does it serve? How is it regarded by the families whose children attend it? How is it regarded by teachers at the elementary school the program graduates attend? Prepare and present a short oral report of the information you have gathered. (Section 3)

THINKING CRITICALLY

1. **Evaluate.** What might cause a parent to have trouble expressing love for his or her own child? How do you think a parent should try to deal with this difficulty? Do you think the parent should focus on the source of his or her own problem or focus on changing his or her behavior? Why? Some parents who have difficulty showing affection say, "It's all right—the kids know I love them, no matter what I say or do." Do you agree? Why or why not?
2. **Compare.** React to this statement: "It doesn't really matter what kind of discipline parents use, as long as they teach their children how to behave." Compare your response with your classmates.
3. **Analyze.** Discuss and defend your ideas in response to these questions: Do you believe children really want parents and other caregivers to set limits? If so, at what age do you believe people no longer want limits imposed by others? If not, why do you think parents and other caregivers continue to set limits?

CROSS-CURRICULUM CONNECTIONS

1. **Science.** Research B. F. Skinner's classic studies on operant conditioning. Write a brief report on these studies, noting particularly how they relate to effective discipline techniques.
2. **Speaking.** Read *The Montessori Method* by Maria Montessori, or read a summary of Montessori's educational theories. Then visit a Montessori preschool, and observe the children and teachers. Prepare and present an oral report, discussing the concepts of Montessori preschools and the application of those concepts in the school you visited.

OBSERVING AND PARTICIPATING

Guiding Children

Parents and caregivers have the opportunity to guide children's behavior through their words, actions, and tone of voice. You will notice that children respond best when parents and caregivers are relaxed and confident around them.

Select one of the following activities, and spend some time observing or participating with children. Write about your observations in your journal, and discuss your ideas with classmates.

- **Observing.** Observe young children and their caregivers in a public place, such as a park, a playground, or a shopping mall. Notice instances in which caregivers encourage appropriate behavior by using positive reinforcement. How often do you see this technique being used? How successful does it appear to be?
- **Observing.** Observe young children in a public place, such as a fast-food restaurant, a shopping mall, or a park. Notice examples of behavior that you consider inappropriate. What seems to cause that behavior? How do parents and caregivers respond to that behavior? With what effect?
- **Participating.** Take care of a five- or six-year-old for an afternoon. Discuss discipline and limits both with the child's parents and, as appropriate, with the child. What limits is the child expected to observe? How does the child seem to respond to these limits? How easy—or difficult—is it for you to enforce those limits?

CHAPTER 4

Teen Pregnancy and Parenthood

Linda stared blankly out the window and faintly heard her mother calling in the background. "Come on, Linda, you'll be late for school."

"That's the last place I want to be," grumbled Linda without moving.

She thought about her class yesterday and could hear her social studies teacher, Mr. Adams tell the class, "The teen years are supposed to be the best time of your life. They are a time for exploring possibilities, interacting with many different groups of people, and making choices about the future."

"Sure. Maybe for some teens, but not for me!" Linda mumbled. "My life has become so complicated—ever since I met Tim. He has me confused. He said he would respect my decision. So, yesterday I finally tell him 'No' and now he won't talk to me. I know his friends are laughing at me. It's going to be a miserable day."

"Linda," called her mother.

"Yeah Mom, I'm coming," Linda said as she left her room.

SECTION 1

Making Responsible Decisions

OBJECTIVES

- Discuss what sexuality does—and does not—involve.
- Explain the relationship between values and sexuality.
- List the steps in the decision-making process.
- Discuss how teens can approach decisions about sexual activity.
- Explain how pregnancy can be prevented.

TERMS TO LEARN

abstinence
consequences
contraception
hormones
peer pressure
sexuality
values

Teenagers have to make many decisions. Some decisions seem very important; a teen may devote a lot of time and energy to selecting the "right" choice. Other decisions may seem insignificant and go almost unnoticed, such as which clothes to wear or what movie to see. However, the kinds of decisions that will have an important impact on the rest of a teenager's life and on the lives of other people should be carefully considered.

Teen Sexuality

Many decisions a teenager makes relate in some way to his or her **sexuality**—*a person's concept of himself or herself as a male or a female*. Sexuality involves much more than physical maturity or the ability to be sexually active. Sexuality involves a person's regard for himself or herself, as well as that person's sense of responsibility and understanding of other people. Thus physical, intellectual, emotional, and social development are all aspects of sexuality.

Individuals express their sexuality in various ways. They show their maleness or femaleness in the way they walk, talk, move, dress, dream, and laugh.

Teenagers are in the process of establishing their own sexual identity—that is, they are developing their own sense of themselves as male or female individuals. This process is influenced by a number of powerful factors. Teens undergo dramatic physical changes, many of which are part of achieving sexual maturity. At the same time, changing **hormones**, *body chemicals*, often cause mood swings or emotional ups and downs. Learning about these processes can help teens cope better with their physical and emotional changes. These changes usually cause social changes. Teens often find themselves attracted to new friends, pressured by peers, or involved in new kinds of interactions with family members.

A teenager adjusting to these changes makes daily decisions about how to behave and how to interact with other people. Many of these decisions reflect the teen's self-esteem or attitude toward himself or herself; at the same time, these decisions help establish that teen's understanding and expression of his or her sexuality.

During this crucial period, teens face many kinds of pressure relating to sexuality and sexual activity. This pressure comes from the media—television, radio, music, movies, and commercials—that often imply sexual activity is necessary for mature sexuality. Teens also face **peer pressure**, *the influence of people one's own age*. Teens may pressure one another to engage in an activity that is inappropriate or not in keeping with an individual's values. "Everyone is doing it—what's wrong with you?" they may ask or imply.

In the face of these pressures and confusion, it is essential for teens to understand that sexual intercourse and other forms of sexual activity are not a necessary part of sexuality.

The teen years should be a time of enjoyment. How can an early pregnancy affect the teen years?

Values and Sexuality

Any decision a person makes may reflect that person's **values**, *the principles a person considers important and uses to guide his or her life*. All people have values; familiar examples include trust, self-respect, respect for others, commitment, and loyalty.

During the early years, a person's values are shaped by his or her family. For example, a parent who values honesty passes this value on by example and is likely to discuss the importance of honesty with a child. A child's values are also influenced by other caregivers, by teachers and others at school, by friends, and often by organizations, such as religious groups or community clubs.

During adolescence, teens may question the values of their parents, of other family members, and of society. This questioning and evaluating is part of the process by which teens decide what they believe and what values they want to uphold during the rest of their lives. In other words, it is part of becoming mature and establishing identity.

Everyday teens are bombarded by media and peer pressure, which can make them confused about values and goals.

A teen's values influence the way he or she thinks about and responds to questions that relate to sexuality: Who am I? What does it mean to be a male or a female? Is sexual activity an essential part of my being a man or a woman? What are some of the possible consequences of sexual activity? Who may be affected by my sexual activity? What responsibilities am I willing to accept for the effects of my sexual activity?

Using the Decision-Making Process

Some say the teen years are the best years of your life. However, teenagers face decisions that may have long-lasting effects on their lives as teens and even as adults. Some of these decisions relate directly to sexuality and to sexual activity. Every teen who has sexual intercourse—even the teen who says, "Well, it just seemed like the thing to do," or "I don't know quite how; it just happened"—has made a decision. Decisions about sexual activity are too important to make casually. These decisions deserve careful consideration, because they can have **consequences** —*the results that come from a decision*—that will last throughout life.

All decisions have consequences for the person who makes the decision; many also have consequences for other people. Thinking about and analyzing the possible consequences is an essential part of making responsible decisions.

Making a decision should be a process, not a single, impulsive act. Understanding and using the six basic steps in the decision-making process can help people of all ages make responsible decisions.

1. **Identify the decision to be made.** The first step in the decision-making process is to recognize that a decision needs to be made and to identify exactly what that decision is.

2. **Identify the alternatives.** The second step involves identifying all the possible choices. Sometimes there may be only two options; sometimes there may be many. Often, one of the options is to avoid doing anything. It is important to remember, however, that doing nothing is itself a decision that has specific consequences.

3. **Consider the consequences of each alternative.** What results is each possible choice likely to have? What are the positive consequences of each option? What are the negative consequences? Are there differences between the short-term consequences and the long-term consequences? If so, what are those differences? Thoroughly examining the responses to these questions is the third step in the decision-making process.

4. **Choose the best alternative.** Once all the options have been carefully considered, it is time to make a choice. The decision-maker's values usually play an important role in determining which results are worth pursuing, and which should be avoided.

5. **Act on the decision.** Once a decision has been made, it should be carried out. Even the most thoughtfully considered decision cannot be meaningful until it is acted on.

6. **Evaluate the decision.** It is always useful to review and analyze the results of a decision: Did the decision have the expected results? Why or why not? Would the decision-maker act on the same choice again? Why or why not? Taking time to respond to these questions can help improve decision-making skills and lead to responsible decisions in the future.

Teens who follow the steps of this decision-making model are able to make responsible choices about all kinds of issues. It may seem easy to use the process in dealing with everyday issues: Should I stay in the library to study with my friends, or should I go home and study by myself? Should I audition for a part in the school play?

Everyday practice can make it easier to apply the decision-making model to choices that may seem more significant: Should I go out with this person? Should I marry this person? Should I have sex with this person? How should I protect myself and my partner from the possibility of pregnancy? What steps should I take to protect myself and my partner from sexually transmitted diseases? Clearly, these are difficult questions. Taking the time to follow the steps of the decision-making process can help teens approach these decisions responsibly.

The process can be very effective in making decisions about sexual activity. However, making a decision with this process takes time and rational consideration. It's not reasonable to expect yourself—or a partner—to use the decision-making process in the heat of passion. In that situation, emotions may override rational thinking.

Decisions About Sexual Activity

The decision to become sexually active is precisely that: a decision. It is best made by each individual, following the steps of the decision-making process. In using this process, it is often helpful to discuss alternatives and consequences with other people. Peers can be good listeners and share their own experiences. However, it is always helpful to discuss important questions with trusted adults as well—a parent or older family member, a teacher, a doctor, a member of the clergy, or an adult friend.

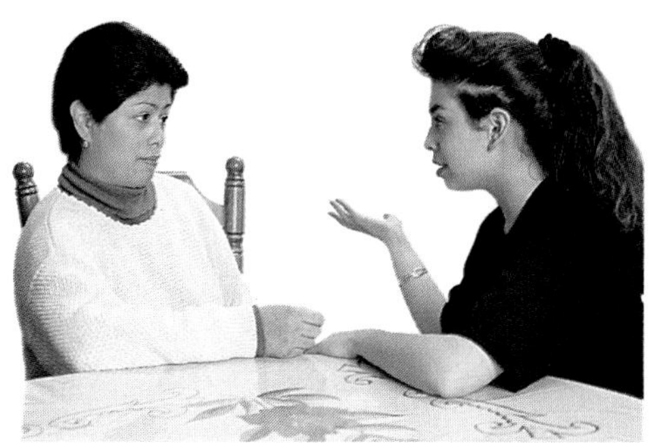

Telling a friend or relative can help you think through the decision-making process and make the decision that will be best for your life.

Consequences of Sexual Activity

To make responsible decisions about sexual activity, it is essential to understand the consequences of sexual intercourse. Some of these consequences may be very personal: How will you feel about yourself—and about your partner—after you have become sexually involved? Only you can know your answer to that question. Remember, though, that you will know your answer in advance only if you take time to think about it. You may want to talk with friends or trusted adults about the emotional consequences of sexual activity. You should also talk to your partner about these consequences. Most people agree that if two people can't talk about the possible consequences of having sexual intercourse together, they aren't ready for that level of involvement.

Whenever you consider becoming sexually involved with someone, the two of you should also discuss possible health consequences of intercourse. Pregnancy is one possible consequence of intercourse. Intercourse also involves the risk of infection with an STD (a sexually transmitted disease) such as gonorrhea, syphilis, chlamydia, herpes, or genital warts. Another possible consequence is transmission of HIV, the virus that causes AIDS.

These physical consequences can have far-reaching effects on a teen's life. No one can make a responsible decision about sexual activity without considering these effects.

Avoiding Pregnancy

Abstinence, *avoiding or abstaining from sexual intercourse*, is a choice that everyone can make. It is the only completely reliable means of protecting oneself from pregnancy and STDs.

Those who choose to be sexually active and choose not to use any protection are taking risks. Health officials advise individuals who decide to be sexually active to use **contraceptives**, *devices or methods that prevent pregnancy*. When used correctly and consistently, contraceptives such as condoms, oral contraceptives ("the pill"), sponges, foams, and diaphragms can dramatically reduce the risk of pregnancy. In addition, condoms can decrease the risk of transmitting STDs.

SECTION 1 REVIEW

CHECK YOUR UNDERSTANDING

1. Define the term *sexuality*.
2. What are values?
3. List the six steps in the decision-making process.
4. When teens are making decisions about sexual activity, with whom should they discuss their alternatives and the consequences of those alternatives?
5. List three possible health consequences of having sexual intercourse.
6. What are hormones?
7. What is the only completely reliable method of preventing pregnancy?

DISCUSS AND DISCOVER

1. How can teens in your community learn more about sexual activity, contraceptives, and the prevention of STDs? With a group of classmates, compile a list of classes, hot lines, clinics, and other sources of information and assistance. Publish your list in a brochure, a poster, or another convenient format.
2. List five specific values that you consider important in your own life. Then discuss your list with a group of classmates. How are the lists alike? How and why are they different? How do you think the values you listed were formed and became important to you?

SECTION 2

Realities of Teen Pregnancy and Parenting

OBJECTIVES

- Describe the decisions that pregnant teens must make.
- List possible sources of help available to pregnant teens.
- Discuss the alternatives available to pregnant teens.
- Describe the consequences of teen parenthood.

Every year in the United States, about one out of nine girls between the ages of fifteen and nineteen becomes pregnant. Each girl's pregnancy is a consequence of decisions she and a sexual partner made. Each pregnancy also raises a number of decisions that the teen—and, if possible, her partner and her parents or other family members—must make.

Identifying the Decision

Unless a teen has planned and hoped to become pregnant, she may have trouble believing and acknowledging the symptoms of pregnancy. A girl who fears she might be pregnant may try to ignore the symptoms. This kind of avoidance, though completely understandable, makes it impossible for the girl to begin responding to the question: How will I deal with this pregnancy?

Teens who are sexually active should be aware of the early signs of pregnancy. (They are discussed in Chapter 6.) As difficult as this may be, a teen who suspects she might be pregnant should discuss her concerns with someone she feels close to—her boyfriend, a parent or other family member, a trusted friend, or a special teacher or counselor. She should also see a physician, who can tell her definitely whether or not she is pregnant.

Once her pregnancy has been confirmed, a teen can begin the process of deciding what to do. In order to make a responsible decision, she will have to consider all her alternatives; she will also have to think about the consequences of each alternative. Pregnant teens are faced with important, difficult decisions. Fortunately, they do not have to go through the decision-making process alone.

Sources of Help

As she works through the decision-making process, a teenage girl may be helped by many different people, including the father-to-be, her parents, a member of the clergy, a member of the school staff, and a family planning counselor.

- **Fathers-to-Be.** Whenever possible, the partner of a pregnant teenager should be an active participant in decisions made about the pregnancy. The father of the unborn baby has rights and responsibilities, just as the mother does. No matter what decision is finally reached, the pregnancy will have a long-lasting effect on his life. He will have to face the consequences of the decision, no matter which alternative is finally chosen.
- **Parents.** Most pregnant teens are reluctant to discuss their situation with their parents. Parents are often hurt or angry when they first learn of the pregnancy. However, the teens' own parents are often uniquely able to help them think through the meaning and implications of pregnancy and parenthood. The emotional support that the parents of a teenage girl and her partner offer can be critical in helping the teens through the stresses of reaching a decision and living with its consequences.

Parents are often the best source of help, reassurance, and comfort when a teen finds out she is pregnant.

Each year about 20,000 unwed teenage girls decide to give their babies up for adoption. These girls decide that adoption will be the most beneficial situation for themselves and for their children.

- **Clergy.** Teens who feel uncomfortable talking with their parents may be able to discuss the pregnancy with a minister, priest, or rabbi. A member of the clergy is usually able to help teens think through their readiness for pregnancy and parenthood. In many cases, he or she can also help teens discuss the pregnancy with their own parents. Frequently, the clergy member can serve as a source of support for both the teenagers and for their parents.
- **School Personnel.** School personnel can be another source of support for pregnant teens and their partners. A teacher, counselor, or nurse can offer advice and assistance when teens feel frightened or confused. Although rules in schools do vary, conversations with school personnel can generally be kept confidential, unless a teen's life or health is in danger.
- **Family Planning Counselors.** Nonprofit and privately funded agencies, as well as public agencies such as county departments of social services, have trained counselors. These counselors help individuals and couples consider all the options in making decisions about unplanned pregnancies. They can also help teens connect with other agencies that provide financial and medical assistance during the pregnancy, or baby clothes, food supplies, and furniture when the baby arrives. Many adoption agencies also provide such services, even when one or both parents are uncertain about giving up their child for adoption or foster care.

Considering the Alternatives

A pregnant teenager should carefully consider her alternatives. She can become a single parent. She can marry and, with her husband, become a parent. She can continue the pregnancy but give the baby up for adoption, or she can terminate the pregnancy. However, some teens may have strong, clear values that eliminate at least one of these alternatives.

Single Parenthood

Having a tiny baby to cuddle and love can seem very attractive. In fact, it can be rewarding to care for someone who is helpless and dependent. However, caring for a newborn is a huge responsibility, and becoming a parent is a lifetime commitment. Anyone who is considering becoming a parent, either alone or with a spouse, should carefully consider the responsibilities, challenges, and rewards of parenthood. (See Chapter 2.)

Single parents face special parenting challenges because they must assume complete responsibility for raising their children, as well as for household chores, financial obligations, and decision making. All these responsibilities can be draining—especially for an adolescent. Burnout or depression may become a problem for many single teen parents.

Many teenage parents have to juggle school, a job, housework, and child care. They become overwhelmed by the emotional and financial costs of being a parent along with the natural demands a baby makes.

Teens who are considering single parenthood should be as realistic as possible. How much help—emotional and financial—can the teen mother expect from the baby's father? From her own parents and other family members? A teen who is considering single parenthood must be especially careful to avoid romanticizing her situation. A teenage partner who was not interested in marriage during her pregnancy is unlikely to change his mind once the baby is born, for example. Parents, counselors, and other adults can help teens develop realistic expectations for their own situations as single parents.

Marriage

For many pregnant teens, marriage and parenthood are appealing alternatives. It is important to recognize, however, that teens who marry because of a pregnancy face many difficulties. Statistics show that early marriages have the following results:

- Divorce rates for females who marry between the ages of fourteen and seventeen are twice as high as the divorce rates for females who marry at age eighteen or nineteen; they are three times as high as the divorce rates for females who marry between the ages of twenty and twenty-four.
- About 80 percent of teens who marry because of a pregnancy divorce within six years.
- Teens who marry are likely to have low incomes and little education; both these factors are associated with increased likelihood of divorce.
- In many teen marriages, neither partner completes high school; couples without high school diplomas are more likely to divorce than couples in which both partners have college degrees.

The prospect of getting married may seem exciting, but married teens face many problems. As the early excitement wears off, and as the strains of responsibility set in, many teen marriages deteriorate. In addition, it is not unusual for married teens to feel socially isolated. They no longer fit in with their single friends, but their interests and activities are not the same as those of most other married couples.

Teens who marry because of a pregnancy face an additional problem. They have to adjust to parenthood while they are still adjusting to marriage.

ASK THE EXPERTS

Managing the Stress of Teen Parenting

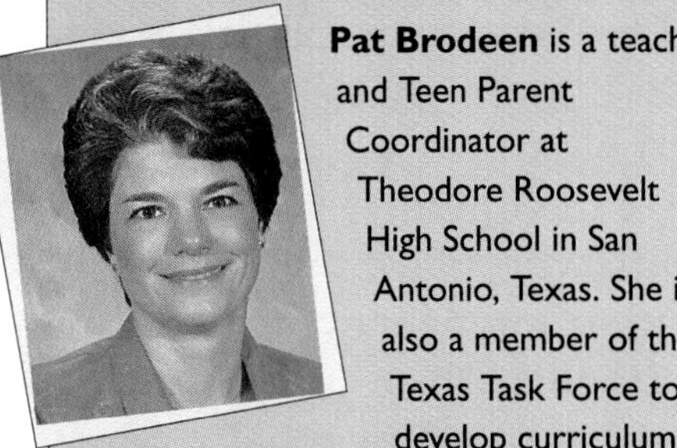

Pat Brodeen is a teacher and Teen Parent Coordinator at Theodore Roosevelt High School in San Antonio, Texas. She is also a member of the Texas Task Force to develop curriculum for School Age Parenting courses.

I have a beautiful four-month-old son. I really enjoy him, but sometimes I feel so tense and angry I'm actually afraid to pick him up. We live with my mom, who takes care of Josh while I'm in school. I'll get my diploma in a few months, and then I'll have to start working—though I have no idea what kind of job I'll be able to get. Sometimes I just feel completely overwhelmed—can you help me help myself?

Of course you feel overwhelmed— you're doing a lot, and I can tell by your question that you're taking your responsibilities seriously and trying very hard. It's great that you're enjoying your baby—that's very important for both of you! At the same time, you should recognize that having a child has added a lot of stress to your life.

You can make your life—and your baby's life—easier and more enjoyable by learning techniques for managing stress.

My first suggestion may sound contradictory to you. I know you feel you already have too much to do, but you'll handle stress better when you find time to take good care of yourself. Here are some specific things you should try to do:

- Exercise every day. Even taking a short walk will help keep you physically healthy. It will also encourage good emotional health.
- Eat a balanced diet. Every time you skip a meal or grab a cola and some chips instead of a sandwich and some fruit, you're undermining your health and making yourself more vulnerable to stress.
- Take time every day to relax. Try to learn some relaxation techniques, including deep, slow breathing.

You'll be more comfortable handling stress if you have a network of supportive friends. Now that you're a parent, you may find you no longer have so much in common with your old friends. Make an effort to establish friendships with other mothers your age, as well as with teens and adults who understand your responsibilities and support you in your efforts to be a good parent. When you feel tense and angry—or simply overwhelmed—make contact with a friend you can count on. Even a phone conversation can be a big help!

I can tell that you're working to keep a positive attitude. That's an important part of handling stress, but it can be hard to do on your own. Don't hesitate to let your friends help you keep your spirits up.

Another important part of managing stress is making plans for the future. You'll be more comfortable with the present if you know what lies ahead. Ask a counselor or teacher to help you explore your employment options. Perhaps there's a special class or program that will help prepare you for an interesting job. If you need more advice or more details than your current school can offer, contact a local community college or a public vocational school.

Pat Brodeen

Pat Brodeen

EDUCATION: A KEY TO SURVIVAL

Teen parents who drop out of school are more likely to commit themselves and their children to a lifetime of economic dependency. The commitment to children often leads to an abandonment of educational goals. Without a high school diploma, teens have little hope for rising above minimum wage level. With the added financial responsibilities of children, minimum wage just isn't enough. Also, the divorce rate is higher for couples who are in the poverty range and have little education.

Fortunately, most cultural groups offer examples of men and women who educate themselves and break out of the poverty cycle. They are models to teens who want to ensure a better future. Teen parents improve the long-term opportunities for themselves and their children if they stay in school.

Adoption

Another alternative for pregnant teens to consider is adoption. Adoption involves the termination of all rights and responsibilities for both the biological mother and the biological father; another family takes on all the rights and responsibilities of raising the child. Many teens who choose adoption feel they are giving their child an opportunity for more care, guidance, and love than they can provide at this stage of their lives.

It is important for teen parents who place their child for adoption to choose a reputable adoption agency or program. Adoption should involve professionals who carefully screen prospective parents and prepare them for a new baby. Many agencies also offer biological parents counseling and health care. Some agencies also give the biological mother an opportunity to select prospective adoptive parents from a pool of applicants. Teens can find reputable adoption agencies by requesting information from their county department of human services, from a member of the clergy, from a school official, or from a health department official.

Pregnancy Termination

Many pregnant teens consider the alternative of terminating their pregnancy. They think about having an abortion, a medical procedure that ends a pregnancy. Since laws governing abortion vary from state to state, teens should get legal and counseling assistance.

The values of teens—and of their parents and other family members—may cause conflict when the option of abortion is considered. There are no easy answers to the questions raised by abortion. However, it is important for pregnant teens to examine their own ideas and feelings about abortion and to respond to this alternative, recognizing that they will have to deal with the consequences of their decision long after the procedure is—or is not—performed.

Consequences of Teen Parenthood

Some pregnant teens decide to raise their children, either as single parents or with a marriage partner. It is important for teens considering these alternatives to examine thoroughly the consequences of parenthood.

The teenage years are a time of choices and changes. They are a time of learning to be responsible for self, of developing a style for interacting with others. Teens are involved in an important process—getting to know and understand themselves, planning

Although teen fathers may not marry the mother of their child, they can be required to pay child support. What are some of the other challenges partners in a teenage marriage must confront that older couples do not face?

what they want to do with their lives, and taking advantage of educational opportunities. In almost every case, teen parenting interferes with this important process.

Teens who become parents find they have fewer options available to them. They also have to face health risks, financial difficulties, changes in educational plans, and emotional and social stresses.

Early Pregnancy—Fewer Choices

Teens who are raising children have important and demanding responsibilities. Caring for a baby or young child takes time—time that other teens may be spending studying, participating in school or community events, playing sports, or just hanging out.

Teen mothers and fathers often find that they are too busy taking care of children or working to attend school. Plans to complete high school or to go on to college may have to be postponed or even abandoned.

Many teens drop out of school when they recognize that they are pregnant. Other teen mothers and fathers drop out soon after the baby is born. Of the teen mothers who leave school, nearly half never return to complete their education. This lack of educa-

tion makes finding a job difficult; it is not unusual for a teen mother to be unable to support herself and her child.

In response to these problems, some schools now have special parenting classes for teen parents. Some even provide in-school child care programs, where children receive care while parents attend classes.

Social and athletic options are similarly restricted by parenthood. A teen parent who is able to continue in school or return to school rarely has the opportunity to join a school sports team, sing with the school choir, or participate in after-school clubs. Being a responsible parent means spending time with an infant or child—time that cannot be spent in the activities most teens enjoy.

Health Risks

Pregnancy during the teen years presents special health risks for both the teen mother and her baby. Before the age of twenty, a young woman is still growing. Her body may not be ready for the stresses of pregnancy. Because her own nutritional needs are high, she may be unable to provide the nutrients her developing baby needs.

Teen mothers are more likely than mothers in other age groups to suffer from toxemia and from iron deficiency. They are more susceptible to urinary tract infections, and they are more likely to have prolonged labor.

The baby of a teenage mother also faces special health risks. Babies born to teen mothers are more likely to die before their first birthday, more likely to be premature, and more likely to have low birth weight. Both prematurity and low birth weight have been linked to other problems, including epilepsy, birth defects, blindness, and learning deficiencies.

Financial Problems

The cost of having a child does not end with the bills for medical care during pregnancy and for the baby's delivery. The financial responsibilities of raising a child typically last 18 years or more, until the child becomes independent and begins to support himself or herself. For teens, undertaking these major, long-term financial obligations can be especially overwhelming.

Often, teens leave school in order to work or care for a baby, so their educational preparation for work is limited. Without an education, it is difficult to find a good job. Teen parents who are able to find jobs also face the task of finding—and paying for—dependable child care.

For many adolescent parents, the financial responsibilities of childbirth and child rearing become overwhelming. The stress of dealing with these obligations may strain the teen parent's relationship with his or her spouse or other family members, or even with the baby.

Emotional and Social Stresses

Adolescence is a period of changes and choices. Adding the responsibilities of parenthood to adolescence can be very stressful. Teen parents must make emotional adjustments as they learn to accommodate the needs and interests of their babies. At the same time, they must deal with their own emotional responses to pregnancy and parenthood and, in many cases, a new marriage. Social stresses result from adjustments in relationships with parents, other family members, friends, classmates, and others in the community.

Most people want to provide the best possible care, attention, love, food, clothing, safety, and protection for their children. They want to give their children the best opportunities to grow and thrive in the best environment. When a child is planned, expected, and wanted, these goals are more easily achieved.

SECTION 2 REVIEW

CHECK YOUR UNDERSTANDING

1. List four sources of help to which a teenage girl might turn when she suspects she is pregnant.
2. What special challenges do single teen parents face?
3. List three statistics about teen marriages. What is the implication of these statistics?
4. What additional problem must teens who marry because of a pregnancy face?
5. What rights and responsibilities do biological parents give up when they allow another family to adopt their child?
6. How do the responsibilities of raising a child limit the opportunities for teen parents?
7. What are the special health risks that the baby of a teenage mother faces?

DISCUSS AND DISCOVER

1. What rights and responsibilities do you believe a teenager has when his sexual partner becomes pregnant? How—if at all—does the role of the father-to-be differ from that of the mother-to-be? If you believe there are differences, what accounts for those differences?
2. With a group of classmates, find out about family planning counselors at private and public agencies in your community. Which of these agencies would you recommend to a pregnant teen? Why?
3. How would you respond if your 17-year-old sister told you—in confidence—that she was pregnant? What advice would you give her? What practical kinds of help would you offer? How would your response change if your sister were 15 years old? If she were 13 years old?

SUMMARY

- Sexuality is a person's concept of himself or herself as a male or a female.
- Responsible decisions, including decisions about sexual activity, can best be made using a six-step process.
- The possible consequences of sexual intercourse include pregnancy, transmission of STDs, and infection with the virus that causes AIDS.
- The four main alternatives for pregnant teens are single parenthood, marriage, adoption, and termination of the pregnancy.
- The consequences of teen parenthood include fewer educational and recreational options, health risks to both mother and baby, financial problems, and emotional and social stresses.

REVIEWING THE FACTS

1. List three kinds of changes to which teens have to adjust.
2. What are two sources of pressure on teens to engage in sexual activity?
3. During the teen years, how do many people regard the values with which they were raised? Why?
4. What are consequences?
5. What is the sixth step in the decision-making process? Why is it important?
6. When should teens consider the consequences of sexual intercourse? Why?
7. What is abstinence?
8. What are contraceptives? List three different kinds of contraceptives.
9. What often makes it difficult for a teen to begin the decision-making process about how to handle an unplanned pregnancy?
10. How might a member of the clergy be able to help pregnant teens?
11. What special health risks do pregnant teens face?
12. Why does becoming a single parent seem attractive to many teens? What are the major difficulties in single teen parenthood?

EXPLORING FURTHER

1. Select one form of media—television, radio, music, movies, or commercials. Analyze the way sexuality and male and female roles are portrayed in this media form. What does the media imply about sexual activity? What does it imply about male and female roles? Do you think some people prefer the days when sex roles were more rigidly defined? Explain. (Section 1)
2. With a partner, plan a skit showing one of these situations: a teenage girl tells her boyfriend she is pregnant; a teenage boy tells his parent he is going to be a father; a teenage girl tells her parent she is going to be a mother; a teen tells a friend he or she is going to become a parent. Together, act your skit out for the rest of the class. (Section 2)
3. With a group of classmates, gather information about the pregnancy rate among teens in your school, your school district, your town, or your county. How many teen pregnancies are reported in that population? Which alternative do most teens choose in response to pregnancy? What are the implications of your findings? (Section 2)
4. Interview students and adults who have strong opinions about abortion. Listen carefully to their ideas, and try to understand both points of view. Then discuss your interviews with classmates. (Section 2)

THINKING CRITICALLY

1. **Analyze.** How do you think teens can benefit from discussing the alternatives and consequences of sexual activity with their peers? What qualities would you want in peers with whom you seriously discuss those alternatives and consequences? Why would you look for those qualities? What do you consider the particular benefits of discussing the alternatives and consequences with adults? With which adults would you be comfortable discussing these aspects of sexual activity? Why?
2. **Evaluate.** Discuss your ideas about this statement from the text: "If two people can't talk about the possible consequences of having sexual intercourse together, they aren't ready for that level of involvement." Rephrase the statement in your own words. Do you agree or disagree with the statement? Why? Do you think there are any exceptions? If so, what are those exceptions?
3. **Analyze.** In recent years, increasing numbers of pregnant teens have chosen single parenthood. What do you consider the significance of this trend? What does it imply about the needs and interests of teenage girls? Of teenage boys? What do you think the trend means for the babies of teen parents?

CROSS-CURRICULUM CONNECTIONS

1. **Health.** Read about the symptoms, the transmission, the methods of prevention, and the current available treatments for a specific STD. Share your findings with the rest of the class, either in a brief oral report or in a clear, complete chart.
2. **Reading.** Read at least two magazine articles about the experiences of pregnant teens or of teen parents. With a group of classmates, share and discuss your reactions to the articles.

OBSERVING AND PARTICIPATING

Teen Parenting

All parents have important responsibilities toward their children. For teens, these responsibilities can seem even more demanding.

Select one of the following activities, and spend time observing teen parents or participating with children of teen parents. Write your observations in your journal, and then discuss your observations and reactions with classmates.

- **Observing.** Spend at least an hour observing a teen parent and his or her child, either in a public place such as a park or in the teen's home. What does the parent have to do to meet the child's physical needs? How much of the parent's time does this take? How does the child respond to the parent's attention and care?
- **Observing.** Observe two or more teen parents as they care for their children, either individually or in a group setting. How do the parents communicate with their babies and children? How do they use language to communicate? How do they use physical contact and gestures to communicate? What attitude do you think each parent communicates toward his or her child? How do the parents guide their children's behavior? How do they nurture their children? What similarities do you see between the approaches of the parents? What individual differences do you notice?
- **Participating.** Spend an hour or more volunteering in an on-campus child care program. What are the special needs of the babies and children there? How are those needs met? What are the special needs of the parents of the babies and children? How does the program meet the needs of those parents?

UNIT 2

Pregnancy and Birth

SOME THINGS DON'T MAKE
ANY SENSE AT ALL

My mom says I'm her sugarplum.
My mom says I'm her lamb.
My mom says I'm completely perfect
Just the way I am.
My mom says I'm a super-special terrific little guy.
My mom just had another baby.
Why?

Judith Viost

CHAPTER 5

Prenatal Development

Katie sat by her mother's side, playing doctor with a toy stethoscope. "Listen to this!" she cried. "A baby!"

"Not just *a* baby, Katie," her mother told her. "That's *your* baby brother or sister." She patted her stomach and added, "The baby is going to be happy to have a sister like you."

"Oooo, do you think so?" asked Katie.

"Yes, the baby can't wait to see you and play with you," replied Katie's mother.

"Really?" asked Katie. "

"Absolutely. The baby will see your lovely dark hair, your big brown eyes, and your sparkling smile. What a lucky baby this is going to be."

Katie smiled happily, as she hugged her mother.

SECTION 1

Forty Weeks of Preparation

OBJECTIVES

- Name the three stages of pregnancy.
- Describe the prenatal development during each of the three stages of pregnancy.

During pregnancy, a single cell grows and develops into a human being capable of independent existence. This amazing process takes place over a period of 40 weeks (or about nine months).

TERMS TO LEARN

amniotic fluid
conception
embryo
fetus
ovum
placenta
prenatal
sperm
umbilical cord
uterus
zygote

Prenatal Development

Prenatal development is the development of a baby *during the period before birth.* Prenatal development is usually considered in three stages: the period of the zygote, the period of the embryo, and the period of the fetus. The chart on pages 118-119 shows how the unborn baby develops during these three periods. It also shows corresponding physical changes in the mother.

Conception

Once each month, an **ovum**—*a female cell or egg*—is released by one of a woman's ovaries. The egg moves through the Fallopian tube to the **uterus,** or womb, *the organ in a woman's body in which a baby develops during pregnancy.* This short journey takes about two or three days. It is only in the Fallopian tube that fertilization can take place.

When the egg reaches the uterus, it usually disintegrates and is flushed away with the menstrual flow. However, if the egg meets and is fertilized in the Fallopian tube by a **sperm**, or *male cell,* **conception**—*the union of an ovum and a sperm, resulting in the beginning of pregnancy*—takes place. This union is called a zygote.

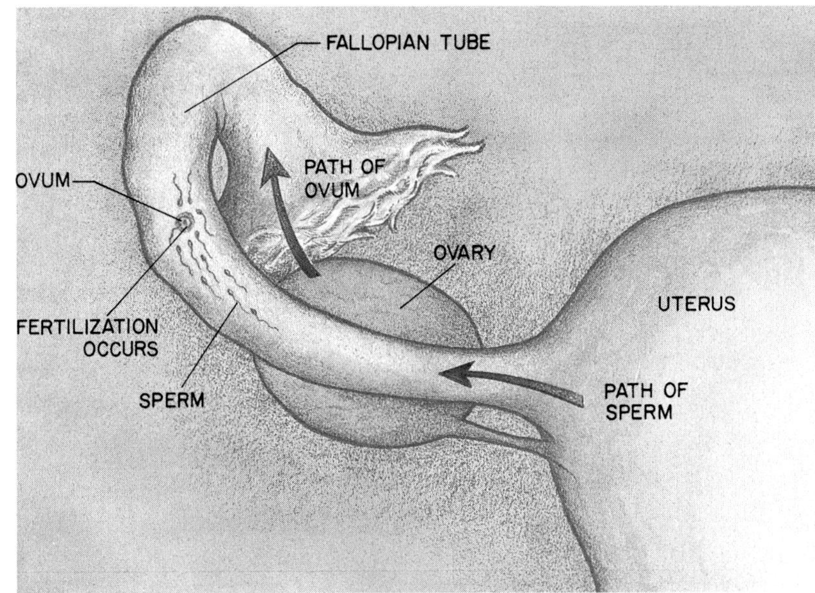

Conception–the beginning of pregnancy–occurs when an ovum is fertilized. The ovum is about the size of the dot over a printed letter i.

Period of the Zygote

The first stage in the development of a human baby is called the period of the **zygote**, or *fertilized egg*. It lasts approximately two weeks.

When the fertilized egg reaches the uterus, it attaches itself to the thickened lining of the uterus and begins to grow. Since the lining is needed to nourish the fertilized egg, it cannot be shed in menstruation as usual. Therefore, menstruation does not take place. The woman's menstrual periods stop and will not begin again until after the baby is born.

The thickened lining of the uterus provides both a soft, warm bed and food for the fertilized egg. It grows by a process called cell division. This single, complete cell divides and becomes two. Two cells become four and so on, until there is a mass of cells. In spite of the remarkable growth during this period, at the end of two weeks, the zygote is still only the size of a pinhead.

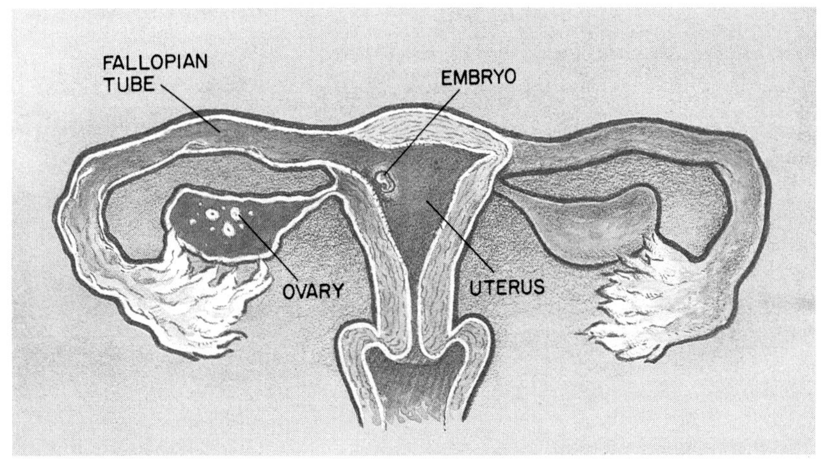

The embryo has made its home by attaching itself to the inner lining of the uterus. The uterus is about 3 inches long at this stage. The embryo is still smaller than a grain of rice.

PRENATAL DEVELOPMENT MONTH BY MONTH

Keep in mind that growth patterns and reactions are individual. Not all babies develop at exactly the same rate, nor does every pregnant woman experience all of the effects described here.

	PRENATAL DEVELOPMENT	EFFECTS ON MOTHER
During the First Month	• Cell multiplication begins. • The fertilized egg attaches itself to the lining of the uterus. • Internal organs and the circulatory system begin to form. The heart begins to beat. • By the end of the month, small bumps indicate the beginning of arms and legs.	• Missed menstrual period. • Other signs of pregnancy may not yet be noticeable.
During the Second Month	• At five weeks, the embryo is only about ¼ inch (6 mm) long. • Face, eyes, ears, and limbs take shape. • Bones begin to form. • Internal organs continue to develop.	• Breasts begin to swell. • Pressure on bladder from enlarging uterus results in need to urinate more frequently. • Possible nausea ("morning sickness"). • Fatigue is common.
During the Third Month	• As this month begins, the fetus is about 1 inch (25 mm) long. • Nostrils, mouth, lips, teeth buds, and eyelids form. • Fingers and toes are almost complete. • All organs are present, although immature.	• Breasts become firmer and fuller and may ache. • Nausea, fatigue, and frequent urination may continue. • Abdomen becomes slightly larger. The uterus has grown to about the size of an orange. • Weight gain totals 2-4 pounds (0.9-1.8 kg).
During the Fourth Month	• At the beginning of this month, the fetus is about 3 inches (76 mm) long and weighs about 1 ounce (28 g). • The fetus can suck its thumb, swallow, hiccup, and move around. • Facial features become clearer.	• Size change continues slowly. • Most discomforts of early pregnancy are usually gone by this time. • Appetite increases.

(Continued on next page)

PRENATAL DEVELOPMENT MONTH BY MONTH

	PRENATAL DEVELOPMENT	EFFECTS ON MOTHER
During the Fifth Month 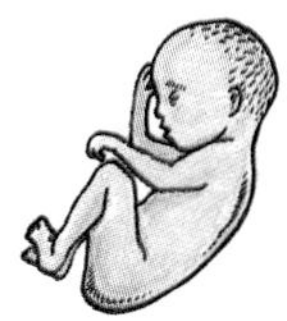	• As this month begins, the fetus is about 6 ½-7 inches (16-18 cm) long and weighs about 4-5 ounces (113-142 g). • Hair, eyelashes, and eyebrows appear. • Teeth continue to develop. • Organs are maturing. • The fetus becomes more active.	• Enlarged abdomen becomes apparent. • Slight fetal movements are felt. • Fetal heartbeat may be heard through a stethoscope. • Increased size may begin to affect posture.
During the Sixth Month 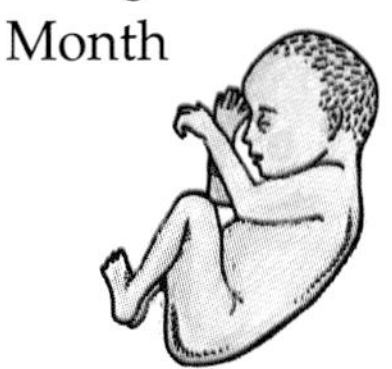	• The fetus is now about 8-10 inches (21-25 cm) long and weighs about 8-12 ounces (227-340 g). • Fat is being deposited under the skin, but the fetus still appears wrinkled. • Breathing movements begin.	• Fetal movements are now sensed as strong kicks, thumps, and bumps. Some may be visible. • Weight gain by the beginning of this month may total 10-12 pounds (4.5-5.4 kg).
During the Seventh Month	• The fetus is about 10-12 inches long and weighs about 1½-2 pounds (680-907 g). • Periods of fetal activity are followed by periods of rest and quiet.	• Increased size may begin to affect posture.
During the Eighth Month 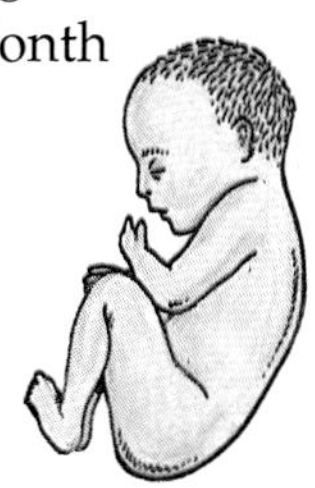	• Weight gain continues rapidly. The fetus is about 14-16 inches (36-41 cm) long and weighs about 2 ½-3 pounds (1.0-1.4 kg). • The fetus may react to loud noises with a reflex jerking action. • In most cases, the fetus moves into a head-down position.	• There may be discomfort as size increases. Backache, leg cramps, shortness of breath, and fatigue are common. • Fetal kicks continue to be felt; they may disturb the mother's rest. • At the beginning of this month, weight gain totals about 18-20 pounds (8.2-9.1 kg).
During the Ninth Month 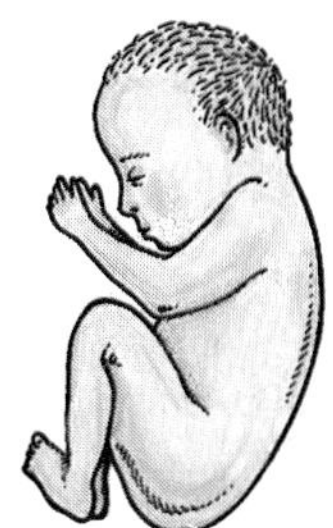	• At the beginning of the final month, the fetus is about 17-18 inches (43-46 cm) long and weighs about 5-6 pounds (2.3-2.7 kg). Weight gain continues until the week before birth. • Skin becomes smooth as fat deposits continue. • Fetal movements decrease as the fetus has less room to move around. • The fetus acquires disease-fighting antibodies from the mother's blood. • The fetus descends into the pelvis, ready for birth.	• "Lightening" is felt as the fetus drops into the pelvis. Breathing becomes easier. • Other discomforts of late pregnancy may continue. • A total weight gain of 24-30 pounds (10.9-13.6 kg) is typical. The uterus is the size of a small watermelon by the time of birth. • False labor pains may be experienced.

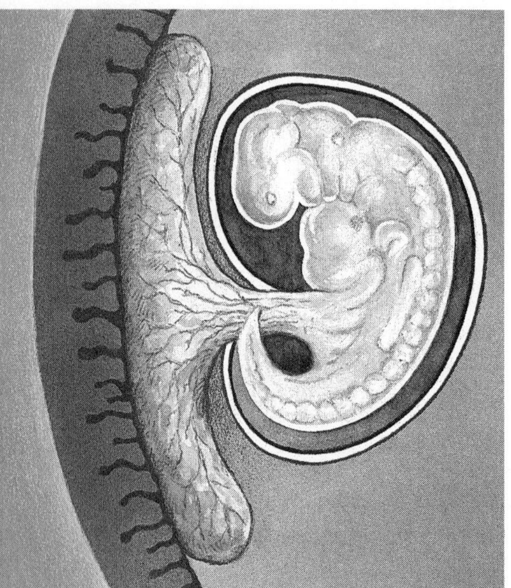

At three weeks after conception, the embryo is surrounded by a sac of amniotic fluid (show in dark gray). Between the amniotic sac and the uterine lining is the membrane that will soon develop in the placenta. The heart is the largest organ so far and has already begun to beat.

Period of the Embryo

The second stage of pregnancy is the period of the embryo. The **embryo** is *the developing cluster of cells in the uterus during about the third through eighth weeks of pregnancy.* In the course of this period, an amazing change occurs as the mass of embryonic cells develops into all the major organ systems of the human body.

Throughout this stage, the embryo grows rapidly. It becomes firmly attached to the inner lining of the uterus. By the end of this stage, the **placenta**, *the tissue that connects the sacs around the unborn baby to the mother's uterus,* has developed. The **umbilical cord**, *a long tube that connects the placenta to the unborn baby,* has also developed. Nourishment and oxygen from the mother's bloodstream are carried from the placenta to the developing baby through the umbilical cord.

The umbilical cord is uniquely formed to supply nourishment to the baby and to take waste products away from the baby. The cord contains three blood vessels. It is usually stiff and firm, like a garden hose filled with water. Usually, it is not flexible enough to loop around the fetus, although this may occur in rare cases. Only after the baby is born does the umbilical cord become limp and ropelike.

The growing embryo is soon surrounded by a bag of liquid called **amniotic fluid**, *a special fluid that surrounds and protects the developing baby during pregnancy.* The amniotic fluid acts as a cushion to protect the embryo, even through minor bumps or falls of the mother. The baby remains within this sac of liquid until just before birth.

Period of the Fetus

The third and last stage of pregnancy begins about the eighth or ninth week and lasts until birth. This stage is called the fetal period, or the period of the **fetus**, *the unborn baby from about the eighth or ninth week of pregnancy until birth.*

By the beginning of this period, the embryo has developed the beginnings of all organs and body parts. The cells are now recognizable as a developing human. Arms, legs, and even fingers and toes have developed. Facial features are also forming. All the internal organs are present, but they are not ready to function yet. They continue to develop in the remaining months of pregnancy.

Sometime during the fourth or fifth month, the kicks and other movements of the fetus touch the wall of the uterus. These fluttering movements are faint and infrequent at first. Gradually, they become stronger and more frequent. This sensation of feel-

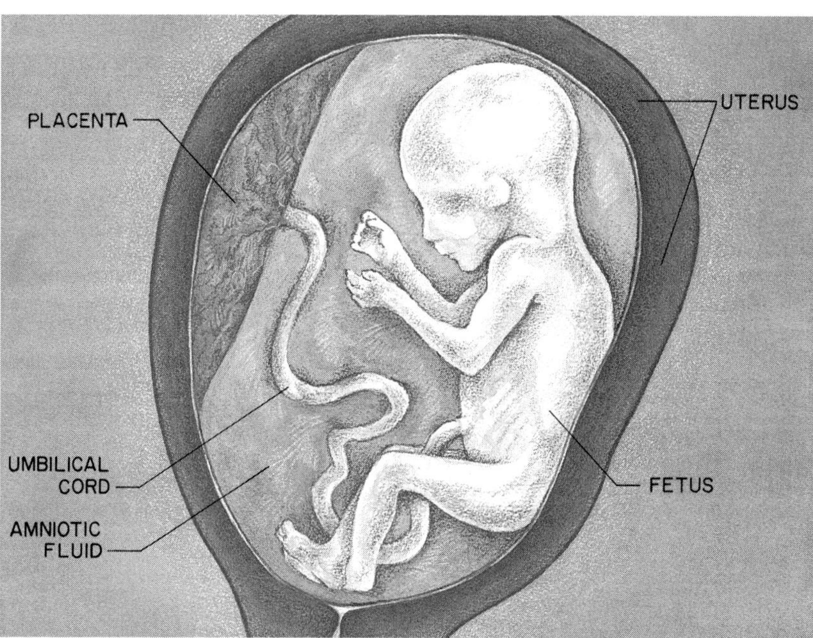

By the fourth month, the fetus looks more like a baby. The eyelids will remain shut until about the sixth month.

ing life, sometimes called quickening, tells the mother that she does, indeed, carry a live child within her. Actually, the baby has been very active long before this time.

Her doctor usually asks the expectant woman when she first felt life. Knowing this helps the doctor estimate the baby's fetal age and project a more accurate delivery date. The fetus's heartbeat can usually be heard before movement is felt.

As the fetus grows, so does the volume of the surrounding fluid. The uterus expands, too, and the woman's abdomen grows. Just before delivery, the amniotic fluid decreases as the baby becomes more active and swallows it. As the fetus grows, it no longer has the room to stretch out. The developing baby curls up in what is called the fetal position.

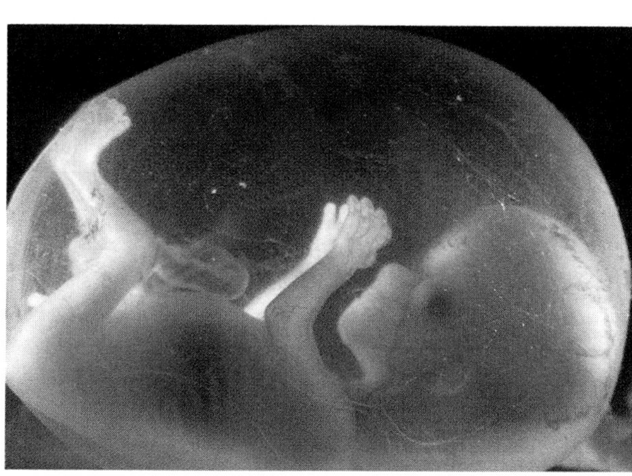

The fetus floats comfortably within the amniotic sac. After brief active periods, the fetus spends long hours resting. The same will be true of the baby after birth.

By the seventh month, most fetal development has already taken place. The fetus is capable of living outside the womb, but not without a great deal of medical help. Now the fetus's main task is to get ready for independent life outside the womb. In these remaining months, the major organs become ready to function without the assistance of the mother's body. The fetus also gains weight rapidly. Fat deposits, which will help the baby maintain body heat after birth, are added under the skin. Gradually, the fetus, which had been thin and wrinkled, takes on the smoother, rounder appearance of a baby. During these final weeks of pregnancy, the fetus also stores nutrients and builds immunity to diseases and infections.

The fetus can do a surprising number of things—suck its thumb, cough, sneeze, yawn, kick, and hiccup. A baby can even cry before birth. In almost all cases, the crying is soundless.

Sometime during the ninth month of pregnancy, the baby's weight seems to shift down and the mother feels noticeably more comfortable in her upper abdomen. Lightening has occurred. This means that the baby has dropped into the birth canal. Birth is not far off. With a first baby, lightening may take place several days—or even weeks—before labor begins. If the mother has given birth before, lightening may occur just before the beginning of labor. Sometimes lightening is accompanied by slight abdominal pains, which first-time mothers may mistake for the beginning of labor.

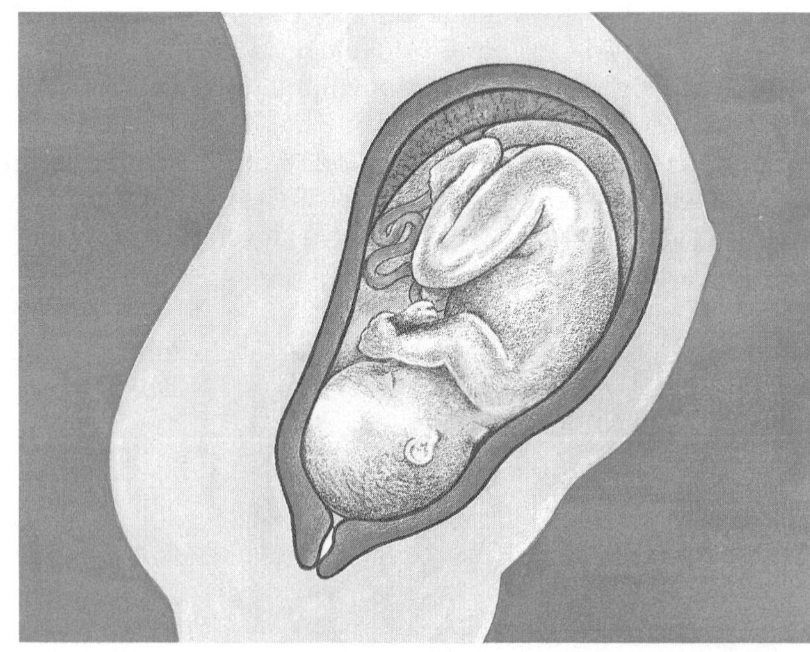

At full term (after nine months of development), the baby has put on weight and settled into the pelvis. The desired position is head down.

At this point in the pregnancy, the fetus is usually upside down, with the head nestled in the pelvis. This is the easiest and safest position for birth. The baby is less active than in previous weeks, because there is so little space in which to move.

The skin of the mother's abdomen appears stretched to capacity. The abdominal muscles are stretched, too. Both are capable of remarkable stretching—and contracting. The muscles of the uterus and abdomen can be stretched up to 60 times their original size during pregnancy, yet they return to nearly their original size within a month or so after the birth.

The nine months of pregnancy bring many changes, both in the pregnant woman and the developing baby. For family members, the signs are clearly evident and their anticipation of a new family member is usually greeted with enthusiasm. After about 40 weeks of preparation, the baby is ready to be born.

SECTION 1 REVIEW

CHECK YOUR UNDERSTANDING

1. What is conception? Where does it take place?
2. During what period of pregnancy do the placenta and umbilical cord develop? Why are they important to the developing baby?
3. What is amniotic fluid? Why is it important to the developing baby?
4. What is a fetus?
5. What is quickening? When does it usually first occur?
6. What are the most important changes that take place in a fetus during the last two months of pregnancy?
7. What is lightening? When does it usually occur?

DISCUSS AND DISCOVER

1. What emotional changes do women experience during pregnancy? Read about these changes, or discuss them with women who are or have been pregnant. Do all women experience the same emotional changes? How do you think a woman's emotional responses to pregnancy vary according to her situation? How do you think a woman's age, marital situation, and economic situation affect her emotions during pregnancy?
2. With a group of other students, collect photographs (from magazines or from other sources) of pregnant women. Then discuss what the photographs show. About how many months pregnant do you think each woman is? What physical changes make the pregnancy apparent? How do women at about the same stage of pregnancy look different? How do they look alike?

SECTION 2

A Closer Look at Conception

OBJECTIVES

- Describe how personal characteristics are inherited.
- Explain how multiple births occur.
- Discuss possible solutions for infertility.

TERMS TO LEARN

chromosomes
dominant
genes
infertility
recessive
surrogate

Pregnancy is the 40-week period of preparation that begins with conception, when the sperm and egg meet to form a new life. In that meeting of sperm and egg, many of the baby's future characteristics are determined.

The Genetic Package

Every individual inherits characteristics from previous generations. Inherited characteristics include such traits as these:

- Physical build.
- Skin color.
- Hair texture and color.
- Color and shape of the eyes.
- Shape and size of ears, hands, and feet.
- Blood type.
- Some medical conditions.

Heredity—the passing on of these and other characteristics—has been observed since ancient times. However, only in the last century has science begun to understand how heredity works.

At the moment of conception, every human baby receives a total of 46 **chromosomes**, *tiny threadlike particles in the nucleus of every cell that carry hereditary characteristics.* The father's sperm provides 23 of these chromosomes; the other 23 come from the mother's ovum. Each chromosome contains thousands of **genes**, *the units that determine inherited characteristics.* Genes make up chromosomes as beads make up a necklace. These genes determine all the characteristics—from facial features to coloring to physical size—that each of us inherits.

Hair color is an example of a characteristic that is genetically determined. Each of these parents contributed one recessive gene for red hair to their son. As a result the child's hair is redder than that of either parent.

For every inherited characteristic, an individual receives two copies of a gene—one from the mother and one from the father. When both copies are the same—for example, both for blue eyes—the child is certain to have that characteristic. However, an individual who receives two different genes for a given characteristic—such as one gene for blue eyes and one gene for brown eyes—will have the trait dictated by the **dominant,** or *stronger,* gene. In this example, the gene for brown eyes is dominant and the gene for blue eyes is **recessive,** or *weaker;* the child will have brown eyes. These terms refer only to the relationship of the gene copies to each other. Blue eyes are not weaker than brown eyes.

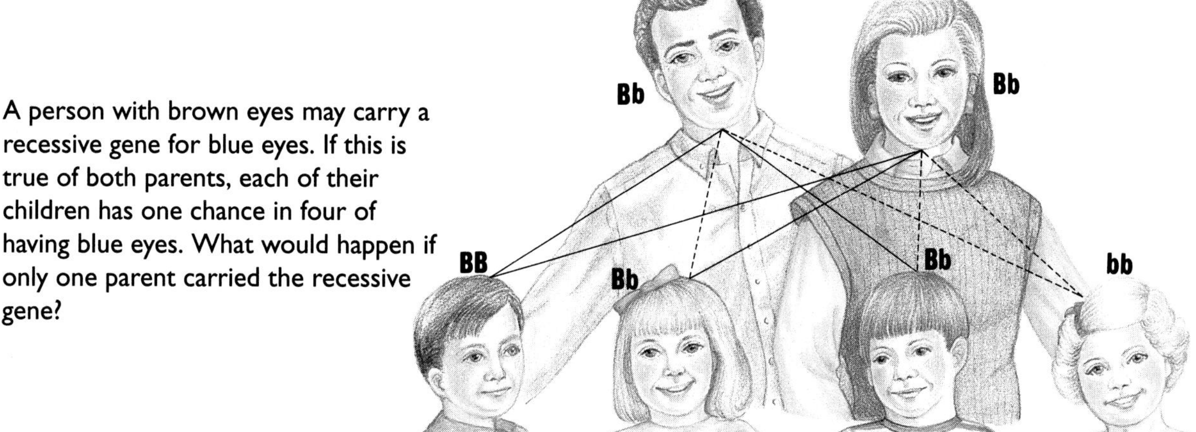

A person with brown eyes may carry a recessive gene for blue eyes. If this is true of both parents, each of their children has one chance in four of having blue eyes. What would happen if only one parent carried the recessive gene?

Heredity explains why brothers and sisters often resemble each other. It also explains why they can look quite different. Of the father's 46 chromosomes, only half go into the sperm cell—one from each of his 23 pairs. Which chromosome from each pair is used? This is a matter of chance. The same is true of the mother's egg cell. Thus each sperm or egg cell contains a different combination of chromosomes and of genes. The uniting of each sperm and egg creates a unique individual.

At conception, the fertilized egg inherits all the physical traits its parents can ever give it. Though it is less than one-fourth the size of a pinhead, the fertilized egg has its own complete genetic blueprint. This may include its father's brown eyes; its mother's dimples; a grandfather's tall, lean build; and a grandmother's clear, sweet singing voice. These traits—and many, many others—are determined by the particular combinations of genes brought together at conception.

Sex Determination

The sex of a child is also determined at the moment of conception. It is determined by the special chromosomes that come in two types, X and Y. Each ovum from the female contains an X chromosome. Each male sperm contains either an X chromosome or a Y chromosome. If the sperm that fertilizes the ovum carries an X chromosome, an XX combination results and the child is a girl. If the sperm carries a Y chromosome, an XY combination results and the child is a boy.

Multiple Births

As you know, a fertilized egg starts growing by dividing into two cells. These cells continue to divide until there are millions of cells.

Sometimes the growing mass of cells splits apart soon after fertilization. Each of these two clumps of cells continues to divide and grow into a separate embryo. This is the process by which identical twins are produced. Identical twins are always the same sex and always have very similar characteristics, because the two babies have developed from one zygote. Why the zygote splits apart is still a mystery of nature.

Unlike identical twins, fraternal twins develop when two eggs are released at the same time and each is fertilized by a different sperm. They grow side by side in the uterus. Fraternal twins can be either the same sex or opposite sexes. They are no more alike in appearance than any other brothers and sisters.

Identical twins share the same genetic pattern. That is why their appearance is so similar. Since a child's sex is determined by the genes, identical twins are always the same sex.

In multiple births of more than two, the babies may be identical or fraternal or a combination of identical and fraternal. Triplets, for example, are identical if the single zygote splits into three parts, each of which continues to develop independently. They are fraternal if three separate ova are fertilized by three different sperm. If the triplets develop from two zygotes, one of which splits apart, there are two identical babies and one fraternal baby.

Multiple births of more than two are usually quite rare, but births of twins are not that rare. In the United States, one birth in approximately 87 is a twin birth. (Identical twins occur only one-fourth as frequently as fraternal twins.)

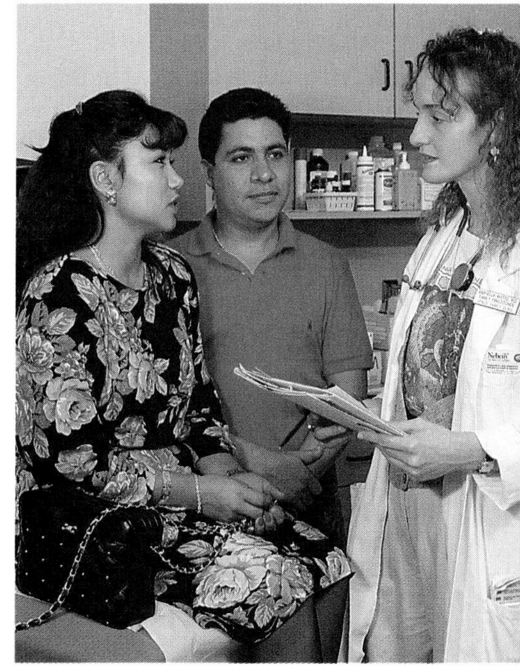

Infertility can be a difficult problem for couples who want to have children. They may decide to undergo a fertility analysis. In many cases, the doctor is able to determine the cause of the infertility and suggest a course of treatment.

Infertility

Not all couples who want to have children are able to conceive. A couple's **infertility,** or *inability to conceive children,* may have many causes. Many couples seek medical advice when they suspect they are infertile, typically after a year of trying without success to conceive. A doctor usually makes a fertility analysis, a detailed physical study of both the man and the woman. The analysis includes taking medical histories and giving both partners thorough physical examinations.

Often, the fertility analysis reveals that the man, the woman, or both have physical problems that prevent pregnancy. Surgery or medication may solve the problem. For example, the woman's ovaries may not be releasing an egg each month. In this case, the doctor may prescribe fertility drugs, compounds that stimulate a woman's ovaries to release eggs. Fertility drugs, however, have several drawbacks, as do all drugs. Some women who take them are troubled by serious side effects, such as lung problems, abdominal pain, nausea, diarrhea, or dizziness. Also, it can be difficult to determine how much of a fertility drug an individual woman should be given. If she takes too little, there will be no pregnancy. If she takes too much, there may be multiple births. Two or three—or even eight or more—eggs may be released and fertilized at one time. The uterus was not designed to carry so many babies, and they have little chance of survival.

Males also account for a large percentage of infertility problems. Drugs can often be used to assure a man is making enough healthy sperm for conception to occur.

Despite the problems associated with infertility treatment, it is estimated that half of all couples who would otherwise have been childless are able to conceive after medical treatment.

People who are unable to have children often feel, that they aren't normal, that they are less masculine or feminine than others, or that they are alone in facing this situation. Medical and counseling support are usually very important.

INTERNATIONAL ADOPTIONS

American families wishing to adopt a child will often explore international adoptions. One reason is the more liberal adoption policies of some foreign countries, another is the speed in which the adoption can be processed. Still other families want to share their homes and lives with someone in great need. As with all adoptions, families follow a procedure. First a reputable agency is contacted and a search is made for a suitable match for the family. Next, arrangements must be made for the release of the child and his or her entry into the United States.

International adoptions have been highly successful for many American families. Today, American parents have become interested in helping their adopted children to understand and think about the country and people that are a part of their heritage. Maintaining a link with their background has helped young people appreciate their past as well as their present way of life.

Options for Infertile Couples

A couple who cannot conceive a child themselves may consider several other options.

- **Adoption.** Couples who cannot become parents biologically may choose to adopt. Adoption can be a means of providing a loving home for one or more children who would not otherwise have one.
- **Artificial insemination.** This is the process of injecting sperm into a woman's uterus with a special needle. A doctor does this during the woman's fertile period. The sperm may be from the woman's husband or from another male, usually unknown to the couple, called a donor. Donor sperm is sometimes used by couples in which the man has a history of inherited disorders.
- **In vitro fertilization.** A woman whose damaged Fallopian tubes prevent pregnancy may have a doctor remove a mature egg from her ovary. The egg is placed in a small glass dish containing a special solution, to which her husband's sperm are added. If fertilization takes place, the doctor then

inserts the zygote into the woman's uterus. There, the zygote may attach itself to the lining of the uterus, and a normal pregnancy can proceed.

- **Ovum transfer.** This procedure is sometimes called adoptive pregnancy. An egg obtained from a female donor is fertilized by the man's sperm with in vitro fertilization and then implanted in the uterus of an infertile woman. Ovum transfer is sometimes used by women who lack working ovaries or who have a history of inherited disorders.
- **Surrogate mother.** A **surrogate**, or *substitute*, mother is a woman who carries and delivers a baby for another couple. In some cases, the surrogate carries a couple's fertilized egg, which is removed from the biological mother because she is unable to carry a pregnancy to term. Other surrogates are artificially inseminated with sperm from the husband of an infertile woman. Such options are usually managed through legal arrangements or according to various state laws.

As technology continues to advance, there may soon be other options available. However, the alternatives that science makes possible are not always considered acceptable by everyone. Procedures such as ovum transfer and surrogate motherhood are controversial. They raise many philosophical questions that society has not had to face before.

SECTION 2 REVIEW

CHECK YOUR UNDERSTANDING

1. List at least five traits that an individual inherits from previous generations.
2. What is a chromosome?
3. How many chromosomes does each person have? How many genes does each chromosome contain?
4. What is the difference between a dominant gene and a recessive gene?
5. How is the sex of a baby determined?
6. Explain the difference between identical twins and fraternal twins.
7. What is infertility? List three options for infertile couples who want to have children.

DISCUSS AND DISCOVER

1. Discuss the physical traits you think you inherited from previous generations of your family. If possible, make a display of photographs, showing you and various other family members from whom you think you inherited certain traits.
2. What adjustments do you think parents and other family members have to make when multiple births occur? How might a multiple birth affect a family's financial resources? How could it affect relationships among family members? How would the effects of the birth of twins differ from, for example, the effects of the birth of quadruplets?

SECTION 3

Problems in Prenatal Development

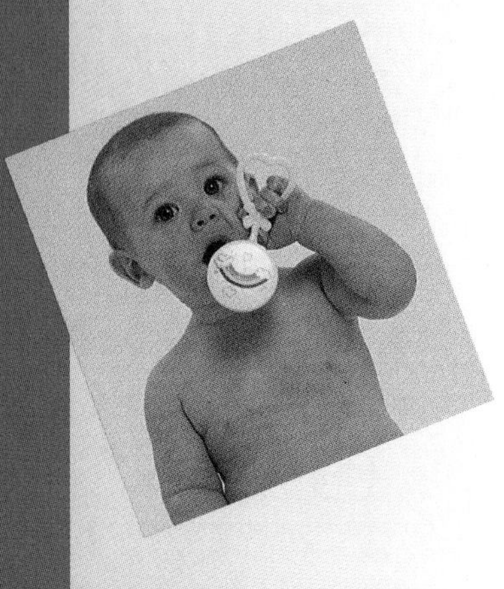

OBJECTIVES

- Name and describe specific types of birth defects.
- Discuss the causes of birth defects.
- Describe how birth defects can be diagnosed and prevented.

TERMS TO LEARN

amniocentesis
birth defect
chorionic villi sampling
miscarriage
premature
stillbirth
ultrasound

Will the baby be all right? This is a major concern for nearly all parents-to-be. Fortunately, most babies develop normally and are born healthy. For a variety of reasons, however, prenatal development does not always proceed normally.

Birth Defects

Premature babies are *born before their development is complete.* This usually means that the pregnancy was less than 36 weeks. These babies have not had time to gain weight, as weight gain usually takes place during the last month of pregnancy, so they often weigh less than 5 ½ pounds (2.5 kg). (A full-term baby usually weighs between 7 and 8 pounds [3.2 and 3.6 kg]). Babies can also weigh less than 5 ½ pounds (2.5 kg) even though they were born on time. These babies are said to be low birth weight babies. Premature babies and low birth weight babies must be given special care. Their small size and incomplete development make them vulnerable to infection, lung ailments, and other problems.

Prematurity is one example of a **birth defect**—*an abnormality, present at birth, that affects the structure or function of the body.* Strictly speaking, almost everyone is born with some type of imperfection. Most, such as birthmarks, are relatively minor. However, some babies are born with more serious kinds of problems, referred to generally as birth defects. In any pregnancy, no matter what the situation, there is a chance the baby will have a birth defect.

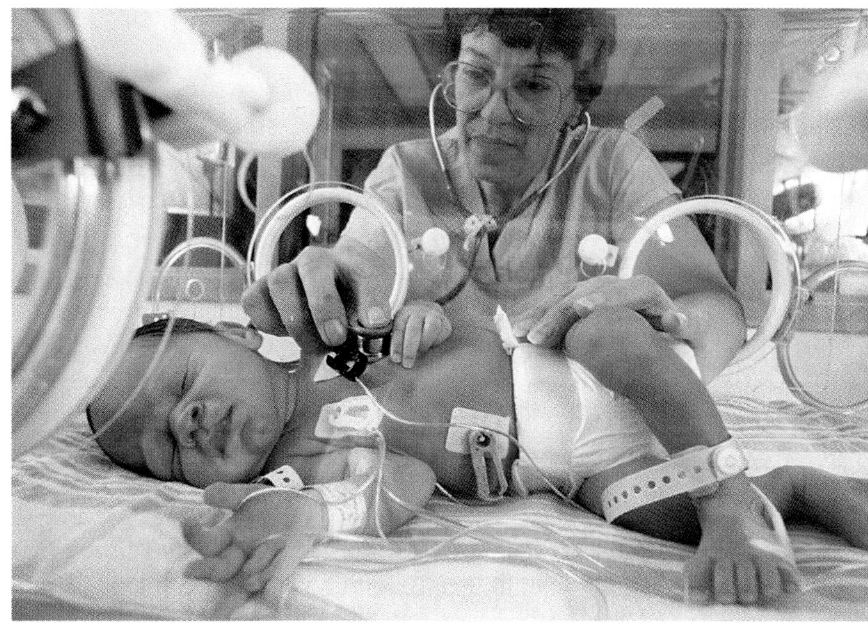

Sometimes a baby is born with a serious health problem. Medical science is constantly working to find not only better ways of treating these problems, but ways to prevent them.

Types of Birth Defects

There are hundreds of kinds of birth defects, with widely differing symptoms and effects. Most, however, are quite rare.

Some birth defects affect the shape or size of the body or of certain parts of the body. For instance, a child may be born with a misshapen foot or an extra or a missing finger. Other birth defects involve a part or system of the body that does not function properly. Blindness, deafness, and mental retardation are examples.

Not all birth defects are apparent at birth. Sometimes the abnormality does not cause problems until months—or even years—have passed.

Birth defects vary widely in their severity. Some are mild or can be readily corrected. Others result in severe lifelong disabilities or even death.

In some cases, if prenatal development is not proceeding normally, a **miscarriage**—*the natural ending of a pregnancy before the embryo or fetus could possibly survive*—occurs. A **stillbirth** is *the natural ending of a pregnancy after 20 weeks.* Usually, these losses happen by accident and are not the fault of either the father or the mother.

As soon as they find out they are pregnant, most couples start making plans for their baby. Thus, when they lose that pregnancy, either by miscarriage or by stillbirth, for most, it is the same as losing a child who had been born. They go through stages of grief, as does anyone who has had a family member die. There are special services and support groups for people who have had a pregnancy loss.

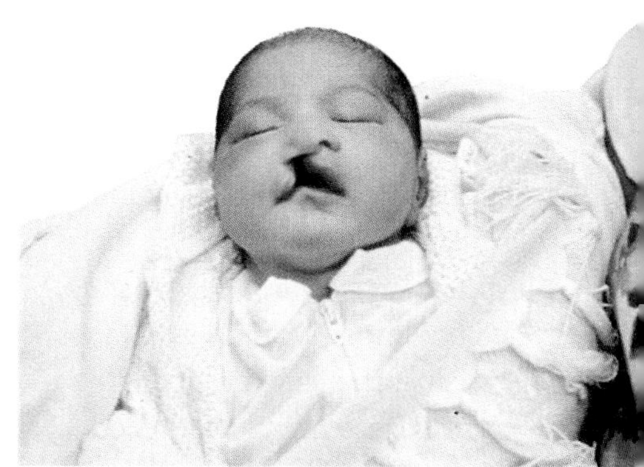

Prenatal development is a complex process. When something interferes with it, a birth defect may result. The development of this baby's lip was not completed the way it should have been.

Causes of Birth Defects

Just as the types of birth defects differ, so do the causes of birth defects. Some are inherited from one or both parents. Others are caused by factors in the environment. Researchers believe that most birth defects result from a combination of environment and heredity. However, the exact causes of many birth defects are not yet fully understood. Some seem to happen totally by chance—not caused by any environmental exposure, and not inherited.

Environmental Causes

As you have learned, prenatal development takes place very rapidly. In just a few weeks, a baby develops all the bodily systems needed for survival and a normal life. During this prenatal period, the developing baby is completely dependent on the mother's body for nourishment and oxygen.

Many choices the mother makes—as well as many conditions of which the mother may be unaware—can affect the development of her baby. These are some of the environmental factors that can influence the development of a baby:

- The nutritional balance of the mother's diet.
- Any diseases or infections the mother has during pregnancy.
- Harmful substances, such as alcohol, tobacco smoke, and drugs, including some medicines that would ordinarily benefit the mother.
- Exposure to outside hazards such as radiation, especially early in pregnancy.

People once thought that the placenta was a barrier that protected the baby from many dangerous substances. However, we now know this is untrue.

Everything a pregnant woman takes into her body—pills, injections, food, tobacco smoke, coffee, and alcohol—may affect her unborn child. The placenta may act as a partial barrier, and certain substances may have difficulty crossing to the child. It is now clear, however, that most substances reach the embryo or fetus. If the concentration of any substance in the mother's blood is high enough, some will surely leak across the placenta and reach the fetus.

As you can see, how the mother takes care of herself during pregnancy is crucial. An important part of taking care of herself is seeking medical care. A woman should see a doctor as soon as she suspects she is pregnant, and she should follow the doctor's advice to stay healthy.

HEALTH TIP

We do not know a "safe level" for possible harmful substances. The best course is to avoid all these substances during pregnancy. Since most women don't realize they are pregnant until the embryo is formed, the ideal is to plan a pregnancy and avoid all possibly harmful substances before becoming pregnant.

Hereditary Causes

Everyone has five or six imperfect recessive genes among the thousands that make up his or her personal blueprint. A single copy of these genes will have no effect on the development of the person with the gene or of a baby to whom it is passed on. However, if each parent passes on the same defective recessive gene, the baby will then have two copies of this gene and therefore will not have a normal gene for the trait determined by this gene. Depending on how important this trait is, there may be a high risk of a birth defect.

Normal genes are usually dominant over defective genes, which are most often recessive. A recessive gene usually produces an effect only when transmitted by both parents. Very often parents do not learn that they carry recessive genes for a particular defect until they have a child born with that defect. If both parents have a recessive gene for the same disorder, *each* of their children has one chance in four of developing that disorder. Sickle-cell anemia, a blood disease, is one kind of birth defect that is passed on in this way. So is cystic fibrosis, a lung disease.

Not all hereditary defects are passed on this way. For example, some inherited conditions affect only males. Hemophilia, a condition that prevents the blood from clotting, and color blindness are such conditions. Other defects and conditions are passed straight through families from one affected person to some of their children and grandchildren.

A positive, encouraging approach can help children with Down syndrome make the most of their abilities.

Interaction of Heredity and Environment

Most birth defects are believed to result from a combination of heredity and environment. For example, sometimes the structure of the heart is defective at birth. Such a defect is usually the result of two factors working together. First, there was an inherited tendency for a heart defect. Second, the defect was triggered by some factor in the environment, such as a drug or a virus. If only one of these conditions had been met, the heart would probably have been normal. This type of interaction between heredity and environment is probably the cause for cleft lip, cleft palate, and spina bifida.

Errors in Chromosomes

A few types of birth defects are linked to a problem with the affected baby's chromosomes. For example, there may be too many—or too few—chromosomes in each cell of the body. Although this type of defect involves genetic material, it is not the same as a hereditary defect. The child does not inherit the

ASK THE EXPERTS

Sources of Support for Special-Needs Children

Jackie Mault is the Director for the Toppenish School District where she develops special programs for children from birth through high school.

Our neighbors' baby was born with Down syndrome. Having a special-needs child so close makes me wonder— where can the parents of young children with special needs go for various kinds of help and support?

Raising a special-needs child places unusual demands on a family. Special-needs children require extra medical attention; most also require other kinds of professional help in dealing with particular physical, social, or educational problems. In addition, parents and other members of families with special-needs children usually benefit from support in coping with the stresses related to their responsibilities. Fortunately, services that offer specific help and general support are increasingly available to the parents of young children with special needs.

In nearly all cases, the first source of help is the child's pediatrician or the family's general physician. Physicians are able to refer babies and young children to medical specialists. More and more, physicians are also able to refer families to other helpful resources within the community. Parents who suspect their child may have special needs or who feel their child is not developing normally should discuss their concerns with the pediatrician or family practitioner.

In many communities across the country, the public school has become an important source of assistance. Most public schools have special programs for special-needs children between the ages of three and five. Services may include center- or school-based preschool classes and home-based instruction. Public schools usually provide not just instructional programs but also such services as speech/language therapy, physical therapy, occupational therapy, counseling, and transportation. Many of these public school programs emphasize providing parents with the skills to help their developing child.

Some public schools also provide services for special-needs babies and toddlers. These services may include assessment and support for children from birth to age three, focusing on objectives that address each child's unique needs.

For emotional support, many parents turn to their own extended families. In addition, they may benefit from association with specific support programs, often affiliated with a local hospital, the department of social services, or the local, county, or state health department.

Jacqueline L Mault

Jackie Mault

defect from the parents. Researchers are still working to understand why chromosomal errors occur.

The most common type of chromosomal error is called Down syndrome. One child in every 650 births has this condition. The risk increases as the mother gets older. A child with Down syndrome has an extra chromosome 21, as shown in the photograph on page 137. Because each chromosome carries hundreds of genes, the defect can interfere with development in many ways.

SELECTED BIRTH DEFECTS

CEREBRAL PALSY

- **Description:** Cerebral palsy is a general term for a variety of motor system disorders. The symptoms can include lack of coordination, stiffness, jerkiness, difficulty in speech, and paralysis.
- **Causes:** Cerebral palsy results from brain damage before, during, or shortly after birth. The causes of the brain damage vary.
- **Detection:** The symptoms usually become recognizable sometime during the first year of life.
- **Treatment:** The brain damage associated with cerebral palsy is irreversible. However, physical therapy, speech therapy, occupational therapy, surgery, and medication can minimize the disabilities in many cases.

CLEFT LIP AND/OR CLEFT PALATE

- **Description:** A gap in the upper lip and/or palate causes problems with eating, swallowing, speech, and appearance.
- **Causes:** Often the cause is unknown; it may be hereditary and/or environmental.
- **Detection:** Both cleft lip and cleft palate are apparent at birth.
- **Treatment:** Surgery can correct the gap and eliminate the problems associated with it.

CYSTIC FIBROSIS

- **Description:** Cystic fibrosis is a functional defect that involves the respiratory and digestive systems. Many of those affected die before reaching adulthood.
- **Cause:** This is a hereditary condition, carried on a recessive gene. An affected child has two copies of the defective gene, one from each parent.
- **Detection:** Tests can identify carriers of the gene and can diagnose an affected child or fetus.
- **Treatment:** There is no known cure for cystic fibrosis. Those affected can be helped by special diets, lung exercises, and treatment of any complications.

DOWN SYNDROME

- **Description:** Down syndrome is a group of associated defects that may include mental retardation, delayed development, heart defects, and other characteristics.
- **Cause:** Down syndrome is caused by a chromosomal error. For reasons not yet understood, there is an extra chromosome 21.
- **Detection:** The syndrome is detected by an analysis of the chromosomes. Amniocentesis or chorionic villi sampling can detect the syndrome in a fetus.
- **Treatment:** Those affected benefit from special therapy and schooling and, in some cases, from corrective surgery.

MUSCULAR DYSTROPHY

- **Description:** There are many different types of muscular dystrophy; all involve a progressive weakness and shrinking of the muscles. The most common form begins between the ages of two and six.
- **Causes:** Most types of muscular dystrophy are hereditary. The most common form is transmitted by female carriers of the gene but affects only males.
- **Detection:** The disease is apparent at its onset. Genetic counseling can identify carriers.
- **Treatment:** There is no known cure. Physical therapy can minimize the disabilities.

SELECTED BIRTH DEFECTS (cont'd.)

PKU

- **Description:** PKU is a condition in which the body is unable to process and use a specific protein. Mental retardation can result.
- **Cause:** This is a hereditary condition, carried on a recessive gene. An affected child has two copies of the defective gene, one from each parent.
- **Detection:** Newborns are tested for PKU, as required by law in all states.
- **Treatment:** There is no known cure for PKU. If it is diagnosed early, a special diet can reduce or prevent brain damage.

SICKLE-CELL ANEMIA

- **Description:** Malformed red blood cells interfere with the supply of oxygen to all parts of the body. The symptoms include tiredness, lack of appetite, and pain. Sickle cell anemia can lead to early death.
- **Cause:** This is a hereditary condition, carried on a recessive gene. An affected child has two copies of the defective gene, one from each parent.
- **Detection:** Sickle-cell anemia can be detected by blood tests. Amniocentesis or chorionic villi sampling can identify anemia in a fetus. Genetic counseling can identify carriers.
- **Treatment:** There is no known cure for sickle-cell anemia. Medication can treat the symptoms.

SPINA BIFIDA AND/OR HYDROCEPHALUS

- **Description:** Spina bifida is a condition in which an incompletely formed spinal cord causes partial paralysis. Spina bifida often occurs with hydrocephalus, a condition in which an excess of fluid surrounds the brain, which can lead to brain damage.
- **Causes:** Both hereditary and environmental factors may cause these conditions.
- **Detection:** Both conditions are apparent at birth. A combination of tests of the mother's blood, amniocentesis, and ultrasound can reveal suspected cases in a fetus.
- **Treatment:** Any paralysis or brain damage associated with these conditions is permanent. Corrective surgery, physical therapy, and special schooling can minimize disabilities. Hydrocephalus can often be controlled by an operation performed shortly after birth.

TAY-SACHS DISEASE

- **Description:** Babies born with Tay-Sachs disease lack a specific chemical in their blood, resulting in an inability to process and use fats. Tay-Sachs leads to severe brain damage and to death, usually by the age of two or three.
- **Cause:** This is a hereditary condition, carried on a recessive gene. An affected child has two copies of the defective gene, one from each parent.
- **Detection:** Blood tests can identify carriers and can test for the disorder in a newborn. Amniocentesis or chorionic villi sampling can identify Tay-Sachs disease in a fetus.
- **Treatment:** There is no known cure or treatment for this disease.

Prevention and Diagnosis of Birth Defects

In the past, little could be done to improve the chances of having a healthy baby. Today, organizations like the National Foundation/March of Dimes fund ongoing research into the cause, prevention, and treatment of all types of birth defects. Some causes of birth defects, such as infections, drugs, and alcohol, can be controlled. Although most birth defects cannot yet be prevented, tests can sometimes determine the probability that specific defects will develop. Advances in the detection of defects before birth make early treatment possible.

It is difficult for a child born with a serious medical problem to lead a normal life. The rest of the child's family is necessarily affected by the emotional and financial strain the defect causes. Responsible couples do everything they can to minimize the possibility of birth defects.

Genetic Counseling

Some hereditary or chromosomal defects can be predicted by genetic counseling. This service combines a knowledge of heredity and birth defects with laboratory tests. It tells parents in advance the statistical odds that their children will have certain diseases or defects. The couple can then use this information to plan their pregnancy. Genetic counseling does not tell people what to do; it only explains the options and risks. Most people who seek genetic counseling do so because they are aware of a specific possible problem.

Although genetic counseling may be provided by family doctors, it is best provided by a genetic specialist. Genetic counselors are individuals specifically trained to understand genetic disorders. They have good communication skills, so they

Some genetic defects can be identified by making a photograph of chromosomes from the person's tissues. In the case of Down syndrome, there are three, rather than two of chromosome 21 (bottom row).

Raising a child who has a serious birth defect involves many challenges. Parents are faced with the drain on their finances, emotions, time, and energy. At the same time, family members should treat the child as normally as possible. They need to help the child gain confidence and overcome feelings of being "different."

can explain the situation to the family, and help family members deal with the emotional and financial impact of their specific situation. Genetic doctors are usually specialists either in recognizing and diagnosing genetic conditions or in performing specialized prenatal care. The most specialized testing is done at major medical centers in large cities, but most states have regional services so that genetic counseling is readily available close to home for families throughout the United States.

A genetic counselor begins by obtaining a complete family medical history from the patients. The patients could be a couple who are concerned about their chances of having a child with a serious birth defect or a couple who, because they already have a child with a problem, want more information. Both the husband and the wife are asked for information relating to diseases and causes of death of all their close relatives. They are also questioned about events during this pregnancy and during any previous pregnancies, and they are asked for other relevant information.

The patients—and, in some cases, other family members—may be given thorough physical examinations. If necessary, special laboratory tests are also performed.

When all the questionnaires and tests are completed, the counselor is usually able to tell the couple whether genetic problems are present. The couple may also be told their mathematical chances of having a child with a serious birth defect. The genetic counselor explains the findings and describes alternative courses of action. The genetic counselor does not tell the family which course of action to take. That is always a personal decision for the family.

Prenatal Tests

If a woman is already pregnant and she or her doctor suspects that a birth defect may be likely, special prenatal tests can be given. These tests determine whether specific birth defects are present. No tests will tell whether a baby will be normal. Some tests may alert the physician to a condition in the baby that must be treated before or immediately after birth. Blood testing to estimate the risk for some defects is common. Although it will not be possible in the foreseeable future to test for all birth defects, new methods of prenatal diagnosis are constantly being developed. Three of the most useful diagnostic procedures are ultrasound, amniocentesis, and chorionic villi sampling.

- **Ultrasound** is *a technique of using sound waves to make a video image of an unborn baby to check for specific health problems.* It can show whether the fetus is developing on schedule. Certain defects, especially those involving the skeleton and other organs, can also be detected by ultrasound.

  Researchers are still studying possible risks of ultrasound. For this reason, most experts advise that ultrasound be used only as part of necessary medical tests. When it is used in

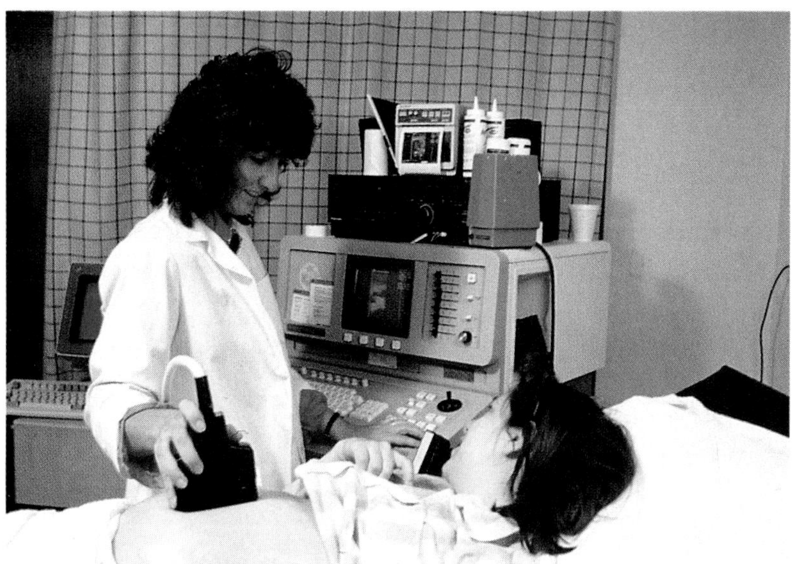

An ultrasound scan produces a picture of the fetus that can give the doctor information about its development.

this way, ultrasound often provides additional information that can be reassuring or helpful to both the parents-to-be and the physician. It can help verify the baby's due date. In addition, ultrasound may reveal the sex of the developing baby or the presence of twins.

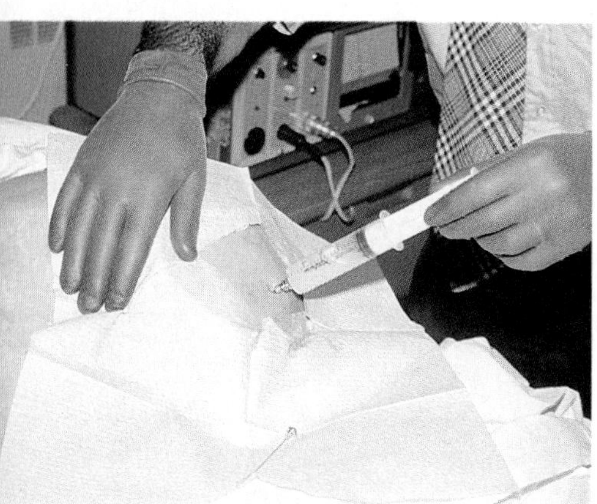

Amniocentesis can detect a number of rare genetic defects. It is performed in the fourth month of pregnancy or later, but only if they suspect a problem.

- **Amniocentesis** is *the process of withdrawing a sample of the amniotic fluid surrounding an unborn baby with a special needle and testing that fluid for indications of specific birth defects or other health problems.* The doctor withdrawing the fluid uses an ultrasound image as a guide when inserting the needle. Some of the cells from the fetus are contained within the sample of amniotic fluid. These cells are tested for evidence of birth defects.

  The most common use of amniocentesis is as a test for Down syndrome when the expectant mother is over age 35. Because the procedure involves some risks, including the possibility of miscarriage, it is performed only when there is a valid medical reason. It is always the woman's decision whether or not to have genetic amniocentesis.

- **Chorionic villi sampling** is *the process of testing for specific birth defects by sampling small amounts of the tissue from the membrane that encases the fetus.* Guided by an ultrasound image, a doctor inserts a catheter, or small tube, through the vagina into the uterus. There, samples of the villi—fingers of tissue that protrude from the chorion, the membrane encasing the fetus—are snipped or suctioned off for analysis.

  Chorionic villi sampling is used to test for the same disorders as amniocentesis, but the sampling can be done earlier in a pregnancy. Unfortunately, the risks that chorionic villi sampling will cause miscarriage or birth defects are much greater than the risks involved in amniocentesis. It is performed only after careful consideration of the medical reasons and risks. It is always the woman's decision whether or not to have chorionic villi sampling.

More than 100 kinds of birth defects can now be diagnosed prenatally. In some cases, the problem can be treated before the baby is born. For example, the first child of a Boston woman died at three months of age from a hereditary condition. During her second pregnancy, the woman underwent amniocentesis. The test results indicated that this child also had the condition. A biochemical defect would cause mental retardation in the developing child. Vitamin therapy was administered to the mother, and thus through the placenta to the fetus, to correct the problem, and the baby was normal at birth.

Several other methods of prenatal diagnosis are now in the experimental stages. These may someday provide more accurate information at earlier stages of development. For example, it has become possible to view the fetus directly through a special instrument, obtain samples of fetal blood and tissue, and even perform surgery on an unborn child. The testing is currently quite dangerous. Further breakthroughs may make these procedures safe enough for widespread use.

Currently in common use are some blood test screenings to estimate the risk for certain birth defects. The information from these blood tests can be helpful to a woman and her doctor when deciding whether there is a valid medical reason to perform one of the diagnostic procedures described above.

SECTION 3 REVIEW

CHECK YOUR UNDERSTANDING

1. What is a birth defect? List three kinds of birth defects.
2. Under what circumstances is a baby considered premature? What special problems does a premature baby face?
3. What is a miscarriage?
4. What is the cause of Down syndrome? What is one factor that increases the risk of Down syndrome?
5. What is the purpose of genetic counseling?
6. What is the purpose of ultrasound testing during pregnancy? What kinds of defects can be detected by an ultrasound?
7. What is the difference between amniocentesis and chorionic villi sampling? What risks are involved in each procedure?

DISCUSS AND DISCOVER

1. Read about the rate of premature births in your community or in your state. Then investigate programs designed to help mothers have healthy, full-term pregnancies. Work with other students to make posters or fliers promoting these programs.
2. What stresses do you think are involved in adjusting to life with a healthy new baby? How do those stresses compare with the stresses involved in adjusting to life with a baby who has a serious birth defect? How do you imagine the birth defect affects the baby's parents? Siblings? Grandparents?
3. Why do you think some couples might have trouble deciding whether or not to seek genetic counseling? What are the advantages of using genetic counselors? Are there any disadvantages? If so, what are they? Do you think a genetic counselor would—or should—tell a couple whether or not they should have children? Why?

SECTION 4 Avoiding Environmental Hazards

OBJECTIVES

- Identify the hazards that alcohol and other drugs pose to prenatal development.
- Discuss other environmental hazards that should be avoided during pregnancy.

TERMS TO LEARN

fetal alcohol effects
fetal alcohol syndrome

In *every* pregnancy, the mother-to-be is responsible for taking the most important step in increasing the chances of having a healthy baby: She must take care of herself and keep herself safe and healthy. One important part of good prenatal care is understanding the harmful effects of environmental hazards such as alcohol and other drugs, smoking, X rays, and infections.

Alcohol

Though many people still avoid realizing this fact, alcohol is a drug—and it can be a dangerous one. Ever since ancient times, writers have commented on the poor mental and physical health of children born to alcoholic women. Modern medicine has confirmed these observations. Women who drink alcohol during pregnancy often bear children with a variety of birth defects, some of which can be fatal.

A woman who drinks during pregnancy risks having a child with **fetal alcohol syndrome,** *a condition of physical deformities and cognitive problems resulting from a mother's consumption of alcohol during pregnancy.* Almost all babies born with fetal alcohol syndrome are mentally retarded. This is because alcohol interferes with tissue growth and development, and brain tissue is most easily injured by this interference. Many childern born with fetal alcohol syndrome also have other problems, such as slow growth, poor coordination, behavior problems, heart defects, and facial disfigurement.

Children whose mothers drink less alcohol during pregnancy may suffer from **fetal alcohol effects**, *a less severe condition involving some, but not all, of the symptoms of fetal alcohol syndrome.* There is no safe amount of alcohol that a woman can drink during pregnancy without taking the chance of causing harm to her unborn child.

The degree of damage to the child is usually directly related to the amount of alcohol the mother consumed during pregnancy. It may also be affected by the stage of the pregnancy during which she drank and by the presence of other drugs in her system. Because the damage is done before birth, there is no cure for fetal alcohol syndrome or fetal alcohol effects.

Although fetal alcohol syndrome and fetal alcohol effects can't be cured, they can be prevented. Doctors do not yet know just how much alcohol presents a danger to the developing baby. For this reason, most health professionals recommend that pregnant women safeguard the health of their babies by avoiding alcohol altogether when they plan a pregnancy, as well as during pregnancy.

Other Drugs

Many doctors believe that drugs taken during pregnancy are among the major causes of birth defects linked to environmental factors. The drugs of which pregnant women should be especially aware include the following:

- Alcohol, as you have just read.
- Medicines that doctors prescribe.
- Over-the-counter remedies such as aspirin, cold medicines, nose drops, and vitamins.
- Chemicals such as caffeine, found in some foods and beverages, and nicotine, found in tobacco.
- Illegal drugs such as heroin, LSD, marijuana, crack, and other forms of cocaine.
- Inhalants—fumes that are inhaled into the lungs.

Over 62,000 nonprescription drugs and other environmental hazards carry warning labels for pregnant and nursing women.

Prescription and Over-the-Counter Drugs

Every pregnant woman should remember that there is no such thing as a completely safe drug. Even over-the-counter drugs, such as aspirin, cold remedies, and antihistamines, can be dangerous for the unborn child. One extreme example is thalidomide, which was considered a safe drug for relieving the symptoms of morning sickness in pregnant women during the late 1950s. Thalidomide caused severe birth defects in more than 5,000 infants before its effects were discovered.

HEALTH TIP

It is almost always impossible to predict the effect that any particular dose of a specific medication will have on a developing baby. For this reason, a woman who even suspects she may be pregnant—or who intends to become pregnant—should avoid medicines and other drugs altogether.

Medicines or infections that reach the fetus through the third month of pregnancy will have their most devastating effect. Any drug a pregnant woman takes reduces the flow of nutrition-bearing blood to the baby. During these months, the body systems, organs, arms, and legs are being formed, so the chances of malformation are greatest during this period. Brain development is also at a critical period, and mental retardation can be caused.

In the last six months of pregnancy, harmful substances that reach the fetus usually cause slow growth, infections, or abnormal bleeding at birth. Drugs taken just before delivery will still be in the baby's body at birth and may cause serious problems.

Doctors advise strict limits on the use of medications during pregnancy. A pregnant woman should not take any medicines—even aspirin or vitamins—unless they are specifically prescribed by her physician.

Drugs that are necessary in managing serious conditions, such as diabetes and high blood pressure, can be taken under a doctor's direction. However, a pregnant woman should be encouraged to give up medications for complaints like headaches and hay fever; avoiding such medications can be a worthwhile contribution to the normal development of her baby. In fact, any woman who is likely to become pregnant would be wise to avoid taking unnecessary drugs. Usually, a woman does not know she is pregnant until several weeks after conception has taken place.

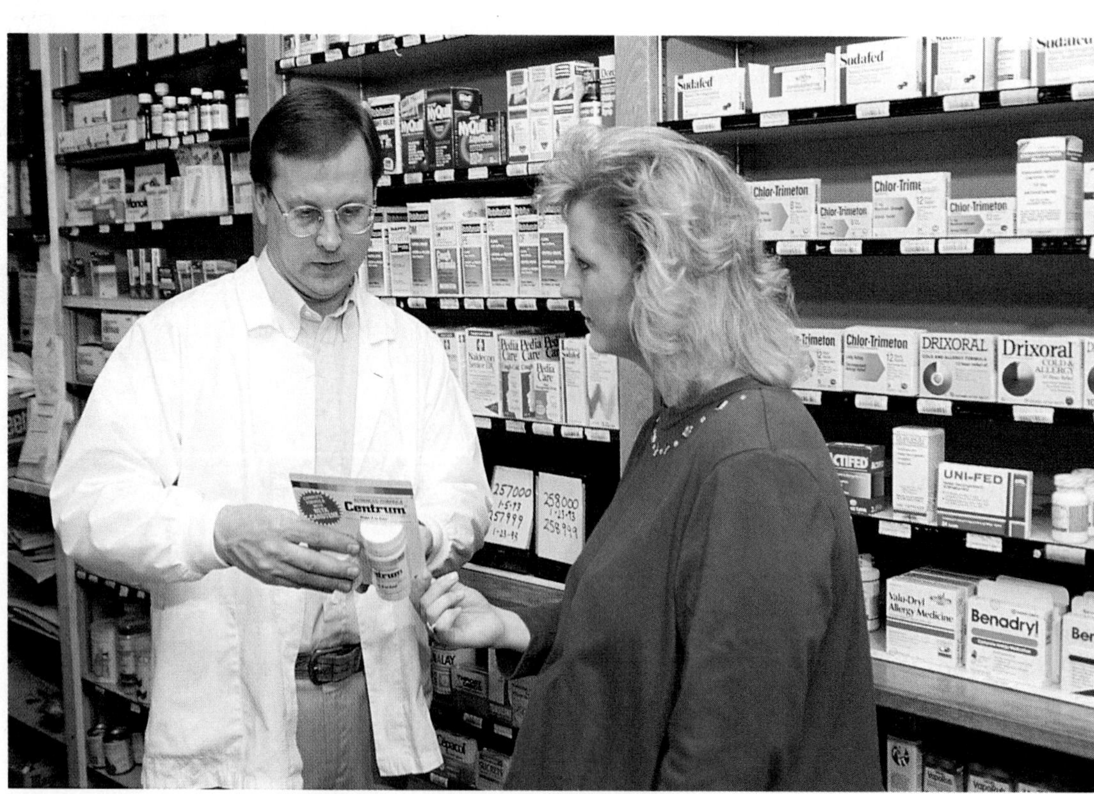

An expectant mother should not take any medication unless it is prescribed or recommended by a doctor who knows of the pregnancy. Even vitamin supplements can pose a risk to the unborn baby unless taken under a doctor's advice.

PARENTING IN ACTION

Decisions Affecting the Unborn

Five-year-old Susan and her four-year-old sister Emily are playing together in their quiet backyard. Emily runs to hide behind a tree. Her movements, however, are slower than those of other four-year-olds. Susan tries to chase Emily. However, instead of running directly to the tree, she stumbles past it.

The girls' mother, Char, sits on a lawn chair and watches them sadly. She recognizes that both her daughters have below-average intelligence, little strength, and, at times, no muscle control. She also sees that, although both girls are quite pretty, slight irregularities in their facial features indicate abnormalities.

For Char, the worst part of her daughters' problems is the knowledge that she herself is the cause of those problems. Char married when she was eighteen. Since her husband was serving in the army, the couple had to move from one military base to another. Char found it difficult to make new friends, knowing that in a few months she would have to start all over again somewhere else. She began drinking to relieve her loneliness and boredom. Char continued drinking throughout her two pregnancies.

Susan's ailments did not become apparent until after Emily was born. Several months later, the specialists gave the verdict: Both the girls had defects resulting from their mother's drinking during pregnancy.

Char explains, "I'd do anything for my girls. Of course I would have quit drinking—if only someone had told me!" Char did stop drinking, but the change came too late for Susan and Emily.

THINK AND DISCUSS

1. Why did Char drink during her pregnancies? Why do you imagine no doctor discussed the problem with her? Why do you think her husband and other family members might have avoided discussing it?
2. What could Char have done to overcome her loneliness and boredom instead of drinking?
3. What do you think Char can do now to help her family?
4. Where would you go if you had a drinking problem? What—if anything—would you say to a friend who had a drinking problem?

Caffeine

Of all the compounds that have been investigated as possible causes of birth defects, none has been so completely taken for granted as caffeine. Caffeine is widely found in beverages such as coffee, tea, cocoa, and many soft drinks, as well as in some foods and many medications. Because it is so common, caffeine is often not considered a drug. However, pregnant women—and those likely to become pregnant—should be cautious. Women who take in moderate amounts of caffeine probably don't need to worry about birth defects. It is known, however, that feeding large doses of caffeine to pregnant mice and rabbits causes birth defects in their offspring. Doctors usually advise women to be cautious about drinking coffee, tea, and cola during pregnancy.

Tobacco

The nicotine in cigarettes is also a drug—and a potentially dangerous one. The more a mother smokes, the smaller her baby is likely to be. This is important because the weight of the newborn is a critical factor in the ability to survive. Heavy smoking is also believed to cause premature birth. Doctors advise smokers that they should try to stop smoking before becoming pregnant. If they cannot quit smoking, they should at least cut down during pregnancy.

Illegal Drugs

Increases in the use of cocaine, marijuana, and other "street drugs" have presented physicians with new problems in preventing birth defects.

A mother who is addicted to drugs at the time of delivery usually passes her addiction on to her baby. Immediately after birth, these addicted infants must go through a period of withdrawal—painful illness resulting from the body's dependence on drugs. Some addicted babies even die as a result of severe withdrawal symptoms. For the babies who survive withdrawal, the future is uncertain. Experts are concerned that the long-range effects of this prenatal addiction may be serious, possibly affecting a child's learning ability and behavior. Many of these children seem unorganized; they are able to follow only very simple directions and are often unable to understand school classes.

Little is known about the specific effects of such drugs as marijuana, cocaine, barbiturates, and amphetamines on a developing fetus. However, considering the fact that even over-the-counter medications are cause for concern, you can see the potential danger of these drugs. Cocaine is known to cause miscarriage, stillbirth, prematurity, and birth defects. Similar results are suggested in studies on marijuana. While this kind of research continues, the best advice is to avoid taking *any* drugs before or during pregnancy.

X Rays

X rays present another potential danger to the unborn baby. Radiation from X rays or other sources can cause birth defects. A pregnant woman who is in an accident or who is sick should inform medical personnel of her pregnancy. They can then take special precautions if X rays are necessary. For the same reason, she should also be sure her dentist or orthodontist is aware of her pregnancy. It is also important to avoid unnecessary X rays before pregnancy. Both men and women should request abdominal shielding during routine X rays.

Rubella

The terrible effect of certain infections on unborn children was highlighted by the epidemic of rubella (sometimes called German measles) that swept the country several decades ago. Thousands of unborn babies were affected when their mothers came down with German measles during pregnancy. Although most of the women had few or even no symptoms of illness, the effects on the developing babies were devastating. Because of their mothers' infection with rubella, babies were born with deafness, blindness, heart disease, and/or mental retardation.

A vaccine for rubella is now available, and millions of children have been vaccinated. The vaccine may be dangerous, however, for women who are pregnant or who become pregnant shortly after receiving it. A woman who is unsure whether she has been vaccinated can check her health records. If records are unavailable, she can consult a doctor, who will be able to determine her immunity with a simple blood test. Every woman should be sure she is immune to rubella before she considers pregnancy.

Sexually Transmitted Diseases (STDs)

Like rubella, sexually transmitted diseases, or STDs, are infections that can have dreadful effects on unborn babies. All the following are sexually transmitted diseases:

- Syphilis.
- Gonorrhea.
- Genital herpes.
- AIDS (acquired immune deficiency syndrome).

- Group B streptococcus.
- Chlamydia.

These and other sexually transmitted diseases can affect prenatal development or be passed on from an infected mother to the developing baby. They can result in serious illness, deformity, or even death.

It is possible for a person to be infected with a sexually transmitted disease without realizing it. For this reason, special measures are often taken to protect unborn babies against the effects of sexually transmitted diseases. Most doctors routinely test pregnant women for syphilis. Such tests are required by law in many states. In addition, doctors usually treat the eyes of newborns with a solution to kill gonorrhea germs that could otherwise cause blindness. The laws of many states make this kind of treatment mandatory.

Drugs and treatment can cure syphilis and gonorrhea and can relieve the symptoms of herpes in adults. Untreated, these diseases can affect the heart, brain, reproductive system, and spinal cord, and can eventually lead to death. No drug can cure the damage to the newborn that results from a delay in diagnosis and treatment. Any pregnant woman who suspects she could have a sexually transmitted disease should discuss the condition frankly with her doctor.

AIDS, a viral infection that attacks the immune system, is a particularly dangerous sexually transmitted disease. There is no cure, and AIDS is invariably fatal. Like other STDs, it can be spread by unprotected sexual intercourse. In addition, individu-

AIDS is a deadly disease with no known cure. Health organizations have developed educational campaigns to inform the public about the realities of AIDS and other sexually transmitted diseases.

als can be infected with AIDS by sharing infected needles or through contact with infected blood. A fetus can be infected with AIDS by the mother. The AIDS virus may lie hidden in a person for many years before causing symptoms, so there is no way to tell whether someone is infected just by looking at him or her. If a woman who has AIDS gives birth to a child, there is a 20 to 50 percent chance that her baby will also develop AIDS and die.

Not all infections in a pregnant woman pose a threat to the developing baby. However, a pregnant woman should tell her doctor about any illness, no matter how mild it may seem.

Genetic Counseling

Genetic counselors can provide information and answer questions for women who have been exposed to any of the above substances or diseases. A genetic counselor can provide information in response to questions such as these: What is the chance that this substance or disease will cause a problem? Is there any special care needed during pregnancy? Should any special tests be considered?

SECTION 4 REVIEW

CHECK YOUR UNDERSTANDING

1. What causes fetal alcohol syndrome? List three kinds of problems associated with fetal alcohol syndrome.
2. During what period of pregnancy are the harmful effects of medications on a fetus most severe? Why?
3. List two problems that can be caused by smoking during pregnancy.
4. How might a pregnant woman be exposed to radiation? What effect can radiation have on a developing baby?
5. List three problems that may result for the developing baby if a pregnant woman is infected with rubella.
6. List four sexually transmitted diseases.

DISCUSS AND DISCOVER

1. With a group of classmates, compile a list of over-the-counter medications that you—and others you know—take routinely. Which of these medications is considered safe to take during pregnancy? Why? What specific risks might be involved in taking these medications during pregnancy?
2. The use of alcohol can result in a variety of fetal abnormalities. The defects seem to be related to the degree of alcohol consumption by the mother. What suggestions would you give to someone who has a drinking problem and is pregnant?
3. It is reported that passive smoking (inhaling others' smoke) has an effect on the unborn child similar to the effect of actually smoking cigarettes. What should a pregnant woman do to protect herself and her developing baby from these harmful effects?

BUILDING POSITIVE ATTITUDES

Whenever you spend time with a young child—as a parent, a teacher, or a caregiver—you have the opportunity to help that child feel good about himself or herself. As you continue to study child development, and as you gain experience observing and participating with young children, you will learn many specific techniques to use in guiding children toward positive attitudes. However, you should also keep in mind the importance of your own attitudes and your own self-esteem: In order to develop positive feelings in children, you need positive feelings about yourself. These positive feelings are possible only if you assume responsibility for your own good health.

How can maintaining your own good health help you take better care of children? When you feel healthy, you enjoy life—and the people around you. Young children respond to that enjoyment with positive attitudes of their own; your good attitude can help children enjoy you, their

environment, and—most important—themselves. An essential aspect of maintaining good health is taking care of your physical well-being. These are some reminders about keeping yourself physically healthy:

- **Eat a balanced diet.** Include a variety of nutritious foods in your diet.
- **Get regular exercise.** Choose sports and other activities that you enjoy, either on your own or as part of a team or other group.
- **Get plenty of sleep.** Remember that eight hours per night is a minimum requirement for most teens.
- **Learn safety rules**—and remember to follow them.
- **Take care of your health and your appearance.** Shower or bathe regularly, keep your hair and nails clean and neat, and brush and floss your teeth daily.
- **Avoid harmful substances.** Harmful substances include tobacco, alcohol, and drugs.

Another essential aspect of maintaining good health is caring for your emotional well-being. Every individual has emotional needs, including the need to give and receive love, the need to

experience a sense of belonging, and the need to feel worthwhile. You can foster good emotional health by recognizing your own emotional needs and seeking out situations, activities, and relationships that meet those needs.

In addition, every individual experiences a wide range of emotions. Part of maintaining emotional health is recognizing and accepting all your emotions, and finding safe and appropriate outlets for expressing those emotions.

A third essential aspect of maintaining good health is assuming responsibility for your own social well-being. You probably think of your social life as involving your friends—and they can make an important contribution to your social health. Your relationships with family members, neighbors, teachers, and others with whom you come in daily contact are also important to your social health. If you enjoy most of these relationships and feel both supportive of and supported by the people around you, you are developing your own social good health.

Your social health involves your sense of yourself within the society as a whole. You can foster good social health by playing an active part in your community—perhaps by volunteering at a local recycling center or at a shelter or even in a child care center.

Remember that as you care for yourself, you are also preparing yourself to help care for others. Beyond that, you are setting a good example for the young children with whom you come in contact.

SUMMARY

- Prenatal development begins with conception. It progresses through three stages: the period of the zygote, the period of the embryo, and the period of the fetus.
- Chromosomes carry the genes that determine all inherited characteristics.
- Infertility problems can sometimes be solved through treatment; if treatment is unsuccessful, couples can consider other options.
- Birth defects have a variety of causes.
- Genetic counseling and prenatal tests can predict some birth defects.
- To minimize risks to her unborn baby, a pregnant woman should avoid environmental hazards such as alcohol, other drugs, and tobacco.

REVIEWING THE FACTS

1. What is prenatal development? In what three stages does it take place?
2. Which two cells are necessary for conception?
3. What is a uterus?
4. How do unborn babies receive their nourishment?
5. List at least four things a fetus can do.
6. How many chromosomes does each human have? What are the two sources of those chromosomes?
7. Briefly describe how fraternal triplets develop.
8. What is the difference between a miscarriage and a stillbirth?
9. List four kinds of environmental factors that can influence the development of a baby.
10. List three prenatal tests that can be used to test for birth defects.
11. Why should a woman avoid alcohol during pregnancy?
12. What are the potential dangers of street drugs to an unborn child? Why should all drugs—including over-the-counter and prescription drugs—be avoided during pregnancy?

EXPLORING FURTHER

1. Investigate one local agency or office through which babies or children can be adopted. How can adults qualify to adopt? Are the qualifications for adopting a newborn different from those for adopting an older child? What fees should adoptive parents expect to pay? What other costs may be involved in the adoption? Share and discuss your findings with other students in your class. (Section 2)
2. Gather pamphlets and other resource materials on birth defects from the March of Dimes or from another organization. Read and discuss the materials. Then make them available to pregnant women, perhaps by giving them to a prenatal clinic. (Section 3)
3. With a partner or a small group, plan and act out a skit about teens being offered alcohol or other illegal drugs. In your skit, demonstrate effective ways to say "no" to drugs. Perform your skit for your classmates. (Section 4)
4. Prepare three hot drinks that a pregnant woman could enjoy in place of coffee. Be sure that none of your drinks contains any caffeine. Serve the drinks to classmates, and ask them to share their reactions. (Section 4)

THINKING CRITICALLY

1. **Analyze.** How do you think a woman is affected by the physical changes that take place during pregnancy? How do you imagine most husbands react to these changes? What effects might her husband's responses have on a woman's emotions during pregnancy? On her physical well-being?
2. **Analyze.** How do you think infertility affects a couple? What effects might a diagnosis of infertility have on the relationship between husband and wife? On their relationships with other family members and friends? Why?
3. **Evaluate.** What do you consider valid reasons for prenatal testing? Why? Do you think some women undergo prenatal tests for inappropriate reasons? If so, what are those reasons? What questions do you think prospective parents should ask themselves before prenatal testing? After they get the results of prenatal tests?
4. **Analyze.** What effects do illegal drugs have on unborn babies? Why, given these effects, do some mothers continue to use drugs such as cocaine and heroin during pregnancy? What, if anything, do you think should be done to help these women? What, if anything, do you think should be done to punish them?

CROSS-CURRICULUM CONNECTIONS

1. **Science.** Research recent developments in the use of fertility drugs. How has the safety of these drugs been improved? What advantages and disadvantages are associated with the use of fertility drugs? Summarize your findings for the rest of the class.
2. **Reading.** Read *The Broken Chord* by Michael Dorris. Summarize the book for your classmates, and discuss your reactions to it.

OBSERVING AND PARTICIPATING

Prenatal Development

The nine months before the baby is born is a time of important development both for the parents and, of course, for the baby. The parents make many decisions and come to terms with many factors, all of which will have an important effect on their child. These decisions and factors relate to conception, heredity, maternal health and nutrition, and environmental hazards.

Choose one of the following activities. Write about your observations in your journal, and compare your ideas with those of other students.

- **Participating.** Watch a film about sexual reproduction and fetal development. Work with a group of classmates to develop a script that can be acted out for junior high school students explaining the process of conception. If possible, obtain permission from the school administration and present your play to these students.
- **Observing.** Take time to notice any twins you see in public places. Also think about the twins you know, have met, or have seen. How are the twins in each pair alike? How are they different? Are they identical twins or fraternal twins? How can you tell? If you are acquainted or friendly with any twins, how do the personalities of the two differ? How are their personalities alike?
- **Observing.** Visit a class or care center for children with severe birth defects. What kinds of problems does each child deal with? How does he or she cope with those problems? What special skills is each child learning? Why?

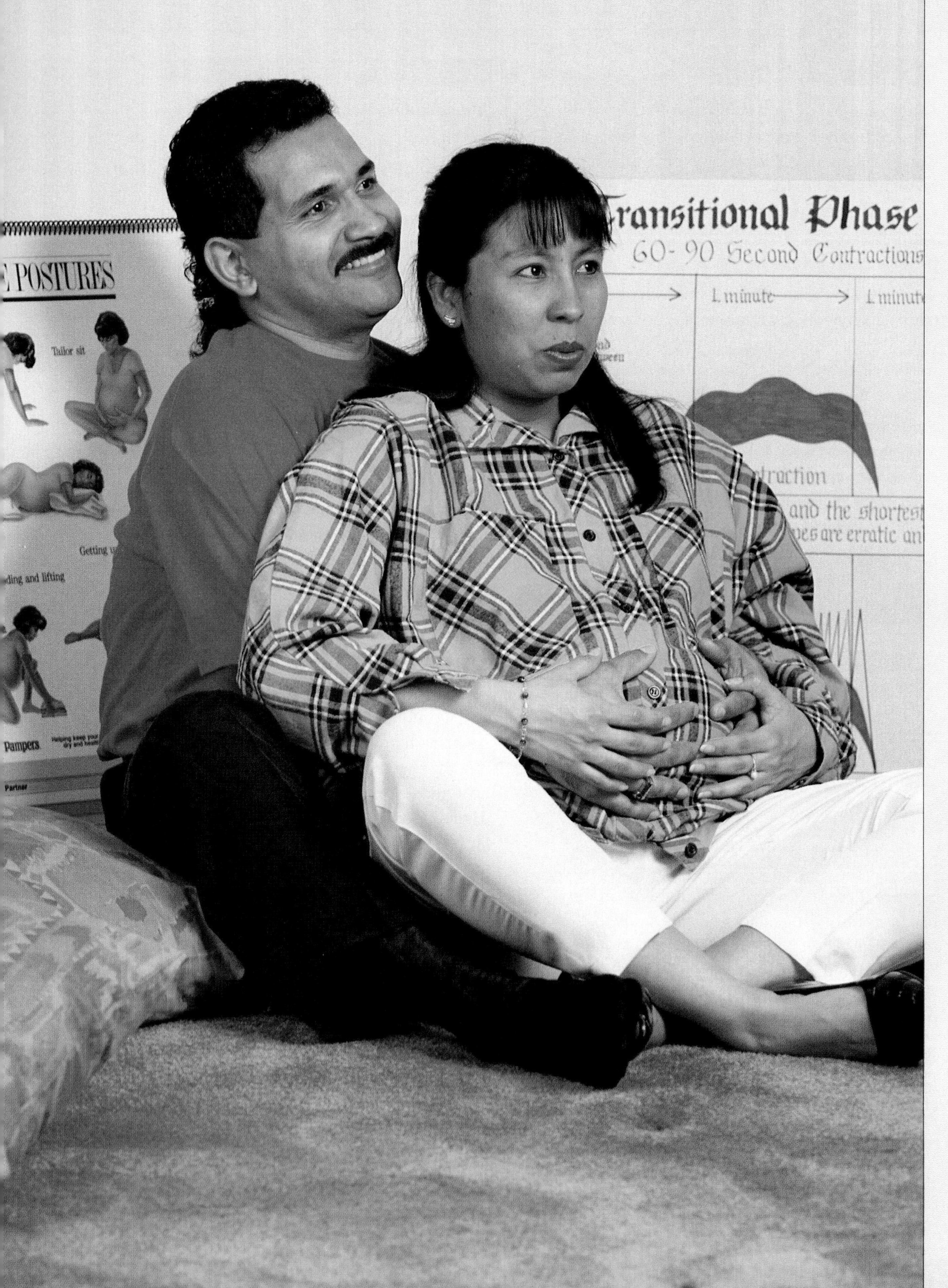

POSTURES
Tailor sit
Pampers
Partner
Transitional Phase
60-90 Second Contractions
1 minute
and the shortest

CHAPTER 6

Preparing for Birth

Elizabeth squeezed Omar's hand as Amelia, the Lamaz instructor, began the class.

"As birth coaches, your partner will be relying on you for emotional support and guidance. During these classes, you'll learn relaxation and breathing techniques that you can practice at home. Then, when the day comes, you'll be better prepared to cope with the birth process," instructed Amelia.

"I can't believe, we're having a baby," Elizabeth thought to herself. She wondered if it would be a boy or a girl, and how the pregnancy would change their lives.

"Don't worry, I'll be there for you," Omar whispered to Elizabeth. "I've coached baseball teams. It shouldn't be any different coaching you. Come on, let's get started. We have breathing exercises to do."

"Okay, coach," teased Elizabeth. "And you'd better be a good coach. If not, I'm going to make you get up with the baby every night for the first two months!"

SECTION 1

A Healthy Pregnancy

OBJECTIVES

- List the early signs of pregnancy.
- Explain the importance of early and regular medical care during pregnancy.
- Explain the importance of nutrition during pregnancy.
- Give recommendations for a pregnant woman's diet, activities, and personal care.

TERMS TO LEARN

anemia
obstetrician
pregnancy test

Pregnancy is a time of change and preparation. As the baby grows and develops within the uterus, the mother-to-be undergoes many physical changes. During this time, the pregnant woman's most important responsibility is to stay in good health.

Early Signs of Pregnancy

How does a woman know that she is pregnant? There are no immediate signals that conception has occurred. However, within several weeks of conception, a woman will probably recognize one or more of these early signs of pregnancy:

- Usually, a missed period is the first indication of pregnancy. This sign is particularly reliable for women who have regular menstrual cycles.
- The woman may have a mild ache or feeling of fullness in her lower abdomen.
- She may have a sense of fatigue, be drowsy, or occasionally feel faint.
- She may need to urinate more frequently than usual.
- She may have discomfort or tenderness in her breasts.
- She may have periods of nausea, especially early in the day.

Any of these physical symptoms can be caused by something other than pregnancy. A woman who notices one—or even several—of these early signs should not conclude that she definitely is pregnant. Rather, she should have a **pregnancy test**, *a test to determine whether or not a woman is going to have a baby.*

Unusual sleepiness, when combined with other signs, can be a clue that a woman might be pregnant. She should confirm the suspicion with a visit to the doctor for a pregnancy test.

Medical Care During Pregnancy

As soon as a woman suspects she is pregnant, she should consult a doctor. She may begin by visiting her own general physician. Many women prefer to see an **obstetrician,** *a doctor who specializes in pregnancy and birth.*

The pregnant woman and her doctor will have an important relationship over the next nine months. The woman will make regular office visits for checkups, and she should discuss any questions or problems openly with her doctor. The doctor who monitors her pregnancy will also assist in the birth of her baby. For these reasons, it is important for an expectant mother to select a doctor she likes and trusts.

Once a woman's pregnancy has been confirmed, her doctor usually performs a thorough examination which includes the following:

- Blood pressure, pulse, respiration, and initial weight are recorded.
- Pelvic measurements are taken to determine whether the birth passageway is wide enough to allow a normal-sized baby to be born without difficulty.
- An analysis of urine checks the condition of the kidneys, which carry a heavier burden during pregnancy.
- A blood test provides valuable information about the woman's health. For example, it tells whether there is a tendency toward **anemia,** *a condition caused by lack of iron, which results in poor appetite, tiredness, and weakness.* The blood test is also used to identify the woman's blood type in case a transfusion is necessary.

SAFETY TIP

For a completely reliable pregnancy test, a woman who suspects she is pregnant, should consult a doctor, who can use laboratory tests of her blood or urine to determine whether or not she is pregnant. Simplified versions of these tests are available for home use, but pregnancy should always be verified by a physician.

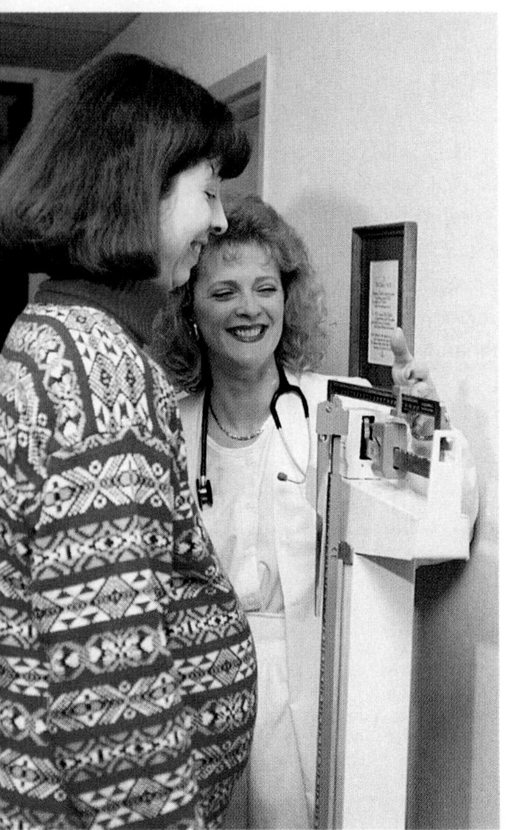

Regular medical checkups are an important part of prenatal care. Checking the baby's heartbeat and recording weight gain are routine parts of each visit.

- A history of past illnesses and operations is recorded. These may reveal conditions that require special treatment or observation.

Doctors usually schedule regular checkups for pregnant women. The examinations during these office visits may seem fairly routine. They are important, however, in monitoring the development of the baby and in making sure that the woman remains healthy. Typically, an expectant mother has a checkup once a month until the sixth or seventh month of pregnancy. Then most doctors schedule two visits a month until the ninth month, when the pregnant woman has a checkup once a week.

When will the baby be born? This is one of the first questions a prospective mother asks her doctor. To answer this question, the doctor makes a simple calculation, based on the date on which the woman's last menstrual period began. The doctor adds nine months and one week to that date to find the approximate date on which the baby will be born.

Discomforts of Pregnancy

Pregnancy is a condition, not an illness. Many women go through pregnancy without any problems or complications. In fact, some women find pregnancy a time in which they feel particularly healthy. Other women may be mildly affected by some of the common discomforts listed here. Although these discomforts usually do not indicate serious problems, a woman who experiences any of these symptoms should discuss them with her doctor.

- Nausea is the most common complaint among pregnant women. It is commonly called morning sickness, although some women experience it in the evening and others feel it all day long. Snacking on soda crackers and eating smaller, more frequent meals can help relieve nausea for many women. Fortunately, nausea rarely lasts beyond the fourth month of pregnancy. A woman who suffers severe and prolonged nausea should contact her doctor.
- Sleepiness is a fairly common symptom during early pregnancy. Unusual fatigue results in part from hormonal changes in the woman's body. Because pregnancy affects every system and organ in the body, some women feel unusually tired throughout pregnancy. For many women, fatigue decreases during the middle months of the pregnancy but may recur during the final months.
- Pregnant women often suffer from heartburn, a digestive disturbance not associated with the heart. A woman with heartburn should ask her doctor about the safest source of relief.

- In the late months of pregnancy, a woman may feel short of breath. This is caused by pressure on the lungs from the growing uterus.
- Some pregnant women develop varicose (swollen) veins from pressure on the blood vessels in their legs. A woman with varicose veins should rest with her legs and feet elevated whenever possible. She may also find elasticized stockings and certain exercises helpful.
- It is not unusual for pregnant women to suffer muscle cramps in their legs. These cramps can be relieved by rest and gentle stretching. A diet rich in calcium may prevent these cramps.
- During the last months of pregnancy, many women experience lower back pain. For back comfort throughout the pregnancy, pregnant women should wear low-heeled shoes and be sure to bend their knees when lifting. Certain exercises can help relieve backache.

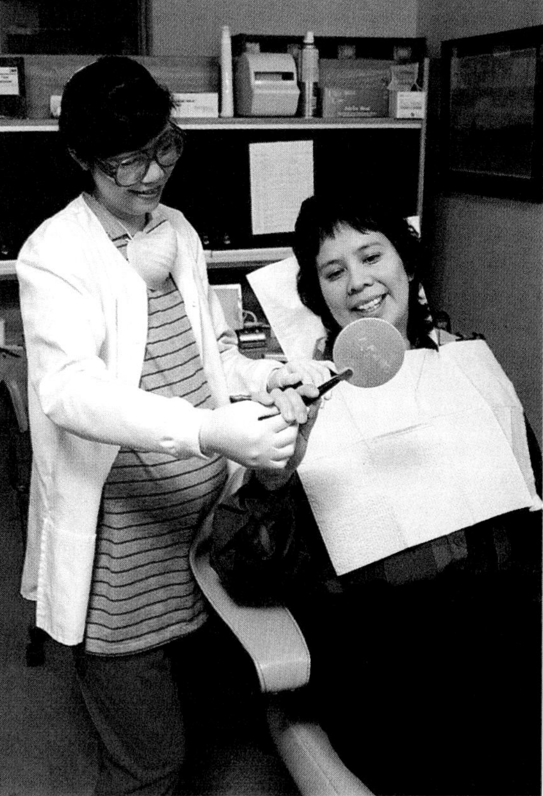

If no unusual problems develop, a woman can keep up her normal activities during pregnancy. Balancing work, rest, and recreation will help her feel her best.

ASK THE EXPERTS

The Myths of Pregnancy

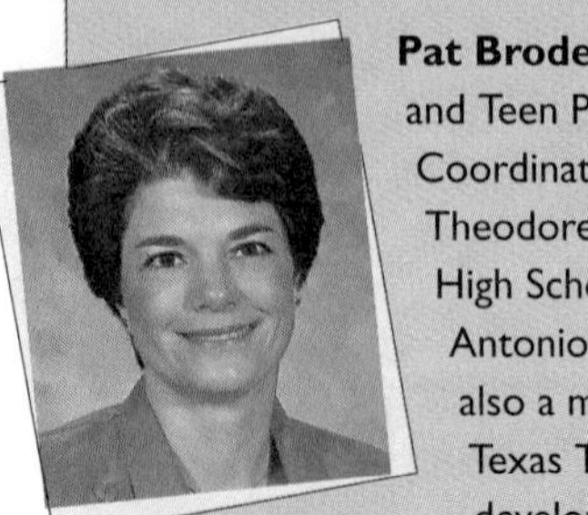

Pat Brodeen is a teacher and Teen Parent Coordinator at Theodore Roosevelt High School in San Antonio, Texas. She is also a member of the Texas Task Force to develop curriculum for School Age Parenting courses.

I'm confused! I've heard so many stories about what women eat and do during pregnancy—now I'm not sure which are facts and which are myths. How can I unravel the myths associated with pregnancy?

I'm glad you realize that not everything you hear about pregnancy is true. Some of the stories you hear reflect the particular experiences of individual women. Other stories pass down cultural beliefs or expectations. Still other stories actually do give information or reliable advice about pregnancy.

Have you ever heard these tales about pregnancy?

- If a pregnant woman sleeps too much, the baby will stick to her backbone.
- A car ride on a bumpy road will end a woman's pregnancy.
- A pregnant woman who sees something frightening will have a baby with an ugly birthmark.
- A woman may cause a strawberry-colored birthmark to appear on her baby's face if she eats strawberries while she's pregnant.
- If a pregnant woman lifts her arms above her head, the umbilical cord may strangle her baby.

All these stories are completely false. The developing baby is safely cushioned within the mother's body. Normal activities cannot affect the baby's safety. Nor will what the mother sees or eats affect the baby's safety or appearance—as long as the mother has a nutritious, balanced diet.

Some age-old adages about pregnancy are at least partially true. Maybe you've heard people say this:

- A woman loses a tooth for every baby she has.

This is another pregnancy story that's untrue, but it does have a clear basis. A pregnant woman may lose some calcium from her bones (not her teeth) if her daily diet does not provide enough calcium for the baby's development. In addition, a woman may have problems with her teeth during pregnancy because hormonal changes sometimes cause gum inflammations; these changes make oral hygiene especially important.

You're right—there are many different stories about pregnancy and pregnant women. Some of them, of course, are true. How can you know which those are? A pregnant woman has an excellent source of information—her physician or other care provider. During her regular checkups, she should discuss her questions and concerns openly with that person. Books written by doctors, nutritionists, or other health professionals are also good sources of information about pregnancy. You can also rely on teachers or librarians to help you find and evaluate information.

Pat Brodeen

Pat Brodeen

Possible Complications

A few women experience more serious complications during pregnancy. A pregnant woman who has any of the following symptoms should report them to her doctor immediately:

- Vaginal bleeding.
- Unusual weight gain.
- Excessive thirst.
- Reduced or painful urination.
- Severe abdominal pain.
- Persistent headaches.
- Severe vomiting.
- Fever.
- Swelling of face, hands, or ankles.
- Blurred vision or dizziness.
- Prolonged backache.
- Increased vaginal mucus.

Nutrition During Pregnancy

Good nutrition is the single most important factor in prenatal care. By eating a balanced diet, a pregnant woman helps her baby develop properly. She also helps maintain her own health.

Doctors once thought that a developing baby took whatever it needed from the mother's body. We now know that this is not true. The fetus may take certain nutrients, such as calcium, from the mother's system. However, the mother is responsible for providing, through a healthy diet, almost all the nutrients the baby needs, as well as all the nutrients her own body needs.

Because of the importance of the mother's diet to prenatal development, any woman who might become pregnant should establish healthy eating habits before conception.

A well-balanced diet is important both before and during pregnancy. A variety of nutritious foods should be eaten daily.

The Role of Nutrients

A healthy diet contains all the food nutrients: protein, vitamins, minerals, fats, and carbohydrates. Each nutrient performs very special functions and forms an essential part of a healthy diet.

- **Protein.** This nutrient can be obtained from meat, fish, poultry, eggs, milk, cheese, and beans. Protein is vital for the growth of the baby. It also helps keeps the mother's body in good repair. Because of the added needs of the growing fetus, a woman should have additional protein during pregnancy. A diet lacking in protein is generally lacking in other nutrients, too.

- **Vitamins.** Vitamins promote general good health, protect against infection and disease, and regulate body processes. A woman needs more vitamins during pregnancy. If her diet is lacking in vitamins, there is an increased risk that her baby will be born with birth defects.

  A woman needs additional vitamin A during pregnancy to assure proper development of her baby's eyes. She also needs extra B vitamins to assure healthy fetal development. B vitamins release the energy in foods, build the nervous system, keep the digestive system working well, and promote healthy skin.

  A woman should also increase her intake of vitamin C during pregnancy. It helps build healthy teeth and gums, and helps make the material that holds body cells together. She also needs additional vitamin D, which aids in the development of strong bones and teeth.

  Vitamin-rich foods are usually those that are also rich in other nutrients. Fresh fruits and vegetables, whole-grain breads and cereal products, and fortified milk are especially rich sources of vitamins.

An expectant mother should drink plenty of milk. The calcium and phosphorus in milk help keep teeth and bones strong, both for the mother and for her unborn baby.

- **Minerals.** These nutrients are needed for sturdy bones and teeth, healthy blood, and the regulation of daily elimination. Many different foods are rich in minerals. If a pregnant woman needs mineral supplements, her doctor will prescribe them.

  Pregnant women have a particular need for iron. Iron helps prevent anemia in the mother. It also helps the developing fetus build its own blood supply. In addition, extra iron is stored in the baby's liver to be used for several months after birth, during the period when the baby's diet lacks iron. Meat is a good source of iron, especially organ meats such as liver and kidney. Other sources include beans, peas, spinach, raisins, and dates.

  Calcium and phosphorous are other minerals especially important during pregnancy. They help build the baby's bones and teeth. The mother's body also has a greater need for calcium and phosphorous during pregnancy. Milk supplies much of the calcium and phosphorous a pregnant woman needs.

- **Carbohydrates and fats.** These nutrients are necessary for heat and energy. Good sources are fruits, vegetables, whole-grain breads and cereal products, and vegetable oils. However, too much fat and sugar are not part of a healthy diet.

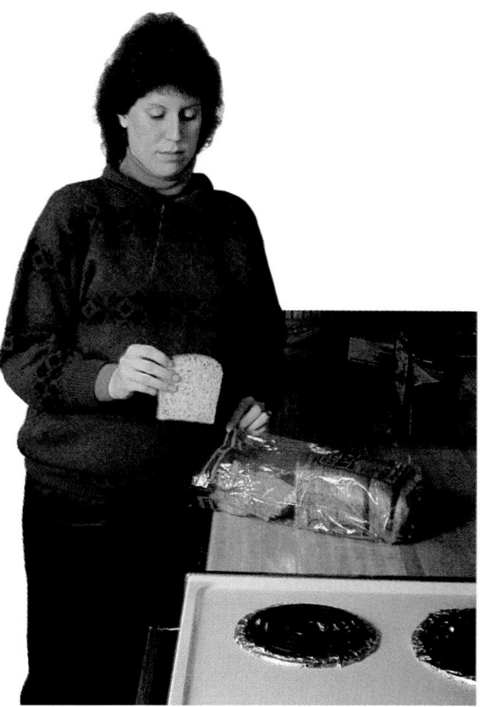

The Food Guide Pyramid

Planning a daily diet that provides all the food nutrients can be quite simple. Everyone can eat a well-balanced diet by choosing foods from the basic food groups in the Food Guide Pyramid. The Food Guide Pyramid recommends various amounts from each group for children and adults, with special recommendations for pregnant women.

- **Milk, Yogurt, and Cheese Group.** A pregnant woman should drink four to five glasses of vitamin D fortified milk each day. She may choose whole milk, low-fat milk, skim milk, or buttermilk, depending on her own preferences, her particular need for calories, and her desire to limit fat. She may also substitute cheese, yogurt, and ice cream for some of the milk.

- **Meat, Poultry, Fish, Dry Beans, Eggs, and Nuts Group.** The foods in this group include all types of meat, poultry, and fish and seafood, as well as eggs, nuts, dry beans and peas, and lentils. A pregnant woman should eat three or more servings from this group every day, and she should include both fish and liver in her diet at least once a week.

- **Vegetable Group.** A pregnant woman should eat three to five servings of vegetables every day. At least one of these servings should be a deep yellow or dark green, leafy vegetable. She should also try to include vegetables high in vitamin C, such as cabbage, in her diet on a regular basis.

- **Fruit Group.** Two, three, or four servings of fruit should be included in the daily diet of a pregnant woman. One or more of these servings should be a fruit high in vitamin C, such as citrus fruit, berries, and melons.

- **Bread, Cereal, Rice, and Pasta Group.** A pregnant woman should eat six to eleven servings of these grain products every day. These may include whole-grain or enriched breads, cereals, and other grain products, such as rice, macaroni, and noodles.

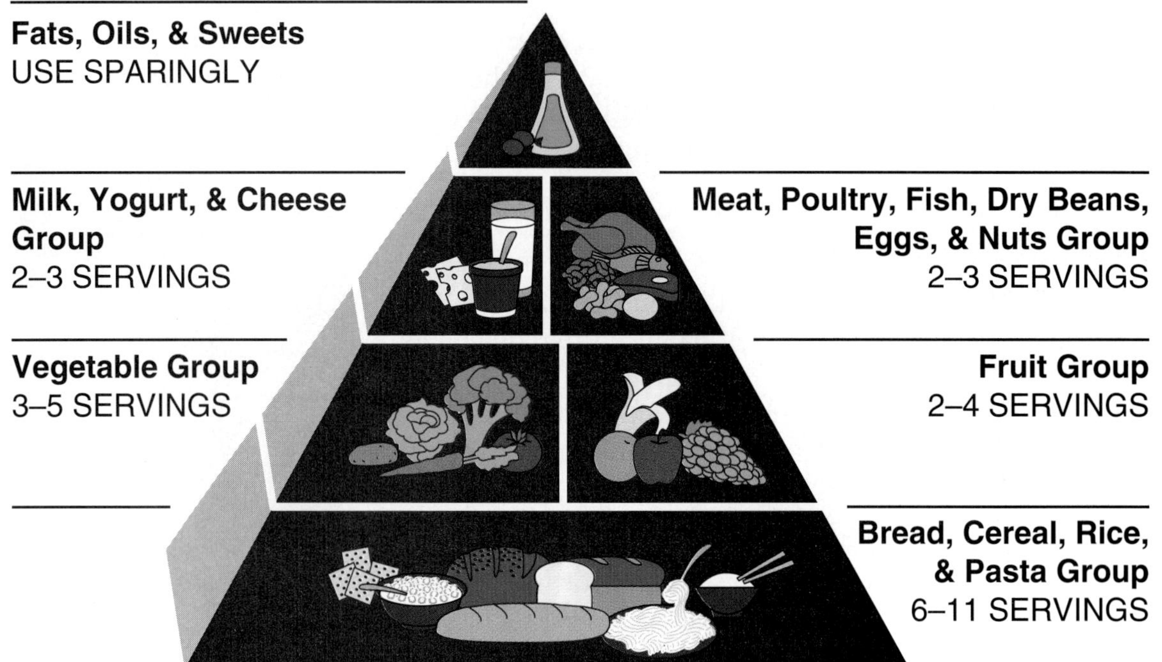

The Food Guide Pyramid shows the number of servings of each group that a person needs each day. Women who are pregnant or breast-feeding, teenagers, and young adults to age 24 need 3 servings of the milk group.

- **Fats, Oils, and Sweets Group.** The foods in this group, such as margarine and sugar, are generally high in calories and low in nutrition. They are not considered part of a healthy diet and should be used sparingly.

If a woman breast-feeds her baby, her need for extra nutrients continues after the birth. The chart above shows the Food Guide Pyramid's recommended amounts for different age groups, for pregnant women, and for nursing mothers.

There are other important dietary recommendations for pregnant women. They should drink six to eight glasses of water daily. They should also avoid rich and fried foods, which are often hard to digest and usually provide few nutrients.

Teenage Diets

In order to have a healthy baby, a woman herself must be healthy. Her diet throughout her life plays an important role in establishing her health—and the health of any babies she will have. A crash nutrition program during pregnancy, or even just before pregnancy, cannot make up for years of poor eating habits. For this reason, the diet of teenage girls is especially important. Teenagers should try to cut back on low-nutrition snacks and eat balanced meals, following the recommendations from the Food Guide Pyramid.

Improving Eating Habits

A woman who is pregnant, or who wants to become pregnant, should consider her eating habits carefully. How does her current diet compare with the recommendations of the Food Guide Pyramid? Then she should decide what changes are necessary to improve her chances of having a healthy baby.

In most cases, just a few changes can make a great difference. A woman who does not like milk, for example, can choose foods made with milk, such as yogurt, cottage cheese, or creamed soups. She may want to get some of her calcium from other foods, such as broccoli, kale, sardines, and tofu.

Protein is an especially important nutrient during pregnancy. Meat, poultry, and eggs are high in protein and other nutrients. Dried beans and peas are also good protein sources, especially when eaten in combination with enriched breads, grains, and seeds.

Weight Gain During Pregnancy

A woman usually gains about 24 to 30 pounds (10.9 to 13.6 kg) during her pregnancy. This gain is not due solely to the baby, who typically weighs 7 to 8 pounds (3.2 to 3.6 kg) at birth. The chart below shows how added weight is usually distributed.

DISTRIBUTION OF WEIGHT GAIN DURING PREGNANCY

	Pounds	Kilograms
Weight of average baby at birth	7-8	3.2-3.6
Placenta	1-2	0.45-0.9
Amniotic fluid	1½-2	0.7-0.9
Increased size of uterus and supporting muscles	2	0.9
Increase in breast tissue	1	0.45
Increase in blood volume	1½-3	0.7-1.4
Increase in fat stores	5	2.3
Increase in body fluids	5-7	2.3-3.2
Total	24-30	11.0-13.65

Gaining at least 20 pounds (9.1 kg) is an essential part of ensuring a healthy baby. There is an increased risk of fetal death among pregnant women who gain less than that amount. Also, mothers who gain less than 20 pounds (9.1 kg) during their pregnancy are twice as likely to give birth prematurely.

Many doctors recommend that a woman gain no more than 30 pounds (13.6 kg) during a pregnancy. However, it is never a good idea for an expectant mother to restrict her intake of nutritious foods. Pregnancy is not the time to go on a weight-loss diet. Moderate exercise and a diet that excludes sugary, fatty foods can help a woman keep her weight gain within the recommended levels.

Personal Care and Activities

In addition to practicing good nutrition, an expectant mother should take good care of herself in other ways. She should avoid alcohol, tobacco, and all drugs or medications. She should also make a point of getting plenty of rest and of exercising regularly but moderately.

- **Rest.** The need for rest varies from individual to individual. To maintain a feeling of well-being, a pregnant woman should get ample rest. Because schedules often prevent naps during the day, frequent breaks may be very refreshing. It is important for a pregnant woman to take such breaks or naps and to get plenty of sleep each night.

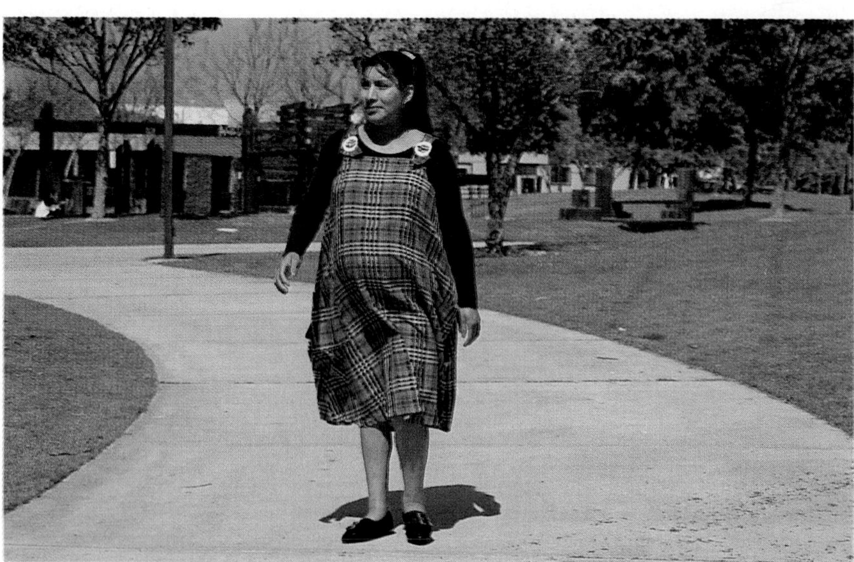

Regular exercise can help a pregnant woman stay fit and feeling well. As long as she is careful not to tire herself out, she can continue most of the physical activities she enjoys.

- **Exercise.** Moderate exercise can help keep an expectant mother in good physical condition. It can also maintain appropriate weight gain and make the pregnancy more comfortable.

  Many doctors recommend exercise such as walking, swimming, or biking during pregnancy. Special programs of prenatal aerobics are offered in some communities. Hobbies such as tennis and golf can also be continued. However, pregnancy is not a time to begin any strenuous new activities.
- **Hygiene.** Daily baths or showers are especially important during pregnancy. The skin helps maintain correct body temperature and eliminate waste, so it should be kept clean. Just before bed is a good time for a bath or shower, because the warm water encourages relaxation and sleep.
- **Other activities.** A pregnant woman usually maintains the same work routines she had before pregnancy. If she works outside the home, she can continue to do so as long as she wants, unless her doctor advises differently. She can also continue to do daily household activities.

The most important point for a woman to remember is that her lifestyle should not change radically during pregnancy. Moderation may be necessary in some circumstances, but on the whole, she should continue her life as before.

Maternity Clothes

By about the fourth or fifth month of pregnancy, a woman usually needs special clothing. Attractive maternity clothes need not be expensive, but they must be comfortable. They should be loose enough to allow for freedom of movement and for good circulation. For her own health and the health of her developing baby, a pregnant woman should always avoid wearing tight clothing.

Simple garments are the best choices in maternity wear. An expectant mother should consider how each garment will fit in the last month of pregnancy. Cotton knit fabrics stretch to allow room for the growing baby. Skirts and pants may include a stretch panel for comfort.

Comfortable, low-heeled shoes with good support are recommended throughout pregnancy. A pregnant woman should avoid wearing high heels. They throw the body out of balance and increase the risk of falling.

By shopping carefully, an expectant mother can put together a basic wardrobe of mix-and-match items that will see her through many different occasions.

BUILDING SELF-ESTEEM

Emotional Support During Pregnancy

Too much stress or too many emotional upsets are not healthy for anyone. An expectant mother should talk over any upsetting problems or situations with members of her support team, including her partner, friends, nurse, childbirth educator, or physician. She should turn to professionals for assistance with prolonged feelings of anxiety, depression, or stress.

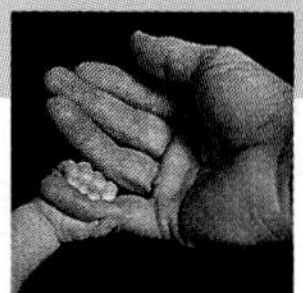

Emotional Health During Pregnancy

Pregnancy is a time of emotional adjustments for both the expectant mother and the prospective father. It is normal for both parents-to-be to have some concerns about the baby's arrival. Talking over their concerns with each other and with family members can be reassuring.

Many of the mother's emotional changes may be related to her own physical changes. Pregnancy causes hormonal changes, and these may result in mood swings. A pregnant woman may shift unexpectedly from happiness to distress—and then back again, for no apparent reason. It is natural for even the most even-tempered woman to feel upset and worried at times during her pregnancy. It is important for the couple to discuss these emotional swings, to share their feelings, and to make plans for stress reduction.

In general, however, a pregnant woman who takes good physical care of herself—especially by exercising moderately and relaxing often—is helping assure her mental and emotional health, as well as her physical health and the health of her developing baby.

SECTION 1 REVIEW

CHECK YOUR UNDERSTANDING

1. List three early signs of pregnancy.
2. What is the most reliable way for a woman to determine whether she is pregnant?
3. List two discomforts pregnant women sometimes have. List two symptoms that may indicate serious complications during pregnancy.
4. What are the basic food nutrients? Which of these does a woman need during pregnancy?
5. Why does a woman need extra iron during pregnancy? Which foods are good sources of iron?
6. Why is weight gain important during pregnancy? What is the recommended weight gain?

DISCUSS AND DISCOVER

1. Do you think an unmarried teenager faces any special problems in having a healthy pregnancy? If so, what are those problems? How would you recommend that she cope with them? If not, why not?
2. Gather information about prenatal exercise programs in your community. Discuss your findings with a group of other students. Together, evaluate the programs and make posters advertising those you feel are most appropriate for pregnant women. (If your community does not have any prenatal exercise programs, work together to design an exercise routine that might be part of such a program.)

Getting Ready for the New Arrival

SECTION 2

OBJECTIVES

- Describe how parents-to-be can plan for a baby's care.
- Discuss the purchases and other preparations parents-to-be should make.
- Give examples of how to estimate and reduce the expenses of having a baby.

TERMS TO LEARN

budget
fixed expenses
flexible expenses
formula
maternity leave
paternity leave
postnatal period

The nine months of pregnancy provide parents-to-be with an opportunity to consider and adjust to the changes that are taking place in their lives. During this time, the expectant parents should make plans and decisions as they prepare for the arrival of a new family member.

Roles, Responsibilities, and Decisions

During pregnancy, every couple must decide how they will meet the responsibilities of child care. They need to consider many factors—each partner's goals, skills, schedule, and personal characteristics, as well as the financial needs of the family.

In many families, both parents work outside the home. For these couples, decisions about arrangements for child care are especially important.

Many new mothers who work outside the home take a **maternity leave**, *time off from a job allowing a woman to give birth, recuperate, and care for her new baby.* A woman's employer may offer leave ranging from a few weeks to several months. During her leave, a new mother is able to care for her baby full-time before returning to her job. Some employers offer **paternity leave**, *time off from a job allowing a father to care for his new baby.* These leave arrangements allow parents to spend time with their baby during the important early stages of development.

IT'S MORE THAN A NAME

The imagery and beauty of Native American names is a treasure worth preserving. Traditionally, Hopi newborns are given a name in a ritual that begins before dawn twenty days after birth. With all relatives assembled, the grandmother washes the baby then rubs the head four times with a perfectly formed ear of corn. The same rite is performed on the baby's paternal aunts who each suggest a name based on the father's clan. As dawn approaches, the grandmother chooses a name, then takes the infant outside where they both pay homage to the rising sun. A grand feast follows.

Later, when the child has reached the age of initiation, another name is added to symbolize a new birth. Today, babies are often given Christian names and the father's last name.

If their finances permit it, a couple may decide that one parent will stay home to care for the child on a long-term basis. In most of these situations, the mother is the one who becomes the primary caregiver. Some couples reverse the traditional roles either temporarily or permanently. The father stays home to care for the house and children, and the mother becomes the primary wage earner.

Regardless of who is primarily responsible for daily care tasks, every parent should know the basics of child care. This allows the parents to share the work—and the special joys—of providing routine care for their baby.

In many families, neither parent stays home to care for the baby after the first few months. A couple may decide that both must work to provide enough income for the family; a couple may decide that both want the satisfactions of employment outside the home; a single parent may discover that he or she must work outside the home to support the family. Whatever the reasons for this decision, parents are then faced with another decision: Who will take care of the baby? Some parents can arrange to work at different times, so that they can take turns caring for the baby. Other parents arrange to have a relative or other caregiver stay with the baby, either in the baby's home or in another home. Other parents choose to take their baby to an infant care center. Parents need to consider all their options carefully.

Some parents must find someone to care for the baby while they return to work. Infant care centers are one option. It is best to consider this decision early so that any necessary arrangements can be made in advance.

Preparing for Parenthood

Most parents-to-be wonder whether they will be able to take good care of their child. Considering all the different ideas about children and parenting they have probably heard, it is not surprising that expectant parents are concerned. Even the most confident mothers and fathers worry about doing the right thing.

A couple should discuss their ideas about parenting methods with each other before the baby is born. For example, they might share their ideas about questions such as these: What attitudes and approaches to discipline do we want to use? What part will organized religion play in our children's lives? How will we share the responsibilities for earning money and for caring for our children? What goals and aspirations do we have for our children? Of course, parents cannot plan what they will do in every possible situation. As they become experienced in parenting, some of their ideas may change. However, by agreeing ahead of time on general philosophies of raising children, parents can reduce conflict later on.

Preparing for parenthood also involves anticipating changes in the other roles parents fill. Parents may be spouses, family members, workers, students, volunteers, and citizens. As they undertake new responsibilities in caring for children, parents may find they have less time and energy available for their other responsibilities. Couples should discuss their concerns and problems about these roles with each other and with friends or family members. They should also strive to use good management practices in balancing their roles.

Other Children in the Family

Many parents are aware that a new baby will require some adjustments for the other children in the family. The reactions of an older child to a new sibling depend largely on how well prepared the child was before the arrival of the newborn. During pregnancy, parents should include the older child in discussions about the pregnancy and about plans for the baby. Giving the older child opportunities to help get the room ready will make the child feel involved.

Parents should be prepared for a wide range of attitudes toward the new baby. It is normal for the older child to respond with feelings of jealousy and confusion, as well as excitement and love. These feelings will come and go as the baby grows and changes. Many parents find that open communication and acceptance of each child's feelings will help foster a positive relationship between siblings.

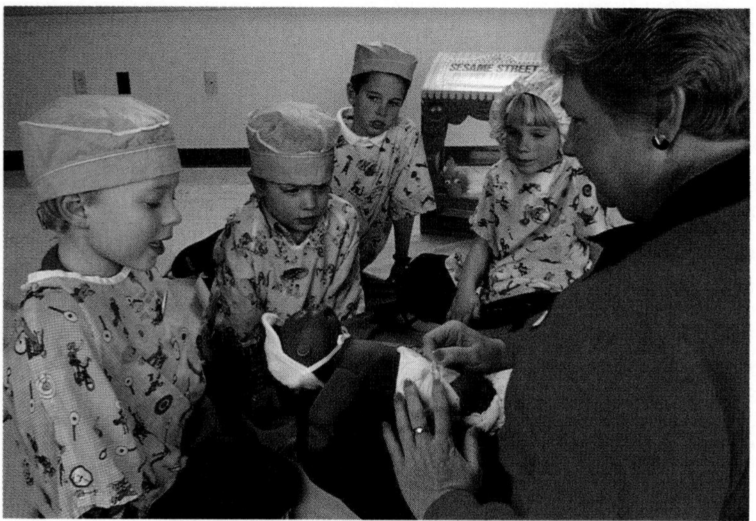

Many hospitals offer special programs for young children who will soon be welcoming home a new baby brother or sister. This helps the youngsters understand and feel part of what is happening.

Feeding is a time for establishing close bonds with baby. Whether breast-feeding or bottle-feeding, allow plenty of time in a relaxed, unhurried atmosphere.

Decisions About Feeding

Will the new baby be breast-fed or bottle-fed? This is one of the significant decisions parents make before the arrival of the baby. Many parents discuss their ideas and reach a decision during pregnancy.

When choosing a method for feeding their baby, parents should be aware that experts consider breast-feeding the best source of nutrition for human infants. On the basis of research that proves the benefits of breast milk for the baby, medical experts recommend breast-feeding whenever possible, for as long as possible.

Breast-feeding has many advantages. Breast milk is best suited to the nutritional needs of a baby. It also provides immunity against many diseases. In addition, experts feel that the physical closeness of breast-feeding helps create a special bond between mother and child. Parents who decide to bottle-feed their baby can achieve this same closeness, too, by holding the baby close and providing caring attention during every feeding.

Bottle-feeding with formula is a convenient alternative to breast-feeding. **Formula**, *a mixture of milk or milk substitute, water, and nutrients*, provides nearly the same nutrition as breast milk. It may be mixed at home or purchased in a variety of convenient forms. Powdered, concentrated, and ready-to-use formulas are available.

The decision to breast-feed or bottle-feed is a personal one. It will depend on the mother's anatomy, schedule, and lifestyle.

Many mothers successfully breast-feed for certain feedings and supplement with bottles at other feedings. However parents decide to feed their baby, they should remember that the baby responds to the feeling and care that accompany each feeding.

The chart below lists some of the pros and cons of both feeding methods.

COMPARING BREAST-FEEDING AND BOTTLE-FEEDING

BREAST-FEEDING

ADVANTAGES

- Creates a bond through physical closeness with the mother.
- Provides some natural immunity against diseases.
- Speeds the return of the mother's uterus to normal size.
- Causes fewer digestive upsets.
- Is conveniently available at all times.
- Reduces baby's risks of allergies.

DISADVANTAGES

- Prevents father from participating in feeding.
- Limits medications the mother can safely take.
- May be painful for some mothers.
- May be difficult because of work schedule.
- May become difficult if anxiety or illness interferes with production of milk.

BOTTLE-FEEDING

ADVANTAGES

- Allows father to participate in feeding.
- Allows mother to have a more flexible schedule.
- Permits baby to be fed by anyone, anywhere.

DISADVANTAGES

- Can be expensive.
- Involves greater chance of allergies.
- Involves risk that baby may not be given close physical contact during feeding.

SAFETY TIP

Automobile accidents are the leading cause of death among young children; a secure safety restraint is the best protection a baby or child can have against injury or death in a car accident. These facts make an infant car seat a necessity for any baby who rides in a car. Beginning with the ride home from the hospital or birthing center, an infant should be buckled into an appropriate car seat every time he or she is taken out in a car.

Clothing and Equipment Needs

Basic supplies for a baby include clothing, bedding, feeding equipment, bathing supplies, and travel equipment. Wise parents begin with only a minimum number of the basic items that the baby will need at birth. The family may receive some of these items—as well as later necessities—as gifts or as loans.

As a rule, the most appreciated baby gifts are practical items. Family members and friends who plan to buy baby gifts should be encouraged to ask the parents about their particular needs. In many cases, a dozen extra diapers or a simple sleeper will be more welcome than a fancy outfit.

The chart on pages 175-176 shows basic needs for a typical baby. This list merely suggests possibilities. Expectant parents may get specific suggestions from a doctor or from family and friends. Advice is also given at the hospital and at classes for new parents.

Baby's Room

Every baby needs a special place to sleep. If it is available, a separate room for the newborn is best. During the first six months, most babies sleep for 15 to 18 hours every day.

Of course, many families cannot provide a new baby with his or her own room. Parents should remember that love and pleasant conditions are more important than a spacious home. If the baby cannot have a separate room, a quiet corner of a room can be made into the baby's special place. A room divider can be used to provide the baby—and other family members—with a sense of privacy.

Adequate and convenient storage in the baby's room makes daily routines easier. Clothing and supplies can be kept in many types of storage areas–closets, drawers, stacking cubes, or shelves, for example.

BASIC BABY SUPPLIES

DIAPERING NEEDS

- Disposable diapers. (Quantity depends on whether they will be for regular use or occasional use.)
- 3-4 dozen cloth diapers (if chosen for regular use).
- Diaper pins (for cloth diapers).
- 4-6 waterproof pants (for cloth diapers).
- 6-10 washcloths.
- Diaper-rash ointment.
- Covered diaper pail.
- Clothes basket or hamper.

CLOTHING

- 6-8 undershirts.
- 4-6 one-piece footed sleepers.
- 4-6 gowns.
- 6 cotton receiving blankets.
- 1 warm outer wrapping blanket.
- 1 sweater and cap set.
- 1-2 sun hats or bonnets.
- 1 dress-up outfit (optional).
- Coat (optional).
- Mittens (optional).

FEEDING EQUIPMENT

- 6-8 large bottles (8-ounce or 237-mL) if the baby is bottle-fed.
- 2-3 large bottles (8-ounce or 237-mL) if the baby is breast-fed.
- Breast pump and pads.
- Plastic bottles for storing breast milk.
- 2-4 small bottles (4-ounce or 118-mL) for water and juice.
- Nipples (the same number as bottles, plus a few extra).
- Bottle caps (the same number as bottles).
- Bottle and nipple brush.
- Saucepan for hot water to warm bottle (optional).
- Bibs.
- High chair.

(Continued on next page)

BASIC BABY SUPPLIES (cont'd.)

BEDDING/BEDROOM

- 4 fitted crib sheets.
- Waterproof mattress cover.
- 2-4 absorbent pads.
- 2 lightweight blankets or spreads.
- 1 heavier crib blanket.
- Bumper pad (fits around inside of crib just above mattress; keeps baby's arms and legs in, drafts out).
- Storage space, such as a chest of drawers.
- Wastebasket.

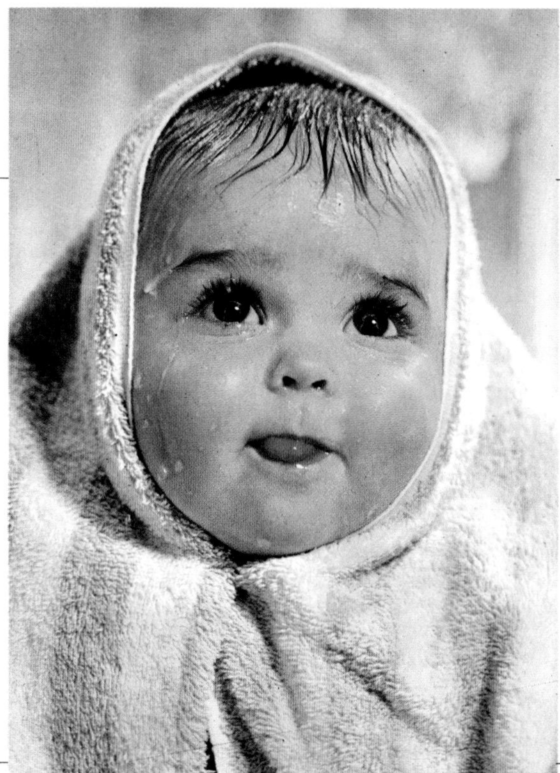

BATHING AND OTHER SUPPLIES

- Baby bathtub or other container.
- Mild, pure soap.
- Baby shampoo.
- Several soft washcloths.
- 2 soft cotton bath towels.
- Cotton balls.
- Baby oil and baby lotion.
- Blunt-tipped nail scissors.
- Baby comb and brush set.
- Thermometer.

TRAVEL EQUIPMENT

- Car seat (safety approved).
- Tote bag for carrying supplies.
- Stroller, carriage, or infant carrier (optional).

The baby's first bed does not need to be a crib, or even a bassinet. A clothes basket, long and wide enough to allow the baby to stretch out, will do nicely. With slight padding to protect against rough sides, and extra padding on the bottom to function as a firm "mattress," the basket can serve as a good, inexpensive portable bed. See Positive Parenting Skills "Safety Guidelines for Baby Equipment" on pages 188-189.

Basic Supplies: The Diaper–Changing Area

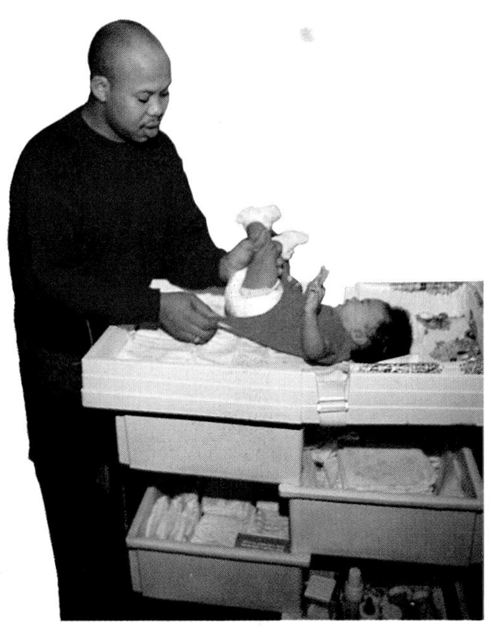

Parents need to plan a place where the baby can be changed and dressed. Special changing tables are available for this use. However, any surface that is a convenient height and that is padded with blankets can serve the same purpose. The top of a chest of drawers can be used as a changing table if it is the correct height and size. A crib with adjustable mattress height also works well. Whatever changing area is used, all caregivers must never leave the baby unattended on it. They should pay constant attention to protect the baby from a fall and possible injuries.

Secondhand Equipment

Baby supplies and equipment need not be new, even for a first baby. Many parents-to-be are able to reduce their expenses significantly by borrowing major items or by buying secondhand items. Relatives and friends often share needed supplies among themselves. Expectant parents can frequently find bargains at neighborhood yard sales, rummage sales, and secondhand clothing stores. Cribs, bedding, and baby clothes are all available secondhand for only a fraction of the cost when new. These items may show little wear, because babies outgrow things quickly.

Everything that is borrowed or purchased secondhand should be thoroughly washed, even though it may appear clean. Special caution should be taken with equipment. Secondhand or borrowed cribs, playpens, car seats, and other items should meet current safety standards.

Estimating Expenses

The financial aspects of having a baby are a concern for most parents. The costs do not end with the hospital bill for birth, or even with the first few years. They continue until the child can live independently. A couple who understands all the costs involved can plan early to meet the expenses of having a child.

The expenses of having a baby begin with the pregnant woman's first appointment with a physician. Many doctors charge a lump sum that covers prenatal care, delivery, and the **postnatal period**—that is, *the time after the baby's birth.*

The hospitalization fee is another major expense of birth. Costs for a hospital stay vary, but they usually depend on the type of delivery the mother has, the medical needs of the baby, and the length of time the mother and baby stay in the hospital. Extra charges are often made for laboratory tests, medicine, and supplies. Expectant parents can check with local hospitals for current rates and policies.

Because costs change so rapidly and are not the same in all parts of the country, it is difficult to estimate the cost of having a baby. In addition to doctor and hospital fees, parents should consider these costs:

- Maternity clothes.
- The clothing, equipment, and supplies listed on pages 175-176, as well as any other items the parents want to provide.
- Formula and baby foods.
- Medical care for the baby.
- Furnishings for the baby's room.
- Child care services, if needed.

In addition, parents should recognize that, with another family member, they may need larger living quarters. They must also consider the costs of raising the child in the years ahead. Food, clothing, medical care, and education will all be major expenses during the many years in which the child needs to be supported. Parents should have a clear idea of the total expenses involved and of how they will manage those expenses.

Reducing Expenses

As parents plan for the birth of a baby, they should consider ways in which they can reduce the expenses involved in raising a child. Many parents are able to reduce or even eliminate certain expenses by having good health and hospitalization insurance and by shopping carefully.

The medical costs of pregnancy and birth are high. Expectant parents should make sure they have adequate health insurance and find out exactly what is covered.

Health Insurance Coverage

Health insurance can enable parents to meet the major expenses involved in the birth of a baby. Newly married couples should immediately make certain that they are covered by a good health insurance plan. If they already have insurance, they should review the hospital and medical coverage to see what it includes. Couples should review and, if necessary, improve their insurance coverage before they begin a pregnancy. It is also a good idea for couples to find out whether their insurance company will pay hospital bills directly or reimburse the parents after they have paid the hospital.

Some large hospitals have free or special-rate clinics to help those without insurance who are unable to pay the full fees. Social workers are often able to help expectant parents with budgeting problems and financial arrangements.

Careful Shopping

With nine months' advance notice, expectant parents have plenty of time to comparison shop on the items they need. Every few months, most stores and mail-order catalogs have special sales. The same item may be sold at three different prices in three different stores.

Cost comparisons are also useful when choosing between alternatives. For example, the costs of diapering an infant vary, depending on whether the family uses disposable diapers, a diaper service, or cloth diapers washed at home. Each method has advantages and disadvantages that must be weighed against the differences in cost.

When buying items for the baby, it pays to shop carefully. Both cost and quality are important considerations. Reading consumer magazines and comparison shopping can help expectant parents find out what features to look for.

PARENTING IN ACTION

Paying for Prenatal Care

Julie and Steve were both pleased when they realized that Julie was pregnant with their first child. They wanted to take good care of their baby, but they also wanted to save money. Julie was in good health, and she came from a large, healthy family, so she did not anticipate any problems with her pregnancy. The couple decided that they should save the cost of monthly checkups by consulting a doctor only toward the end of her pregnancy.

Julie and Steve were in for a real surprise. When, in the seventh month of her pregnancy, Julie tried to make an appointment, she learned that all the doctors in their community charged a lump sum for pregnancy care. The fee was the same, whether it covered nine months or nine days.

THINK AND DISCUSS

1. How could Julie and Steve have avoided the unpleasant surprise they received?
2. Even if Julie and Steve had been able to save money by postponing medical care, would it have been a wise choice? Why or why not?
3. How could Julie and Steve's decision have affected Julie's health? How could it have affected the health of their unborn baby?

Making a Budget

Do you keep a personal budget? A **budget** is *a spending plan.* Its purpose is to help people set financial goals and work toward those goals in steps. Everyone can benefit from this kind of spending plan. Expectant parents find a budget especially useful as they plan for the added expenses of having and raising a baby.

In preparing a budget, parents-to-be should begin by considering where their money currently goes. **Fixed expenses** are *the costs of items that cannot be changed, such as rent, mortgage payments, taxes, insurance payments, and loan payments.* **Flexible expenses** are *costs for items over which people have some control and which can be cut back if necessary.* Usually, this category includes food, household maintenance, recreation, clothing, and similar expenses.

Next, expectant parents should get an idea of the added expenses they will soon face. How much of their medical expenses will be covered by insurance? Which items will they need to buy rather than borrow? Another important consideration is whether there will be any income lost if one of the parents plans to take time off from a paying job.

Once they have a clear idea of their new expenses, the parents can plan how to meet them. The expenses involved in having a baby must be budgeted like any other expenses. The couple has to recognize that the additional money spent on having a baby must be subtracted from another part of their budget. Often, flexible expenses have to be cut back.

Parents who have set aside some savings will find it easier to meet the early, large expenses of having a baby. Although, it is often difficult to set aside money for the future, having a budget can make this process easier. It is a good idea for the prospective parents to include a regular savings plan in their new budget. Even a few dollars set aside each month can help pay for the baby's future needs.

SECTION 2 REVIEW

CHECK YOUR UNDERSTANDING

1. Why is it important for the family that parents have either maternity leave or paternity leave? What is the difference between the two?
2. What can parents do to help prepare other children for the arrival of a new sibling?
3. List three questions that parents-to-be should ask themselves when deciding whether to breast-feed or bottle-feed their child.
4. List three ways that parents can reduce expenses when outfitting the nursery.
5. What is a budget?
6. What is the difference between a fixed expense and a flexible expense? Give two examples of each kind of expense.

DISCUSS AND DISCOVER

1. What factors do you think influence a mother's choice to breast-feed or bottle-feed her baby? Which of these factors is probably most important for teen mothers? Why?
2. Check to see whether your state has a law requiring family health insurance policies to include coverage of newborn infants. If so, when was it passed? If not, what efforts have been made to pass such a law? Share and discuss your findings with other students.
3. Choose one piece of baby equipment—crib, stroller, car seat, or high chair—and evaluate the safety of the equipment. If you were a parent, would you purchase the equipment you evaluated? Why or why not?

SECTION 3 Childbirth Choices

OBJECTIVES

- Discuss the childbirth choices available to most parents.
- Describe how parents can make decisions and prepare for childbirth.

TERMS TO LEARN

alternative birth center
delivery
labor
lay midwife
nurse-midwife
prepared childbirth

Not many years ago, birth practices in all hospitals were very similar. Today, there are many options from which to choose. Expectant parents must make arrangements for someone to deliver the baby. They should also decide on a place for the birth and on the methods or procedures they prefer.

What Is Prepared Childbirth?

Prepared childbirth, sometimes called natural childbirth, is *a method of giving birth in which pain is reduced through the elimination of fear and the use of special conditioning exercises.* Though a woman's body knows instinctively how to give birth, most women find childbirth education classes helpful in preparing them for this event. There are many different types of prepared childbirth classes, including Bradley and Lamaze methods. In recent years, however, there has been a blending of these styles, so that most classes offer similar information.

During a childbirth preparation course, class members learn what happens during **labor**—*the process by which the baby gradually moves out of the uterus into the vagina to be born*—and **delivery**—*the birth itself.* Class members see films of childbirth and receive reading material. Typically, they also take a tour of a hospital maternity department.

Much of the class time is spent learning skills to cope with the discomforts of labor, such as relaxation techniques and patterned breathing. The father, or anyone else the mother chooses to serve as a partner or childbirth coach, learns along with the mother. She depends on her partner for emotional support and guidance in practicing the exercises. The partner is also prepared to be an active participant throughout the labor and delivery.

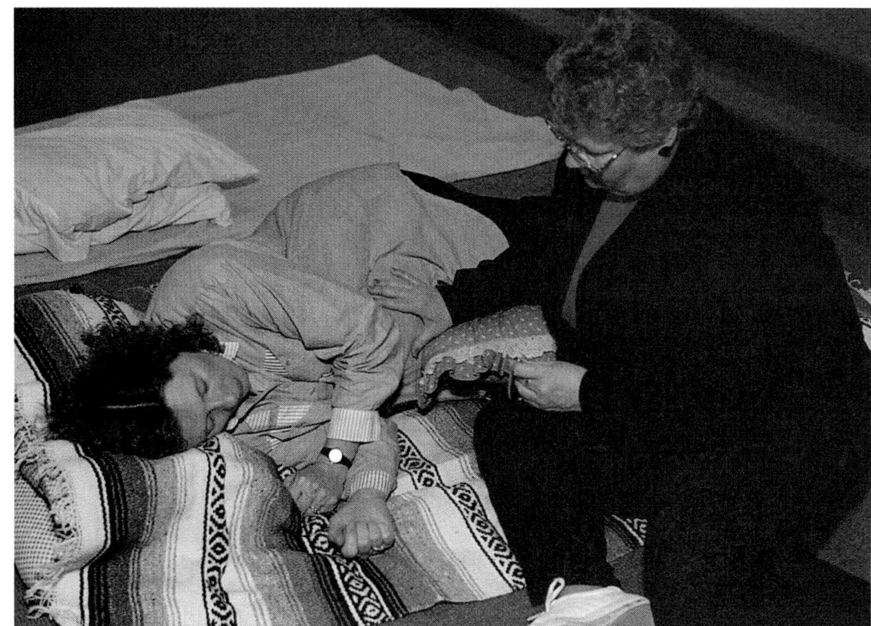

In Lamaze classes, the expectant mother learns special breathing techniques to use during labor. The coach's role will include keeping track of the breathing.

Who Will Deliver the Baby?

Most babies are now delivered either by an obstetrician or by a family doctor. Another option for women who expect a normal, uncomplicated delivery is a nurse-midwife.

- **Obstetricians.** These doctors specialize in prenatal and postnatal care of the mother and baby. They are qualified to handle any emergencies or special situations that may arise.
- **Family doctors.** Some general-practice doctors also deliver babies and provide prenatal and postnatal care. If complications arise during pregnancy or delivery, a family doctor may need to call in an obstetrician.
- **Licensed midwives.** The laws governing the practice of midwifery vary from state to state. There are two types of licensed midwives, each with different educational backgrounds. A certified **nurse-midwife** is *a registered nurse with advanced training in the care of normal, uncomplicated pregnancy and birth.* Nurse-midwives must pass a special licensing exam before they can establish a practice. A **lay midwife** is *a person who has special training in the care of pregnant women and uncomplicated deliveries but does not have a nursing degree.* Like nurse-midwives, lay midwives must pass a special exam before they can be licensed to practice.

How do expectant parents choose their birth attendant? They can get recommendations from their family doctor, the county medical society, or a local hospital. They should visit and talk with each doctor or licensed midwife they are considering. The

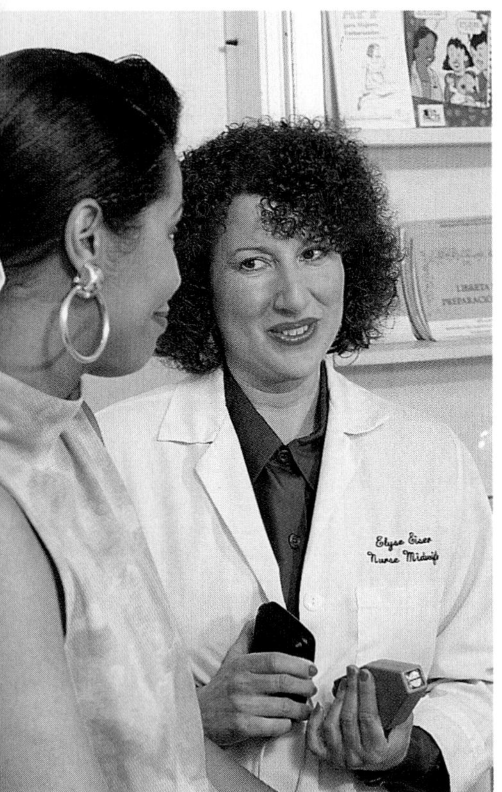

A licensed midwife is qualified to give prenatal care and to supervise routine, normal births. If complications arise during pregnancy or delivery, an obstetrician will be called in.

parents will want to be sure the person they choose is not only well qualified, but also makes them feel comfortable and can answer their questions clearly.

The parents should find out how emergency calls will be handled at night and on weekends. Another consideration is whether the doctor or licensed midwife is affiliated with a particular hospital or medical center, as most are. The parents should find out what programs and facilities that hospital has. They will also want to know whether the birth attendant's preferences toward delivery procedures agree with their own.

Although the mother-to-be should get medical care as soon as she is pregnant, she may not feel ready to make a decision about the delivery at that time. There is no reason she cannot switch to a different doctor or nurse-midwife during pregnancy if she wishes. The sooner a final decision is made, however, the better prepared both the parents and the birth attendant will be.

Where Will the Baby Be Born?

Until this century, almost all babies were born at home. Today, most American births occur in hospitals. There, sanitary conditions, trained personnel, and special equipment help make the birth process as safe as possible.

In recent years, hospitals have begun to offer a variety of services designed to meet the various needs and preferences of expectant mothers and their families. These services, often referred to as family-centered maternity care, include:

- Childbirth and parenting classes help the parents prepare for delivery and for caring for an infant.
- Special programs help young children prepare for their new baby brother or sister.
- Fathers and other family members are encouraged to help the mother through labor and to be present during delivery.
- "Birthing rooms" provide a homelike atmosphere for both labor and birth. The need to move from a labor room to a separate delivery room is eliminated. Medical equipment is kept out of sight, but is ready for use at a moment's notice.
- Mothers may be able to choose their preferred position for labor and delivery. Instead of lying flat, a woman may be encouraged to walk, rock in a chair, lie on her side, sit propped up, or even shower or soak in a tub. Many women find that these positions are more comfortable and make labor easier.
- Special procedures are often allowed to make the birth special for the family. For example, the lights in the delivery room may be dimmed so that the newborn can open his or her eyes without discomfort.

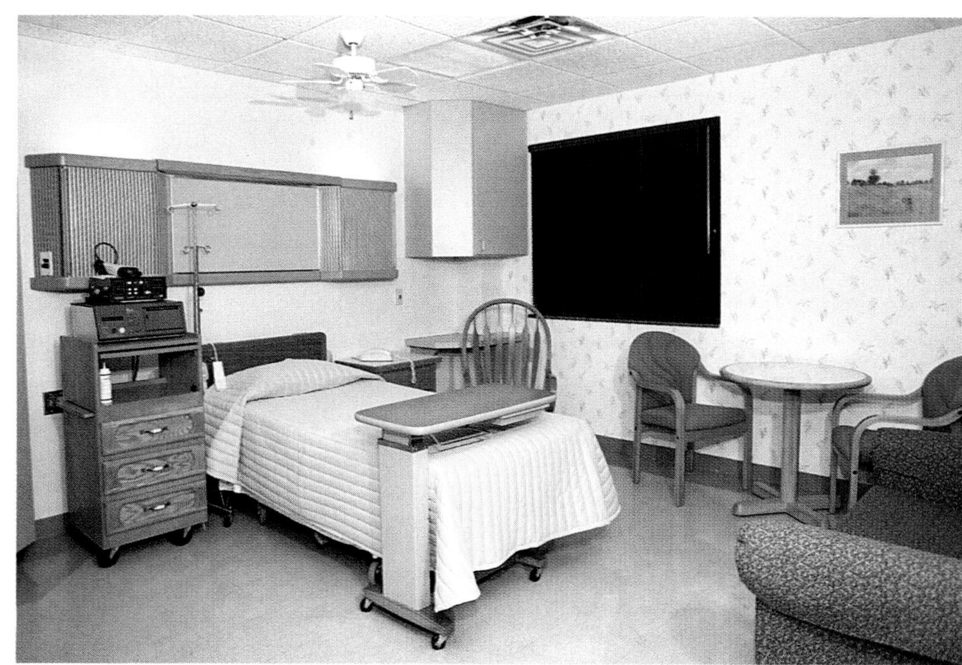

Many hospitals offer birthing rooms that combine a comfortable, homelike setting with full medical facilities. Both labor and delivery take place in the same room, and mother and baby can stay there together.

- The mother and her baby remain together for all or most of the hospital stay, instead of being kept in separate rooms.
- Some hospitals offer the new LDRP concept. In this special unit, the woman labors, delivers, recovers, and spends her postpartum stay all in the same room. The baby stays with the mother; often the father is invited to stay, too.

Expectant parents should take the time to explore the various services offered by local hospitals. Many offer tours of their maternity department, which can be both informative and reassuring. After gathering information, the couple should discuss which services seem most appropriate for their needs.

Some couples choose not to use a hospital at all, but instead go to an **alternative birth center**, *a homelike facility, separate from any hospital, for giving birth.* Alternative birth centers emphasize prepared childbirth and offer many of the nontraditional approaches that are part of family-centered maternity care. Mothers are often assisted during labor and delivery by licensed midwives. Most alternative birth centers accept only low-risk mothers. However, a hospital is usually nearby, and mother and baby can be transferred there if necessary.

The costs of family-centered hospital maternity care or alternative birth centers are usually less than those of traditional hospital maternity care. The time spent at the facility is also usually much less. If there are no complications, parents usually leave the hospital or birth center within 24 hours of delivery, compared with the two- to three-day stay for traditional births.

PARENTING IN ACTION

Choosing an Appropriate Birth Setting

Ashley and Phil were surprised when they visited the new birthing rooms at a local hospital. They liked the setting—a place that looked and felt like home but could handle any emergency. The room was a large lounge with comfortable furniture, lamps, TV, and a stereo.

It was more than the atmosphere, however, that drew them to this kind of birth experience. As Phil explained, "We wanted to have our baby right there with us. We didn't want to be separated."

Ashley and Phil chose that hospital's birthing room setting for the delivery of their daughter, Megan. They were especially pleased because the nursing staff helped them learn to take care of Megan. After less than two days in the hospital, Ashley and Phil took Megan home, feeling very satisfied with their birth experience and increasingly confident in themselves as parents.

THINK AND DISCUSS

1. Why do you think staying with the baby after birth helps new parents feel more confident?
2. What might be some other effects of this kind of birth experience?

Couples have many decisions to make as they prepare for the birth of their child. Where to have the baby is one of these major decisions. Whether the couple decides to have the baby delivered in a hospital, alternative birth center, or at home, safety for both the mother and the baby is the primary concern. Couples should discuss the advantages and disadvantages of each delivery option with their health care provider. Then they should make the decision that is best for them and their baby.

Some women may choose a health care provider who is willing to deliver their baby at home. This setting for delivery has gained popularity during recent years. The family that chooses a home delivery must carefully weigh the benefits and risks. This option is generally possible only for women with uncomplicated pregnancies. A special transport system should be available in case of an emergency.

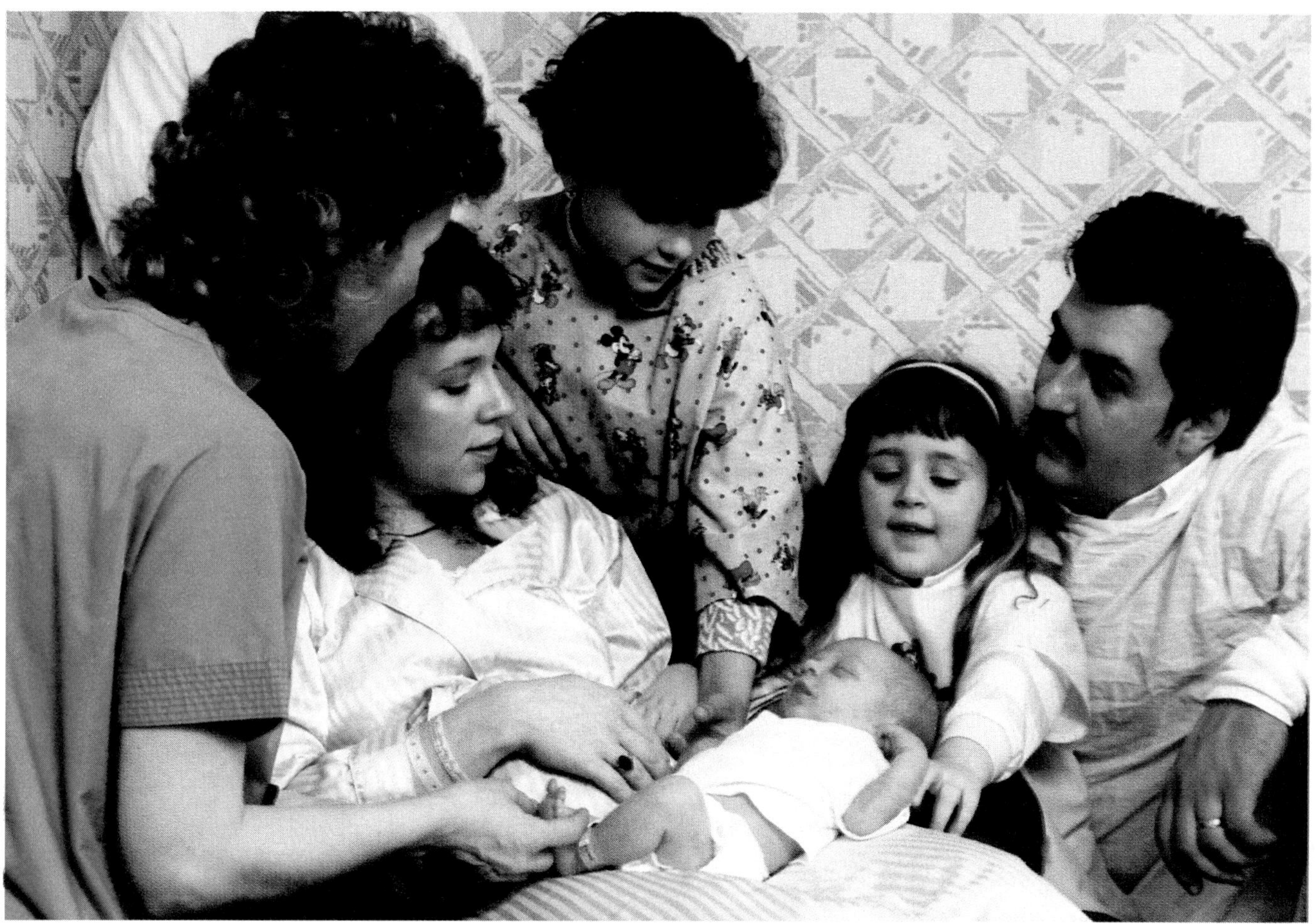

Alternative birth centers emphasize family participation and a relaxed atmosphere.

SECTION 3 REVIEW

CHECK YOUR UNDERSTANDING

1. What is prepared childbirth? List three main points emphasized by most prepared childbirth courses.
2. What is labor? What is delivery?
3. What are the differences between an obstetrician and a licensed midwife?
4. List two questions an expectant couple might ask a doctor or licensed midwife they are considering choosing as their birth attendant.
5. List three services that are often part of family-centered maternity care in a hospital.
6. What is an alternative birth center?

DISCUSS AND DISCOVER

1. Under what circumstances do you think women might prefer traditional maternity services to family-centered maternity care? Why? What pressures do you think these expectant mothers might feel to use the current, more popular procedures of family-centered care?
2. Work with a group of other students. Together, gather information on the various maternity services offered by hospitals and alternative birth centers in your community. Make a poster or bulletin board display comparing the different kinds of services.

SAFETY GUIDELINES FOR BABY EQUIPMENT

Two of the most important pieces of baby equipment are the car safety restraint, which is needed immediately, and the crib, which many parents acquire weeks or even months after the baby has been born. Whether these pieces of equipment are purchased new or used, borrowed or handed down, each should be carefully checked for safety.

CAR SAFETY RESTRAINTS

Everyone needs to be buckled up in a moving vehicle. Because of their size, children under the age of four need special safety restraints. Regular adult seat belts do not fit or restrain young children properly. There are two types of safety restraints for young children in cars: rear-facing restraints and forward-facing restraints.

Rear-facing Safety Restraints

Rear-facing safety restraints are specially designed to keep infants safe. Any baby who weighs less than 20 pounds (9.1 kg) or is less than 26 inches (66 cm) long should ride in one of these bucket-type carriers. The infant should face backwards in a reclining position. A harness in the carrier holds the baby in position, and the carrier is secured with a car seat belt.

Forward-Facing Safety Restraints

Around the age of nine months, most children are ready to sit up and face forward in a safety seat. Some rear-facing safety restraints can be converted to forward-facing seats, but a variety of other types are available.

★ Seat with harness. A harness comes over the child's shoulders and up between the child's legs. The seat is secured by the car seat belt.

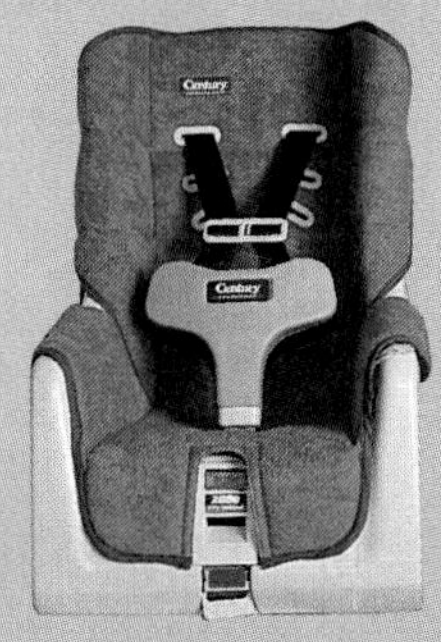

★ Seat with protective shield. A padded surface protects the child if he or she is thrown forward by an impact or by sudden braking. Look for seats with extended, padded shields around the head. The child is held in place by the car seat belt and sometimes by a harness as well.

★ Booster seat. This is a strong seat without a back. It is used

with the car seat belt and a special harness fastened permanently to the car. Booster seats are designed for young children who have already reached a weight of 40 pounds (18.2 kg) or a height of 40 inches (102 cm). When a child wears a seat belt, either with or without a booster seat, it is important to check the fit of the belt. The lap belt should fit snugly over the child's hip bones, not across the stomach. The shoulder belt should be used only if it does not cross the child's neck or face.

CRIB

When choosing a crib, parents should consider the safety and comfort of the baby, as well as conveniences for themselves. These are some important points to use in evaluating and selecting a crib:

- Adjustable sides and adjustable mattress height eliminate unnecessary bending for the baby's parents or caregiver. Some cribs have sides that can be dropped or removed when the child is old enough to get in and out of bed alone. This is a good feature to look for when considering cribs.
- A baby's crib should have a firm spring and mattress. Doctors advise against using a pillow in the crib. A pillow is bad for the baby's posture and creates a risk of suffocation.
- The bars or slats of the crib must be no more than 2⅜ inches (6.0 cm) apart.
- Corner posts should be no higher than ⅓ inch (8.5 mm) above end panels or side panels. (Canopy cribs are an exception.)
- The top of the crib sides should have a plastic covering, sometimes called a teething rail.
- If the crib has drop sides, check to see whether the mechanism is likely to be accidentally released.
- The higher the sides of the crib when raised, the less chance that an older baby can climb out.
- There should be no rough edges or exposed bolts.
- Cribs and mattresses vary in size. Be sure there is no space between the edge of the mattress and the crib.

SUMMARY

- A woman should visit a doctor as soon as she suspects she might be pregnant, and she should have periodic checkups throughout her pregnancy.
- Good nutrition is very important for both the developing baby and the mother.
- A pregnant woman needs plenty of rest and moderate exercise.
- Expectant parents should prepare by discussing child care and parenting, deciding on a method of feeding, and assembling the basic items needed for the baby.
- Parents-to-be should estimate the expenses of having a baby, look for ways to reduce those expenses, and make a budget to meet their financial needs.
- Prepared childbirth classes help the expectant mother become physically and mentally ready for labor and delivery.
- Expectant parents must choose who will help deliver their baby and in what setting.

REVIEWING THE FACTS

1. What should a woman who notices one of the signs of early pregnancy do? Why?
2. List four steps that are usually part of a doctor's examination of a woman at the beginning of pregnancy.
3. During which part of pregnancy is a woman likely to feel short of breath? Why?
4. What are the basic food groups in the Food Guide Pyramid?
5. How much weight does a woman usually gain during her entire pregnancy? List three factors, other than the weight of the baby, that contribute to the mother's weight gain.
6. List two advantages of breast-feeding. List two advantages of bottle-feeding.
7. Why is it especially important for expectant parents to have a budget?
8. What methods of reducing pain are taught in childbirth preparation classes?
9. List three kinds of health care professionals who help deliver babies.
10. Are alternative birth centers and home births an option for all pregnant women? Why or why not?

EXPLORING FURTHER

1. Prepare two nutritious snacks that might be part of a healthy, balanced diet for a pregnant woman. Serve these snacks to your classmates. Together, evaluate the snacks in terms of nutrition and appeal. (Section 1)
2. Plan a baby shower for a young couple expecting their first child. Make an invitation for the party, and include general gift suggestions on the invitation. Also write a schedule for the party, noting what activities will be included and what foods will be served. (Section 2)
3. Imagine the feelings a young child might have when his or her mother goes to the hospital for several days and then returns home with a new baby—a baby who becomes the center of everyone's attention. Write and illustrate a small book that could help prepare a child for this event. (Section 2)
4. Investigate three childbirth preparation courses offered in your community. Find out who gives each course, where and when it is given, and what fees, if any, are involved. Share your information with a group of classmates. Together, discuss the apparent advantages and disadvantages of the different courses. (Section 3)

THINKING CRITICALLY

1. **Analyze.** How do you think a woman's emotional responses to her own pregnancy might affect her symptoms of physical discomfort? What effect, if any, do you think her physical discomfort may have on her feelings about her pregnancy and her developing child?
2. **Compare.** Why do you think some women might try to gain less than 20 pounds (9.1 kg) during a pregnancy? Why do you think others might gain more than 35 pounds (15.9 kg)? What risks are these groups of women running? Do you think the women in either or both of these groups should be helped? If so, how?
3. **Evaluate.** High-risk mothers are not offered the option of a birthing room. Why might mothers be considered high-risk? Why are the birthing rooms not offered to them?

CROSS-CURRICULUM CONNECTIONS

1. **Writing.** Imagine that you have just received a postcard from a friend who is young, newly married, and far from her familiar neighborhood. Your friend writes that she thinks she is pregnant, but she's not positive. She's also not sure how she feels about being pregnant now. Write your friend a letter, expressing your response and giving her some advice.
2. **Math.** Select twelve items from the list of Basic Baby Supplies on pages 175-176. Visit stores, check newspaper ads, or look in catalogs for prices on those twelve items. Record prices from three sources for each item. Then use the lowest price for each item to write a spending plan for purchasing those twelve items.

OBSERVING AND PARTICIPATING

Preparing for Birth

During pregnancy, a woman experiences a series of physical changes that may affect her attitudes and emotions. She and her partner are also faced with a number of important decisions that will affect both of them, as well as their new baby and any other children they may have.

Choose one of the observation activities below. When you have completed the activity, record your observations in your journal. Share your journal entry with other students, and discuss what you have learned.

- **Observing.** Over the course of a week, take time to observe pregnant women in public places, such as malls, parks, and grocery stores. What kinds of activities do pregnant women undertake? Does each woman's pregnancy appear to affect her activities? If so, how?
- **Observing.** Visit a child care center. How many children are in the center? How old are the children? How many adults are available to care for the children? How attentive do the adults seem to be? Do you feel the children are receiving personal, loving care? Would you be comfortable leaving an infant in this child care center? Would you be comfortable leaving a three-year-old in this center? Why or why not?
- **Observing.** If possible, arrange to visit either a prepared childbirth class or a hospital tour for maternity patients. Listen carefully to the teacher or the tour guide, and observe the reactions of the prospective parents to what is being said. How do the parents seem to feel about this activity? What feelings do the parents express about pregnancy and birth?

CHAPTER 7

The Baby's Arrival

Baby Jakia had just awakened from a nap and she felt hungry. Beatrice and Gerald, Jakia's mom and dad, were in the kitchen when they heard her start to cry. They went to Jakia's room together.

Beatrice picked up baby Jakia and said, "Hello, Little Jakia. What's wrong? Are you hungry?"

"We love you, Jakia. Don't cry. Mommy and Daddy have waited a long time for you to join our family. You're such a beautiful baby," crooned Gerald.

Jakia knew their voices already, and liked it very much when Mom or Dad held her close. She stopped crying as her eyes scanned the loving faces hovered so near. Beatrice carried Jakia into the kitchen and Gerald followed. When Beatrice started feeding Jakia, the baby made happy grunting noises that made both parents smile with contentment.

SECTION 1 The Birth Process

OBJECTIVES

- Recognize the ways in which labor may begin.
- Outline the three stages of labor.
- Describe a newborn's physical changes and appearance at birth.

TERMS TO LEARN

cervix
cesarean birth
contractions
dilates
fontanels
forceps

When a woman labors to bring her child into the world, it is an experience like no other. Labor brings powerful sensations and emotions. It is a challenging experience for most women, but it is a challenge with a very special reward.

The Beginning of Labor

During the last weeks of pregnancy, women often become anxious to finally meet the new baby. Time seems to pass slowly as they watch for any sign that labor is about to begin.

There are many changes that occur in the last days of pregnancy. However, these changes may be very subtle, and the timing of the changes varies a great deal from woman to woman. Even when a woman notices some of these signs, it is still difficult to predict when her labor will actually begin.

One sign that labor is approaching occurs when the baby settles deep into the mother's pelvis, preparing for his or her journey into the world. This settling is often called lightening; it may also be referred to as the baby's dropping.

There are some definite signals that the baby is coming. One is commonly called show or bloody show; it may also be referred to as losing the mucus plug. Throughout the pregnancy, the **cervix**, *the lower part of the uterus*, which serves as a kind of door, is closed and sealed with mucus. This mucus helps prevent bacteria from moving up from the vagina into the uterus where it might cause an infection. As the woman's body prepares for birth, this mucus begins to liquefy. The woman may notice a few drops of blood or a slight pinkish vaginal staining.

In some women, the onset of labor is signaled by a trickle—or even a gush—of warm fluid from the vagina. This indicates that the membrane holding the amniotic fluid surrounding the baby has broken. In most women, this membrane does not rupture until she is at the hospital or birthing center, in active labor.

When the membrane breaks, the woman should note the time, the amount of fluid, and the color and odor of the fluid, and should report this information to her doctor or midwife. He or she may want to deliver the baby within 24 to 48 hours after the membrane has broken, to protect the baby from infection.

Though researchers still do not know exactly what causes labor to begin, it appears that the mother's hormones, her uterus, the placenta, and the baby all play an important role. During the final days of pregnancy, each system undergoes changes in preparation for the birth.

Though there are many clues that a woman is entering into labor, the only clear sign that labor is underway are **contractions**, *the tightening and releasing of the uterine muscle.* Many women wonder what these contractions will be like: "Will they hurt? How will I know I'm having one?" When the uterus contracts, it—like any other muscle—gets shorter and harder. Bend your right arm toward your shoulder while making a tight fist. Feel the muscle in your upper arm become thick and hard. Now, slowly relax and lower your forearm. Feel the muscle stretch and soften. With each contraction of labor, the uterine muscle shortens and gets harder, holds that hardness for a short time, and then relaxes and rests for a few minutes.

The contractions of true labor have a characteristic pattern. Over time, they get longer, stronger, and closer together. Many women find it helpful to have their partner use a watch or clock to time their contractions for a while to see whether they follow this pattern. If they do, the woman should contact her health care provider, who will want to know how long the contractions are lasting, how frequently they are occurring, and how she is feeling.

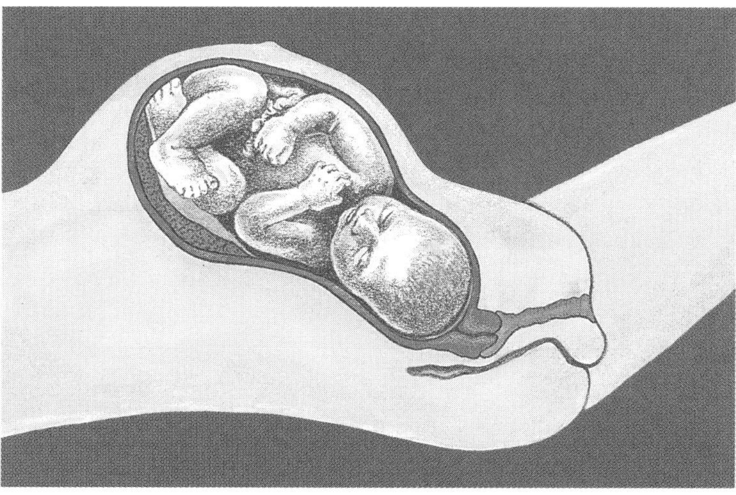

This drawing shows the baby at the end of nine months of pregnancy, before labor begins. The cervix (between the baby's head and the birth canal) is its normal size and shape. On the following pages you will see how the cervix becomes wider and thinner as labor progresses.

Stages of Labor

When actual labor begins, it progresses through three stages:

- In the first stage, contractions open the cervix.
- In the second stage, the baby is born.
- In the third stage, the placenta is expelled.

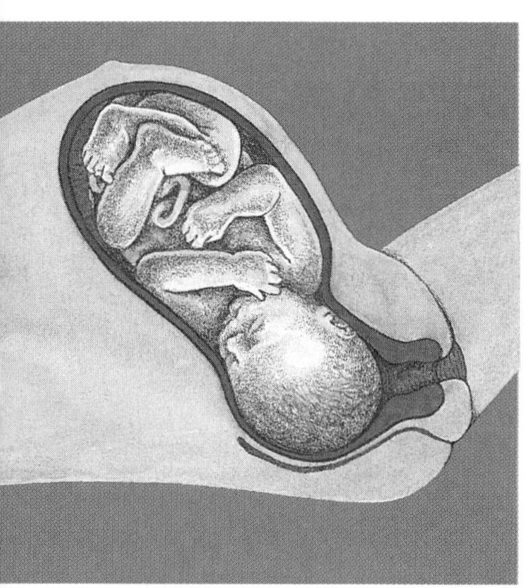

During the first stage of labor, the cervix begins to dilate or widen. The baby's head moves lower in the pelvis.

The First Stage

Each time the uterus contracts during the first stage of labor, something very special occurs. As the muscles of the uterus shorten and thicken, they gently pull up on the cervix, slowly thinning and opening it until it is wide enough for the baby's head to slip out of the uterus into the birth canal. Ordinarily, the cervix is nearly completely closed. During the first stage of labor, the cervix **dilates**, or *widens*, to form an opening about 4 inches (10 cm) in diameter. Before the cervix can dilate completely, it has to become thinner. It changes from its usual thickness of about 3⁄4 inch (19 mm) to become as thin as a sheet of paper. This process is called effacement.

As labor progresses, the contractions get longer (about 60 seconds), stronger, and closer together (5 to 6 minutes apart). As the contraction pattern intensifies, the woman begins to turn inward, searching for the strength to deal with the sensations of labor. She becomes more serious and focused on the labor, and she needs increasing support from her partner. During this time, the woman usually checks with her doctor or midwife by phone. The birth attendant will tell her when she should go to the hospital or birth center.

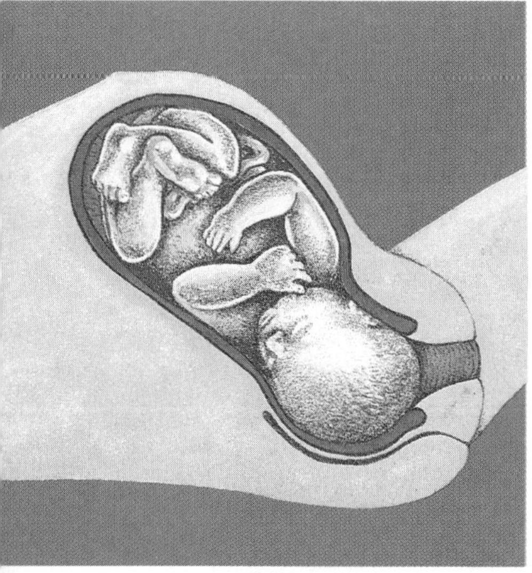

The first stage of labor ends with the cervix fully dilated. The opening of the uterus is now 4 inches (10 cm) wide.

As the cervix opens, the baby usually moves down into the lower pelvis, getting ready for birth. In most cases, the baby is head down, but occasionally, babies are in other positions. Some enter the pelvis with their feet, buttocks, or knees first. These positions are called breech presentations. Babies in these positions may have a difficult time moving through the mother's pelvis for birth. An obstetrician will carefully evaluate each situation to determine whether a vaginal delivery is possible or whether a cesarean birth would be safer.

Throughout this first stage of labor, the mother should try to relax as completely as possible, both between contractions and during contractions. Fear and tension cause the muscles of the body to tighten, and tightened muscles can slow labor down and make it more uncomfortable. A mother who has taken a prepared childbirth course may have learned special breathing exercises she can do with her partner. These exercises encourage relaxation, distract the mother from the discomfort of the contractions, and help the labor progress. Most mothers may safely assume any positions they find comfortable during the first stage of labor—lying, sitting, standing, walking.

As the first stage of labor comes to an end, the contractions become very strong. They last longer (up to 90 seconds) and come more frequently (2 to 3 minutes apart) than those of early labor. With these last contractions, the cervix stretches and opens until it is fully dilated to 4 inches (10 cm). This part of labor is called transition. It is usually the most difficult part of labor to cope with. A woman's partner needs to be very supportive at this time. The partner can use touch and reassuring words to guide the woman through these last difficult contractions of the first stage.

HEALTH TIP

If the mother finds the first stage of labor very long or difficult, she may choose to use medication to reduce the discomfort. Various kinds of medications are available; their effects vary from changing the woman's perception of pain to completely numbing an area so that no painful sensations are felt. All medications have potential benefits and risks. The possibility of side effects in both the mother and the baby must be considered.

The Second Stage

Once the cervix is completely dilated and the baby's head has slipped out of the uterus into the vagina, the second stage of labor has begun. The contractions of the second stage are very different from those of the first. They no longer stretch the cervix open. Instead, the contractions work to move the baby down through the pelvis and out the vagina. The second stage of labor may be as short as a few minutes, or it may last up to three hours. It culminates in the event for which the parents have been waiting—the birth of the baby.

You might wonder how a baby could ever fit through what seems to be such a narrow space. Actually, the bones of the pelvis are joined together by ligaments, which are like rubber bands. At the time of delivery, these ligaments are very stretchy, as a result of the influence of a special hormone. The bones of the pelvis gently stretch open as the baby passes through. The vagina is also very stretchy from the effects of the same hormone, so that the baby can safely pass through to be born.

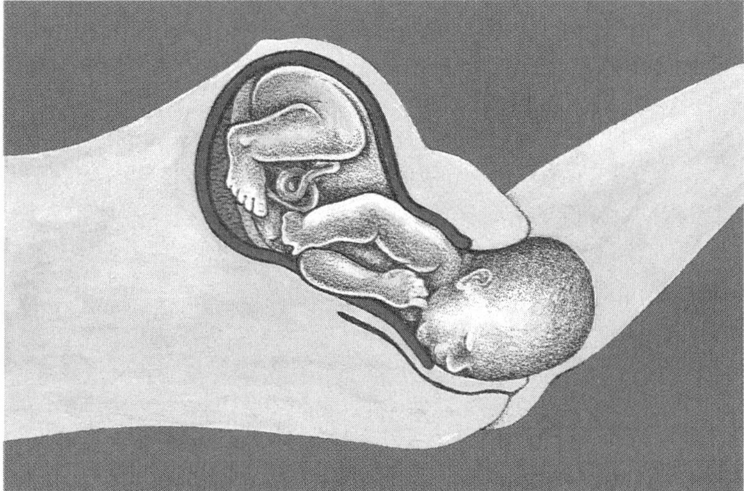

During the second stage of labor, strong contractions push the baby out of the uterus and down the vagina, or birth canal. Notice that the baby begins to rotate to a facedown position.

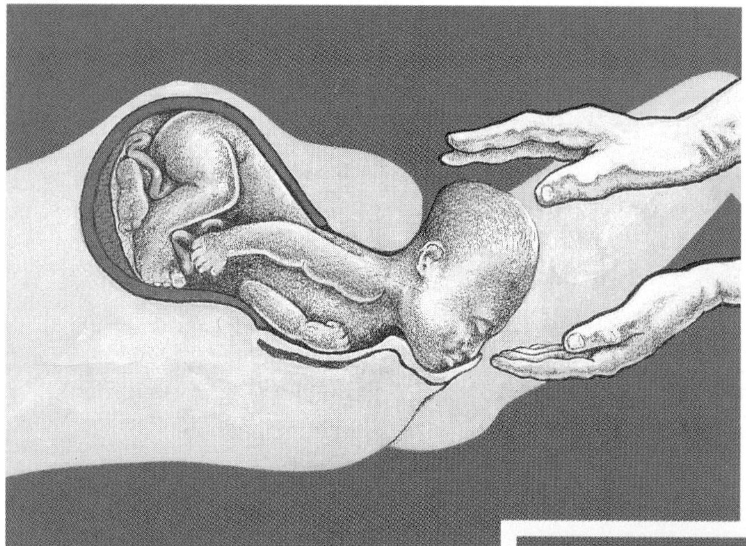

As the head emerges, the baby stretches out. The head may seem "molded" into an odd shape after traveling such a narrow passageway. This is normal and temporary.

Almost there... Getting the head and shoulders out is the "tricky" part of the delivery. After that, the rest of the body slips out easily.

The body of the unborn baby is specially adapted for the journey through the pelvis and the vaginal canal. The skull is soft and flexible, so that the baby's head can become longer and narrower than normal. The skull consists of five separate bones. These bones can overlap each other to allow the baby's head to fit through the pelvis and vagina.

If the birth attendant decides that the fit between mother and baby is not perfect, he or she may use a special procedure to assist in the delivery. One option is to widen the vaginal opening with a surgical incision called an episiotomy. Episiotomy may be used to speed the delivery of the baby in the event of a problem or to prevent tearing of the woman's tissue. Although the procedure was performed routinely in the past, many doctors and midwives now work with women to avoid episiotomy. The woman must be willing to relax the muscles of her bottom and to follow the direction of her birth attendant, so that the vaginal tissues have time to stretch open around the baby's head.

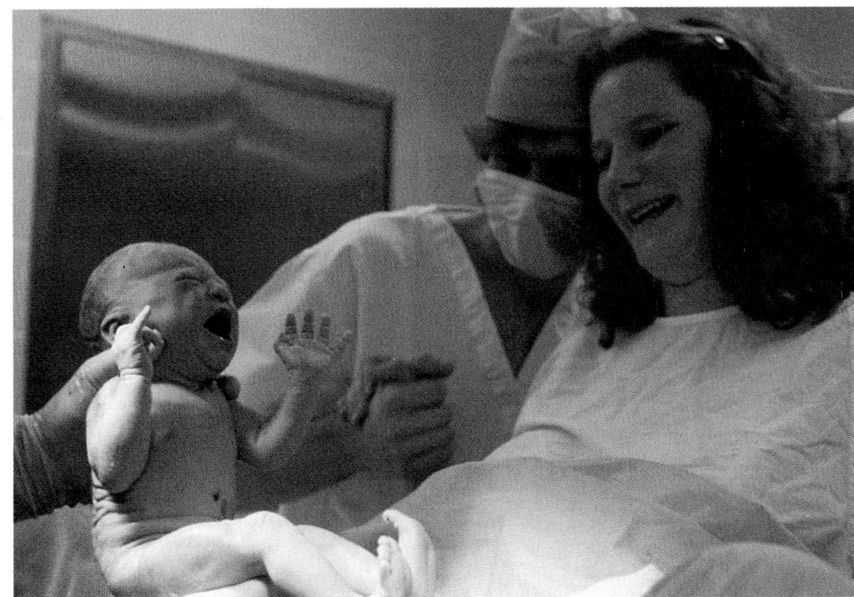

Success! Though she may have felt tired and discouraged earlier in labor, the mother experiences a great surge of energy just before delivery. She is ecstatic and eager to hold her baby.

By bearing down during contractions, the mother begins the delivery of her baby. Women can give birth in a variety of positions. Often women choose a semisitting position in the special birthing bed, with the legs apart and the knees bent. Some women choose squatting, sitting in a birthing chair, lying on the side, or even kneeling on hands and knees for the delivery. If a woman is moved to a traditional delivery table, her legs may be supported by stirrups or foot rests.

As the baby moves down the birth canal, the top of the head appears first. The birth attendant provides gentle support as the head is delivered. The head is followed by one shoulder, and then the other. Then the baby slips out into the world.

Sometimes a doctor uses **forceps**—*specialized tongs made from bands of surgical steel that are molded to fit the shape of a baby's head*—to guide the baby's head during delivery. The forceps enable the doctor to control the movement of the head, helping the baby emerge more quickly—or more slowly—if necessary.

The Third Stage

During the third stage of labor, the uterus gives birth to the placenta. This final stage may be as brief as two minutes, or it may last half an hour. After a period of rest, the mother may again feel some contractions and an urge to push. She usually feels very little discomfort with the contractions of the third stage. These contractions help the placenta separate from the wall of the uterus. The placenta is soft and comes away easily. When the mother pushes and delivers the placenta, the birth process is complete.

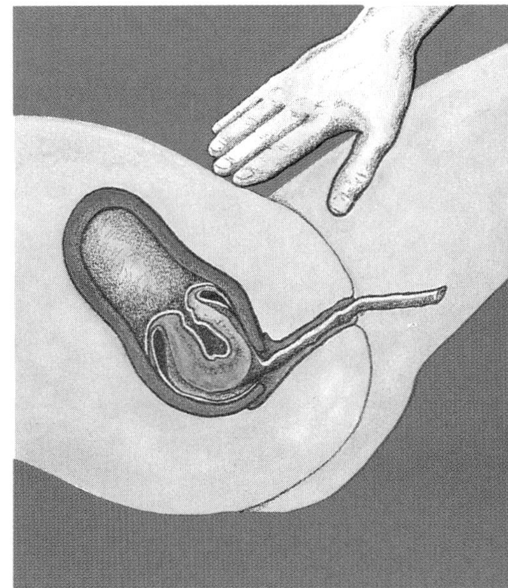

The placenta–no longer needed to nourish the baby–is expelled from the body in the third stage of labor.

THE BIRTH OF CESAREAN

Julius Caesar was one of the most important leaders of ancient Rome. The doctors who attended his birth (probably in 104 B.C.) realized that Caesar's mother was dying in labor. They performed a radical surgery to save her baby—and tiny Julius Caesar was delivered by the procedure that now recalls his name: cesarean birth.

Cesarean Birth

Not all births progress through these three stages of labor. If complications arise during the pregnancy or during labor, a **cesarean birth**—*delivery of a baby through a surgical incision in the mother's abdomen*—may be necessary. Depending on which type of medication is given, the mother may remain awake during cesarean surgery. The father or coach may also be present, with the doctor's permission.

In pregnancies where a cesarean birth is likely, a special cesarean childbirth education class may be recommended to help the parents prepare for the event. After the surgery, the mother and baby usually stay in the hospital for about four days.

The Newborn at Birth

In the hours of labor, the baby undergoes amazing changes. For the first time, the newborn is not completely dependent on the mother's body for life support.

During its development in the uterus, the baby's lungs are filled with fluid. The pressure of being squeezed down the birth canal forces much of the fluid out. When the baby finally emerges, the pressure is released and the baby's lungs automatically expand. The baby takes his or her first breath.

Usually, the breathing reflex continues on its own, and the newborn baby breathes naturally. If the baby needs help, the doctor or nurse-midwife may gently rub the baby's back to get the process started. Any fluid that remains in the airways or mouth is gently suctioned out.

Once the lungs have begun to take in oxygen, the baby's circulatory system changes. A valve in the heart closes and, over the next few days, becomes permanently sealed. Blood now circulates to and from the lungs, rather than bypassing the lungs as before. The umbilical cord, through which the baby has received oxygen and nourishment, is no longer needed. Within a few minutes of birth, the cord stops pulsing and begins to shrink. The cord is clamped, tied, and cut off.

How Does the Newborn Look?

What will our baby look like? When parents imagine their answers to this question, they usually picture a sturdy baby of about six months. They do not often recall that a newborn has a unique appearance.

The newborn's head is wobbly and large; it accounts for one-fourth of the baby's entire length. The head may appear

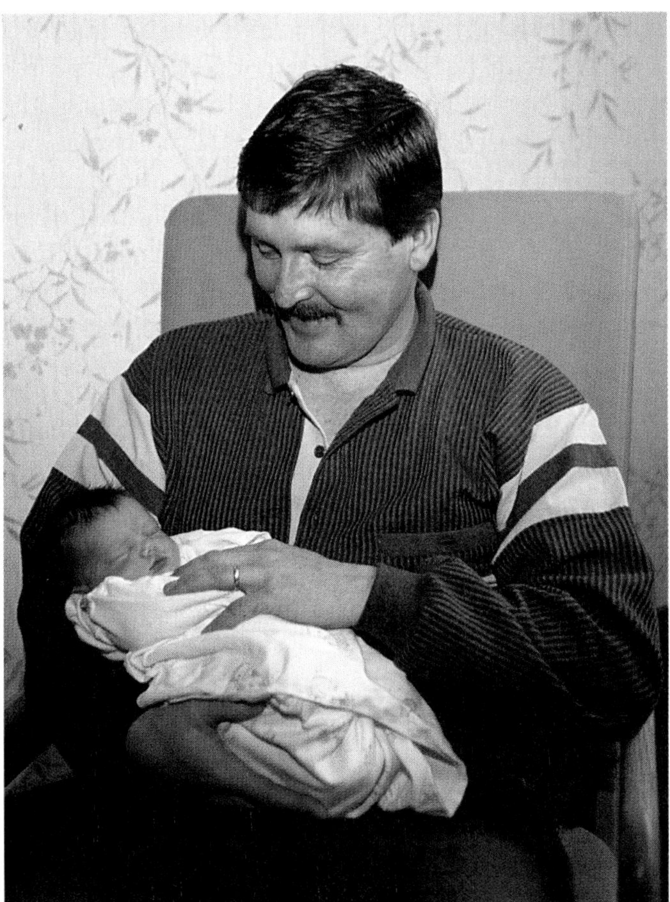

The newborn may have a full head of hair or no hair at all. Red marks on the skin are common. Can you see how the newborn's facial features make sucking easier?

strangely lopsided or pointed from the passage through the birth canal. The bones of the baby's skull are not yet tightly knitted together, so they can be molded together during birth without harm. Any lopsidedness is only temporary.

The baby's head has two **fontanels**, *open spaces where the bones of the baby's skull have not yet permanently joined*. The larger of these "soft spots" is just above the baby's forehead. The other fontanel is toward the back of the skull. These spaces allow the bones of the baby's skull to move together during birth. As the baby grows older, usually between the ages of six and eighteen months, the bone structure comes together to cover the spaces completely. In the meantime, the soft spots are protected by skin that is as tough as heavy canvas.

The newborn typically has fat cheeks; a short, flat nose; and a receding chin. These features make the baby's face well adapted for sucking, because the nose and chin are out of the way.

At birth, a baby's eyes are nearly adult-sized. They are usually dark grayish-blue at birth. The baby's permanent eye color becomes apparent within several months.

At the time of birth, the newborn is often a dusky color. Very quickly after the baby begins to breathe, his or her color improves. It takes some time for the circulatory system to adjust to life outside the womb. As a result, some babies' fingers and toes remain dusky and slightly cooler than the rest of their body for up to 24 hours. Wrapping the baby well and covering his or her head with a cap helps keep the baby warm and comfortable.

Newborns have many unique characteristics that new parents may not be prepared for. Some babies, particularly those born early, have fine, downy hair over their forehead, back, and shoulders. This hair disappears as the baby grows.

While in the uterus, the baby bathes in warm amniotic fluid. To protect their skin from constant exposure to the fluid, babies are covered with a rich, creamy substance called vernix. After the birth, most newborns have some vernix in the folds of their skin, particularly around their ears and neck and under their arms. During the baby's bath, it can be gently removed with warm water and a washcloth.

Many babies have tiny white bumps scattered over their nose and cheeks. These bumps are called milia, or baby acne. They are simply plugged oil ducts, caused by stimulation from the maternal hormones, which remain in the baby's system for a short time after delivery. The milia will disappear in a week or two.

SECTION 1 REVIEW

CHECK YOUR UNDERSTANDING

1. What are contractions?
2. What is the cervix? How does it change during labor?
3. What happens in the second stage of labor?
4. What are forceps? How may they be used?
5. What happens in the third stage of labor?
6. What is a cesarean birth?
7. What causes a newborn to begin breathing?
8. What are fontanels? What purpose do they serve?

DISCUSS AND DISCOVER

1. Why is it important for a mother to relax during labor? What factors can make relaxing especially difficult? What do you think a mother's birthing partner can—and should—do to help her relax?
2. Read more about the experiences of first-time mothers during the three stages of labor. Then draw a time line showing how long each stage typically lasts and what happens during each stage.

The Postnatal Period

SECTION 2

OBJECTIVES

- Describe common hospital procedures following a birth.
- Give recommendations for the postnatal care of the mother.
- Explain the special needs of a premature baby.

TERMS TO LEARN

Apgar scale
bonding
colostrum
incubator
rooming-in

The moment of birth signals the end of nine months of preparation and anticipation. Of course, the moment of birth is also a beginning. In a short time, the newborn—also called a neonate—and his or her parents will go home to begin their new life together. First, however, the staff at the hospital or birthing center must make sure the new family gets off to a good start.

Examining the Newborn

Shortly after delivery, the neonate is usually checked according to the **Apgar scale**, *a method of evaluating a newborn's physical condition*. The infant is given a rating from 0 to 2 in each of these five areas: pulse, breathing, muscle tone, reflex to stimulation, and skin color. A total score of 6 to 10 is considered normal. A lower score is a sign that the baby needs special medical attention. Usually, the Apgar evaluation is given one minute after birth and then again at five minutes after birth. The baby is also given a brief examination to check for any conditions that might require special care.

Within 60 minutes of delivery, drops of silver nitrate or an antiseptic ointment are put into the baby's eyes to guard against infection. The baby is weighed, measured, and, in some cases, cleaned up. A permanent copy of the baby's footprints is made for public record. Two bands giving the baby's family name are clamped to the wrists or ankles. The mother wears a bracelet with the same information. These identification procedures are completed before the baby leaves the delivery room or birthing room to avoid any confusion later.

THE APGAR SCALE

	SCORE 0	SCORE 1	SCORE 2
HEART RATE	Absent	Under 100	Over 100
BREATHING	Absent	Slow, irregular	Good, crying
MUSCLE TONE	Limp	Some movement of extremities	Active motion
RESPONSIVENESS (Baby's reaction when nose is irritated)	No response	Grimace	Cough or sneeze
COLOR	Blue or pale	Body limbs pink, not blue	Completely pink

(The chart above shows the color scale for a white child. An infant of dark-skin color who is grayish and pale scores a 0 on the color scale. If the dark-skinned infant has a strong body color, but grayish limbs, the score is 1. A score of 2 is given to a dark-skinned newborn who has strong color, pink lips, and pink palms and soles.)

Bonding and Attachment

In recent years, researchers have focused increasing attention on the emotional needs of the newborn. Many experts feel that it is natural for lifelong emotional ties to be formed between parents and the newborn soon after birth. Facilitating **bonding**—*the process of forming lifelong emotional ties*—has become a goal in many hospitals and birthing centers. Most facilities now delay such procedures as cutting the umbilical cord, cleaning the infant, and giving eyedrops so that parents have the opportunity to begin bonding with their newborn right away.

Immediately after birth, a healthy baby may be placed in the mother's arms or on her stomach. The baby can feel the mother's skin and hear her familiar heartbeat and voice. The newborn instinctively focuses on the mother's face. In turn, the mother—and the father, if he is present—enjoys stroking and talking to the baby.

If the baby will be breast-fed, the mother may nurse the baby within minutes after birth. The baby knows instinctively what to do. Many hospitals have specially trained professionals who assist the nursing couple at these first feedings to ensure success. The mother's breasts supply *the first breast milk*, called **colostrum**. The colostrum is easy for the newborn to digest and rich in antibodies to protect against disease. It is sometimes thick in consistency; it may be clear or yellow in color.

Bonding takes place as the parents and baby interact through sight, sound, and touch. This process is important for the baby's development. It also brings out the parents' natural desire to love and care for their baby.

The Hospital Stay

The process of birth is a momentous undertaking for both mother and baby. The newborn must adjust to a whole new world. The mother, too, needs time to adjust. In a matter of hours, her body has gone through many physical changes, from pregnancy to labor and birth and back to the nonpregnant state. Although she probably feels thrilled and excited, she also needs to rest and recuperate.

After delivery, the medical staff monitor the new mother's blood pressure, pulse, and other vital signs until all body functions have stabilized.

Nationally, there are differences in the length of time mother and baby are expected to stay in the hospital. At a minimum, the mother needs a chance to eat, bathe, and rest. She and her infant must also be medically checked, to make sure everything is going well. In some hospitals and birthing centers, a mother and baby who are both healthy may go home if that is where the mother feels she can recuperate best. This may be as soon as 12 hours after the birth. In other hospitals, the average stay for mother and baby following birth is two or three days.

Getting to know your new baby brother is easier when you can visit Mom in the hospital and even hold the baby yourself.

Rooming-In

Many hospitals have a **rooming-in** program, *an arrangement in which the baby stays in the mother's room, rather than in a hospital nursery, after birth.* In most cases, the baby stays at the mother's bedside both day and night.

Rooming-in allows the new family to be together. It is a natural beginning to family unity and warm parent-child relationships. With rooming-in programs, fathers are allowed to visit whenever they wish.

Rooming-in programs have important advantages for all family members. They provide a homelike atmosphere in which grandparents and older brothers and sisters can visit, hold, and get to know the new baby. Couples benefit by having an opportunity to get to know their baby and practice caring for the baby before going home. The baby can be fed whenever he or she is hungry, rather than on a set schedule. In a good rooming-in program, parents enjoy a head start in getting to know their newborn, and babies seem more content.

Birth Certificate

All new parents should make sure their baby has a birth certificate. Usually, the birth certificate is issued free of charge soon after the baby is born.

Getting a birth certificate when a baby is born is a rather simple process. The parents simply need to fill out a form provided by the hospital or birthing center, at which time a temporary certificate is issued. In many states, the official birth certificate can be applied for by the family or by the hospital on behalf of the family. In our society, a birth certificate is considered the most important piece of personal identification anyone has; it is required for entrance into school.

Postnatal Care of the Mother

Rest and exercise are important to a new mother. A good time to rest is as the baby naps.

After the baby is brought home, it is natural for most of the attention to be focused on the new family member. However, care of the mother is just as important as the baby's care. A new mother has special physical and emotional needs, which continue for several weeks or months after the birth. A doctor or nurse will explain and discuss these needs before the mother and baby go home.

Physical Needs

Physically, the mother needs to recover from pregnancy and childbirth and to regain fitness. She must also take good care of herself so that she is able to care for her child. The best way to accomplish these goals is through rest, exercise, nutrition, and a medical checkup.

- **Rest.** During the first few days and weeks following the birth, the mother is likely to feel tired. She should try to sleep whenever the baby does. This will help her get the rest she needs, even with late-night feedings. Many couples especially appreciate having a relative or friend help with household chores or with baby care during this early period.
- **Exercise.** As soon as the mother feels able and her doctor approves, she should begin mild exercise. At first, this may be just a few simple stretches while lying down. Gradually, the mother can add other exercises to this simple routine. Postnatal exercise helps the woman return to her normal figure and correct posture.
- **Nutrition.** Eating right is just as important after pregnancy as during pregnancy. A mother who breast-feeds her baby should be sure to eat the number of servings recommended by the Food Guide Pyramid for nursing women. She should also drink plenty of water and other liquids. Just as before the birth, the food she eats is supplying the nutrients for the baby as well as for her own needs. Even if the mother is not breast-feeding, good nutrition helps her feel good and regain her energy.

- **Medical checkup.** About four to six weeks after the birth, the new mother should have a postnatal checkup. At this appointment, the doctor makes sure that the woman's uterus is returning to normal and that there are no unusual problems. This is also an opportunity for the mother to discuss any questions or concerns she has about adjusting to parenthood and about birth control.

Emotional Needs

Having a baby is a joyous event, but also a stressful one. Many new mothers go through a few days of mild depression sometime after the birth. They may have feelings of disappointment, loneliness, or resentment. No one knows for certain why the "baby blues" occur, but they are very common. Actually, new fathers often have these feelings, too.

New parents should expect to experience some unhappy moods after the birth. It helps to talk over their feelings with each other and with empathetic relatives or friends. If possible, the parents should arrange to take some time away from the baby for short periods—even just a few minutes a day. Taking good care of themselves, seeking support, and avoiding isolation helps parents minimize the blues.

The "baby blues" usually clear up in a few days. In the meantime, friends and relatives can help take some of the pressure off the new parents.

Caring for Premature Babies

Premature babies—those born before prenatal development is complete—require special care. They are smaller than normal at birth. Prematurity can happen for many reasons, not all of which are understood. Any newborn who weighs less than 5 ½ pounds (2.5 kg) or who is born before 36 weeks is considered premature and may need special medical attention. The more the baby weighs at birth and the closer the pregnancy comes to full term, the better the baby's chances of healthy survival.

Premature babies are not ready to live outside the mother's body. Their systems for heat regulation, breathing, and sucking and swallowing are not yet mature. To minimize these problems, a premature baby is usually placed in an **incubator**, *a special enclosed crib in which the oxygen supply, temperature, and humidity can be closely controlled.*

BUILDING SELF-ESTEEM

Meeting the Needs of Premature Babies

Modern medicine is also concerned about the emotional needs of premature babies. In some hospitals, the babies are gently stroked within their incubators. Many hospitals encourage parents to spend time with their babies, touching them within the incubator or holding them outside the incubator for short periods. In one experiment, a tiny, heated waterbed was designed to simulate the warmth and free-floating sensations the baby experiences before birth. In addition, the sounds of the mother's heartbeat, her voice, and soft music were played for the infant. These measures soothed the premature babies, allowing them to save precious energy for growth.

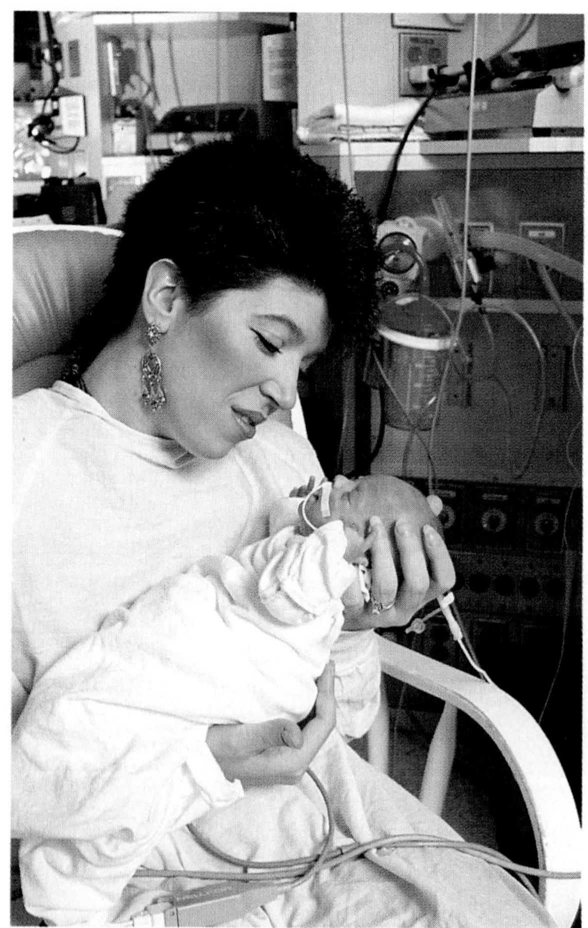

Today, advanced medical technology is combined with a recognition of the premature infant's emotional needs, including close contact with parents when possible.

PARENTING IN ACTION

Caring for Premature Babies

Four-year-old Erica scrambles happily up the climbing equipment in the preschool play yard. She is a sturdy, cheerful child, and she fits in well with her preschool classmates. Looking at her today, you would never guess that Erica was born six weeks early.

Erica weighed only 3½ pounds (1.6 kg) at birth. However, she had no physical problems other than her low birth weight.

As a newborn, Erica became part of a special study. She was one of 79 babies that weighed 2 to 4 pounds (0.9 to 1.8 kg) at birth but were otherwise healthy. Half of the babies in the study were kept in the hospital for standard treatment. The others were sent home 11 days earlier and given intensive nursing services at home.

Erica was one of the babies sent home early. With loving care from both parents and frequent checkups from the medical team, Erica gained weight steadily and developed no health problems.

The medical study was completed when Erica was almost a year old. According to the report, the average costs for the babies discharged early, including home nurses' fees, were almost $20,000 less per infant than the costs of standard hospital treatment. These babies experienced no more medical complications than did the babies kept in the hospital.

THINK AND DISCUSS

1. How do you think Erica's emotional development might have been affected by the kind of care she received?
2. If you were the parent of a premature baby like Erica, would you prefer to have your baby come home early or stay in the hospital? Why?

In the incubator, the baby's heart and lungs are electronically monitored. Special medical procedures and medications may be needed to combat infection, breathing difficulties, and other problems. Advances in medical technology allow many premature infants—even those weighing as little as 1 pound (454 g)—to survive and become healthy.

When they become healthy enough to leave the incubator, premature babies are moved to an open bassinet. Before being allowed to leave the hospital, the baby must achieve the ability to control his or her body temperature and gain weight at the same time.

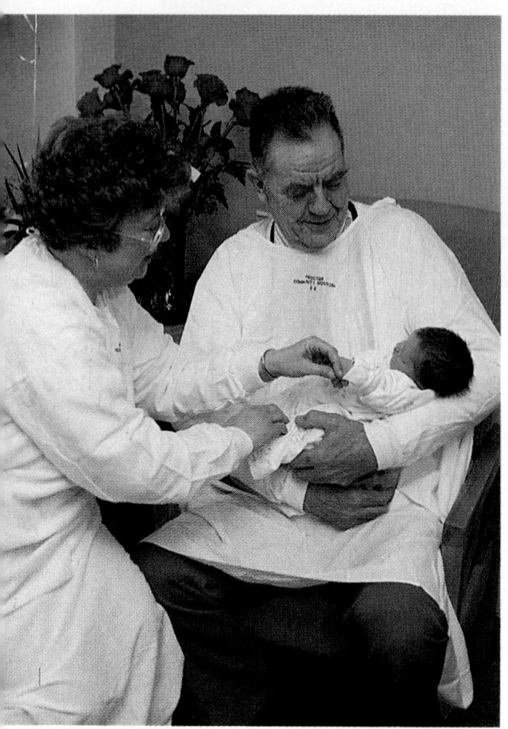

These proud grandparents were able to see and hold the baby just one day after birth.

Medical science continues to work at increasing the survival rate of premature and low birth weight babies. Efforts are also being made to reduce the rate of such births. One way to reach this goal is through educating the public in the importance of good nutrition, good health practices, medical care during pregnancy, and an understanding of the warning signs of premature labor. Helping young people recognize the dangers of teen pregnancy is also important. Researchers continue to explore other factors that increase the risks of prematurity and low birth weight.

If premature labor is recognized soon enough, the mother can be given medication that may stop the contractions before they progress to delivery. A small device that monitors uterine contractions has become available recently. A woman considered at high risk for premature delivery can wear this device for short periods, beginning in about the fifth month of pregnancy. If premature labor begins, the device detects it and the woman's doctor can be quickly alerted.

SECTION 2 REVIEW

CHECK YOUR UNDERSTANDING

1. What is the Apgar scale? When is it used?
2. What is bonding? When does it take place?
3. What is colostrum?
4. List two advantages of rooming-in.
5. How soon after birth should a mother begin to exercise?
6. What are the "baby blues"? Who can suffer from them?
7. What is an incubator? How is it used?

DISCUSS AND DISCOVER

1. Do you think parents and their babies who do not have an opportunity to bond immediately after birth are at a disadvantage? Why or why not? Do you think parents who have cesarean births or who adopt might have trouble bonding with their babies? If so, what kinds of problems could they have? If not, why not?
2. Find out whether any local hospitals have special volunteer programs that provide extra handling and attention for premature babies. If so, what is the specific purpose of the program? How is it conducted? Who can volunteer for the program? Share your findings with the rest of the class.

A New Family Member

SECTION 3

OBJECTIVES

- Describe babies' basic needs.
- Discuss how babies' needs can best be met.

For the first few months of life, every baby is considered "new." The baby's family, too, is newly expanded, with new relationships to establish. Welcoming this tiny person home and getting to know him or her are exciting aspects of adjusting to life with a new baby.

TERMS TO LEARN

grasp reflex
reflexes
rooting reflex
startle reflex
temperament

The Amazing Newborn

Newborn babies are amazing, born with remarkable capabilities. Recent research has shown that newborns can focus their eyes, hear, smell, and vocalize to communicate.

A researcher at Harvard University discovered that babies less than a day old could follow a pattern printed on paper and rolled before their eyes. Other studies show that newborns seem to select certain outlines, such as edges and angles, for attention. Newborns also prefer human faces to other shapes. Hearing is also present at birth, though it takes a few days for the neonate's auditory canals to clear of the amniotic fluid and for the hearing to become fully functional. Infants selectively respond to human sounds, particularly the female human voice—especially the mother's. Newborns can hear many sounds and distinguish between different pitches. Taste, smell, and touch are also present right from birth.

The newborn can breathe independently. The newborn can also cry to signal a variety of needs, such as the need for food, attention, or a dry diaper.

Reflexes

Babies must be able to handle certain of their own needs involuntarily until they learn to do things voluntarily. **Reflexes**—*instinctive, automatic responses, such as sneezing and yawning*—make this possible. These coordinated patterns of behavior help the baby's body function. For example, a sneeze helps clear the baby's nose of lint. Swallowing lets the baby eat without choking.

Some reflex actions, such as sneezing and swallowing, continue throughout life. Others are temporary; they last only until voluntary control develops and takes over. Three of a newborn's temporary reflexes are the rooting reflex, the grasp reflex, and the startle reflex.

- **Rooting reflex.** This is *a newborn's automatic response, when touched on the lips or cheek, of turning toward the touch and beginning to suck.* The rooting reflex, which is completely automatic, helps the baby find his or her food. When babies become aware of their surroundings and use their eyes to search for the bottle or mother's breast, around four months of age, the rooting reflex stops.
- **Grasp reflex.** The **grasp reflex** *is the automatic response of a newborn's hand to close over anything that comes in contact with the palm.* The grip is often so strong that the newborn can be lifted off the bed. However, the baby lets go without warning. When, at about three months of age, the baby begins to reach for objects, the grasp reflex weakens; it disappears by one year of age.
- **Startle reflex.** This is *a newborn's automatic physical response—legs thrown up, fingers spread, arms extended and then brought rapidly back to the midline while the fingers close in a grasping action—to a loud noise or to a touch on the stomach.* The startle reflex disappears when the baby is about five months old.

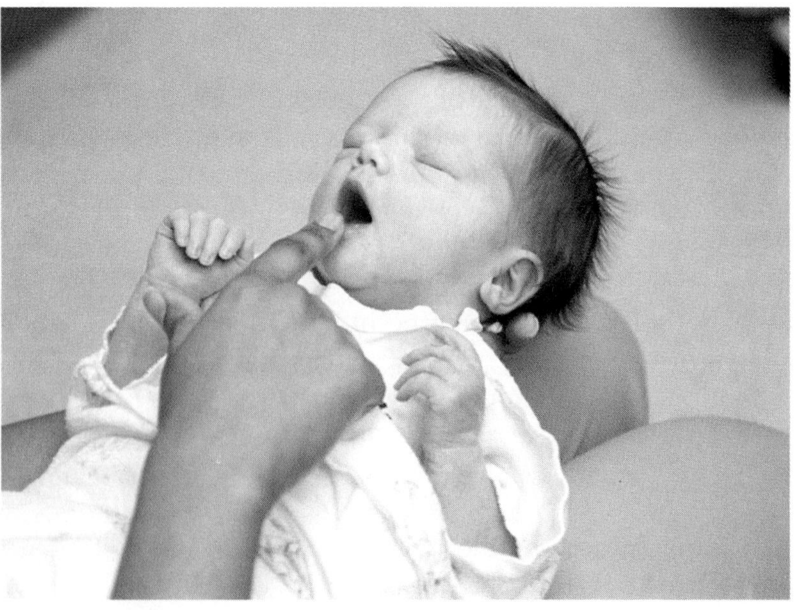

Baby demonstrating rooting reflex.

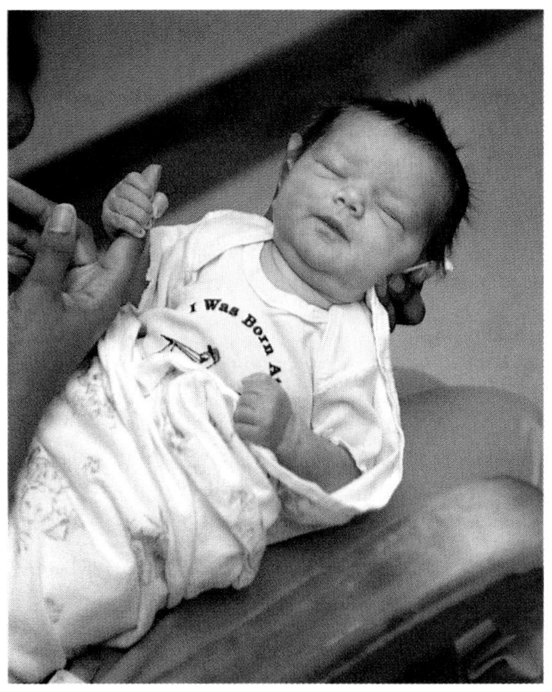

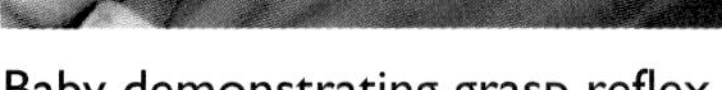
Baby demonstrating grasp reflex.

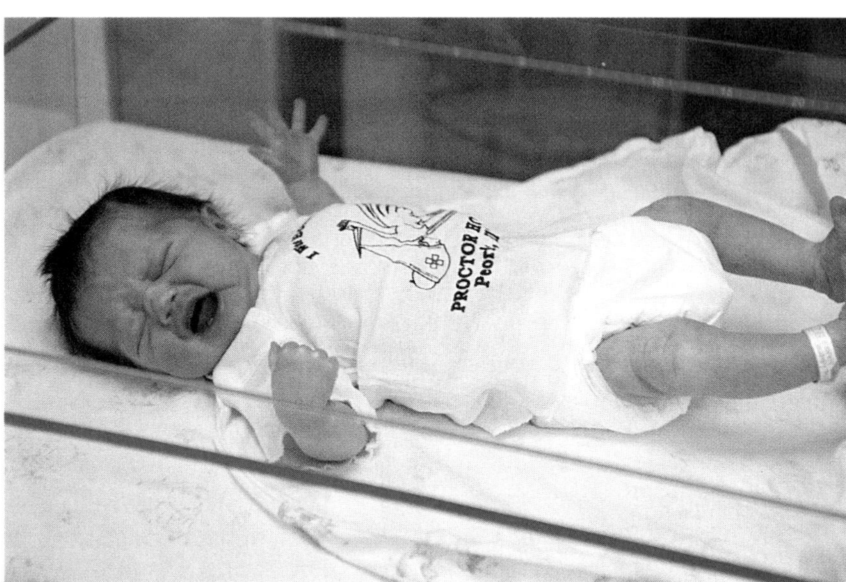
Baby demonstrating startle reflex.

Learning to Care for the Newborn

At first, it may take some time for new parents to feel comfortable caring for the baby. Soon, they gain confidence and become attuned to the baby's way of communicating. They learn how to recognize the baby's needs and how to adapt their responses to the baby's individual style.

What Do Babies Need?

Adapting to parenting begins with understanding the baby's needs, the needs of parents, and the needs of the entire family. Later chapters in this book present more detailed information about caring for a baby. Here, however, are babies' basic needs:

- **Babies need food.** A hungry newborn is hungry with his or her whole body. The baby squirms about, mouth searching for the mother's breast or a bottle nipple. Crying is the most effective way for a newborn to signal his or her hunger.

  Newborns want food immediately when they are hungry, and it is important to give it to them—right away. Having their needs met in this way helps babies learn that they can trust the world.

- **Babies need sleep.** Newborns sleep and wake throughout the day and night. Most young babies take short naps around the clock, waking at night between one and three times for feeding. A newborn sleeps an average of 15 hours a day, typically in six to eight separate sleep periods. However, the level of alertness or drowsiness varies from baby to baby. Every baby is different; what is normal is normal for that individual baby. It is very important for parents to avoid comparisons.
- **Babies need exercise.** In their brief wakeful periods, newborns wave their arms and legs. This activity helps their muscles and nervous system develop. Before a feeding, babies usually become very active, moving all parts of their body. They can kick freely while being diapered, as long as someone watches them closely. Splashing or wiggling during a bath is another good way for small babies to get exercise.
- **Babies need to be kept safe, clean, and warm.** Diapering and bathing soon become a familiar part of the new parent's routine. The parent must also protect the baby from anything that might be harmful. When he or she is awake, a baby should always be under the watchful eye of a responsible person. Anything the baby might come in contact with—a toy, a crib, a garment—should be checked for safety, and any potentially harmful objects should be kept away.

When parents set aside "play time" with their baby, they are helping to fulfill the baby's needs for exercise, stimulation, and close contact.

ASK THE EXPERTS

Sudden Infant Death Syndrome

Dr. Van D. Stone has served as Chief of Pediatrics at Baptist Medical Center in Little Rock and is in private practice in Tupelo, Mississippi.

We have just learned that our cousins' two-month-old baby died suddenly, apparently a victim of crib death. It's sad for all of us, but it must be just devastating for the baby's parents. Can you help me understand this terrible event?

The death of a baby is a terribly sad loss for parents, for other family members, and even for friends.

What you call crib death is known medically as Sudden Infant Death Syndrome, or SIDS. The loss of a baby to SIDS can be especially difficult to accept, because the death is so sudden and so mysterious. The victims are usually healthy infants between the ages of two weeks and six months. They die in their sleep, with no warning, no cry, and no evidence of pain.

Researchers are continuing to investigate the possible causes of Sudden Infant Death Syndrome; so far, no cause or prevention has been discovered. However, it is understood that the parents and other caregivers are not at fault when a baby dies of SIDS. Nothing they did do—and nothing they failed to do—caused the baby's death.

Parents and other relatives of SIDS victims can often benefit from counseling as they deal with their grief over a baby's death. The baby's pediatrician or another physician can usually refer families to clinics or to social workers or other therapists who are specially trained in this field.

Parents can also benefit from support groups such as the National Sudden Infant Death Syndrome Foundation. This foundation has local chapters in cities all over the country; each chapter sponsors group meetings for parents who have gone through the heartbreaking experience of SIDS.

If you have more questions about SIDS, you can call the Sudden Infant Death Syndrome Foundation; the telephone number is 1-800-221-SIDS. Your cousins may want to use that same number for information about local chapters and support-group meetings.

Van D. Stone, MD

Dr. Van Stone

- **Babies need medical care.** Throughout the first year, an infant will have periodic well-baby checkups to make sure he or she is healthy and developing normally, and to receive immunizations. A baby may be cared for by a family doctor or by a pediatrician, a doctor who specializes in the care of babies and young children.
- **Babies need things to look at, touch, listen to, and play with.** Interesting, stimulating surroundings help babies learn. However, they do not need expensive toys. In fact, an infant's favorite thing to look at is a human face, and a gentle voice is a baby's favorite music.

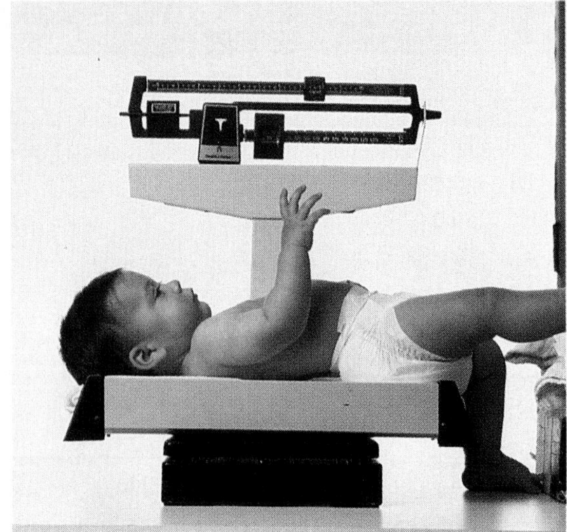

Weighing in to check the baby's physical growth is a routine part of each visit to the doctor.

- **Babies need love.** Just like everyone else, babies want to be near the people who love them. Newborns need close contact with warm, affectionate adults. Love is as important as food and sleep to babies.

  There is no one way to love a baby. Every newborn is different—and so is every parent. Each parent should express love for his or her newborn naturally, in the ways that are personally comfortable. Love is one of the strongest forces affecting every person's life. When a healthy baby senses that he or she is loved, the infant is at ease and feels secure.

What Do Parents Need?

Parents of newborns are often so concerned about caring for their babies that they neglect to consider their own needs. New parents have special needs of their own, which—like the baby's needs—must be met for good physical and emotional health. These are some of the things that parents of newborns need:

- Knowledge of how to care for an infant.
- Resources to turn to for answers to their questions.
- Information about normal occurrences and emotions they experience with their newborn.
- Time to fill their many roles—spouse, parent, family member, worker, student, and citizen.
- Emotional support from a network of family and friends.
- Financial planning.
- Reassurance and confidence that both parents are capable and needed.
- Agreement about parenting and household responsibilities.
- Personal health, rest, and nutrition.
- Privacy and time alone.

Adjusting to New Routines

During the first few weeks, both parents and babies have to adjust to new patterns of life. A newborn typically needs at least several weeks of trial-and-error before he or she can settle into any predictable pattern of eating and sleeping. Parents must adjust their schedule to the baby's needs. That means feeding the baby whenever hunger strikes, day or night.

Receiving attention and care whenever he or she needs it cannot "spoil" a newborn. At this early stage in life, the baby needs to learn that he or she is important and that his or her needs matter—and will receive attention. Later, when the baby is more mature, he or she can begin to learn other ways to communicate and to get those important needs met.

Of course, every newborn benefits from order in life. Soon certain daily patterns emerge to manage the baby's hunger, sleepiness, and wakefulness. It takes about a month, for example, to establish a fairly predictable feeding and sleeping routine. Meanwhile, the key to the baby's happiness is the parents' flexibility.

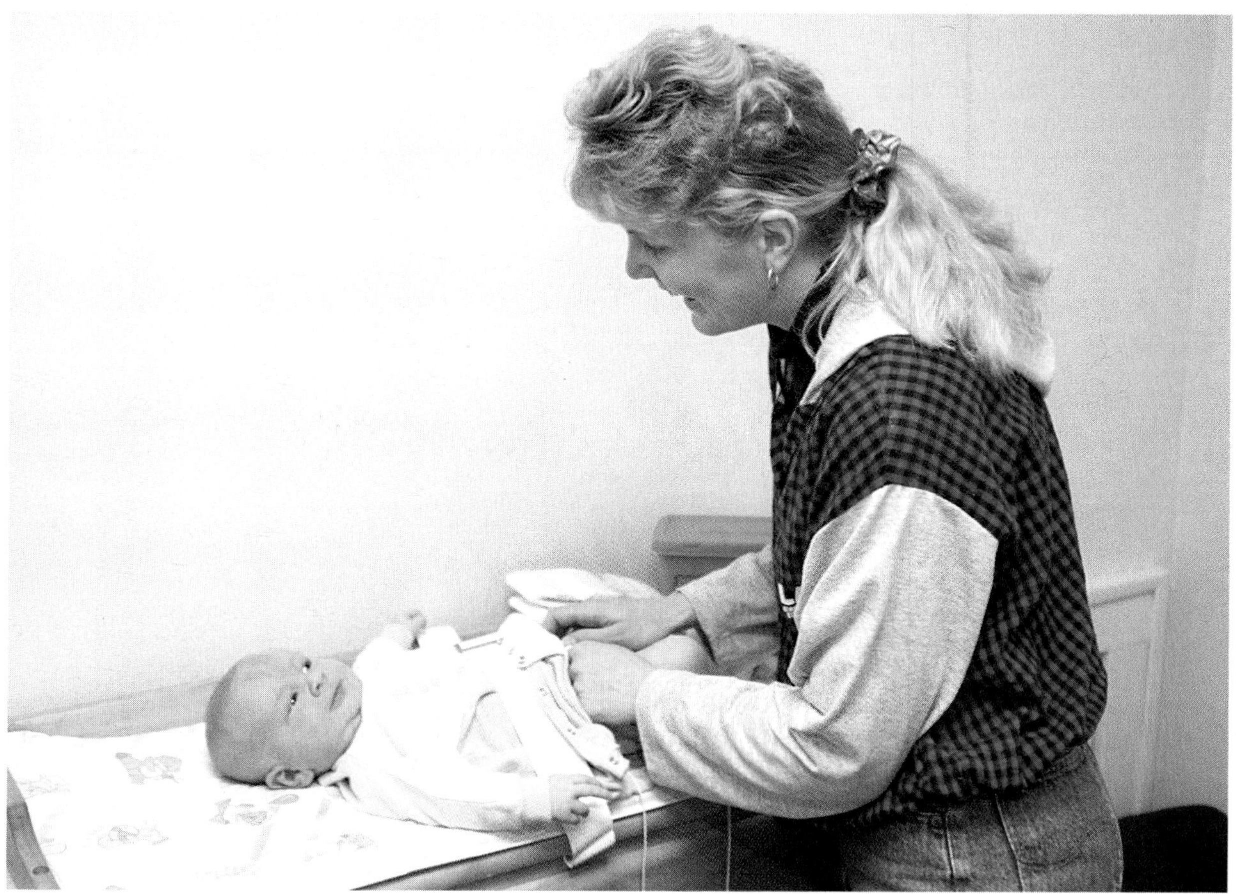

Newborns set their own pace at first, and parents must respond to it. This is how infants learn that their world is safe and dependable. As the baby grows a little older, daily routines will fall into a comfortable pattern.

BUILDING SELF-ESTEEM

Responding to Baby's Needs

Newborn babies often stop crying when they are picked up and held close. The constant reassurance of being picked up by parents and other caregivers comforts the baby and makes him or her feel important. Being held can help relieve the baby of annoying gas. It also provides a chance to hear the comforting sound of a parent's heartbeat.

If a parent or other caring person responds whenever a baby cries, the baby feels secure. He or she soon learns that the person who responds to the crying will help the baby feel better, usually by feeding or comforting the baby. A baby cannot be spoiled by this kind of attention.

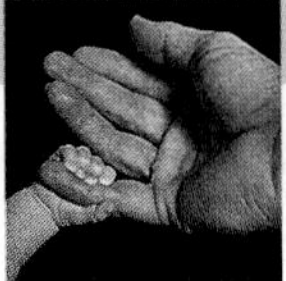

Understanding the Baby's Language

Babies have one way to communicate with the world—by crying. Although newborns never cry for fun, their reasons may often be far less serious than the worried new parents imagine. Hunger is usually the reason that newborns cry. Sometimes babies cry because they are too hot or too cold. Sometimes they cry because they are lying in an uncomfortable position and need to be moved. Other reasons for crying are fatigue and loneliness, and sometimes a baby cries for no reason at all. The average amount of crying for a newborn is one hour per day, but individual babies may cry much less or much more than that. A baby's crying seems to have nothing to do with the quality of parenting he or she is receiving. Parents soon learn to recognize their baby's different cries—one for hunger, another for discomfort, and so on.

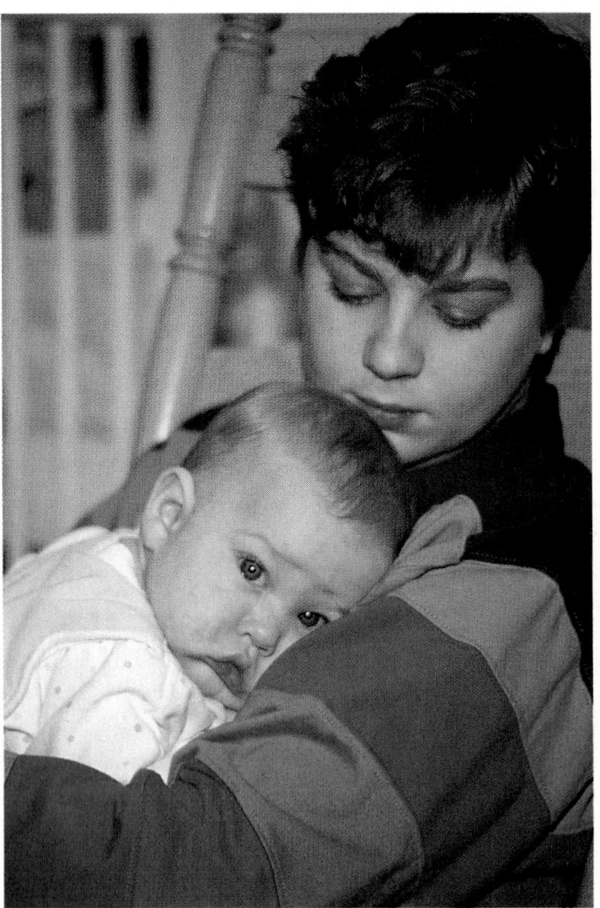

Every baby has a unique temperament. Parents and other caregivers soon become attuned to these individual differences.

Early Temperament

Babies differ markedly in their inborn **temperament**, or *style of reacting to the world and of relating to others.* For example, one baby usually moves from sleep to wakefulness with a startled jump and a cry. Another awakens gradually and quietly looks around the room. Some babies may be so easily upset that extra-gentle handling and a smooth routine are necessary to maintain happiness. Others can be handled more playfully without objection. Just as no two babies look exactly alike—even identical twins—no two react in just the same way.

Parents—and others who care for a baby—need to be sensitive to the baby's own style. The baby, too, learns to adapt to the style of his or her parents. Studies have shown that babies as young as two weeks of age adjust their reactions, depending on how parents handle and talk to them. When parents are very gentle and soothing, the baby tends to respond with soft cooing and gentle motions. When parents relate to the baby more playfully, the baby tends to react with excited grunts and active motions. These natural adjustments help parents and babies feel at ease with each other.

SECTION 3 REVIEW

CHECK YOUR UNDERSTANDING

1. What is a reflex? What purpose do a newborn's reflexes serve?
2. What is the rooting reflex? When does this reflex stop?
3. List at least five things newborns need.
4. List at least five things parents of newborns need.
5. How does an infant communicate?
6. What is a person's temperament?

DISCUSS AND DISCOVER

1. How does a baby's temperament affect the baby's parents? How do the parents' temperaments affect the baby? What adjustment problems do you think might be caused by differences between the temperaments of parents and baby? How do you think parents should try to deal with those problems?
2. Read more about SIDS, sudden infant death syndrome. When and how does it occur? How do families react? Then work with a partner or a small group to plan and perform a short, informative skit about SIDS.

STRENGTHENING FAMILY BONDS

It is important to remember that bonding is a process, not a moment. The emotional bond between infant and parent continues to grow and strengthen as the parent holds, cuddles, talks to, and cares for the newborn. In fact, the process of bonding is carried out in different ways throughout life; the parent and child revise and solidify their emotional relationship as the child progresses through infancy, childhood, adolescence, and into adulthood.

The following approaches can help parents and other caregivers encourage the bonding process with children of various ages.

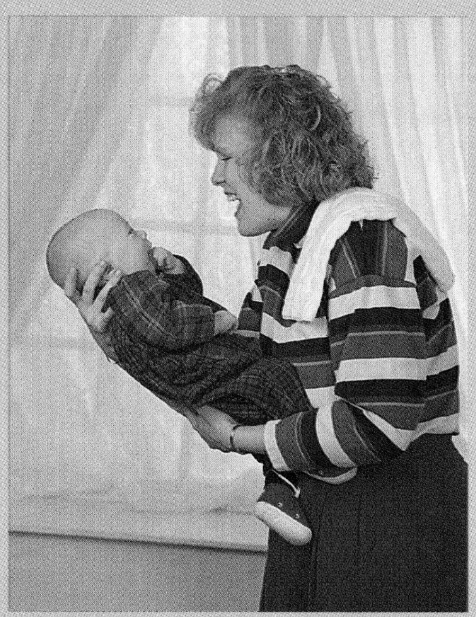

INFANTS

- **Keep the baby close and comforted.** Babies feel warm and secure when they are physically close to a caring parent or caregiver. Look for ways to hold the baby that are comfortable for both of you. Try keeping the young baby close in a sling or front carrier. As the baby grows and becomes more interested in the rest of the world, you may both prefer a backpack-type carrier.
- **Take time to touch the baby.** Touching is a primary key in early bonding; during feeding, changing, and bathing, stroke or pat the baby gently. You may also want to try massaging the baby by gently kneading his or her arms, legs, and back. Notice the baby's response to each kind of touch, and continue with the touching the baby finds most comforting and pleasant.
- **Be responsive to the baby.** Which tone of voice does the baby find most soothing? What music evokes a pleasant response? What colors and shapes does the baby enjoy looking at? How does the baby prefer to be held or cuddled?

  Remember that every baby is an individual. Take the time to notice and respond to the baby's individual preferences.
- **Play with the baby.** You can turn routine activities into games for the baby simply by singing, talking, and making caring eye contact. Try making funny faces or imitating the baby's sounds, and see how the baby responds. You might also select toys or other safe objects that catch the baby's attention.

TODDLERS AND PRESCHOOLERS

- **Continue to play with the child.** Seek out activities that you both enjoy. Sharing a book or a walk can be special for both of you. At least occasionally, join enthusiastically in the child's favorite activities, both imaginative and active. Also make a point of finding some

regular activity that all the family members can enjoy together.

- **Continue using touch to express your affection and caring.** Most young children enjoy kisses, hugs, and other embraces from parents or other important caregivers.
- **Continue to respond to the child as an individual.** Remember that each child is an individual—and that each child grows and changes. Be thoughtful in noticing the child's development and in responding to the child's changing needs and interests.

SCHOOL AGE CHILDREN

- **Continue to be physically affectionate.** Giving and receiving physical signs of affection can strengthen emotional bonds throughout life. However, parents and other important caregivers should be careful to respond to the child's changing needs. For some older children, a pat on the back or an arm around the shoulder is more comforting and acceptable than the familiar hugs that were essential in earlier years.
- **Talk to the child, and encourage the child to talk to you.** Remember that communication involves both talking and listening. Ask the child questions, and listen attentively to his or her responses. When the child brings up a sensitive or troubling issue, take the time to pay close attention.
- **Value the child's opinion.** Encourage the child to form and express his or her own opinions, and respect those opinions as fully as possible.
- **Don't stop playing with the child.** Your emotional bond is strengthened whenever you are enjoying one another's company. Seek out games, sports, or other activities that are fun for both of you.

SUMMARY

- Labor is the process by which the baby is expelled from the mother's body. A normal birth includes three stages of labor.
- A cesarean birth is performed when medically necessary.
- Physical adjustments in the newborn's body make life outside the uterus possible.
- Bonding is the formation of emotional ties between parent and child.
- To recover from childbirth, a woman needs rest, exercise, proper nutrition, medical checkups, and attention to her emotional needs.
- Premature babies need special care.
- Reflexes help a newborn's body function until voluntary actions take over.
- Babies need food, sleep, exercise, medical care, safe and interesting surroundings, and love.

REVIEWING THE FACTS

1. List three possible indications that labor is beginning.
2. What purpose do contractions serve in the first stage of labor? In the second stage of labor? In the third stage of labor?
3. How does a baby's circulatory system change once the baby's lungs have begun taking in oxygen?
4. Briefly describe a newborn's facial features. How are these features adapted to sucking?
5. List the five areas of a baby's physical condition that are measured by the Apgar scale.
6. What is rooming-in? Who can benefit from a rooming-in program?
7. Why is good nutrition important for the mother after birth?
8. When and why should a new mother have a postnatal checkup?
9. List three of a newborn's temporary reflexes.
10. Why is it important to respond to a newborn's crying?

EXPLORING FURTHER

1. Prepare a small kit of items that an expectant couple might find useful or reassuring during labor. Display your kit, and explain your reasons for choosing those items. (Section 1)
2. Survey three or four mothers who have recently given birth and find out their length of labor. Ask them to talk about their condition after the birth. Does there seem to be a relationship between the length of labor and the mother's condition after birth? (Section 1)
3. How should older children behave around a newborn sibling? Think of two or three guidelines. Then compose a simple song or make up a chant that a three- or four-year-old would enjoy, encouraging the child to follow your guidelines. (Section 2)
4. How often should babies have medical checkups during the first year of life? What immunizations should they be given? What other kinds of medical care should they receive? Make a colorful poster or create a short brochure sharing the responses to these important questions. (Section 3)

THINKING CRITICALLY

1. **Compare and contrast.** With a group of classmates, brainstorm a list of the emotions you think mothers and fathers experience during labor. Then discuss your list. Which of the emotions seem contradictory? How are they contradictory? Is it reasonable to expect that such contradictory emotions will arise during this event? Why or why not?
2. **Analyze.** Why do you think some people feel reluctant to hold a newborn baby? What would you say to help someone overcome this reluctance?
3. **Synthesize.** Why do you think so many parents experience at least some symptoms of mild depression following the birth of their baby? Why do you think mothers' depression is more commonly discussed than fathers'? If you had a close friend who was about to become a parent for the first time, would you discuss the "baby blues" with your friend? If not, why not? If so, what would you say?
4. **Analyze.** Why do you think parents of newborns need time alone? Do you think it is more important for each parent to spend time independently or for the two parents to spend time together, apart from the baby? Why?

CROSS-CURRICULUM CONNECTIONS

1. **Social Studies.** Research the practices for handling labor and delivery in this country—or in another country of your choice—100 years ago. How were they different from modern practices? How do you think the differences affected babies? Parents? Write a brief report of your findings.
2. **Writing.** Read Frederick Leboyer's book *Birth Without Violence*. Then write an essay expressing your reactions to the philosophy and practices described in the book.

OBSERVING AND PARTICIPATING

The Amazing Newborn

Newborn babies have amazing abilities. They can see, hear, eat, and even communicate. Perhaps most important, they can respond to caring parents and family members, and begin to participate in relationships.

Choose one of the following observation or participation activities. When you have completed the activity, record your observations in your journal. Then discuss your observations with a group of classmates.

- **Observing.** On the basis of information in this chapter, write a list of the physical characteristics of newborns. Then observe a newborn baby, either in a hospital nursery or at home. Which of the listed physical characteristics do you observe? Do you think the baby had all the typical newborn characteristics? If not, why not?
- **Observing.** Spend time observing parents and small infants in a public place, such as a park or a mall. How do parents show their love and affection for their babies? How are the methods of demonstrating love similar? How are they different? How do parents respond to their babies' crying? What effects do those responses have on the babies?
- **Participating.** Spend at least four hours taking care—or helping take care—of a newborn baby. How often does the baby cry during that period? What seems to be the cause of the baby's crying? How do you feel when you are easily able to comfort the baby? How do you feel if you have trouble comforting the baby?

UNIT 3

The Baby's First Year

THINKING OF BABY

Baby awake is a mischievous elf
Who can keep you busy
In spite of yourself!
A rollicking, frolicking, gurgling sprite
Who may sleep half the day …
(And cry half the night)!
And yet when you're humming
A last lullaby,
And the sandman has come
And closed each little eye …
Gone is the elf, and you find out instead
You've just tucked a tired little angel in bed.

Anonymous

CHAPTER 8

Physical Development During the First Year

SECTION 1 Growth and Development During the First Year

SECTION 2 Providing Care for Infants: Handling and Feeding

SECTION 3 Other Infant-Care Skills

Linda was washing dishes when four-year-old Benjamin ran into the kitchen. "Quick, Mommy— Daddy wants you!"

Without turning around, Linda asked, "What's the problem?"

"It's not a problem. It's a surprise," Benjamin answered.

Linda saw the excitement in her son's face and smiled at him. "Here I come," she said, drying her hands and following him into the baby's bedroom.

Linda looked questioningly at her husband and immediately saw the "surprise." There was baby Carolyn, standing up on her own feet—and looking very happy and proud!

"Wow!" laughed Linda as she hugged Benjamin. "Look at your little sister. Thanks for bringing me in to see this great surprise!"

SECTION 1

Growth and Development During the First Year

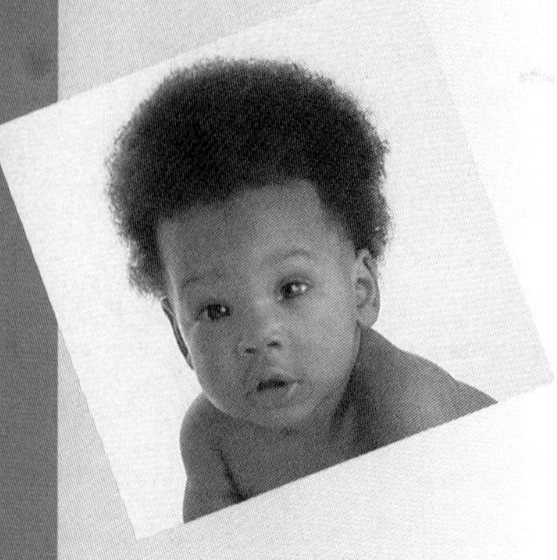

OBJECTIVES

- Explain the three basic patterns that physical development follows.
- Describe physical growth during the first year.
- Describe the development of senses and skills during the first year.

TERMS TO LEARN

audiologist
depth perception
hand-eye coordination
motor skills
primary teeth
proportion

Would you recognize a baby you had seen first as a week-old infant and next on the child's first birthday? If you have ever watched the development of a baby, you know that many changes occur from week to week and from month to month. In the first twelve months, most babies change so much that they would be difficult to match up with pictures taken in the first weeks of life.

Development and growth during the first year are the most rapid of any time in life. In twelve months, the baby who begins as a helpless newborn triples his or her birth weight, learns to stand alone, and may even begin to walk.

Patterns of Physical Development

As you already know, all development follows an orderly sequence. It proceeds step-by-step in about the same order for every baby. Physical development is no exception. You will find it easier to observe physical development if you understand the three basic patterns it follows. Physical development proceeds from head to foot, from near to far, and from simple to complex.

- **Head to foot.** Long before birth, the baby's head takes the lead in development. Two months after conception, the head is about half the size of the entire fetus. The arms and legs do

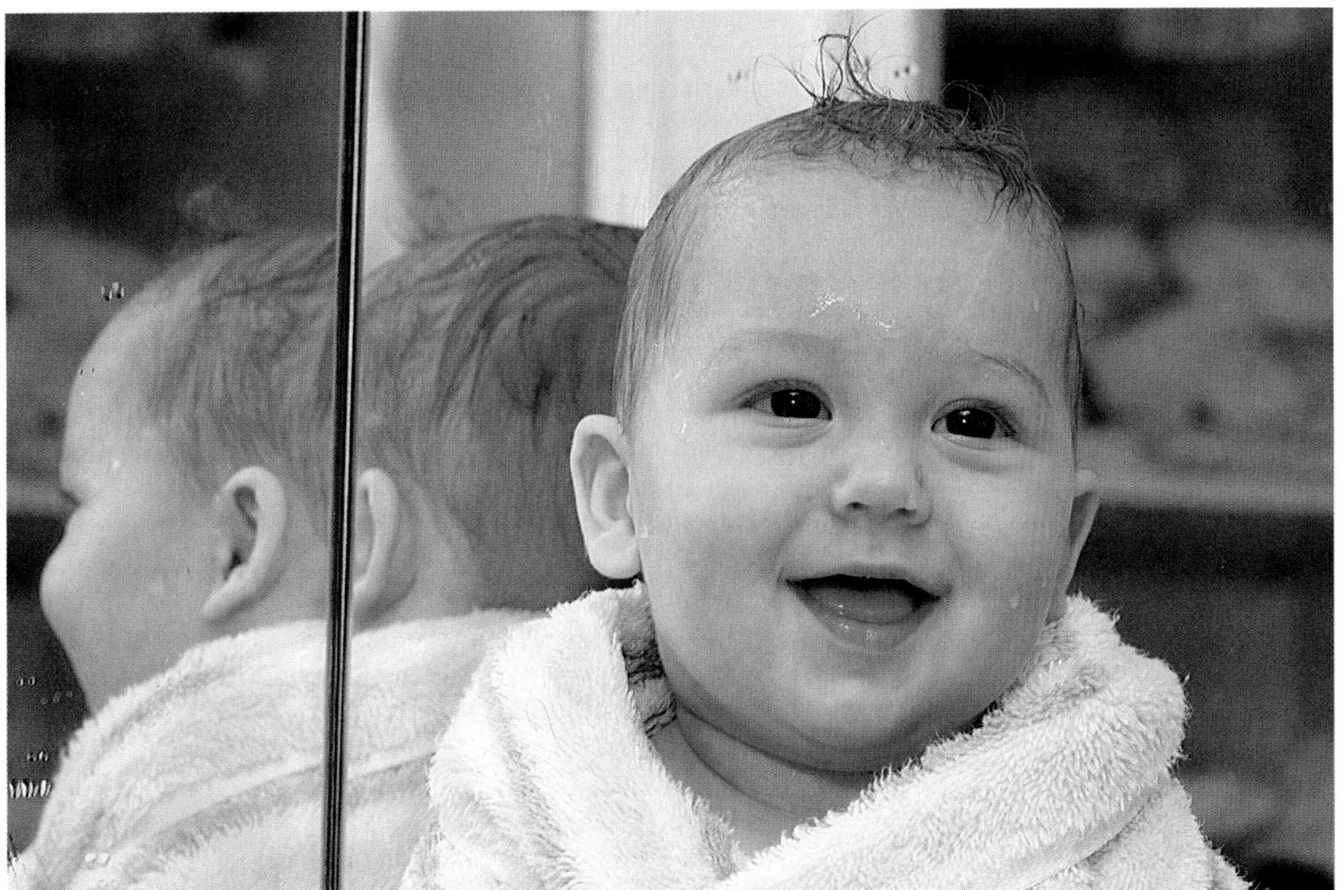

Both appearance and behavior give clues to a baby's health. A healthy baby is generally happy, active, and curious.

not catch up until later. A newborn's head is still large in proportion to the body. The same head-to-toe pattern continues after birth. First, babies learn to lift their heads to see an interesting object. Later, as the development proceeds down toward their arms and hands in the middle of the body, they will be able to pick that object up. Still later, when development has continued downward to the feet, they can walk to it.

- **Near to far.** Development starts at the trunk of the body and moves outward. First, babies simply wave their arms when they see an object they want. Later, they are able to grab at an object with the palm of the hand. Finally, babies learn to pick up small objects with their thumb and fingers.
- **Simple to complex.** At first, babies' main activities are sleeping and eating. Gradually, they learn more complicated tasks. From being fed, they progress to eating with their fingers. Eventually, they are able to use a spoon and fork for eating.

Growth During the First Year

You also know that children grow and develop at individual rates. Charts are available that show average weight, height, and abilities at certain ages. These charts help give a general understanding of child growth and development. Remember, that these charts are based on averages.

Few babies are precisely average. Unless a child is significantly above or below average, there is no need for concern. All babies grow and develop at their own rate.

Weight

In babies, weight gain is one of the best indications of good health. Most babies experience a slight weight loss just after birth. From then on, they gain weight rapidly. For the first six months, a healthy baby gains 1 to 2 pounds (0.45 to 0.9 kg) per month. During the last half of the first year, the average weight gain is 1 pound (0.45 kg) per month. This means that the baby's weight usually doubles within the first few months. By the first birthday, a baby has typically tripled his or her birth weight.

The weight of year-old babies varies widely. The average weight is 20 to 22 pounds (9 to 10 kg). An individual baby's weight and pattern of weight gain may be influenced by heredity, by feeding habits, and by levels of physical activity.

Height

Growth in height is steady during the first year. You know that the average newborn is 20 inches (51 cm) long. By one year of age, the average infant is about 30 inches (76 cm) long.

Heredity has a stronger influence on height than on weight. If both your parents are tall, you are more likely to be tall than is a child of two short parents. This does not mean that tall parents always have tall children. Since human beings carry a mixture of genes, the results of a child's particular mixture cannot be predicted.

Proportion

Proportion is *the size relationship of one thing to another.* In child development, proportion refers to the size relationship between different parts of the body. Compared with adult proportions, a baby's head and abdomen are large. The legs and arms are short and small.

The head grows rapidly during the first year to provide room for the swiftly developing brain. Over half the total growth of the head occurs at this time. The fontanels provide for this growth of the head. The fontanels, which are sometimes visible in the growing infant, close by about age eighteen months.

Development During the First Year

Although the terms *growth* and *development* are often used to mean the same thing, there is a difference. *Growth* refers to measurable change in size. *Development* refers to an increase in physical, emotional, social, or intellectual skills. Growth and development are both rapid during the first year.

If you observed a group of teens, you could probably tell the older teens from the younger ones, but it would be difficult to identify the exact age of each individual. A fifteen-year-old and a sixteen-year-old look and act much alike. In contrast, it is easy to tell a newborn from a one-year-old. A healthy baby not only grows bigger, but also develops many observable skills during the first year of life.

Sight

Development of sight in the unborn baby is limited by lack of bright light. The fetus's eyes, however, do open and shut before birth.

A newborn's eyes are closed most of the time. When they are open, you may wonder whether the eyes are clearly focused. Uncoordinated muscles cause the eyes to blink separately or to look in different directions. A newborn's eyes may—or may not—produce tears when the baby cries; both conditions are normal.

Eyesight improves rapidly. An infant's vision is blurry at first. Within a week or so, the newborn is increasingly aware of his or her surroundings and can focus on objects that are 7 to 10 inches (17.5 to 25 cm) away. The infant's eyes begin to work together. By about three and one-half months, a baby's vision is almost as good as a young adult's.

Depth perception is *the ability to recognize that an object is three-dimensional, not flat.* Depth perception is not recognizable in babies until the second month. By the third month, babies prefer to look at three-dimensional or real objects rather than flat pictures of objects.

Hand-eye coordination is *the ability to move the hands and fingers precisely in relation to what is seen.* Babies develop this coordination gradually. Around the age of three or four months, babies begin to reach for objects they see; this is an important milestone. Hand-eye coordination continues to develop throughout childhood. It is necessary for many skills, such as eating, catching a ball, coloring, and tying shoes. It continues into adulthood, with the abilities to thread a needle, keyboard, and play sports, for example.

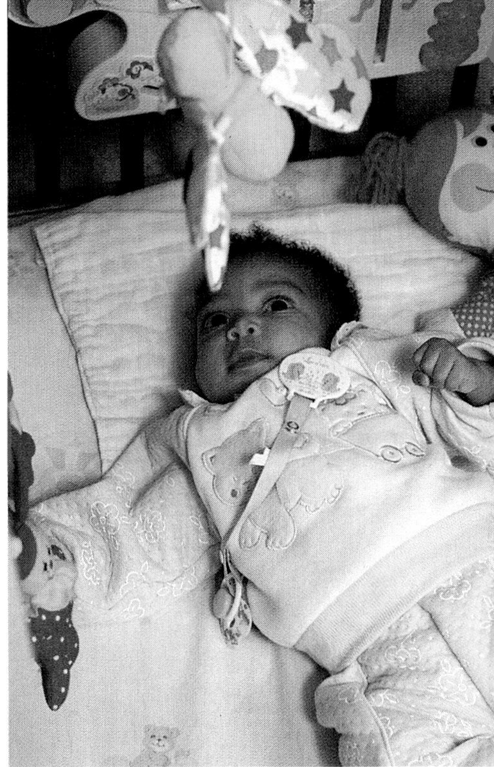

During the first two months this baby will focus on objects 7-10 inches from her nose. By two and one-half months, the baby will be able to follow a moving object with her eyes. By three months she will begin to swipe at it.

HEALTH TIP

Be alert for these signs of hearing problems:

- A newborn is not startled by a sharp clap.
- A three-month-old never turns toward the source of sounds.
- A baby is not awakened by loud noises, does not respond to familiar voices, and pays no attention to ordinary sounds.

These warning signs should be discussed with the baby's pediatrician. The pediatrician will probably refer the baby to an **audiologist,** *a professional specially trained to test for, diagnose, and help treat hearing problems.*

Hearing

The sense of hearing develops even before birth. In fact, babies still in the uterus often respond to sounds with altered heart rates or with changes in activity levels. At birth, a baby can already tell the general direction a sound comes from.

Newborns respond to the tone of a voice rather than to the words themselves. A soothing, loving voice calms them. A loud or angry voice alarms them. Remember the importance of your tone of voice when you are caring for any child—especially a newborn.

Hearing is essential for normal language development. Listening to words and gradually associating meaning with those words is the first step in learning to speak. Because hearing and listening are so important to a child's development, many physicians recommend that babies have a hearing test by about six months of age. This is especially important if the baby has had frequent ear infections.

Smell and Taste

Since a baby is surrounded by amniotic fluid until birth, the sense of smell does not have much chance to develop. Studies at Brown University have shown, however, that even newborns respond to disagreeable odors. For example, the babies in the study turned away from teddy bears that smelled like vinegar, but responded eagerly to teddy bears with a sweet vanilla scent. During the first few days of life, infants become sensitive to less noticeable smells and adjust quickly to familiar odors. Within ten days they can distinguish by smell their own mother from another person.

The sense of taste develops rapidly. In research studies, two-week-old babies have shown, through their sucking behavior, that they can taste the differences between water, sour liquids, sugar solutions, salt solutions, and milk. Even at this early age, babies show a preference for a sweet taste.

Voice

The newborn's cry, initially quite shrill, becomes softer as the baby's lungs mature and the voice is used. This change in the baby's voice also results from the physical growth of the throat muscles, tongue, lips, teeth, and vocal cords. The tongue and interior of the mouth change in shape and proportion during the first months of life.

These physical changes also affect feeding. At first the infant is able only to suck liquids. Later in the year, when the baby is able to swallow and digest foods more easily, solid foods may be added to the diet.

Growth of the mouth, vocal tract, and related areas also affects speech development. Distinct speech depends on that growth. Teeth are necessary to produce some sounds, so even babies who speak early are unable to make certain sounds.

Although young babies cannot speak, they communicate their needs with distinct types of crying. For example, one cry may express a baby's pain and a different cry may express that baby's boredom. Babies also prepare for speech by making word-related sounds. They begin babbling vowel sounds, such as "ooh," "ah," and "au," as early as three months of age.

Many babies are physically ready for speech by the end of the first year. However, children learn to speak at different rates, and many do not say any words until after their first birthday.

Teeth

The development of a baby's teeth actually begins about the sixth week of pregnancy. However, the **primary teeth** or "baby teeth," *the first set of teeth a baby gets,* usually do not appear until six or seven months of age.

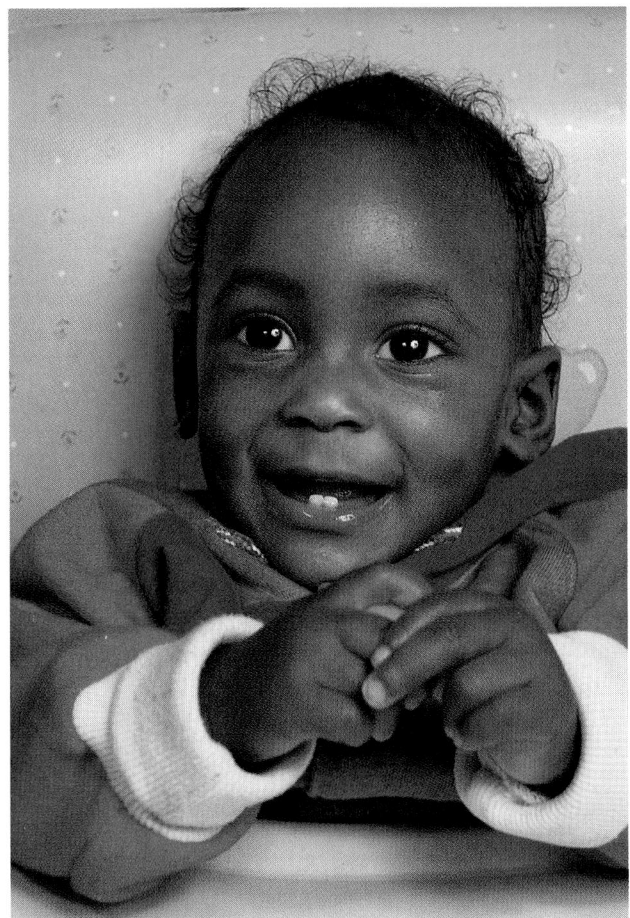

At six or seven months, the two lower front teeth are the first to come in. By age two or three, most children have a full set of 20 primary teeth.

BUILDING SELF-ESTEEM

Music to a Baby's Ears

Within hours after birth, babies respond to the sounds around them. Quiet, musical sounds can calm a baby; loud, high-pitched sounds can excite or even frighten a baby.

Within weeks, babies recognize the voices of people in their world, such as, parents, grandparents, siblings, or other caregivers. By three months of age, babies can be observed to awaken from a nap, cry out, and listen for someone to walk toward their room.

Babies also respond with smiles and movement when a parent or other caregiver talks to them, repeats their baby sounds, and stays near them. Apparently, human voices are like music to a baby's ears.

HEALTH TIP

It's never too early to start caring for a baby's teeth. Even before the first tooth appears, an infant's mouth should be cleaned after each feeding. Just wipe the gums gently with a piece of clean, dampened gauze. This cleaning method can be continued even after early teeth have come in.

Teething is an entirely normal process, but often a painful one for the infant. The teeth must force their way up through the baby's gums. As they do, they stretch and tear the tender gum tissues. This often causes pain and swelling. During teething, a normally contented infant may suddenly become cranky, restless, and wakeful. Some babies refuse food and drool a lot. Teething can also cause other symptoms, including an increased desire for liquid, coughing, and fever.

Discomfort usually lasts from two to ten days for each tooth. You may find these methods helpful for dealing with a teething baby:

- Teething babies like to bite down hard to relieve the pressure on their gums. Offer teething biscuits or teething rings.
- Since cold is a good painkiller, try chilling a liquid-filled teething ring in the refrigerator.
- Rubbing an ice cube on the baby's gums may ease the pain temporarily.
- Commercial medications specifically for teething pain are available. These liquids are rubbed onto the swollen gums to reduce pain. Read and follow all directions.
- If teething pain persists or other serious symptoms develop, consult a doctor.

The teething process continues periodically for about two years, until all 20 primary teeth have come in. The order in which primary teeth appear is fairly predictable. The timing, however, varies widely.

Motor Skills

Much of a baby's development during the first year is in the area of motor skills. **Motor skills** are *abilities that depend on the use and control of muscles.* Although motor skills seem to be signs of physical development, mastering them requires intellectual, social, and emotional development as well. This is because development in each area affects all other areas.

One of the first motor skills infants acquire is control of the head. At birth, the head is large and heavy; the neck muscles are weak. By age one month, babies placed on their stomach can lift their head slightly. By two to three months of age, they can also lift their chest. At this age they can keep their head steady when propped in a sitting position.

The chart on pages 235-236 shows other motor skill accomplishments during the first year.

AVERAGE MOTOR SKILLS DEVELOPMENT

BIRTH TO TWELVE MONTHS

ONE MONTH

- Lifts chin when placed on stomach.

TWO MONTHS

- Lifts chest well above surface when placed on stomach.

THREE TO FOUR MONTHS

- Reaches for objects, but unsteadily.
- Holds up head steadily.
- Rolls from side to back and from back to side.
- Has complete head control when sitting on an adult's lap.
- Holds head erect when carried.

FIVE TO SIX MONTHS

- Sits alone briefly.
- Reaches and grasps successfully, but awkwardly.
- Turns completely over when laid on back or stomach.
- Prefers to sit up with support.
- Uses hands to reach, grasp, crumble, bang, and splash.

(Continued on next page)

AVERAGE MOTOR SKILLS DEVELOPMENT (cont'd.)

SEVEN TO EIGHT MONTHS

- Reaches for spoon.
- Pulls self up while holding on to furniture.
- Sits up steadily.
- Propels self by arms, knees, or squirming motion.
- Eats with fingers.
- Picks up large objects.

NINE TO TEN MONTHS

- Walks when led.
- Reaches for and manipulates objects with good control.
- Picks up medium-sized objects as well as larger ones.
- Stands holding on to furniture or other supports.
- Is more skillful with spoon.
- Crawls on hands and knees.

ELEVEN TO TWELVE MONTHS

- Stands alone.
- May be walking alone.
- Shows preference for one hand over the other.
- Holds and drinks from a cup.
- Fits blocks, boxes, or nesting toys inside each other.
- Picks up small objects using thumb and forefinger.

As the baby grows older, the ability to support and control the head improves.

SECTION 1 REVIEW

CHECK YOUR UNDERSTANDING

1. List the three basic patterns that physical development follows.
2. How much weight does an average healthy baby gain each month during the first six months of life?
3. Explain what proportion is. How do a baby's proportions compare with an adult's proportions?
4. What is depth perception? When is it first noticeable in babies?
5. What is hand-eye coordination? When and how does hand-eye coordination develop?
6. What signs would indicate a possible hearing problem in a baby?
7. List at least three motor skills that the average baby develops at seven to eight months.

DISCUSS AND DISCOVER

1. What activities would you suggest parents and caregivers might use to help stimulate hand-eye coordination in their infants?
2. Discuss how speaking—which might be described as a physical ability—requires a combination of physical, emotional, social, and intellectual growth and development.
3. Evaluate at least three different teething toys and explain how an infant uses each toy. What makes the toys effective? What foods might serve the same purpose for a baby?
4. How are the symptoms of teething similar to the symptoms of common illnesses?
5. Why may one baby's motor skills develop much more slowly or much more quickly than average?

SECTION 2

Providing Care for Infants: Handling and Feeding

OBJECTIVES

- Explain how to hold and feed a baby.
- Identify nutritional needs during infancy.

TERMS TO LEARN

malnutrition
strained foods
weaning

When you take care of an infant, you will spend much of your time responding to the baby's physical needs. Many of your activities will involve lifting, holding, and carrying the baby. Feeding the baby will also be an important concern. With understanding and practice, you will soon develop the skills to handle the baby gently and efficiently, and to recognize and respond to the baby's own special personality and needs.

Handling a Baby

You will find that a baby needs to be lifted and held for all sorts of reasons—to have diapers changed, to be fed, to be dressed, to be bathed, to be moved. There are two more reasons, equally important, for handling a baby—to comfort the baby and to give the baby your attention. When you pick up and hold an infant, for any reason, you have an opportunity to strengthen the bond between you and the baby and to help the baby feel secure and happy.

All babies need to be handled gently and carefully. The lack of head control in younger babies requires more careful handling than is needed by a more mature baby who can support his or her head. You may also find that a baby's temperament influences your handling.

Of all babies, newborns require the greatest care when you are picking them up, carrying them, or holding them. Whenever you handle a newborn, remember that the baby's neck muscles cannot yet support the head. You'll need to keep your hand or arm under the baby's neck and head at all times.

To lift a newborn, slide one hand under the baby's buttocks, and slide the other hand under the shoulders and head. Use your forearm to support the neck and head as you raise your hands together to lift the newborn. Remember to move smoothly and gently so that you do not startle the baby.

There are two basic positions for holding a newborn safely and comfortably. You may want to hold the baby upright, cradled in the curve of your arm against your body. In this position, your arm supports the baby's head and neck, and you can easily maintain eye contact with the baby. You may also want to hold the baby against your chest, so that the baby faces—or peeks over—your shoulder. In this position you need to use your hand to support the baby's neck and head.

When you lay a newborn down, continue to support both the neck and head and the body. Bend over, keeping the baby close to your body until the baby comes in contact with his or her next support system. Again, move smoothly and gently so that the baby continues to feel comfortable and secure.

As the baby grows older and stronger, his or her head needs less support. However, it is still important to handle the baby gently and to hold the baby close, to ensure a sense of security.

When you are handling a baby of any age, it is important to avoid shaking and jiggling. These actions can be surprisingly dangerous; they can cause bleeding in the baby's brain and may lead to lasting brain damage.

SAFETY TIP

With all the stresses involved in caring for a baby, it is sometimes natural to feel anger or frustration—perhaps with the world, perhaps even with the baby. You don't need to worry about feeling angry occasionally, but you *do* need to worry about handling the baby when you are upset. If you feel yourself becoming very angry, try the following:

- Put the baby down in a safe place (the crib, for example) and go into another room.
- Ask a friend or relative to stay with the baby for a while.
- If there is no one available to help, try looking out a window, taking a few deep breaths, slowly drinking a cool glass of water.

You can easily have skin to skin contact with your cheek and baby's face by holding the baby against your shoulder. Be sure to gently support the neck and head with one hand. Supporting the infant in the curve of your arm lets you stay face-to-face.

Feeding a Baby

Mealtime provides a baby with much more than physical nourishment. It is also a time for enjoying close contact with other people and for learning more about the world. Especially for a newborn, the cuddling, body contact, and nurturing words that go with feeding are as important as the food.

Feeding Schedules

A newborn's schedule of eating and sleeping is unpredictable at first. Newborns need to eat about as much as they want and as often as they want. In the first few weeks of life, a baby feeds six to eight times—or more—in 24 hours. These frequent feedings are necessary because a newborn's stomach can hold only a small amount at a time.

By the second or third month, a regular pattern generally emerges. The baby may wake for a feeding every three or four hours around the clock. Eventually, the baby will no longer need a late-night feeding. By the time a baby reaches 12 pounds (5.4 kg), he or she can usually sleep through the night, because at that size, the stomach can hold more milk or formula. As the baby grows, the schedule will continue to change. At the end of the first year, most babies eat three meals a day, plus snacks.

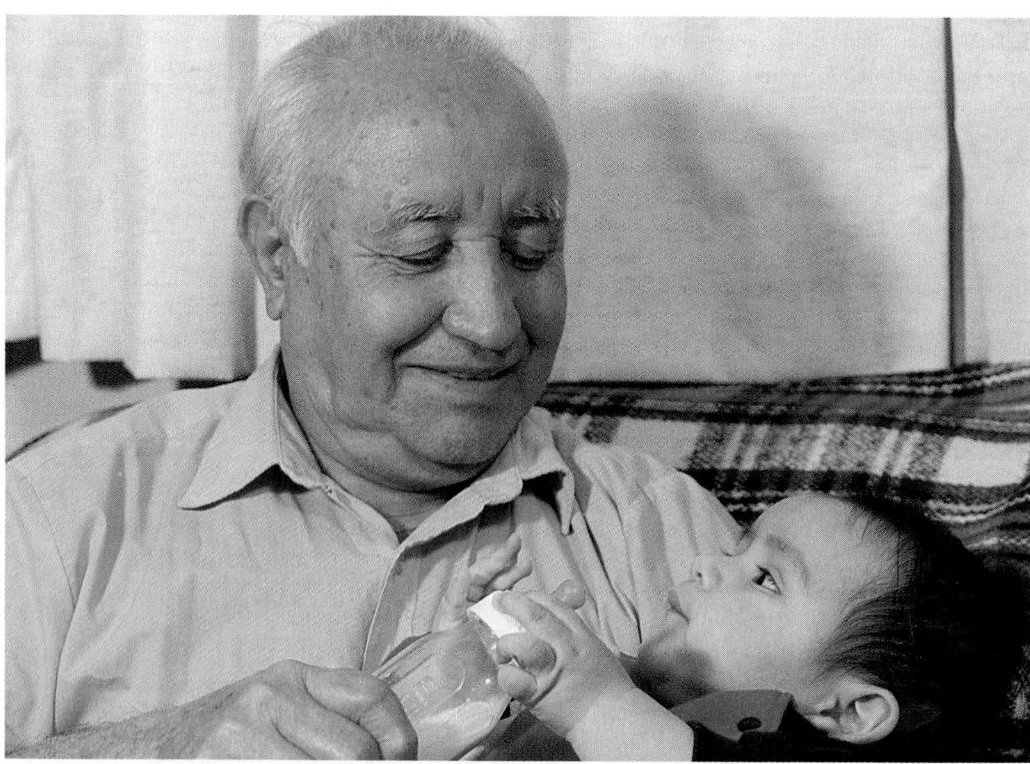

During a feeding, it is important that a baby feel loved and cared for.

To burp an infant, hold the baby either upright against your shoulder or lying down across your knees. (Protect your clothes with a clean diaper or cloth.) Then pat the baby gently on the back several times.

Mealtime Methods

A mother who breast-feeds can expect to receive feeding instruction and help while she is still in the hospital, or from the midwife if she has delivered her baby at home or at an alternative birth center. Information and assistance are also available from La Leche League, an organization that promotes breast-feeding. Another good source of assistance is a pediatrician or nurse-practitioner, who can offer advice or can help the mother contact a national organization or another nursing mother.

Whenever you feed an infant from a bottle, hold the baby close in a semi-upright position. Remember that the young baby's head and neck need to be supported, and the head should be held well above the level of the baby's stomach. Hold the bottle at an angle, so that the baby can suck comfortably and so that the nipple remains full of milk. If the bottle nipple isn't kept full of milk, the baby will swallow too much air.

Whether you breast-feed or bottle-feed, continue the feeding until the infant seems satisfied. Healthy babies usually eat the amount they need.

Whichever method of feeding you use, you should take time to burp the baby at least twice—once during the feeding and once when the feeding is over. Burping involves holding the baby in a position in which he or she can comfortably expel air swallowed during feeding. Don't be surprised if the baby doesn't actually burp each time; the baby needs the chance to burp but may not always have extra air to expel.

SAFETY TIP

Disease-causing bacteria can grow quickly in a baby's formula. It is important to discard the formula that a baby doesn't drink during a feeding. Trying to save and reuse the formula could lead to illness.

Any bottle from which a baby drinks should be carefully sterilized, either in boiling water or in a dishwasher cycle with very hot water. The nipples, bottle rings, and bottle caps should be sterilized in the same way.

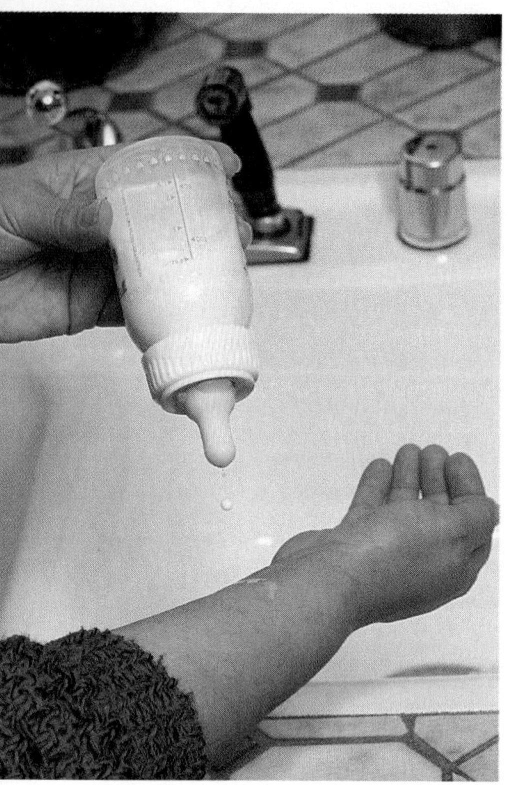

Before you feed the baby, shake a drop of formula onto your wrist or inner arm to check the temperature. The formula should feel lukewarm, not hot.

Many parents prefer to give their baby a warm bottle, although this is not really necessary. If you want to warm the baby's formula, fill the bottle and place it in a pan of water on the stove; heat the water in the pan until it makes the formula lukewarm. You can also use a special bottle warmer. You should not, however, heat the formula in a microwave oven. Microwave heating may create "hot spots," dangerously hot portions in a bottle of formula that seems to be lukewarm. When you are away from home, you can warm the bottle by holding it under hot running water, periodically shaking it and checking to see whether the formula is warm.

No matter how busy or rushed you feel, you should never leave a bottle propped up so that a baby can drink from it without your help. The formula typically gushes from a propped bottle; this can cause digestive problems and ear infections. In addition, the baby misses out on the physical contact and attention you provide when you hold the baby for a feeding.

Introducing New Foods

Around the age of six months, most babies are ready to begin adding other foods to their diet of breast milk or formula. The baby's pediatrician will recommend when these "solids" should be introduced. Maturity, or readiness, is as important in feeding as it is in learning to sit or stand.

With most babies, there is no rush to introduce new foods. Choose a time when the baby and the caregiver are both well, content, and happy. Don't begin solids, for example, if the infant has been sick or the family is moving. You don't need to worry about postponing new foods for a while; breast milk or formula will continue to provide all the nutrition the baby needs.

Usually, a baby's first solid food is cereal—one of several special baby cereals prepared to a smooth and runny consistency. Once the baby has become accustomed to cereal, you can gradually add **strained foods**, *solids processed to make them smooth and runny*. You can prepare strained fruits, vegetables, and meats in small quantities at home or buy them as baby foods in jars or in packages to be mixed for each meal. As you expand the baby's diet, be sure to add only one new food every fourth or fifth day. That way, if a certain food causes a skin rash or digestive trouble, you will be able to identify which food is causing the problem.

Cereal and strained foods present the baby with unfamiliar tastes and textures. Don't be surprised if the baby spits back the first spoonfuls of a new food. Remember to be patient as the baby adjusts to this new experience. Following these feeding tips will help make the experience safe and enjoyable for both the baby and you:

- For the first feedings, hold the baby comfortably in a fairly upright position.
- If the baby is used to warm formula, heat solid foods to lukewarm, too. To avoid dangerous hot spots, do not use a microwave to heat a baby's food. Check the temperature of warmed foods by placing a drop on your wrist.
- Be prepared for messy feedings, especially at first. Put a large bib on the baby, and be sure your own clothes are either easily washable or protected.
- Realize that the baby may spit out an unfamiliar food. It may be that the baby dislikes the food. In this case, reintroduce the food later, or try combining it with a favorite food to make it more palatable.
- Especially at first, make the baby's cereal very runny, diluting it with either breast milk or formula. Runny cereal seems more familiar to a young baby—like the breast milk or formula he or she is used to. The cereal should be offered on a spoon, however, not in a bottle, because solid matter in the bottle may cause the baby to choke.
- If you are using baby food from a jar, take out a small portion and place it in a bowl. Then close the jar and refrigerate it immediately. Do not feed the baby directly from the jar. Bacteria from the spoon will multiply rapidly in the food and cause any leftovers to spoil.

Weaning

Sometime around the first birthday, many babies are ready for **weaning**, *a process of changing from drinking from the bottle or breast to drinking from a cup*. Weaning is an important sign of the baby's increasing independence.

There is no precise age at which a baby should be weaned. Nine months is common, but the age varies greatly. The baby usually shows some signs of readiness for weaning, such as playing or looking around while sucking, pushing the nipple away, or preferring to eat from a spoon. It is always best not to force weaning on an unwilling baby; instead, wait until the baby is ready and accepts weaning naturally. Forced weaning may result in other feeding and behavior problems for the child.

Self-Feeding

When babies can sit up steadily, usually around the age of eight or ten months, they start to eat with their fingers and to reach for the spoon. They open their mouth when they see a spoon coming. Before long they want to hold the spoon themselves. These are signs that the infant is ready to begin feeding himself or herself.

SAFETY TIP

Finger foods must be chosen carefully. Remember that the baby may have no teeth at all—and cannot be counted on to actually chew with any teeth he or she does have. Avoid giving the baby foods that are difficult to chew or that, without chewing, might block the baby's breathing passage. Avoid giving the baby foods such as cut-up raw vegetables, nuts, whole grapes, candy, chips, pretzels, popcorn, slices of hot dog, chunks of cooked chicken or meat—or any other food that looks to you like it could cause choking. Be sure that the food has been cut into small pieces. Then give the baby just a few pieces at a time. Some babies try to stuff their mouths full of food.

Around the age of eight to ten months, infants show an interest in self-feeding. What developmental skills has this baby mastered in order to feed himself?

To encourage the baby's self-feeding, provide "finger foods," such as strips of dry toast, small pieces of cheese or banana, or small squares of flavored gelatin. Choose nutritious foods that the baby can grasp easily.

The baby's first efforts at self-feeding with a spoon will probably be important and fun for the baby, but they may not result in much actual eating. You can help by using a separate spoon and placing bits of food in the baby's mouth now and then.

You will probably find that it takes patience—and, at least on some occasions, a sense of humor—to encourage a baby's self-feeding. You and the baby will both benefit if you allow plenty of time for each meal. Then encourage the baby's efforts and enjoy the baby's delight in these new accomplishments.

Nutritional Concerns

Feeding a baby involves more than mastering the necessary techniques. Part of the responsibility of parents and caregivers is making sure that babies' nutritional needs are being met. Fortunately, this is usually not difficult if the child receives formula or breast milk until he or she is eating a good variety of cereals, vegetables, fruits, and meats. However, problems can result if the baby is given too much food, too little food, or the wrong kinds of food.

Overfeeding

For years, nutritionists and physicians have been debating the proper weight for babies; they continue trying to determine whether overfeeding in infancy contributes to weight problems in adulthood. There are still no final answers. However, it is clear that eating habits are established very early in life. A baby who is encouraged to overeat is likely to continue overeating during childhood and adulthood. A baby who is frequently given sweet snacks instead of nutritious foods is more than likely to continue choosing sweets later in life. Infancy is the time to begin a lifetime of healthy eating.

Bottle-fed babies have a greater risk of overfeeding than breast-fed babies. Parents and caregivers may be tempted to urge the bottle-fed baby to take any formula left in the bottle. Nursing mothers, on the other hand, can follow their baby's lead when the baby stops sucking.

Malnutrition

Infants have very specific nutritional needs. To be healthy, a baby needs the following:

- Enough calories to provide for rapid growth.
- Food that contains needed nutrients, such as protein, iron, B vitamins, vitamin C, and vitamin D.
- Food that is easy to digest.
- Adequate amounts of liquid.

Until solid foods are well established in the diet of the child, a baby's main source of nutrition is breast milk or formula. Cow's milk alone does not provide the nutrients a baby needs; it is mostly protein and does not contain the carbohydrates a baby requires for energy. However, cow's milk can be added to a baby's diet, usually after the first solid foods have been introduced.

Babies whose diets do not meet the listed requirements may suffer from **malnutrition**, *a lack of enough food or a lack of the proper type of food.* Malnutrition is not a problem faced only by developing countries in other parts of the world. Malnutrition is a problem in this country, as well. Some parents do not have enough money to provide their babies with an adequate diet. Other parents risk infant malnutrition because they do not know about babies' special food needs or because they feed their children high-calorie, low-density foods.

Some parents, for example, put their infants on diets very low in fat and cholesterol during the first year. They use low-fat milk or skim milk to prepare formula and later for drinking. While cholesterol has been linked to adult heart disease, low-fat and skim milk do not provide enough calories for normal infant growth; in addition, they put a strain on a baby's kidneys. There is also no clear evidence that limiting cholesterol in early childhood prevents adult health problems. Breast milk, considered the ideal food for infants, is itself high in cholesterol.

Malnutrition in infancy can cause lasting physical problems. Severe malnutrition is also linked to poor brain development and learning problems.

Many government and community programs try to eliminate infant and childhood malnutrition. Some of these programs provide food; others teach parents about the nutritional needs of children. The federal government's Women, Infants, and Children Program (WIC) helps meet the special food needs of new mothers and young children. Other programs in your area may be funded by state and local governments.

SECTION 2 REVIEW

CHECK YOUR UNDERSTANDING

1. Which part of a newborn's body do you always need to support when lifting or holding the baby? Why?
2. Describe the position in which a baby should be held for bottle-feeding.
3. Should parents put a bottle in the crib so that the baby can suck and drift off to sleep more comfortably? Why or why not?
4. What are strained foods? When do most babies begin to eat them?
5. What is weaning? What is a common age for weaning?
6. What is the main source of nutrition for babies during most of the first year?
7. What is malnutrition? Who can suffer from infant malnutrition?

DISCUSS AND DISCOVER

1. Discuss the kinds of feeding frustrations that parents of young babies may face. What options do you think frustrated parents have? Which responses would you recommend? Why?
2. Explain how a newborn's feeding schedule might affect other family members. What problems might arise in a specific family situation, such as a family with a single parent, two employed parents, other small children in the family, or twin newborns? What approaches would you suggest to resolve those problems?
3. Find out which programs in your own community help meet the special food needs of new mothers and young children. How are those programs funded? How do people find out about those programs? How many people use their services?

Other Infant-Care Skills

SECTION 3

OBJECTIVES

- Demonstrate how to bathe, dress, and diaper a baby.
- Tell how to encourage good sleep habits.

Taking care of a baby can—and should—be fun. A caregiver who is competent and confident in carrying out basic care routines can enjoy the baby and contribute to the baby's appreciation and enjoyment of the world. These routines include bathing, dressing, and diapering. Proper sleep habits are also important for the baby's health.

TERMS TO LEARN

cradle cap
diaper rash
sleeper

Bathing a Baby

A bath helps keep a baby clean and healthy. As is the case when learning other care skills, confidence in bathing a baby comes from knowing what to do and from having a bit of practice. Any time is fine for a bath except right after feeding. Then the baby needs to sleep and digest the meal.

A newborn is given sponge baths until the navel heals. This takes about two weeks. After that, a tub bath—first in a basin of water or a baby bathtub and later in the family tub—may be given. Both require the caregiver's careful attention to ensure safety.

Sponge Baths

Many of the same basic supplies are needed for both sponge baths and tub baths. These include:

- Two soft bath towels.
- A soft washcloth.
- A diaper.
- Mild soap.
- Baby shampoo.
- Cotton balls.

BUILDING SELF-ESTEEM

A Loving Touch

Parents are usually eager to hold and stroke their newborn babies. With these early touches, the process of bonding begins.

Bonding continues as parents and other caregivers hold and touch the baby. Stroking the baby's arm or leg, holding the baby's hand, gently circling the fingertips on the baby's cheek or chest—all these touches send messages of love.

After bathtime, a caregiver can massage baby lotion onto the baby's back, moving the fingertips gently back and forth, up and down, or round and round. After the lotion has been absorbed, turn the baby over and apply a little more lotion to the baby's chest and tummy in the same way.

Before bathing a baby, assemble these articles and the baby's clean clothes in a warm place with no drafts. The temperature of the room should be 70° to 80° F (20° to 26° C). Choose a room with a good work surface—usually the bathroom, kitchen, or baby's room. Place a soft bath towel over the work area for the baby's comfort and safety.

For sponge baths, it is often most convenient to put the bathwater in a basin on the work surface. Test the water with your elbow. (The skin there is more sensitive than that on your hands or wrists.) The water should feel lukewarm, about 98° F (37° C).

Remove the baby's clothes and place the infant on the towel. Lay another towel on top of the baby's body. Begin by washing the baby's face with clear water and a soft washcloth, while supporting the baby with your other hand. Then pat the baby's face dry. A young baby's skin is very tender, so never rub it with a towel.

Wash the rest of the body with baby soap and water, one area at a time. Rinse thoroughly. Pay particular attention to the skin creases. They should be gently separated, washed, and thoroughly dried.

It is not necessary to clean the inside of the baby's mouth, ears, eyes, or nose. Nature takes care of this. Never use cotton swab sticks. Babies move very suddenly and can easily be injured by them. Just wipe the outer ears, and use a clean washcloth to remove any visible mucus from the nose.

Wash the baby's scalp with tear-free baby soap or baby shampoo once or twice a week. On other days, just wipe the scalp with clear water and pat dry.

Sometimes babies develop **cradle cap**, *a skin condition in which the scalp develops patches of yellowish, crusty scales*. To treat cradle cap, apply baby oil or lanolin to the scalp at night. In the morning, gently loosen the scales with a washcloth or a soft hairbrush (not a stiff one!) and shampoo the hair.

You may want to apply baby powder or lotion to the baby after a bath, but neither is really necessary. You must be careful if you choose to use powder. If it accumulates in skin creases, powder can cause irritation. If the powder is inhaled, the baby can develop breathing problems or even suffocate. Never let a baby play with the container of powder. If you do decide to use powder, choose a cornstarch-based product. Apply it by shaking it first into your own hand and then rubbing it onto the baby's skin.

Tub Baths

With proper handling, even a two-week-old baby can be bathed in a tub if the navel has healed. At first the "tub" can be a large dishpan or special baby bathtub. At age six or seven months, the regular tub can be used.

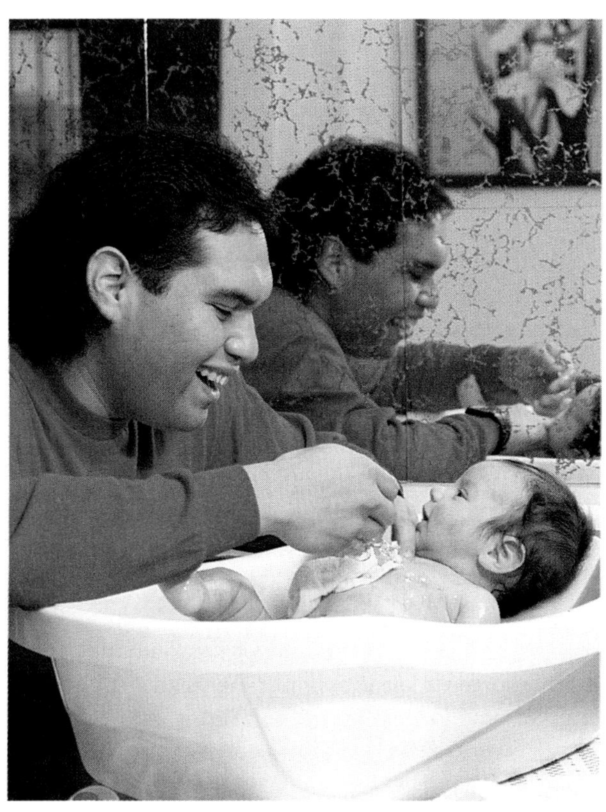

Bathing a baby can be fun for both parent and baby, but safety is very important. For a young infant, a special baby bathtub placed on the counter allows the baby to lean back and enjoy the experience.

Place a rubber mat or a towel in the bottom of the tub to make the baby comfortable and to prevent falls. Add lukewarm water to a depth of about 2 to 3 inches (5 to 8 cm). Assemble the other equipment and the baby's clean clothes before starting the bath.

Begin by washing the baby's face with clear water and patting it dry. Then lift the baby into the tub with a secure grip. Slide one hand under the baby's shoulders; hold the baby securely under the arm, using your wrist to support the baby's neck and head. Slide your other hand under the baby's thighs, and hold the farther leg securely just above the knee. Be especially careful to hold the baby firmly—yet as gently as possible.

While the baby is in the tub, continue to hold the baby under the arm, with your wrist supporting the baby's back and head. You can use your other hand to wash and rinse the baby. Then lift the baby from the water with the same secure grip. Place the infant on a clean towel, and immediately wrap the towel around the baby to prevent chilling. Then pat the baby dry.

Most older babies enjoy baths, especially when they are able to sit by themselves in the tub. They love to splash and play in the water. A few floating toys add to the fun. Don't forget, however, that safety is the primary concern when bathing a baby of any age.

SAFETY TIP

The bathtub can be a dangerous place for babies, so keep these safety precautions in mind:

- Never leave the baby alone during a bath, even "just for a second." A baby can drown very quickly, even in very shallow water.
- Keep the baby seated in the tub. Standing or climbing can lead to falls.
- Always check the water temperature before you put the baby into the tub.
- Faucets present a double hazard. They are hard, sometimes sharp, surfaces. They may also be hot. Keep the baby away from the faucets.
- Don't let the baby drink the bathwater or suck on the washcloth. Try offering the baby a drink of fresh water instead, or give the baby a teething toy to suck on.

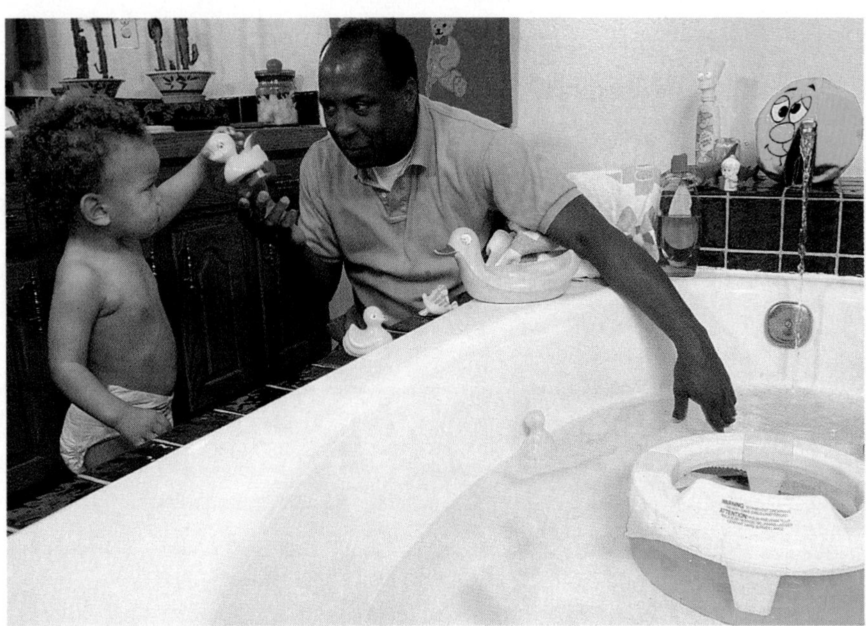

As babies get older, they can sit up in a bathroom tub in a small amount of water. A safety ring in the bathtub and adult supervision helps ensure the baby's safety. Bathtime is a good time for playing and socializing with baby.

Dressing a Baby

When you are choosing the clothes a baby will wear indoors, consider the temperature in the home rather than the season of the year. A good rule of thumb is to check your own clothing needs. An infant does not need to be warmer than you do. Since a newborn's hands and feet often feel cool to the touch, check the baby's body temperature by feeling the arms, legs, or neck. Babies who are too cold usually begin to fuss. Babies who are too warm perspire and become cranky.

The Newborn

A newborn's clothing needs are minimal. Many babies wear a **sleeper**, *a one-piece stretch garment with feet*, for both sleeping and waking, or the baby may be dressed in a cotton undershirt and a gown. In warm or hot weather (if there is no air conditioning), the baby may wear only a diaper and perhaps a short-sleeved undershirt. When taking the baby outdoors in cool weather, add warm outer garments or blankets.

Socks and booties are usually not necessary for everyday wear. They may bind, and babies often get them wet or kick them off. The newborn's feet usually stay covered by a sleeper or blanket. If the baby's feet feel cool to the touch, they should be covered with sleeper feet or with stretchy socks, which stay on the feet better than regular socks or booties.

Older Babies

When babies begin to creep and crawl, they need different kinds of clothing. Overalls, especially those with legs that snap open for easy diaper changes, are good for crawling babies. Very active or determined crawlers may need pants with padded or reinforced knees. Soft, cotton knit shirts are comfortable. For bed, a sleeper keeps the baby covered even if blankets are kicked off.

Shoes are not really necessary until the baby is able to walk outdoors. Many physicians feel the best way to learn to walk is barefooted. This leaves the toes free to grip the floor and gives the ankles flexibility. If the baby is learning to stand and walk indoors on cold floors, slippersocks or nonskid socks will keep the feet warm and the baby safe. Once the baby is ready for shoes, either sneakers or leather shoes are satisfactory.

Dressing Tips

Whenever you dress or undress a baby, take the time to give special attention to the baby—not just to the clothing. Dressing and undressing provide ideal opportunities for extra strokes, pats, hugs, and kisses. This is also a good time for songs, simple rhymes, or "conversations," in which you name the baby's body parts or discuss the clothes you are putting on the baby.

As you dress or undress a baby, do your best to work smoothly and quickly without being rough. Quick, jerking movements often frighten babies. Try following these steps to dress the baby in various kinds of infant garments:

- **Pullover garments.** These garments have a small, but stretchable, neck opening.
  1. Gather the garment into a loop and slip it over the back of the baby's head.
  2. Stretch the garment forward as you bring it down past the forehead and nose. This keeps the face and nose free so that the baby does not feel smothered.
  3. Put the baby's fist into the armhole and pull the arm through with your other hand. Repeat with the other arm.

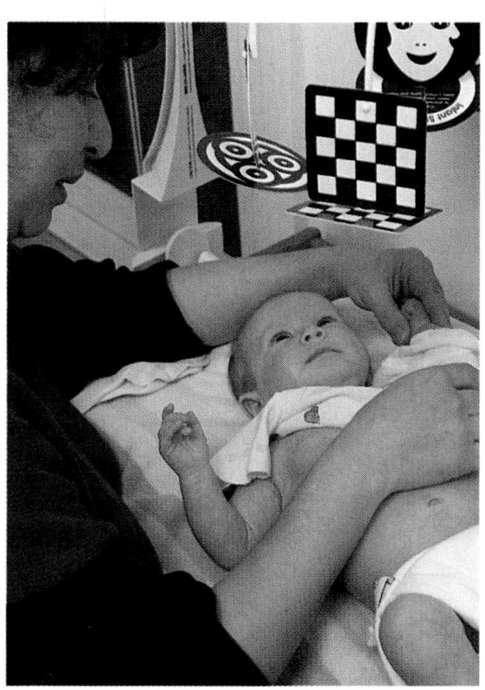

- **Slipover gown or shirt.** If the garment has a larger neck opening than a pullover, use this method.
  1. Gather the garment into a loop, and place it around the baby's face like an oval frame.
  2. Slip the garment down the back of the baby's head.
  3. Put the baby's fist into the armhole and pull it through with your other hand. Repeat with the other arm.
- **Open-front shirt.** The "secret" of this method is first laying the baby facedown. This helps the baby feel secure.
  1. Place the baby on his or her stomach.
  2. Open the shirt and lay it on the infant's back.
  3. Gently turn the baby faceup so that the shirt is underneath.
  4. Put the baby's arms through the sleeves.

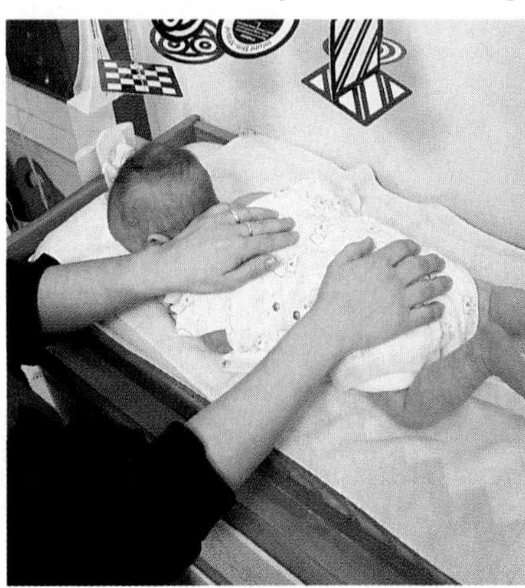

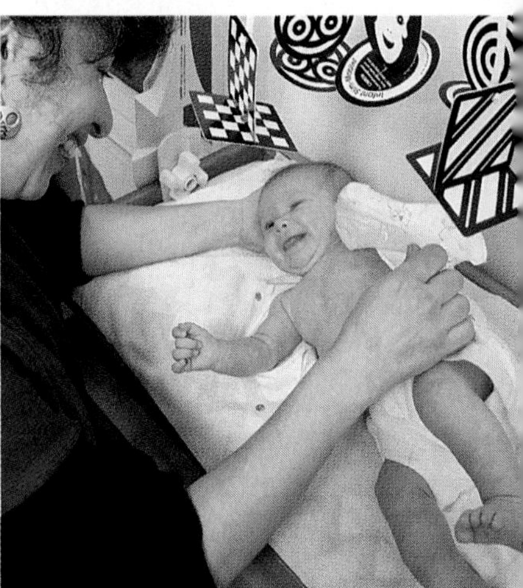

- **One-piece garment with feet.** Putting on this type of garment is easier when the zipper or the snaps go from neck to toes.
  1. Put the bottom part of the garment on first.
  2. Roll the baby onto one side and pull the garment up under the baby's shoulders.
  3. Roll the baby back onto the garment. Then gently pull the sleeves over the baby's arms.

You can follow the same tips for taking each kind of garment off a baby. Just reverse the order of the steps. For example, to remove a pullover top, first take the baby's arms out of the sleeves. Gather the garment into a loop as it lies around the neck. Stretch the garment up and over the baby's face, and slip it off toward the back of the head.

As babies get older, they are better able to help with dressing; for example, they can sit up while you are putting on a shirt, and they can stretch their own arms through short sleeves. However, you may often find that even a capable baby is uncooperative. Sometimes distracting the baby with a toy or a song can help make dressing easier.

Choosing Clothes

When choosing baby clothes, keep in mind that both comfort and ease in dressing are important. Since clothing is expensive, it is wise to look for clothes with generous hems and extra buttons on shoulder straps and waistbands to allow for rapid growth.

The clothing available today is much better suited to babies' needs than was the case in the past. Clothes are simple and comfortable. Many are made of knit fabrics that contain nonirritating fibers and provide both ease of movement for the baby and ease of care for the parents.

The size of infant wear is indicated by both weight and age of baby. Weight is the more reliable guide. It is usually best to buy nothing smaller than a six-month size for a newborn. At first, the infant will probably "swim" in the shirts and gowns. Babies grow quickly, however, and the tiniest sizes soon become too small. You can simply fold up the hems of large garments for the first few weeks until the baby catches up with the clothes.

Diapering a Baby

Diapers are the most essential part of a baby's wardrobe. Parents have a number of diapering options. Cloth diapers, the traditional favorite, may be the least expensive if home laundry facilities are available. Disposable diapers offer throw-away convenience. They are, however, more expensive than cloth diapers, and they contribute significantly to the country's environmental problems. Commercial diaper services are available in some areas. These services deliver clean cloth diapers and pick up used diapers. These services are convenient and may not be much more expensive than other options.

When you care for a very young baby, you will probably find yourself changing diapers twelve to fifteen times each day. A newborn wets several times an hour, but in small amounts that do not require changing with each wetting. An older baby may need fewer diaper changes each day—and is more likely to let you know when a clean diaper is required.

If you keep your diapering supplies organized and handy, you can turn diaper-changing time into a period of pleasant and interesting interaction with your baby. When the baby seems fussy or sleepy, try singing or humming a soothing tune. When the baby seems alert, talk about what you are doing. A young baby will enjoy listening to your voice—and may even babble an answer to your questions.

Keep your diapering supplies near a sturdy, padded surface (such as the crib or a changing table). Cloth diapers must be folded to the correct size. (The illustration [right] shows a good

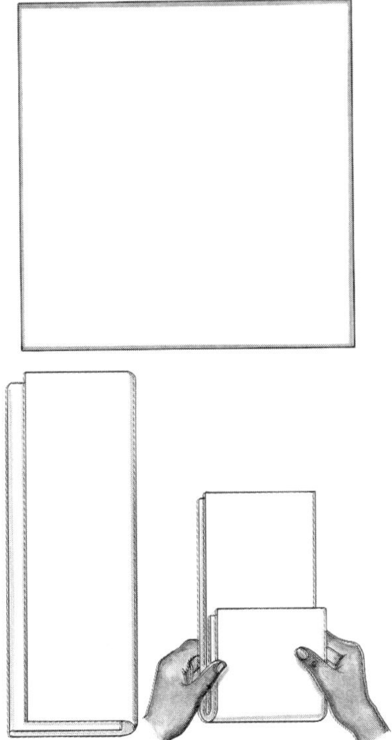

Fold a square diaper in thirds lengthwise so that it is a little wider than the baby's hips. Then turn up one end of the diaper part way.

SAFETY TIP

Once you have put the baby down on the work surface—whether it is a changing table, a counter, or any other raised area—you must pay constant attention to the baby. Always keep at least one hand firmly on the baby. If you need to leave the work surface, for however short a time, take the baby with you. No one knows when the ability to wriggle, kick, or even roll will develop enough to endanger the baby. Falls from changing tables and other work surfaces cause serious injuries and infant deaths every year.

method.) Disposable diapers come in several sizes, with thicker diapers available for nighttime wear. In addition to the diaper, you will need a wet washcloth, soft tissues or toilet paper, cotton, and baby oil; or you may choose to use special disposable baby washcloths.

Follow these steps to change a diaper. As you change the diaper and clean up, remember that it is never safe to leave a baby alone on a changing table or other raised surface.

1. **Remove the diaper, and clean the baby.** If the diaper was merely wet, clean the baby with cotton and baby oil. If the baby had a bowel movement, use soft tissue or toilet paper to remove the soil from the baby. Then wash with a washcloth and apply baby oil.
2. **Put on a fresh diaper.** Hold the baby's ankles, and lift the body enough to slide the diaper under. If you are using cloth diapers, place the extra thickness in the back for girls, in the front for boys. If you are using disposable diapers, be sure the adhesive tabs are under the baby. Bring the diaper up between the baby's legs. Use the adhesive tabs to fasten a disposable diaper. Use large safety pins or special diaper pins to fasten a cloth diaper. To protect the baby, place the pins crosswise, keeping your finger between the diaper and the baby's skin as you pin. Waterproof pants may be added over the cloth diaper.

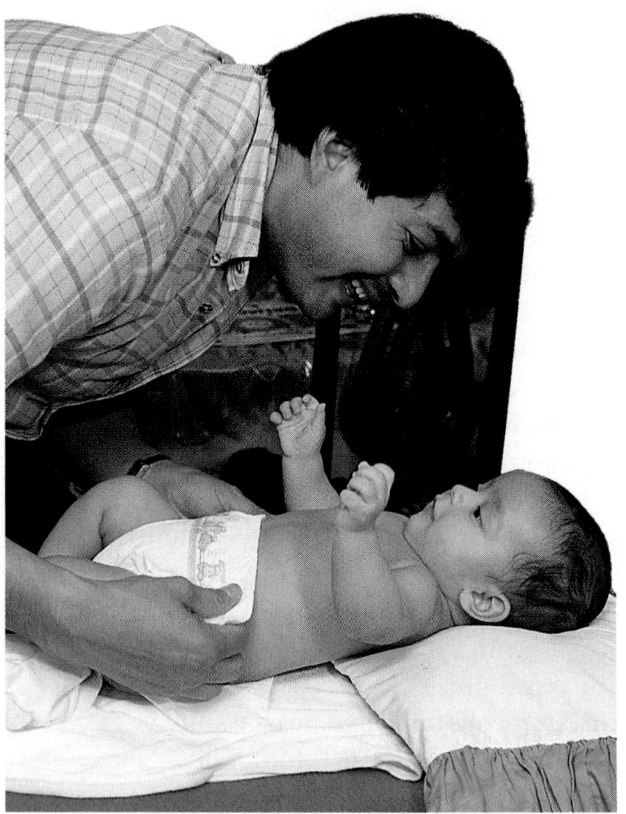

This baby enjoys the attention that comes with changing a diaper. All infant-care routines can be turned into social times by talking or singing to the baby.

ASK THE EXPERTS

Which Kind of Diapers?

Dr. Van D. Stone has served as Chief of Pediatrics at Baptist Medical Center in Little Rock and is in private practice in Tupelo, Mississippi.

We are expecting our first child in less than a month, and we still haven't decided which kind of diapers to use. Can you help us make up our minds?

This is a good question, and I'm glad you're prepared to give it careful consideration. There are some obvious advantages to both cloth and disposable diapers.

Cloth diapers are soft and comfortable against a baby's tender skin. Because you will use the same diapers over and over, you will have to make an initial investment in cloth diapers—but then your only expenses will be those of running a washing machine and, perhaps, a dryer.

Disposable diapers are also comfortable for most babies, and they are clearly more convenient. However, they are also significantly more expensive than cloth diapers. In addition, disposable diapers contribute to the growing environmental problems that our country—and our world—must face.

I hope you will agree that the most important consideration is the comfort and safety of your baby. For that reason, I advise most parents to begin using cloth diapers on their newborn babies. Using cloth diapers for the first few months gives you the chance to see just how sensitive your baby's skin is. It also lets you judge how much extra work may—or may not—be involved in using cloth diapers. After two or three months, parents usually decide to continue using cloth diapers most—but not all—of the time. They often want to use disposable diapers during daytime outings, so they can change the baby quickly and conveniently. Disposable diapers are also a common choice for traveling with a baby.

If you decide to begin with cloth diapers, you may want to check into diaper services in your area. If diaper services are available, investigate their prices and compare them to the investment in cloth diapers and in disposable diapers. If you are lucky, friends, relatives, or co-workers may ask you to suggest an appropriate gift for your new baby—a month of diaper service might be just the thing!

Van D. Stone, MD

Dr. Van D. Stone

3. **Dispose of used supplies.** Cleanliness is important in diapering. Promptly dispose of used tissues, cotton, and other soiled supplies. Drop solid waste from a disposable diaper into a toilet. Then roll the disposable diaper up and place it in a covered trash container. (Never flush disposable diapers down a toilet. They will clog the plumbing.) Place a wet cloth diaper in a covered container filled with a mixture of water and borax or vinegar. Rinse a soiled diaper before placing it in the container. A good method for rinsing is to hold the diaper firmly in a clean, flushing toilet. Then wash your hands with soap and hot water after changing the diaper.

Washing Cloth Diapers

Washing a baby's cloth diapers requires special care. Washing machines do not always wash out all the bacteria, and bacteria can cause skin problems. It is important always to wash diapers in the hottest water and with a mild soap. (Cold or warm water leaves too many bacteria in the fabric.) You may also want to add special laundry sanitizers to the wash to destroy bacteria. Always wash diapers separately, never with other clothing. Be sure, too, that the diapers are thoroughly rinsed. Soap left in diapers can irritate a baby's skin. Diapers may be dried in a dryer. However, drying them outdoors in the sunshine destroys even more bacteria.

Diaper Rash

Controlling bacteria in diapers is important because babies may develop **diaper rash**, *patches of rough, irritated skin in the diaper area*. Sometimes diaper rash includes painful raw spots. Bacteria from wet or dirty diapers or improperly washed diapers are the usual cause. A sensitivity to disposable diapers can cause similar symptoms.

You can treat a mild case of diaper rash without consulting the baby's pediatrician. Change the baby's diapers more frequently, and clean the baby thoroughly after a bowel movement. Try using one of the products containing zinc oxide and cod liver oil, designed to protect against diaper rash and help it heal more quickly. Also, expose the diaper area to the air as much as possible, and avoid putting waterproof pants on the baby. If the baby's rash continues or gets worse, ask a pediatrician for help.

Sleep

All babies need sleep in order to grow and develop. However, the amount of time an infant spends sleeping decreases considerably during the first year. A newborn may sleep from 12 hours a day to almost continuously. By one year, however, a baby often has as few as two or three sleep periods, including naps.

The amount of sleep needed also depends on the individual baby. An active baby needs more sleep than an inactive one, just as active babies need more food. Babies also require more sleep on some days than on others.

Preparation for Sleep

Putting the baby to bed for the night should be a relaxed and pleasant experience—both for you and for the baby. Begin by

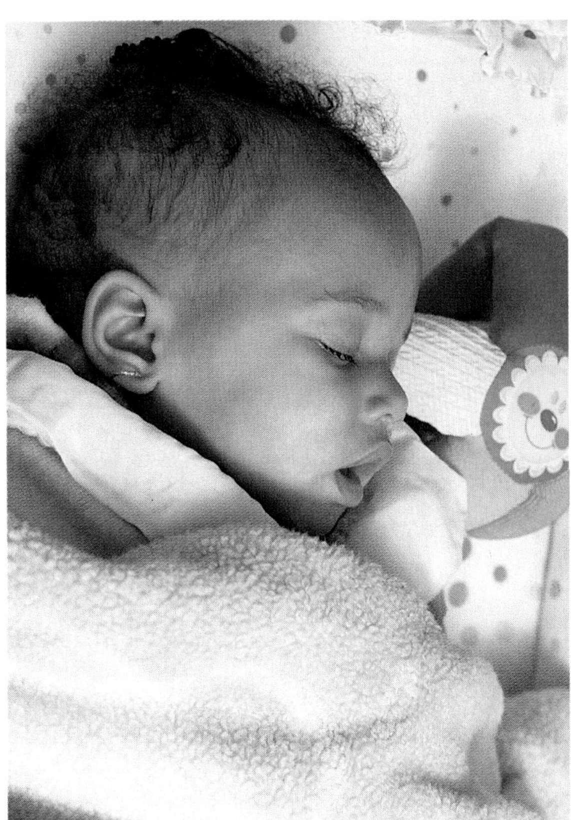

Sleep lets infants regain energy after their brief active periods. During sleep, the body repairs itself and builds new cells for growth.

washing the baby's face and hands and by changing the baby's diaper and clothes. Specific sleeping garments remind the older baby that it is time to go to bed.

Then spend a few minutes rocking the baby or singing a soothing lullaby. This will be comforting and reassuring for the baby. As you put the baby to bed, keep your manner calm and unhurried, even if you don't feel that way. Otherwise, the baby will pick up your feelings and will probably not settle into sleep as well as usual.

Finally, put the baby down in bed with adequate covering. (Never let a baby sleep in a draft, even in very hot weather.) If the infant is too young to roll over independently, you will probably find that the baby sleeps best on his or her stomach.

Try to follow the same simple routine every night. You will find that the baby soon learns the signals for bedtime and is likely to find comfort in the consistency of the ritual. For example, you and the baby might say "goodnight" to favorite toys in the room, or you might read or tell a simple bedtime story. As the baby grows older, you can change the ritual gradually to suit the baby's age.

Sleep should never be brought about by the use of drugs or sleep medicines of any kind. Consult the baby's pediatrician if sleep problems continue.

Cultural Exchange

THE STORY OF "ROCK-A-BYE-BABY"

It is reported that the author of the well-loved lullaby, "Rock-a-Bye-Baby" was a pilgrim who sailed on the Mayflower. The Wampanoag Indians, who became friends to the pilgrims carried their infants in cradleboards on their backs. In temperate weather, the Indians suspended the cradles from tree limbs so that passing breezes could rock the babies while their mothers tended the maize and beans. Nursery rhymes remain popular in families today. Perhaps the gentle lilt and inflection soothes some children. Perhaps, too, the familiar nursery rhymes reminds youngsters of the cuddling, holding, and reassurance they felt as a young child.

PARENTING IN ACTION

Who Is Training Whom?

Rachel's parents are concerned—and exhausted—by her bedtime routine. Laurel and Reggie put Rachel, who has just had her first birthday, down for the night around 7:30. Then the fussing and crying begin. If no one responds, Rachel's cries turn into screams. Eventually, either Laurel or Reggie gets up with a sigh of resignation and goes to Rachel.

Rachel stops crying when one of her parents picks her up and soothes her. As soon as she is put back down in her crib, however, Rachel starts screaming again. This can go on for quite a while, but it always ends the same way. One of her parents brings Rachel out into the living room, where Laurel and Reggie like to relax before going to bed. Rachel finally falls asleep in her parent's arms and is—at last—put back to bed for the night.

Last week Laurel and Reggie mentioned this problem to Rachel's pediatrician. The doctor asked a few questions and then responded, "Rachel's got you trained, not the other way around. You've given in to her crying so long that the habit will only get worse. Bedtime problems usually develop when parents aren't firm enough."

The doctor smiled reassuringly at Laurel and Reggie. "It won't hurt Rachel to cry herself to sleep. If you don't pick her up, she'll soon learn that screams won't help her get her way. It'll be tough for a while—for all of you—but she'll soon learn that when she's put down for the night, she'll stay there. Babies don't keep up behavior that doesn't work."

Laurel and Reggie intend to start following their doctor's advice—soon. For now, however, they both agree that they just can't stand to hear their baby screaming.

THINK AND DISCUSS

1. How is Rachel's bedtime behavior affecting her parents?
2. How is her parents' behavior affecting Rachel?
3. What questions do you think Laurel and Reggie should be asking themselves, and to whom should they turn for answers?
4. If you were in Laurel and Reggie's position, would you follow the doctor's advice? Why or why not? If not, what would you do about Rachel's bedtime routine?

Bedtime Problems

Babies—especially active babies—often become restless while they sleep. During the night, they may waken partially and suck their fingers, cry out, or rock the crib. It is best not to respond to these activities. If you do respond, your presence may become a necessary part of the baby's pattern for getting back to sleep. Infants need to learn to use their own resources for returning to sleep. Of course, this does not mean you should ignore a baby who needs feeding or a diaper change. A baby whose restlessness develops into crying also needs your attention.

SECTION 3 REVIEW

CHECK YOUR UNDERSTANDING

1. What should you do if you have to leave the room while you are giving a baby a sponge bath? Why?
2. Explain what cradle cap is. What should you do to treat cradle cap?
3. List two important considerations in choosing clothes for a baby.
4. List the three main steps in changing a baby's diaper.
5. Explain what diaper rash is. List two things you can do to treat diaper rash.
6. List two things you should do before putting a baby in bed to sleep.

DISCUSS AND DISCOVER

1. Using actual garments or magazine pictures, select four items of children's clothing, ranging in size from newborn to twelve-months. Evaluate each item for comfort, practicality, ease in dressing the baby, and required care. Of all the items you selected, which garment ranks highest on your list?
2. What are some ways to calm a baby down or to help a restless baby fall asleep? Discuss why it is a poor idea to give a baby medicine to cure sleeping problems.
3. Explain why consistent bedtime routines can be beneficial for both the baby and the caregiver. Name three bedtime routines you would suggest for first-time parents.

SPENDING QUALITY TIME WITH BABY

Many newborn babies spend most of each day sleeping. When they are awake, they need to be fed, changed, bathed, talked to, rocked, and held. You can turn all these routine activities into "quality time" by focusing on the baby and by doing your best to understand and respond to the baby's signals.

As the baby gets a bit older—and as you become more confident in caring for the baby's daily needs—you will find more and more opportunities to play games with the baby. There are many different games that can both delight and stimulate babies. Here are a few suggestions:

LOOKING GAMES

* **Funny faces.** Shake your head; stick out your tongue; make funny faces. Even babies a few days old often respond to or imitate facial expressions.
* **Light games.** Shine a flashlight on the walls and ceiling of a partially darkened room. Make shadow designs by placing your fingers in front of the beam.
* **Mirrors.** Sit with the baby in front of a mirror. Point to the infant's eyes, nose, mouth, and other features, and name each feature. Do the same with your own features. Eventually, the baby will also point to the features you name.

LISTENING GAMES

* **Musical games.** Play or sing music and nursery rhymes. Encourage the older baby (three months and up) to respond by swaying or humming.
* **What's that?** Point out everyday sounds, like running water, the washing machine, and the telephone. Name the sound, and then help the baby see what is making it.
* **Mimic.** Make fun sounds—car noises, animal noises, motorcycle noises, and so on. See whether the baby will imitate you.

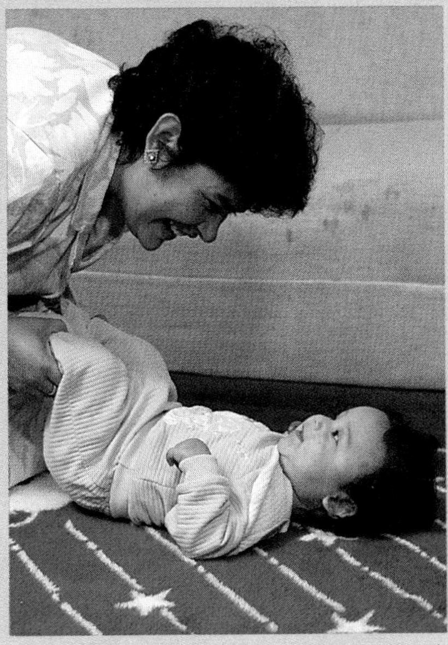

BABY EXERCISES

- **Bicycle.** Lay the baby faceup, and gently hold both his or her ankles. Revolve the baby's legs as if riding a bicycle.
- **Tug-of-war.** Grasp one side of a large rubber ring, and let the baby grasp the other side. Gently play tug-of-war. Remember—the baby gets to win. However, if the baby is sitting up, don't let go entirely of the rubber ring, or the baby will tumble backwards.
- **Airplane.** Playing airplane can help strengthen the back and neck muscles of a baby who can already hold his or her head steady. Hold the baby just above the waist, and then slowly lift the baby above your face. Avoid a sudden lift, which could cause the baby's head to wobble. The baby's back will arch and the arms and legs will stretch out. You'll probably want to add some airplane noises, too.

OLD FAVORITES

- **Peek-a-boo.** Establish eye contact with the baby. Quickly turn your head away, and then turn back again, saying "peek-a-boo." For older babies, cover your eyes and then uncover them. Don't forget to say "peek-a-boo"!
- **Hide and seek.** Make a toy disappear behind your back. Let the baby crawl to find it. Help the baby find toys that you have hidden. Try hiding from the baby yourself—and reappear quickly.

SUMMARY

- Development and growth are most rapid during the first year of life.
- Physical development proceeds from head to foot, from near to far, and from simple to complex.
- Development of motor skills depends on physical, intellectual, social, and emotional development.
- Daily care routines include feeding, bathing, dressing, and diapering.
- During the first year, eating habits change from breast- or bottle-feeding to self-feeding a variety of foods.
- Clothing should be easy to put on and take off, should suit the activity of the baby, and should "grow" with the baby.
- Bedtime should be handled with a soothing, familiar routine.

REVIEWING THE FACTS

1. What is the difference between growth and development? Give at least two examples of growth and two examples of development.
2. Which of a baby's senses is most fully developed at birth? Which senses are less developed at birth? Use what you know about prenatal development to account for these differences in development.
3. What are three common symptoms of teething? List at least three things you might do to help a teething baby feel more comfortable.
4. Why shouldn't parents and caregivers prop bottles up for young babies?
5. What are four types of food that might be included in a baby's diet during the first year? List those foods in the order that they should be introduced to the baby. Why is the order important?
6. What are two signs that a baby is ready to be weaned? How should parents respond to these signs?
7. Should parents and caregivers encourage babies over the age of about eight months to feed themselves? Why or why not?
8. Why is infancy the best time to begin learning good eating habits?
9. What is the difference between a sponge bath and a tub bath? Which is safe for newborn babies? Why?
10. Briefly describe an outfit that would be good for an active ten-month-old. Why would that outfit be appropriate for a baby of that age?

EXPLORING FURTHER

1. Take a survey of students in the class. How do their heights compare with the heights of their parents? Give some possible reasons for differences. (Section 1)
2. Hold a 10-pound (4.5-kg) sack of flour in the crook of one arm while you perform various routine activities, such as writing a check, preparing a bottle, opening the mail, opening an umbrella, and tying a shoe. Discuss your experience with classmates. Which activities were easiest for you? Which were the most difficult? How was holding the sack of flour similar to holding a baby? How would your experiences have been different if, instead of the flour, you had been holding a baby? (Section 2)
3. Make a booklet of lullabies to share with others. Perform and teach each one to the class. Try writing a poem that could be used as a lullaby for babies. If possible, set your poem to music, using a guitar, keyboard or piano. (Section 3)
4. Compare the use of cloth diapers, disposable diapers, and a diaper service. Make a chart showing the advantages and disadvantages of each, as well as the costs involved. Calculate the costs per week, per month, and per year. (Section 3)

THINKING CRITICALLY

1. **Analyze.** What do you consider the three most important guidelines for the care of infants? Why?
2. **Synthesize.** What can parents and caregivers learn about infants from growth charts or from lists of average motor skills development? What are the possible dangers in referring to such charts and lists?
3. **Evaluate.** How can a parent's attitudes toward eating and sleeping affect a baby? What do you consider the most helpful attitudes toward eating and sleeping? Why?

CROSS-CURRICULUM CONNECTIONS

1. **Math.** Choose three different types of infant formula—ready-to-use, liquid concentrate, and powdered. Calculate the cost per 4-ounce (118-mL) baby bottle of each kind of formula.
2. **Reading.** Look for ideas on preventing and solving bedtime problems in the book *Solving Your Child's Sleep Problems,* by Richard Ferber, M.D. Share what you learned with the class.

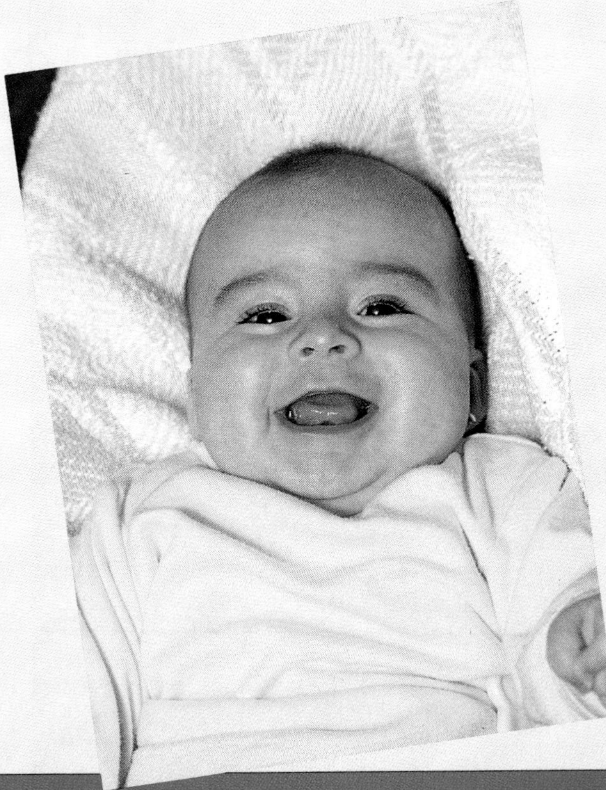

OBSERVING AND PARTICIPATING

Infant Care

When you are observing infants, learn to look at them objectively. Try to see them without ideas that you may have had before working with them or observing them. Avoid thinking about what they should be doing or guessing why they are doing something. Instead, look for details that indicate the babies' stage of development. For example, instead of stating, "Susie was crying because she missed her mother," record, "Susie began to cry when her mother handed her to the caregiver."

Choose one of the activities below, and spend some time observing or interacting with an infant. Then write your observations in your journal, and compare them with those made by other students. Discuss how the ages of the babies affected your observations.

- **Observing.** Observe an infant to identify signs of sensory development. Do you think the baby can hear, see, smell, taste, feel, and make sounds? What signs indicate development in each area? What changes have been made in the environment to help stimulate the baby? What other changes could be made?
- **Participating.** Feed—or help feed—a baby who has started eating solids. How does the baby respond to different foods? How does the baby show his or her interest in self-feeding?
- **Observing.** Observe as parents or caregivers dress and undress babies of various ages—one just a month or two old, the other nearly a year old. How are the babies' garments appropriate to their ages and activities?

CHAPTER 9

Emotional and Social Development During the First Year

Robert gently dances with his seven-month-old son Robbie. The baby squeals with delight and laughs as he swings him around, hugging him close.

Robbie squirms, clearly communicating that he wants more play. Again, Robert twirls him and sways with the music. Then he puts the baby down onto the floor. "There you go, Robbie," he says cheerfully. "Now you can play with your toys, and Daddy will read his book."

"Badabadabada," Robbie answers, pulling himself up to a standing position by grabbing Robert's pant leg.

Robert stares into his open book for a moment, trying to ignore his son's insistent chatter. Then he closes the book, grabs the baby playfully, and says, "You win, Robbie. Let's dance together some more."

SECTION 1

Emotional Development During the First Year

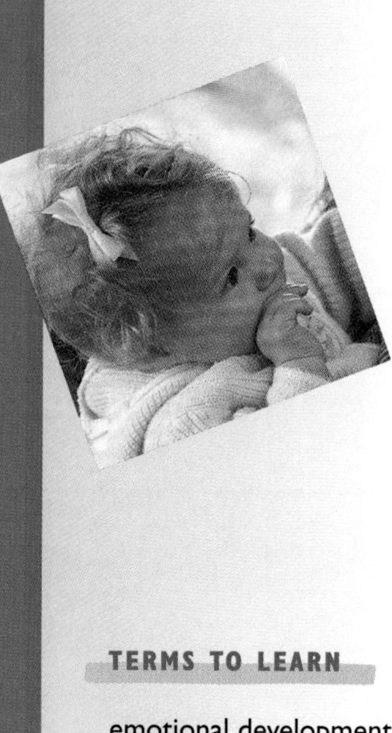

OBJECTIVES

- Recognize signs of emotional development in babies.
- Explain how a baby's care affects emotional development.
- Describe how emotions change during infancy.

TERMS TO LEARN

emotional development
pacifier
social development

An infant's physical development is rapid and impressive during the first year. For healthy infants, emotional development and social development are also impressive, but these important kinds of development can be harder to observe and measure.

Distinguishing Between Emotional and Social Development

Emotional development is *the process of learning to recognize and express one's feelings and learning to establish one's identity and individuality.* Healthy emotional development in children is important because it results in an adult who has self-confidence, can handle stressful situations, and displays empathy toward others.

Social development is *the process of learning to interact with others and to express oneself to others.* Healthy social development results in an adult whose actions display a tolerance for others and who has an ability to interact peacefully with others. A socially healthy adult listens to all points of view before acting, communicates accurately with others, and treats both himself or herself and other people with respect and dignity.

Observing and understanding a baby's feelings and relationships with others are important tasks for parents and other caregivers. Succeeding at these tasks requires the ability to recognize and respond to each child's age level and maturity. It is also important to remember that emotional and social development are closely interwoven; a child's feelings about self and a child's behavior toward others are dependent on one another.

Understanding Emotional Development

Emotional development begins at birth and continues throughout life. Like physical development, emotional development follows predictable patterns but progresses according to each baby's individual timing.

Every baby copes with life in a very personal way. This is because each baby brings his or her own individuality to a situation. For example, all babies react to a sudden shaking of the surface on which they are lying. However, one baby may respond by screaming, while another baby may simply squirm a bit and quickly settle down again.

Emotional development depends on other factors besides the child's individuality. The type of care the baby receives and the atmosphere of the home are two important influences on an infant's emotional development.

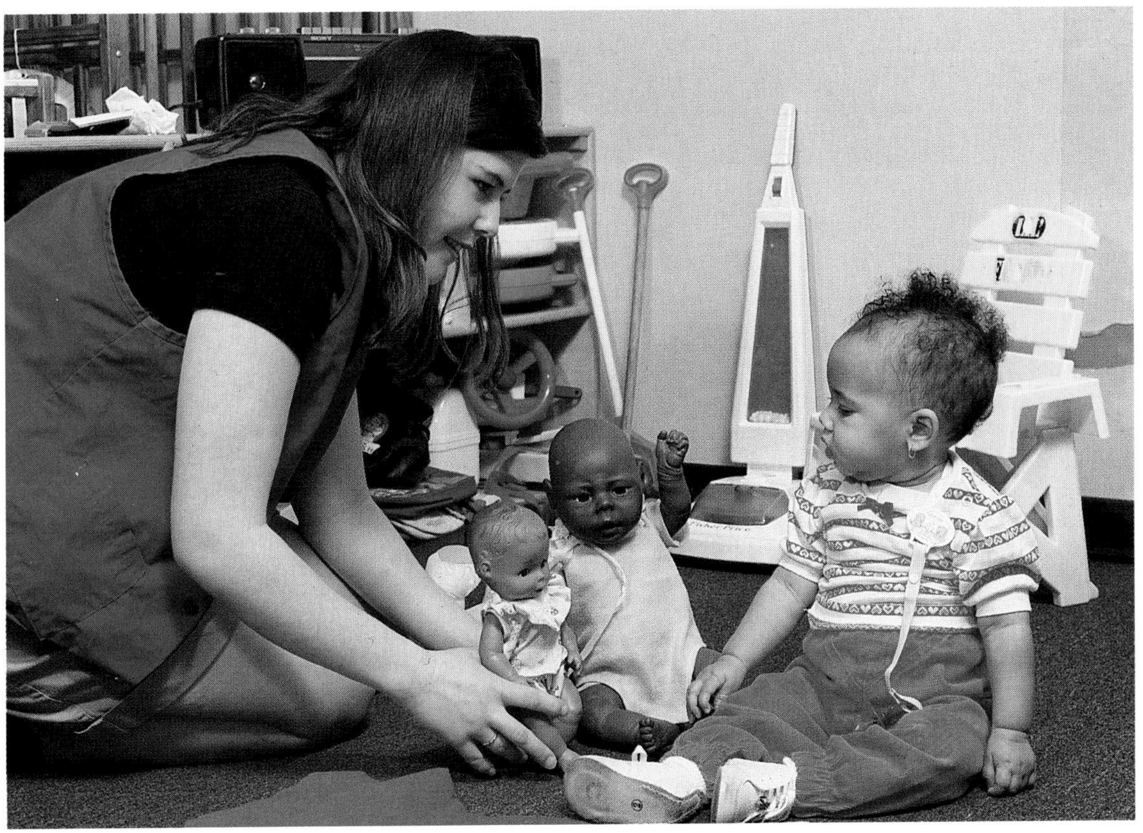

At this age, children can't tell you what they are thinking or feeling. It takes understanding to interpret their moods and the meaning of their behavior.

BUILDING SELF-ESTEEM

Holding Baby Can Build Trust

Before birth, a baby has been kept close and secure within the mother's body. After birth, most babies find close, gentle contact very comforting. They feel secure when a caring parent or caregiver holds, strokes, and pats them.

Holding the baby during feedings, rocking the baby when he or she is fussy, and taking the baby for a walk around the house can help the baby develop a sense of comfort and trust. As the baby grows older, he or she begins to count on the presence of parents or caregivers—reliable people who will offer help when the baby needs it, comfort when the baby feels frightened, and companionship when the baby feels lonely.

Building Trust Through Care

The world is a strange new place for newborns. Depending on a baby's early experiences, the world may be a comfortable, secure place—or a confusing, difficult place. The attitudes that newborns develop about their world depend on how well their needs are met.

If the newborn is kept warm and dry, and is fed when hungry, soothed when fussy, and talked to when awake, the infant comes to feel that this world is a comfortable place and develops a sense of security.

On the other hand, if the newborn is made to conform to a rigid schedule of feeding, and crying brings no comfort or adult response, the baby learns that this world is not a very friendly place. The same attitude develops when parents and other caregivers are inconsistent in their care or in their responses to the infant. If schedules are changed often, or if parents and caregivers are sometimes gentle and loving and other times sharp and impatient, the baby has difficulty building trust.

Building trust in infancy is essential for a person's emotional and social development. A baby who learns to trust parents and caregivers will grow into a child who can trust himself or herself and into an adult who can establish and maintain caring relationships with others.

A baby who experiences a world of caring people and interesting things has a good start in life. How do these influences help build trust?

Establishing a happy, loving home environment is one of the best and most important ways in which parents can provide for their children.

Emotional Climate of the Home

Affection and harmony between parents, caregivers, and all family members are the foundation of successful family life. If the family members and caregivers also love and understand each child as an individual, the conditions are ideal for emotional and social development.

Undoubtedly, you have days when you are grumpy. Have you ever noticed how contagious such feelings are? If you snap at someone, the chances are that person will snap back at you—or at someone else. Babies react the same way. Long before they know the meanings of words, babies catch the tone of adults' feelings. Nervous, worried parents and caregivers are likely to be tense or awkward in handling their baby. They may cuddle the infant in a way that is more anxious than soothing; they may rush the baby through a feeding. The baby senses the person's nervousness and, in turn, becomes irritable and fussy.

Every family has its normal ups and downs, and a baby adapts to these. However, it is essential for the baby to feel that genuine, warm affection and caring are the basis of the family's interactions. Continuing bitterness and mistrust can interfere with the baby's healthy development.

PARENTING IN ACTION

Adjusting to Parenthood

Jess and Twana were thrilled when they learned they were going to be parents. However, now that the baby, Ashley, is here, they are having difficulty adjusting.

After Ashley was born, Twana quit her job to stay home with the baby. She sometimes feels "trapped" at home and watches sadly as Jess sets off for work every morning. "I miss my job," she explains. "I miss being with my friends at work. Ashley is fun—but I want some time with adults, too."

Jess, on the other hand, feels left out of the life Ashley and Twana share. He also worries because he is now responsible for earning all the money that the family needs.

When Jess comes home from work—often late—he and Twana are both tired. On most nights, they feel angry and end up arguing. Then Ashley wakes up and starts to cry. Her parents, both tense and angry, have trouble comforting her. Last night, when Twana picked her up, Ashley cried even harder. Frustrated, Twana pushed the baby into Jess's arms and shouted, "Here, you take care of her for a change!" Then she ran into the bedroom and slammed the door.

THINK AND DISCUSS

1. How has the emotional climate of Jess and Twana's home changed since Ashley's birth? What are the causes of that change?
2. How do you think Jess feels about Twana? About Ashley?
3. How do you think Twana feels about Jess? About Ashley?
4. What questions do you think Jess and Twana should be asking themselves? What should they be asking each other?
5. If you were in a position to help Jess and Twana, what would you suggest? Why?

Crying and Comforting

The most obvious sign of an infant's emotions is crying. Newborns vary greatly in the amount and the intensity of their crying. Some babies cry infrequently, and they are usually easy to comfort. These are what parents call "easy" or "good" babies. Other babies cry often and loudly, and it is usually hard to comfort them. These babies can be considered "difficult," because being able to comfort and help a crying baby provides a sense of satisfaction—and parents of inconsolable criers often miss out on that satisfaction. Instead, they may develop a sense of frustration at not being able to calm the baby or to remedy the problem.

A young baby who is crying needs attention and care. The first step is to check for any physical problem. Is the baby hungry or in need of a diaper change? Is the infant too cold or too hot? Perhaps there's a burp left over from the last feeding. If none of these is the cause of the crying and the baby doesn't seem ill, then you must assume that the baby needs something else—your company, your cuddling, or your comforting. Remember that these are real needs, too. As you and the baby get to know each other, you will probably discover which comforting measures work best. Here are a few to try:

- **Cuddle up with the baby in a rocking chair.** The combination of being held and rocked often soothes a crying baby. You can provide a similar combination by holding the baby close as you walk around. A frontal baby carrier that fits over the shoulders and across the back may assist you in keeping the baby close, comfortable, and soothed by your gently moving.
- **Move the baby to a new position.** Perhaps the baby wants to lie in a different position but isn't yet strong enough to roll over. Perhaps the baby wants to sit in an infant seat and feel involved with the rest of the family.
- **Talk softly to the baby, or sing to the baby.** Don't worry—you don't have to be a great singer. The tone and rhythm of your voice, and the attention they indicate, may comfort the baby.
- **Offer a toy to interest and distract the baby.**
- **Place the baby facedown across your legs as you sit in a sturdy chair.** Support the baby's head with one hand while gently rubbing the baby's back with the other.

Babies also develop their own techniques for comforting themselves. The most common comforting technique is sucking—on a thumb, a fist, or a **pacifier**, *a nipple attached to a plastic ring.*

Many babies also comfort themselves with a soft object such as a certain blanket or stuffed toy. They develop a special attachment to this object and use it for comfort when they are sleepy or anxious. Other babies may comfort themselves by twisting their hair or by rocking themselves back and forth in their crib.

The baby's special self-comforting technique is an indication of his or her individuality and development. Children typically outgrow their need for such techniques and, when they are ready, give up these habits without a problem.

Emotions in Infancy

Think about all the different emotions you experience. You may feel happy, angry, anxious, fearful, or excited. Babies, however, only gradually develop such specific emotions.

SAFETY TIP

During the first few months, a pacifier can help satisfy the baby's need to suck and may even help eliminate some of the air in the stomach. However, in order to be safe for the baby, pacifiers must be used carefully. *Never* tie the pacifier on a string around the baby's neck. To keep the pacifier from falling, use a pacifier ribbon, which snaps on the pacifier at one end and attaches to the baby's clothing at the other end. These ribbons are available in most baby stores. Check the baby's pacifier frequently for cuts and tears in the surface. A pacifier that is old or torn can fall apart and become a health and safety hazard.

ASK THE EXPERTS

Babies and Crying

Jean Illsley Clarke is the director of J.I. Consultants in Minneapolis, Minnesota where she designs and conducts workshops on self-esteem, parenting, and group dynamics

We're exhausted! Our month-old baby cries and cries each evening, and nothing seems to help. Friends have suggested that we should just leave her alone and let her "cry it out." What do you think?

This is a good question—and a very natural one. Most babies between the ages of three and twelve weeks have a fussy period at the end of the day. They seem to be overloaded, and they apparently need to fuss before they can settle themselves for the night. This fussy period (sometimes called colic) is a trying time for parents, who are usually tired themselves by the end of the day.

My answer to your question really depends on what you mean by letting your baby cry it out. Some parents let their babies "cry it out" by completely ignoring them. These parents believe—mistakenly—that a baby's crying is pointless and that it is not necessary to respond to an infant's cries. This approach to crying is never appropriate.

Other parents let their babies "cry it out" during a fussy period by trying various methods of comforting the baby, one method at a time. Then they leave the baby alone for a short period—perhaps five minutes—between attempts to provide comfort. With this approach, the parents might try feeding, rocking, singing, talking, patting, carrying, adding more covers, removing covers, bundling, and loosening clothing all in turn, with short periods in which the baby can cry and can perhaps start learning to comfort himself or herself. As the baby grows and gains experience, he or she will learn to use a thumb, a pacifier, a special blanket, or a soft toy to ease the distress. This approach to crying it out can help both the baby and the baby's parents.

The approach that parents and other caregivers take to crying can be crucial to a baby's development. When parents hover and jump at the slightest whimper, babies are likely to become discouraged and fretful. These babies often end up crying more, rather than less. On the other hand, babies whose parents consistently ignore their crying are likely to lose confidence in themselves.

Crying is a baby's method of letting parents and other caregivers know about his or her needs. When the baby cries, they should be willing to listen, to respond by trying to figure out what the baby needs, and to meet the baby's need as directly as possible.

Jean Illsley Clarke

Jean Illsley Clarke

At birth the range of emotions is limited to pleasure or satisfaction, during which the baby is quiet, and pain or discomfort, during which the baby cries. This is why crying does not necessarily indicate pain in a newborn; it may indicate boredom or some other form of discomfort. By the second month, however, babies produce different cries to express different feelings. These more specific responses continue to develop as babies connect their feelings with inner sensations and outer experiences.

HOW EMOTIONS DEVELOP

PLEASANT EMOTIONS

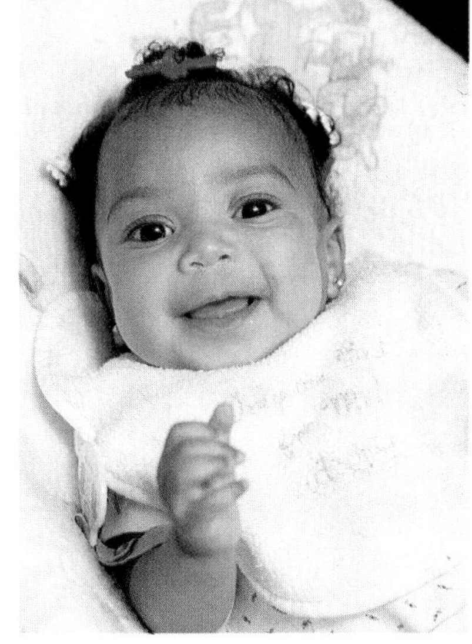

DELIGHT

Beginning at about two months, babies show delight by smiling, perhaps in response to an adult who is making funny faces at them.

ELATION

By seven or eight months, babies show the high spirits of elation.

AFFECTION

At about nine months, babies begin to feel affection for those who provide security and care. Affection for other children comes later.

(Continued on next page)

HOW EMOTIONS DEVELOP (cont'd.)

UNPLEASANT EMOTIONS

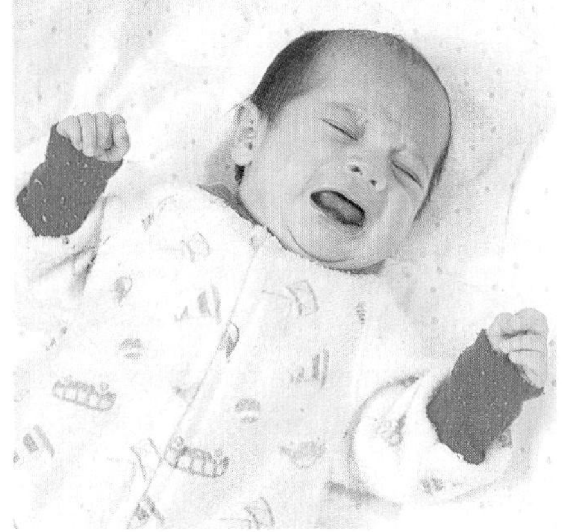

DISTRESS

Very young babies express any discomfort or unhappiness in the same way—by crying.

ANGER

By about four or five months, babies show their anger when they don't get their own way. Older babies show anger at objects as well as at people. They may throw their toys or push something away.

DISGUST

Disgust can also be observed at about four or five months of age. Babies show their dislikes very clearly.

FEAR

Until around the age of six months, babies do not show fear because they cannot recognize threatening situations. Fear of strangers begins at about eight months of age.

Building an infant's sense of trust has long-term benefits for all. By the time she is six to nine months old, she will learn to comfort herself with a thumb, a pacifier, a blanket, or a soft toy.

SECTION 1 REVIEW

CHECK YOUR UNDERSTANDING

1. What is emotional development?
2. What is social development?
3. How should parents and caregivers respond to a baby's needs in order to help the baby build a sense of trust?
4. Does it matter to a baby how the adults in the baby's family treat each other? Why or why not?
5. List at least four needs that might cause a baby to cry.
6. What are two measures that might comfort a crying baby?
7. Which of a baby's emotions require attention from a parent or other caregiver? Why?

DISCUSS AND DISCOVER

1. Discuss what parents can do to provide consistency in the care and attention their babies receive. What issues should parents discuss with each other? What issues should they discuss with their baby's other caregivers?
2. Talk with at least five experienced parents or grandparents. Find out what special techniques each uses for comforting a crying baby. Share your findings with the class.
3. Explain how the following factors can affect the emotional climate in a home: the emotional maturity of parents; education; unemployment; substance use and abuse.

SECTION 2

Social Development and Personality

OBJECTIVES

- Recognize signs of social development in babies.
- Explain the importance of attachment to emotional and social development.
- Describe how behavior is learned.
- Define *personality* and describe how it develops.
- Recognize different personality types in babies.

TERMS TO LEARN

aggressive
attachment
consistency
failure to thrive
personality
placid
self-concept
sensitive
stranger anxiety

A baby's social development is closely related to his or her physical development and emotional development. Even a newborn responds to other people in ways that encourage those people to satisfy the baby's physical and emotional needs. As the baby develops physically, he or she becomes more capable of involvement and interaction with other people. As the baby develops emotionally, his or her feelings about self become an integral part of the baby's relationships with other people.

Signs of Social Development in Infancy

Like physical and emotional development, social development follows a predictable pattern. The following list shows the common signs of social development for babies during the first year. Like all such lists and charts, this one is designed to indicate typical development for many babies; it should be considered a general guide—not a checklist—for helping you understand individual babies.

- **The first days of life.** From birth onward, babies respond to human voices. A calm, soothing voice will quiet a baby; a harsh or loud voice will upset a baby.

- **One month.** Most babies stop crying when they are lifted or touched. A baby's face brightens when he or she sees a familiar person—usually a parent.
- **Two months.** Babies begin to smile at people. Now their eyes can follow moving objects, and they especially enjoy watching people move about the room.
- **Three months.** Babies turn their head in response to a voice. Now they want companionship as well as physical care.
- **Four months.** Babies laugh out loud. They look to other people for entertainment.
- **Five months.** Babies show an increased interest in family members other than their parents. They may cry when they are left alone in a room. At this age, babies babble to their toys, dolls, or stuffed animals, or to themselves.
- **Six months.** Babies love company and attention. They delight in playing games such as peek-a-boo and pat-a-cake.
- **Seven months.** Babies prefer their parents over other family members or strangers.
- **Eight months.** Babies prefer to be in a room with other people. Many babies this age can move from room to room, looking for company.
- **Nine and ten months.** Babies are quite socially involved. They creep after their parents and are often underfoot. At this age, babies love attention. They enjoy being chased; they like to throw toys over and over again—with someone else picking the toys up each time.
- **Eleven and twelve months.** Babies are most often friendly and happy at this age. They are also sensitive to the emotions of others. They know how to influence and adjust to the emotions of the people around them. At one year, babies like to be the center of attention. They like to play games with other family members and are usually tolerant of strangers.

Social development is a natural part of being with parents and other family members.

Attachment

Around the age of six months, a baby comes to understand that he or she is a separate person. The baby then works to develop an **attachment**, *a special strong bond between two people*, to parents or other important caregivers. This attachment is a strong emotional bond; it also represents the baby's first real social relationship.

BUILDING SELF-ESTEEM

The Lasting Benefits of Hugs

Infants have a basic need for physical contact—holding, cuddling, rocking, or just being near. Physical contact communicates a clear message to an infant: "You are special to me, and I care about you."

Hugging a baby is one special way to communicate this message. Hugging also shares feelings of excitement, happiness, reassurance, or pleasure with the infant. A hug can be a celebration of happiness after an infant has taken his or her first few steps; or a hug can provide reassurance that you will return after leaving the baby in the crib for his or her nap.

Research studies indicate that physical contact is important for all infants. It helps them develop positive, caring relationships with other people. Hugging does not spoil a child—instead, it shows the child that he or she is loved.

Researchers have discovered that physical contact is an important factor in this attachment. In one famous experiment, an American experimental psychologist, Harry Harlow, used substitute "mothers," monkey-shaped forms in either chicken wire or soft cloth, to raise baby monkeys. All the baby monkeys clung to the soft "mothers," regardless of which kind of "mother" held their feeding bottles. Clearly, the monkeys needed the feeling of physical closeness in addition to the nourishment of their feedings.

However, attachment requires more than physical contact. Once the baby monkeys were grown, it was clear that Harlow's experiment had had a profound effect. These monkeys did not know how to relate to other monkeys; they did not develop normal social relationships. Harlow believed this was caused by the lack of interaction between the babies and their "mothers."

Human babies, of course, are quite different from monkeys, but such research can give us clues to the process of human social development. Interaction with adults seems critical to human development as well.

All babies need lots of love. Even very young babies can experience loneliness. If a baby is left alone most of the time except for physical care, the infant begins to fail to respond to people and objects.

Social relationships are important for many animals as well as for humans. A famous example is Koko the gorilla's attachment to her favorite kitten.

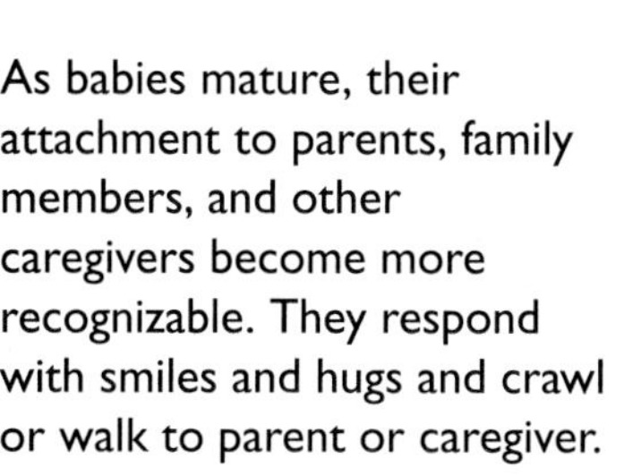

As babies mature, their attachment to parents, family members, and other caregivers become more recognizable. They respond with smiles and hugs and crawl or walk to parent or caregiver.

This problem is most likely to develop in certain kinds of institutions, where babies may receive physical care but no emotional support or social practice. However, the problem can also develop in families if the parents or caregivers consistently lack the time, energy, or ability to become emotionally and socially involved with the baby. When normal, demanding infants get so little attention and encouragement from parents or caregivers, their cries weaken, their smiles fade, and the babies become withdrawn and unresponsive.

For some babies, a lack of love and attention may result in **failure to thrive**, *a condition in which the baby does not grow and develop properly*. Failure to thrive may be caused by a physical problem, such as heart disease or the lack of proper food. However, failure to thrive can also be a physical symptom of poor emotional and social care. In these cases, parents and caregivers must be given instruction and support so that they can help the baby recover and grow. If these babies are not helped, they become unattached. Throughout development into adulthood, they will be unable to develop caring, meaningful relationships with other people.

Most parents and caregivers, however, can identify signs that the baby is making healthy attachment as he or she matures. Babies who cry to communicate various needs, gaze into the eyes of parents or caregivers, track the movements of parents or caregivers with their eyes, snuggle, cuddle, and become quiet when comforted are showing positive signs of growing attachment. As babies mature and their attachments continue to develop, they vocalize with their parents or caregivers, embrace parents or caregivers, and eventually crawl or walk to parents or caregivers.

HEALTH TIP

Failure to thrive is a specific condition that doctors can—and do—diagnose. It is, in fact, relatively uncommon. Much more common are babies' erratic growth spurts. You may feel that the baby has "stopped growing" or is not growing this month as rapidly as he or she did last month. As a rule, you should not feel worried by such changes. However, if you are concerned that the baby might be suffering from failure to thrive, it is best to take the baby to a pediatrician and discuss all your concerns openly with him or her.

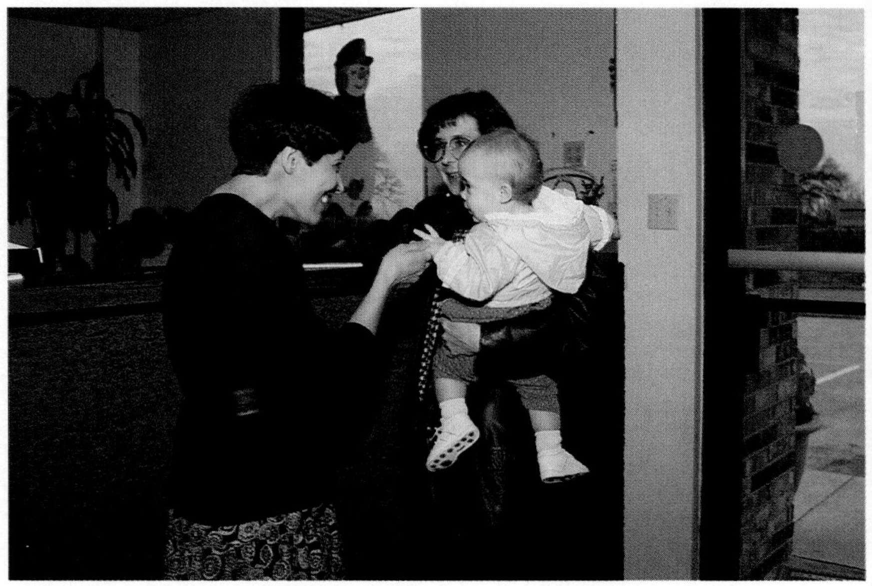

Improved memory allows older babies to realize whether they are in a familiar place with familiar people. Stranger anxiety may be less of a problem if the child is given opportunities to grow used to being around others.

Stranger Anxiety

Parents and caregivers may recognize and enjoy many signs of a baby's social development. The baby smiles brightly at a familiar face. The baby reaches up to be held. The baby laughs as she drops the ball once more and waits eagerly for her big brother to pick it up again.

Another important sign of social development is not so immediately heartwarming, but it is nonetheless a significant stage for each baby. During the second half of the first year, often around the age of eight months, babies develop **stranger anxiety**, *a fear, usually expressed by crying, of unfamiliar people.* During this period, a baby who used to sit cheerfully on anyone's lap suddenly screams and bursts into tears when an unfamiliar person approaches.

Stranger anxiety is an indicator of the baby's improving memory. At this age, the child is better able to remember the faces of parents and beloved caregivers; these are the people who provide comfort and security. Most other faces suddenly seem strange and make the baby feel fearful.

You can help a baby through this stage by reminding new people to approach the baby slowly and to give the baby time to adjust. You may also want to keep the baby's routine as regular as possible; if you can avoid it, this is not the time to introduce sudden changes in activities or caregivers. If you find the baby's stranger anxiety troubling, you can reassure yourself that this is just a stage for the baby—and it indicates a healthy social development.

Cultural Exchange

KNOWING A STRANGER

Experiments throughout the world—in American cities, isolated Guatemalan highlands, towns in Israel, and remote areas of the African Kalahari Desert—have shown that all babies experience stranger anxiety. It appears to be universal, regardless of the child's personality or the nature of child-rearing practices.

How Behavior Is Learned

An infant learns to behave in certain ways through his or her relationships with other people. What kind of behavior the baby learns depends primarily on the attitudes and expectations of the baby's parents and other caregivers.

Babies learn some behavior through their daily routine. Running water may signal bath time; the rattle of keys may mean a ride in the car. A baby begins to respond to these clues with predictable behavior.

As babies mature, they learn that certain kinds of behavior are rewarded with positive responses, such as smiles, hugs, or praise. Because love is very important to them, they begin to repeat behavior that brings approval. Babies also learn to avoid behavior that provokes negative responses, such as frowns or scoldings.

Babies are more sensitive to attitudes than to words. For example, if a mother says "no" as her ten-month-old blows food all over the high-chair tray, yet laughs at the same time, the baby thinks she approves. This kind of mixed message can be very confusing.

To help a child understand what behavior is expected, parents and caregivers must provide **consistency**, *repeatedly acting the same way*. Their responses, both verbal and nonverbal, should be consistent and should convey the same meaning. A baby will be confused if the same behavior provokes a positive response one time and a negative response the next, or if he or she continually receives mixed messages. Children react best to definite expectations. Parents and caregivers who often change their mind about expectations or who frequently switch moods make learning appropriate behavior difficult for their children.

To a very young child, everything is meant to be explored and played with. Only gradually does the child learn that not all behavior results in praise or approval.

Influences on Personality

As babies develop emotionally and socially, their personalities become increasingly evident. **Personality** is *the total of all the specific traits (such as shyness or cheerfulness) that are consistent in an individual's behavior*. To be consistent, the trait must be present over a period of time and in a variety of activities. For example, babies who always pick themselves up after a tumble and try again can be said to have the personality trait of determination or persistence.

There are many personality traits. Each trait can have many degrees. For example, a person might be described as somewhat shy or very shy. With all the possible traits and all the degrees of each, you can see why no two people are exactly alike!

Some personality traits seem to be inborn. If you observed a group of newborns for a few weeks, you would see striking differences. One baby, for example, might be very active whenever she is awake; she waves her arms and legs and squirms almost constantly. A second baby might be very different; he lies quietly but cries at the slightest change in his surroundings. A third baby may be different from both of the others; he sleeps quietly, looks around, and rarely cries except when he is hungry.

Family and environment also play an important role in shaping a child's personality. Children tend to pattern themselves after their parents. They adopt some of their parents' likes and dislikes, many of their interests, and some of their ideas. Children may imitate their parents' mannerisms and share many of their attitudes.

In spite of this strong parental influence, a wide range of personalities is possible among children in the same family. Why? Part of the reason is that each child has a unique heredity and so responds in his or her own way to the same environment. Another part of the reason is that the family environment is slightly different for each child. Family experiences for the oldest child are clearly different from those for the youngest child. Middle children, too, have different and unique experiences.

Each child's personality is also influenced by his or her **self-concept**, *a person's feelings about himself or herself.* Self-concept, in turn, is strongly influenced by the way parents and other people regard and treat the child. Babies who are cared for, praised, and admired for their individual strengths are likely to develop positive self-concepts. Babies who are belittled or are often negatively compared with other children risk developing negative self-concepts.

Every baby seems to have a unique way of reacting to the world. Inborn differences may be part of the reason, but environment has a great deal of influence.

Common Personality Traits

Each person has his or her individual personality, composed of a unique set of personality traits. However, it is common for certain clusters of personality traits to occur together. For this reason, people are sometimes considered as belonging to one of three main groups reflecting three general personality patterns. A baby's activity and behavior during the first months of life do not necessarily predict the adult personality that will develop. Still, understanding these personality patterns can help you understand and provide effective care for individual children.

The Sensitive Child

A **sensitive** child is one who, when compared with other babies, is *unusually aware of his or her surroundings and of any changes in those surroundings*. Sensitive children are often quite fussy and irritable as babies; they are more likely to cry and be difficult to comfort than other babies. Babies who cry a great deal, as sensitive babies usually do, need more than the average amount of love and tenderness. Unfortunately, their behavior often causes parents to withdraw rather than to respond with extra attention.

A baby who is easily startled and frightened is likely to become fearful of new experiences. Parents should encourage sensitive babies to explore and try new things. At the same time, parents should be especially patient and understanding with sensitive babies. In these ways, they can help their babies establish self-confidence.

The sensitive child needs more reassurance when introduced to new situations.

The Placid Child

A **placid** child is one who, when compared with other babies, is *remarkably easygoing and accepting of his or her surroundings*. The placid child is, for most families, the easiest personality type to live with. Placid children are less easily upset by changes in schedules and the demands of family life than any other personality type.

When a placid child gets older, he or she is usually cheerful and patient or simply quiet and willing. Placid children adjust easily to new people and situations. They make friends readily and seem to handle life with a minimum of fuss and upset.

Sometimes placid children can be "forgotten." Parents need to remember that these children need as much attention as sensitive and aggressive children.

The Aggressive Child

An **aggressive** child is one who, when compared with other babies, is *unusually strong-willed and determined*. The responses of aggressive babies are extreme. They eat more heartily, cry more

Aggressive babies have a way of reaching out and letting family members and caregivers know exactly what they want. These babies are usually more determined to have their own way.

Ethan seems content to examine a toy while he waits for his snack. How would you describe his personality?

loudly, and kick more strenuously than sensitive or placid babies.

Aggressive babies love activity. They enjoy trying new things and are less likely than other babies to be concerned about failure. They simply pick themselves up and try again.

Aggressive children are especially likely to express anger when they do not get their own way or are frustrated. Parents and caregivers should try to react unemotionally to these outbursts and keep the child from hurting himself or herself and from hurting others. For example, substitute a soft toy for another object the child might want to throw, and keep your voice calm and reassuring. This is when a sense of humor really helps. "Oh my! What a silly clown—angry at everything!" Sometimes the tone of the adult's voice can help calm the child, too.

As time passes, you will want to acknowledge the baby's feelings, rather than discounting them, and help the child express anger and frustration with less extreme behavior.

Parents should remember that aggressive children need love, praise, and immediate attention—usually they can't wait. They also need help in becoming aware of the feelings and interests of other people.

SECTION 2 REVIEW

CHECK YOUR UNDERSTANDING

1. What are two signs of social development that many one-month-old babies exhibit?
2. What is attachment? What kinds of development do early attachments represent?
3. What is failure to thrive? What are two possible causes of failure to thrive?
4. What is stranger anxiety?
5. How do parents' smiles and frowns help babies learn good behavior?
6. What is personality? What are two important influences on personality?
7. What are the three general personality patterns that can be observed in babies? What is one characteristic of each pattern?

DISCUSS AND DISCOVER

1. Collect at least three photographs (from magazines or other sources) of babies who exhibit various types of social interaction. Label the pictures with appropriate captions. Then display them, and explain how the caption relates to the infant's social development.
2. Talk with adults who remember you as a baby or a young child. Which type of personality did you seem to have then? What specific behaviors indicated that personality type? Do you think you still have the same personality type? Why or why not?

HELPING BABY DEVELOP A SENSE OF TRUST

In the first year, babies are almost entirely dependent on other people. The kind of care they receive determines how babies begin to view themselves and the world around them. For every baby, the foundation of a strong, healthy self-concept is trust.

RESPONSIVE CARE

A sense of trust begins to develop in newborns when they feel that their needs are being met. One of the most obvious ways to promote trust is to feed a baby who is hungry. Understanding and responding to the baby's emotional needs is just as important.

An infant who is upset or fussy needs to be soothed. However, a baby needs attention when he or she is content, as well. Here are some ways to let a baby know that you are responsive to his or her needs and wants:

- Hold and cuddle the baby often. Carry the baby close to you as you walk, both indoors and outdoors.
- When the baby is able to crawl, don't rely solely on a playpen. Give the baby the freedom to explore independently in a safe, accessible environment.
- Answer the baby's babbles and "funny noises" with your own noises, words, and sentences.
- Let the baby sense your caring and love in your facial expression, your voice, and your touch.
- Learn to read the baby's signals. When the baby smiles and coos, he or she might mean, "Let's play." Turning or looking away may be the baby's way of saying, "That's enough—time to rest."
- Calm an unhappy baby with close contact, rhythmic movement, and soothing sounds.

Your responsive care will help the baby feel secure. It lets the baby know that the world can be a satisfying place.

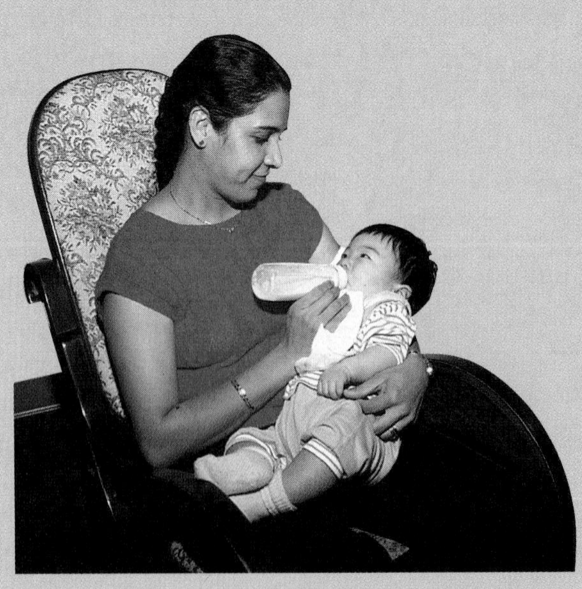

FAMILIAR ROUTINES

Following a consistent schedule is another way to encourage the baby's sense of trust. Babies seem to need a predictable daily routine in order to thrive. Start with the baby's unique pattern of eating, sleeping, and waking. Then you can work out a routine that makes sense for you and for the baby. For example, if you always hold the baby and sing to him or her after a feeding, the baby begins to learn what to expect. He or she will accept and look forward to that pattern of dependable care.

NEW FACES, NEW PLACES

Although it is important for babies to have a consistent routine, they must also learn to accept new situations. A parent or trusted caregiver can soothe away fears and help the baby feel secure in unfamiliar surroundings.

Most babies go through a stage of fearing strangers. During this period, don't force a baby to sit on an unfamiliar lap. Instead, give the baby some time to get used to the new person's presence. Stay close by and show the baby that you trust this person.

You can help the baby get used to strangers by taking him or her to stores, parks, and other places where young children play. Talk to the baby about what to expect and about what is happening. Speak in a calm, reassuring voice.

Babies who have been helped to develop a sense of trust are happy, loving, and secure. They have the confidence to explore and to learn with enthusiasm. When babies have their physical, emotional, social, and intellectual (see Chapter 10) needs met in a caring and responsive manner, they feel secure and learn to trust their caregivers, their environment, and themselves.

SUMMARY

- Emotional development deals with feelings. Social development deals with relationships.
- The type of care a baby receives and the atmosphere of the home are major influences on emotional development.
- Babies' emotions gradually become more specific and recognizable.
- Babies develop socially to satisfy their physical and emotional needs.
- Physical closeness, interaction, and a strong attachment to parents or other caregivers are necessary for normal social development.
- Behavior is learned through relationships with others. Consistency on the part of caregivers aids this process.
- Each baby has an individual personality, although general personality patterns can be identified.

REVIEWING THE FACTS

1. What is the difference between emotional development and social development? How are the two kinds of development related?
2. How can a baby's feeding schedule affect his or her emotional development?
3. What can parents do to create the best possible climate for their children's emotional and social development?
4. Why do babies cry? How should parents and caregivers respond to a baby's crying?
5. How do babies learn about feelings? What emotions or feelings do they express? How do they express them?
6. Do babies show signs of social development during the first days of life? If so, what are the signs? If not, why not?
7. What did Harry Harlow's experiment with baby monkeys show?
8. How do human babies respond when they are denied emotional support and social interaction?
9. Why is stranger anxiety a sign of a baby's social development? What else does it indicate about the baby?
10. What is consistency? Why is it important in helping babies and children learn appropriate behavior?
11. What is self-concept? How can parents and caregivers help a baby develop a positive self-concept?
12. How would you expect a sensitive baby, a placid baby, and an aggressive baby to respond to a new, noisy toy?

EXPLORING FURTHER

1. Work with a partner to write "A Baby's Bill of Rights," a list of everything babies have the right to receive from their parents. Consider making your list into a poster and hanging the poster in a location where parents might see and read it. (Sections 1 and 2)
2. Gather at least five photographs of babies who seem to be expressing various emotions. Mount the photographs on posterboard. Label each picture with the words you think the baby might be saying—if only he or she could talk. (Section 1)
3. Work with a group of classmates to consider and discuss your responses to this question: How can parents select caregivers and child care centers that will encourage babies' emotional and social development? After you have all shared your ideas, work together to write a checklist that parents might use when they are evaluating caregivers and child care centers. (Sections 1 and 2)

THINKING CRITICALLY

1. **Analyze.** What do you think happens to a person who has never learned to build trust? How do you think that lack of trust affects the person's behavior when he or she is a school-aged child? A teenager? An adult? What special problems does he or she face in becoming an effective, loving parent?
2. **Evaluate.** Who do you think is best able to encourage a baby's emotional development—the mother, the father, another relative, or a nonrelated caregiver? Why? What particular advantages do you think each person has in encouraging a baby's emotional development? What disadvantages does each have?
3. **Interpret.** Why do you think the placid child is usually considered the easiest personality type to live with? What might be the characteristics of parents who would find raising a sensitive child more satisfying? What might be the characteristics of parents who would prefer to raise an aggressive child?

CROSS-CURRICULUM CONNECTIONS

1. **Health.** What happens to babies when their parents abuse alcohol or other drugs? Specifically, what effects does the parents' substance abuse have on babies' emotional and social development? Read at least three articles about substance abuse and its effects. Then consider what impact substance abuse typically has on family life and, in particular, on young children. Give a short oral report on your findings.
2. **Writing.** Write a short essay about your own personality. In the essay, identify the most significant traits within your personality. Also include your responses to these questions: Which of your personality traits do you consider inborn? Why? How do you believe your family influenced your personality? How do you believe other aspects of your environment influenced your personality?

OBSERVING AND PARTICIPATING

Infant Emotional and Social Development

When you are observing a baby, try to stay out of the baby's line of vision, and avoid interacting with the baby's parent or caregiver. In other words, do your best to allow the adult and the infant to interact naturally—as though you were not there. When you are participating, interact with the baby as naturally as possible; focus your attention on the baby and his or her responses.

Choose one of the following activities, and spend some time observing or participating with an infant. Write a journal entry about your observations. Then discuss your observations with other students.

- **Observing.** Visit a center where several infants are cared for. Notice what techniques the caregivers use to comfort the babies when they cry. How does the technique used for each baby seem to suit that baby's particular needs?
- **Observing.** Spend some time watching babies in a shopping mall, a park, or some other public place. What signs of social development do you notice in each baby?
- **Participating.** Play a few simple games with a baby who is approaching his or her first birthday. Notice how the baby responds to familiar games and toys and to new games and toys. What do the baby's responses indicate about his or her personality type?

CHAPTER 10

Intellectual Development During the First Year

Five-year-old Martrez watches Brandon, his baby brother playing happily on the floor. Brandon giggles as he pushes and tosses the colorful balls in the air.

After a moment, Martrez is bored by Brandon. He climbs into his father's lap and asks, "Daddy, when will Brandon start going to school?"

"Oh, Martrez," his father laughs, "Brandon is just a baby. He can't go to school until he's a big boy—like you are."

"You mean he has to wait and wait until he can start learning things?"

"Well, he has to wait a long time before he can learn the things you are learning now in school, "Martrez's father explains. "But Brandon's already learning right now."

"Um-hum," says Martrez, not quite convinced. "But I didn't have to do it that way, did I, Daddy?" he asks.

"Of course you did, Martrez. You were a baby once, too, and that's how babies learn."

SECTION 1

Understanding Intellectual Development

OBJECTIVES

- Give examples of signs of intellectual growth in infants.
- Describe how a baby learns.
- Identify and give examples of Piaget's stages of learning.

TERMS TO LEARN

attention span
cause and effect
central nervous system
concrete operations period
cortex
egocentric
formal operations period
object permanence
perception
preoperational period
sensorimotor period
symbolic thinking

Babies grow and develop especially rapidly during the first year of life. Along with his or her physical, emotional, and social development, a young baby experiences rapid intellectual development.

Learning Abilities During the First Year

Right from birth, babies have a number of capabilities. Newborns can hear, see, taste, smell, and feel. They use these abilities as the building blocks of learning.

Researchers still do not fully understand the complex process of learning. They have, however, discovered a great deal about how quickly and efficiently infants learn. Understanding the basics of the learning process will help you care for babies more effectively.

Consider the differences between a newborn and a one-year-old. The newborn knows virtually nothing; the one-year-old has an impressive store of knowledge. By the age of one year, the baby has learned how to:

- Move to a desired location by creeping, crawling, or walking.
- Understand some words and perhaps even say a few words.
- Make his or her wants known, primarily by gestures.
- Play simple games, such as peek-a-boo.
- Handle objects skillfully and manipulate them—put one object inside another, for example.

The Mind-Body Connection

Newborns learn about the world primarily through their senses—sight, hearing, smell, taste, and touch. The blanket feels soft and fuzzy. A fist or a finger tastes different from milk. Mother's heartbeat sounds familiar.

For babies, as for all humans, information is transmitted from the senses through the nerves into the **central nervous system**, which consists of *the spinal cord and the brain.* The sensory information moves through the spinal cord into the brain.

The brain is the key to intellectual development. It receives and interprets the messages from the body. Gradually, the brain also develops the ability to send messages to the body, telling the body what to do. (In general, the responses of a newborn are physical reflexes; they do not originate in these kinds of messages from the brain.)

The brain is divided into distinct sections, each controlling specific functions. The major sections are identified in the diagram below. By the second or third month, the baby's **cortex**, *the outer layer of the brain, which permits more complex learning*, is clearly better developed than it was at birth. **Perception**, or *learning from the senses*, has improved, too.

Memory also begins to develop in the first few months of life. The information from the senses can be crudely interpreted

HEALTH TIP

Most babies love to be rocked, and rocking has a variety of benefits—including a benefit for the baby's brain. Gentle rocking stimulates the cortex of the brain. This stimulation helps the baby gain weight, develops the baby's sight and hearing, and promotes regular sleep habits.

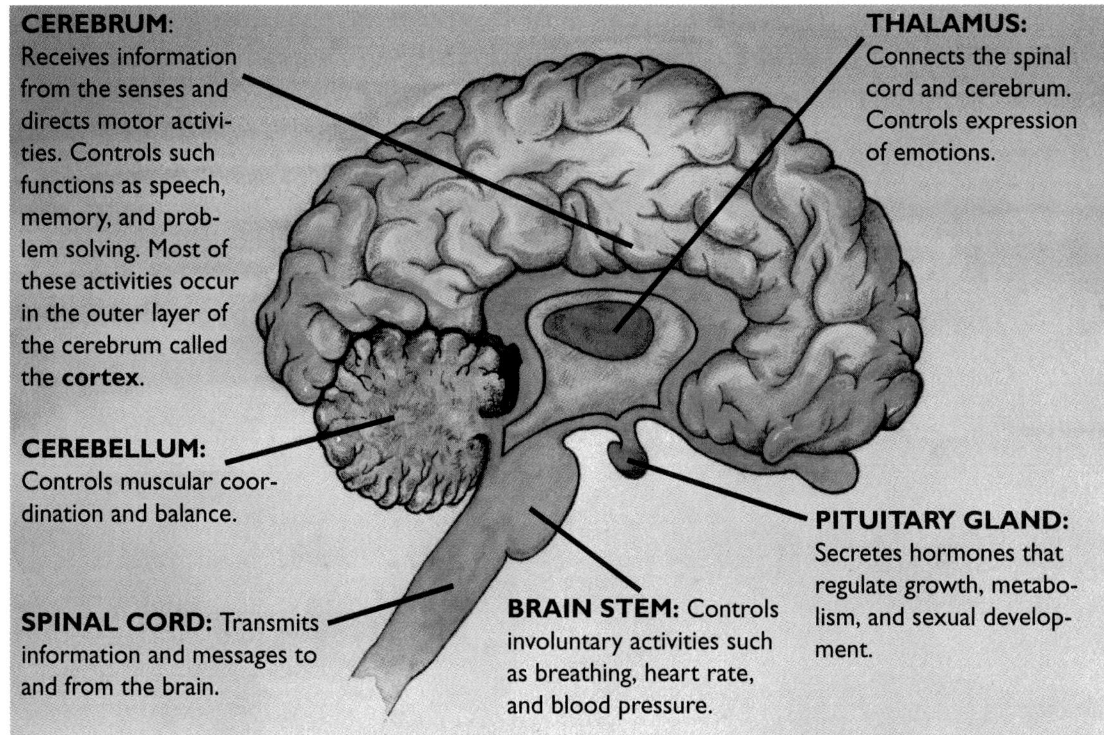

Each area of the brain has specific functions to perform.

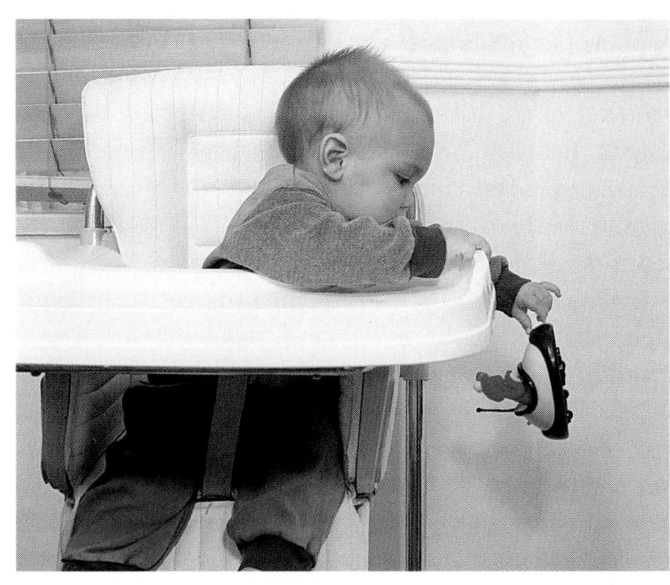

By seven months old, babies have an understanding of cause and effect. They will drop objects and delightfully watch them fall to the ground.

in light of past experiences. A two- or three-month-old baby may stop crying when someone enters the room because the baby knows that he or she is now likely to be picked up and comforted. This simple act—the baby's ceasing to cry—also indicates association. The baby associates his or her parent or other caregiver with receiving comfort.

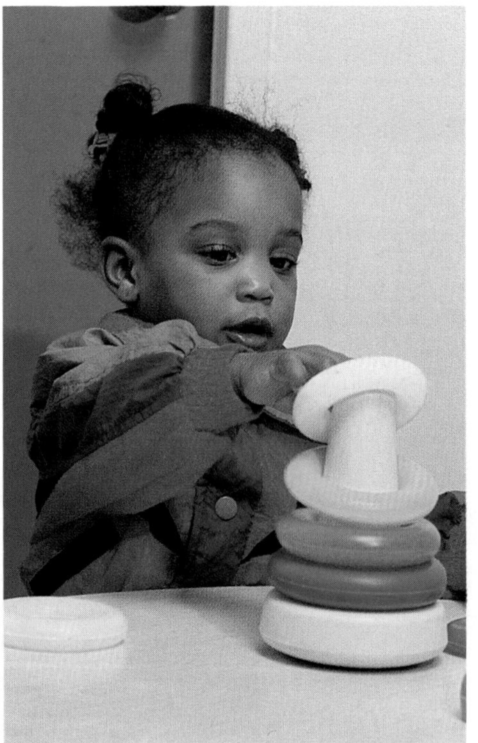

When this little girl was six months old, she would have used these colorful rings to suck on and squeeze. Now that she is older, she begins to recognize similarites and differences and can stack the rings according to size.

In these first few months, babies also begin to develop an understanding of **cause and effect**, *the concept that one action results in another action or condition.* When a baby closes his or her eyes, it gets dark. When the baby opens them again, it gets light. A baby can reach out a hand and feel a soft, warm surface. Sucking causes milk to flow. If the baby stops sucking, the milk stops. In short, when the infant does something, something else happens, and it happens consistently. Gradually, the baby develops some awareness of such control.

As babies' motor skills develop, cause-and-effect learning changes. By seven or eight months, babies can throw things deliberately. They can pull the string on a toy and make the toy move. At this age, babies have a better understanding of their own power to make certain things happen.

A baby's **attention span**—*the length of time a person can concentrate on a task without getting bored*—gives valuable information about his or her intellectual development. If the same object is presented over and over again, the baby's response to the object will eventually become less enthusiastic. The baby's diminishing response is a way of saying, "That's old stuff. I've seen it before." Generally, very bright babies have a short attention span; they tend to lose interest sooner than babies of average or below-average intelligence. (However, beyond infancy, bright children typically have a longer attention span than others their age.)

AVERAGE INTELLECTUAL DEVELOPMENT

BIRTH TO TWELVE MONTHS

ONE TO TWO MONTHS

- Follows moving objects with eyes.
- Gains information through senses.
- Prefers faces to objects.
- Cries to indicate needs.
- Can distinguish between familiar and unfamiliar voices.

THREE TO FOUR MONTHS

- Recognizes caregivers' faces.
- Can distinguish between familiar and unfamiliar faces.
- Grasps objects that touch hand.
- Tries to swipe at objects.
- Interested in own hands and feet.
- Practices making sounds.
- Responds when caregiver talks.
- Smiles and laughs.

FIVE TO SIX MONTHS

- Is alert for longer periods of time, up to two hours.
- Reaches for objects and grasps them with entire hand.
- Studies objects carefully.
- Looks for objects that are dropped.
- Plays peek-a-boo.
- Recognizes own name.
- Distinguishes between friendly and angry voices.
- Makes sounds to indicate pleasure and displeasure.

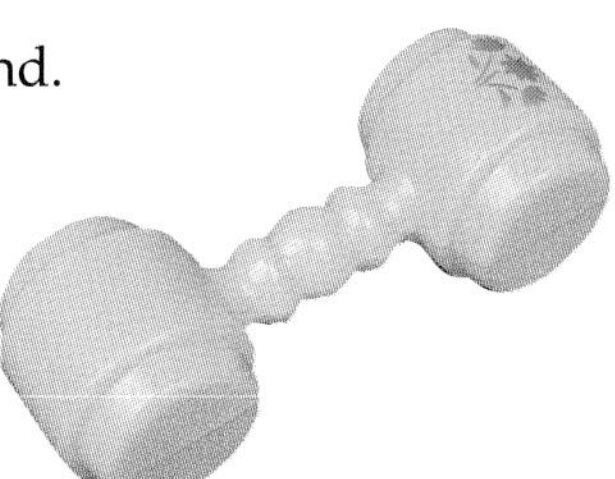

(Continued on next page)

AVERAGE INTELLECTUAL DEVELOPMENT (cont'd.)

SEVEN TO EIGHT MONTHS

- Imitates the actions of others.
- Begins to understand cause and effect.
- Remembers things that have happened.
- Smiles at self in mirror.
- Sorts objects by size.
- Solves simple problems.
- Recognizes some words.
- Babbles, imitating inflections of speech.

NINE TO TEN MONTHS

- Searches for hidden objects.
- Handles medium-sized objects skillfully.
- Takes objects out of containers and puts them back in.
- Plays pat-a-cake.
- Responds to some words.
- May say a few words.
- Obeys simple commands or directions.

ELEVEN TO TWELVE MONTHS

- Manipulates objects skillfully.
- Likes to look at picture books.
- Fits blocks or boxes inside one another.
- Knows parts of body.
- Can pick up small objects with forefinger and thumb.
- Recognizes many words.
- Speaks some words regularly.

Piaget's Theories

Jean Piaget, a Swiss psychologist who died in 1980, had a remarkable influence on what we know about how children learn. His theories of learning and the research they inspired have helped us better understand and appreciate infants and children.

While investigating the development of intelligence, Piaget found that children's responses fell into patterns according to their age. This timetable seemed to control the development of intellectual skills. Piaget believed it suggested that the capacity for logical thought is not learned, but is determined—along with such characteristics as eye color and sex—in the genes. These capacities do not mature, however, until they are used.

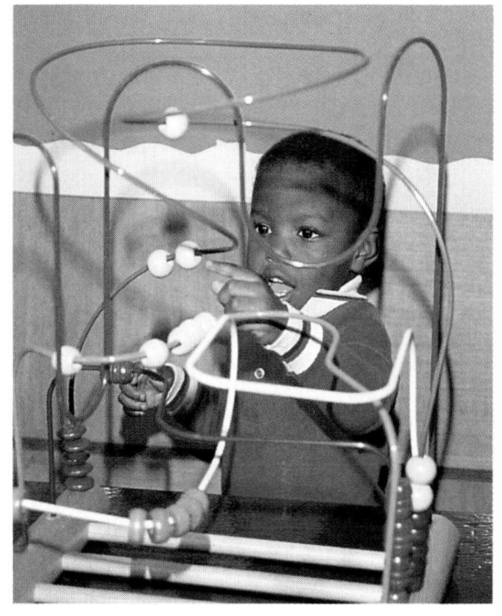

Children cannot be forced by parents or teachers to develop understanding any faster than their abilities mature. This is why, in nearly every case, it is a waste of effort to try to teach a two-year-old to read. On the other hand, children who do not get the chance to apply their developing abilities and test their limitations may never reach their full intellectual ability.

According to Piaget, learning stages appear in the same order in all children. What differs is the ages at which the stages develop, although average ages can be given. He identified four major periods of development and gave them these names: sensorimotor period, preoperational period, concrete operations period, and formal operations period.

The Sensorimotor Period

The **sensorimotor period** is *Piaget's first stage of learning, lasting from birth until about the age of two, during which babies learn primarily through their senses and their own actions.* During this period, a baby is completely **egocentric**, *thinking only about himself or herself.*

During the sensorimotor period, usually around the age of ten months, a baby develops the concept of **object permanence**, *an understanding of the fact that objects continue to exist even when they are not in sight.* At four months, Maria drops her rubber ring toy and it rolls behind her. She shows no concern; she looks for something else to play with. By eleven months, Maria's memory has improved a great deal. When her ball rolls out of sight, she actively looks for it. She also looks for her favorite stuffed animal when she feels lonely. It is clear that she has learned the concept of object permanence.

The sensorimotor period can be broken down into six shorter stages. At each stage, a baby has specific intellectual abilities. The chart on page 298 explains the stages within the sensorimotor period. It will help you better understand how early learning occurs.

SAFETY TIP

During the later stages of the sensorimotor period, babies' curiosity often leads them to put things into their mouths and to try opening whatever is closed, including doors, drawers, and cabinets. Although curiosity helps the baby learn, safety is of the utmost importance. Anything dangerous must be kept out of a baby's reach. During this period, it is especially important to keep dangerous or poisonous materials locked away; baby-proof locks should be added to most other cabinets.

When a toy is out of sight, an infant will simply find a new interest. By four months, however, the memory has improved and the baby will actively look for favorite objects.

THE SENSORIMOTOR PERIOD

BIRTH TO AGE TWO

STAGE	APPROXIMATE AGES	CHARACTERISTICS
Stage 1	Birth to one month	• Practices inborn reflexes. • Does not understand self as separate person.
Stage 2	One to four months	• Combines two or more reflexes. • Develops hand-mouth coordination.
Stage 3	Four to eight months	• Acts intentionally to produce results. • Improves hand-eye coordination.
Stage 4	Eight to twelve months	• Begins to solve problems. • Finds partially hidden objects. • Imitates others.
Stage 5	Twelve to eighteen months	• Finds hidden objects. • Explores and experiments. • Understands that objects exist independently.
Stage 6	Eighteen to twenty-four months	• Solves problems by thinking through sequences. • Can think using symbols. • Begins imaginative thinking.

The Preoperational Period

The **preoperational period** is *Piaget's second stage of learning, lasting typically from age two to age seven, during which children think about everything in terms of their own activities and in terms of what they perceive at the moment*. Since their intellectual processes are not fully developed, during the preoperational period children may believe that the moon follows them around, or that dreams fly in through the window at night. A child in this stage may think that 8 ounces (237 mL) of water becomes "more to drink" when it is poured from a short, wide glass into a tall, thin glass. The child sees that the water is higher in the second glass and concludes that there must be more of it.

In the preoperational period, children begin to understand abstract terms like *love* and *beauty*. Concentration, though, is limited to one thing at a time. A child cannot think about both pain and the softness of a kitten at the same time, for example. Children this age tend to solve problems by pretending or imitating, rather than by thinking the problems through. You can observe many examples of this "pretending" behavior in children this age. For example, if a toy has been broken or the water has been left running, a young child may blame the mistake on an imaginary friend, saying with complete conviction, "Georgia did it." In many cases, children at this period may not even be aware of what is real and what is make-believe.

Children in the preoperational period love to act out situations like playing fire fighter. However, they have trouble thinking about things that they aren't experiencing at the moment.

Pretending and imitating are the tools that young children use to understand their world.

The Concrete Operations Period

The **concrete operations period** is *Piaget's third stage of learning, lasting usually from seven to eleven years of age, during which children are able to think logically but still learn best from direct experiences.* When problem solving during this stage, children still rely on actually being able to see or experience the problem. However, logical thinking is possible. Children understand that pouring water from one container to another does not change the amount of water. They can also comprehend that operations can be reversed. For example, subtraction will "undo" addition, and division is the reverse of multiplication. During this stage, children also learn to make more complex categories, such as classifying kinds of animals or types of foods.

The Formal Operations Period

The **formal operations period** is *Piaget's fourth stage of learning, lasting from about age eleven through adulthood, during which children become capable of abstract thinking*. In other words, people in this stage are able to think about what might have been the cause of an event without really experiencing that cause. This ability allows problem solving just by thinking. Abstract thinking also allows adolescents to make more realistic future plans and goals. They do not automatically accept everything that they hear or read; instead, they are able to think things through critically and logically. Adolescents can also form ideals and understand deeper, less obvious meanings or subtle messages.

Applying Piaget's Ideas

Although Piaget's theories have been criticized by some for setting boundaries of learning stages too rigidly, his work revolutionized our understanding of child development. He focused attention on the intellectual development of infants, an area of study previously ignored. He drew attention to the importance of developmental steps that researchers continue to study today.

Piaget's work shows that adult intelligence has its origins in infancy. However, his work also shows that attempts to impose adult ideas or understanding on children are bound to fail. Why? Older children can learn through **symbolic thinking**, *the use of words and numbers to represent ideas*. Younger children, who have not yet developed symbolic thinking, rely on concrete experiences. For example, the statement "I have three balls" means nothing to a young child. The child has to see the balls. A further example is the fact that a three-year-old will hold up three fingers when asked how old he or she is, even though the child may say the words, too. The preschool child needs lessons presented with objects or activities, not just symbols. Verbal instruction from a teacher or parent has only a minor role in learning during the early years.

The abstract concept of "three" has no meaning for a young child unless it is associated with something concrete—like three balls or three fingers.

ASK THE EXPERTS

Infants' Perception

Dr. Asa Hilliard is a Fuller E. Callaway Professor of Urban Education at Georgia State University.

I am fascinated by babies. I enjoy caring for them, and I love to watch them. Recently, I have begun to wonder how much babies actually understand about what goes on around them. What can you tell me about how infants perceive their world?

This is an especially interesting question, and our response to it is changing. When I did my first child development work, students learned either that infants saw the world as a big, buzzing confusion or that infants didn't really notice the world around them until they were about six months old. Of course, current research shows that neither theory is accurate.

Now we recognize that infants come into the world with the ability not only to see and hear what goes on around them, but also with the ability to organize the information they receive from their senses. Young babies are clearly able to select from their environment the things they find interesting; they are further able to operate on those things until they become familiar with them. Infants demonstrate a definite pattern of seeking order in their environment.

Emotionally, infants who are cared for and nurtured apparently feel very comfortable and very free. These feelings encourage the babies' expressiveness and exploration. It's important to remember that, before birth, a baby has been very well cared for—protected and nourished—within the mother's body. If this same care is extended to the baby after birth, then we know children do quite well emotionally.

Parents and other family members must provide the infant with enough comfort and enough stimulation to allow the baby to feel trusting. When parents allow themselves to respond openly and lovingly to their baby, when they trust their own instincts in caring for their baby, they can provide an incredible push to the infant's awareness and opportunity to learn.

Asa Hilliard, Ph.d.

Heredity Versus Environment

As you know, there is continuing disagreement about the influences of heredity and environment on the development of children. Much of the heredity-environment debate focuses on intelligence. In the past, intellectual ability was thought to be determined mainly by a child's inheritance—bright parents had bright children. However, findings now indicate that a child's environment can actually increase or decrease his or her intelligence.

It is true, however, that limits for intelligence are present at birth. Even the most stimulating environment cannot raise a person's intelligence beyond that limit. Most people, though, never develop or use their full potential (the highest level of learning possible for an individual). Understanding how intellectual development progresses and how babies learn can help you guide children toward fulfilling their potential.

Both heredity and environment influence intelligence. The influence of heredity is determined before birth. Environmental influences begin before birth, but continue to affect development throughout life.

SECTION 1 REVIEW

CHECK YOUR UNDERSTANDING

1. List at least three things that the average one-year-old child can do because of the learning process.
2. What is the central nervous system? What is its most important function?
3. What is perception? How does a baby's perception change during the first year of life?
4. Explain what an attention span is.
5. What is the name of Piaget's first stage of learning? How do babies learn during this period?
6. What is the name of Piaget's fourth stage of learning? What is the most significant accomplishment during this period?
7. What did Piaget's work show about adult intelligence?

DISCUSS AND DISCOVER

1. Using either baby books or magazines, collect photographs of infants at different ages. Share the photographs with another student. Together, discuss what behaviors you see that indicate a specific learning ability.
2. Define and then discuss the importance of object permanence. How do you think the development of object permanence affects a baby's behavior? How do you think it affects the baby's parents or caregivers?
3. Explain how Piaget's description of intellectual development can be compared with motor skills.

SECTION 2

Helping Babies Learn

OBJECTIVES

- Discuss ways parents and caregivers can help babies' intellectual growth.
- Identify toys appropriate for a baby's age.
- Explain how babies develop communication skills.

Like physical, emotional, and social development, intellectual development of an infant is closely linked to the responsiveness of others. That is, babies learn more and learn faster when parents and caregivers comfort them, smile at them, talk to them, and play with them. A baby treated this way is likely to be brighter than a similar child who does not receive loving, attentive care. Parents are babies' first and most important teachers.

Providing Care

Even the youngest babies learn about the world from the care they receive. A newborn who feels hungry expresses that feeling by crying. When a parent hears that cry, picks up the baby, speaks soothingly, and feeds the baby, that uncomfortable hunger goes away. If parents and caregivers respond this way whenever the baby feels hungry and cries, the infant learns that all these events are related. There is a consistent pattern—discomfort, crying, parent or caregiver, feeding, and comfort.

If this pattern is not established, the baby senses no relationship between his or her expression of discomfort and the comfort provided by a parent or caregiver. Perhaps the baby's hunger cries are often ignored. Perhaps the baby is fed on a strict schedule decided by someone else and not related to the baby's own sensations. In these cases, there is no predictable pattern for the baby to learn.

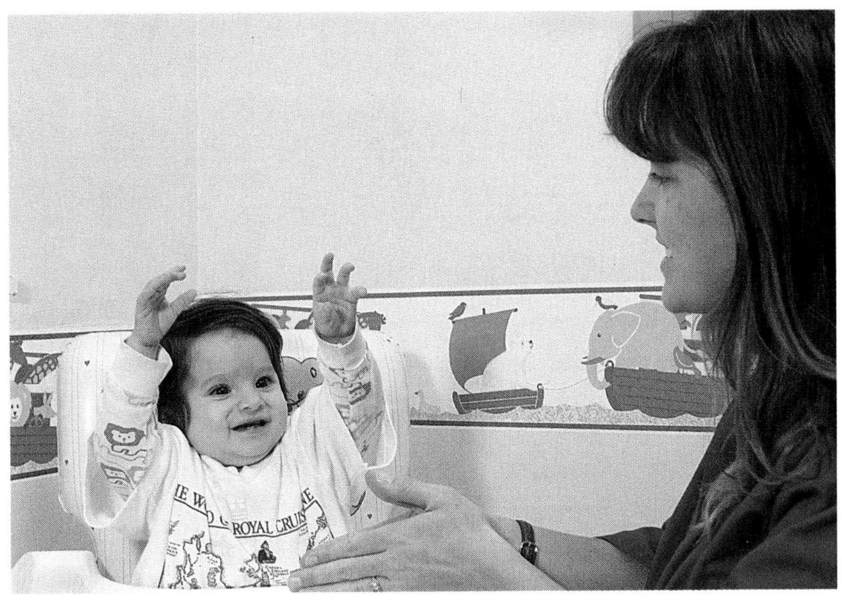

Babies who receive loving care and attention are more likely to approach their full potential, in learning as well as in other areas of development.

When babies receive attentive care in response to their individual needs, they learn that their behavior has consequences, that they can affect and change their environment. This care and learning, in turn, motivates babies to learn more about the world.

Encouraging Learning

Those who care for children have a real influence on the children's intellectual development. Encouraging learning does not require money or special toys. Rather, it depends on the attention, knowledge, and time of parents and other caregivers. Here are some specific suggestions for encouraging learning:

- **Learn about child development.** Understanding how an average child develops can help you provide learning experiences that are appropriate for the age and individual needs of a child.
- **Give your time and attention.** No baby needs attention every waking moment. However, you can help a baby thrive—and learn—just by talking to the baby and playing simple games with him or her.
- **Provide positive feedback.** When the baby demonstrates a new skill or tries out a new activity, show your pleasure and respond with praise. Your reaction will encourage the baby to keep trying new things.

BUILDING SELF-ESTEEM

Encouraging Safe Exploration

Babies need a secure environment in which they can explore freely. Parents and other caregivers should encourage this exploration. However, their first consideration should be that the baby is safe from dangerous situations and materials. You can use the Positive Parenting Skills "Keeping Children Safe and Healthy" on pages 344-345 to make sure that a home or living area is safe for an infant.

Take a look at everything that is going on in this scene. What sights, sounds, and other sensations does the child experience? How does taking a child to new places enrich learning?

TOYS ACROSS TIME AND CULTURES

Toys are more than "just fun" for children. Throughout time and across cultures, toys have helped children learn and kept them entertained. Even cultural differences can be noted in toys from several hundred years ago. Balls are a good example. Prehistoric children amused themselves with smooth, rounded stones. The Egyptians made balls from painted wood, or colored leather or reeds. The Celts made balls filled with air from bladders of sheep. The Japanese used tissue paper and string to construct their balls. The materials common to the region where the families lived were used to make the toy. In each case, a child's cultural environment influenced the type of ball constructed.

- **Express your love.** Use your personal style to show your love for the baby. You'll be helping the baby grow self-confident and encouraging him or her to try more—and to learn more.

To encourage learning, allow the baby as much freedom of movement at home as possible. In the first few months, this may involve moving the baby from room to room to be with the family. A baby who spends times in different rooms and has the companionship of family members can experience and learn more than a baby who is kept in a crib most of the time. Older babies who can crawl or walk should not be restricted to playpens for long periods of time. It is better to childproof as much of the home as possible and to monitor the child's activities. Learning occurs best when children can explore and try new things.

The Positive Parenting Skills on pages 312-313 presents more ideas for creating a stimulating environment and helping babies learn.

Toys—The Tools of Learning

Ten-month-old Beth sits on the kitchen floor, thumping a spoon against the bottom of a saucepan. She has discovered her own "educational toy." With it, she learns that a certain action will produce a particular sound. She delights in the sound and in her own power to produce it.

For children, play is work as well as pleasure. Researchers have found that playtime is not aimless or wasted. Rather, playtime is essential to intellectual development. Toys are the tools with which a child learns.

Play is also a physical necessity through which growth and development take place. When a baby shakes a rattle, stacks blocks, throws a ball, or chews on a teething toy, the activity is not just for amusement. These are serious, absorbing tasks through which babies strengthen their muscles, refine their motor skills, and learn about the world.

Infants are just as happy to be playing with simple household objects like these as expensive toys. Be sure, however, that all playthings are safe and suitable for the baby's age.

Different Toys for Different Ages

Because babies mature and change rapidly during the first year, their toys need to change, too. Here are some ideas about appropriate toys for different stages:

- **Birth to three months.** A baby at this age can do little except look and listen. Bright colors and interesting sounds stimulate development of the senses. A mobile hung above the crib is interesting for the baby to watch. The baby's random arm and leg movements can set the objects in motion and produce sounds. Brightly colored crib liners, wallpaper, and pictures also provide interest.
- **Four to six months.** The sense of touch is important during this period. Babies need things to touch, handle, bang, shake, suck, and chew. Choose toys that are small enough to handle easily but too large to swallow. All items and pieces should be at least 1½ inches (3.8 cm) across. Teething rings, cups, rattles, and plastic toys are good choices. Stuffed toys are fun to touch, and toys that squeak give results for the baby's actions. At this age, babies like simple picture books. Choose washable books with colorful pictures of familiar objects.
- **Seven to nine months.** Babies still need things to handle, throw, pound, bang, and shake. Anything that makes a noise fascinates babies of this age. They enjoy blocks, balls, large plastic beads that pop apart, and roly-poly toys. Safe household items are just as interesting as store-bought toys. Stacking toys, pots and pans with lids, and plastic containers make great playthings.
- **Ten to twelve months.** Babies of this age need things to creep after. Those who are already walking like toys to push or pull. During this period, children especially enjoy toys to manipulate. Baskets, boxes, and other containers are fun. Babies like to put things into them and then dump them out again. Simple books are good for looking at alone or for brief storytimes during the day or before bed.

Choose toys that are appropriate for the child's age and development. Once children start to walk, they enjoy push toys.

When choosing playthings for a young child, look for toys that encourage participation and use. Younger children need simple toys. As a baby's abilities increase, toys can be more complex.

Toys, especially those labeled "educational," can be expensive and may be limited in their function and usefulness. You can provide a baby with as much fun and learning by making common household items available. Try offering the baby items such as these: plastic measuring spoons, a set of plastic or metal measuring cups, a clean bucket, a set of plastic bowls, a metal pan or mixing bowl and a large spoon, a large cardboard box with a "window" cut in it. You may be surprised at the variety of ways young children play with these items.

When you do buy toys, try to choose those that will remain interesting and appropriate for a number of years. A set of blocks is a good example. At the age of six months, Reuben grasped and inspected his blocks. By his first birthday, he could stack several blocks into a tower. At age three, he used the blocks to make roads for his cars. Now, at age six, Reuben creates elaborate houses and castles, using every available block.

SAFETY TIP

Common household objects often make the best toys for babies, but they must be chosen carefully. Never allow a baby or young child to play with plastic bags; small objects that could be swallowed; any objects that might splinter, tear, or break; or any sharp or pointed objects.

Developing Communication Skills

One of the major tasks for infants is to learn to communicate effectively with others. This skill depends on development in all areas—physical, emotional, social, and intellectual. There are wide differences in the rate of development from baby to baby. However, a normal baby should show steady improvement in communication skills.

PARENTING IN ACTION

Learning in the Park

Seven-month-old Tina sat in a playpen beside a park bench. Her mother was nearby, helping Tina's four-year-old sister play on the swing and the slide.

Tina watched them from time to time, but she gave most of her attention to a red plastic cup. She turned the cup over and over, staring at it intently. Then she started chewing on the bottom, the rim, and the handle of the cup. Occasionally, she stopped chewing for a minute and banged the cup on the bottom of the playpen.

After a while, Tina grew tired of chewing and banging. She dropped the cup and began pulling herself up to a standing position. When she succeeded, she clung to the edge of the playpen and laughed happily. Tina's mother turned and smiled appreciatively. "Look at you, Tina," she called.

Tina sat down suddenly. She looked for a moment as if she might cry. Then, she reached up and tried to stand again. Over and over, she pulled herself up, stood for two or three minutes, and then lost her balance.

Finally, Tina sat down with a particularly loud thump. She had had enough of standing, and there was nothing new to play with. Bored, Tina began to cry.

"I'm coming, Tina," answered her mother. A moment later, she was lifting Tina out of the playpen and chatting happily about the swings and slides. "Look, Tina, there goes Laurel down the slide. See what your big sister learned today? One day you'll learn to go down the slide, too."

THINK AND DISCUSS

1. What were Tina's learning experiences in the park? What stage of the sensorimotor period do her experiences reflect?
2. What toy did Tina play with? How did that toy facilitate her learning?
3. What did Tina's mother do to encourage Tina's learning? What else do you think she should have done? Why?
4. Compare what Tina learned during her time in the park with what her older sister Laurel learned.

Communicating Without Words

Babies communicate long before they are able to talk. By the end of the first year, even without words, they can effectively make most of their needs and wants known.

Crying is a baby's first means of communication. Discomfort automatically causes crying. Someone usually responds to the baby's cries and attempts to relieve the discomfort. Within a month or so, the baby's crying takes on a pattern. A cry is followed by a pause to listen for reactions. If no response is obvious, the baby resumes crying.

The baby soon develops different cries for different problems. A cry indicating hunger is interrupted by sucking movements. A cry of pain may include groans and whimpers. Those providing care can usually identify the baby's problem by the type of cry.

A baby also communicates by making special sounds. Some noises just provide practice in the use of the voice. The nonsense syllables of babbling, for instance, help the baby learn to make sounds needed for speech. Other sounds, such as giggles, grunts, and shrieks, carry obvious messages.

Babies also communicate effectively with movements and gestures. It's clear a wiggling baby just does not want to get dressed. An eleven-month-old who pushes away a bowl of usually favorite food has had enough to eat. A baby who clings with both arms to a parent's leg is showing a sure sign of fear or shyness. The use of gestures continues into adulthood, but they are used more to reinforce words than as a substitute for words.

BUILDING SELF-ESTEEM

Talking Is Fun!

When parents and caregivers spend time talking with infants, they are helping infants to learn about their environment. Talking together is a wonderful way to build feelings of security, too. During the first few months of life, infants seem to enjoy the attention and close contact involved in having adults talk to them. As they grow older, infants begin to focus more on the words they hear. They may begin to respond to language with their own sounds and babbling. A back-and-forth pattern of talking and listening can develop between a caregiver and an infant. This pattern encourages the baby's language development.

Learning to Speak

Before a baby can learn to talk, he or she must learn to associate meanings with words. This is a gradual process. It depends on the parents and other caregivers talking to the baby, even when the baby doesn't appear to respond. For example, when you take a baby for a walk, you can talk about what you see. Use simple words, but not baby talk. Tell the baby the names of

When you talk to an infant and identify names of objects, you are laying a good foundation for the child's speech development.

everyday objects. Although the infant won't understand much of what you say, you are beginning to establish an important habit. Listening to other people talk—especially directly to him or her—is essential for an infant's language development.

A newborn, of course, is physically unable to speak. Over the first year, physical changes take place that allow the baby to make the sounds necessary for speech.

Babies get ready for real speech by babbling—repeating syllables and sounds. You may have heard babies endlessly repeating consonant and vowel sounds such as "mamamamamama" or "gogogogo." This kind of babbling is a baby's preparation for saying recognizable words. Adults can encourage this babbling—and thus encourage language development—by responding to and imitating the baby's sounds.

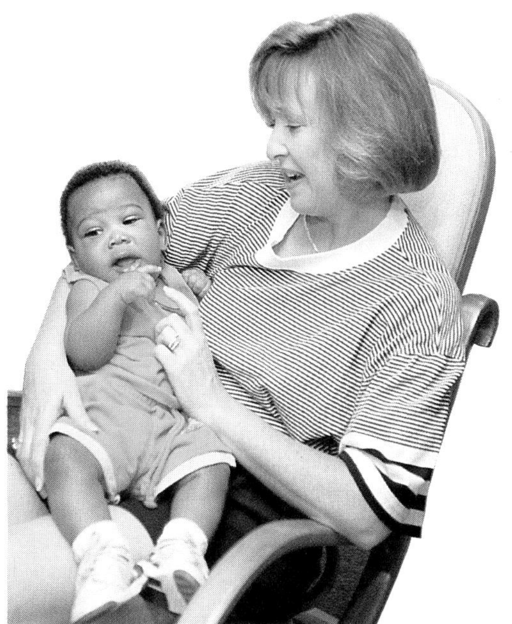

A child's first real words are usually understandable between the ages of eight and fifteen months. Because the infant typically has been babbling and coming close to real word sounds for some time, it isn't easy to know exactly when a specific word is purposely spoken. First words are usually common, simple words that have special meaning for the baby, such as "mama," "dada," or "bye-bye." Most children don't have a large vocabulary or combine words into simple sentences until after their first birthday.

SECTION 2 REVIEW

CHECK YOUR UNDERSTANDING

1. What do very young babies learn when they receive consistent, attentive care?
2. How does expressing love for a baby help that baby learn?
3. What kinds of toys are appropriate for babies from birth until around the age of three months? Why?
4. What do babies around the ages of ten to twelve months enjoy doing? What kinds of toys are appropriate for them?
5. Before they learn to talk, do babies communicate? If so, how? If not, why not?
6. What is babbling? What is its purpose?

DISCUSS AND DISCOVER

1. Visit toy stores or look through catalogs, and identify six different toys for infants. Evaluate and compare the toys, considering appropriateness, appeal, and price. Which of the toys would you buy for a baby? Why?
2. Why is consistent, attentive care so important for a baby? Do you believe babies who spend time in child care centers or with babysitters can receive that kind of care? If so, how? If not, why not? Discuss your ideas with other students.
3. Explain how communication skills are related to a child's physical, social, emotional, and intellectual skills.

CREATING A STIMULATING ENVIRONMENT

Babies begin learning the moment they are born. Parents and other caregivers influence both what and how a baby learns. They can offer a variety of appropriate experiences that will help the baby use his or her natural learning abilities fully. Here are some suggestions for helping infants develop their senses and abilities.

Establishing a good learning environment is a natural part of providing loving care for an infant. Holding, cuddling, gentle stroking, and soft singing all stimulate an infant's senses. They also communicate a message of love to the baby.

Very young babies should have something interesting to look at, but just one or two things at a time. Simple shapes and bright or contrasting colors attract babies' interest. If you are decorating a special room or area for a baby, try to use colorful decals, posters, pictures, crib sheets, or wallpaper.

A mobile hung over the crib provides both color and movement for the baby to watch. You can also hold a bright toy not far from the baby's face and then move the toy slowly, letting the baby's eyes follow it.

Infants like human faces even better than colorful pictures or toys. Let the baby look into your eyes as you hold and play with him or her—and enjoy looking back into the baby's eyes!

You can also stimulate learning by surrounding the baby with interesting things to touch. Offering a variety of textures is more important than providing a great number of toys. Stuffed toys can have different textures, from a furry teddy bear to a simple cotton beanbag. Different shapes encourage the baby to touch and explore, too. Small plastic squeeze bottles and empty plastic containers with secured lids are both educational and inexpensive.

Babies learn from listening, too. The familiar voice of the primary caregiver is the first sound a baby learns to recognize. The different voices of other family members and caregivers provide other listening experiences. Rattles and squeak toys introduce different kinds of sounds.

Babies delight in music, whether it comes from a wind-up toy, a recording, or a caregiver's singing. The rhythm of some music is exciting; so is "dancing" securely in the arms of a caring adult. The rhythm of other music is soothing— especially when a parent or caregiver cuddles the baby and rocks gently in a rocking chair.

As babies begin to experiment with their voice, they soon learn that their own sounds bring responses from an attentive caregiver. When you care for a baby, talk to him or her. Imitating each other's sounds can be fun for both of you. Reading to a baby is also a good way to help the infant become familiar with the sounds of words.

A stimulating environment can help babies learn about their own abilities to move. As the baby starts to reach and grasp, reinforce these skills by encouraging the baby to reach for a special toy. Let the baby have attractive objects, such as a shiny spoon or a set of colorful blocks, that motivate the use of small muscles. As the baby's large muscle skills develop, gently pull the baby into a sitting or standing position on your lap. Once the baby is ready to take a few steps, be sure your hand is there for the baby to hold—providing both stability and security.

SUMMARY

- Babies first learn through their senses, but they gradually develop memory, learn cause-and-effect relationships, and develop a longer attention span.
- Jean Piaget, a Swiss psychologist, developed important theories of learning; he asserted that all children go through the same four stages of learning.
- Both heredity and environment influence learning.
- An infant's intellectual development is linked to the responsiveness of others, especially of parents and other important caregivers.
- Babies need a safe, stimulating environment for learning. Toys are tools for learning.
- In the first year of life, learning is a combination of intellectual ability and motor skill development.
- Communication skills depend on development in all areas—physical, emotional, social, and intellectual.

REVIEWING THE FACTS

1. What is the cortex? What kinds of learning does it permit?
2. Briefly describe how an infant might begin to develop an understanding of cause and effect.
3. What are three signs of intellectual development that can be observed in most babies three to four months old?
4. What are the four learning periods identified by Piaget?
5. During which learning period do children begin to understand abstract terms? About how old are children during this learning period?
6. During which learning period do children begin to learn through symbolic thinking? About how old are children during this learning period?
7. Who are a baby's most important teachers? Why?
8. What is a baby's first means of communication? What are two messages a baby can communicate this way?
9. Do newborns talk? Why or why not?
10. Should parents and other caregivers respond to babies' babbling? If so, how? If not, why not?

EXPLORING FURTHER

1. Watch an educational television program, such as *Sesame Street*. List the teaching techniques used in the show, and analyze those techniques in terms of Piaget's theories. Discuss your ideas with a group of classmates. (Section 1)
2. Design and make a simple toy for a baby. Present your toy to a group of other students. Let them evaluate the toy in terms of safety, appeal, and appropriateness. (Section 2)
3. Select a specific "educational toy" for infants. Discuss the purpose of the toy. Then explain how babies could use common household objects to achieve the same purpose. (Section 2)
4. Read about a company that provides "learning experiences" for infants. Examine the company's advertising, and, if possible, visit some of its classes. Would you recommend that parents use the services of the company for their babies? Why or why not? (Section 2)
5. Make up at least two songs or chants that would be fun to use in encouraging an infant's babbling. Write your songs or chants and then perform them—if possible, for a baby. Share your experience with the class. (Section 2)

THINKING CRITICALLY

1. **Evaluate.** Why is a short attention span a sign of relatively high intelligence in an infant? What do you think a short attention span indicates about a school-aged child? Why?
2. **Interpret.** Why do you think most people never develop or use their full potential for learning? Do you think people should strive to fulfill their intellectual potential more completely? If so, how? If not, why not?
3. **Synthesize.** Why do you think some parents try to teach their babies to recognize letters and words or to play musical instruments? How would you expect a normally intelligent child to respond? Would you expect a different response from a child with an unusually high intelligence? Why or why not?

CROSS-CURRICULUM CONNECTIONS

1. **Reading.** Read about the Bayley Scales of Infant Development. What is it? When and by whom was it created? How is it used? Discuss your findings with other students.
2. **Science.** Ask three or more young volunteers (in the range of two to ten years old) to help you with an experiment. Let each child watch as you pour water from a short, wide glass into a tall, narrow glass. Ask the volunteers: "Is there more water in this tall glass than there was in the short glass?" Record the children's responses. Then discuss whether and how your results agree with Piaget's theories.

OBSERVING AND PARTICIPATING

Intellectual Development

When you observe an infant, don't start by considering the baby's exact age. Instead, watch how the infant behaves and reacts. Try to determine the baby's stage in the sensorimotor period. Then you may want to check the baby's age and see whether it corresponds, at least roughly, to the age given for the stage you observed.

Choose one of the activities below, and spend time observing or participating with an infant. Record your observations in your journal. Then compare them with the observations of other students.

- **Observing.** Observe a parent or caregiver playing with a six- to nine-month-old. What does the adult do to engage and encourage the baby? How does the baby respond? What is the baby learning?
- **Participating.** Select a simple, sturdy book that you think an older infant might enjoy. Read the book to a ten- to twelve-month-old. How does the baby respond? Which parts of the experience does the baby seem to enjoy most? How does he or she express that enjoyment?
- **Observing.** Watch as an infant explores and begins to play with a new toy. How does he or she respond to the toy? What does he or she try to do with it? With what results? How long does the baby remain interested in the toy?

UNIT 4

The Child from One to Three

EVERYBODY SAYS

Everybody says
I look just like my mother.
Everybody says
I'm the image of Aunt Bea.
Everybody says
My nose is like my father's.
But I want to look like ME.

Dorothy Aldis

CHAPTER 11

Physical Development from One to Three

At age fourteen months, mealtime was Tess's favorite time of the day. But her mother, Sue, had come to dread the struggle and mess. One night at dinner she described that day's lunchtime to her husband, Tom.

"It all started out peacefully enough except Tess didn't want to sit in her high chair. You know how she always wants to stand up to eat."

"I sure do," replied Tom. "I never did get her into the high chair yesterday for breakfast."

"For Tess's lunch," continued Sue, "I fixed her favorites—turkey, peas, mashed potatoes, and melon balls. When I tried to feed her some turkey, she took a few bites and then grabbed the spoon. Instead of eating her peas with her fingers like she usually does, she kept trying to get them onto her spoon. Whenever she did succeed in corralling one, she would usually turn the spoon over on the way to her mouth and lose it. She finally lost interest and started eating her mashed potatoes—with her hands."

Tom chuckled, "You must have had quite a clean-up job."

"It was a mess! I was just getting ready to scold her when I happened to glance at the mirror. There Tess and I were, covered with food. I had to laugh instead, and of course, she was laughing!"

SECTION 1

Physical Growth and Development from One to Three

OBJECTIVES

- Describe the changes in an average child's height, weight, proportion, and posture from ages one to three.
- Identify habits that influence tooth development and care.
- Distinguish between large and small motor skills, and give examples of each.

TERMS TO LEARN

circumference
large motor skills
manipulation
small motor skills
toddlers

The time between the first and fourth birthdays is one of many physical changes. During this period, the baby learns to walk, to pick up small objects with thumb and forefinger, and to throw objects. By the age of three, the child is running, jumping, building block towers, and using a fork and spoon. The transition from babyhood to childhood is dramatic!

Toddlers

Actual physical growth slows considerably after the first year. However, the child's physical skills show dramatic improvement. Most children begin to walk a few unsteady steps about the time of their first birthday. In fact, the term **toddlers** is frequently used for *children from the age of first walking, usually about twelve months, until the age of three years.* Their skills develop so remarkably that, by the time children turn four, they not only walk steadily, but also hop, jump, and run. Similar advances are made in most other areas of physical development.

As physical skills develop, toddlers need lots of space to walk and run. They need time set aside each day for active play so they can exercise their muscles and use their stored up energy. Children this age become bored easily, so it may be necessary to change games and activities frequently.

Walking is related to growth and changes in posture.

Height and Weight

The toddler's growth in both height and weight is slower than the baby's. A toddler gains only about ½ pound (0.2 kg) per month. That is less than half the average monthly weight gain during the first year of life. Growth in height also slows by about half. The chart on page 322 shows average heights and weights for children one through three.

Hereditary and environmental influences on height and weight are more noticeable during this period. Toddlers show more variation in size than babies usually do. Some toddlers are much larger than average; others are much smaller. Height differences are particularly significant. A tall two-year-old will probably grow to be a tall adult. An unusually short toddler will probably be shorter than average as an adult.

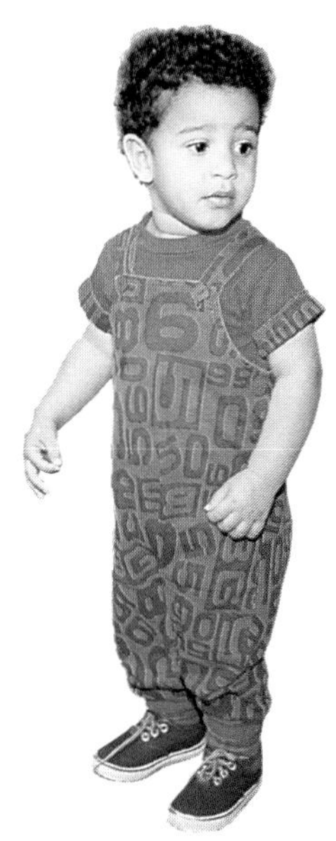

Proportion and Posture

Because of changes in proportion, posture improves during the period from one to three. Until age two, a child's head, chest, and abdomen all have about the same **circumference**, *or measure-*

AVERAGE HEIGHTS AND WEIGHTS

AGES ONE TO THREE

AGE	HEIGHT		WEIGHT	
	Inches	Centimeters	Pounds	Kilograms
One year	29.8	75.7	22.5	10.2
Two years	34.0	86.4	27.7	12.6
Three years	37.7	95.8	32.4	14.7

ment around. All three grow at the same rapid rate. Between ages two and three, however, the chest becomes larger than the head and abdomen. The arms, legs, and trunk grow rapidly during this time. These changes in proportion help improve the toddler's balance and motor skills.

By two years of age, the child stands straighter. The abdomen still protrudes, and the head is somewhat forward. The toddler's knees and elbows are still slightly bent.

By the third birthday, the toddler's posture is more upright. The spine has strengthened, so the back is straighter. The child has lost some—but still not all—baby fat.

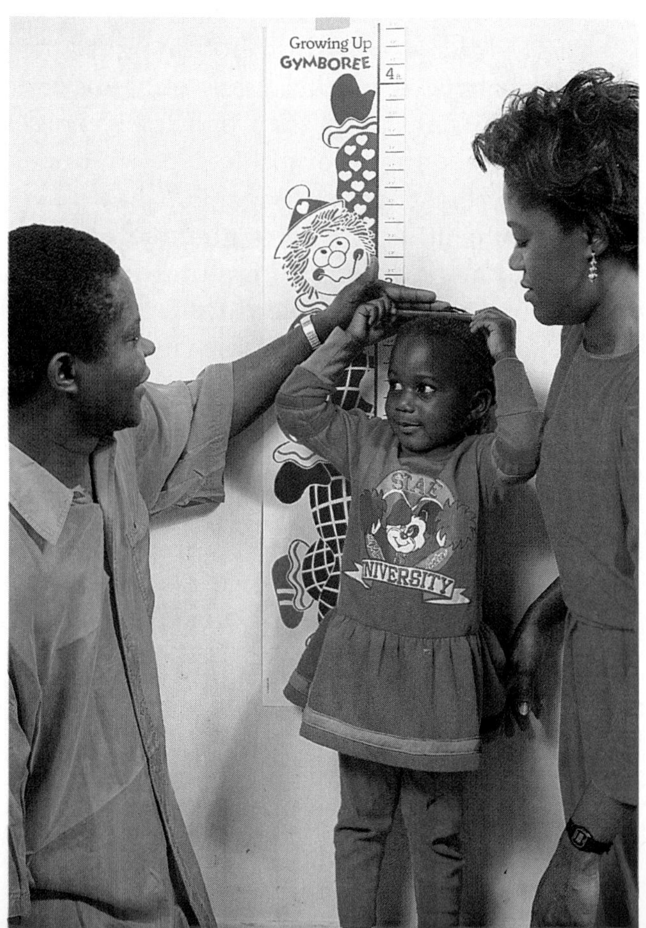

Children undergo dramatic changes in height, weight, and proportion between their first and fourth birthdays. They are proud of "growing up".

Drinking plenty of milk helps build strong teeth that are more resistant to decay. What else influences the health of the teeth?

Teeth

One-year-olds have an average of eight teeth. There is a great deal of variation, however; many children have more than eight or fewer than eight. During the second year, eight more teeth usually come in. For most children, the last four back teeth emerge early in the third year. That makes a complete set of 20 primary teeth.

The quality of a child's teeth is greatly influenced by diet. The diet of the mother during pregnancy and the diet of the child during the first two years lay the foundation for a lifetime of good—or poor—teeth. Dairy products, which are rich in calcium and phosphorus, are especially beneficial. The vitamin D in milk also contributes to the development of strong and healthy teeth and bones.

Heredity also appears to play a role in tooth quality. Dentists have identified a protective mechanism that discourages decay. Some children inherit this mechanism from their parents; others lack this form of natural protection.

HEALTH TIP

You can help a child build strong teeth not only by providing healthy foods, but also by limiting the foods that promote tooth decay. Avoid giving the child sweet treats, especially candy. Also avoid offering sugar-coated cereals, which often stick between the child's teeth.

Motor Skills

You may recall that physical development proceeds according to these patterns: from head to foot, from near to far, and from simple to complex.

BUILDING SELF-ESTEEM

Praising Children's Accomplishments

As children succeed in developing their large and small motor skills, they need special praise from the important adults in their lives. Simple, sincere praise can help children recognize their accomplishments and feel good about themselves.

Parents and other caregivers who recognize and praise developing skills can help in another way, too. They can be sure the child has a variety of experiences that will allow him or her to practice using and developing that skill. With practice and praise, the child learns this important lesson: I can keep trying, and I can do it!

When you compare the skills of children at age one and at the end of the third year, these patterns are easy to see. Hand skills are a good example. At thirteen months, a child stacks only two blocks. By the fourth birthday, the same child uses blocks to make high towers, houses, and roads.

Motor skills are often divided into two types. **Large motor skills** are *abilities that depend on the use and control of the large muscles of the back, legs, shoulders, and arms.* Walking, running, and throwing balls are all examples of large motor skills. **Small motor skills** are *abilities that depend on the use and control of the finer muscles of the wrists, fingers, and ankles.* Many small motor skills such as, completing single knob puzzles, grasping colors and paintbrushes, turning pages on cardboard books, and stringing beads, require hand-eye coordination, the ability to move the hands precisely in relation to what is seen.

Children do not acquire physical skills as predictably during the period from one to three as they did during the first year of life. Most toddlers learn some skills earlier than "average" and other skills later than "average." Such variations can be caused by differences in children's physical size, health and diet, interests, temperament, opportunities for physical play, and many other factors. As you learn more about average development for a particular age, remember that many children develop more slowly or more quickly.

Both large and small motor skills become increasingly well developed as children grow. What type of motor skills is this little girl using?

ASK THE EXPERTS

What Does Developmentally Appropriate Mean?

Linda Espinosa is the Director of Primary Education for the Redwood City School District in California, and is Treasurer of the National Association of Education for Young Children.

I often hear the caregivers in our school's child care center use the term "developmentally appropriate." Teachers and parents use the term, too. Can you help me understand what they mean?

Developmentally appropriate is an important term for caregivers, teachers, parents—in fact, for everyone who is involved with children. Activities for any group of children should be developmentally appropriate. A baby's toys should be developmentally appropriate. So should the explanations and guidance that a parent gives a child. In addition, teachers and other professionals sometimes evaluate a child's behavior to see that it is developmentally appropriate.

Since this term has such widespread use and importance, it is vital to understand the meaning of *developmentally appropriate. Appropriate,* of course, means "suitable" or "right." An activity or behavior that is developmentally appropriate, then, is suitable for the development of an individual child or a group of children.

In considering development to determine developmentally appropriate behaviors and activities, there are two essential factors. One is the age of the child or children involved. Age alone, however, does not determine developmental appropriateness. The other factor is the individual interest of the child or, in a group setting, of each child. What are the special needs of this child or this group of children? What are the particular abilities of this child or this group of children? Both these questions must be answered before developmentally appropriate activities can be selected.

A developmentally appropriate approach is relevant to the particular child or group of children. It takes into account both the age of the children and the individual needs, interests, and abilities of the children.

Linda Espinosa

Linda Espinosa

Large Motor Skills

Physical exercise and repeated practice of actions are necessary for the development of motor skills. An individual child's improvement in any one skill is typically slow but steady, and follows a predictable pattern.

As you know, most children begin to walk shortly before or after their first birthday. This is an important accomplishment. It gives the child a feeling of pride—and much more mobility for exploration. At first, the toddler walks by holding on to furniture. The child's first steps are wobbly, with toes pointed outward and arms held out for balance. After a few shaky steps, the child collapses into a sitting position. The child's constant practice of this new skill brings improvement in steadiness, balance, and body control.

Climbing skills follow a similar sequence. Even children who have learned to walk continue to climb stairs on their hands and knees for a while and slide backward when going down the stairs. Then they begin walking up stairs with help, placing both feet on each step. Next, they try walking up and down stairs on their own, holding on to a railing. They continue placing both feet on each step. Most children do not begin alternating feet on stairs until about age three.

Climbing is not limited to stairs. Nothing is safe from the climbing toddler—furniture, counters, ledges, and sometimes even people are conquered like mountains! This activity, of course, makes safety an important concern for parents and other caregivers. The Positive Parenting Skills feature on pages 344-345 gives suggestions for making areas safe for young children's explorations.

Small Motor Skills

Between their first and second birthdays, children learn to feed themselves and to drink from a cup fairly well. At first, poor hand-eye coordination causes many spills. With practice, however, their success and neatness improve. One-year-olds usually enjoy playing with blocks, large pop beads, and pyramids of different-sized rings. They also like jack-in-the-box toys, musical rolling toys, and toy pianos. Activities with these toys help develop small motor skills.

Crayons, large stacking blocks, clay beads to string, blunt scissors, and modeling dough are some of the toys that help toddlers improve their small motor skills. For these young children, how is play like toddler's work?

AVERAGE MOTOR SKILLS DEVELOPMENT

AGES ONE TO FOUR

AGE	LARGE MOTOR SKILLS	SMALL MOTOR SKILLS
1 to 1 ½ years	• Improves from walking a few unsteady steps to walking well. • Slides down stairs backwards, one step at a time. • Stoops to pick up toys.	• Turns pages of a book, several pages at a time. • Picks up small objects easily, using thumb and forefinger. • Scribbles.
1 ½ to 2 years	• Runs fairly well. • Stands on one foot. • Learns to walk up and down stairs, holding on, both feet on each step. • Throws objects overhand.	• Buttons large buttons. • Pulls down zippers. • Turns doorknobs. • Stacks several blocks to form a tower.
2 to 2 ½ years	• Walks with more coordination and confidence. • Climbs, even in unsafe places. • Jumps off bottom step. • Pushes self on wheeled toys.	• Turns pages of a book, one at a time. • Strings large beads. • Builds towers of about six blocks.
2 ½ to 3 years	• Runs, but may not be able to stop smoothly. • Alternates feet going up stairs, but not going down. • Throws ball overhand, but inaccurately. • Kicks balls.	• Builds towers of about eight blocks. • Draws horizontal and vertical lines; draws circles. • Screws lids on and off containers.
3 to 4 years	• Jumps up and down in place. • Walks on tiptoe. • Rides a tricycle. • Catches a ball with arms straight.	• Builds towers of about nine or ten blocks. • Makes a bridge from three blocks. • Cuts with scissors. • Draws recognizable pictures. • Uses a fork and spoon with little spilling.

Two-year-olds show improved **manipulation,** or *skillful use of the hands and fingers*. They can turn the pages of a book one at a time, peel a banana, and turn on a faucet. They enjoy using crayons—typically with a happy abandon that results in marks running haphazardly off the paper and onto the table or floor. They build towers of blocks, which usually reach a maximum height of five or six blocks before the tower topples.

Three-year-olds show considerably more skill. They typically delight in taking things apart and putting them back together again. Children this age can draw circles as well as horizontal and vertical lines.

The chart on pages 327 shows average large and small motor development between the first and fourth birthdays.

As small motor skills improve, a child's random scribbles gradually become more recognizable lines and shapes.

SECTION 1 REVIEW

CHECK YOUR UNDERSTANDING

1. What are toddlers?
2. Why does a child's posture improve during the period from one to three?
3. What is the number of primary teeth in a complete set? At about what age do most children have a complete set of primary teeth?
4. Why are milk and milk products especially important for the development of healthy teeth?
5. List at least two large motor skills.
6. List at least two small motor skills.
7. What is manipulation?

DISCUSS AND DISCOVER

1. Cut out at least three pictures of favorite toys for young children, aged one to three. Display the pictures and label each with a list of the motor skills involved in playing with that toy.
2. How do safety concerns in the home change as the baby grows into a one-year-old, a two-year-old, and then a three-year-old? Why do the safety concerns change as the child grows? Discuss your ideas with other students.

Providing Care for Children from One to Three

SECTION 2

OBJECTIVES

- Plan meals appropriate for young children.
- Explain how to help children learn and practice personal hygiene habits.
- Discuss how to encourage children to feed and dress themselves.
- Identify desirable characteristics in children's clothing.
- Describe common bedtime problems, and discuss how they can be minimized.
- Discuss the process of toilet training a child.

TERMS TO LEARN

natural fibers
sphincter muscles
synthetic fibers
training pants

Caring for a one-, two-, or three-year-old is quite different from caring for a baby. By their first birthday, children are already beginning to do things for themselves. If they are encouraged to try out and practice their developing skills, children are capable of a surprising amount of self-care by the time they are three. They may be able to put on their coat, brush their teeth, and butter their toast.

Feeding

Between the first and fourth birthdays, children acquire food habits and attitudes that influence their eating throughout life. They also learn to feed themselves, an activity which both depends on and helps improve their small motor skills.

It is important to understand what toddlers of various ages can—and like to—eat.

- **The one-year-old.** The one-year-old eats a variety of baby foods and many simple foods from the family table. Family foods may include such things as mashed or boiled potatoes,

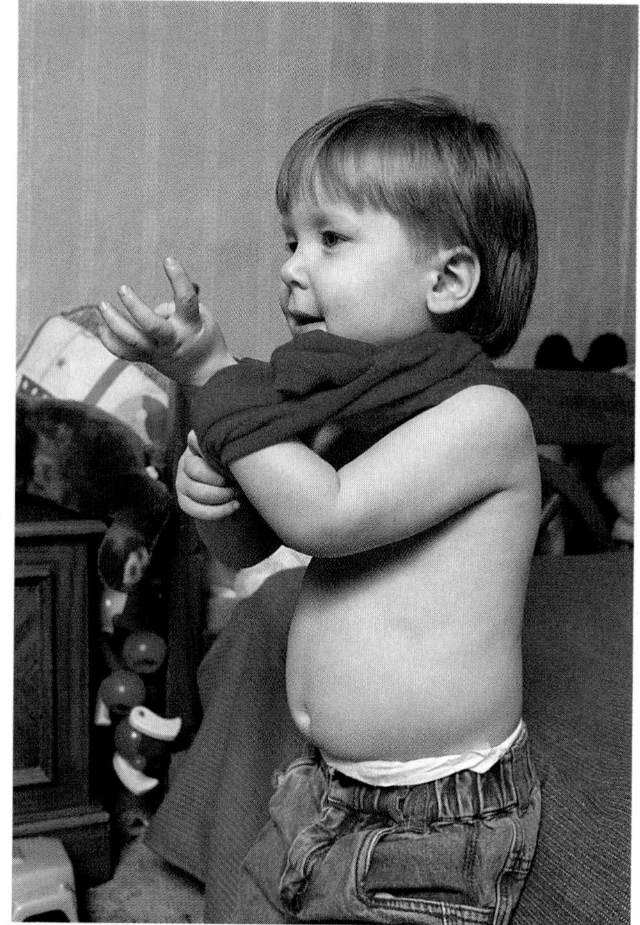

As toddlers grow, they become more independent and capable of doing many things for themselves. How do you think this child feels about his new sense of independence?

rice, cooked vegetables, soups, toast, fresh fruit pieces, yogurt, and puddings. In the early months, most foods should be finely chopped. As more teeth come in and the child's ability to chew improves, foods can have a coarser texture.

Finger foods are popular with most young children. For one-year-olds, finger foods improve coordination and encourage self-feeding. Appropriate finger-foods for one-year-olds include cheese chunks, peas, cooked carrot slices, melon or banana pieces, and scrambled eggs.

The transition from being fed to self-feeding is a long process. Babies begin trying to use a spoon before their first birthday. However, most are eighteen months or older before they can use the spoon to feed themselves with little spilling. By the time they are approaching their second birthday, most children can also drink from a cup fairly well.

During the second year, meals can become a battle of wills between parent or caregiver and toddler. One-year-olds want not only to feed themselves, but also to choose what they will eat. They often develop strong food dislikes, though these usually don't last long. Rather than forcing the child to eat a particular food, it's better to wait until the next meal or snack, when you can offer the child a different food that meets the same nutritional needs. In a few weeks, the sweet potatoes that were rejected so vehemently will probably be a favorite food again.

- **The two-year-old.** Two-year-olds vary greatly in their eating habits. Some are easy to please. Others are very finicky eaters. Most, however, do have specific likes and dislikes; they often refuse to eat certain foods.

  Two-year-olds can usually feed themselves without any help. Some are usually neat eaters; others are usually quite messy. At this age, a child can be taught to use a fork.

  Be patient. It is important to remember that children often take a long time to eat. Eating not only provides nutrition but also allows children to experiment with new textures.

  Conversation during a meal may distract the toddler from eating. For this reason, many families choose to feed the young child before the family meal, but socialization at meals is important. Whenever possible, try to schedule your meals so the young child is able to eat with the rest of the family.

- **The three-year-old.** By three years of age, a child can eat the same foods as the rest of the family. With a full set of primary teeth, chewing foods is not a problem. However, meats and other tough foods should still be served in small pieces.

  Three-year-olds are very active and need food for both growth and energy. They should have three meals a day plus nutritious snacks. The amount that an individual child eats will vary considerably from day to day, depending on the appetite level and the amount of activity he or she has had.

  At this age, it is still best not to make an issue of food likes and dislikes. Children should be encouraged to try new foods, but they should not be forced to eat large amounts of foods they dislike. Substituting foods with similar nutrient value still works at this stage. For example, a child who refuses a cup of plain milk will probably eat milk in cereal, soup, and pudding. If a child is offered nutritious foods, and high fat and sugar foods are not given, most children will eat a well-balanced diet.

Choosing Foods for Children

Parents and other caregivers must consciously choose healthful, nutritious foods for young children. Like adults, children need a variety of nutritious foods daily. The best way to make sure a child gets this variety is to plan meals using the Food

BUILDING SELF-ESTEEM

Responding Positively to Messes

Children from one- to three-years-old are busy little people as they move from one activity to another. At times, they move quickly and do not watch what their hands reach for or where their feet lead them. This is when messes can, and do often happen!

Spilling a glass of milk, dropping a bowl of cereal, or knocking over a plant are common messes that children this age can make. However, the way adults respond to these messes can affect how a child feels about himself. An adult's response can also affect whether a child will try to help with or avoid activities in the future.

Use the incident as a time for teaching. Children can help clean up a mess and can be gently reminded to move the object away from the edge next time, or wait for help.

By responding positively, adults teach children that it is alright to make mistakes or to cause messes. This sends a message to the child that they are OK and still loved.

Guide Pyramid. The chart on page 164 shows the food groups and the number of servings from each that young children should eat each day.

The primary concern in preparing food for young children is nutrition. It is important to be cautious in serving adult convenience foods to children. Many of these foods are less nutritious than other alternatives. In addition, these foods may contain a great deal of salt and a variety of preservatives, colorings, and artificial flavoring agents. Choose fresh foods when possible. Use the nutrition labels on frozen, canned, and dried foods to help you make nutritious choices.

In addition to considering nutrition, parents and other caregivers should strive to present meals that are appealing in terms of color, texture, shape, temperature, and ease of eating.

- **Color.** A variety of bright colors adds interest to a meal. For example, a meal consisting of cream of chicken soup, applesauce, milk, and vanilla pudding may be nutritious, but it looks boring. Substituting fresh sliced apples for the applesauce would make the meal more visually appealing. Further variety could be added by substituting flavored yogurt topped with granola for the vanilla pudding.
- **Texture.** Think of all the adjectives you might use to describe foods. Applesauce is smooth, a cracker is crunchy, and a strawberry is seedy. Children usually enjoy a meal consisting of foods with a variety of textures.
- **Shape.** Foods with a variety of shapes appeal to young children. For example, you can cut sandwiches into rectangles or squares—or triangles. Then you can help the

Meals need to be nutritious, appealing, and easy for young children to eat. How does this meal satisfy those requirements?

child identify the shape before he or she begins to eat. You can even use a cookie cutter to cut special shapes from the bread before you assemble the sandwich.

- **Temperature.** Young children are very conscious of the temperature of food. Check the temperature of all foods before serving them to children. If a food has been cooked or warmed in the microwave, stir it thoroughly to disperse the heat evenly. This stirring prevents "hot spots" that can burn the child's mouth.
- **Ease of eating.** Certain foods are easier than others for young children to eat. For example, ground beef is easier to chew and swallow than steak. Spaghetti is often a favorite, but children can handle it on their own more easily if it is cut into short pieces.

Mealtime Tips

Planning and preparing nutritious, appealing meals for young children is a challenge. However, mealtimes are important events in every toddler's day; they provide a chance to practice skills, experience independence, explore the feel and texture of foods, socialize with others—and have fun. The following guidelines can help you make mealtime enjoyable, both for the child and for yourself:

- Keep the child's mealtimes, including snacks, on a regular schedule. It is difficult for children to wait, especially when they are hungry.
- Keep the atmosphere at meals pleasant. Praise the child, and avoid criticism. Remind yourself that the child's table manners will improve with age.
- Use a sturdy, unbreakable dish or plate with sides for serving the child's food. This will encourage self-feeding; the child can scoop food up against the sides of the plate or dish.
- Choose a cup that the child can hold easily and that does not readily tip.
- Provide child-sized eating utensils. Young children have trouble handling full-sized forks and spoons.
- Let a young toddler sit in a high chair for meals. When the child starts sitting at the family table, use a high stool with a back or a booster seat on a regular chair.
- Never use food as a punishment or a bribe. Eating healthy food should be considered expected behavior. If you say, "You can't have a cookie until you finish your vegetables," you give the impression that vegetables are bad and cookies are good.
- Remember that children imitate others. Set a good example in food choices and in table manners.

By age three, a booster seat makes it easier for children to reach the table.

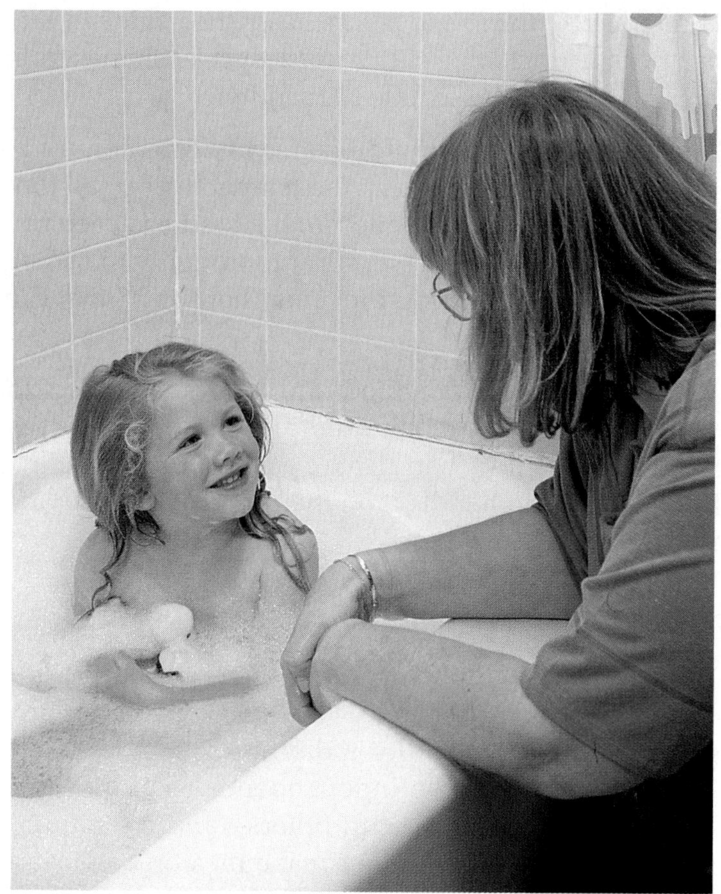

As children grow older, they need less adult help while bathing. However, for safety's sake, a young child should not be left unattended in the bath.

Bathing

During the years from one to three, children establish important attitudes about personal hygiene. Parents and other caregivers need to help young children develop both good attitudes and good hygiene skills.

At this age, most children take baths. Evening baths are usually most practical, and a bath can become an enjoyable part of a child's getting-ready-for-bed routine. Toddlers typically have fun in the bath, which they consider more a place for playing than a place for getting clean.

In the bath, one-year-olds begin to wash themselves. At first, this means merely rubbing the washcloth over the face and stomach. By age two, however, most children can wash, rinse, and dry themselves fairly well, except for the neck and back. By age three, children can bathe themselves with a minimum of supervision.

All young children need attention and supervision while they are in the bath. For children under the age of two and a half, the supervision must be constant. Even a minute away to answer the phone or get clean clothes can have disastrous results. As the mother of a two-year-old relates, "I just left the

SAFETY TIP

As children become more active and independent in the bath, it is essential to keep the tub a safe place. To prevent dangerous slips, be sure the bottom of the tub has ridges or rough plastic stickers. If the surface is smooth, you can place a rubber mat—or even an old towel—on the bottom of the tub during a child's bath time.

room for a second to get Denny's shoes. He was bathed and fully dressed for the day. When I came back, he was sitting in the tub again—with all his clothes on—playing with his toys in the bath water!" This situation may sound humorous, but the child could have drowned during the short time his mother was away.

Caring for the Teeth

Around the age of eighteen months, most toddlers have several teeth—enough to begin brushing on their own. To encourage independent brushing, give the toddler a small, soft toothbrush and a bit of toothpaste. The child's first attempts will not be very successful, but the opportunity to try is important. Even three-year-olds often only swish the front teeth a few times with the toothbrush. Children of this age still need adult help. In fact, many dentists recommend that parents should also begin flossing the child's teeth and showing the child how to hold and use dental floss.

HEALTH TIP

According to many dentists, eighteen months is the recommended age for a child's first dental checkup.

Dressing

Toddlers are eager to learn dressing skills; adults and other caregivers should encourage self-dressing whenever a child begins to show interest. It is important to remember, however, that dressing involves a number of large and small motor skills, and each of these skills must be learned one step at a time. Patience is important during this long process.

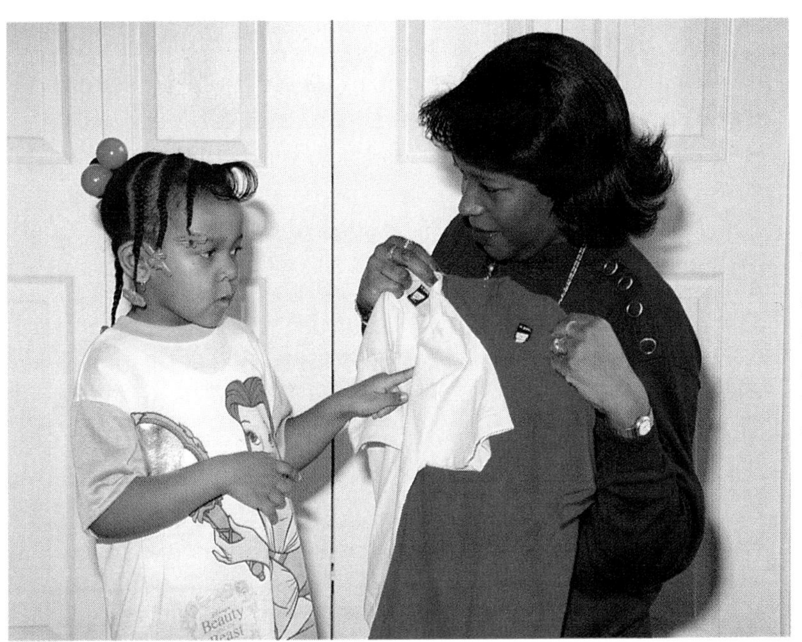

Young children take pride in being able to dress themselves and assist in the clothing decisions. Avoid clothing with fasteners or tight openings. They will only frustrate the child.

Soon after his or her first birthday, a child begins pulling clothing off. At first, it may be just a sock or hat. Between eighteen and twenty-four months, the toddler learns to undress completely, unless his or her clothes have unusually difficult fasteners.

A child usually starts trying to help with dressing around the age of thirteen or fourteen months. He or she may hold out an arm for the sleeve of a shirt, for example. Next, the toddler may learn to actually push his or her own arm through a shirt sleeve. By two years, the child can pull up pants, but putting on shirts continues to be difficult. At this age, children often end up with their garments inside out or backwards. By the age of three, the child can dress independently, except for some help with buttons, other difficult fasteners, and shoe laces.

You can encourage a child's interest in dressing by providing clothing that is easy to put on and take off. Self-dressing helps develop independence, responsibility, cooperation, and self-esteem. This period requires patience on the part of parents and other caregivers. With a relaxed attitude, you can share the child's fun and satisfaction in learning.

Choosing Clothing

Comfort, durability, and economy are the most important characteristics to look for in clothing for young children.

- **Comfort.** Clothes that allow freedom of movement are the most comfortable. Knit clothes that stretch as the child moves are good choices. Fabrics that are stiff or scratchy do not provide comfort, especially for young children.

  Choosing the best clothing size is important in providing comfort. Clothes that are too small restrict movement. Clothes that are too big can also be uncomfortable. Too-long pants can cause a toddler to trip. A shirt with sleeves so long that they cover a child's hands makes it difficult to play. Remember that different articles of clothing labeled with the same size may not fit the same way. Whenever possible, let a child try on clothing before you buy, and remember to allow for some shrinkage.

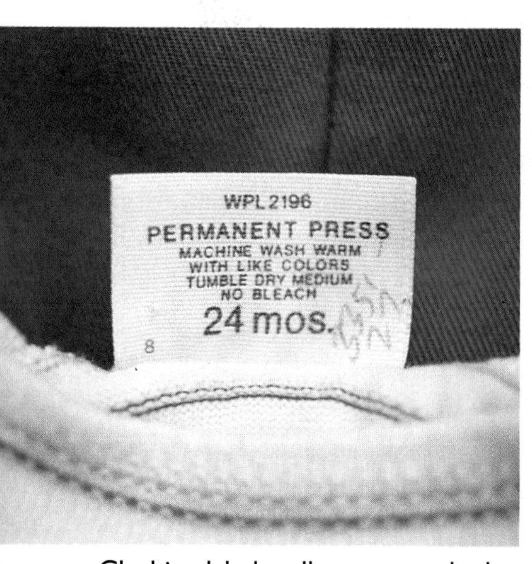

Clothing labels tell you not only the fiber content of the garment, but how it should be cared for. Why is care an especially important consideration for children's clothing?

- **Durability.** Children's clothes must withstand both hard wear and repeated laundering. Durability is influenced by the quality of the fabric and by the quality of the construction of the clothing. Denim, for example, is a durable fabric; children's jeans and overalls are usually made from denim. In checking the construction of clothing, look for close, even stitching with strong thread. The stitching should be reinforced at points of strain. All fasteners and trims should be firmly attached.

PARENTING IN ACTION

Developing Self-Care Skills

Three-year-old Michael cannot dress himself. He wants to dress himself, and he is certainly capable of learning. However, Michael has not had an opportunity to develop and practice dressing skills.

Michael has three older sisters. To make the household run smoothly, each family member has assigned tasks. Dressing Michael is one of twelve-year-old Maria's duties.

Maria took over this job when Michael was still a baby. She learned to dress him quickly and efficiently. Now, when Michael tries to find a shirt in the dresser drawer, Maria invariably pulls out her own choice and says, "Here, Michael, you can wear the red one today. It's all ready for you," and slips it over his head. Maria doesn't let Michael pull up his own pants, button his own shirt, or put on his own shoes. She can do it all much faster herself.

THINK AND DISCUSS

1. What self-dressing skills do other three-year-olds have? Why hasn't Michael developed those skills?
2. What effect does Maria's help have on Michael? How do you think his inability to dress himself affects the way he feels about himself?
3. If you were Michael's parent, what goals would you establish for Michael? How would you help Michael meet those goals?

Cotton is a good fabric choice, especially for T-shirts and underwear. Cotton wears well, launders well (though some cotton fabrics shrink), and does not irritate the skin. Since it absorbs moisture, cotton is also comfortable to wear. Cotton is one of the **natural fibers**—that is, *fibers that come from plants or animals*—from which clothing is made. Other natural fibers are wool, silk, and linen.

Synthetic fibers, also called manufactured fibers, are *fibers manufactured from chemicals rather than natural sources.* Polyester, nylon, and acrylic are synthetic fibers often used in children's clothes. Fabrics made from synthetic fibers have several advantages. They are durable, wrinkle-resistant, and quick-drying; they require little or no ironing. However, unlike natural fibers, synthetic fibers do not absorb moisture well. They tend to hold heat and perspiration against the body.

A blend of natural fibers and synthetic fibers is often a good fabric choice. A blend offers the benefits of both kinds of fibers.

By law, all clothing must have a label that identifies the fibers used. Checking clothing labels can also help you determine how to care for each garment.

- **Economy.** Since young children continue to grow rapidly, they outgrow their clothes often. Many parents exchange outgrown clothes to cut costs. Others find good used clothes at yard sales, secondhand clothing stores, and thrift shops.

  Children's clothes are most economical when they can expand a bit to allow for growth. Look for deep hems or cuffs that can be altered after the child has grown. Check that the straps on overalls or jumpers are long enough to allow the buttons to be moved.

  Whenever possible, allow the child some choice in clothing selection. Children usually love brightly colored clothes. In fact, young children choose their clothes more by color than by anything else. Other clothing favorites include "picture clothes"—clothing made from fabrics printed with animals, toys, or story characters, or garments with a picture on the front.

Sleeping

As the second birthday approaches, the sleeping habits of most children undergo a significant change. Children at this age usually require less sleep than before, and they may not sleep as easily or as willingly.

By age two, most children no longer take a morning nap. They do, however, sleep all night and continue to take an afternoon nap. Most three-year-olds require slightly less sleep; many give up regular naps.

Emotionally, a two-year-old appears more dependent on adults than he or she was during the previous year. Typically, the two-year-old calls his or her parents back repeatedly at bedtime. He or she may ask for a drink of water, another story, and one more trip to the bathroom; clearly, what the child really wants is someone near. Children of this age often use self-comforting techniques at bedtime, such as thumb sucking, rocking the crib, or cuddling a favorite blanket or soft toy.

Love and understanding are essential during this period. At bedtime, parents should be sure that the child's physical needs have been fully met. Establishing a consistent bedtime routine and following it will help.

Cultural Exchange

SLEEPING WITH TEDDY BEAR

According to a survey cited by Peter Bull in *The Teddy Bear Boo,* 45 percent of British bear-owning children call their bears "Teddy." Prior to 1903, American children referred to their toy bears as "Bruin." Austrian bears are called "Brum" bears, and the French bears go by the name of Martin.

Forcing a child to sleep in the dark is not likely to eliminate fear. A night-light may be needed, along with the caregiver's patience and reassurance.

It is not unusual for three-year-olds to wake in the middle of the night and even get out of bed. Emotional experiences of the day, excitement at bedtime, or nighttime fears may cause the three-year-old to feel insecure at night.

Fear of the dark is common among two- and three-year-olds. There are many possible causes. For example, the child may have overheard conversations or news reports about prowlers, fires, accidents, or other dangers. The child's fears are very real and usually very troubling. Unfortunately, there is rarely a quick solution. A calm discussion of the problem may help some children. Other children may feel more comforted by a night-light. All children who feel afraid of the dark need patience and understanding. Ridicule or shaming the child only makes the problem worse.

Toilet Training

Most children begin the process of toilet training between the ages of eighteen months and three years. There is no set age at which the process should begin. Rather, each child should start toilet training when he or she is physically mature enough and emotionally ready.

To be physically mature enough for toilet training, a child must be able to control his or her **sphincter muscles**, *the muscles that control elimination*. The child must also be able to recognize the body sensations that precede elimination. Only then is the child ready to start learning to control and release the sphincter muscles.

A child can be considered emotionally ready for toilet training if he or she is happily settled into a familiar daily routine. During a family move or any similar event that requires adjustments, the child should not be expected to deal with the further changes involved in toilet training.

HEALTH TIP

Consistent and careful hand-washing is an effective defense against the spread of illnesses. Young children should learn to wash their hands before and after meals, after toileting, and after playing outdoors. By three years of age, most children can handle these tasks independently.

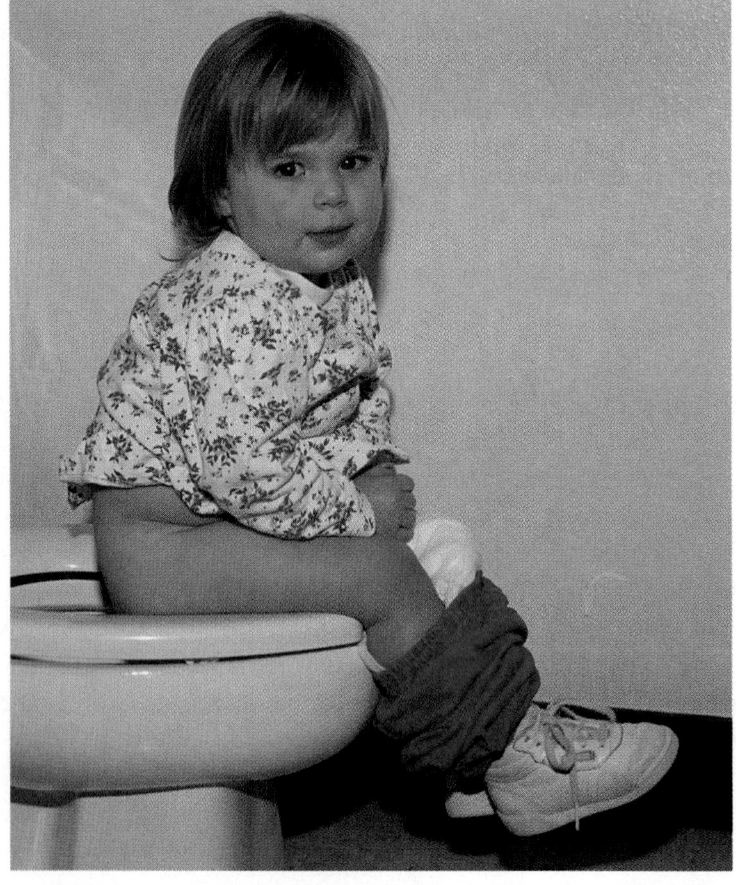

Once the child is physically ready for toilet training and shows an interest in it, the process can usually be accomplished with little trouble.

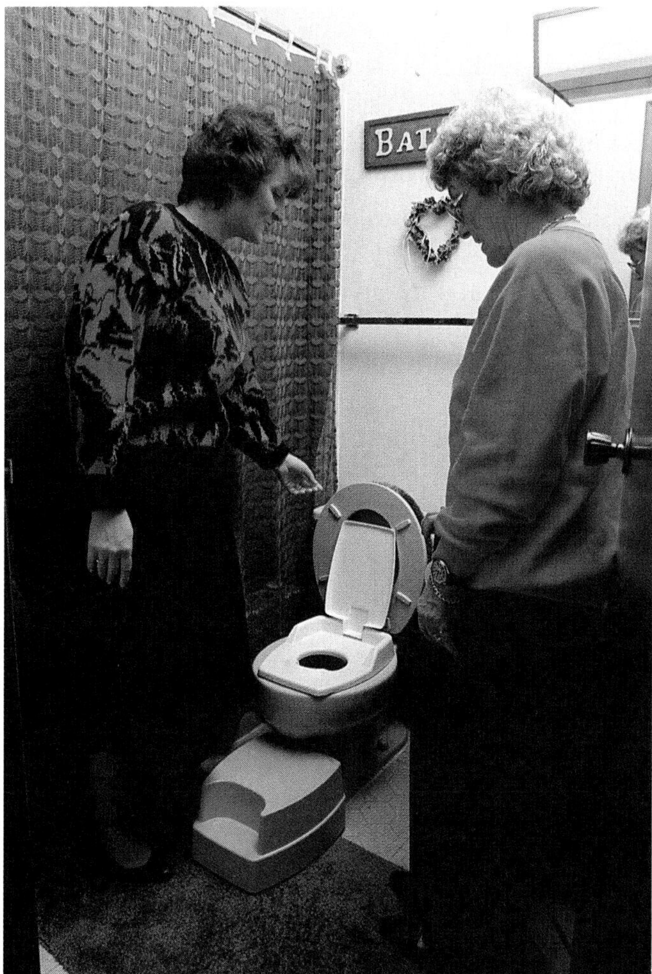

Parents should let other caregivers know about the child's progress so that toilet training is consistent. This mother is explaining the potty chair.

The attitudes of parents and other caregivers toward toilet training are very important. An overly strict approach can make training more difficult and may cause long-lasting emotional problems for the child. Interest and calm encouragement are more effective than rules and punishment. Remember that if the child is physically and emotionally ready for toilet training, he or she genuinely wants to succeed. As is the case with other learning skills, the child needs the chance to practice and to be in charge of his or her progress. It is especially important never to force toilet training. If the child resists, don't insist or even urge. Simply abandon all attempts at toilet training for several weeks; then try again.

When the child begins trying to use the toilet, he or she will need either a special child seat on the toilet or a separate potty chair. Using a child seat eliminates the need for another adjustment later, when the child is ready to graduate from a potty chair to the toilet. On the other hand, using a potty chair allows the young child more independence than a special seat on top of the toilet.

Remember that some children are frightened by the flushing of a toilet. Unless the child is particularly interested in the flushing, it may be better to flush the toilet after the child has left the bathroom.

Bowel training usually comes before bladder training. The child is probably ready when he or she shows an awareness that a bowel movement is imminent. When you recognize this awareness in the child's facial expressions or gestures, you can suggest that he or she might try sitting on the special toilet seat or on the potty chair. Be available and encouraging, but remember that being too forceful or demanding will make toilet training more difficult both for the child and for you. Some children seem naturally to follow regular patterns of elimination; these children are more easily trained than those who have irregular bowel movements.

Bladder training typically begins several months after bowel training, although some children learn both at about the same time. The child who is ready for bladder training has a less frequent need to urinate—sometimes as long as from one meal to the next. Other signs that a child is ready include indicating that his or her diapers need changing and expressing a clear understanding that he or she is the cause of that puddle on the floor.

A child's urination habits are often irregular. They are affected by liquid intake, weather, temperament, and excitement. However, the parent or caregiver should take note of the pattern and encourage the youngster to try the toilet or potty for short periods at specific times. These times should include before and after meals, bath, and sleep.

Many young children are encouraged in toilet training by the opportunity to wear **training pants**, *heavy, absorbent underpants*, in place of diapers. Wearing training pants makes it possible for a young child to use a potty independently. Most children also recognize that wearing underpants instead of diapers is a significant sign of maturity.

Even after bowel and bladder training seem to be well established, parents and other caregivers should expect—and accept—accidents. Like other skills, toileting skills develop along a predictable pattern, but at the rate appropriate to the individual child.

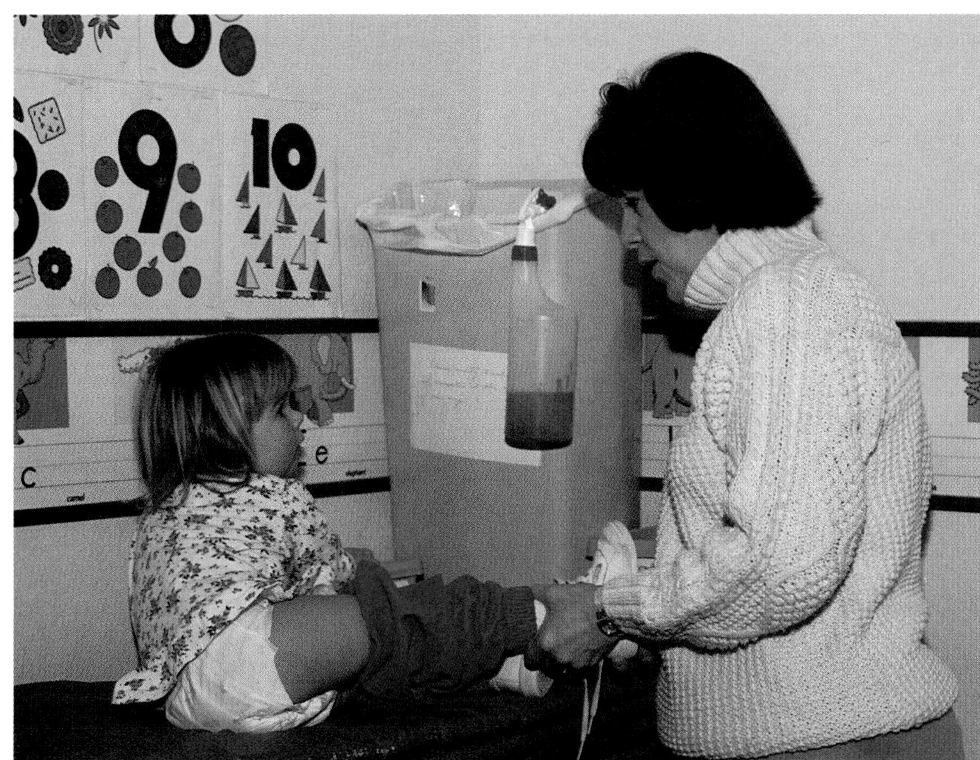

When the child is taking a nap, sleeping at night, or going on a trip, it is best to use diapers. This prevents the child from experiencing too many "discouraging" failures.

SECTION 2 REVIEW

CHECK YOUR UNDERSTANDING

1. List two benefits of providing finger foods for one-year-olds.
2. What is the most important consideration in preparing meals and snacks for young children?
3. How do toddlers usually respond to taking a bath?
4. What should toddlers do to care for their own teeth? What should parents or other caregivers do to care for the toddler's teeth?
5. What is the difference between natural fibers and synthetic fibers?
6. How should parents and caregivers respond to a young child's fear of the dark?
7. At what age should a child begin toilet training?

DISCUSS AND DISCOVER

1. Plan and write out a two-day menu for a young child. Include meals and snacks, and note the quantities of each food you would offer, taking into account the possibility that the child might not eat everything provided. Present your menu to other students, identifying the specific age of the child. Ask the other students to help you evaluate your plan.
2. With a group of other students, select three or four children's outfits, and evaluate the quality and durability of the garments. What are the advantages of each garment? Are there disadvantages to any of your choices?

KEEPING CHILDREN SAFE AND HEALTHY

As children grow and mature, they are capable of—and interested in—exploring more and more of their home environment. Toddlers walk and climb. They open drawers and cabinets. They turn knobs and stick their fingers into tiny holes. Children try all these things so that they can learn more about the world, but they often put themselves in danger while they're learning.

It's not fair to the child—or to the parents and caregivers—to spend the day saying "no." The best solution is to make the home as safe as possible for the young child. This is called" child-proofing" your home. One suggestion is to crawl around your house at the child's current level, and observe situations that may present a safety hazard. Notice what is accessible to the child. Then use the following tips to help you keep toddlers safe from falls, burns, and other hazards.

FALLS

- Keep the floor and all the stairs free of toys and other objects that children—or adults—might trip over.
- Wipe up spills immediately—before someone slips and falls.
- Use a rubber mat or adhesive strips in the tub or shower.
- Use safety gates to block off the top and the bottom of each stairway. Be sure the gates meet current requirements for narrower spaces between the bars.
- Always use the seat belt when the child is in a high chair.
- Be sure that all open windows have secure screens. Windows in high-rise buildings pose a particular danger; they should have special safety latches.
- Once the child begins to walk, remove loose rugs and furniture that might tip easily.

BURNS

- As early as possible, teach the child that the stove is hot and must not be touched.
- Always turn the handles of pots and pans toward the center of the stove.

★ Put safety caps on electrical outlets when they are not in use.

★ Keep small appliances, such as toasters and irons, unplugged and out of reach when they are not in use.

★ Check the temperature of the hot water from the taps. The temperature should be no higher than 120° to 130° F (49°to 54° C) to prevent burns. If the water is hotter than that, lower the thermostat on the home water heater.

OTHER HAZARDS

★ Keep all dangerous materials, such as cleaning supplies, medicines, paints, and insecticides, securely out of the child's reach. Remember that many toddlers like to climb, so keeping these materials on a high shelf is not enough; they should be stored in locked cabinets or containers.

★ Keep sharp knives, razor blades, sharp scissors, and matches securely out of the child's reach. Many of these items can be conveniently stored in a drawer that has been secured with a sturdy child-proof latch. Use "child-proof" latches on any cupboard you don't want accessible to the child.

★ Lock unused refrigerators and freezers, or remove their doors.

SUMMARY

- For children from one to three years of age, physical growth proceeds more slowly than during the first year of life.
- Posture improves as a child's body proportions change.
- By the age of three, most children have a full set of baby teeth.
- Both large and small motor skills improve greatly during this period.
- Children this age are developing lifetime eating and cleanliness habits.
- Children learn gradually to feed and dress themselves.
- Bedtime problems are common during this stage.
- Toilet training should not be started until a child is physically and emotionally ready.

REVIEWING THE FACTS

1. Define *circumference*. Explain how the circumference of a child's chest changes between the ages of two and three.
2. What role does heredity play in tooth quality?
3. How are large motor skills and small motor skills different?
4. List at least four large and small motor skills that most one-and-one-half- to two-year-olds have.
5. Why are the attitudes that toddlers develop toward food so important?
6. How should parents and other caregivers respond when a toddler refuses to eat a particular food?
7. What is the best way for parents and other caregivers to teach toddlers good table manners?
8. Around what age should children begin having regular dental checkups?
9. What are two approaches that might help a young child who feels afraid of the dark?
10. What are training pants? How can training pants help children during toilet training?

EXPLORING FURTHER

1. Collect several photographs of yourself taken between your first and fourth birthdays. Make a display, showing the photographs in chronological order and labeling the physical development noticeable at each stage. (Section 1)
2. Watch at least four different commercial television shows directed at very young children. Notice the food products that are advertised during those shows. Then discuss those ads with other students: What foods do they show young children? How do you think those foods might affect the physical growth and development of young children? (Section 2)
3. Plan and prepare lunch—or another meal—for a two-year-old. Include an appropriate variety of foods; concentrate on including a variety of shapes that would interest and appeal to a young child. (Section 2)
4. Design an article of clothing—or an outfit— for a toddler. Sketch your design, and note the kinds of fabrics and fasteners to be used. Also note the kind of activity for which the clothing is intended. Display your sketch, and invite other students to critique your design. (Section 2)

THINKING CRITICALLY

1. **Synthesize.** Why do you think a toddler typically uses excuses to call his or her parent back at bedtime? Would it be easier for the child if he or she expressed the fear or anxiety directly? Why or why not? Would that be easier for the parent? Why or why not?
2. **Analyze.** Why do you think toilet training is such an important issue in many families? What do you think toilet training represents to a young child? To a child's parents? What attitudes and approaches do you think are most important in dealing with toilet training?
3. **Analyze.** Investigate and evaluate at least four potty chairs and child-sized toilet seats. What special advantages does each offer? What are the disadvantages of each? How much does each cost? If you were preparing to toilet train a toddler, which would you buy? Why?

CROSS-CURRICULUM CONNECTIONS

1. **Math.** Weigh and measure at least ten three-year-olds in a child care center or other group care setting. Calculate the average weight and height of the children in your group. How do the averages for your group compare with the national averages given in the chart on page 322?
2. **Writing.** Plan, write, and illustrate a short story, appropriate for toddlers, about tooth brushing. Read your finished book to a young child or to a small group of children.

OBSERVING AND PARTICIPATING

Motor Skills

Motor development includes the child's increasing ability to control body parts and body movements. Muscle control depends upon the maturity of the nerves, bones, and muscles as well as changes in body proportions. Learning and control cannot occur until the child is mature enough. Motor development follows a predictable pattern having different stages. There are individual differences in the rate of motor development.

Choose one of the activities below, and spend some time observing or participating with a child. Then write your observations in your journal. Compare your observations with those made by other students, and discuss what you have learned.

- **Participating.** Volunteer to play with a group of two or three toddlers in a child care center. Plan an interesting and fun activity that uses the toddlers' large motor skills such as kicking a ball, walking backward, throwing a ball, running, or marching. How interested are they in the game? What differences did you notice in the childrens' abilities and the tasks they could accomplish?
- **Observing.** Observe one- to two-year-olds playing in a group setting, such as a child care center or a park. What differences in large and small motor skills do you notice? How do those differences affect the activities the toddlers enjoy?
- **Participating.** Interact with a group of two or three toddlers to see how each child demonstrates small motor skills. Let the children demonstrate small motor activities by putting puzzles together, stringing beads, or hammering pegs. Construction paper, crayons, and scissors may also be included on the table. Evaluate each child's hand-eye coordination and his or her use of small motor skills.

CHAPTER 12

Emotional and Social Development from One to Three

Justin sat on the carpeted floor and played contentedly with pegs and rings. He liked going to preschool on Tuesdays and Thursdays. It was always fun to see his friends, Melissa, John, and Jason, and to play with all the different toys.

Just then, Melissa arrives and races over to the block area where Justin is playing. "Hi, Justin," announces Melissa, "what are you doing? Can I play too?"

"Sure," replies Justin. "I'll show you what to do."

"This is my plane," instructs Justin. "You drive the plane by moving the rings. The rings can make the plane go faster or slower, or go up and down."

"But I want the blue ring," explains Melissa. "Blue is my favorite color."

"Wait! That will make the plane go backwards," insists Justin.

Melissa continues, "Please, can't I have the blue ring? I'll be your friend forever."

"Oh, okay," Justin slowly agrees, "we'll back up and then drive around the block."

SECTION 1

Emotional Development from One to Three

OBJECTIVES

- Describe the general patterns of emotional development in children from ages one to three.
- Identify the common emotions of young children and the changes in how those emotions are expressed.

TERMS TO LEARN

negativism
self-centered
separation anxiety
sibling rivalry
temper tantrums

It is easier to observe emotional development in early childhood than during any other stage in life. During the period from their first to their fourth birthdays, children develop new emotions, such as jealousy, that they did not feel as young babies. Young children display their emotions very clearly, first through their actions and later through their words. At the end of this period, children also begin to control their emotions or to show their emotions in more socially acceptable ways.

General Emotional Patterns

The time between the first and fourth birthdays is one of emotional ups and downs. The child experiences periods of negativism, and rebellion, but also periods of happiness, calmness, stability, and inner peace.

Throughout childhood, emotional development tends to go in cycles. This cyclical pattern can be observed in the predictable emotional stages most children go through. However, it is important to remember that each child is an individual. Jane may not go through the negativism of age two and one-half until she is three years old. Manuel, with his calm and sunny disposition, may not seem to go through it at all. Generally, however, you will find the following characteristics in children at about the ages given.

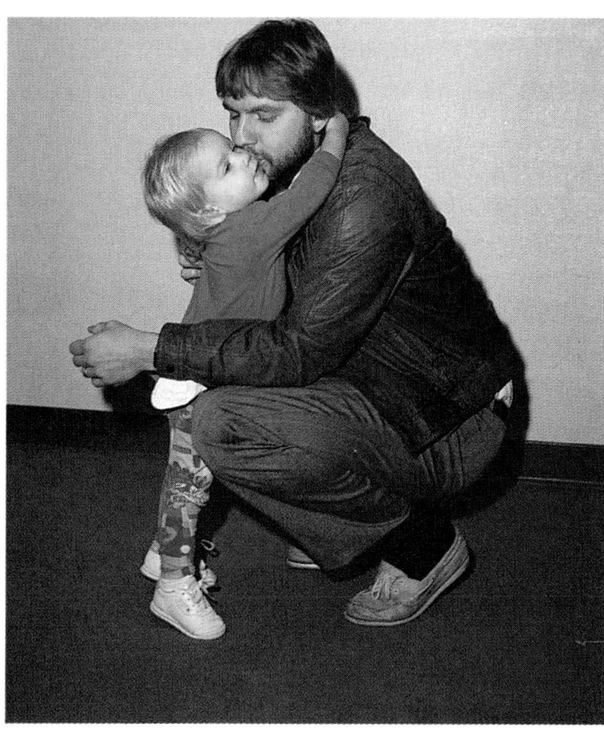

Toddlers show their feelings by their facial expression and their actions. Both smiles and tears are common.

Eighteen Months

Eighteen-month-old children are primarily **self-centered**, that is, *thinking about their own needs and wants, not those of others.* This is not surprising. During infancy, the child's needs and desires are promptly met by parents and other caregivers. At eighteen months, however, parents and caregivers are beginning to teach the child that some desires won't be met immediately and others will never be met. This is a difficult and long-term lesson for a child. An eighteen-month-old is only beginning the process of learning it.

Parents' and caregivers' spoken instructions are usually not very successful at this age. The toddler is likely to do the opposite of what is requested. The child's favorite response—no matter what the question or request—is "no." A request to "give it to me" typically prompts the eighteen-month-old to run off with the object instead.

Being negative is a way for toddlers to prove that they don't always have to follow along with the desires of others.

Negativism, or *doing the opposite of what others want*, is a normal part of development for the toddler. It has a number of causes. One is the child's desire for independence. Saying "no" to parents and other caregivers is merely a way of saying, "Let me decide for myself sometimes." The child may even say "no" to things he or she would really like to do—just for the chance to be in charge of the decision.

Another cause of negativism is simply the frustration that toddlers feel. Their bodies are not developed enough to obey their wishes, and they don't have sufficient language skills to express their feelings. The result is anger or frustration.

At this age, a child also finally realizes that he or she is a separate person. This realization is both exciting and frightening. The child likes the power of being a separate person but misses the close bond with his or her mother, father, or other primary caregiver.

It is important to remember that negativism is a normal stage in emotional development. Understanding its causes makes it easier to deal with. One of the best ways to combat negativism at this age is simply to eliminate as many restrictions as possible. For example, rather than asking an eighteen-month-old not to touch certain things in the home, remove everything that is dangerous, breakable, or especially valuable. As the child gets older, the objects can gradually be returned.

At this age, distraction can be an effective way of coping with inappropriate behavior. Instead of saying "put that down," for example, you might open a picture book and talk about what you see, or start noisily arranging the child's blocks into an interesting pattern. The child will soon leave the undesirable activity to join you.

It also helps to give the child reasonable choices whenever possible. If the child can choose between a pear and a banana for lunch, it won't matter quite so much that there is no choice about taking a nap. It is best to limit choices to two alternatives, however. Toddlers cannot think about three or four things at the same time.

Around the age of eighteen months, many children start to have **temper tantrums,** *incidents in which children release their anger or frustration by screaming, crying, kicking, pounding, and sometimes even holding their breath.* Children typically have occasional temper tantrums until the age of three or four. At some points, even seemingly minor frustrations can cause temper tantrums.

Two Years

Emotionally, the two-year-old is less at odds with the world than he or she was at eighteen months. The child's speech and motor skills have improved, relieving much of the previous frustration. The child also understands more and is able to wait for longer and longer periods of time for his or her needs to be met.

The two-year-old expresses love and affection freely and actively seeks approval and praise. Though the child still has occasional emotional outbursts, they are fewer and less intense. The child is easier to reason with. Relationships with parents and other children have improved, for the two-year-old tends to be outgoing, friendly, and less self-centered.

BUILDING SELF-ESTEEM

The Game of Offering Choices

Even very young children feel better about themselves when they make their own choices about daily activities. Whenever possible, offer children the opportunity to choose. Cleaning up can become a game when the caregiver asks, "Which should we do first—put these books on the shelf or put these toys into the toy box?" Getting ready for bed is more fun if the child gets to make simple choices—"Do you want to wear your yellow pajamas or the red pajamas tonight?"

However, there are some circumstances under which children should not be asked to make decisions. A child who is very tired or who is in a new situation should not be given choices; the parent or caregiver should guide the child's activities in these situations. Also, parents and caregivers should avoid offering choices if they are unwilling to accept the child's decision.

Two and One-Half Years

Just as parents and caregivers begin to adjust to a smoother, less intense toddler, the child enters a new stage. In some ways, this period is more difficult for parents and other caregivers than the eighteen-month-old stage, because toddlers at two and one-half are not so easily distracted.

At two and one-half, children are learning so much that they often feel overwhelmed. Their comprehension and desires exceed their physical abilities. For example, they may want their blocks and dolls placed just so, but they succeed only partially before accidentally knocking them over. Two-and-one-half-year-olds work hard at talking. They know what they want to say, but they don't always succeed in making themselves understood. If parents or other caregivers answer with an absent-minded "uh-huh" or ignore their efforts to communicate, toddlers at this stage often become even more frustrated.

Toddlers' drive for independence causes them to resist pressures to conform. They are sensitive about being bossed, shown, helped, or directed. Independence and immaturity clash head-on during this stage. At two and one-half, children are sometimes stubborn, demanding, and domineering. However, their moods change rapidly, and within a short time, they can become lovable and completely charming.

One characteristic of this age is the child's desire for consistency; he or she wants the same routines, carried out in just the same way, day after day. This is the child's way of coping with a

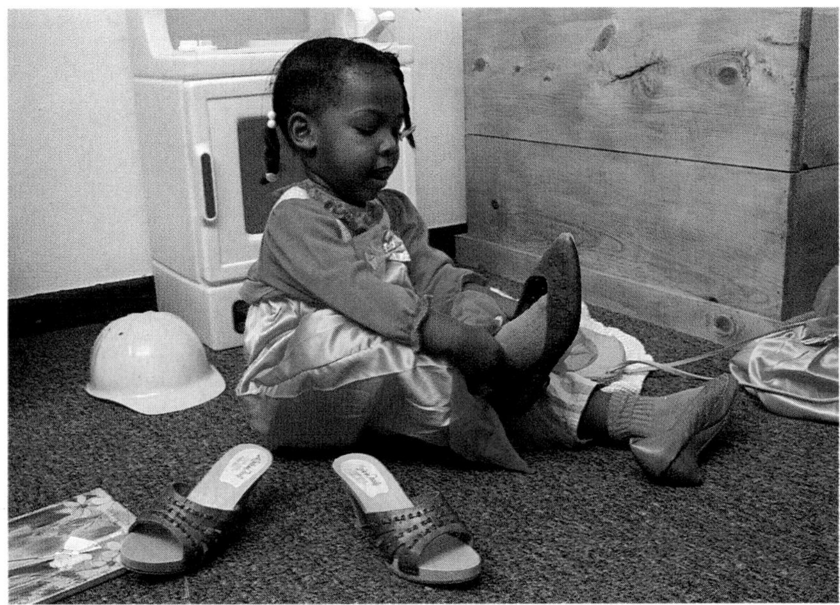

At two and one-half, children sometimes want to be grown-up but aren't sure of their ability to do so. At other times, they look for reassurance that they can still be babied when they want.

BUILDING SELF-ESTEEM

Temper Tantrums—Responding Appropriately

In handling a tantrum, there are two main goals. First, you must prevent the child from being hurt or hurting anyone else. Second, you must enforce the limits you have set. If you give in to the child's demands, tantrums are more likely to be repeated.

If a tantrum occurs at home, the behavior sometimes simply can be ignored. Putting the child in his or her room or in a chair away from others often helps.

When a tantrum occurs in a public place, move the child to a quiet spot to cool down, or just go home.

Always remain calm. Acknowledge the child's feelings while reemphasizing the reason his or her demands can't be met. "I know you are upset that you can't go outside and play. It's getting dark now and you can't play in the yard after dark. Tomorrow morning you can go out and play."

confusing world. The child feels that tasks must be done in exactly the same way and objects must be in exactly the same place. Maintaining a consistent schedule and environment helps build feelings of security and confidence.

At two and one-half, toddlers are part independent, part dependent. Sometimes they seek comfort and help; at other times, they assert their independence and want to do it themselves. Parents and other caregivers can help children of this age most by giving them much love and a great deal of patience—especially when the children are neither lovable nor patient. Two-and-one-half-year-olds need more flexible and adaptable limitations rather than hard-and-fast rules.

Three Years

Most three-year-olds have made remarkable strides in emotional development. They are again generally sunny and cooperative and are learning to be considerate. Since three-year-olds are more physically able to do things, they do not have to deal with as many frustrating situations as the toddler.

Three-year-olds take directions from others with little of their previous resistance. They follow instructions and take pride in the tasks they can perform for others. Three-year-olds are eager for praise and affection, and they are willing to modify their behavior in order to achieve those responses from adults. At three years of age, children generally have fewer and less violent temper tantrums than they may have had earlier.

At three, children love to talk, and they are much better at talking. They talk to their toys, to their playmates, to their imagi-

Using a real or toy telephone is a favorite activity for three-year-olds. Children this age are finally able to express themselves clearly by talking.

PARENTING IN ACTION

Adapting to Change

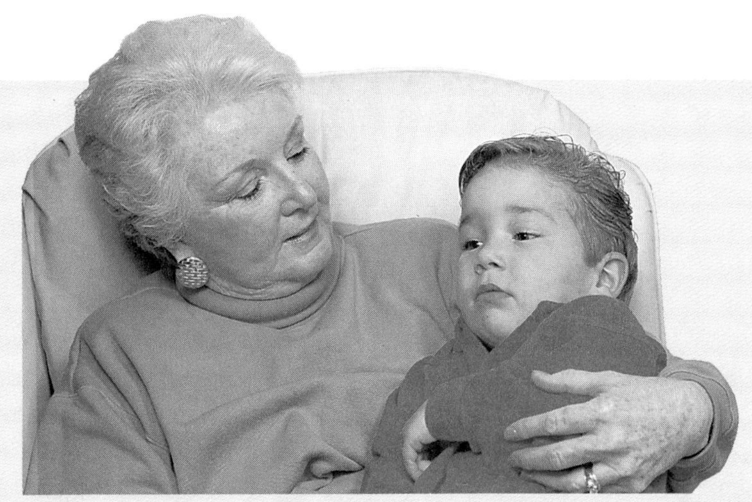

Andy, age three and one-half, had been staying with his grandparents while his parents were out of town for a few days. The surroundings were familiar and, aside from an uncharacteristic quietness, Andy seemed to be coping well.

On the third evening, however, just before Andy's bedtime, a neighbor stopped by unexpectedly to visit Andy's grandparents. As soon as the neighbor stepped into the living room, Andy buried his head against his grandmother, covered his eyes, and cried, "I don't want to see anybody!"

THINK AND DISCUSS

1. What particular aspects of the situation influenced Andy's response to the neighbor?
2. How did Andy try to control his environment?
3. Do you think Andy's reaction to the situation—and to the stay at his grandparents' home—would have been different had he been two and one-half? If so, how? If not, why not?

nary companions, and to themselves. They derive emotional pleasure from talking. They also respond to others' talking; they can be reasoned with and controlled with words.

Three and One-Half Years

The self-confident three-year-old is suddenly very insecure at three and one-half. Parents may feel that the child is going backward rather than forward emotionally.

Fears are common at this age. The child may be afraid of the dark, lions and tigers, monsters, strangers, or loud noises—even though none of these were frightening before.

Emotional tension and insecurity often show up in physical ways, too. Some children may exhibit tensional outlets such as thumb sucking, nail biting, or nose picking. Others may stumble or stutter.

At three and one-half, children try to ensure their own security by controlling their environment. They may issue insistent demands, such as "I want to sit on the floor to eat lunch!" and "Talk to me!"

Specific Emotions

Children express their emotions openly until the age of two or three. As they mature, they begin to be affected by the cultural demands for more control of emotional expression. The three-year-old begins to learn socially acceptable ways of displaying feelings. For example, three-year-old Jonathan uses words to express his anger. His fifteen-month-old sister, Marta, expresses her anger by kicking and screaming.

Children's emotions become more specific as they grow older. Some of the most common emotions of one- to three-year-olds are anger, fear, jealousy, affection, and sympathy.

Anger

The crying and screaming of temper tantrums are most common at about two to three years; then they begin to decline. When an eighteen-month-old has a tantrum, he or she is not hostile toward any particular person or thing—just easily angered. Between the ages of two and three, the object or person responsible comes under attack. For example, the ten-month-old who is intent on getting a ball is concerned only with that ball. A two-year-old, however, may attack the person who is holding the ball.

Outgoing, confident children tend to display their anger more aggressively, such as by hitting or kicking. Shy, passive children are more likely to cry and seek comfort from an adult.

These primitive expressions of anger gradually disappear if they do not bring the desired results. Children's reactions become less violent and explosive. Physical attacks begin to be replaced by threatening, name-calling, pouting, or scolding.

As children get older, their anger becomes focused on the person or thing that is causing the problem.

Even though the frequency of anger decreases with age, the intensity of anger changes as the child gets older. Children become capable of lasting hostility. Three-year-olds think about "hitting back" when someone makes them angry.

A number of factors can cause a child to be angry more often than normal. Anger is more frequent in anxious, insecure children. The child who has not learned self-control also tends to have frequent outbursts. Children whose parents are overly critical or inconsistent become frustrated easily and show anger. There are also some common temporary causes of bad temper. When a child is sick, uncomfortable, tired, or hungry, he or she will become angry much more easily than usual.

Frequent, intense outbursts of anger are destructive and disturbing to both parent and child. Parents should recognize and respond to the child's bewilderment and anxiety, rather than reacting angrily themselves. Parents should make sure that the demands on the child are both limited and reasonable as they try to help the child learn self-control.

Fear

Every phase of a child's development has its particular fears. A one-year-old may be frightened of high places, strangers, and loud noises. A three-year-old might be afraid of the dark, animals, and storms. Some fears are actually useful, since they keep the child from dangerous situations. Other fears must be overcome for proper emotional and social development.

Some children have more fears than others. These differences are related to such factors as physical condition, mental development, temperament, feelings of security, and ability to cope with daily life. Thoughtless adults sometimes build fears to ensure obedience. They may say, for example, "Stay on the sidewalk or the police will get you."

Adults often communicate their own fears to children. Even if the fear is never discussed, a child may sense it. For example, a child may pick up fear of dogs simply from the alarmed call of a parent whenever a dog comes near.

At one time or another between the first and fourth birthdays, many children suffer from **separation anxiety**, *a fear of being away from parents, familiar caregivers, or their normal environment*. Nicole cried when her parents left her with a new baby-sitter; Eli cried when his mother first left him on his own at the child care center; Darnell cried when his father left on the first day of preschool. All these tears are signs of separation anxiety.

A child's separation anxiety can be disturbing for the parents. Parents should be careful to avoid communicating their own concerns to the child; it may be helpful for parents to recall that they have chosen a safe, secure caregiver or care center for

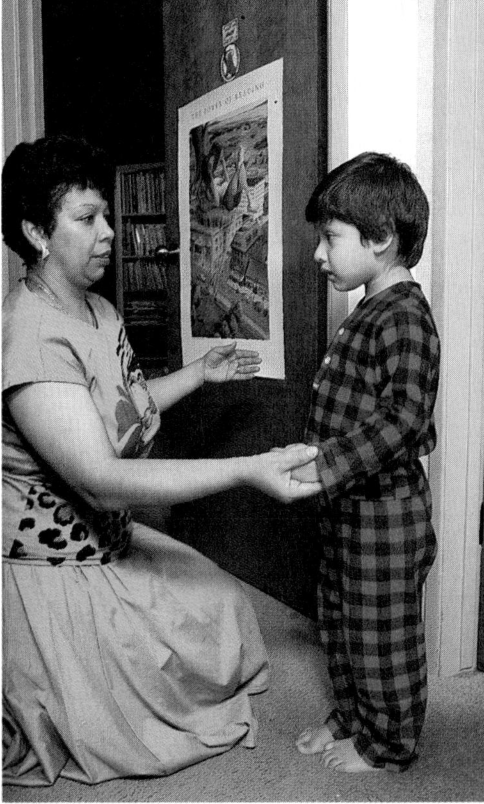

Age three and one-half often brings fears and insecurity, such as a fear of the dark. Parents should be calm and reassuring.

the child. Parents can also help both the child and themselves by spending special time with the child at home.

Some of a toddler's generalized fears can be identified as caused by specific incidents. For example, a toddler who is frightened by a loud barking dog may develop a generalized fear of all dogs. Some children may develop fears about sirens, men with beards, or loud noises. When a young child has an experience that seems likely to produce fears, it is best to try to talk with the child about it right away. When the child experiences the "trigger," talk them through it—"See it is just a man with a beard. He is just like your daddy but he has hair on his face." Otherwise, the child's imagination may blow the experience out of proportion.

Fears depend a great deal on individual experience. A child with a pet dog will probably not be afraid of other dogs. However, unfamiliar situations are likely to prompt fears at first.

Parents and other caregivers should be patient in their responses to the fears of young children. The following suggestions will help you deal with the fears of one- to three-year-old children:

- Be careful to avoid shaming a child for his or her fears.
- Encourage the child to talk about his or her fears, and listen seriously and attentively to the child. Recognizing and admitting fears may diminish their impact.
- Offer honest, understandable explanations for events and situations that have frightened the child.
- Nightmares are common at this age; help the child separate reality from fantasy.
- Make unfamiliar situations more secure with your presence. A first visit to the dentist, for example, goes more smoothly in the company of a familiar adult.
- Being unprepared for a situation is one of the chief causes of fear. Discuss new experiences and events in advance; help the child know what to expect.
- Teach the child how to control frightening situations. For example, if the child is afraid of the dark, teach him or her how to turn on the light.
- Be supportive and understanding.

Jealousy

Jealousy becomes a recognizable emotion sometime in the second year. The one-year-old shows no jealous reactions, but by eighteen months, jealousy is very pronounced. It reaches its peak at age three and then declines as outside relationships begin to replace the close ties to home and parents.

Resentment of affection between parents is one of the most common causes of jealousy in early childhood. The very young child may not understand that parents have enough love for everyone.

Jealousy of a new baby can lead an older child to return to babyish habits.

Sibling rivalry, or *competition between brothers and/or sisters for their parents' affection and attention*, is another common cause of jealousy. This is often particularly evident when there is a new baby in the family. Suddenly, all the attention is focused on the baby rather than on the older child.

Children between the ages of eighteen months and three and one-half seem to be most jealous of a new baby. They may try to hurt the infant or demand that the baby be "taken back." Some children respond by trying to get attention. They may show off, act inappropriate, or revert to babylike behaviors, such as bed-wetting, thumb sucking, or baby talk.

If parents act shocked or threaten not to love the toddler anymore, they only make the problem worse. The feeling of loss of love caused the negative attention-getting behavior to begin in the first place. Instead of expressing displeasure with the older child's behavior, parents and caregivers need to realize that what the child needs is more affection and reassurance.

The following suggestions are helpful in encouraging a young child to develop a good relationship with his or her new sibling:

- Arrange special time alone with the older child.
- Compliment the youngster on his or her appropriate behavior whenever possible.
- Point out the advantages of not being a baby and all the things he or she can do.
- Acknowledge and label the feelings the child may have—be specific. "It bothers you when he cries." Let the child know that you are trying to understand how he feels and that his feelings are important to you.
- Give the older child extra love and attention.

SAFETY TIP

When a new baby arrives, parents must expect anger, jealousy, and other kinds of upset in a young child who has suddenly been assigned the role of "big brother" or "big sister." For this reason, it is never safe to leave a toddler "in charge" of the baby—even for a few minutes. Many experts recommend not leaving a toddler alone with a baby at all.

BUILDING SELF-ESTEEM

Encouraging Children to Love Themselves

Young children show emotions in simple and direct ways. They may appear to be quite independent one moment, yet quite helpless the next. Though they want to do things for themselves, they have not yet learned to complete all tasks safely or responsibly.

Adults can help young children to handle those times when they are having difficulty. This can be accomplished by helping children to like themselves and realize that they are capable. Children see themselves through the eyes of people around them. When children hear adults say, "David is a happy boy," or "Kristin helps set the table," children see themselves as being happy or helpful. Children who hear these words feel good about themselves and learn to love themselves.

- If the older child must change bedrooms, make the move months in advance.
- Prepare the child for the baby's coming. Instill the feeling that the new baby is a baby brother or a baby sister and that parents will need the older child's help.
- Ask the child to help with small tasks in caring for the baby. For example, an older child can bring a clean shirt for the baby or help with feeding. Such positive tasks make the child feel like a useful part of the family.

Love and Affection

The relationships that children have with others in their early years form the basis of their capacity for love and affection in later life. Young children must learn, through experience and practice, to love.

First comes "love" of those who satisfy the baby's physical needs. If one person is the baby's primary caregiver, he or she is preferred above all others. Gradually, the baby's affection expands to include other caregivers, siblings, pets, and people outside the home.

Relationships between parents and children should be strong, but not smothering. A child who is overly dependent on his or her parents and other caregivers has difficulty forming other relationships.

A warm positive relationship between parent and child will foster the child's ability to form good relationships with others.

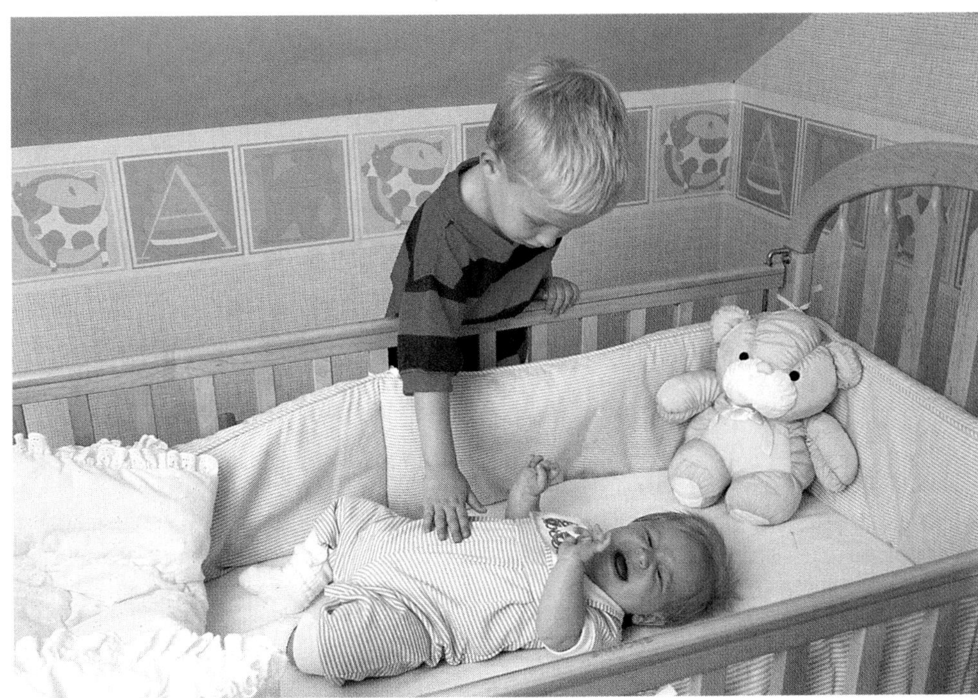

Older toddlers may try to comfort someone who appears distressed. However, they don't always know the best way to go about it. Why not?

Sympathy

Most children show little evidence of sympathy until about age two. To feel sympathy, the child must be able to understand that a situation can be upsetting for someone else even though he or she does not feel upset. The child must also be able to relate to other people emotionally. A well-adjusted, happy child is more inclined to be sympathetic than a child whose relationships are less satisfactory.

A child's first sympathetic responses are limited to crying when—and because—another person is crying. Around the age of three, the child first tries to comfort the other person and even tries to remove the cause of that person's distress. A three-year-old may pat and talk to an unhappy baby, or push all his or her own toys into the crib of a crying baby brother or sister. The ability to actually understand the feelings of others develops later.

Evaluating Emotional Adjustment

How can parents tell whether their child is developing well emotionally? Between the first and fourth birthdays, the single most important clue is the harmony of the parent-child relationship. The early pattern established between parents and child is never outgrown. It will have a significant influence on the child's later relationships in life—relationships with his or her spouse, own children, co-workers, and friends.

These are important signs of a healthy relationship between parent and child:

- The child seeks approval and praise from parents.
- The child turns to parents for comfort and help.
- The child tells parents about significant events so that they may share in the joy and sorrow.
- The child accepts limits and discipline without unusual resistance.

Another important indicator of emotional adjustment is a child's relationship with his or her siblings. (When the child is slightly older, friends and outside relationships also become important.) Quarreling with brothers and sisters is not always a sign of poor adjustment. Arguing is a normal pattern in some families. However, the child who is continuously and bitterly at odds with brothers and sisters, in spite of parents' efforts to ease the friction, may need professional help.

SECTION 1 REVIEW

CHECK YOUR UNDERSTANDING

1. Explain what it means to be self-centered.
2. What is negativism? What does negativism in a toddler indicate?
3. What kinds of emotions do toddlers release during temper tantrums?
4. Briefly describe the emotional stage typical for a three-year-old.
5. How does a child's expression of emotions change around the age of three?
6. List three factors that may influence the number of fears a young child has.
7. What is the most notable cause of jealousy in children between the ages of eighteen months and three and one-half years?

DISCUSS AND DISCOVER

1. Discuss your own ideas about how parents should deal with sibling rivalry. What goals should parents have in dealing with this kind of jealousy? What are reasonable steps for parents to take toward achieving those goals?
2. Collect photographs, or cut pictures from magazines, showing one- to three-year-olds expressing anger, fear, jealousy, affection, and sympathy. Display the pictures, and discuss which emotion you think each child is expressing. Do other students agree with you?

Social Development from One to Three

SECTION 2

OBJECTIVES

- Describe the general patterns of social development in children from ages one through three.
- Describe how young children gradually learn to play with each other.
- Explain the importance of a positive self-concept, and identify ways it can be developed.

TERMS TO LEARN

cooperative play
negative self-concept
parallel play
positive self-concept
socialization

Between the ages of one and four, children develop social attitudes and skills that remain with them throughout their lives. Early experiences in the family must teach a child how to cooperate and adapt to the needs of others.

General Social Patterns

Young children gradually learn to get along with other people, both in their own families and in other groups. This is the beginning of **socialization**, *the process of learning to get along with others.*

Social development is related to emotional, intellectual, and physical development. Certain social characteristics and tasks can be expected at different ages. Remember that individual differences may influence these patterns.

Eighteen Months

The primary socialization goal of children at eighteen months is to begin developing some independence from the family. For most children, the closest relationships are—and will remain—those with family members. However, toddlers need to begin learning about the outside world. This may mean trips to the playground or other opportunities to be with children and adults who are not part of the family.

The younger the children, the less likely they are to interact while playing.

SAFETY TIP

Eighteen-month-olds are usually not ready to share; struggles and even fights over specific toys are not uncommon. It is important that a parent or caregiver resolve such fights for young children. Fighting won't help the children learn about sharing, and one—or both—of the children might be hurt.

At about eighteen months, children begin to notice the presence of other children in play situations. However, there is little real interaction between children at this age.

Parallel play—*playing independently near, but not actually playing with, another child*—is characteristic of this age. The participation between children varies. One child may simply watch another child play with a toy. A different child might grab the toy away. Still another child may seem to pay no attention to the other children at all.

Eighteen-month-olds often seem to treat other people more as objects than as human beings. At this stage, the toddler is intent on satisfying strong desires without regard for anyone who interferes. There may be conflicts over toys that result in screaming, hitting, biting, or hair pulling.

Two Years

By age two, children already have an impressive list of social skills. A two-year-old is especially good at understanding and interacting with his or her primary caregiver. The child can read the caregiver's moods and gauge what kind of behavior he or she will accept. As speech develops, the young child is increasingly able to communicate with others.

Two-year-olds find it is fun to have someone to play with. They enjoy being with other children, although they usually engage only in parallel play.

Most two-year-olds are still not able to share or take turns. However, they like to please other people. Occasionally, they are willing to put the wishes of someone else (usually an adult) above their own wishes.

Two and One-Half Years

The negativism characteristic at age two and one-half carries over into children's social relationships. During this stage, a child who refuses to do anything for one person may perform tasks willingly for another person. The reasons for these responses are often impossible to understand.

At this age, children are beginning to learn about the rights of others. Social play is still parallel and works best with only two children. Squabbles are frequent, but brief. Children forget about them quickly and resume their play.

Three Years

Most three-year-olds are relatively sunny and agreeable. This shows in their relationships with others. People are important to children of this age. A three-year-old will share, help, or do things another person's way—just to please someone.

Three-year-olds begin **cooperative play**, *actually playing with one another, interacting and cooperating*. They build sand castles together, push toy tractors down the same roads, and park their toy cars side by side in the same garage—all without friction. They can also work together in small groups to build with blocks, act out events for doll families, and fit puzzles together.

Parents, though still very important to three-year-olds, are no longer all-powerful in children's social lives. Most children this age seek friends on their own. They may prefer some companions over others.

At three, children are more sure of themselves, and they are less easily frustrated than at earlier stages. Experience gives them confidence in themselves and in their relationships with others.

By age three, children are able to play together, not just next to each other. This is called cooperative play.

BUILDING SELF-ESTEEM

Helping Toddlers Make Friends

It is not uncommon for toddlers to have difficulty playing with other children. Although they may quickly respond to adults, they may be less inclined to do so with other children. Sometimes they seem more content to watch, rather than play with others. However, you will notice their social skills develop daily.

Toddlers may find it difficult to share playthings, playspace, or people, but as they reach three years old, social changes can be observed. The possessiveness and the grabbing of toys gives way to sharing and playing with other children, at least for short periods of time.

Adults can help toddlers make friends in several ways. First, adults can serve as a positive role models and demonstrate ways to talk, share, and take turns. Next, adults can praise the toddler's attempts of sharing with others. Finally, adults can limit play to short time spans, allowing youngsters to play alone with their toys, though in the presence of another child.

Three and One-Half Years

By the age of three and one-half, children are experienced in cooperative play; their play becomes more complex and includes more conversation. Disagreements with playmates are less frequent. Because three-and-one-half-year-olds enjoy companionship, they realize that they must share toys and put up with some things they do not like while playing with other children.

There is an increasing ability to evaluate friendships. For example, a three-and-one-half-year-old may say, "I don't like to have Kevin come here. He doesn't play nice." Close friends begin to exclude others, although friendships are not always long-lasting and often change rapidly depending on the needs of the child.

Friendships help young children learn to enjoy companionship, consider other people's desires, and handle disagreements.

Making Friends

Friendships are important to normal social development. They may also be a sign of good social progress. A child who is comfortable and friendly with others and who has at least one friend at a time is usually developing normally. However, if a child is unable or unwilling to make friends, it is important to discover the cause and take steps to help. Remember that this is a crucial stage for developing lifelong social skills.

Enjoying activities with a friend doubles the fun. Children learn social skills that can last a lifetime.

It is important to expose even very young children to other people. The give-and-take of socializing is needed throughout life. Children who begin to play with others early are not likely to be afraid of other children. They learn to cope with the occasional blows and snatching of other one- and two-year-olds.

Parents often have to make a special effort to arrange playtimes with other children for a first or only child in a family. This is important, though, because children who grow up with only adults for companionship may have difficulty interacting with children their own age. Since adults are more polite and considerate than children, a child who does not experience and learn to enjoy the rough-and-tumble companionship of other children until school age may face a difficult adjustment. At five or six, the child's feelings are more easily hurt, and the socialization process takes longer.

What about the child who does not get along with playmates? Remember that all children sometimes have disagreements and arguments. Whether or not the parent or other caregiver should intervene depends on the situation. Children need to learn how to solve such disagreements. If two children are relatively evenly matched and there is no physical or emotional harm being done, the caregiver can simply observe the situation. If this is not the case, the caregiver will probably need to step in and help the children solve the problem. Talking about the feelings of others, seeking options, and urging compromise helps children learn problem-solving skills that they will need in social situations throughout life.

Developing a Good Self-Concept

Your self-concept—the way you feel about yourself—affects your relationships with other people. The formation of self-concept begins at birth and continues throughout life. However, a person's basic attitudes about self are formed in early childhood. In general terms, a person may have a **positive self-concept**—*an inclination to see oneself as good, worthwhile, and capable*—or a **negative self-concept**—*an inclination to see oneself as bad, unimportant, and incapable.*

A child forms his or her self-concept in response to the actions and attitudes of other people. Parents usually spend the most time with the young child, so they have the strongest influence on the child's self-concept. A child who is treated with love and respect usually develops a positive self-concept.

Even in the first days of life, a newborn is beginning to form his or her self-concept. If, when the infant cries, the parents respond willingly and quickly with food or comfort, the baby begins to feel like a worthwhile person.

Soon the baby begins to explore his or her surroundings. These explorations give the child a chance to experience different sights, sounds, smells, tastes, and feelings; the child learns about the world and gains a sense of accomplishment.

Parents and other caregivers may—intentionally or unintentionally—discourage the baby's early attempts at exploration. Instead of creating an environment that is safe for exploration, they keep the baby confined to a playpen. This limits the baby's opportunities for successful experiences, and such experiences are essential for developing a positive self-concept.

As children begin to understand language, they are increasingly influenced by what people say to and about them. Children also reveal their image of themselves in their own language and their actions. For example, three young boys were playing together at a neighborhood playground. Two of them scrambled to the top of a log fort. They called to their friend still on the ground, "C'mon up here, Teddy. See how high we are!" Teddy watched them without moving and answered, "I can't. I'm too little. Mommy says I'll fall and get hurt."

UNDERSTANDING NONVERBAL CUES

Raising your eyebrows briefly, called the "the eyebrow flash," indicates friendliness—at least if you are European, Balinese, Papuan, Samoan, or American. However, the Japanese regard the gesture as indecent. Children learn to recognize body language as quickly as spoken language. Most nonverbal communication is not consciously relayed, and, as the examples above demonstrate, may differ from one social group to another. What is common to nonverbal methods is that all cultures teach their members to perceive communications in different ways.

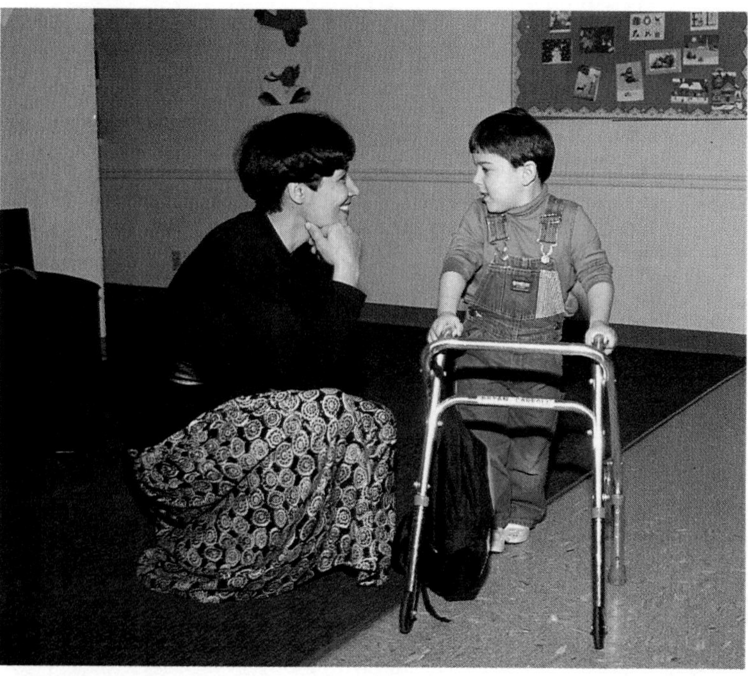

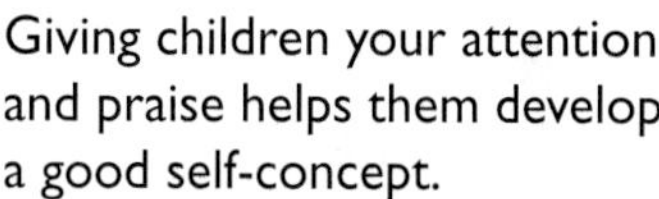
Giving children your attention and praise helps them develop a good self-concept.

Too many "don'ts" hurt a child's self-confidence. Sensible limits protect children, help them learn what they are able to do, and encourage success.

Some parents unintentionally act in ways that hurt a child's self-concept. For example, three-year-old Jackie set the table. Her mother smiled at her and said, "You did a very nice job, Jackie!" Then, however, the mother moved the dishes and silverware to their correct locations. This showed Jackie that her efforts weren't worth much. A better approach would have been for Jackie's mother to avoid making any changes. Then at dinner she might have said, "Jackie set the table tonight. Didn't she do a nice job? She already knows where the knives and spoons go."

Children who have a positive self-concept usually get along well with other people. They don't have to show off or boss other children to prove themselves. They are generally confident and outgoing. When they need help, they can usually ask for it and accept it readily.

Establishing a positive self-concept early in life is essential. Young children accept what others say about them as true. If children believe they are good, they try to act the part. However, if they constantly hear that they are "bad" or "stupid," they will live up to that image. The strong influence of adults' words and actions doesn't diminish until children are older and can judge their own actions. By that time, however, the self-concept and matching behavior are already well established.

SECTION 2 REVIEW

CHECK YOUR UNDERSTANDING

1. What is socialization?
2. What is parallel play? At what age do children typically engage in parallel play?
3. How do two-and-one-half-year-olds often show negativism in their social relationships?
4. What is cooperative play? At what age do children usually begin to engage in cooperative play?
5. Why is it important to give young children opportunities for forming friendships and for playing with friends?
6. What is a positive self-concept? How should parents and other caregivers treat a child to help him or her develop a positive self-concept?

DISCUSS AND DISCOVER

1. Discuss your ideas about this situation: A three-year-old boy appears to have no friends. He seems happy on his own, but he almost never seeks out the companionship of other children—and other children leave him alone, too. Does the boy have a problem? If so, how should he be helped? If not, why not?
2. Collect at least five toys—or pictures of toys—commonly used by two- and three-year-olds. Explain how each toy could be used in parallel play by younger children and later in cooperative play by older children.

SECTION 3

Personality Patterns and Behavior from One to Three

OBJECTIVES

- Discuss the three basic personality types of young children.
- Describe effective discipline techniques.

TERMS TO LEARN

discipline
self-discipline

An individual's personality is the combination of all the behavior characteristics usually shown by that person. Everyone has a unique personality (unlike that of anyone else), but these three general personality types can be identified in young children: the sensitive child, the placid child, and the aggressive child. An individual's personality type may change from infancy through adulthood.

Respecting Individual Personalities

It is important for parents to recognize and respect their child's individuality. Parents often want their child to be like themselves. Outgoing, assertive parents, for example, may try to make their shy child more outgoing. This doesn't work. Remember that a young child's self-concept depends on how well the child feels accepted—as himself or herself—by other people.

Parents do have a responsibility to guide their children, but this guidance should help each child develop within his or her own personality. For example, a sensitive child needs experiences that will encourage adapting to new people and situations. An aggressive child needs to learn consideration for others.

Descriptions of three basic personality types among one-, two-, and three-year-olds follow. Remember that these descriptions deal with children who are extremely sensitive, placid, or aggressive. The personalities of most children are not so extreme; many children show characteristics of more than one type.

The Sensitive Child

Sensitive, self-restrained toddlers prefer to be alone much of the time. They generally have a longer attention span (the length of time spent without boredom on one activity) than other children. The sensitive child rarely asks, "What can I do now?"

Sensitive children often lack the assertiveness to stand up for their own rights and desires. They tend to be dominated by others. They are less adventurous and often hold back from new experiences, watching until they feel more sure of themselves. They also seem to have less tolerance for conflict than other children do.

Parents and other caregivers must help sensitive children meet new situations with less reluctance. Overprotecting sensitive children makes life easier, but it does not encourage independence. Young children of this personality type should be allowed to explore and achieve slowly. Small tasks that can be successfully achieved help build confidence. Whenever possible, tell the sensitive child what to expect from a new situation. If, for example, the child has learned about the animals and the sounds they make, a trip to the zoo will be more successful and more enjoyable.

New experiences should be presented at a pace appropriate to the individual child. Do not hurry sensitive children into feeding or dressing themselves or into toilet training. Define goals within the individual child's ability. One playmate at a time is best; allow the sensitive child to adjust gradually to groups of children. Sensitive children usually play best with children their own age or younger.

Some sensitive children are especially frightened of strangers. These children need opportunities to learn how to get along without their parents or customary caregivers. The transition should be gradual, not forced. Prepare them for an outsider's care by emphasizing the enjoyment they can expect from the experience. For example, you might say, "Sally's going to help you make soap bubbles while I'm gone," or "Jeff is bringing along a new story about dinosaurs. He's going to read it to you this afternoon."

The Placid Child

Placid toddlers take things as they are. These children are most often at peace with their world. Placid children typically play happily with brothers, sisters, and friends. They are outgoing and respond easily to other people. Placid children usually take guidance well. They often enjoy accepting responsibility for routine tasks; they may make games out of eating, dressing, and bathing.

Placid children usually play well with others, but are also content to amuse themselves.

Like all other children, placid children need encouragement and praise. Parents and other caregivers should be alert to the needs of these "easy" children and should be careful to offer them plenty of time, attention, and care.

The Aggressive Child

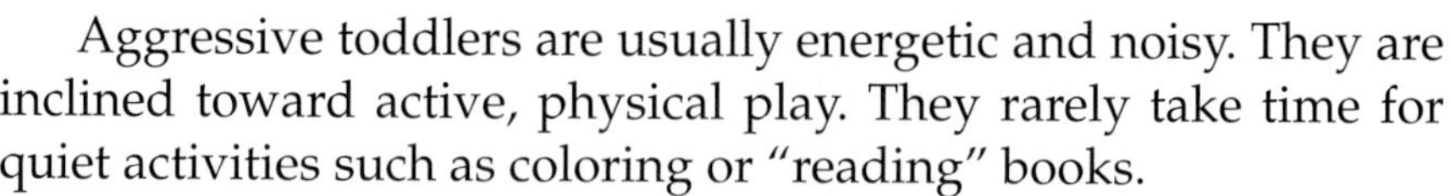

Aggressive toddlers are usually energetic and noisy. They are inclined toward active, physical play. They rarely take time for quiet activities such as coloring or "reading" books.

Aggressive children often simply take the toys they want from other children. If caregivers insist that the toys be returned, the children soon learn to trade toys rather than grab them. Aggressive children often kick, bite, or hit to get their own way. As a last resort, they cry or have a temper tantrum.

Praise is especially useful for guiding aggressive toddlers. When an aggresive child behaves in unacceptable ways, it is best to point out the negative consequences of his or her actions. Physical punishment is not an effective method of discipline and especially ineffective in discouraging excessive aggression; in

Children with an aggressive personality are even more active and adventurous than most toddlers. They need to be kept within the bounds of safe, acceptable behavior without being punished for their assertiveness.

fact, it generates more hostility and actually encourages further excessively aggressive behavior.

Self-assertive children are usually leaders rather than followers. They set examples—either appropriate or inappropriate—for other children. For this reason, parents and other caregivers should be especially careful to clarify desirable and acceptable behavior goals for aggressive children.

Discipline

Discipline is *the task of helping children learn to behave in acceptable ways* on their own, without the help of the adult. It is a subject that concerns many parents. They realize the need to teach children to control their behavior, but parents worry about how to handle discipline effectively.

Most experts agree that the long-range goal of discipline is to help children develop **self-discipline**, *the ability to control one's own behavior*. There will not always be someone around to tell a child what is right and wrong. Each child must acquire and follow his or her own standards of responsible conduct.

There is no single best approach to discipline. Parents should consider the individual personality of each child, as well as their own personal beliefs, in deciding how to handle discipline. They should also consider each child's age and stage of development, recognizing that different approaches to discipline may be especially effective at various ages.

- **Eight to twelve months.** Children at this age can usually be controlled by distraction. If the baby is chewing on a newspaper, for example, you might jingle a bright rattle in front of the child. As the rattle catches the baby's attention, you will have the chance to remove the newspaper quietly.
- **Twelve to fifteen months.** During this period, remove as many problem or unsafe objects as possible from the baby's reach. Distraction and physically removing the child from forbidden activities or places work best at this age. For example, Jared was fascinated by the lawn mower and tried to follow it around the yard. His older sister picked Jared up and took him into the house, saying, "Let's see if we can find the book about the teddy bear."
- **Fifteen to twenty-four months.** Children this age require distraction, removal, and spoken restrictions. Twenty-month-old Richard started playing with toy cars on the driveway, where a repair truck was parked. Richard's father said, "Let's take your cars into the backyard. You'll have more room there, and maybe we can make another garage for your cars. There are better places to play than our driveway. Driveways are only for big cars and trucks."

Discipline—or establishing some limits on behavior—is often necessary to keep children out of danger. How should you handle this situation?

ASK THE EXPERTS

Time-Outs

Jackie Mault is Director of Special Services for the Toppenish School District where she develops special programs for children from birth through high school.

I'm convinced that time-outs are the most effective method of guiding children's behavior. However, I'm still not confident enough about the time-out procedure to actually use them. Can you explain when and how time-outs work best?

I agree—using a time-out is the best way to discipline a child and to encourage the development of that child's self-discipline. A time-out is essentially a cooling-off period during which the child is removed from opportunities for interaction and activity.

Time-outs should be used when children's behavior is very disruptive, violating a specific set of rules. In either the classroom or the home, both adults and children should have a clear understanding of the kind of behavior that will result in a time-out. These are two rules commonly used in administering time-outs:

- If you hurt anybody, you will have to go to time-out.
- If you damage or destroy another person's property, you will have to go to time-out.

Like any other form of discipline, time-outs should be used consistently and calmly. To ensure that a time-out is effective, it is critical that the adult remain calm and reasonable.

These are the three basic steps of using time-outs:

1. State the rule and the consequences. It is important to remind the child of the rule that he or she has broken. It is also important to avoid discussing this rule or the child's behavior; any further talk actually rewards the child with attention.

2. Ignore the child's responses. Some children may try to avoid the time-out consequence by protesting the rule or explaining details of their behavior. Others may try to distract the adult with unusual behavior; some may have tantrums. It is important to show the child, calmly and clearly, that his or her behavior has resulted in a time-out; no words or actions can change that consequence.

3. Follow through quickly. Begin the time-out promptly, in direct response to the child's behavior. This helps the child understand that his or her behavior has consistent consequences.

The time-out setting should be an area free of distractions and rewarding activities. Often a time-out chair can be placed in a quiet area. The setting should be safe and easy for an adult to monitor. Any dark, enclosed, or especially lonely area is unsuitable; the purpose of a time-out is to discourage inappropriate behavior, not to frighten the child.

Jacqueline L Mault

Jackie Mault

- **Two to three years.** By the age of two, children have become better at responding to spoken commands and explanations. With their improved knowledge, two-year-olds can more easily understand adults' reasoning. Parents and other caregivers who explain their reasons get better results than those who only issue sharp commands. When she saw that her two-and-one-half-year-old was still not dressed, Kari's mother said, "Kari, you need to get dressed now because Grandma will be here soon to go shopping with us. We can't go unless we are ready."
- **Three to four years.** Three-year-olds take reasonable, loving discipline more readily than children of other ages. They like to please, and they may remind a parent that they were obedient. Three-year-old Marcus came inside on a rainy day and said, "I remembered to wear my boots today, didn't I? See my clean shoes? I'm a good boy, right?"

Discipline Tips

In the long run, desired behavior can best be taught through example. Parents and other caregivers who serve as positive role models in their daily lives have the most lasting influence on young children.

When you are selecting and using specific techniques of discipline, keep these suggestions in mind:

- Make relatively few requests, and be sure those requests are reasonable and age appropriate.

Once children are old enough, simple explanations can help them understand why they must follow rules.

- Be consistent. Don't laugh at the child's behavior one day and punish the child for the same behavior the next day. Parents should discuss their ideas about discipline and agree on methods.
- Let the child know that you mean what you say. Carry out all your promises and/or follow through with the appropriate natural or logical consequence. Use the "when" and "then"approach. For example, *when* your coat is on, *then* you can go outside.
- Look at situations from the child's point of view. When a three-year-old pulls a flower plant out of the garden, he or she may simply be trying to figure out what makes the plant grow or may want to please you by bringing you a flower.
- Respond to misbehavior by telling the child these things:
  This is not a good choice because...
  Why it is not a good choice.
  What he or she should do or try instead.
- Keep explanations simple and brief. Remember that a child's vocabulary and attention span are limited.
- Be prepared to repeat—over and over again. Toddlers have difficulty transferring learning. They don't realize that what applies to one situation also applies to another, similar situation.
- Discipline should not be an outlet for an adult's anger.
- Remember that all children need love and guidance.

SECTION 3 REVIEW

CHECK YOUR UNDERSTANDING

1. What is personality?
2. How should parents or other caregivers prepare a sensitive toddler for a new situation?
3. What general outlook does a placid toddler seem to have?
4. What kinds of activities are typical of aggressive toddlers?
5. What is discipline? What is the long-range goal of discipline?
6. What method of discipline is usually most effective in controlling the behavior of a two-year-old?
7. When responding to a toddler's misbehavior, what three things should you tell the child?

DISCUSS AND DISCOVER

1. Do you think that all the children in a given family are likely to fit into the same personality pattern? Why or why not? How do you think the similarities or differences between siblings might affect their parents and the parents' responses to the children?
2. Draw a picture or write a description of a two-year-old child who is behaving in a clearly inappropriate way. Share your picture or description with other students. Together, discuss your ideas about how a parent or caregiver could best respond to the child.

ENCOURAGING INDEPENDENCE

Between the ages of one and three, children long to feel and be more independent. At the same time, they fear independence. Parents and other caregivers must be careful to guide young children in feeling both independent and secure.

The following suggestions will help you encourage children to develop self-help skills and to grow, at their own rates, toward independence.

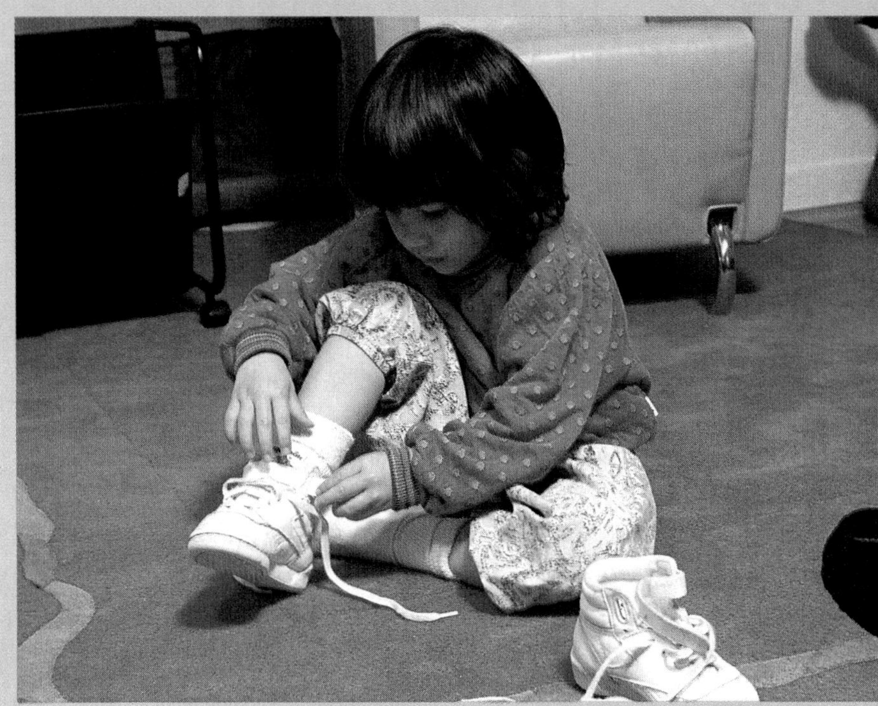

SELF-FEEDING

- Don't expect a child who is just learning to feed himself or herself to be neat. Minimize the mess with unbreakable dishes and a child-sized spoon and fork and small servings. A cup with a spill-proof lid helps during the learning stage.

- Choose foods that are easy to handle and eat. Cut food into bite-sized pieces before serving. Remember that attractively served food with a variety of colors, shapes, and textures encourages the child's interest.
- Be sure the child is comfortable. For eating at a table, use a high chair with the tray removed or a booster seat to raise the toddler to the right height.

SELF-DRESSING

- Choose clothes that are easy for the child to put on and take off. Look for roomy shirts that slip on easily. Elastic waistbands make pants, skirts, and shorts easier to handle. Dresses with buttons or zippers in the front are much more convenient than those with back openings.
- Fasteners often cause problems. Velcro fasteners, large buttons, and zippers that don't come apart at the bottom are easiest for toddlers to manage.

* If a dressing task is too difficult for the child to do completely, let him or her do at least one part of the task. Pulling up a zipper or slipping a foot into a shoe can be the first step to learning a more complex task.
* Praise the child's efforts as well as his or her accomplishments.

GROOMING SKILLS

* Provide the child with his or her own towel, washcloth, brush, comb, and toothbrush. Be sure that all are within easy reach.
* A small stool can help toddlers cope with adult-sized bathrooms.
* Establish grooming routines, and help the child follow them every day.
* Set a good example yourself. The child is more likely to wash hands before eating if he or she sees you washing your hands, too.

HELPING OTHERS

* Putting away toys can start as a game and can be encouraged with praise. Be sure there is adequate storage space within the child's reach.
* Toddlers love to imitate. Let them help with simple chores, such as sweeping, carrying or folding laundry, and setting the table.

* Keep directions short and clear. Younger children can remember only one step at a time.
* Be patient. A child's efforts will always be slower and less efficient than your own, but learning can't take place without practice.

SUMMARY

- The period between the first and fourth birthdays is a time of emotional ups and downs.
- Negativism is a normal part of toddlers' development.
- Children's emotions become more specific as they grow older.
- The parent-child relationship is an indicator of a child's emotional development.
- Many lifetime social attitudes are developed between the first and fourth birthdays.
- A child needs a positive self-concept in order to develop well emotionally and socially.
- Children with different personality types need different types of guidance.
- The goal of discipline is to help the child develop self-discipline.

REVIEWING THE FACTS

1. Why might a young child insist on unchanging routines?
2. List three reasons a toddler might be angry more often than normal.
3. Why might some fears be helpful? Give an example.
4. Who is the first person a baby loves? What other people gradually are included in a young child's affections?
5. What is sibling rivalry?
6. What is the difference between parallel play and cooperative play? At what ages are children likely to engage in these kinds of play?
7. Identify two ways in which a person with a positive self-concept differs from a person with a negative self-concept.
8. How are the preferred activities of a sensitive child likely to differ from those of an aggressive child and a placid child?
9. What is the best way to teach a child desired behavior?
10. What kind of discipline is especially effective with children between the ages of three and four? Why?

EXPLORING FURTHER

1. Work with several other students to brainstorm a list of childhood fears. Then discuss your experiences with those fears and your ideas about them. Which of those fears did you have as a child? Which have you seen in young children you know or remember? How do you think adults can best help young children deal with each of the fears? (Section 1)
2. Investigate toddler play groups (sometimes called mommy-and-me groups) in your community. Who attends these groups? What kinds of activities are involved? How appropriate do you feel the programs are? Why? Discuss your ideas with other students. (Section 2)
3. Observe parents or caregivers in a store or park. Describe an episode when the adult was required to discipline the child. Was the discipline technique suitable for the inappropriate behavior? Was it a reasonable form of discipline and age-appropriate? (Section 3)

THINKING CRITICALLY

1. **Compare and contrast.** Do you think adolescents and adults ever have temper tantrums? If so, how do they differ from the tantrums of a toddler? If not, why not?
2. **Analyze.** When a child is suffering from separation anxiety, what questions do you think his or her parents ask themselves? What other questions do you think they should ask themselves? What are parents' options in dealing with separation anxiety? What do you think is the best response to this kind of fear? Why?
3. **Analyze.** Why do you think parents often feel so worried about disciplining their children? What could help parents overcome these worries?

CROSS-CURRICULUM CONNECTIONS

1. **Writing.** Should young children be allowed to hear stories and watch television shows that deal with frightening topics? Do you think that kind of exposure can help children deal with their own fears, or do you think such stories and shows only create fears in children? Write a short essay explaining and supporting your ideas.
2. **Social Studies.** What are the acceptable methods of expressing common emotions, such as anger, fear, jealousy, affection, and sympathy, in our culture? In which cultures are acceptable expressions of those emotions different? What are the "right" ways to express those emotions in those cultures? Research some facts on this topic, and present a short oral report on your findings.

OBSERVING AND PARTICIPATING

Social Skills

The ability to get along with others begins to develop at an early age. Parents and other caregivers influence a child's social skills, and the child starts to learn what to expect from others. Children learn by imitation and modeling. This makes it important to set examples that encourage children in appropriate social skills.

Choose one of the activities below, and observe or participate with a toddler. Write your observations in your journal. Then compare your observations with those made by other students, and discuss what you have learned.

- **Observing.** Observe one or more groups of one- to three-year-olds playing in the same area, such as a park or a child care center. Which children are engaging in parallel play? What are they doing? How do they appear to be interacting, if at all? Which children are engaging in cooperative play? What are they doing together? How are they interacting and cooperating?
- **Participating.** Spend some time engaging a three-year-old in a quiet activity, such as reading, painting, or working with play dough. How does the child respond to the activity? How does the child respond to your suggestions, instructions, and encouragement? On the basis of this interaction, what do you think the child's personality type is?
- **Observing.** Observe two or more children playing under the supervision of a parent or a caregiver. How often does the adult intervene to direct or correct the children's behavior? Would you have intervened more often or less often? Why? What guidance techniques does the adult use? With what success?

CHAPTER 13

Intellectual Development from One to Three

SECTION 1 Understanding Learning and the Mind

SECTION 2 Encouraging Learning from One to Three

Grandpa Bill looks forward to spending time with his grandson, Steven. He was so proud of him and he was glad that Steven was getting older so they could do more things together.

"Take the dirt with the shovel, Steven, and put a little into the bottom of the pot."

"Like this, Grandpa?" asks Steven.

"Yes, that's right," replied Grandpa Bill. "It's okay if you spill a little. It won't hurt the table and we can clean it up afterwards."

"Will this plant grow really big?" Steven wonders aloud.

"It sure will," his grandfather explained. "As a matter of fact, it will probably grow as fast you you! We'll put it in a nice, sunny place. As long as you water it everyday, it will grow into a beautiful sunflower."

"Can we plan some more seeds?" begs Steven.

"That's a good idea, Steven. The next time you come to visit me you can plant some seeds right in my garden. You can plant some vegetables, like carrots and radishes, and how about some pretty flowers for your mom?"

SECTION 1

Understanding Learning and the Mind

OBJECTIVES

- Describe various methods of learning.
- Explain how children develop concepts.
- Explain the seven basic elements of intellectual activity.

TERMS TO LEARN

concepts
creativity
directed learning
imitation
incidental learning
intelligence
trial-and-error learning

Learning is a complex and exciting process. This process begins on the first day of life and continues throughout a person's lifetime.

The Role of Intelligence

Intelligence, as you know, is the capacity to learn. However, a more precise definition of intelligence will help you as you read about intellectual development between ages one and three. **Intelligence** is *the ability to interpret or understand everyday situations and to use that experience when faced with new situations or problems.*

A person's intelligence is determined by both heredity and environment. Everyone is born with certain possible limits of intellectual development. Some people have more intellectual potential than others. However, the extent to which an individual's potential is actually developed is greatly influenced by that person's environment.

Environmental experiences, such as interactions with family members, the availability of playthings, and personal encouragement, are especially important during the first years of life. During this early period, the foundation for later learning is formed. During this period, children also establish their attitudes toward learning. If curiosity about everything (a natural toddler's quality) is encouraged and enhanced, the child develops a positive attitude about learning.

Methods of Learning

Children learn in a variety of ways, some of them rather unexpected. Learning doesn't take place just in schools and school-like situations; it is an ongoing process. Children learn on their own through everyday experiences and through play. Researchers have classified children's learning methods into four groups: incidental learning, trial-and-error learning, imitation, and directed learning.

Although toys can aid learning, the encouragement of caregivers is far more important.

Incidental learning is *unplanned learning*. A small baby happens to push both feet against the bottom of the crib and discovers that this motion moves his or her body forward. When this happens accidentally a number of times, the baby understands the cause-and-effect situation. After this incidental learning has taken place, the baby may choose to push against the crib on purpose, in order to experience the forward movement. Here's another example of incidental learning: A three-year-old sets an open bottle of bubble liquid down on its side. When she picks the bottle up again to blow some bubbles, she finds all the liquid has poured out. Next time, she will be careful to put the bottle down upright.

A close-up view of a fish tank opens the door for learning opportunities.

HEALTH TIP

Research shows that good nutrition is essential in helping children develop to their full intellectual potential. Children need protein for building and repairing tissues and cells. They also need carbohydrates for energy.

Trial-and-error learning is *learning in which a child tries several solutions before finding out what works.* Pete, for example, uses trial-and-error learning as he tries to fit four pieces into a new puzzle board. He picks up one puzzle piece and tries fitting it into each hole on the board until he finds the right one. Janet also uses trial-and-error learning when she wants to play with the truck her younger brother is using. First, Janet grabs the truck from her brother, but he screams and her mother makes her give the truck back. Next, she tells her brother to go outside and play, but he doesn't want to. Finally, Janet offers to let her brother use her play dough if she can play with his truck. He agrees, and Janet gets what she wants.

Imitation is *learning by watching and copying others.* Perhaps you have been annoyed by a younger brother or sister who copied everything you did. Did you realize that he or she was trying to learn from you? Children—and adults—often learn by imitating others. Three-year-old Ben gives a doll a bath because that's what his parents do with his baby brother. "There, doesn't that feel good?" Ben asks the doll, using the same tone of voice his mother uses with the baby. Both skills and attitudes are learned by imitation.

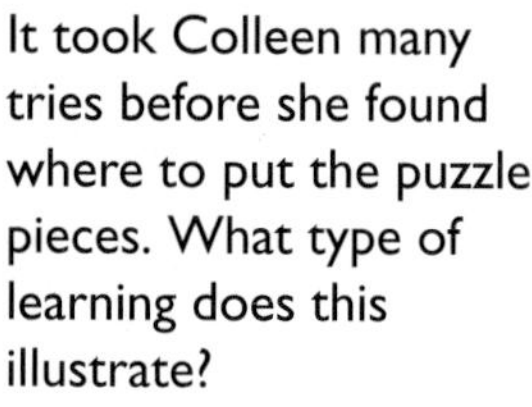

It took Colleen many tries before she found where to put the puzzle pieces. What type of learning does this illustrate?

You might not think pretending is an example of learning, but it is. Much of a child's behavior comes from watching and imitating others.

Directed learning is *learning from being taught, either formally or informally*. His first-grade teacher helps six-year-old Umberto learn to read, step by step. That's directed learning. Her mother shows two-year-old Monica how to point to her eyes, her nose, and her mouth. That's directed learning, too—it's just a less formal process. Directed learning begins in the early years and continues throughout life.

Concept Development

As they learn to think effectively, young children begin to organize the information they receive from their senses. They start to form **concepts**, *general categories of objects and information*. Concepts range from categories for objects such as "fruit," to qualities such as color or shape and to abstract ideas such as time.

As a child matures and learns, concepts become more refined and more accurate. Young babies begin by distinguishing two broad concepts, "me" and "not me." Toddlers and preschoolers make very broad distinctions between people and things. For example, all women are "mama" and all men are "dada." Later, the concepts of "woman," "man," "girl," and "boy" begin to have meaning. Similarly, the child learns that this is a table and that is a chair. Tables have flat surfaces and no backs. They may be small or large, and they vary in color. They are used to eat from or to put things on.

This three year old can sort objects by colors or shapes. He will also begin to recognize shapes in everyday objects.

Young children also learn to categorize objects by shape, color, and size. Balls are round, and so are biscuits and plates. Grass and trees are both green. When shown balls of three different sizes, most two-year-olds cannot identify the middle-sized ball. By age three, they can do so easily. However, the relationship between two items—"big" and "little"—may be recognized as early as eighteen months. At that time, the larger cat in the picture is called the "mama kitty" and the smaller one, the "baby kitty."

Concepts of life and time are not learned until later. A young child believes that anything that moves or works is alive. This includes clouds, mechanical toys, dolls, and the washing machine. Later, the child will be ready to learn that only plants, animals, and people are alive.

Concepts of time improve slowly during the second and third years. Two-year-olds may be more patient than before because they know that "soon" means something will happen. They know the difference between "before" and "after." However, "today," "tomorrow," and "yesterday" may not be completely grasped until a child is in kindergarten.

The Mind at Work

Intellectual activity is a complex process that coordinates the many elements of the mind. The most basic elements of intellectual activity are attention, memory, perception, reasoning, imagination, creativity, and curiosity. All these elements show remarkable development in children from one to three, but they continue to develop throughout life.

Attention

Every moment, the five senses are bombarded with information. This moment—as you are reading—is a good example. You see the words on the page. At the same time, you are also aware of such things as the size, shape, and color of the book and the amount of light in the room. You can probably hear pages being turned; perhaps you also hear someone walking in the hall or a fly buzzing around the room. You may be able to smell lunch being prepared in the cafeteria, or you might smell fresh wax on the floor. Your skin is telling you that the paper of the book is smooth and cool; it may also be telling you that there is a small rock in your shoe.

Fortunately, you are able to block out most of this sensory information and focus only on the book. You can concentrate. A baby is not able to concentrate. The infant's attention flits from one bit of sensory information to another.

As children mature, they gradually develop the ability to ignore most of the information their senses provide and to concentrate on one item of interest. One- to three-year-olds have short attention spans. However, a three-year-old can focus on one activity for much longer than a one-year-old.

Memory

Without memory, there would be no learning. If an experience left no impression, it would not affect future behavior. A child reacts to a situation by remembering similar experiences in the past. A one-year-old who was frightened by a dog may be afraid of all animals for a time. A three-year-old can remember the particular dog and compare it with others to judge their character.

Memory begins with the routine of a baby's life. The comfortable familiarity of parents is one of a baby's earliest memories.

By age two, a toddler has a fairly good memory. A two-year-old can deliver simple messages. The child can also remember a parent who has been absent for several weeks, repeat bits of favorite stories, and relate experiences after returning from an outing.

Can you explain how playing this "piano" involves attention, memeory, perception, and reasoning?

A three-year-old typically remembers simple requests or directions, uses numbers as if counting (although 14 may come directly after 6), and identifies most colors when asked to point to a specific color.

Perception

Perception is the ability to receive and use information from the senses. This ability develops gradually throughout childhood.

A newborn receives a great deal of sensory information but is unable to interpret much of it. Gradually, a baby develops the ability to make broad distinctions between people. These distinctions become more refined with experience.

Parents and caregivers can encourage the development of perception by answering, cheerfully and accurately, the frequent questions common among two- and three-year-olds—"Why?" "What is that?" "How does it work?" They can also encourage learning by making descriptive observations that the child can understand and expand on. For example, when passing a store window, you might say, "Look at the blue coat. Your shirt is blue, too. Let's see what other blue things we can see as we walk." Commenting on the environment and answering questions helps improve a child's perception and aids his or her concept development.

A child whose questions are ignored or brushed aside, on the other hand, loses opportunities for learning. If adults usually respond with an absent-minded "Uh-huh" or "Don't bother me right now—I'm busy," the child eventually stops asking questions.

Reasoning

Reasoning is basic to the ability to solve problems and to make decisions. It is also important in recognizing relationships and forming concepts.

Babies show the beginning of problem-solving ability at about four to six months of age. Around this age, the baby first pushes away one toy in order to get at another.

Later, the child solves problems by actually trying out all possible solutions. For example, young children often enjoy playing with a box in which objects of various shapes can be dropped through matching holes. A fourteen-month-old child will pick up a triangle and try to fit it into all the holes until one works.

By about two or three years of age, problem solving becomes more mental. A child can think through possible solutions to a problem and eliminate those that won't work without actually trying out each possibility.

BUILDING SELF-ESTEEM

Nature—An Educational Playland!

The outdoors can be an educational playland! Children learn through their senses and nature has different smells, sounds, textures, and tastes.

When children are outdoors, they discover that sticks make wonderful tools for scratching designs or letters in the earth or sand, and rocks come in a variety of sizes and shapes.

When children are surrounded by nature, there are many things to discover, compare, and think about. Flowers have different scents; some birds enjoy the water; the bark of trees can feel rough or smooth. Caregivers can help children in these discoveries by talking about nature and providing opportunities for children to explore and ask questions.

Decision making is closely related to problem solving. In fact, a decision can be considered a kind of problem. Gradually, children learn to follow the five basic steps in problem solving by mentally responding to these questions:

1. What is the problem?
2. What do I already know about it?
3. What are the possible solutions?
4. Which is the best solution?
5. Did I make the right choice?

Parents and caregivers can help children learn to make good decisions. One way is to give the child a chance to make real decisions. At first, these decisions should be based on limited choices, and a poor decision should not cause any harm. "Would you rather wear your yellow shirt or your green striped shirt with these brown pants?" "Would you like chicken soup or vegetable soup for lunch?" This kind of practice helps the child avoid making snap decisions. Eventually, the child will learn how to focus on the choices and to make thoughtful decisions on his or her own.

Imagination

Imagination begins to become evident at about two years of age. Actually, babies may also have active imaginations, but there is no way of knowing since they cannot speak. An active imagination is an important part of learning.

BUILDING SELF-ESTEEM

Helping Children Make Decisions

If a difficult situation is beyond the toddler, you can give just enough help to prevent discouragement. Show the child a possible solution, and then allow the child to continue. For example, you might say, "Let's see. This piece of the puzzle has green grass on it. Maybe it fits on that side of the picture where everything is green." Remember that children need successful experiences to gain perseverance, self-confidence, and the willingness to test their own reasoning ability.

Children can be and do almost anything through imagination. An empty box makes a good house. Another day it might become a spaceship or fort.

Imagination allows the child to try new things and to be different people—at least in the mind. Chairs become trains, boxes are buildings, and closets are caves. The child becomes a ferocious lion or a busy mail carrier. Many children of this age also have imaginary playmates.

Children use their imaginations to connect what they see and hear with themselves. A child may see an airplane and wonder, "Will I fly in a plane someday?" A child may hear about death and ask, "Will I die, too?"

Unfortunately, adult responses often stifle a child's imagination. When three-year-old Emma makes up a story, she isn't lying—she's using her imagination. In fact, until about the age of five, children are simply not sure where reality ends and imagination begins. However, if Emma's mother says, "Don't be silly. You know that didn't really happen," Emma will be discouraged from using her imagination, and her options for learning will be limited.

Creative activities are a way for children to express themselves. They also help children feel good about their accomplishments.

Creativity

Imagination is closely related to **creativity**, *the use of imagination to produce something.* The product is usually something others can see, such as a finger painting. Daydreams are also products of creativity, as is creative dramatic play where different roles are assumed—mother, baby, firefighter, and so forth.

Creativity, which is an asset throughout life, is most readily developed in early childhood—if children are given opportunities and encouragement. Here are some ways to promote creativity:

- Encourage play activities that depend on exploration, imagination, and creativity. Drawing, playing with clay, building things, dressing up in grown-up clothes or hats, and telling stories are opportunities for creative expression.
- The process of creating is more important than the product. Don't insist on conformity in every aspect of life. The message that being different is always bad stifles creativity. To encourage creativity, you might respond to a child's drawing this way: "Wow, Martin, I've never seen a cat with three eyes before or a purple cat! I wonder what it would be like to have a purple cat, or to have three eyes, or to have a purple cat with three eyes?"
- Praise the child's efforts, with deeds as well as words. Display that new picture of a three-eyed purple cat on the refrigerator and tell other people significant to the child about the picture.

Curiosity

Babies are curious about the world around them. That curiosity is the source of learning and should increase with age. However, parents sometimes stifle a child's curiosity by over-

SAFETY TIP

Parents and other caregivers need to remember that curiosity stimulates learning, but it can also be dangerous. Young children should be encouraged to explore—once hazards have been removed from their environment and as long as adults check on them frequently. You may want to review the ideas for toddler-proofing presented in Positive Parenting Skills on pages 344-345.

Learning should be fun. Sharing new experiences with caregivers helps give a child confidence.

PARENTING IN ACTION

Learning by Pretending

Jane Rodriguez was expecting several people for a neighborhood committee meeting. Three-year-old Jessica was underfoot, so her mother suggested she let the neighbors in as they arrived. Jessica greeted each person politely and proceeded to tell about her upcoming trip to visit her grandmother.

"This is my suitcase. I am taking the bus to Nana's. Mommy and Daddy are taking me to the bus. They will put my suitcase on the bus and put me in a bus seat and then go home. I'll go on the bus alone till I get to Grandma's house."

Surprised, each adult asked the same question: "Are you really going alone?"

"Yup. I'm going all by myself. I'm big enough now. I can do things by myself," she answered confidently.

The details were so complete that the adults accepted Jessica's story. As they gathered around the table for their meeting, however, one of them said doubtfully, "Jane, are you sure you want Jessica to go on a bus to Cambria by herself? She's only three! I wouldn't even let my ten-year-old do that!" The other neighbors agreed.

Jessica's mother laughed in surprise. "Oh, you mean Jessie's trip to her grandmother's! Of course, she's not going. She's just pretending she is. Two days ago, we sent Jenny, Jessica's twelve-year-old sister, on the bus to visit her grandmother. It's a nonstop ride, and her grandmother was there to meet her when the bus arrived. Jessie heard all the planning and instructions we gave Jenny. She went with us when we took Jenny to her seat on the bus. Now Jessie is imagining that she's going to make the same trip by herself."

THINK AND DISCUSS

1. What had Jessica learned? By what method had she learned it?
2. Which elements of intellectual activity can you identify in Jessica's "game"?
3. How do you think her parents encouraged those elements of intellectual activity?
4. Do you think there are any potentially harmful elements in Jessica's "game" about going to Grandma's? If so, what? If not, why not?
5. If you had been Jessica's parent, would you have handled the situation differently? Why or why not?

protecting the child—or by overprotecting the home. Parents and caregivers should remember that children are educating themselves while they are creating clutter.

Young children seem to be into everything. They poke into every corner and closet. They handle and examine everything within reach. It is impossible for caregivers to anticipate what a two- or three-year-old may do next. Surprised parents may find a doll or a truck in the washing machine because "it was dirty." A plastic horse may stand in the center of the mashed potatoes as the child explains, "Horsey eat, too."

It doesn't take much effort to turn everyday activities into learning experiences. This boy is finding out about where the food he eats comes from and how it grows.

SECTION 1 REVIEW

CHECK YOUR UNDERSTANDING

1. What is intelligence?
2. Which method of learning is based on watching and copying others? Who uses this method?
3. What is a concept? List at least three examples of concepts.
4. Why could there be no learning without memory?
5. What is perception? When and how does it develop?
6. What are the five basic steps in problem solving?
7. What is curiosity? Why is it important?

DISCUSS AND DISCOVER

1. Discuss your own responses to the four methods of learning: Which do you find most useful and enjoyable now? Why? Which do you think you found most useful and enjoyable as a three-year-old? Why?
2. Select a single concept that a three-year-old child might be ready to learn. Devise a simple game or make a simple toy that would help teach that concept to a young child. Share and discuss your game or toy with other students.

SECTION 2

TERMS TO LEARN

articulation
flammable
speech therapist

Encouraging Learning from One to Three

OBJECTIVES

- Suggest ways to encourage young children to learn.
- Select safe, appropriate toys that promote learning as well as physical and social skills.
- Describe how children develop speech patterns.
- Identify common speech problems.

Parents and other caregivers inevitably have an effect—either positive or negative—on a child's learning. Adults who provide a relaxed, accepting atmosphere and a variety of experiences encourage young children to learn. On the other hand, adults who are overly harsh, who are too busy with their own lives, or who show children that they do not really care discourage learning.

Readiness for Learning

Children can learn a new skill only when they are physically and intellectually ready. As an extreme example, it would be a waste of time trying to teach a six-month-old to pull a zipper closed—the baby has neither the physical maturity nor the intellectual maturity necessary for that skill. In the same way, nearly all three-year-olds lack the physical and intellectual maturity to learn to print words. When adults push children toward learning for which they are not ready, the children cannot succeed. In such situations, a child's sense of failure often causes him or her to learn more slowly rather than (as the adult intended) more rapidly.

Just as it is important to avoid pushing children into learning skills too early, it is also important to avoid delaying skills that children are ready to learn. For example, Ben's mother put Ben's shoes on for him every time he struggled with the task, but she discovered that this kind of "helping" caused problems later.

When Ben was well past the age when he should have succeeded in putting on his own shoes, he continued to bring them to his mother for her to put on.

Guiding Learning

These suggestions will help you as you guide the learning of young children:

- **Give your time and attention.** Children learn best when they are encouraged by someone who cares about them. That doesn't necessarily mean teaching them lessons. Going places together or sharing a game teaches, too. Reading to children can be a very special way of giving your time.
- **Allow time for thinking.** Toddlers need time to consider choices and make decisions. Remember that problem solving and decision making are new experiences for a toddler. When you offer a young child a choice, be prepared to offer time for decision making, too.
- **Give only as much help as the child needs to succeed.** If a toddler is struggling to pull on his or her own socks, don't take over. Instead, just help slip the sock over the child's heel before it gets caught. Then the child learns how to put on socks and enjoys the accomplishment—"I did it myself!" If at all possible, let the child do the final step in any task they may be struggling with.
- **Encourage children to draw their own conclusions.** "Let's find out" is better than an explanation. Seeing and doing helps reinforce learning. For example, let a child help plant a few seeds in a pot of soil. The child can help care for the seeds and watch as they grow into plants.
- **Show how to solve problems.** When a toddler's tower of blocks keeps toppling, demonstrate that stacking one block directly on top of another provides balance. Then remember that building the block tower is the toddler's project—don't try to take it over. Instead of building the tower, you can watch and encourage as the child tries again.
- **Maintain a positive attitude.** Encourage learning by letting the child know that you have confidence in his or her abilities. This may involve offering praise—"What a good try! You really worked hard on that."
- **Keep explanations simple and on the child's level.** When a toddler asks about the fish in the aquarium, you might say, "The fish are in the tank because fish live in the water. People live outside the water. We need air to breathe."

ASK THE EXPERTS

Reading to Children

Dr. Asa Hilliard is a Fuller E. Callaway Professor of Urban Education at Georgia State University.

I love reading, and I certainly hope my child will become a skilled and enthusiastic reader. When should I begin reading to him?

It's never too early to start reading to a child. In fact, I think parents should start reading to their babies even before the babies are born. This kind of reading is an extension of the natural conversing that parents do with their children, both before and after birth. It is a special affirmation of the baby as a human being, rather than an object.

Reading is much more than a method of communicating information to a young child. Reading is a social event, and reading to a young child can help establish close emotional bonds. When you read to a young child, you have an opportunity for a special kind of communication and relationship.

The sense of competency and accomplishment that children gain from reading begins long before they start reading for themselves. They enjoy being part of the close relationship of adult and child and like to be a participating member of a story circle as the preschool teacher reads aloud. As the child grows and develops, these accomplishments help prepare him or her to become a capable independent reader.

Parents who, like you, especially enjoy reading, offer their child another special gift by reading aloud: They have the opportunity to demonstrate and share a valued behavior. Of course, parents who are not themselves avid readers should not feel at a disadvantage in this situation. Whenever they take the time to read to young children and to enjoy sharing books and pictures together, they are also developing both attitudes and skills that will benefit their children. Even parents whose own reading skills are limited can participate in these activities. They can look at books with young children, talking about the pictures and, when the children are old enough, encouraging their comments and questions. They can also enjoy reading-related games and activities with their children.

Whatever the age of the child, and whatever the reading skills of the adult, the most important aspect of reading to young children is enjoyment. Don't rush, and don't make reading a daily chore. Instead, enjoy sharing books, and enjoy sharing time together.

Asa Hilliard

- **Allow children to explore and discover.** Recognize the benefits of letting children roll in the grass, climb trees, and squeeze mud through their fingers and toes. This is part of learning, too. Constantly saying "Don't do this" and "Don't touch that" inhibits sensory and motor experiences. Remember, children learn through all their senses and through play.

- **Help children understand the world and how it works.** Take young children along, even on routine errands, whenever possible. The library, the supermarket, and the gas station can all be places of learning. Wherever you go, talk about what is happening, and why it is happening, in that place. Encourage children to participate at home, too. Let them use small garden tools to help rake fallen leaves; call attention to the different colors and to the crackling sounds, and discuss the changing seasons.

Play Activities and Toys

A child's play can be compared to an adult's work—it is the basic task of that stage of life. Toys are an important part of play. They allow children to experience imaginary situations and act out different roles. They encourage the development of both large and small motor skills. They also help children learn to share and cooperate with others. Today, with thousands of toys to choose from, it is important to know how to choose wisely. When you are selecting a toy, ask yourself these questions:

- Is the toy safe?
- Is it well made and durable?
- Will it be easy to care for?
- Will it encourage the child to use his or her imagination?
- Is it colorful?
- Will it be easy for the child to handle?
- Is it appropriate for the child's age?

SAFETY TIP

Safety should be the most important consideration in choosing toys. This is especially true for toddlers. Remember that toys receive hard use. They should not break easily, have any sharp edges, have small parts that a young child could swallow, or be **flammable**—that is, *easily burned.* Be sure that no lead-based paints are used on the toys, because these paints are poisonous. Read all labels carefully before buying. The Food and Drug Administration and the Consumer Product Safety Commission have the power to recall toys that are unsafe. However, sometimes the danger is not known until a child is seriously injured or even killed by a toy.

A shovel, a pail, and sand are simple toys, yet think of how many areas of development they benefit: creativity, motor skills, cooperative play. What else would you add this list?

CULTURALLY-DIVERSE DOLLS

Dolls hold a special fascination for children. Today, as distances shrink, dolls are a way for people of one culture to learn about others. Two examples from Africa illustrate this point. A Ndebele mother makes a ceremonial initiation doll for her daughter when the young girl comes of age. The doll symbolizes a new beginning.

During idle winter months, Zulu women make dolls from fabric, discarded clothing, and decorative items that have been collected all year. Culturally-diverse dolls give insight into the creative spirit of the individuals who create them and convey a better understanding of diverse cultural backgrounds.

There is nothing more discouraging for a child—or an adult—than having a toy break the first time it is used. When you are buying a toy, think about the child or children who will be using it. How will the toy be used? Is it made of materials that will withstand that kind of use? Are all the parts firmly attached? Choose only toys that will give good value and service for their price.

Many people do not think about care when they are selecting a toy, but it is an important consideration. A stuffed bear that takes a ride through a mud puddle may be ruined unless it can be washed. Similarly, books with wipe-clean covers are the most practical choice for young children.

Many toys for sale today do everything for the child. Although such toys may look inviting, they do not help the child develop an imagination. Simple toys that can be different things or can be used in a variety of ways are better. A child may be able to push a button and make a talking doll say five phrases; that same child can make a nontalking doll say anything he or she wants it to say. Toys that lend themselves to many uses allow toddlers to work out their own ideas and develop self-confidence.

Colorful toys are important. Children—especially young children—respond more readily to colorful objects. Later, bright toys encourage children to learn color names.

When you are buying toys, it is also important to take the size of the child into consideration. A toy that is too large for the youngster to handle alone cannot be played with easily. The excitement of a new tricycle is quickly lost if the child's legs are too short to reach the pedals. A doll that is too big for the toddler to cuddle and carry cannot receive the attention and care the child probably wants to give.

Similar problems can occur when toys are not appropriate for the child's developmental stage. Infant toys are usually not challenging enough for most three-year-olds. Neither will an older child's toys amuse most fourteen-month-olds for long. It is important to know the capacities and interests of children at various ages in order to choose appropriate toys.

- **One to two years.** At this age, a child practices body control and learns through exploration. Many toys can be items found in the home, such as pie tins, wooden spoons, and plastic storage containers. Anything that allows the child to use large muscles is usually popular. This may include swings, small wagons, rocking horses, riding toys with wheels, balls, boxes, and low furniture. Children of this age also enjoy small dolls and animals, sturdy books, and containers of all sorts. Stacking toys, simple puzzles, and toy cars are also popular. Be careful to avoid small toys or toys with small parts that a young child might swallow.

- **Two to three years.** A child's coordination and understanding improve markedly during this year. In addition, the child wants to do what he or she sees adults doing. This desire to imitate suggests a variety of toys: a child-sized broom, a small shovel, plastic or wooden tools, play dishes, empty food containers, and other similar items. Crayons, clay, large beads to string, books, large blocks, and blunt scissors are popular. A sandbox can provide hours of enjoyment, and some children may be ready for a small tricycle.

- **Three to four years.** At this age, children continue to enjoy many of the same toys they liked as two-year-olds. In addition, their improved motor skills and imagination increase their interest in toys requiring the use of their hands. Dolls to dress, trucks, trains, and similar toys are popular. Children of this age love to color, paint—especially with finger paint, and play with play dough. Three-year-olds also spend longer periods with books and enjoy listening to records or cassettes. They will work and rework simple puzzles, and they are enthusiastic about using playground equipment such as ladders, swings, and slides. Most three-year-olds love the freedom and mobility of a tricycle.

Two-, three-, and four-year-olds need safe opportunities to run, jump, and climb.

Speech Development

Babies begin learning to say words by repeating sounds. Gradually, they discover that some combinations of sounds—words—have specific meanings. Then, as one-, two-, and three-year-olds, these children acquire speech patterns and learn about grammar simply by listening to other people speaking.

The ability to speak depends on all areas of development—physical, emotional, social, and intellectual. A problem in any one area can slow or even prevent speech development. However, even children without any such problems vary greatly in learning to speak.

Between their first and second birthdays, children work at learning new words. They like to learn the names of everything, and they enjoy listening to the sounds the words make. During this period, most children use one word rather than a whole sentence to express a thought. For example, a child might hold out a cup and say "water"—meaning, quite clearly, "I want a drink of water."

An individual child's language development is strongly influenced by the way adults and older children speak to that child. For example, Jason's mother usually used baby talk with him: "It's time for mommy's itsy-bitsy boy to go night-night. Does little Jason want his ba-ba first?" Not surprisingly, three-and-one-half-year-old Jason still has trouble speaking plainly enough for others to understand him. Amy's parents rarely talked to her when she was a baby. When a neighbor asked them about their silence, Amy's father explained, "I'd feel silly talking to Amy. She can't understand what we're saying." Amy started talking much later than average. Both Jason's and Amy's parents probably contributed to their children's speech difficulties.

You can encourage language development and learning in children aged one to three simply by talking to them, clearly and engagingly, about their daily lives. For example, you can take the time to describe—and guide the child in talking about—whatever he or she is seeing and doing. "My, Cindy! Look at the big bite you've taken out of that shiny red apple. Can you hear the crunch it makes when you put your teeth into it?" "Jake, can you point to the white chicken in the story? Where are the chicken's eggs? Let's count them together. You had an egg for breakfast this morning, didn't you?"

You can see that Cindy and Jake are being encouraged to learn. They hear correctly spoken English that helps them organize and understand what they are experiencing.

At about age two, the child usually starts combining two or three words to make short sentences: "Doggie bark." "Jimmy fall down." At this stage, the child typically calls himself or herself by name.

The sun is in the sky. Can you make a s-s-s sound? Some words and sounds are difficult for young children to articulate. With time and practice, however, most children eventually master them.

Children usually find pronouns (such as *I, you, me,* and *they*) confusing at first. Two-year-old Katie spent several weeks demanding, "Help you!" and "Change you!" She had been listening to her parents say, "I'll help you," and "I think it's time to change you." She had quite logically concluded that *you* was another word for *Katie.*

At about age two and one-half, children begin to learn some of the rules of grammar. They learn by listening to other people talk rather than by any formal teaching. For example, a child begins to add an *s* to words to make them plural; the child applies this rule to all words. At two and one-half, *foots* and *tooths* make as much sense as *hands* and *eyes*. It is the English language—not the young child—that fails to follow the rules. Gradually, the child will learn the right plural forms by hearing older children and adults speaking correct English.

Speech Difficulties

Many parents are concerned about "late talkers." Delayed speech shouldn't be considered a problem before the age of three if the child understands what others say and if other areas of development are normal. Some parents make the mistake of pressuring the child who talks late or unclearly. Most often, this pressure just makes the child aware of the problem and may result in an exaggeration of the problem.

A child who does not seem to understand what is said and does not speak or speaks very little should have a thorough physical examination. It is important to identify, as soon as

Most children eventually grow out of their minor speech problems. Sometimes, however, an examination reveals a physical problem affecting speech. The help of a trained professional may be needed.

possible, any physical problem that may be hindering the child's language development. Poor hearing is one physical problem that interferes with speech development. Mental retardation, learning disabilities, and emotional problems may also slow a child's speech.

Many children continue to have problems with **articulation**, or *the ability to use clear, distinct speech,* until they are three or four—or even older. Some children have trouble only with certain sounds. Other children skip syllables or leave off the endings of words. These problems usually correct themselves as the child grows older.

It is best to avoid frequent corrections of a child's pronunciation. Instead, be careful to set a good example with your own speech. If the toddler says "ba" and reaches for a bottle, hand the bottle over, saying, "Bottle. Tommy wants his bottle."

Stuttering is a more serious speech difficulty for young children. However, many adults mistake normal speech hesitations for stuttering. A child may repeat whole words or phrases: "Johnny... Johnny... Johnny. He... he... he hit Collin!" This is not true stuttering. The child's speaking and thinking abilities are still immature. The youngster simply cannot get the words out as rapidly or as smoothly as necessary. The same thing happens when a child who has been offered a choice of colored balloons says, "I ah... ah... ah... I... ah... I want this green one." The child is thinking and waiting for the right words to come. Some hesitation and repetition are common to all preschool children; they are not a sign of real stuttering.

A true stutter can be identified by the rhythm, pitch, and speed of speech. It is rapid, forced, and short and sharp in sound. Usually, the child repeats only the beginning sound of a word: "I c—c—c—can't g—g—g—go outside." The child usually shows tenseness in some way—gasping, sputtering, or rapid blinking.

The cause of stuttering is still not clearly understood. Most children outgrow it without special help. Some children, however, need the help of a **speech therapist**, *a professional trained to diagnose and help correct speech problems.* Patience and understanding are very important.

No matter what speaking difficulties a child may have, parents must let the child know that it does not affect their love. Such an attitude will help the child cope with—and perhaps even overcome—the problem.

SECTION 2 REVIEW

CHECK YOUR UNDERSTANDING

1. What is required before a child can learn a new skill?
2. Why is it important to give a toddler only as much help as he or she needs in practicing a new skill?
3. Which kinds of development does playing promote?
4. What should be the most important consideration when choosing toys for children? Why?
5. List at least four toys that are appropriate and fun for toddlers between the ages of one and two.
6. What should parents and caregivers do to encourage language development in young children?
7. What is a speech therapist? What kinds of problems might indicate that the help of a speech therapist is needed?

DISCUSS AND DISCOVER

1. Identify at least three local activities or events appropriate for young children. Discuss why you would take one- to three-year olds to these activities or events, what you would expect to do with children there, and what you anticipate children would learn from them.
2. Interview a speech therapist who works with young children, or arrange to have the therapist visit your class. Ask the speech therapist to explain his or her work and to make specific suggestions for parents and caregivers who work with young children.

READING TO CHILDREN

Sharing a book with a child can be a special experience, both for you and for the child. Books—both fiction and nonfiction—are wonderful learning tools. In addition, reading to a child nourishes close relationships, encourages language and listening skills, and helps the child separate reality from fantasy. Children who learn early in childhood that books are fun are more likely to remain readers throughout life.

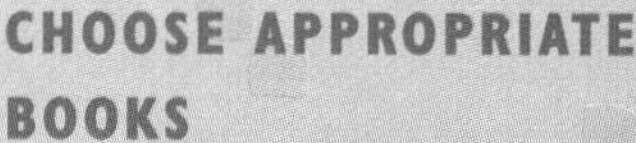

CHOOSE APPROPRIATE BOOKS

Children of different ages respond best to different types of books. Understanding their interest will help you choose books they will like.

One-year-olds need short, simple books with large, uncomplicated pictures. They like picture books with objects they can name. Books with rhymes are also popular. Some books have different textures on each page to stimulate the toddler's sense of touch.

Two-year-olds prefer simple stories they can relate to. Books about families and familiar experiences are good choices. Like one-year-olds, they never tire of hearing their favorite stories again and again.

By age three, children can enjoy longer stories (up to 10 or 15 minutes) with more of a plot. They like realistic stories about children, but also ones that help them use their imagination. Look for books that help them learn how things work and why things happen.

BECOME A MASTER STORYTELLER

Reading a story is much like putting on a play—a play in which you portray all the characters. Vary the tone and rate at which you read to create excitement and interest. Give each character a different voice. For example, a bear's voice might be low and growly. A princess's voice might be either shy or commanding. Use your own gestures and facial expressions to reinforce the content of the story.

If you are reading to one or two children, snuggle up close and hold the book so they can see. If you are reading to a group, the children should be in a semicircle facing you. Read loudly enough for everyone to hear. Take time to learn the story beforehand so you can keep the pictures facing the children.

ENCOURAGE PARTICIPATION

Long before they can read, children can participate in stories. Active involvement helps increase learning and fun.

- Even very young children can turn the pages. This gives practice in hand-eye coordination.
- Relate the action and pictures in the book to the child's own life. "You have a red ball, too, don't you?" "In the story, Peter has a baby sister. You have a baby brother."
- Ask questions as you read. "What do you think Melissa will find when she opens the box?" "What color is the dog?" "How would you feel if you were lost in the store? What would you do?"
- With familiar books, let the child play the part of one character. Don't expect word-for-word accuracy. Provide clues, when necessary, to keep the story moving.

- With older children, practice recognizing letters and the sounds they make. Point out the words for familiar objects.
- Encourage children to dramatize a story, either by acting it out of by putting on a puppet show. Let children draw their own pictures to go with favorite stories.
- Remember to keep your focus on the child—not on the story. Reading together should be fun. If the child has stopped enjoying a story, put the book away. It's not necessary to finish every book.

SUMMARY

- Intelligence is determined by both heredity and environment.
- Children learn on their own, as well as by being taught.
- Children learn to organize the information they receive from their senses by gradually developing concepts.
- Many elements of the mind are continuously developing.
- Play promotes all aspects of development.
- Toys should be safe, appealing, and appropriate to a child's age.
- The rate of speech development varies greatly.
- The way in which adults and older children speak to a young child greatly influences the child's language development.
- Some young children have difficulties with articulation or stuttering.

REVIEWING THE FACTS

1. What major factors determine an individual's intelligence? How?
2. What is the difference between incidental learning and trial-and-error learning?
3. How do concepts change as a child matures and learns?
4. What is reasoning?
5. What is the difference between imagination and creativity?
6. How do young children usually respond when they are pushed toward learning for which they are not ready?
7. What is the most important consideration in choosing toys for young children?
8. Why should toys for young children be colorful?
9. What is articulation? How should parents and other caregivers respond to a child's problems with articulation?
10. What is the difference between speech hesitations and stuttering? Why is it important to identify the difference?

EXPLORING FURTHER

1. Plan a game or activity for toddlers that requires attention, memory, perception, and reasoning. Discuss the game or activity with other students. Then, if possible, try the game or activity out with a very small group of two- or three-year-olds. (Section 1)
2. Select a simple, appealing food that a three-year-old could help prepare. (Be sure it is a food that a three-year-old might enjoy eating, too.) Write out a recipe for that food, including specific directions that will guide a caregiver in encouraging a child to participate in the preparation. (Section 1)
3. Using a doll to represent a one- or two-year-old, demonstrate how daily routines can be used as language-learning opportunities. For example, you might help or encourage the child to put on a jacket and hat before going outdoors, or you might shop for some fresh vegetables together. As you act out the activity, speak as you would to a young child. Be sure the subject of your conversation and the level of your language are appropriate to the child's experience. (Section 2)
4. Working in small groups, research ideas on ways to store toys. What ideas would be helpful when space is limited? What techniques might help children learn to put away their toys? (Section 2)

THINKING CRITICALLY

1. **Analyze.** Why do some very young children develop poor attitudes toward learning? Do you think such negative attitudes can be overcome? If so, at what age and how? If not, why not?
2. **Synthesize.** What are the most important influences on parents' attitudes toward learning and education? How do parents pass those attitudes on to their children? What is the significance of this transfer of attitudes?
3. **Analyze.** How do you think a parent or other caregiver can judge how much assistance a child needs in any situation? How could the adult's attitudes and interests interfere with making a good decision? What do you think are the results of giving a young child too much help? Too little help?

CROSS-CURRICULUM CONNECTIONS

1. **Art.** Take a series of photographs or draw a series of pictures expressing a child's actions and feelings as he or she engages in imaginative play.
2. **Writing.** Find out about various local events and activities for young children. Select the events you consider most appropriate in providing fun and learning for one- to three-year-olds. Then make a brochure for parents, describing the events and activities and encouraging families to participate in them.
3. **Math.** Choose a specific age child and make a list of toys that would be sutiable and safe for that age. Price these toys and total the cost. Then make suggestions for lower-cost substitutes for the recommeded toys.

OBSERVING AND PARTICIPATING

Communication Skills

In learning to speak, the child faces some major developmental tasks that are interrelated. These tasks include comprehending or understanding the speech of others, pronouncing words, building a vocabulary, and combining words into sentences.

Language development requires social contact. As children interact with others and hear language being used, they learn what words mean. They learn how to say and use words. Children depend on other people to provide models for their language development.

Choose one of the following activities, and spend some time observing or participating with a young child. Then make a detailed entry in your observation journal; discuss your observations with other students and compare your responses to the situations.

- **Observing.** Observe a toddler and the child's parent or primary caregiver, interacting with the child during play. In what ways is the parent or caregiver modeling good language? Does the play situation provide a relaxed environment for the child?
- **Observing.** Observe several two-year-olds at play with toys. What words do the children use to name and describe the toys? At whom are their words directed—themselves, each other, or a parent or caregiver? How do the children respond to one another's use of language?
- **Participating.** Spend time playing with a one- or two-year-old, or let the child help you with some routine tasks. Make an effort to talk with the child in an appropriate and encouraging way. How much of your language does the child seem to understand? How does the child respond to your statements and questions? How comfortable are you in adjusting your language to the child? Why?

39
38
37
3
FEET
36
35
34
33
32
31
30
29
28
27
26
2
FEET
7
6

UNIT 5

The Child from Four to Six

THE END

When I was One,
I had just begun.

When I was Two,
I was nearly new.

When I was Three,
I was hardly Me.

When I was Four,
I was not much more.

When I was Five,
I was just alive.

But now I am Six, I'm as clever as clever.
So I think I'll be six now for ever and ever.

A.A. Milne

Happy Birthday
Happy Birthday
Happy Birthday

CHAPTER 14

Physical Development from Four to Six

Today was Jimmy's birthday and he was having a party with cake, ice cream, balloons, hats, streamers, and paper whistles that unrolled when you blew them. After playing pin the tail on the donkey and musical chairs, they took turns at being blindfolded and hitting the piñata with a long stick. Finally, it broke open and the candy and prizes fell out. The children scrambled to the floor to pick up the fallen treats.

"Time for cake and ice cream!" Jimmy's mom called as she brought the cake to the table. Jonathan ran to stand beside Jimmy calling excitedly, "Yum, yum! My favorite kind of cake!"

Jimmy's mom smiled at him and gently teased, "Jonathan, I think any kind of cake would be your favorite!"

"Tolani and Jonathan stand close to Jimmy and blow your whistles while I take a picture," said Tolani's mom.

SECTION 1

Physical Growth and Development from Four to Six

OBJECTIVES

- Describe the changes in an average child's height, weight, proportion, and posture from ages four to six.
- Describe motor skill development in children from ages four to six.

TERMS TO LEARN

ambidextrous
dexterity
permanent teeth

Children of four, five, and six are known for their activity. They run instead of walk and they wiggle when they sit, yet there is a purpose behind all this activity. The period between the fourth and seventh birthdays is a time of practicing and refining physical skills.

Height and Weight

The rate of physical growth from ages four to six is only slightly slower than from ages one to three. The average yearly increase in height from four to six is 2½ to 3 inches (6.4 to 7.6 cm). You may remember that, in general, children double their birth length in five years. Thus, a shorter-than-average baby is likely to be shorter than most children at age five. Height and weight charts give average measurements. Many children are smaller or larger than the averages but are still considered to be developing normally.

Differences in height and weight increase as children grow older. You can see this when you look at a group of kindergartners—or even when you consider the students in your own class.

In general, children tend to be taller and heavier than their parents. Improved diet and health habits, enriched foods, and advances in medicine have combined to make children today the largest and healthiest in history.

The chart on page 415 shows average heights and weights for four- to six-year-olds. Most children gain about 4 to 5 pounds (1.8 to 2.3 kg) per year during this period. However, larger or smaller gains are quite common. Boys are often slightly taller and heavier than girls.

AVERAGE HEIGHTS AND WEIGHTS

AGES FOUR TO SIX

AGE	HEIGHT		WEIGHT	
	Inches	Centimeters	Pounds	Kilograms
Four years	40.7	103	36.0	16.3
Five years	43.5	110	40.5	18.4
Six years	46.0	117	45.0	20.4

Proportion and Posture

Between the fourth and seventh birthdays, a child's body becomes straighter and slimmer. The protruding abdomen of babyhood flattens. The shoulders widen and are held more erect. The chest, which was round at birth, remains so until about age three. Then it broadens and flattens. The neck also becomes longer.

The legs lengthen rapidly, growing straighter and firmer. The child's balance and coordination improve, so the arms are held nearer the body when the child walks or runs.

The movements of arms, hands, and fingers become more coordinated, and the ability to do more precise work is seen each year.

At this age, children seem to be always in motion.

Teeth

At about age six, children begin to lose their primary teeth. They are gradually replaced by **permanent teeth**, *the set of 32 teeth that will not be naturally replaced.*

The six-year-old molars, or "first molars," are the first of the secondary teeth to appear. There are four of these molars—two upper and two lower—positioned in back of the 20 primary teeth. These molars appear before the front teeth are replaced and act as a lock to keep all the teeth in position. Later, as the child's front teeth are replaced by larger secondary teeth, the molars prevent the new front teeth from pushing other teeth farther back in the jaw.

In general, the primary teeth are lost in approximately the same order as they came in. The two lower front teeth are usually the first to be replaced, followed by the two upper front teeth.

Thumb sucking

Some four-, five-, and six-year-olds continue to suck their thumb. Like younger children, they use thumb sucking as a self-comforting technique. Most children learn that it is not socially acceptable; they give the habit up entirely or limit it to home.

For children who continue to suck their thumb, the habit may cause other problems. Heavy or strong sucking several times a day or all night can affect the position of the permanent teeth and the shape of the jaw.

Only a professional can diagnose the seriousness of a child's thumb sucking. It is wise to consult a dentist, who can examine the child and make specific recommendations. The dentist may be able to recommend positive methods of stopping the habit. Scolding or punishing the child usually only prolongs the habit.

Learning to bat a ball requires large and small motor skills, hand-eye coordination, and lots of practice.

Motor Skills

During this period, most basic large motor skills, such as walking, running, and climbing, become well developed. Small motor skills, such as drawing, cutting, and stringing beads, also show significant improvement.

Four-, five-, and six-year-olds are very energetic. Their favorite activities are usually physical—jumping, climbing, rapid tricycling, and turning somersaults. At four, children are learning to throw and catch both large and small balls. Five-year-olds show improved speed and coordination in all their activities.

Four- and five-year-olds show improved **dexterity**, *the skilled use of the hands and fingers.* At this age, children have steady hands as they stack blocks to create towers and buildings. Four-year-olds usually learn to lace their shoes, but most children cannot tie shoes until about age five. Five-year-olds pour liquids from a pitcher into a glass, showing improved hand-eye coordination. They like to cut and paste, and can print some letters, but often, not words.

The motor activities and interests of six-year-olds remain much the same, but children of this age show even greater ease and skill. Their movements are smoothly coordinated. Their increased mental abilities lend judgment to throwing, catching, building, and drawing. Six-year-olds enjoy balancing activities, such as walking a curb or riding a two-wheeled bicycle. Rhythm intrigues them. They like to keep time to music and jump rope to chanted jingles.

Children have many opportunities to practice and improve small motor skills when parents, caregivers, and teachers provide activities such as coloring, drawing, painting, tracing, cutting, and writing.

The chart on page 418 summarizes average motor abilities by age. The timing of motor skills development may vary because children have different abilities and interests.

Writing the alphabet is not only an intellectual skill, but a physical one. Can you explain why?

BUILDING SELF-ESTEEM

Encouraging The Development of Skills

From four to six years of age a child loves physical activity, and an increasing skill in motor activities will make the child feel confident about trying new challenges.

During this time children begin comparing themselves with their friends. They may begin to refuse to be involved in activities with other children when they see themselves less competent than their peers.

It's difficult for children to understand that everyone develops skills at different times. However, it is important for caregivers to encourage children in their attempts at activities. Caregivers need to point out those areas in which a child excels, and remind the child that everyone has different skills and interests.

AVERAGE MOTOR SKILLS DEVELOPMENT

AGES FOUR TO SIX

FOUR YEARS

- Gallops and hops.
- Laces shoes.
- Dresses and undresses self.
- Cuts on line with scissors.
- Jumps forward as well as in place.
- Throws overhand with body control.

FIVE YEARS

- Ties shoelaces.
- Draws recognizable person.
- Skillfully picks up very small items.
- Writes alphabet letters.
- Stands and balances on tiptoe for short period and skips, alternating feet.
- Buttons, snaps, and zips clothes.

SIX YEARS

- Throws and catches ball with more ease and accuracy.
- Builds block towers to shoulder height.
- Cuts, pastes, molds, and colors skillfully.
- Writes entire words.

Hand Preference

By about age five, most children consistently use either the right hand or the left hand for most activities. The hand that is used most often becomes the more skillful. Only a few people are **ambidextrous**, *able to use both hands with equal skill.*

Actually, preference for the right or left hand begins before the second birthday. Researchers are still not certain how hand preference is developed. Some point to heredity as the probable source. Others think it depends on which hand parents usually put objects into during the first several years of a child's life.

PARENTING IN ACTION

Encouraging Motor Skills Development

Joanne Simons teaches kindergarten at Monroe Elementary School. Today, she is the guest speaker on motor skills development in the child development class at a local high school.

"You only have to look at my class of kindergartners," says Ms. Simons, "to realize that motor skill development varies greatly from child to child. The children range in age from four and one-half to five and one-half. However, you can't tell which of the children are older by how well they cut or color or jump.

"One of the youngest children in the class has excellent coordination and concentration. He likes to put together puzzles with 75 or even 100 pieces. Another child in the class is almost a year older but can't put together a 35-piece puzzle or draw a circle that's easy to recognize. There's just a lot of individual variation."

"Try thinking back to your own days in kindergarten," Ms. Simons suggests. "I think you'll remember that many of the class activities are designed to help children improve their small and large motor skills. Painting is fun and creative—but it also helps develop hand-eye coordination. So do cutting and coloring. We play games that involve running and jumping and climbing—all large motor skill activities."

Mario raises his hand and asks, "Why are these skills emphasized so much in school? Don't kids learn them on their own at home? Isn't it the school's job to concentrate on teaching reading and writing and math?"

"That's a good question," replies Ms. Simons. "There are really two reasons for emphasizing motor skills. First, we know that children who have good motor skill development will be more successful learning to read and write. Think about writing for a moment. Forming letters takes the same kind of small muscle control and hand-eye coordination as coloring, doesn't it? The second reason we emphasize these activities is that they provide a transition between home and first grade. They resemble the play activities that children are accustomed to, but they are somewhat more structured or controlled. This emphasis helps children prepare for the more formal learning of first grade."

"Your class will be coming to observe my kindergarten next week," Ms. Simons went on. "I think you'll find the children interesting and see that they're very much individuals. If you look closely, you'll also see lots of learning going on—whether the children are jumping rope or listening to a story. After you've seen the children, I'll come back and answer any more questions you may have."

THINK AND DISCUSS

1. Why do you think Ms. Simons was chosen to speak to this child development class? What do you think the students learned from her that they might have missed otherwise? Do you think all kindergarten teachers would have expressed the same ideas? Why or why not?
2. Which kindergarten activities can you recall that provide practice in small motor skills? In large motor skills?
3. Do you think children who have poor motor skill development should be promoted to first grade or spend another year in kindergarten? Why? What other factors might be considered?

Parents, caregivers, and teachers should not attempt to change a child's hand preference. It doesn't really matter whether a child is right- or left-handed, except for the usually minor inconvenience of being left-handed in a world made for right-handed individuals.

SECTION 1 REVIEW

CHECK YOUR UNDERSTANDING

1. List three changes in physical proportion that take place between the fourth and seventh birthdays.
2. What are permanent teeth? Which are the first secondary teeth to appear?
3. What motivates most children to give up thumb sucking?
4. What is dexterity? Give two examples of a five-year-old's improved dexterity.
5. List at least three motor skills that an average five-year-old develops.
6. What does *ambidextrous* mean?
7. How do children develop hand preference?

DISCUSS AND DISCOVER

1. List at least ten games or activities that four- to six-year-olds enjoy. Which of the games and activities use and help develop large motor skills? Small motor skills? Which of the games and activities would be appropriate for children younger than four? Why?
2. Collect and display pictures that four-, five-, and six-year-olds have drawn of themselves and their families. How are the drawings alike? How are they different? What indications of the artist's age can you identify in each picture?

Providing Care for Children from Four to Six

SECTION 2

OBJECTIVES

- Explain the importance of good nutrition for children from ages four to six, and tell how good nutrition can be encouraged.
- Explain how to help children develop good self-care habits.

TERMS TO LEARN

enuresis
group identification
preschoolers

Four-, five-, and six-year-olds need less actual physical care than younger children. However, parents and other caregivers must still remind children and guide their self-care efforts. The biggest change in schedule during this period is the addition of school. The term **preschoolers** is often used for *children aged four and five*, but many four-year-olds go to preschool programs, and most five-year-olds go to kindergarten for a half or full day. Six-year-olds are typically in school for a full day.

Feeding

Like adults, children get their energy from the food they eat. The amount of food a child needs depends on many factors—activities, height, weight, and temperament of the child. For example, running requires more food energy than watching television. Even the time of year can make a difference. People need more food in cold weather to provide energy for keeping warm.

A child who is overweight is eating more food than his or her body can use. This extra food is stored as fat to meet future energy needs. A child who is underweight is not eating enough food to supply his or her energy needs. Neither of these conditions occurs suddenly (except, perhaps, as a result of illness). Overweight and underweight both result from long-term eating habits that are not right for the individual's needs. With the help of parents and other caregivers, children can learn to balance the amount of food they eat with the specific needs of their body.

An apple makes a tasty, healthy, and portable snack. Children who learn to enjoy nutritious snack foods when young will still have these habits as adults.

Snacks

Few children grow up without between-meal snacks. Actually, snacks are not bad—if they contribute to the child's daily nutritional needs. Some snacks, such as candy, cake, and soft drinks, provide the body with energy but fail to supply many of the nutrients (such as protein, vitamins, and minerals) necessary to keep the body healthy. Advertising encourages children to ask for snacks like these. Children who are given too many sweets at an early age often develop a "sweet tooth." On the other hand, children who are given nutritious snacks like fresh fruit and raw vegetables continue to enjoy such snacks when they are teenagers and adults.

Poor Nutrition

Poor nutrition has many causes. Though lack of money to buy healthful food is one cause, it is not the most common. Many children in families with sufficient money have poor diets. Parents in these families may not understand good nutrition, or they may not take the time to make sure their children are eating well. In other cases, children are left with the responsibility of choosing and preparing their own meals. The choices these children make are usually not the most healthful.

Poor nutrition can have a number of bad effects. Children with inadequate diets have less resistance to colds and infections and may find learning more difficult. Poorly nourished children are easily distracted and often lack motivation to learn.

Teaching Children About Good Nutrition

The best way to make sure children have a proper diet is to teach them about good nutrition early in life. Both home and school are part of this educational process. In our society, many meals are eaten away from the family. That means children regularly choose which foods they will eat—and which foods they won't eat.

One research study showed how four- and five-year-olds can be taught better eating habits. The study focused on helping children eat vegetables, which many youngsters dislike. The researchers began by surveying their young subjects to find out which vegetables the children liked best—and least. Then the researchers selected five of the less popular vegetables—asparagus, broccoli, rutabagas, spinach, and turnips—to use in the experiment. The children helped clean, chop, and cook these vegetables for their own meals. They learned about growing, harvesting, and serving the vegetables. Most importantly, the children learned how each vegetable helped them grow and stay healthy. At the end of the three-month experiment, most children ate the vegetables willingly at school. In addition, their parents reported that they were more willing to try new vegetables and other foods at home.

Shopping for fruits is a good way to learn to enjoy eating them. It also teaches children about nutrition and science, and makes them proud of their ability to help you.

Similar learning projects can be carried out at home. Four- to six-year-olds love to help in the kitchen, and everyone benefits when they do. The child learns about various foods, improves his or her motor skills, and is usually more willing to try new foods. The parent has a chance to spend time alone with the child, while encouraging the child in improved eating habits and in self-sufficiency.

What can children this age do to help in the kitchen? They can help put food away after a trip to the grocery store, and they can set the table. They love pulling the husks from ears of corn or tearing lettuce for salads. They can use a small egg beater to help prepare pudding, scrambled eggs, or batter. They enjoy rolling and cutting out biscuits or cookies. For an especially fun project, try making mini pizzas—children can flatten biscuit dough, spread on tomato sauce, and sprinkle on cheese and other toppings.

It is important to teach preschoolers good food habits because at this age, children are forming lifetime eating habits. Children learn quickly. As one four-year-old said as he waved his carrot stick during lunch, "This gives me good eyes, Grandma."

Once children start school, many take a packed lunch. Lunches should be nutritious, but there's no need to fall into a boring routine. Consider these tips for keeping packed lunches interesting and fun to eat:

- Let the child choose his or her own lunch box or reusable lunch bag. Encourage the child to add decorations, too.
- Children like finger foods. Cut chicken, cheese, or meat into bite-sized pieces for easier handling.

When young and older children help prepare meals, they are more apt to enjoy eating nutritious foods.

ASK THE EXPERTS

Promoting Good Eating Habits

Pat Brodeen is a teacher and Teen Parent Coordinator at Theodore Roosevelt High School in San Antonio, Texas. She is also a member of the Texas Task Force to develop curriculum for School Age Parenting courses.

I'm worried about my five-year-old. Sometimes I think all she eats is peanut butter and pizza. How can I encourage her to eat a balanced diet now, and how can I help her build healthy eating habits that will last a lifetime?

Many parents worry about their children's eating habits. It's a natural concern, but worrying isn't part of the solution. The best approach to helping a child develop good eating habits has three steps:

1. Understand children's nutritional needs.
2. Make nutritious foods available and attractive.
3. Set a good example, but don't make eating an issue. Let your child choose what he or she enjoys—and don't worry.

The first step is easy. Become familiar with the Food Guide Pyramid, which establishes recommended amounts of food for children. The pyramid makes it clear that children—like the rest of us—should be eating more pastas, fruits, and vegetables rather than meat. This usually works well, because most children don't especially like meat.

The second step is easy, too—and it can be fun for both parents and children. Involve the children in selecting, preparing, and serving nutritious foods. Together, find ways to enjoy familiar foods, and experiment with new foods. Try making frozen pops from fruit juice—and slip a piece of fruit into the middle as a special surprise. Let children create—and then eat—their own necklaces of oat ring cereal. Cut sandwiches or jellied fruit into appealing shapes. Try broccoli "trees" with a cheese dip, or fresh fruit with a yogurt dip.

For many parents, the third step in this approach is the most challenging. Be confident that you are offering your child nutritious, appealing foods; then let go. Avoid making a child eat a certain food, and don't insist that children eat everything on their plates. Instead, treat your child's food preferences— and your child— with respect. Given opportunities, good examples, and respect, children will be inclined to develop healthy, long-lasting eating habits.

Pat Brodeen

Pat Brodeen

- Sandwiches don't have to be boring. Use a variety of breads and fillings. Cut sandwiches into squares or triangles, or use cookie cutters to cut out fancy shapes.
- Insulated containers make it possible to keep foods hot or cold until lunchtime. Soup, casseroles, and salads are interesting alternatives to sandwiches.
- Muffins, biscuits, rolls, and bread sticks are all good substitutes for slices of bread.

- Pack fruits and vegetables ready to eat. Peel and cut them at home, if necessary. Vegetables can be cut into strips, chunks, or flowers. Try including raw vegetables such as yams, sweet potatoes, broccoli, and cauliflower.
- Lunch "treats" don't have to be cookies or candy. Raisins, peanuts, popcorn, and pumpkin or sunflower seeds are fun to eat and provide more nutrients.

Bathing and Dressing

During this period, children may show a decreased interest in washing, bathing, and dressing. Performing these tasks has already lost its novelty. The three-year-old's satisfaction of accomplishment gives way to boredom and reluctance.

Children need help in maintaining cleanliness habits. Poor habits acquired at this age can continue into adulthood. It is important for the rest of the family to set a good example and provide encouragement.

It is best to set up and maintain routines for bathing, washing hands, and other cleanliness habits. Routines help children accept these tasks as expected behavior, just like bedtime. Praise works better than nagging or scolding. Parents and other caregivers might say, "You always smell so good after your bath!" or "We'll let dinner wait until you've finished washing because it's much nicer when we all sit down together." When the task is done, a comment such as "Terrific—you're nice and clean and ready to eat" helps children feel good about themselves.

Children can be taught at an early age to take pride in their appearance. They will benefit from both good grooming habits and a good self-concept.

Four-, five-, and six-year-olds are usually able to dress themselves independently. Some may need help with complicated fasteners, such as buttons down the back or shoelaces. Many children have difficulty figuring out which clothes match. It's not unusual for preschoolers to choose combinations of prints or colors that clash. In most cases, parents and caregivers should ignore a mismatched outfit and comment instead on how well the child buttoned his or her shirt or how quickly the child was able to get dressed this morning. Parents who are uncomfortable with such outfits should remember that, as a child's matching skills develop, so do his or her skills in selecting clothing.

Choosing Clothes

The guidelines for choosing toddlers' clothes—comfort, durability, and economy—remain important at this age. Knit shirts and jeans are popular and practical for everyday wear.

Four- to six-year-olds have definite likes and dislikes in clothing. Some become as attached to a favorite garment as they do to a particular toy.

Group identification—*the need for a feeling of belonging*—also begins to be important. Wearing the accepted kind of clothing and following clothing fads are an important part of belonging to a group. Within reason, it is important to allow children to make their own clothing choices. Being happy with his or her clothing contributes to a child's self-confidence.

Caring for Clothes

As soon as children begin to care about what they wear, they can begin learning clothing-care habits. This is a long process. Many parents still find it necessary—at least occasionally—to remind ten-year-olds about putting their clothes away.

Children need to be taught that all clothes need care. Parents and other caregivers should show children where and how clean clothing can be hung up or put away, and where dirty clothes belong.

It is important to have adequate storage space that the child can reach, so that putting clothes away is a task the child can accomplish. Hooks just above eye level, low rods, and handy shelves encourage a child to put things where they belong.

Adults should provide consistent guidance, but they should avoid taking over the task. Parents who pick up and put away clothing for their five-year-old should not be surprised when that child expects the same service as a teenager. Parents and other caregivers can best encourage a child to develop good clothing-care habits by offering encouragement, showing patience, and setting a good example.

BUILDING SELF-ESTEEM

Complimenting Children

How do you know when you have completed a task properly? Often, the best indication is that someone tells you so. You are likely to feel especially pleased when someone praises your efforts, skill, or results.

Children feel the same way. However, compliments are even more important for children because they don't yet have the experience to recognize that their efforts are helpful, correct, or even complete.

Compliments can be the reinforcement that helps children feel good about themselves and lets them know that their efforts in attempting or completing a task are appreciated.

Compliments can also encourage children to try more difficult tasks. Compliments are meaningful only when they are sincerely expressed.

PARENTING IN ACTION

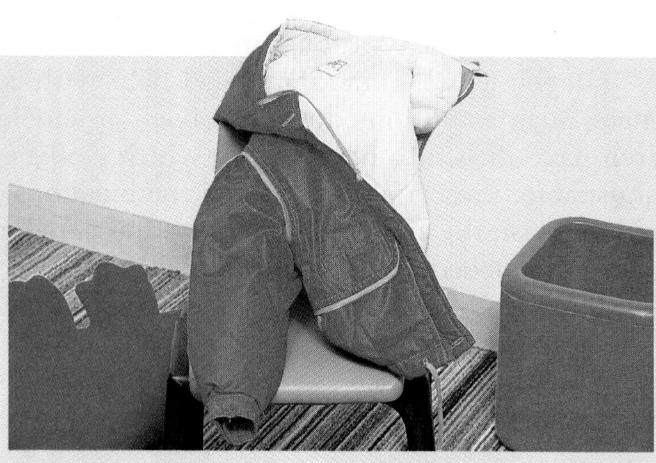

Dealing with Inconsistencies

Six-year-old Sarina lives with her father and stepmother. They have never expected Sarina to pick up her own clothes or put them away. Usually, her stepmother hangs up Sarina's jacket after school and sorts out the clothes she takes off at night. She washes the clothes that are dirty and puts everything away for Sarina.

Every other weekend, Sarina goes to stay with her mother. Her mother feels irritated when she sees Sarina's clothes draped over a chair or dropped onto the floor. Her mother reminds Sarina repeatedly to use the laundry hamper and hang up her clothes, but Sarina seems never to remember.

Sarina wants to please her mother, and she feels upset that taking care of her clothes has become such a problem.

THINK AND DISCUSS

1. Why has being responsible for her own clothes become a problem for Sarina?
2. How could this problem have been avoided?
3. Who should help Sarina with this problem? How?

Sleeping

Sleeping arrangements after the third year usually provide separate rooms for boys and girls, if at all possible. An individual bed for each child usually encourages better sleep habits.

Many four-year-olds do not take an afternoon nap. Although, a few continue to do so until they begin a full day of school.

Most four-, five-, and six-year-olds show less reluctance to go to bed. A few children still use delaying tactics, but many children actually ask to go to bed. After saying good night and perhaps looking at a book or listening to soft music for a while, most go to sleep easily. Some children may need conversation, companionship, or a stuffed toy before going to sleep, and many continue to enjoy bedtime stories.

Taking care of clothes, like anything else, can become a habit if parents and caregivers provide praise and encouragement.

Toileting

By the fourth birthday, most children have few toileting accidents. Four- and even five-year-olds may still have occasional accidents when they concentrate so completely on an enjoyable activity that they postpone going to the bathroom. Sickness—even as minor as a cold—is another common cause of accidents.

When they begin school, some children may suffer from constipation or may occasionally wet their pants. These problems can be caused by the tension children feel in their new school surroundings. The length of time for adjustment depends on the individual child. Most children will adjust within a few weeks. For some children, the problem may reoccur at the beginning of school for several years. Adults can help children with these problems by responding with patience and understanding. In addition, parents and other caregivers should develop a morning routine that allows enough time for relaxation and bathroom use before school. A calm, secure home atmosphere is also important.

HEALTH TIP

It is important to treat toileting accidents casually. Shaming or scolding the child cannot help. **Enuresis,** *a lack of bladder control,* is usually not considered a problem until a child is four—and sometimes it should not be treated as a problem even then. About 10 to 15 percent of normal five-year-olds wet the bed at least occasionally. Parents who are concerned about enuresis should consult a pediatrician for help in identifying the cause of the problem and in understanding the most helpful responses.

SECTION 2 REVIEW

CHECK YOUR UNDERSTANDING

1. What is a preschooler? Do any preschoolers go to school?
2. List at least three specific examples of nutritious snacks. What are two reasons young children should be given such nutritious snacks rather than sweet snacks?
3. List two causes of poor nutrition.
4. What is group identification? What is one way for young children to achieve group identification?
5. What clothing-care responsibilities should four- to six-year-olds be given?
6. How should adults respond to four- to six-year-olds who have toileting accidents?

DISCUSS AND DISCOVER

1. Observe and, if possible, photograph groups of kindergartners or first-graders. Then discuss the children's clothing. In what ways are their outfits appropriate for school activities? Which outfits, if any, are inappropriate? In what ways? What evidence, if any, do you see that the children associate a sense of belonging with any particular item or style of clothing?
2. Imagine that you are the parent of a six-year-old who wets the bed about once a month. How do you think you would feel about this situation? How would you try to respond? Why?

MONITORING TELEVISION VIEWING

Should young children watch television? This is a question that evokes strong—and often conflicting— responses. It is, however, probably not the question that parents and other caregivers should be considering. Much more relevant are these questions: Which TV programs should young children watch? How much TV should they watch? With whom should they watch?

Television can help with many types of learning. Shows like *Sesame Street*, for example, have been specially developed to make learning fun and easy for children. Such shows may teach the alphabet and numbers, help children learn about different cultures, and help them understand their feelings. Nature shows are both entertaining and educational. Programs on space exploration or other special events can help children develop a sense of history and an interest in the current world.

Certainly, some television shows are both fun and beneficial for children. However, letting the TV serve as a child's "electronic babysitter" is probably not healthy. The more a child watches the TV, the less time he or she has for other activities important to physical, social, and intellectual development. The following are some of the negative effects of television:

- Children learn to expect to be continually entertained. This may make their adjustment to school more difficult.
- Children become less active and physically fit.
- Television can stifle imagination and creativity. Children who watch a lot of television may find it difficult to amuse themselves.

Television watching can be an asset or a liability to a child's learning and development. Parents and other caregivers should select shows that are appropriate for the child—musical entertainment, children's stories, or programs that present reassuring images of family life. Whenever possible, adults should watch along with the child to explain things that may be confusing and to help differentiate between what is real and what is fantasy. If violence or other inappropriate behavior is shown, the caregiver and the child can discuss ways it could have been avoided and better ways of handling the situation. These approaches can make watching TV an enjoyable shared activity.

- Children who are over dependent on television don't develop the social skills learned through play with other children.
- Children often have trouble distinguishing between reality and fantasy. They can easily be misled into thinking everything they see on TV is true.

It is important to remember that not all TV programs are suitable for children to watch. Some programs frighten or confuse children. Others present topics that are too mature for them to understand or deal with. One particular problem is the amount of violence depicted on television, even in children's cartoons. Research is still being conducted on the effects of watching TV violence. You may be able to find up-to-date reports on this research in current magazines or journals.

SUMMARY

- Growth in height and weight remains steady from ages four to six.
- Secondary teeth begin to emerge at this age and replace primary teeth.
- Four- to six-year-olds practice and refine their motor skills.
- The amount of food a child needs depends on activities, height, weight, and temperament of the child.
- Establishing good eating habits is an important goal at this age and can influence the child's nutrition habits as an adult.
- Four- to six-year-olds can wash and dress themselves and can help care for their own clothes.
- Enuresis may still be a problem for some children at this age.

REVIEWING THE FACTS

1. Why do children generally tend to be taller than their parents?
2. As a child gets older, do height and weight charts become more or less reliable as guides to healthy growth? Why?
3. What special purpose do six-year-old molars serve?
4. What are two theories about how hand preference is developed?
5. What are four benefits of letting children help prepare meals?
6. What are three ways to help children develop cleanliness habits?
7. What sleeping arrangements should be made, if possible, for children aged four or older?
8. What are three ways to help children become responsible in caring for their own clothes?
9. Why do some children suffer from constipation when they begin attending school? How should parents respond?
10. What is enuresis? How should parents respond to enuresis?

EXPLORING FURTHER

1. Think about how you would teach a five-year-old to tie shoelaces. Make a simple chart demonstrating the best teaching steps. Then, if possible, try using your teaching plan with a child who has not yet learned to tie his or her shoelaces. (Section 1)
2. Collect several jump-rope chants that six-year-olds enjoy. Then make up at least one new chant for children to try. Make an illustrated booklet with these chants. Share the booklet with parents, first-grade teachers, or young children. (Section 1)
3. Plan and practice a five- to ten-minute puppet show that teaches young children about good nutrition. If possible, perform your puppet show for a group of preschoolers. (Section 2)
4. Plan and prepare two after-school snacks for six-year-olds. Eat the snacks with the young children. How nutritious are the snacks? How appealing are they? What might make the snacks more nutritious and/or more appealing? (Section 2)
5. Interview three or four parents to determine whether they think it is important for their children to select their clothes for the day. Do the parents think it makes any difference what the children wear? Why or why not? (Section 2)

THINKING CRITICALLY

1. **Synthesize.** What effect, if any, do you think size might have on a child's personality? How do you think parents and other caregivers should help children cope with concerns about their own stature?
2. **Analyze.** How important do you think it is for families to eat together? Why? What circumstances make such meals difficult for many families? What compromises do you think parents should make? Why?
3. **Synthesize.** How do you think parents should respond to their children's desire to follow clothing fads? Why? What problems might result from allowing children to follow such fads? What problems might result from forbidding children to follow them?

CROSS-CURRICULUM CONNECTIONS

1. **Math.** Help weigh and measure the children in a preschool or kindergarten class. Record all the heights and weights. Then calculate the average height and weight of children in the class. How do the class averages compare with the figures in the Average Heights and Weights chart on page 415?
2. **Computers.** Collect or create recipes for tasty, nutritious snacks for young children. Use computer software to do a nutrient analysis of each recipe. Include serving size, number of calories, and grams of fat, protein, and carbohydrates.

OBSERVING AND PARTICIPATING

Health and Safety

Although four- to six-year-olds are grasping concepts about health and safety, they need encouragement and constant reminders. At this age, children are often playing or attending schools in community settings. This means that caregivers, other children, and the condition of the environment greatly influences the health and safety of the young child.

Choose one of the activities below, and spend some time observing or participating with four- to six-year-olds. Then write your observations in your journal, and compare your observations with those made by other students.

- **Observing.** Observe four- to six-year-olds at play in a park or other public area. How is the outdoor play equipment constructed to ensure safety for the children? Which pieces of equipment, if any, could cause safety problems for the children? Why? Which of the children's activities or behaviors, if any, could cause safety problems?
- **Observing.** Visit a child care center or a school, and observe the children as they eat lunch. What is available for the children to eat? What choices do the children make about their lunch foods? Can you determine why children are making those choices? What suggestions, if any, would you make for improving the children's lunch choices?
- **Participating.** Work with a four- to six-year-old to prepare a snack or a simple meal (or help a group of children in a preschool program as they participate in preparing a snack or meal). Which health habits—such as washing hands before preparing food, avoiding contact with pets while handling food, wiping up spills immediately—does the child follow independently? About which health habits do you have to remind the child?

CHAPTER 15

Emotional and Social Development from Four to Six

Adam and Anna rummaged through the old-clothes box. What a treasure chest of shirts, ties, jewelry, purses, and a lot more! Within minutes they were creating some interesting outfits.

"I'll be the Mom and you be the Dad," announces Anna with authority. "You have to put on a suit and go to work. I'm going shopping." She chooses necklaces from the box and adds a bracelet to match her pretty clothes.

"Okay,"says Adam. "I am going to work at a big building downtown and I'm the boss." He selects a shirt and vest, adds a tie, and then puts on a business-like hat.

Anna looks at herself in the mirror and pretends to put on lipstick. "Now are we ready to go?"

"Let me look," says Adam as he holds the mirror. "Yes I'm off to work," he announces.

SECTION 1

Emotional Development from Four to Six

OBJECTIVES

- Describe general patterns of emotional development in children aged four, five, and six.
- Give examples of the causes of and the responses to anger, fear, and jealousy in children aged four to six.
- Discuss the positive and negative effects of competition.

TERMS TO LEARN

self-esteem

Four-, five-, and six-year-olds must cope with many changes in their lives. Most begin regular school attendance during this period. School takes children away from their home and into a new environment, to be shared with unfamiliar adults and large groups of other children. In addition, children of this age begin to assume the responsibilities of childhood and become aware that they have left babyhood forever. These major steps require many adjustments for four-, five-, and six-year-olds.

General Emotional Patterns

Like children from one to three, children aged four to six often go through characteristic emotional stages. However, each child differs in some ways from others. Emotional development depends on the individual child's personality, family, and experiences.

Four Years

Most four-year-olds seem intent on asserting their independence. They are more self-centered, impatient, defiant, and boastful than they were as three-year-olds. They often argue and compete, and they are bossier than in the past.

Four-year-olds can also be unusually loving and affectionate. They need and seek parental approval. A four-year-old may stamp her foot and scream, "I hate you, Mommy!" Three minutes later she may smilingly offer her mother a shiny stone or a flower as a special present.

The independence of four-year-olds has special benefits, too. At this age, children can wash and dress themselves independently. They are typically proud of their accomplishments, abilities, possessions, and creations.

When children of this age make mistakes or disobey rules, they are likely to deny responsibility for their actions. It is common to hear a four-year-old explain, "A big dog came by and knocked it over" or "Joe made me hit her."

Four-year-olds use their language ability with enthusiasm. They enjoy language in part for its sounds. "Antsy-Wantsy-Nancy"—or some similar nonsense—can send them into hysterical laughter. They enjoy trying out bathroom-related words and seeing reactions from other children and adults. They also want to talk the way adults do, though they do not yet have the language skills for mature conversations. They boast, tattle on their friends and siblings, and tell imaginative stories.

Four-year-olds can sometimes be difficult. However, when they are loveable, it's hard to resist them.

Four-year-olds have trouble separating fact from fantasy. Parents and other caregivers should treat exaggerations with humor, since at this age, children do not tell deliberate lies. It is helpful to let children know what is pretend and what is real. After a wild story about a dinosaur in the backyard, for example, a parent can say, "It's fun pretending there is a dinosaur in our yard."

Four-year-olds enjoy having other people laugh at their jokes, but they are very sensitive about having people laugh at their mistakes. It is important to children this age that they are no longer "babies"—whose mistakes people can laugh at, all in good fun.

Most four-year-olds are in a rather difficult phase of normal emotional development. You can help children of this age by respecting their need to explore and test themselves. Parents and caregivers should make an effort to avoid treating four-year-olds as babies. They should also try to use flexible rules in guiding the behavior of four-year-olds.

Five Years

Five-year-olds enter a quieter period of emotional development, similar to that of age three but at a higher level. Children of five are generally rather practical, sympathetic, and serious. Their improved attention span allows them to finish what they have started, rather than moving from one thing to another. Also, five-year-olds are able to go back and finish uncompleted tasks.

At age five, children are usually willing to cooperate with parents and follow reasonable rules, such as putting away toys. They can stick with a task until it is done.

Five-year-olds have learned that others will not accept tall tales and lies; they are, therefore, increasingly realistic. They are like four-year-olds in their continued enjoyment of slapstick humor. However, their abilities to carry on discussions and ask meaningful questions are noticeably better than those of four-year-olds.

At this age, children conform to rules more easily. They like supervision, accept instruction, and ask permission. They willingly mind their parents and teachers—at least most of the time. However, adult criticism is very hard for five-year-olds to take.

Emotionally, children at age five are more patient, generous, persistent, and conscientious than they were earlier. The occasional anxiety that they feel is usually caused by a desire to achieve acceptable results rather than by general insecurity.

Six Years

Like children of four, six-year-olds are often stubborn and quarrelsome. They resent directions, and they "know everything." They are the center of their own universe—and determined to stay there. Six-year-olds are often at their worst with their own parents.

Can you interpret the moods this boy is experiencing? Note how the moods change the boy's entire appearance.

At six, children have rapidly changing moods. They love and hate, accept and reject, smile and storm—sometimes for no apparent reason. Even a favorite playmate is likely to get a swift whack before being informed, "You bumped into my truck." Of course, a playmate who is also six will probably deliver an immediate blow in return.

Six-year-olds are learning to appreciate humorous situations and jokes. They throw themselves into their fun with the abandon that characterizes all they do.

It is easy to understand why six is a difficult age for children. Many are beginning school full-time; they are faced with the task of developing their status outside the home. This is a time of difficult transitions for most children. It is also a time when children long to feel grown-up—but often feel small and dependent. Six-year-olds crave praise and approval. They are easily hurt, they wilt under criticism, and they are readily discouraged.

Specific Emotions

During the years from four to six, children experience a wider range of emotions—and more intense emotions—than they did when younger. They need guidance in recognizing and expressing all their emotions. Parents and other caregivers of children this age should be careful to accept and help children identify all the emotions they experience.

As children grow older, they find new ways to vent their emotions. Teasing, insulting, and making fun of others are typical of six-year-olds.

Anger

Anger shows more distinct changes during childhood than does any other emotion. Young children show anger freely, without any attempt to restrain themselves. As children grow, they learn to use more subtle means of expressing their anger:

- **Four years.** Four-year-olds may still express their anger by engaging in physical fights. Their anger lasts longer than before. They often threaten and attempt to "get even."
- **Five years.** Five-year-olds often attempt to hurt other children's feelings rather than hurting them physically.
- **Six years.** Six-year-olds are even more stinging with words. They tease, insult, nag, and make fun of others.

The frequency of anger declines during the period from four to six. However, the effects of anger are longer lasting. There are a number of reasons for these changes. A child's tolerance for frustration generally increases as he or she grows older. Also, some sources of earlier frustration are eliminated as the child's motor skills improve. During the period from four to six, a child usually gains a better understanding of the property rights of other people, is able to work well in groups, and begins to learn about and accept the differing personalities of other people.

The most common cause of anger for four- to six-year-olds is disagreements with other children. While quarrels are still loud and verbal, five- and six-year-old children begin to conceal and disguise their feelings. Sometimes their methods of revenge are indirect. They may pretend indifference, sneer, or make sly remarks. Often they make exaggerated threats. Occasionally, they take their anger out on a scapegoat, such as a younger sibling, a pet, a toy, or the furniture.

School-age children begin to understand that other people sometimes try to provoke their anger. One particularly imaginative five-year-old scored a crushing defeat with this reply to a kick: "Aw, that just felt like a little minnow swimming by me!" The child clearly recognized both his opponent's intent to hurt and the frustration that accompanied the obvious failure to cause pain.

Parents are frequently on the receiving end of a school-age child's anger. To children, parents are the source of rules. Often in their anger, they will "punish" a parent by breaking yet another rule. For example, when six-year-old Hanna was told to go to her room for kicking her brother, she retorted, "Okay, I'm not going to hang my clothes up for a week—or maybe a year!"

Children vary greatly in the amount of anger they show and in the ways in which they show it. Some of these variations depend on each child's personality. However, the way parents express their own anger and the way they respond to the child's anger are also important. All caregivers should set an example by sharing and verbalizing—but not acting out—their own anger and by providing a happy and orderly environment for the child. They should also help teach the child self-control early in life before inappropriate expressions of anger become a habit. Parents and other caregivers can encourage children to use words—not their bodies—in expressing anger. For example, they can teach children to use sentences like these: "It makes me mad when you take my truck!" "It hurts my feelings when you don't want to share with me." "My name is Jason—not Dummy!"

Fear

Children from four to six have well-developed imaginations, and many of their fears center on imaginary dangers. They may be afraid of ghosts, robbers, kidnappers, or vampires. Sensitive and insecure children are especially prone to fears. Many children of this age are afraid of the dark. Some may worry about the possibility of being left alone or abandoned.

Many children fear school, but there can be a number of different causes for this fear. Some children are afraid to be without the security their parents offer. Others may fear a bully at school, a stern teacher, or "hard" school work. Taking the child to school—rather than simply dropping the child off or letting him or her go with another adult—can help. Talking about the problem, acknowledging the fear, and offering an understanding explanation may provide all the reassurance some children need.

Anxiety about school is common. Parents or caregivers should be sympathetic, but must help the child understand that going to school is necessary.

As one mother said to her son, "I know you are upset that you have to go to school. Daddy and I go to work. We don't always feel like going, but that's our job. Going to school is your job."

Special fears also arise in four- to six-year-olds. Social acceptance is very important at this age; the threat of its loss is a continual source of anxiety for children.

At this age, children are especially fearful of ridicule. They may not show their other fears openly because they do not want to be ridiculed. Instead, a child may act aggressively, pretend indifference, or deliberately try to distract himself or herself. These kinds of coping are signs of the child's increased maturity.

Parents and other caregivers should not ignore a child's fears. It is usually best to let the child talk about his or her fear. A listening, understanding adult can be especially important to a fearful child. Accept the child's fear by identifying it. Don't tell him or her that the fear does not exist, because it is very real to the child. Guide the child in comfortable actions that will gradually help him or her overcome the fear. Remember that fears won't simply disappear on their own. Unless the child can deal with and overcome the fears, they may pile up and create emotional problems.

Jealousy and Sibling Relationships

Sibling rivalry—jealousy of brothers and sisters—is common during this period. Some parents make the problem of sibling rivalry worse, often without meaning to, by showing favoritism to one child. Another common mistake is trying to improve behavior by comparing one child with another. For example, a father may ask his daughter, "Why can't you be neat and clean

PARENTING IN ACTION

Providing Emotional Support

Every day when Janie came home from school, she seemed to have a list of complaints. Several times, when her mother asked about her day, Janie burst into tears. "The kids don't play with me." "I can't run fast—I'm always last." "Jimmy calls me 'Freckles,' and now the other kids do, too."

Fortunately, Janie's mother took her child's unhappiness seriously. She didn't simply pass the complaints off with a casual, "Oh, the kids will get over it. They'll like you when they get to know you." Instead, she put aside her work and said soothingly, "I think I'll sit down and have some of this snack with you, and we'll talk about it."

During the snack, Janie's mother learned what was causing the child's complaints. Two friends had indeed rejected Janie's attempts to enter their game that day. Her mother hugged her and said, "Well, honey, maybe they already had enough players. It's not that they don't like you. When it happens again, ask someone else to play another game. Other kids like to be asked to do things, just like you do."

Janie had complained about not running fast enough because the swings were all taken by the time she got to the playground after lunch. "You run as fast as most of your friends," her mother said reassuringly. "I've seen you do it. Maybe you just don't start out as soon as some of the other children. You can always play on the climbing platform for a while if the swings are all full. Then, pretty soon, a swing will be empty and you can take your turn."

The nickname Freckles prompted this response from Janie's mother: "I think your freckles are beautiful. Your father has freckles, too. That's one of the things I liked first about him. He's so proud that you look like him. And he loves you very much. I wouldn't change one of your cute freckles for the world!"

Janie's unhappiness soon faded, but her mother decided to make the after-school talks a part of their daily routine.

THINK AND DISCUSS

1. What effect do you think these early sessions between Janie and her mother will have on Janie as she grows older?
2. How long do you think Janie and her mother should continue to spend this kind of time together? Why?
3. Why is talking with another person helpful in easing stress? With whom do you talk when you feel you are under a great deal of stress?

like Jeff? I never have to tell him to wash before meals." Such comparisons rarely improve behavior; they are much more likely to damage a child's self-concept and undermine good family relationships.

At this age, jealousy often takes the form of tattling, criticizing, or even lying. Some children react to their own feelings of jealousy by boasting, while others pretend there is no rivalry. Jealousy may also result in tensional outlets such as nail biting, bed-wetting, and tantrums.

Normally, early childhood jealousy fades as the child matures and develops interests outside the family. However, some children never seem to outgrow it and are jealous even as adults. In such cases, jealousy is often a part of deeper emotional problems.

BUILDING SELF-ESTEEM

Helping Children Cope with Stress

Children—like adults—can feel too much stress. This can happen when a child is given too much responsibility, is expected to deal with too many changes, or is overloaded emotionally.

Do the following to help children cope with stress:

- Spending time with the child. Talking and touching or holding the youngster shows the child that he or she has support.
- During private conversations, encourage the child to talk about the changes in his or her life and to examine and express his or her feelings. Reading a story about a character who is experiencing similar disruptions or responses can also be helpful.

Children and Stress

Stress among teens and adults is a well-recognized problem. Many people, however, fail to realize that children also lead stressful lives. Children may worry about everything from fires to their own popularity, their grades at school, or news about missing children.

As with an adult's stress, a child's emotional stress can lead to physical symptoms. Stomachaches, headaches, moodiness, irritability, and trouble eating or sleeping may be caused by stress, as well as by purely physical ailments.

What should parents and other caregivers do? Hugs help. Other approaches to reducing a child's stress include listening carefully, identifying and showing acceptance of the child's feelings, using a relaxed manner with the child, and building up the child's self-confidence. Talking through problems with the child also helps reduce stress.

Competition—Good or Bad?

People have differing views about the role competition should play in children's lives. Some believe that it helps children excel and prepares them for the competitive world in which adults function. Supporters of competition cite these specific advantages:

- Competition helps a child gain a realistic estimate of his or her own ability in relation to others.
- Competition promotes higher standards.
- Competition stimulates children and adds zest to otherwise dull tasks.
- Competition encourages speed in accomplishment.
- Competition creates an interest in completing tasks.
- Competition stimulates individual effort.

Other people feel that competition discourages cooperation. They believe that, since there are more losers than winners in competitive situations, competition can damage children's **self-esteem**, their *positive sense of self-worth*. These people note the following disadvantages:

- Competition instills in children the idea that success depends on the ability to outdo others.
- Competition leads to hostile relationships with others.
- Defeat in competitive situations may provoke a desire for revenge.
- Those who never win or rarely win may lose interest or quit.
- Competition points out children's inadequacies.
- Competition lowers the status of those who lose.

Sometimes parents' feelings about competition are based on their own desires or experiences. Monica Chavez, for example, wasn't allowed to play on the Little League team as a child, so she pressures her daughter Sara to join the local baseball league. Theo Wills was an "A" student all through school. His son Jess works hard but is an average student. Mr. Wills constantly "encourages" his son to do better. "Don't you want to be at the top of your class?" he asks. Neither parent has really considered the child's interests and abilities.

An added advantage to competitive play is that parents tend to spend time with the child at practice and at their games.

APPRECIATING TRADITIONS

Holiday traditions are an occasion to understand significant aspects of a culture such as religious rites, the celebration of important people, the changing of seasons, or a great event. December is a month for three holidays important to different groups. Families who celebrate Christmas may attend special church services, decorate a Christmas tree, and hang stockings by their fireplaces. Jewish families celebrate Hanukkah by lighting a candle on a menorah each of the eight nights of the holiday. Children play in a game with a top called a dreidel. African-American families observe Kwanzaa, which lasts for seven days. The holiday celebrates family unity and is a chance for families to join and share baskets of fruit and light candles on a kinara.

Most four-, five-, and six-year-olds prefer cooperative play to competitive games. Older children are more likely to be competitive at play. Parents and caregivers can promote cooperation with group projects and noncompetitive games. "Let's help our friends" can be a key phrase for cooperation.

Competitiveness, often spurred on by sibling rivalry, is likely to show up at home. Children may insist, "Holly gets to stay up until eight o'clock. Why can't I?" or "Why can't I cross the street by myself? You let Dominic!"

Children differ in their responses to competition. Some who constantly lead come to think of themselves as superior. Those who usually lose may develop a harsh, unpleasant attitude to cover their feelings of inferiority. Many, though, find competition a stimulating challenge and suffer no harmful effects.

Personality and Behavior

By age four, many behavior patterns are set; children have many of the characteristics they will exhibit as adults. Other characteristics will change in response to new experiences. For example, children who are shy and withdrawn may become more and more outgoing if they receive positive feedback whenever they exhibit outgoing behavior.

At any age, positive or negative changes in personality can occur. This is one reason that adults should not use labels when discussing a child's behavior. That is, a parents should say, "We

All children need to be encouraged and praised for their own unique abilities.

expect you to put all your toys back on the shelf when you finish playing," rather than labeling the child by saying, "You're so messy! Why don't you ever put your things where they belong?" Children tend to live up to—or down to—the ideas other people have about them. They may become messy or lazy or unfriendly simply because adults tell them that they are.

A successful business manager recalled that, when he was a child, his father had continually lectured him about his poor management of his paper route. His father said he was "irresponsible and stupid and unable to do anything right!" As an adult, he realized that he had actually handled his responsibilities with better than average efficiency. However, years of hearing about his shortcoming had made him think of himself as a failure. The man developed a realistic view of his abilities when his own judgment and values matured. Many people are not so fortunate; they continue, even as adults, to believe the negative labels they were given as children.

Understanding and guidance from adults is as important for children from four to six as it was in earlier years. Each child—whether sensitive, placid, or aggressive—should be treated as an individual.

SECTION 1 REVIEW

CHECK YOUR UNDERSTANDING

1. What are two important changes that take place for most children between the ages of four and six?
2. Who is more likely to tell tall tales—a four-year-old or a five-year-old? Why?
3. Why is six a difficult age for many children?
4. What is the most common cause of anger in children aged four to six?
5. List at least three fears common among four- to six-year-olds.
6. List at least three things parents can do to help relieve children's stress.
7. List three advantages and three disadvantages of competition among children.

DISCUSS AND DISCOVER

1. How is a child's stress related to the stress his or her parents feel? How can stress build up within a family? What can be the results of family stress? What resources are available to help parents and children trying to deal with stress?
2. Gather information about local sports programs and other group activities for young children. What official attitude toward competition does each program present? From what you can observe, is that attitude reflected in the children's activities? If not, what accounts for the difference?

SECTION 2

Social and Moral Development from Four to Six

OBJECTIVES

- Describe general patterns of social development in children aged four, five, and six.
- Describe a child's relationship to family at ages four, five, and six.
- Explain how children develop a sense of right and wrong.

TERMS TO LEARN

conscience
moral development
peers

School brings four-, five-, and six-year-olds into contact with many new people. Children must learn how to meet strangers, make friends, work and play in groups, and accept authority from new people.

General Social Patterns

During the preschool and early school years, social skill development is a major task. As a child moves outside the home, he or she learns to get along with **peers**, *other people of one's own age*. Not all children learn social skills at the same rate, but there are general patterns common at each age.

Four Years

Four-year-olds form friendships with their playmates. At this age, children spend more time in cooperative play than in playing alone. They seem to play best in groups of three or four.

By the age of four, children begin to share their toys and to take turns. However, four-year-olds are still often bossy and inconsiderate, and fighting is common.

Although friends are important to four-year-olds, the family is still more important. Children this age request approval by making frequent remarks such as "I'm a good builder, right?" or "Look how high I can climb!" If things go wrong, they still look to adults for comfort.

The preschool years bring more opportunities to develop social relationships outside the home.

Five Years

Most five-year-olds are more outgoing and talkative than they were at age four. They play best in groups of five or six, and their play is more complicated. They prefer friends of their own age. Quarreling is less frequent. When they do quarrel, five-year-olds typically resort to name-calling and to wild threats.

At age five, children have more respect for the belongings of other people. This does not mean that a five-year-old will never snatch a toy from another child. Such behavior, though, is not as common as in earlier years.

As children begin school, social acceptance by peers becomes more important. Children are concerned about what their friends say and do. They don't like to be different.

Six Years

At age six, social relations are often characterized by friction, aggression, threats, and stubbornness. They want everything, and they want to do things their own way. When playing with other children, they may not want to share their own toys; and they are likely to be jealous of other children's toys.

Best friends are usually of the same sex, although six-year-olds play readily in mixed groups. Friendships are closer and longer lasting now than at age five.

At this age, children like the group play and organized teams of school games. As soon as they tire of playing, though, they will drop out of a game with no regard for the team effort.

TREASURES WITHIN A COMMUNITY

Children can be excellent ambassadors of good will. Parents or caregivers know that children quickly become acquainted with adults and other children when they explore their communities.

Regardless of the size of a community, cultural differences within a neighborhood can help children learn about people and appreciate diversity. In some cases, such as gender, race, or language, diversity can be apparent.

Cultural diversity can be appreciated in religious, cultural, and national differences. A simple walk around the neighborhood is a worthwhile experience for all to treasure.

Six-year-olds form close friendships, usually with others of the same sex. However, boys and girls still play together in groups.

BUILDING SELF-ESTEEM

Manners and the Young Child

Children learn their manners from the example set by others around them, either in the home or at school.

Young children are capable of practicing some good manners, but the manners should never be given more importance than the activity or than the children themselves. What can be expected? Most children are able to feed themselves fairly well without making a mess; children this age enjoy eating with the family, but usually have trouble sitting through a long meal. Children can learn to say "please" and "thank-you," but they may be inconsistent about using these words on a daily basis. In addition, children this age enjoy helping; they can be encouraged to hold a door open for others, for example, or to answer a telephone politely.

Family Relationships

During the infant and toddler years, children learn to get along with others by forming strong relationships with their parents and other members of their family. They learn cooperation, fair play, and respect for others. In the preschool and early school years, children start putting these social skills to work in social situations outside the home.

Four-year-olds have a strong sense of family and home. They want to feel important in the family. They are proud to perform household chores. However, they are also apt to quarrel and bicker with their brothers and sisters.

In many ways, the family relationships of five-year-olds are similar to those of four-year-olds. They are proud of their parents and delight in helping. At five, though, children play much better with their younger brothers and sisters. They are usually protective, kind, and dependable with younger siblings.

Six-year-olds are less in harmony with their family members. One reason is that children tend to be more self-centered at six. Their own opinions and needs come first. Arguing with parents is common. At six, children are often rough and impatient with younger brothers and sisters, and they may fight with older siblings.

Family, of course, continues to be important to every child. However, once a child begins to attend school, peers, teachers, and other nonfamily influences become increasingly important.

Moral Development

Moral development—*the process of gradually learning to base one's behavior on personal beliefs of right and wrong*—begins early in life. Parents have a responsibility to help their children develop a moral sense that will guide their behavior.

As toddlers, children begin to learn the rules their parents and other caregivers set. At this age, though, they can't understand the reasons behind the rules or the difference between right and wrong. They just know that some actions—such as hitting a playmate—make their caregivers unhappy with them. They learn to avoid such behavior because they don't want to lose love and approval.

Between the ages of five and seven, children gradually develop the beginning of a **conscience**, *an inner sense of right and wrong that prompts good behavior and causes feelings of guilt following bad behavior*. The rules learned in early childhood form the basis of the conscience in the early school years.

At this stage, children begin to know the difference between truth and lies. However, that understanding is not always accurate. For example, children may think of a mistake as a lie and expect to be punished for it. Children may also fail to realize that their imaginative stories are fantasy, not reality. Caregivers need to help children separate fact from fiction; they should avoid punishing children for using their imaginations.

At about ages seven to ten, children often don't like or even understand all the rules they are expected to obey, but they don't question the rights of the adults in authority to make and enforce those rules. During this stage, children are still motivated to follow rules primarily by their fear of being punished. They don't yet use their own personal beliefs about right and wrong to control their own behavior.

Guidelines for Moral Development

Most parents take their responsibilities for the moral development of their children seriously. However, it can be difficult to know how to help children learn right from wrong. Here are some guidelines:

- **Consider the child's age and abilities.** For example, a preschooler playing at the sensory table full of rice may start tossing the rice into the air and watching it land on the floor.

Relationships with parents, brothers, and sisters are the foundation for social relationships outside the home.

ASK THE EXPERTS

Children and Lies

Jean Illsley Clarke is the director of J.I. Consultants in Minneapolis, Minnesota where she designs and conducts workshops on self-esteem, parenting, and group dynamics.

I've heard people say that young children don't tell lies, but today I watched a four-year-old in the child care center break a toy and then hide the pieces. When the teacher asked the child about the toy, she said very solemnly that she hadn't touched it. Now I feel confused: Do young children lie?

Of course children lie. Children learn about their world by exploring it, by trying it out. So we can expect children to learn about lies by lying.

The dictionary says a lie is a false statement deliberately presented as true. However, young children don't read the dictionary, so their lies are often not deliberate attempts to deceive.

Many children, especially four- and five-year-olds, tell tall tales. Telling such tales helps children develop their imagination and creativity; it may also help them deal with their own fears and frustrations.

Here's an example of tall-tale-telling from my own childhood. As our family drove through farmland, my four- year-old brother told detailed stories about his own life as a farmer. He explained which land he farmed, pointed out which cows he owned, and noted which horses he planned to buy for his farm. This kind of fanciful thinking is worth encouraging.

It's not unusual for young children to mix tall tales with reality. When you need information from a child, you can expect him or her to know the difference. You might explain, "I will listen to your tall tale, and then I need to know what really happened."

Sometimes a statement that sounds like a lie is really the reflection of a child's misunderstanding. "I already did put my book away," Mandy tells her father. When her father said, "Please put your book away now," he meant, "Please put it on the shelf." To Mandy, however, putting something away simply means removing it from the middle of the floor, so she stuck the book under the sofa. Mandy's father does not say, "Don't lie to me!" Instead, he explains, "When we put your books away, we put them on this shelf. Can you get your book and put it here now?"

Children sometimes tell lies simply to get a response from adults. In these cases, it's usually best to give the child more attention at other times, but to avoid special attention in response to the lying. Remember that all children want—and need—to be noticed.

Children may also lie to protect themselves or to please others. I imagine this is what the four-year-old you observed was doing. She probably didn't want to risk an adult's anger or disappointment, so she lied about breaking the toy. Parents and other caregivers can help by encouraging children to accept and deal with their own mistakes or with their own deliberate misbehavior.

As we help children learn when and where and how to tell the truth, we should remember that the development of a conscience as an internal behavior guide takes many years. We should remember, as well, that children learn from our examples.

Jean Illsley Clarke

Jean Illsley Clarke

The teacher will remind the child to keep the rice on the table and then hand the child a broom and dustpan to use in sweeping up the mess. The teacher knows that the child cannot always remember the rules and understands that the child will learn from the consequences of his or her actions.

- **Remember that parents and caregivers teach most effectively by example.** Children receive a mixed message if, for example, they are told that lying is wrong, but they also hear their parents telling lies. If you are around children, you must behave the way you want them to behave.
- **Understand that the process of learning to monitor one's own behavior is a lifelong task.** It is unfair to expect perfection from children. Instead, help children accept and learn from their mistakes.
- **Don't withhold love in response to misbehavior.** It is important for children to know that, although you don't like what they did, you continue to love them.

Both Chapter 3 and the Positive Parenting Skills feature on pages 454-455 present additional suggestions for guiding children effectively.

A developing moral sense helps older children understand the importance of being dependable. Parents can set a good example by the way they approach their own responsibilities.

SECTION 2 REVIEW

CHECK YOUR UNDERSTANDING

1. Who are a person's peers?
2. What kind of play is typical for four-year-olds?
3. Compare the family relationships typical for four-year-olds with those typical for six-year-olds.
4. What is moral development?
5. What is a conscience? What forms the basis of the conscience in children aged four to six?
6. List at least three suggestions for helping children learn right from wrong.

DISCUSS AND DISCOVER

1. Ask at least four different four- to six-year-olds this question: What is a friend? Record each child's answer and, if possible, let the children draw pictures to go with their answers. Display the children's artwork and discuss their ideas about friends. How do their ideas seem to change as the children get older?
2. What is the difference between a four-year-old's imaginative story and a ten-year-old's lie? Are there stages or circumstances in which it might be difficult to distinguish between an imaginative story and a lie? Why?

USING POSITIVE GUIDANCE TECHNIQUES

One of the most important responsibilities that parents and other caregivers undertake is guiding the behavior of young children. Parents and caregivers serve as role models in the words and actions they use. Occasionally, they may also physically restrain children from dangerous or seriously inappropriate behavior. However, much of the direct guidance that parents and other caregivers provide is verbal.

The following suggestions will help you take a positive and helpful approach to guiding the behavior of young children.

* **Before you give a child directions, be sure you have the child's attention.** You should be close enough to the child to speak in a clear and quiet tone of voice, and you should be on a level that makes eye-contact comfortable for both you and the child. Often, you may need to stoop down or sit beside the child.
* **Use positive statements to give a child directions.** Be sure your directions tell the child what behavior you expect—not the behavior you want the child to avoid. For example, imagine that four-year-old Suki is being too rough with a kitten. The direction "Don't pull the kitten's tail" focuses her attention on only one aspect of her rough handling and fails to tell Suki what she should be doing instead. More helpful would be the direction, "Pet the kitten gently with your whole hand."
* **Begin your direction with an action word that tells the child what to do.** A clear verb should be the first word—or at least one of the first words—in a direction to a young child. Beginning with a verb can also help you keep your directions straightforward and simple. For example, the direction "Put your hat back on your head" tells a child just what action is expected. A young child might simply be confused by a direction like this: "I'm afraid that we'll lose your pretty red hat if you keep playing with it, and it's cold out today, so put it back on now."
* **Give a child a direction at the time and in the place you expect the child to carry it out.** When a young child has finished digging in the

garden, for example, you might want to give a direction like this: "Put the trowel back on the shelf in the tool closet. That's where we keep it." A very young child—or a child who hasn't used the trowel before—would probably have trouble remembering this direction if it were given while he or she was still busy digging.

* **Whenever possible, give a child only one direction at a time.** A series of directions can be difficult to remember and hard to follow. It's best to give one direction, let the child carry it out, and then give another direction as necessary.

* **Whenever appropriate, give a simple reason for your direction.** Knowing why he or she has to behave in a certain way can help a child follow directions. It can also help the child begin to develop his or her own sense of acceptable behavior.

* **Reward a child for following your direction.** Often, a special smile is enough to show the child that he or she has done a good job. Don't forget, though, to offer more direct praise, too. "That was quick" or "I like the way you listened to my words" or—perhaps best of all—a hug and a kiss can help a child feel proud of following directions.

SUMMARY

- Beginning regular school attendance requires many emotional adjustments and brings about rapid social development.
- Although four-, five-, and six-year-olds have better emotional control than younger children, emotional development still alternates between positive and negative stages.
- Expressions of anger become more subtle and less physical at this age.
- An active imagination, school, and the need for social acceptance can lead to a variety of fears.
- Competition can have both positive and negative effects on children.
- As children spend more time with their peers, other factors besides the family influences the child
- Conscience and moral values are developed during this period.

REVIEWING THE FACTS

1. What are two things parents and other caregivers can do to help children learn to channel their expressions of anger?
2. List three possible causes of a child's fear of school.
3. List at least three actions that are often expressions of a child's jealousy.
4. What is self-esteem?
5. What three different responses are various children likely to have to competition?
6. At what age is a child's basic behavior pattern usually clearly established? What might cause some characteristics to change after that age?
7. Why should parents and other caregivers avoid labeling a child when discussing the child's behavior?
8. What differences would you expect to observe between a group of four-year-olds at play and a group of five-year-olds at play?
9. How do six-year-olds typically interact with other members of their families?
10. At what age do children begin to develop their own sense of right and wrong? What motivates children to follow rules before that age?

EXPLORING FURTHER

1. Using magazines, newspapers, or other sources, collect photographs of children and adults expressing anger. Present the photos on a poster or bulletin board display. Encourage other students to describe the pictures and discuss whether each shows an appropriate expression of anger. (Section 1)
2. List eight comments or questions that parents might make, intending to correct or remind their children and unintentionally arousing sibling rivalry. Then rewrite each comment or question so that it presents the same question or reminder without causing jealousy between siblings. (Section 2)
3. Make up a noncompetitive board game or other activity for five- and six-year-olds. Share your game or activity with other students, and encourage them to suggest improvements. Then teach the game or activity to a small group of young children. (Section 2)
4. Interview at least five teachers of kindergarten and first grade. Ask the teachers how they help children make the transition into school and what they do to keep communication open between the school and the family. Discuss your findings with your classmates. (Section 2)

THINKING CRITICALLY

1. **Analyze.** In your opinion, is it possible to raise two or more children without sibling rivalry? Why or why not? What do you think parents can do to reduce or eliminate sibling rivalry among their children? Do you think it is possible to treat all the children in a family in exactly the same way? Do you consider that form of equal treatment desirable? Why or why not?
2. **Analyze.** On the basis of your own experiences and observations, do you think competition is good for children during the early school years? Why or why not? If so, what do you think parents can and should do to promote healthy competition for their children? If not, what would you suggest parents do to protect their children from competition?
3. **Analyze.** Why is guiding a child's moral development the responsibility of the parents? What factors might make it difficult—or impossible—for parents to assume this responsibility? How can a lack of such guidance affect a child?

CROSS-CURRICULUM CONNECTIONS

1. **Writing.** Write an original story that begins with the following paragraphs:

   Sandy came home in tears from her first day of kindergarten. Her mother greeted her with a reassuring hug and asked, "Sandy, what's wrong? Didn't you like school?"

   Sandy shook her head and sobbed.

   "What's wrong, honey?" her mother asked. "Did something happen?"

   Sandy shook her head again. "I'm not going back there," she told her mother.
2. **Reading.** Read one of these books by Louise Bates Ames and Frances L. Ilg: *Your Four-Year-Old*, *Your Five-Year-Old*, or *Your Six-Year-Old*. Discuss the book and your reactions to it with other students in the class.

OBSERVING AND PARTICIPATING

Social Development

By the time the child enters preschool, socialization has already begun, and the values and attitudes of the family have been firmly established. Preschool provides a social setting in which children can develop friendships outside the family unit. If the caregivers in this setting encourage humor, kindness, respect for others, and cooperation, these qualities will be imitated by the children.

Choose one of the following activities, and spend some time observing or participating with a child. Write a detailed journal entry about your observations. Then share your observations with a group of other students, and compare your conclusions with those of other group members.

- **Participating.** Collect a few jokes and riddles appropriate for young children, or choose a short book of jokes and riddles. Share the jokes and riddles with several four- to six-year-olds. Notice how each child responds. Which jokes or riddles appeal most to four-year-olds? To five-year-olds? To six-year-olds? How can you account for the differences?
- **Observing.** Observe a group of young children at play. What examples of competition do you see? How do various children react to that competition? What examples of cooperation can you identify? What effect does cooperative play seem to have on the children? How do nearby parents or teachers react to competition? To cooperation?
- **Observing.** Observe a four-, five-, or six-year-old playing with one or more siblings. How does the child appear to treat his or her sibling? How is the interaction between siblings affected by the presence—or absence—of a parent? What values or attitudes is the parent reinforcing?

K L M N O

CHAPTER 16

Intellectual Development from Four to Six

Standing before the big easel, Milagros grabs the brush and begins painting. It is one of her favorite preschool activities.

"What a beautiful painting, Milagros!" remarks Mrs. Schultz the preschool teacher. "I like your strong, bold lines and beautiful choice of colors. Can you tell me about your picture?"

"This is a picture of me," Milagros proudly announces. "Here are my eyes," she says pointing to the middle of the page. She dips her brush deep into the brown paint and splashes on some more color in the middle of the picture. "And this is my hair," she adds with a big grin.

"Oh yes, I can see that," replies Mrs. Schultz. "You really are doing a very good job. When you are done, would you like to hang it on the bulletin board? That way everyone can see your beautiful self-portrait."

SECTION 1

Intelligence and Learning from Four to Six

OBJECTIVES

- Describe the characteristics of intellectual development in children aged four to six.
- Explain what IQ tests are, and discuss their advantages and disadvantages.
- Give examples of ways children can learn from everyday experiences.
- Explain how parents and caregivers can encourage children's interest in reading, art, and music.

TERMS TO LEARN

dramatic play
finger plays
intelligence quotient (IQ)

You may recall that Jean Piaget identified the time between ages two and seven as the preoperational period. Four-, five-, and six-year-olds show by their thinking and actions that they are still in this period.

Preoperational Thinking

These are some signs of preoperational thinking observable in children aged four to six:

- **Use of symbols.** Children learn that objects and words can be symbols—that is, they can represent something else. For example, a child hands the teacher an empty cup and instructs, "Drink the hot cocoa. It has marshmallows in it."
- **Make-believe play.** Children continue to learn through fantasy and through creative play. They also learn through **dramatic play**, *imitating real-life situations, such as playing house or playing school*. One four-year-old, for example, builds a coffin in the block area, and he and his friends act out a funeral; the boy's grandfather has recently died.
- **Egocentric viewpoint.** At four, five, and six, children continue to view the world in terms of themselves. Their words and actions show this self-centeredness. For example, when the mother of a five-year-old arrives at the hospital for

surgery, she finds her daughter's "second favorite" blanket stuffed in her suitcase. The child knows that anyone who has to go away from home—especially to the hospital—needs a blanket.

- **Limited focus.** In the preoperational period, children find it difficult to focus on more than one characteristic at a time. For example, you might place 10 tennis balls—3 white and 7 yellow—in front of a four-year-old. If you ask the child whether there are more yellow balls or more tennis balls, he or she will usually say more yellow balls. The child can't focus on both the color and the type of ball at once. An older child, no longer in the preoperational period, would immediately know that all the balls are tennis balls and only some of them are yellow.

Piaget helped adults realize that children this age do not think like adults and should not be treated like adults. They are prelogical in their thinking, and they need to be respected for who and what they are. Between their fourth and seventh birthdays, children make significant gains in their thinking skills; around the age of seven, they enter into the stage Piaget identified as the operational period.

Fantasy play is a way for children to learn. How does the use of these uniforms show symbolic thinking?

BUILDING SELF-ESTEEM

Promoting Pretend Play

Many aspects of children's play involves pretending. Too often, however, people dismiss make-believe play as "a waste of time" or "just pretending—not really doing anything." However, pretend play is an opportunity for young children to control their environment, to examine their own feelings and ideas, and to develop their thinking skills.

Parents and other caregivers can encourage children by allowing them time and freedom to enjoy make-believe play, and by permitting them to use safe household items as props for their games. See Positive Parenting Skills on page 478-479 for other tips on encouraging make-believe play.

Measuring Intelligence

When they label children as "intelligent" or "unintelligent," adults are often influenced by observations that have nothing to do with intelligence. Maria is considered bright. She has a dimpled smile, dark curls, and appealing manners; she seems to make a favorable impression on everyone. Zach is considered slow. He is large for his age and is often compared with children several years older. He is actually of average intelligence. Traci is so shy that few people see her true ability. It is difficult to separate a child's intellectual ability from such characteristics as curls, size, and shyness.

Educators use formal intelligence tests to more accurately determine the intellectual abilities of children. The test results can help teachers, principals, and learning specialists understand and meet students' educational needs.

The first intelligence test was developed by a French psychologist, Alfred Binet, in 1905. In 1916, Lewis M. Terman of Stanford University made a major revision of the Binet test. Today the test is commonly called the Stanford-Binet, and it is widely used to test children from ages two to sixteen.

Terman devised a way to give a person's intelligence a numerical score. He did this by having many children take the test. Eventually, he was able to determine how well the average

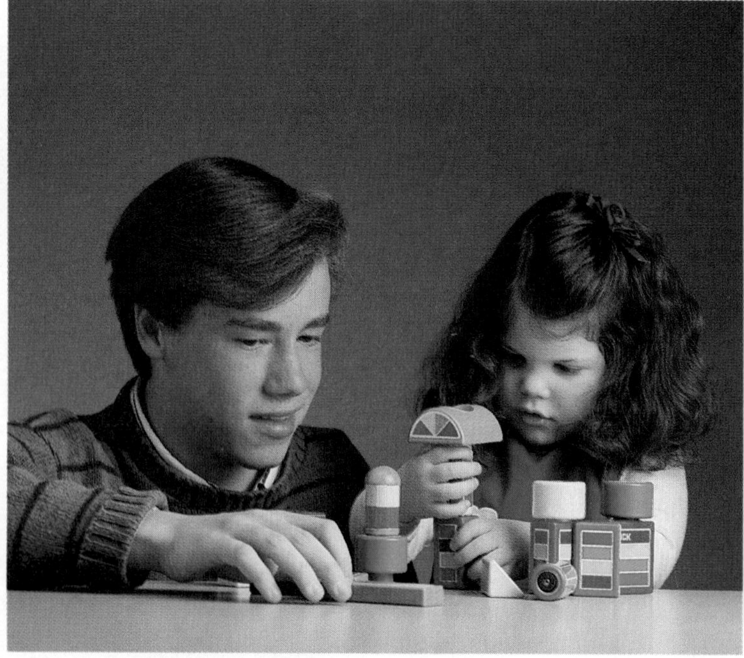

Before entering kindergarten most children are screened by a teacher to determine their developmental stage. A child who has been led by an older sibling may score high on those screenings.

child of a particular age would do. Then he created a simple mathematical formula to calculate a number representing a child's intelligence. This **intelligence quotient**, or **IQ**, is *a numerical standard that tells whether a person's intelligence is average or above or below average for his or her age.* With this method, the average child of any age has an IQ between 90 and 110.

Intelligence tests are composed of tasks and questions. These correspond to the expected abilities of various age levels. Two-year-olds, for example, cannot read. An IQ test for them might include building a tower of blocks, identifying parts of the body, and fitting simple geometric shapes into corresponding holes.

Disadvantages of IQ Tests

Many types of intelligence tests are used today. However, no one test gives an absolutely accurate estimate of an individual's mental ability. Many things can influence test results. A child's physical or emotional state during the test, limited experiences, or unfamiliarity with the language can all affect the child's score.

Most tests depend a great deal on language ability and the experiences of a particular culture. This may penalize those who speak another language at home or have different cultural traditions.

Another problem with IQ tests is that they do not tell much about specific abilities. Two people with the same IQ may have very different strengths and weaknesses. One person may be unusually good at science and math but poor in language skills. Another may have the opposite strengths and weaknesses.

In addition, IQ test results are not always consistent. The same test administered to the same child at two separate times sometimes show a wide difference in scores.

Unfortunately, some parents and children become too concerned about IQ test scores. The Rockefeller Foundation report on quality in education made a good point: "Tests are effective on a limited front. We cannot measure the rarer qualities of character that are a necessary ingredient of great performance. We cannot measure aspiration, purpose, courage, vitality, determination." Neither do tests measure such positive qualities as originality, creativity, self-confidence, and independence.

More commonly used in preschools and kindergartens today are screening instruments that provide an overview of a child's level of development in all areas, not just thinking skills. If the child falls outside the norms of development for a child of his or her age, then an in-depth assessment of skills can be done. These evaluations help identify problem areas and guide parents, caregivers, and teachers in planning appropriate activities to encourage the child's development.

BUILDING SELF-ESTEEM

Questioning Techniques

Asking questions can be a good way to start conversations with children. Although too many questions discourage most children, parents and other caregivers can use questions to help children think about what they are seeing and to begin talking about their thoughts and feelings.

To encourage thinking and talking, questions should ask for more than "yes" or "no" as a response. Questions beginning with "what," "who," "when," and "how" are especially effective. Questions such as "Where does the rain come from?" and "Why did the rock fall faster than the feather?" encourage learning.

Everyday Learning Opportunities

A four-, five-, or six-year-old learns from a wide variety of experiences. However, these experiences provide more learning if a parent or other important caregiver shares them with the child. You can try techniques like those suggested here whenever you are with children.

Look for opportunities to talk with children about what they are doing. A few positive comments, such as "Wow, the building you are making is so tall—and it has so many windows!" can encourage interest. Questions help children think in new ways about what is happening and encourage them to organize their thoughts into answers.

Explanations and suggestions can also be helpful. You might explain in simple terms why water turns to ice. If a child is trying to lift a heavy box full of toys, you could suggest that pushing the box might be easier.

Asking a child's advice is another effective technique for promoting learning. For example, you might ask how the carrot sticks and radishes should be arranged on the serving plate. Following through on such advice helps the child understand that his or her opinions are valued; it improves the child's self-esteem.

Everyday learning can take place in such simple things as playing a game with parents, friends, or family members.

Although books and television programs can be educational, it's always more exciting to learn about the world first-hand.

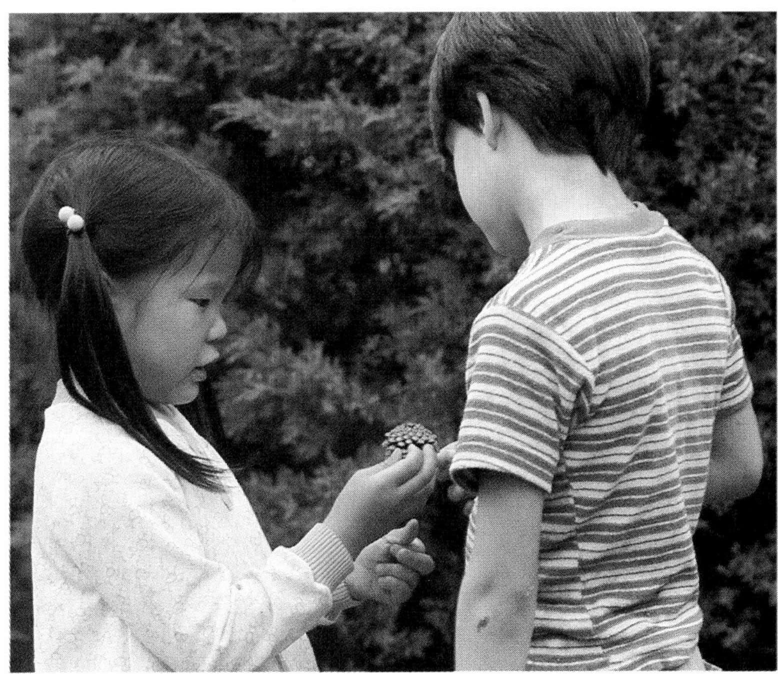

Recreational activities are important to learning. On short car trips, the child can follow the progress on a clearly marked map. A ride on a bus, or plane can be an exciting adventure; encourage the child to discuss what he or she sees and to ask questions suggested by the trip. Nature walks are fun—and free. Everyone in the family can learn by looking closely at leaves, flowers, and birds.

Children need to be included in household tasks such as shopping, cooking, and keeping the home clean. There is much that children can learn from helping with these routine activities. In addition, sharing these tasks strengthens the bonds between family members, and children develop responsibility, maturity, and independence.

Parents and other caregivers should also take time to help children learn and explore. Even preschoolers can participate in experiments. Finding out what objects magnets attract, determining what floats, and learning why a candle goes out when covered with a jar are just a few possibilities. Other activities can encourage creativity and curiosity. The sound of a watch ticking is magnified when you listen through an empty paper towel tube. Oil floats on top of water, but food coloring mixes with it. Learning should be an everyday, family-centered event.

Children of this age are curious to learn more about their own bodies and about where babies come from. Answer their questions in simple terms they can understand, and help them learn the correct names for body parts. Encourage children to have positive attitudes by answering their questions in an unembarrassed, natural way.

ASK THE EXPERTS

Flash Cards and Computers

Linda Espinosa is the Director of Primary Education for the Redwood City School District in California, and is Treasurer of the National Association of Education for Young Children.

We know even very young children can learn a lot, and we want to do our best to help our youngsters. When would you recommend introducing flash cards and computers?

It's wonderful that you want to encourage your children to learn and to explore the world. Before you rush them into specific kinds of "learning activities," however, you should think a bit more about how children learn.

Young children learn by experiencing their world. Every day, in apparently simple activities, children learn about themselves, about other people, about other living things, and about objects.

How do flash cards and computers fit into this kind of learning? In most cases, not at all well.

Flash cards are appropriate for only a very few educational objectives. In my opinion, they are never appropriate for children under the age of five. Flash cards are intended to facilitate the rapid memorization of small bits of information, independent of the natural context of that information. Young children simply do not need this approach to learning. Instead, they need interaction with real objects and people; through these interactions, children can begin to understand concepts, particularly those relating to numbers, series, and categories. Young children need repeated experiences with a variety of objects to begin to internalize such concepts. Flash cards simply cannot provide those kinds of experiences.

A more challenging question is raised regarding the possibilities for learning with new types of interactive computer programs. Certainly computers can and are being used in preschool classrooms, as well as by many young children at home. Whether the computers are being used appropriately and meaningfully is another issue. Many "educational" programs are just a waste of the child's valuable time. For instance, why should a child repeatedly count red dots on a computer screen? The child could learn much more by playing with cubes or small blocks or beads, making counting a natural part of the play.

On the other hand, certain computer programs now allow children to control the images on the screen, to create novel series of events, or to receive immediate feedback to their responses. In these cases, the high visual interest and special quality of a computer-based learning experience may provide some children with an enhanced learning opportunity. Even though these programs may have some usefulness, I feel strongly that they should be given limited use, so that young children are encouraged to learn in the most direct and appropriate ways possible.

Linda Espinosa

Linda Espinosa

Appreciating Reading, Art, and Music

Whether or not children enjoy reading, art, and music depends largely on the attitudes of their parents, caregivers, and other important family members. For many people, these are hobbies that provide pleasure throughout their lives. This early school stage is a period in which many children develop an interest in one or more of these areas.

Reading

Young children love books and stories. If this interest is encouraged and adults take time to read to them, children are likely to enjoy reading as they grow older. Developing an interest in reading is important. Books provide an opportunity to learn about and understand the world and the people in it. Children who enjoy reading will find learning easier—and more fun.

Four- to six-year-olds like stories about events that are different from their own experiences. City children can learn about farm life from books. Children who live far from a large city can "experience" buses, apartments, skyscrapers, and other aspects of city life through books.

Children this age also appreciate humor and unusual situations. They giggle over the picture of a horse in the bathtub or a dog wearing a hat. This shows that children are beginning to be able to separate reality from fantasy.

A public library or school library can be a good source of books for children. Most communities have free public libraries that lend children's books. Many of these libraries also offer story hours for young children. Some schools and preschools have books that children and their families may borrow for limited periods of time.

When you are choosing books for children, these questions can help you make appropriate choices:

- Are the pictures colorful, interesting, and easy to understand?
- Will the story appeal to the child's interests?
- Are the situations and settings familiar to the child?
- Does the story include action that will hold the child's interest?
- Will the child understand most of the words?
- Does the book use descriptive language that brings the story alive?
- Is the story short enough to read in one sitting?
- If you are considering buying the book, is it well constructed to stand up under hard use?

THE VALUE OF FAMILY TRADITIONS

Family traditions add order and stability to our lives. Also, they lay a foundation for lifetime spiritual and emotional development. For example, a Jewish parent will encourage a child to study the Old Testament from an early age. A small drop of honey is placed on the page of a Bible, and the child is encourage to pass a finger over the page and lick the honey from the finger. It is believed that this association of honey and sweetness will cause the child to have a sweet experience while studying the Bible. The practice is repeated until the child begins formal Bible study at a later time.

Children love to express their artistic talents on paper—as well as on their fingers, arms, and smocks!

SAFETY TIP

All the materials children use in their art projects should be carefully checked for safety features. For example, paints, pastes, and other supplies must be nontoxic. Sharp objects, including sharply pointed scissors, should not be made available. Also remember that even carefully chosen materials are not safe unless the children know how to use them safely.

Art

Art helps children express their feelings, learn to control their body, and show their creativity. Four- to six-year-olds should have access to a variety of art materials, such as play dough, crayons, paper, paste, paint, and scissors.

Children should be encouraged to experiment with art materials. Don't offer corrections, ridicule, or "lessons." Children need to enjoy the process of creating art; they should not worry about the production.

Instead of guessing what a child's picture represents, ask the child to tell you about it. Then do your best to praise the child's actions rather than the artwork he or she has produced. For example, you might say, "I really like the bright colors you used for the flowers," instead of "That's a good picture."

Music

A baby beats a rhythm with a spoon, enjoying the sound. A boy holds a stick against a fence as he walks, listening to the rhythm. A girl listens to the beat of her footsteps as she runs. All children imitate the sounds they hear around them. They respond naturally to rhythmical sound, which is a part of music.

Singing and rhythm games are fun, especially for four- to six-year-olds. Many children are introduced to singing by **finger plays**, *songs or chants with accompanying hand motions.* Young children usually enjoy singing, especially simple, repetitive songs.

The opportunity to play simple instruments helps develop children's interest in rhythm. Children enjoy using bells, drums, tambourines, or almost anything that makes a noise. Kitchen pans and mixing spoons provide good substitutes for purchased instruments.

Early, positive experiences with music can lead to a lifetime of enjoyment. Children should have opportunities for creative experiments with sound and rhythm.

SECTION 1 REVIEW

CHECK YOUR UNDERSTANDING

1. List at least three important signs of preoperational thinking.
2. What does an IQ score of 100 tell you about a child? List at least three things the score does not tell you about the child.
3. Why should parents make an effort to spend quality time with their children every day?
4. List at least three questions that will help you select an appropriate book for a child.
5. How should parents and other caregivers respond to a child's artwork?
6. What are finger plays?

DISCUSS AND DISCOVER

1. Should children routinely be given IQ tests? Under what circumstances should individual children be tested?
2. Early childhood professionals urge that all standardized testing of young children be stopped. Why do you think they are interested in preventing such testing? Do you agree with this position? Why or why not?
3. Gather information about children's library services, story times, and other reading-related activities for children in your community. Work with other students to plan and make posters advertising these services and activities.

SECTION 2

Schools Meeting Individual Needs

OBJECTIVES

- Explain what learning disabilities are.
- Discuss the effects of learning disabilities and giftedness on school experiences.
- Describe the speech development of children aged four to six, and identify possible speech problems.

TERMS TO LEARN

attention deficit hyperactivity disorder (ADHD)
dyslexia
gifted children
learning disability
vocabulary

Although a child learns from the moment of birth, many people associate learning with school. Most children begin school sometime between the ages of four and six. Some have their first school experience when they go to a child care program or to a preschool program. Others start by attending kindergarten.

The School Experience

Since children will attend school for many years, it is vital that they develop a good attitude at the outset. Children who have a bad experience with classmates or a teacher can develop negative feelings about school. These bad feelings keep them from learning as well as they might.

There are several things parents can do to help make sure a child adjusts well to kindergarten.

- Make sure the child has had complete medical and dental examinations. Vision and hearing tests are especially important since problems with sight or hearing can severely handicap a child's learning.
- Be sure that the child has appropriate self-help skills. He or she should be able to put on and fasten outer garments and shoes. Of course, independence in such tasks as blowing the nose and taking care of toileting needs is essential.
- Be sure the child knows his or her full name, address, and telephone number.

How well children do in school depends partly on how well prepared they are for the experience.

- Help the child feel confident about his or her ability to follow simple directions.
- Prepare the child by explaining, as fully as possible, what he or she can expect at school. If possible, visit the school together before the child's first day, or take the child to the school's open house day for new students.

Although most children learn well in school, some have special educational needs. Two common causes of special needs—learning disabilities and unusually high intelligence—are discussed here. Chapter 18 presents information about children with physical, mental, and emotional disabilities.

Learning Disabilities

Not all children learn easily. For some, learning is made more difficult by a **learning disability**, *a disorder in psychological processes that prevents a person from using information received through the senses in a normal way for learning*. The New York Institute of Child Development defines a learning disability as a complicated disorder that generally falls into one or more of these four areas of difficulty:

1. How a child receives information from his or her senses.
2. How the brain puts such information together.
3. How the information is stored in the brain as memory.
4. How the information is expressed as written or spoken language.

A severe physical handicap, such as blindness, is not a learning disability. Obviously, lack of sight makes learning more difficult, but blindness is a problem in receiving information through the sense, not a problem in using that information. A person with a learning disability typically can see the writing in a book. However, because of a malfunction in the brain, the person might see every sentence—or perhaps only certain letters—backwards. In this case, the problem is categorized as a learning disability because the brain is not functioning normally to use the information received from the eyes.

In the past, little was known about learning disabilities. Learning-disabled children were simply labeled "dumb" or "lazy," or became "troublemakers" in school. You can imagine the discouragement these children felt. They tried as hard as they could but were still unable to keep up with their classmates.

It is important to note that IQ is unrelated to learning disabilities. Some children with a very low IQ also have one or more learning disabilities. However, so do some children with average or above-average IQs.

There are many types of learning disabilities. Some school children can be diagnosed as having **attention deficit hyperactivity disorder**, or **ADHD**, *a condition involving the inability to control one's activity or to concentrate for a normal length of time.* These children are unusually active and may seem uncontrollable. Some error in their brain may keep them from focusing their attention and controlling their actions.

Other children cannot understand the spatial relationships between objects. They may not understand the difference between "under" and "over" or between "near" and "far," for example. Some children cannot understand what words mean, and others cannot form their own thoughts into speech or cannot write properly. If these and similar problems result from an error in brain processes, they are classified as learning disabilities.

Dyslexia is *a learning disability that prevents a person from handling language in a normal way.* Dyslexia usually causes problems with reading, writing, spelling, and math. Children with dyslexia are often intelligent, but their brains do not process certain kinds of information—especially visual information—normally. Researchers have found that children with dyslexia have difficulty processing series of instructions, such as "Add one to three and then divide by two." They typically have trouble sounding words out and often have a short attention span. Children with dyslexia need special help, particularly during the early school years.

Many of the causes of learning disabilities remain unknown, though research is revealing some answers. Many children with such problems are never identified or helped. Sometimes, too, the label "learning disabled" can be as harmful as the problem itself. Children who have been diagnosed with learning disabilities risk being treated as if they cannot learn. In fact, they can learn—but somewhat differently from most other children. They need special approaches tailored to their special needs. They also need encouragement and praise for their efforts, because they often have to work especially hard in school.

Gifted and Talented Children

It is estimated that 3 to 10 percent of the nation's students are **gifted children**, *children with an IQ of 130 or above.* Children may also be talented in an area that does not show up well on IQ tests. Ramon, for example, has exceptional musical ability. Jennifer, even as a preschooler, shows remarkable artistic talent. Neither has an IQ over 130; both are talented.

Educators once believed that gifted and talented children would thrive in any environment. It is now known that these children have special needs that must be met. Among these are the needs for recognition and acceptance and for challenging pursuits in which they can be successful. Gifted and talented children need to be free from feelings of inferiority, superiority, or "being different." They benefit from play with a variety of children, but they also need time with other gifted or talented learners.

Children with above-average ability—like all children—need challenging opportunities, but should not feel pressured.

EDUCATION BEGINS WITH ATTITUDE

Research indicates that the cognitive (i.e., learning) abilities of American, Chinese, and Japanese children are similar, but large differences exist in the attitudes and beliefs toward their education. Chinese and Japanese children spend more time at school in academic activities. They also spend more time on homework than do most American children. Contrary to some opinions, the high demands placed on Chinese and Japanese children does not result in a dislike of school. Children in these countries appear happy, enthusiastic, and responsive. Possibly, the reason is that education is highly prized in China and Japan. Homework is assigned in each grade, and parents spend considerable time helping their children with their work. It appears, then, that parental and school attitudes contribute to the overall success of education in China and Japan.

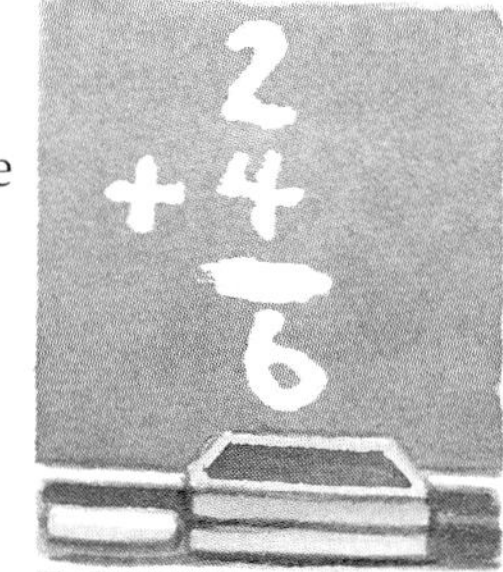

Parents, teachers, and other adults should avoid overwhelming gifted and talented children with unrealistic expectations or goals. Instead, these children need encouragement and opportunities for leadership and creativity.

Gifted children can easily become bored and frustrated in school. They risk being labeled "problem children" because they may not conform to classroom procedures and because they often respond with unexpected answers. Some gifted children who are not challenged at school become poor students.

Most bright children exhibit recognizable signs by age two. They may talk early, using complete sentences, and demonstrate an unusually large vocabulary. Many read before school age—some even by age two and one-half. Gifted children are highly curious and ask challenging questions.

Most schools have special educational programs for gifted students. In small schools, enrichment programs within regular classes are often offered. Large school systems usually have special classes or even special schools for gifted children.

Speech Development

By school age, language ability is one of the most dependable indicators of intelligence. What children say tells much about the way they think. Speech also reveals each child's interests and personality. Remember, however, that there are exceptions. Some children who speak poorly or cannot speak at all have above-average intelligence.

A speech teacher works with children by using games or toys that make sounds the child can identify, such as bells, trains, or animal puppets.

By the time they start school, children have gained an extensive knowledge of language just by listening. They probably do not know what an adjective is, but they can use adjectives confidently and correctly. As children grow older, their **vocabulary**—*the number of words a person uses*—will increase. The sentences they use will become more complex. However, all the basic language forms have already been learned in the preschool period.

Some children with hearing loss are taught to communicate using sign language.

Articulation (clear, distinct speech) improves dramatically. At age three, children typically say only about 30 percent of their words correctly. By age six, that has increased to 90 percent.

Much of this improvement depends on physical development. Some sounds are more difficult to make than others. For example, the sounds represented by *b*, *m*, and *p* are produced simply by moving the lips. By three years of age, most children can make these sounds. Sounds such as those represented by *f* and *v* involve both the lips and the teeth. Children may not master these sounds until age five. The most difficult sounds are those represented by *j*, *ch*, *st*, *pl*, and *sl*. They require the smooth coordination and timing of the lips, tongue, and throat muscles. Some children may be six or seven before "pwease" becomes "please" and "shicken" becomes "chicken."

A child's vocabulary should increase rapidly during this period. A normally developing six-year-old knows about two and one-half times the number of words an average three-year-old knows. This means a six-year-old can understand and use approximately 2,500 words!

Speech Difficulties

When they first send their children to school, parents sometimes worry that the children will talk too much during class. However, many kindergarten and first-grade teachers worry more about the students who don't talk enough. Children who speak very little are not yet comfortable with language. Teachers know that these children will have trouble keeping up with the class. They will not be ready to learn to read until they have more experience with spoken language.

Some children are language-poor in another sense. Although they have plenty of opportunity to listen and speak at home, they hear and use only a limited number of simple words. Children need to hear—and be encouraged to use—language that is specific and rich in detail. For example, rather than using the very general verb *go*, children should be encouraged to use a variety of specific verbs: The cars *roar* up the hill. The boys *race* across the field. The women *jog* every morning. The bugs *creep* down the tree trunk.

Children who speak only a language other than English at home often experience problems when they begin school. They must learn English language skills and, at the same time, keep up with their class. Children who move from one part of the country to another may also have difficulty because of differences in pronunciation.

In all these situations, children may suffer from a communication problem in school. They may not be able to understand the teacher, or they may have difficulty making themselves understood. As a result, learning becomes more difficult for them.

Sometimes these situations can cause emotional difficulties, as well as learning problems, for young children. Classmates are often unkind to a child whose speech is different. The teasing and jokes of other children may add to a child's sense of isolation.

Of course, not all language problems are caused by a child's home environment. Some children have physical problems that prevent normal speech. Some may be mentally deficient. Others may be emotionally immature. These children all require special help, preferably before they begin school.

Most children, however, are able to develop good language skills at home. For these children, parents should remember that they are the child's most influential teacher. Parents who spend time talking with—and listening to—their child are encouraging the child to speak well, and are preparing the child to succeed in school.

Difficulties in school may arise when a child's family speaks a foreign language at home. However, talking with and listening to classmates can help improve the child's English skills.

PARENTING IN ACTION

Promoting Language Development

Jill is an attractive and polite five-year-old. Both her parents work, and Jill spends every weekday with a caregiver, Mrs. Carson. Mrs. Carson is usually busy with household chores, such as cooking and cleaning. She rarely finds time to play or talk with Jill.

When Jill's parents come home from work, they don't seem to have the time or energy to talk with her. Jill usually spends the evening watching television or playing alone in her room.

Recently, Jill started attending a half-day session of kindergarten. Her teacher, Mr. Wiener, is worried about Jill. She is in good physical health and clearly has at least an average IQ. However, Jill speaks only very rarely at school. When she does speak, her pronunciation is noticeably poor.

THINK AND DISCUSS

1. Why does Jill speak so rarely at school? Why is her pronunciation so poor?
2. What do you think Mr. Wiener should do to help Jill at school?
3. Do you think he should also ask Jill's parents for help? If so, what kind of help? If not, why not?

SECTION 2 REVIEW

CHECK YOUR UNDERSTANDING

1. List at least four things parents can do to prepare their children to adjust easily to school.
2. What is a learning disability?
3. What is attention deficit hyperactivity disorder?
4. What is dyslexia?
5. What kind of test can be given to determine whether a child is gifted? What score indicates that a child is gifted?
6. How does an average child's articulation change between the ages of three and six?
7. List three possible causes of a child's speech or language difficulties.

DISCUSS AND DISCOVER

1. When and under what circumstances do you think children should be tested for possible learning disabilities? How does a child benefit when he or she is diagnosed with a learning disability? What problems can such a diagnosis create for the child?
2. Investigate the special programs for gifted and talented children in the elementary schools in your community. How are children screened for the programs? What special learning opportunities are provided? How do the students in these programs seem to respond?

ENCOURAGING MAKE-BELIEVE PLAY

Between the ages of two and nine, children often engage in make-believe play. This kind of play is important to a child's development because it helps make the child aware of the adult world. In fantasy play, children themselves choose what to play, and they create a situation over which they have full control. The real world is brought down to a manageable size. In their pretend world, children can be successful, feel important, and gain confidence. They can make up their own rules and try out new activities without fear of failure or ridicule.

In make-believe play, children often enact situations they observe in the adult world. After watching an adult bake a cake, a child may pretend to bake a cake for a favorite stuffed animal. Old pots and pans, wooden spoons, toy tools, child-sized benches or chairs and tables, and plastic or toy dishes are good props for make-believe play.

Pretend play provides endless opportunities for trying out different roles. A chalkboard and some books can turn a room into a school. Old clothes, jewelry, and shoes for dressing up can make playing house more fun. Many throwaway items can become make-believe treasures.

Within reason, parents and other caregivers should avoid limiting fantasy play. They can, however, let children know how they feel about certain situations. For example, when children are "shooting" each other with pointed fingers or toy guns, a caregiver might explain that he or she doesn't like to shoot people or be shot at. In this way, the caregiver reinforces a set of values without preventing the children from learning about aggressive behavior.

Fantasy play also helps children understand and express their feelings. Stuffed animals, dolls, toy figures, and puppets can all act as good friends—or perhaps enemies to talk to and act out feelings with.

When invited, a parent or other caregiver can take part in fantasy play—by being an audience, by playing a minor role, or even by sampling a slice of pretend apple pie. As soon as possible, however, the adult should leave the play area, allowing the child to create and control the fantasy.

SUMMARY

- Children aged four to six are in the preoperational period of thinking.
- Intelligence tests can help determine a child's intellectual abilities.
- Parents and other caregivers who listen, explain, answer questions, and provide learning experiences help children learn better and faster.
- Children should be encouraged to develop an interest in reading, art, and music.
- Children who are properly prepared for school adjust more easily.
- Learning disabilities result from communication problems within the brain.
- Gifted and talented children need opportunities that will challenge, but not overwhelm, them.
- Between the ages of four and six, children show rapid speech development, especially in vocabulary and articulation.
- Some children have speech and language problems that hinder learning.

REVIEWING THE FACTS

1. What is dramatic play?
2. Define the term *intelligence quotient*.
3. List three disadvantages of IQ tests.
4. What are two ways children can benefit from helping with household tasks?
5. Why should children be encouraged to enjoy reading?
6. What should parents do to encourage children's art activities? What should parents avoid doing?
7. Why should children have medical exams before starting school?
8. What is the difference between a learning disability and a physical disability?
9. Why are gifted children sometimes considered problem students?
10. What is a person's vocabulary? How does an average child's vocabulary change between the ages of three and six?

EXPLORING FURTHER

1. Create a personalized book for a child you know. Write a simple story about the child and his or her family. Use photographs, magazine pictures, or your own drawings to illustrate the story. Share your book with the rest of the class, and then give the book to the child for whom you wrote it. (Section 1)
2. Make up an original finger play that you think will appeal to four- to six-year-olds. Teach your finger play to a group of classmates, and encourage them to discuss and evaluate your work. Make any revisions you consider necessary. Then teach your finger play to at least one child or a small group of children. (Section 1)
3. What community resources are available to help learning disabled children and their families? Plan and prepare a flier with basic information about these programs, and make the fliers available to local parents. (Section 2)

THINKING CRITICALLY

1. **Analyze.** What does the term *culture-free* mean? How is it applied to IQ tests? Do you think IQ tests should be culture-free? Why or why not? Do you believe it is possible to create a truly culture-free IQ test? Why or why not?
2. **Analyze.** What might account for the current trend toward full-day kindergarten programs? What advantages does a full-day program have over a half-day program? What are the disadvantages of full-day kindergartens? Which do you consider better? Why?
3. **Analyze.** Do you think language ability is always an indicator of intelligence? Is it possible that a child who is unusually intelligent and has no physical speech problems might speak very little or even not at all? Why or why not? If so, what might cause the child's speech delay?

CROSS-CURRICULUM CONNECTIONS

1. **Music.** Listen to the recordings of a singer or a group that performs especially for young children. Consider the melodies, harmonies, rhythms, and lyrics the singer or group generally uses. Then compose an original song that would be appropriate for the singer or group to perform. Make your own tape of the song, and play it for your classmates.
2. **Speaking.** Interview an adult who has a learning disability. How did the learning disability affect the person's school experience? When and how was the learning disability diagnosed? How did the diagnosis affect the person's school experience? What effects, if any, does the learning disability have on the adult's daily life? After the interview, plan and present a short oral report of your findings.

OBSERVING AND PARTICIPATING

Creativity in Children

As children play alone or with others, they reflect their creativity. Developing creativity is important because it helps children learn to express themselves and to solve problems. For example, children will use a single toy, such as a teddy bear or a truck, in many different ways. They will imagine changes that make their toys more useful or more fun; for example, their teddy bears may cry and their toy trucks might fly.

Choose one of the activities below, and spend time observing or participating with children. Then make an entry in your observation journal, and compare your observations with those made by your classmates.

- **Observing.** Observe a small group of four- or five-year-olds in the dramatic play area of a preschool or classroom. How do the children begin dramatic play there? How do they decide which role each child will have? What do the children say as they play there? What materials do they use? How long do they sustain their interest in dramatic play?
- **Observing.** Observe as a teacher or librarian reads aloud to a group of preschool or early school-aged children. How does the adult present the book? What special reading techniques or visual additions does he or she make? How do the children respond?
- **Participating.** Select some relatively unusual art materials (such as glue, glitter, and paper) and show a small group of five- or six-year-olds how the materials can be used. Then make the materials available, and encourage the children to create their own artworks. How do the children respond to the new art materials? How freely does each child seem to experiment with the materials? How do the children react to your encouragement?

Vv
Ww
Xx
Yy

UNIT 6

Special Areas of Study

THE BIGGEST PROBLEM
(IS IN OTHER PEOPLE'S MINDS)

My brother Bobby never listens when I talk;
Pays close attention though, and watches like a hawk.
Took some time for my hands to learn the signs,
But now the two of us, we get along just fine.

Bobby's biggest problem is in other people's minds;
We do things we like to do and have a great time.
Some kids stay away, but if they knew him they would find
Bobby's biggest problem really is in other people's minds.

Don Haynie

Fisher-Price

CHAPTER 17

Health and Safety

Jonathan liked riding his brand new tricycle. It made him feel grown-up and very independent. He was even allowed to ride up and down on the sidewalk in front of his house. Jonathan's father, Roland, came out the front door and said, "Jonathan, do you know the rules of crossing the street?"

Jonathan stopped pedaling and looked up at his dad.

Roland knelt beside his son and said, "Let's have a lesson right now." Jonathan nodded in agreement. "First of all, never ride into the street from a driveway or from between parked cars because drivers may not be able to see you in time to stop." Then, pointing at the intersection a few houses down, Roland continued, "When you want to visit your friend, Jerry, always go to the corner where there is a crosswalk. Then stop and look up and down the street very carefully. Make sure there is not traffic coming, and look again before you start across."

"Okay, Dad," said Jonathan as he pedaled away. He was glad to have a dad to teach him about being safe.

SECTION 1

Prevention of Accidents and Illness

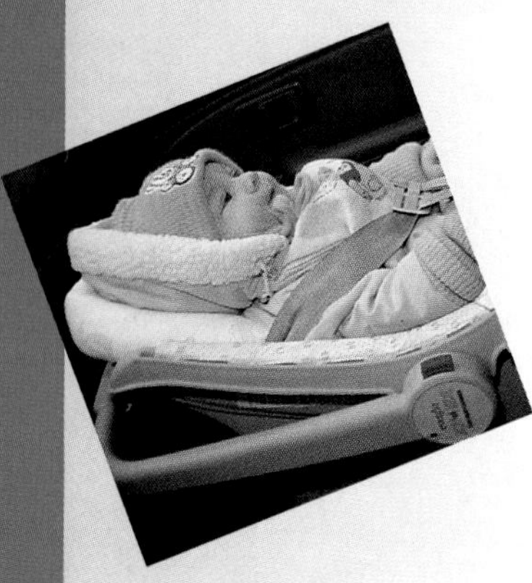

OBJECTIVES

- Identify safety hazards for children of different ages.
- Explain the part immunizations and health checkups play in the prevention of illnesses.
- Discuss what allergies are and how they can be treated.

TERMS TO LEARN

allergy
communicable diseases
immunize
infant mortality rate
nontoxic
vaccine

"An ounce of prevention is worth a pound of cure." That's an old saying that you've probably heard often. The saying is especially true about childhood illnesses and accidents—it's easier to prevent them than to cope with their effects.

Safety

The safety of the child is the most important responsibility of every parent and caregiver. Keeping a child safe requires the following: knowledge of child development; a safe environment; alertness to safety hazards; and, teaching the child safe habits.

Every age has its particular hazards because children of different ages have different abilities and interests. What you know about child development will help you anticipate hazards.

Infants

During the eighteenth century, the American **infant mortality rate**—*the percentage of deaths during the first year of life*—was nearly 40 percent. By the end of the twentieth century, the infant mortality rate in the United States has dropped to about 2 percent. This great improvement is due largely to medical advances. Many infectious diseases that were once life-threatening have now been controlled or even eliminated.

Today, accidents represent the most serious threat to infants. Falls cause the most injuries among babies, and they account for many deaths. Even before an infant can crawl, his or her wiggling can produce enough movement to cause a fall from a bed, a changing table, or an infant seat placed on a table. Such accidents are particularly dangerous because babies tend to fall headfirst. This kind of fall can result in brain damage or other serious injuries. Because of these dangers, no baby should ever be left unattended on any kind of furniture from which a fall is possible.

Babies like to suck and chew on almost anything that comes within reach, so parents and caregivers must be especially careful. Because babies can choke on small objects, anything that could be swallowed—including small toy parts that might be chewed or pulled off—must be kept away from an infant.

Poisoning is another danger for babies. Anything babies could place in the mouth—even the edges of furniture—must be **nontoxic**, or *not poisonous*. Some paints that contain lead are particularly dangerous for children. Plastic bags represent a special hazard. They can cause choking or suffocation. Babies and small children should never be allowed to play with plastic bags. Also, plastic bags should never be used as protective covering for the mattress in a crib or playpen.

A small child should never be left alone near water. Water—indoors in a sink or tub or outdoors in a fish pond, a wading pool, or a swimming pool—can be very dangerous. Drownings happen quickly, even in the time it takes to answer the phone or go to the door.

Although infant walkers are commonly used, they can lead to injury. They can easily tip over or roll down a flight of stairs.

INFANT MORTALITY RATES

According to the Statistical Office of the United Nations, there is a wide range of death rates among infants worldwide. Among their listings are the following number of deaths per 1,000 live births.

Country	
Japan	5.0
Switzerland	6.8
Singapore	7.0
Canada	7.3
France	7.7
United Kingdom	8.8
United States	10.0
Czechoslovakia	11.9
China	12.0
Nigeria	17.6

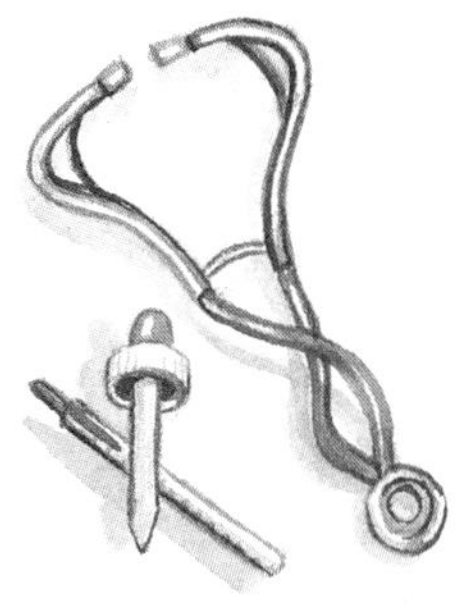

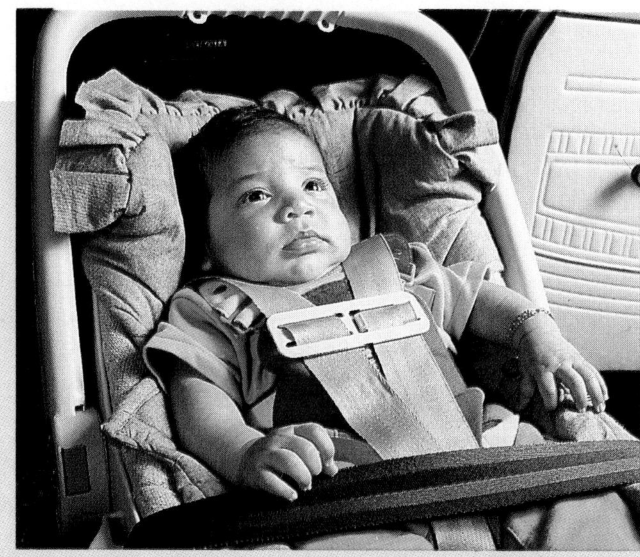

PARENTING IN ACTION

Making Safety Decisions

Fifteen-year-old Nina was spending the day with her older sister Olivia and Olivia's month-old son, Hector. Just before noon, Nina and Olivia decided to drive to a nearby market to get some milk.

As they were getting into the car, Nina asked, "Where's Hector's car seat?"

"Oh, no," sighed Olivia. "I left it in the apartment. Well, it's only a few blocks. You just hold him. This won't take long."

Both sisters put on their own seat belts, and Nina held Hector carefully while Olivia drove. Just before they reached the store, another car pulled out suddenly, and Olivia had to slam on the brakes. Fortunately, she was able to stop the car in time to avoid a collision. However, the force of the sudden stop was enough to tear Hector from Nina's arms. He was thrown against the dash and seriously injured.

THINK AND DISCUSS

1. What would the result of the sudden stop have been if Hector had been in an infant safety restraint? Why?
2. How do you think Olivia feels about Hector's injuries? How do you think Nina feels?
3. How do you think other family members must feel about the accident and its cause? Why?

SAFETY TIP

Children learn best by example. Parents and caregivers can help children learn about safety restraints by using their own seat belts regularly and by making sure that everyone else in the vehicle—young or old—is securely buckled in for safety.

Automobile accidents cause the most deaths among young children. In spite of that fact, many loving parents allow their children to sit or stand in a moving vehicle without any protection. An accident or even a sudden stop can throw the child against the windshield or instrument panel. Most states now have laws that make child safety restraints mandatory, but the laws alone cannot protect children. Every parent and caregiver must be responsible for putting babies and young children into safe car seats for every trip, short or long.

Car seats and restraints must be carefully chosen and consistently used. Regular adult seat belts cannot keep babies or young children safe. The Positive Parenting Skills on page 188-189 gives information on how to choose and use car seats and restraints.

Ages One to Three

One- to three-year-olds need particularly careful supervision. Any area in which they play or spend time should be carefully checked for safety. In addition, no toddler should be left unattended for more than a few minutes; even then they should be within hearing distance. Sometimes it is necessary to be in the garage or outside bringing items from a car while the child is sleeping. Under such circumstances, check on the child periodically or carry a child monitor that transmits sounds from the child's room.

Like babies, toddlers must be guarded against choking. Even very young children should be encouraged to follow these safety guidelines:

- Stay seated while eating.
- Always take small bites.
- Swallow what is in the mouth before taking another bite.
- Do not talk or laugh with food in the mouth.
- Chew all food thoroughly.
- Keep small toys and other small objects out of the mouth.

SAFETY TIP

Parents and other caregivers can help young children avoid choking by following these safety guidelines:

- Cut foods into small pieces, no more than 1/2 inch (1.3 cm) square.
- Avoid serving peanuts, grapes, popcorn, hard candy, fish with bones, or hot dogs to children under age three.
- Always hold a baby's bottle—don't prop it.
- Always keep an eye on a young child who is eating.
- Keep small objects out of the reach of infants and toddlers.

Ages Four to Six

Children aged four to six spend more of their time in unsupervised play. During these years, they need to learn good safety practices. However, you should never rely on young children to remember and follow all the appropriate safety rules. Children need frequent reminders and watchful adults nearby.

Outdoor play equipment, such as a swing set, should be firmly anchored so that there is no danger of its tipping over. When children use this kind of equipment, parents or other caregivers should set and enforce safety rules. One useful rule, for example, is that only one child may be on a swing at a time.

A preschooler should begin learning his or her address and phone number; school-aged children should be able to give this information clearly in an emergency. Children should also be taught how to use a telephone in an emergency, either by calling 911 if it is available in your community or by reaching an operator. Keeping important numbers by the telephone, including the parents' phone numbers at work, can help a child in an emergency.

Children should be taught how to telephone for help before an emergency arises.

Many communities offer safety programs sponsored by the police, fire department, or civic groups. Children can learn traffic rules and other ways to stay safe.

Young children are often fascinated by fire. Even those who have been carefully taught that matches are unsafe may sometimes experiment with matches. As the lighted match burns closer to a child's fingers, the child often becomes frightened. He or she may drop the match or even throw it into a wastebasket to hide the evidence. Many fires start this way. Parents and other caregivers should keep all matches locked away and should remain watchful of children's activities.

When young children begin attending school, they should be prepared for several new kinds of dangers. As children approach school age, parents become increasingly concerned about keeping them safe from crime. To help protect their children, parents should discuss crime openly and honestly with them. However, parents should also avoid frightening children unnecessarily. They should avoid discussing terrible things that have happened to children, and they should not introduce the threat of strangers' stealing children away from their parents.

Parents need to set up safety rules for their children. They need to make it clear, for example, that they will never send a stranger to pick the child up. Parents need to teach children never to go anywhere with a stranger and discuss what children should do if they are approached in a threatening way. If the child walks to school, identify the safest route and be sure the child uses that route every day. If possible, arrange for older children to walk with younger ones.

Some families are unable to provide at-home supervision for children after school. Allowing a young child to return to an unsupervised home is never a satisfactory solution to the problem of child care. In these situations, other, more desirable options should be explored: after-school programs either at the school or in the neighborhood, child care programs that provide transportation from school to the child care center, and neighbors or relatives who are willing to care for the child.

If a child must occasionally stay at home alone, the family should establish special rules. These rules should cover contacting a neighbor for help, keeping doors locked, answering the door and the phone, making phone calls, preparing snacks, and deciding whether friends can visit.

SAFETY TIP

In addition to learning how to get help in an emergency, children must also learn how to recognize a real emergency. One good way to help children with this task is to play the "What If?" game. Ask a child specific questions such as these: What would you do if you woke up at night and smelled smoke? What would you do if you heard a scary noise outside your bedroom window? Use such questions—and the child's responses—to help build an understanding of appropriate behavior in various situations.

Health Care

Everyone should have regular medical checkups. This is especially true for children. A physical can often detect health problems in their early stages. Early treatment can help prevent serious illness or permanent damage to the child's health.

Newborns should be examined frequently during the first year. The baby's physician or clinic will recommend how often.

After the first year, healthy children need checkups less frequently, but at least once a year. Because these checkups are so important, most cities have free or inexpensive clinics that provide good medical care.

Infants can become seriously ill very quickly. If any symptoms of a health problem develop—such as fever, listlessness, prolonged diarrhea, constipation, vomiting, or difficulty in breathing—consult a doctor. In older children, the symptoms of possibly serious illnesses include fever, persistent cough, vomiting, severe headache, and dizziness.

Dental checkups usually begin around three years of age. Fluoride supplementation is often begun at two weeks of age in areas without fluoridated water. Children's secondary teeth can be affected by poor dental care during childhood.

Immunization

To **immunize** is *to protect a person against a particular disease.* People can be protected from many **communicable diseases**—*diseases that are easily passed from one person to another*—by being immunized. Unless people are immunized against them, communicable diseases can easily turn into serious epidemics.

The most common way to immunize people against diseases is with vaccines. A **vaccine** is *a small amount of an antigen introduced to the body, usually by injection, so that the body can build resistance to the disease.* In response to a vaccine, a person's body produces antibodies that fight off the germs for a specific disease. Later, if that person is exposed to the disease, he or she already has antibodies to it. These antibodies ensure that the vaccinated person either will not get the disease at all or will have only a very mild case of the disease.

Every child needs protection from these seven serious diseases: diphtheria, pertussis (whooping cough), and tetanus—often referred to together as DPT; measles, mumps, and rubella (German measles)—often referred to together as MMR; and polio. Many pediatricians also recommend HIB vaccinations, against Haemophilus B, a type of flu associated with ear infections. All these diseases can cause serious illness or even death. The chart on pages 492-494 gives information about the immunizations recommended by the American Academy of Pediatrics and the U.S. Centers for Disease Control. Parents should be sure that their children are immunized according to those schedules and should keep a record of each child's immunizations.

Many states require immunizations for all school children. However, preschool children are most likely to develop complications from the diseases, so parents should not wait until school starts to have their children immunized.

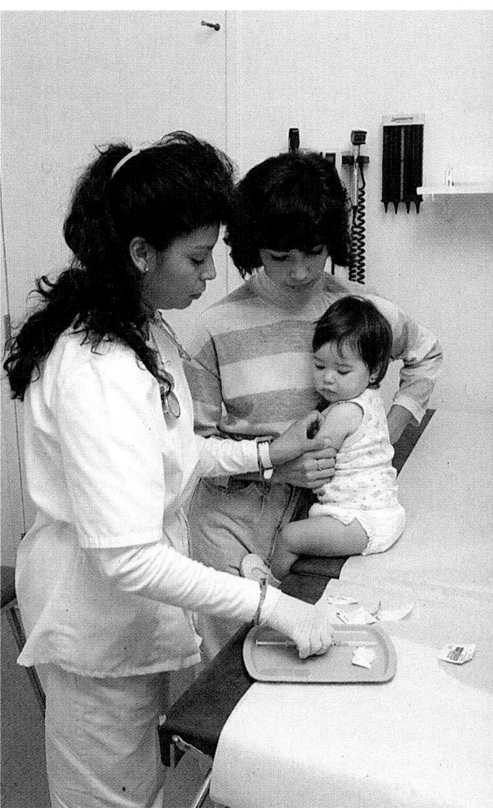

Immunizations have helped many youngsters lead healthier lives.

DISEASE & IMMUNIZATION

DISEASE	IMMUNIZATION	SYMPTOMS	HOME CARE
CHICKEN POX	None available.	A rash of tiny red, raised pimples or blisters appears first. In a day or two, scabs form which fall off in 7 to 10 days. The rash affects the whole body. Fever is either absent or no higher than 102° F (39°C). Rash is irritating but child usually does not feel ill otherwise.	Rest in bed during feverish stage. Fever control is recommended but do not use aspirin. Keep the child cool in loose clothing. Apply talcum powder or calamine lotion to relieve the itching. Recovery is usually within 7 days. Once scabs form, and no new pox have appeared for 2 days, the disease is no longer infectious.
DIPHTHERIA	DPT shots against diphtheria, pertussis (whooping cough), and tetanus are given at 2, 4, and 6 months of age. Booster shots at 18 months and between 3 and 6 years. A combined tetanus and diphtheria shot at age 12 and every 10 years thereafter.	Sore throat, pain in limbs, loss of appetite, swollen neck glands, difficulty breathing.	Child should be under close medical supervision. Hospitalization is usually necessary.
HAEMOPHILUS INFLUENZA (HIB)	Vaccinations are given at 2 years of age. Children 18-23 months of age who attend child care facilities should be vaccinated, as the disease is easily spread. Children should be revaccinated 2-12 months later, but not before 24 months of age.	Most common cause of bacterial meningitis. Symptoms include sudden onset of fever, nausea, vomiting, and intense headaches.	A doctor's care is essential. Patient will need immediate hospitalization. Disease is fatal in 5 percent of meningitis cases in children less than 5 years of age. Causes long-term neurological problems in many others.

(Continued on next page)

DISEASE & IMMUNIZATION (cont'd.)

DISEASE	IMMUNIZATION	SYMPTOMS	HOME CARE
MEASLES	Vaccination at about 15 months. Combination vacines (a Measles/Rubella and a Measles/ Mumps/Rubella are available).	Usually fever, sometimes as high as 105° (41°C). The child may also cough, have a runny nose and inflamed, watery eyes. About 4 days later a blotchy, dusty-red rash appears, often seen first behind the ears or on the forehead and face. On day 6 rash quicky fades and by day 7 all symptoms are gone.	Child should be under a doctor's supervision and kept in bed for the duration of the fever. The disease is most contagious during the few days before and after the rash appears. If patient's eyes are sensitive, the child should be kept in a darkened room and not allowed to read or do other close work.
MUMPS	Vaccine is given at 12 months or thereafter. A parent who has not had mumps may be immunized if his or her child contracts the disease.	Sudden fever, occasional nausea, abdominal pain, and swelling of one or more salivary glands, most commonly those located at the angles of the jaws. Swelling reaches maximum within 24 hours and may last 7-10 days. In boys, infection may also cause painful swelling in the testicles.	A hot-water bottle and analgesics may ease pain. Fluids are easiest to swallow. Mumps is usually a mild disease, leaving no ill effects. However, sometimes deafness occurs.
POLIOMYELITIS	The Sabin vaccine is given orally at 2, 4, and 18 months of age and again at 4 or 5 years.	Sudden fever, headache, vomiting, stiffness of neck. In paralytic cases, the muscles become painful and tender; paralysis follows.	A doctor's care is essential. Patient must be isolated and kept in bed during acute phase. In paralytic cases, even partial recovery takes many months.
RUBELLA (German Measles)	Vaccination between 12 and 15 months of age or thereafter.	Similar to those of a head cold. Mild fever and joint pain are often the first signs, followed by rash on face and head, and later on neck and body. Lymph nodes at back of neck may become tender and swollen.	Child should be kept at home until recovery. The disease is dangerous only for women during pregnancy. It can cause defects in the unborn child.

(Continued on next page)

DISEASE & IMMUNIZATION (cont'd.)

DISEASE	IMMUNIZATION	SYMPTOMS	HOME CARE
SCARLET FEVER and STREPTOCOCCAL SORE THROAT	No prevention. Penicillin or erythromycin helps prevent such complications as rheumatic fever.	Sudden onset, with headache, fever, sore throat. Lymph nodes usually enlarged. In scarlet fever a rash appears, usually within 24 hours, as fine red dots. The rash is seen first on the neck and upper part of the chest, and lasts 24 hours to 10 days. When it fades, skin peels. The rash is the only symptom that differentiates scarlet fever from "strep throat."	Because strep throat and scarlet fever can be followed by or reactivate rheumatic fever, a physician's care is needed. The child should rest in a warm, well-ventilated room. Patient usually recovers in a week's time, but parent should watch for such complications as earache or inflamed neck glands.
WHOOPING COUGH (Pertussis)	See Diphtheria section.	Begins with cough that is worse at night. Symptoms may at first be mild. Characteristic "whooping" cough develops in about 2 weeks, and coughing spasms sometimes end with vomiting.	Child should take antibiotics under a doctor's care. Hospitalization is often required for infants. Rest is important, as is a diet that will not irritate the throat. Keep the child isolated from other children until antibiotics have been taken for at least 5 days.

Allergies

An **allergy** is *an oversensitivity to one or more common substances*. Individuals may have allergic reactions when they eat, breathe in, or touch specific substances, such as grass, molds, milk products, and pollens. Symptoms of allergic reactions may be mild, such as nonitching rash, nasal stuffiness, or a runny nose. Some allergic reactions, however, can be life-threatening and may cause such conditions as constriction of the air sacs in the lungs and severely diminished oxygen intake.

Nearly half of all the children in the United States develop allergies. Specific allergies are not inherited, but the tendency to be allergic is apparently inherited. If both parents have allergies, the chance of their child's developing at least one allergy is about 70 percent.

Although allergies cannot be cured, their effects are often preventable. For example, a child who is allergic to a specific food can avoid eating that food—even in small amounts. Foods that commonly cause allergies in babies and children include milk, cereal grains, eggs, shellfish, nuts, fresh fruit juices, chocolate, and food additives.

A doctor may prescribe medication to help control an allergy. If the allergy causes severe problems, the child may be given a series of allergy tests to determine which specific substances are causing the problems. Then the child can be gradually desensitized to those substances.

A child who is sensitive to animal hair may still be able to have a pet, as long as it is kept outdoors.

SECTION 1 REVIEW

CHECK YOUR UNDERSTANDING

1. List four things necessary to keep a child safe.
2. Define the term infant mortality rate.
3. When should car safety restraints be used?
4. List four things caregivers should do to reduce the risk of choking for babies and young children.
5. Which telephone numbers should young children learn?
6. List the seven illnesses that children should be immunized against.
7. What is an allergy?

DISCUSS AND DISCOVER

1. Check your own home for fire safety. Be sure that your home has one or more smoke detectors, and check to be sure they work. Plan an escape route from your home to be used in case of fire. Draw a simple map showing your plan; share and discuss this map with other students.
2. Design and make a poster to increase parents' awareness of one aspect of child safety. If possible, display your poster in an area where the parents of young children are likely to notice it and stop to read it.

SECTION 2 Handling Emergencies

OBJECTIVES

- Recognize emergency situations and plan appropriate responses.
- Demonstrate appropriate first aid for common ailments.
- Identify basic rescue techniques.

TERMS TO LEARN

artificial respiration
convulsion
CPR (cardiopulmonary resuscitation)
fracture
Heimlich maneuver
poison control centers
sprain

Someday you may have to take care of a child in an emergency. If that happens, you will have to make decisions and take actions that will affect the child's health and well-being—perhaps even the child's life. You can prepare yourself by learning how to act in an emergency and how to give first aid and use rescue techniques.

Guidelines for Fast Action

Accidents often happen because children fail to recognize danger or to understand their own limitations. If a child in your care does get hurt, these five guidelines will help you make good decisions:

1. **Above all, try to remain calm.** A quiet, soothing approach will help reassure the child and help you think more clearly.
2. **Evaluate the situation.** What seems to be wrong? Is the child burned, bleeding heavily, or unconscious? Does the child have an arm or leg in an awkward position?
3. **Make the victim comfortable.** If the injury is serious, keep the child warm with a blanket, jacket, or other covering.
4. **Call for help, if symptoms indicate a need.** If you are not certain what the problem is or how to care for an injury, call for help. Contact the child's parents, a neighbor, a doctor, or emergency room of a hospital; or call for the paramedics or an ambulance. What you say on the phone is as important as making the call. Give the facts as clearly and concisely as possible. You will be able to save valuable time if you keep near the phone a list of phone numbers you might need and a record of the address where you are.

5. **Give the minimum necessary first aid treatment.** Knowing what you should *not* do in an emergency is often as important as knowing what you should do. For instance, some injuries can be made worse just by moving the patient. If you are in doubt about how to handle an injured person, give only the most necessary first aid treatment and seek help from someone better trained.

No one can predict an emergency. However, it is possible to prepare yourself so that you can act quickly if an emergency occurs.

First Aid

It is essential for anyone who takes care of children to be familiar with first aid procedures. The following guidelines are very general. For more information, contact the nearest office of the American Red Cross about first aid training classes.

Animal Bites

Wash the area around the bite with soap and running water. Try to have the animal caught so that it can be tested for rabies. (Wild animals are more likely than pets to have rabies.) The victim should be checked by a doctor. A DPT shot may be necessary.

Bleeding

Stop the bleeding by placing a clean, wet or dry cloth over the wound and pressing hard for about ten minutes without releasing. If the bleeding is severe, send for medical help.

- **Minor cuts or scrapes.** Clean a small cut or a simple scrape with soap and warm water. Apply a mild antiseptic, and cover the wound with a bandage.
- **Deep cuts or wounds.** These may be severe. If the child is pale and bluish and his or her skin is moist, or if the child's breathing is shallow and rapid, send for medical help. Continue to try to stop the bleeding until medical assistance arrives. Elevating the affected area may help. Do not apply a tourniquet. (A tourniquet is a bandage that cuts off the blood supply to a portion of the body.) An improperly applied tourniquet can further harm the victim.
- **Nosebleeds.** A nosebleed may result from an injury, or it may have no apparent cause. Usually, a small blood vessel inside the nose has broken. Have the child sit down and lean slightly forward over a basin or sink. Using the thumb and forefinger, squeeze the child's nose firmly just below the bones in the nose. Continue squeezing for several minutes; then check to see whether the bleeding has stopped. If not,

To stop a nosebleed, have the child lean forward slightly. Firmly press above the nostrils and hold for several minutes.

reapply pressure for five to ten minutes. Sometimes applying cold packs to the nose and forehead also help. If you cannot stop the bleeding, or if the child becomes dizzy or pale, seek medical help.

Bumps and Bruises

Treat bumps and bruises with a cold cloth or ice pack to minimize swelling. An injured arm or leg can be elevated. If the child complains of pain for more than a day, call a physician.

A fall or bump on the head can be serious. Call a doctor if the child loses consciousness, is drowsy or irritable, complains of headache, or vomits.

Burns

How you treat a burn depends on what caused the burn and how bad it is. All but small surface burns are serious because they may cause scarring, infections, or shock. Burns are classified by degree.

- **First-degree burns look red and slightly swollen.** They may be caused by too much sun, hot objects, hot water, or steam. First-degree burns heal rapidly.
- **Second-degree burns are deeper, redder, and blistered.** They remain swollen and somewhat moist for several days. They can have various causes, including very deep sunburn, hot liquids, and flammable products like gasoline. Second-degree burns should be treated by a physician.
- **Third-degree burns destroy the skin.** These burns may look white or charred, or they may resemble second-degree burns at first. There may be little pain at first because the nerve endings have been destroyed. Third-degree burns can be caused by flames, burning clothing, hot water, extremely hot objects, or electricity. The skin is lost and will not grow back. Only scar tissue will cover the area after healing. Third-degree burns are extremely serious and require emergency medical attention. Treat small, surface burns where the skin is not broken with a cold, wet cloth. Apply the cloth several times for short periods to take the heat out of the burn. A burned hand or foot may be placed in a basin of cold water. Then cover the burned area with a clean, loose cloth. Never apply butter or grease to a burn. If the skin has been broken or the burn looks serious, call for medical help. Cover the burn with a clean, dry cloth and keep the patient warm. To help ease the pain, elevate the burned area slightly. The patient should be taken to a hospital as soon as possible.

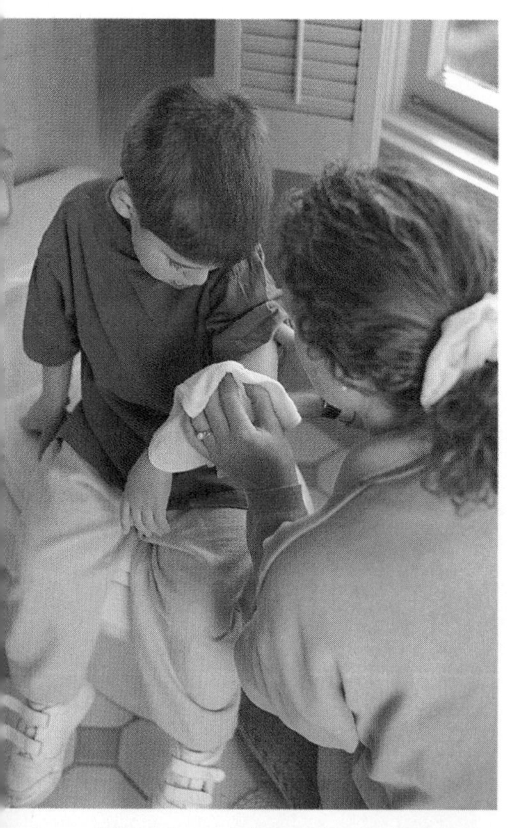

Minor burns should be treated with a cold, wet cloth and covered with a clean, dry cloth. More serious burns require professional medical help.

Household products, such as toilet bowl cleaners, drain cleaners, and disinfectants, can cause chemical burns. Using protective gloves or a towel, wash off the affected area immediately and completely with cold water. Remove any clothing with the chemical on it, unless the clothing is stuck to the skin. Apply a clean bandage, and call a doctor.

Electrical burns may be deep, but they often appear minor, leaving only a small black dot on the skin. Cool the burned area with cold water, and cover it with a clean, smooth cloth such as a handkerchief. Then have the patient lie down with legs elevated and head turned to one side. This prevents shock. (See pages 503 and 505 for more information about shock.) Take the child to a hospital emergency room, or call an ambulance.

Choking

Choking occurs when something is caught in a person's throat. With a child, this may be food or a small object. The danger is that choking can cut off the supply of air. When oxygen is no longer going to the brain, brain damage can occur within a few minutes.

First, recognize the signs of choking: an inability to speak, breathe, or cry; bluish lips, nails, and skin; high-pitched noises or ineffective coughing. If a baby or child is choking, immediately work to help dislodge the object that is blocking the breathing passage. Hold a baby or small child facedown across your lap with the head lowered; for a larger child, kneel on the floor and drape the child facedown over your thighs so that the head is lowered. Use the heel of your hand to give four quick blows between the child's shoulder blades. This often helps get the object out. If this method does not succeed, you can use the **Heimlich maneuver**, a *technique for using pressure on the air within the body to force an object interfering with breathing from the throat*. The diagrams on page 500 show how to administer the Heimlich maneuver to infants and to older children and adults.

Keep in mind that the amount of pressure to use in the Heimlich maneuver depends on the age and size of the victim. Too much pressure, especially on a young child, can be harmful. It is best to get special training in using the Heimlich maneuver—before you need to use it.

If the baby or child has lost consciousness, begin artificial respiration and call for emergency medical help. (See page 506 for information on artificial respiration.) If the child stops breathing, use your thumb and forefinger to try to locate and remove the object from the child's throat; then begin artificial respiration immediately. Continue until help arrives.

Heimlich Maneuver for Infants and Toddlers

1. Turn the infant facedown over your arm.

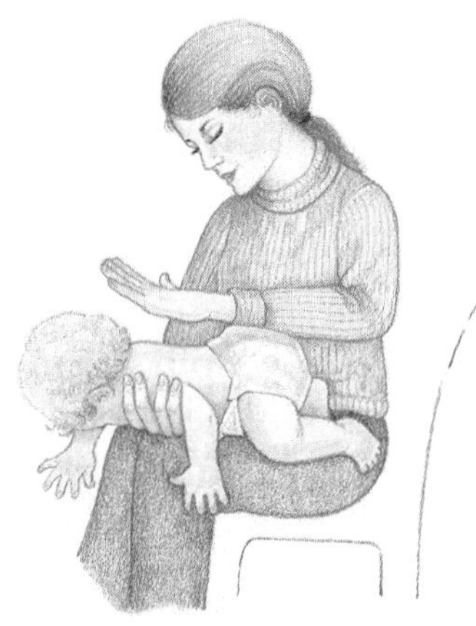

2. Using the heel of your other hand, give four quick blows between the infant's shoulder blades.

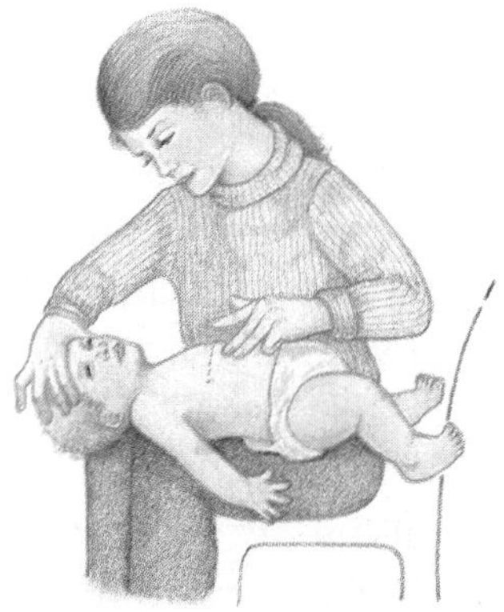

3. Turn the infant over, supporting the head, neck, and back. Position your two middle fingers below the rib cage and above the navel; give four quick thrusts toward the chest. Repeat these three steps, if needed.

Heimlich Maneuver for Older Children and Adults

If the victim is standing or sitting:

1. Stand behind the victim. Clasp your hands with your fists just below the victim's rib cage.

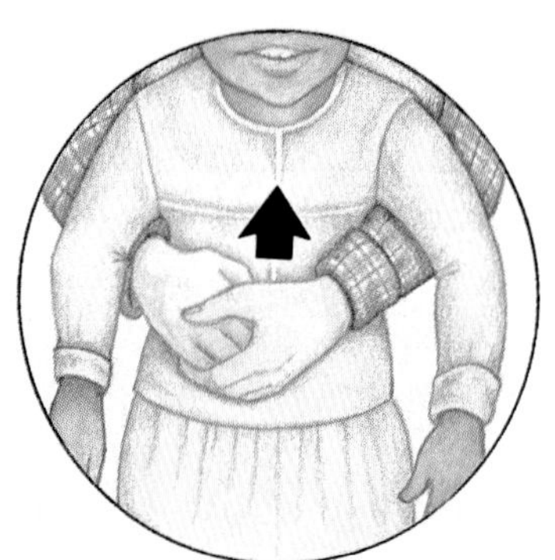

2. Press your clasped hands into the victim's abdomen with a quick upward thrust. Repeat step 2 if necessary.

If the victim has collapsed:

1. Kneel above the victim's hips. Place both your hands, one over the other, on the victim's abdomen. The heel of your bottom hand should be slightly above the victim's navel and below his or her rib cage.

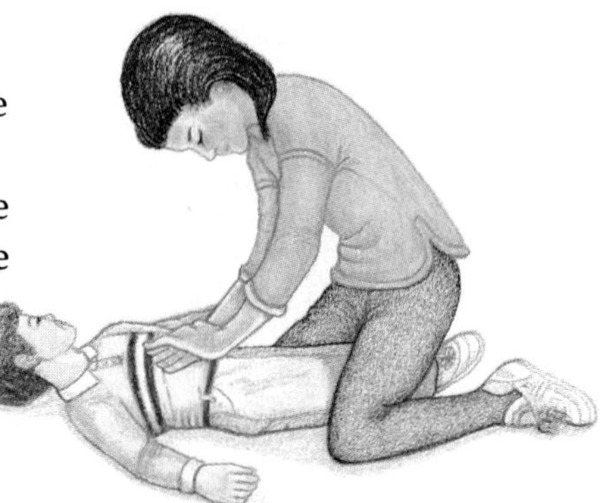

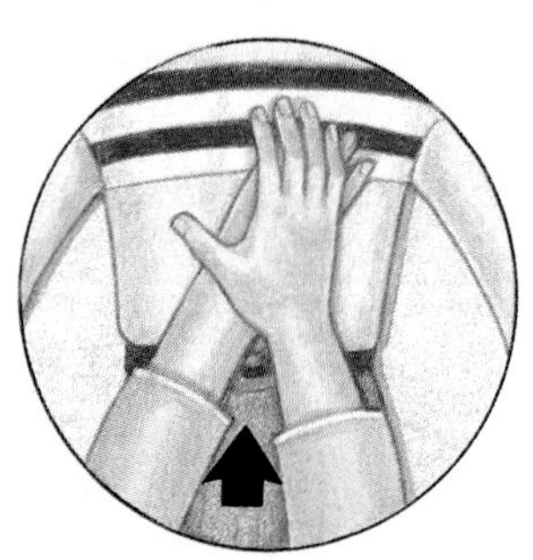

2. Use the force of both hands to press with a quick upward thrust. Repeat step 2 if necessary.

Convulsions

A **convulsion** or a seizure is *a period of unconsciousness with uncontrolled jerking or twitching of the muscles.* There are many causes of convulsions. They occur most often in infants, usually as a result of high fever.

If a child of any age, including an infant, has a convulsion, place the child on his or her side on the floor. Move any hard objects out of the way. Don't attempt to hold the child down, and don't force anything between his or her teeth. After the convulsion stops, be sure the child's head is turned to one side to reduce any risk of choking. Check with a doctor for further instructions. If the convulsion lasts more than 15 minutes, take the child to a hospital emergency room or call an ambulance.

Fainting

Fainting is a loss of consciousness. A child may collapse without warning, or he or she may first experience sweating, cold skin, nausea, or dizziness. A child who is about to faint often looks pale or bluish. Anyone who feels faint should lie down or sit with the head between the legs.

If a child has fainted, loosen any tight clothing. Position the child's head to one side. Check to be sure the child is breathing. If breathing has stopped, begin artificial respiration, and have someone call for medical assistance. (See page 506 for information on artificial respiration.) If the child is breathing, expect him or her to revive from the faint within a minute or two. If the child does not gain consciousness within two minutes, call for help. A child who has had a head injury, has experienced seizurelike movements, or has been unconscious for more than two minutes should be seen by a physician immediately.

Fractures and Sprains

A **fracture** is a *break or a crack in a bone.* A **sprain** is *an injury caused by sudden, violent stretching of a joint or muscle.* Both may cause pain, swelling, and bruising. It is often difficult to tell a sprain from a fracture without an X ray.

If you suspect that a child has a fracture or a sprain, do not move the child until you know how serious the injury is. This is especially important for back, rib, neck, or collarbone injuries. You can cause further damage—even paralysis—by moving the child. Call for qualified medical help, and use artificial respiration if necessary.

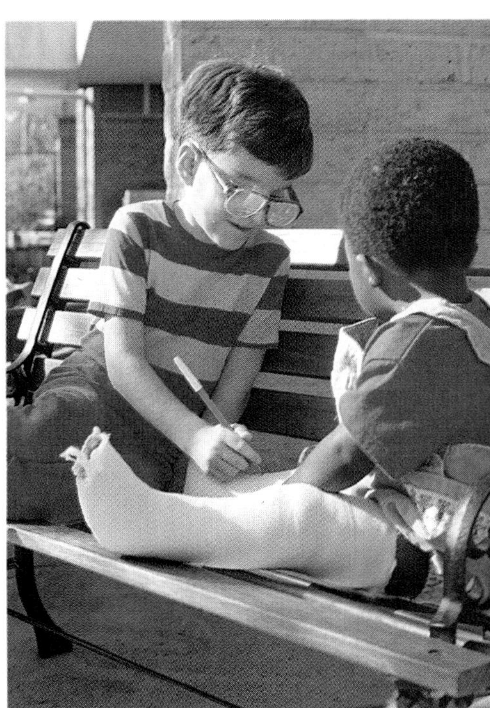

A broken bone must be set by a doctor so that the fracture will heal properly. Children like to have their casts signed by friends.

You can treat a mild sprain by elevating the injured area. Apply cold packs to help reduce swelling. If the pain persists, check with a doctor.

Insect Stings and Bites

If a child has been stung by a bee, wasp, hornet, or yellow jacket, scrape off any stinger. Apply an ice pack or ice water to the affected area. Then cover the area with a paste made from baking soda and water.

Some people are very allergic to insect stings. For them, a single sting can cause serious illness or even death. Anyone with a known allergy to stings must be taken to a hospital or doctor immediately after being stung. In addition, anyone who becomes dizzy, feels faint, has difficulty breathing, shows signs of generalized swelling, or perspires heavily after a sting needs prompt medical attention.

Ticks are small insects that cling to the skin or scalp. They are dangerous because they carry diseases. If you find a tick on a child, don't try to pull it off. Instead, cover the tick with cooking oil (or a similar heavy oil) until it comes loose. Wash the area well with soap and water.

Mosquito, ant, and chigger bites are annoying, but they are usually not dangerous. A baking soda paste or a coating of witch hazel or rubbing alcohol will give relief.

Poisoning

Poisons are one of the greatest hazards for young children. Too often, parents and other caregivers leave poisonous products within a child's reach around the house. Part of the problem is that so many common household products are poisonous. The chart on page 504 lists common household poisons. These items should be kept out of the reach of children, preferably in a locked cabinet.

Recognizing the fact that a child has been poisoned is not always easy. If a toddler is holding an empty vitamin bottle and has a mouthful of vitamin tablet pieces, the situation is clear. Often, however, it is difficult to tell. Here are some symptoms that may indicate poisoning:

- **Swallowed poisons** can cause difficulty in breathing, unconsciousness, fever, burns in the mouth and throat, and vomiting from swallowed poisons or chemicals.
- **Skin-contact poisons** can cause burns or rash on the skin.
- **Eye-contact poisons** can cause burning or irritation of the eyes, or blindness.
- **Inhaled poisons** can cause choking, coughing, nausea, or dizziness from fumes, sprays, and poisonous gases.

If you suspect poisoning, call for help right away. Be prepared to tell what you think caused the poisoning and how much was involved. Have the container with you when you call.

In case a child is poisoned, you should know what to do:

1. Keep emergency phone numbers and addresses posted by all telephones. Include numbers for the doctor, hospital, police, and poison control center. **Poison control centers** are *special hospital units that are equipped to advise and treat poison victims.* If you care for children in someone else's home, take a copy of your emergency phone number list with you.
2. Determine what has poisoned the child. If the child has swallowed something poisonous, determine about how much he or she swallowed.
3. Phone the poison control center or the child's doctor. Have the container of poison at hand as you call, so that you can give complete, accurate information. (Do not rely on the emergency procedures listed on product labels; they are not always accurate.)
4. Follow the directions you receive from the poison control center or the doctor. Act quickly and calmly.

Anyone who has been poisoned must be checked by a physician, even if emergency treatment has already been given and even if there are no symptoms. Be sure to take the poison container or a sample of the poison substance with you. This information helps the doctor give proper treatment.

Shock

When a person's body is threatened, such as by an injury, by the loss of a great deal of blood, or by poisoning, the body goes into shock. Important body functions, including breathing and heart action, are impaired. The symptoms of shock can include a pale or bluish skin color, rapid pulse, clammy skin, shallow breathing, enlarged pupils, a glassy stare, and nausea. Sometimes a person in shock loses consciousness.

COMMON HOUSEHOLD POISONS

KINDS OF POISONS	EXAMPLES	TYPE OF CONTACT
MEDICINES	• Sleeping pills • Aspirin • Tranquillizers • Vitamins • Cold preparations	• Swallowing
CLEANING PRODUCTS	• Ammonia • Automatic dishwasher detergent • Laundry detergents • Bleach • Drain and toilet bowl cleaners • Disinfectants • Furniture polish	• Swallowing • Skin • Eyes • Inhaling
PERSONAL CARE PRODUCTS	• Shampoo • Soap • Nail polish remover • Perfumes and after-shave lotions • Mouthwash • Rubbing alcohol	• Swallowing • Skin • Eyes • Inhaling
GARDENING AND GARAGE PRODUCTS	• Insecticides • Fertilizers • Rat and mouse poisons • Acids of all kinds • Gasoline • Paint thinner • Charcoal lighter fluid • Antifreeze	• Swallowing • Skin • Eyes • Inhaling
PLANTS	• Some wild mushrooms • English ivy • Daffodil bulbs • Rhubarb leaves • Holly berries • Poinsettias • Poison ivy and poison oak	• Swallowing • Skin

Shock can be serious. If you suspect a child is in shock, seek medical help immediately. Until help arrives, be sure the child remains lying down, and keep him or her warm.

Splinters

Although splinters are not dangerous, they do hurt, and they can become infected. Splinters are usually tiny pieces of wood, metal, or glass; thorns may also be treated as splinters.

If part of the splinter is above the surface of the skin, it can be removed with tweezers. Sterilize the tweezers in boiling water or in a flame. If a nonglass splinter is just under the skin surface, it can be carefully taken out with a sterilized needle. Numb the skin over the splinter first with a piece of ice to help dull the pain. After the splinter has been removed, put antiseptic on the wound and cover it with a sterile bandage.

Large or deep splinters and those caused by glass can be more serious. They should be removed by a physician.

Rescue Techniques

When an emergency situation causes the victim to stop breathing and perhaps even causes the victim's heart to stop beating, immediate action is vital. You should become familiar with rescue techniques that enable you to respond quickly to this kind of life-or-death situation.

Artificial Respiration

Artificial respiration is *a procedure for forcing air into the lungs of a person whose own breathing has stopped*. Some emergency situations, including drowning and electrical shock, for example, call for artificial respiration. The technique for giving artificial respiration to infants and small children is slightly different from that for adults. It is shown on page 506. A rescue training class can provide you with more information about the proper way to give artificial respiration and can give you a chance to practice the correct techniques.

CPR

CPR, a short name for **cardiopulmonary resuscitation**, is *a rescue technique used to sustain life when both breathing and heart action have stopped*. Special training from a certified instructor is needed to perform CPR. Many communities offer training programs. To find out where CPR training is offered in your area, call a local chapter of the American Red Cross or the American Heart Association.

Artificial Respiration for Infants and Small Children

1. Turn the child's head to one side. With your finger, carefully clear the child's mouth of any foreign objects or fluid. (However, if the victim is under a year old, do not put your finger into his or her mouth.) If there is an object caught in the child's throat, or to clear the mouth of a young baby, follow the instructions for using the Heimlich maneuver on infants and toddlers, page 500.

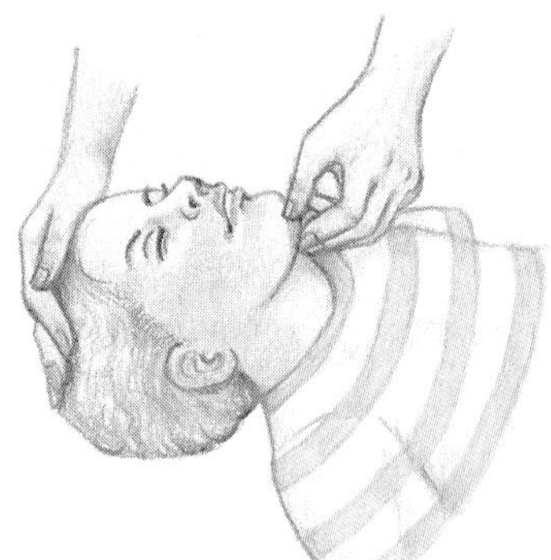

2. Tilt the child's head back slightly. Put two fingers just under the chinbone and lift the jaw into a jutting-out position. Check for breathing.

3. If the child is not breathing, take a deep breath. Seal your lips around the child's mouth and nose. (If you can cover only the mouth, pinch the child's nostrils shut with your fingers.)

4. Blow into the child's mouth and nose. (For an infant, use gentle puffs of air.) When you see the chest lift, remove your mouth and let the air come out. Then blow in again. Repeat 15 to 20 times per minute for a child, or 20 times per minute for an infant. Continue until the child resumes normal breathing or until help arrives.

SECTION 2 REVIEW

CHECK YOUR UNDERSTANDING

1. List the five guidelines for fast action in case of an accident or injury.
2. How should a nosebleed be treated?
3. Briefly describe the three categories of burns.
4. What is the Heimlich maneuver?
5. What is the difference between a fracture and a sprain?
6. What is a poison control center?
7. What symptoms call for artificial respiration? What symptoms call for CPR?

DISCUSS AND DISCOVER

1. Why might it be difficult to remain calm if a child in your care was injured? Why would it be especially important to remain calm? What could you do to help yourself maintain a calm attitude and a clear mind?
2. Read about syrup of ipecac: What is it? Where, and at what price, can it be purchased? Under what circumstances should it be used? When should it not be used? Share your findings with classmates.

Caring for a Sick Child

SECTION 3

OBJECTIVES

- Give basic guidelines for caring for children who are ill.
- Describe the special nutritional needs of sick children.
- Discuss problems involved in the hospitalization of children.

It is never easy caring for a child who is ill. Normal routines are upset. The child may cry often, demand attention, and have a short temper. However, the attitude of the caregiver can be as important as the medical treatment in restoring good health.

The Caregiver's Role

A caregiver should maintain a calm, efficient, confident, and cheerful attitude. It is best to treat the illness matter-of-factly and to discuss it as little as possible.

When a child is ill, the caregiver often has to assume responsibility for entertaining the child. A child who is very ill does not have much energy for play and may spend most of the time sleeping. However, during mild illness or the recovery stage of a serious illness, the child may be easily bored. Reading books, playing with puzzles, and other quiet activities are suitable for the recovering child.

Children of different ages may have different needs during illness.

- **Infants.** Infants who are ill sleep much more than usual. They tend to be cranky and may want a lot of physical comforting. Comforting is important because the baby cannot understand what is wrong. Gently rocking the baby, talking softly, singing, and holding the baby close (perhaps in a cloth carrier) can help the baby feel calm and comforted.

- **Ages one to three.** Young children may need more help than older children in keeping comfortable and occupied during an illness. Young children are usually very physically active, and staying in bed is difficult for them. Doctors often do not

Infants may need to be sung to and rocked to distract them from an illness.

insist on keeping toddlers in bed. A child who is warmly dressed can play quietly around the house. For toddlers, quiet play may include listening to stories, building with blocks, and playing simple games.

- **Ages four to six.** Older children handle ordinary illnesses much better than toddlers usually do. Preschoolers and, especially, school-age children can help care for themselves. Four- to six-year-olds can usually enjoy playing quietly with storybooks, stickers, puzzles, and games.

Because of medical advances, childhood illnesses are viewed differently today. One hundred years ago, people took longer to recover from illness. Today, however, antibiotics and other medical treatments prevent many illnesses from becoming serious. Children are usually up and about in a few days. Often recovery involves no more than keeping the child inside and quiet for a while; it may also be important to keep the child away from other children during the contagious period of an illness.

Of course, serious illnesses or injuries may necessitate additional treatment and a long period of recovery. In these cases, the understanding and cooperation of the entire family are required. The child needs to remain, as much as possible, an active and contributing part of the family.

The chart on pages 492-494 lists the symptoms, immunizations, and care for common childhood illnesses.

Medical treatment keeps many childhood illnesses from becoming serious. Having companionship and fun things to do helps the child feel better, too.

ASK THE EXPERTS

Nutrition During Illness

Dr. Van D. Stone has served as Chief of Pediatrics at Baptist Medical Center in Little Rock and is in private practice in Tupelo, Mississippi

One of my own children seems prone to flu and other illnesses, and I often help out friends and neighbors by caring for their children during minor illnesses, so the parents won't have to miss work. Can you give me any tips about feeding children who aren't well?

I'm sure you already know that taking care of a sick child is an important—and sometimes a demanding— job. By providing good nutrition during an illness, you can help a child feel more comfortable and often even encourage the child's recovery.

It's usually important to offer a sick child plenty of water and other liquids. A child with a fever should be encouraged to drink as much as possible; sometimes using a special cup or a fancy straw can encourage the child to drink throughout the day.

However, if the child's stomach is upset, even water may cause vomiting. Then it's best to let the stomach rest for at least an hour. After that period, offer the child very small amounts of water or of clear carbonated soft drinks—just a sip or two at first. You might find you can help a child get started with liquids by letting him or her suck on chips of crushed ice.

With some illnesses, the child's doctor may recommend a specific diet. In this case, of course, you should follow the doctor's suggestions as closely as possible. In all other cases, it's best simply to offer the sick child small amounts of regular foods. Remember, though, that children often lose their appetite during even minor illnesses, and it is never a good idea to force a child to eat. Once the child is feeling better, he or she will resume an interest in eating.

In certain cases, a child's doctor may recommend a bland diet or a liquid diet. A bland diet consists of soft, smooth, mild-flavored foods. If this has been the doctor's recommendation, you might offer the child soups, hot cereals, puddings, gelatin desserts, eggs, and mild cooked vegetables. A liquid diet provides foods in liquid form that can be more easily used by the body. If a pediatrician recommends a liquid diet, offer the child fruit juice,carbonated soft drinks, milk, broth, cream soup, ice cream, and pudding.

Van D. Stone, MD

Dr. Van D. Stone

Hospitalization

A hospital stay is an emotional crisis for almost every child. Child psychologists agree that no experience is more emotionally upsetting to a child than suddenly being separated from home and family. In the hospital, the youngster is surrounded by unfamiliar people, unusual routines, strange noises and smells, and frightening machines.

PARENTING IN ACTION

Dealing with Hospitalization

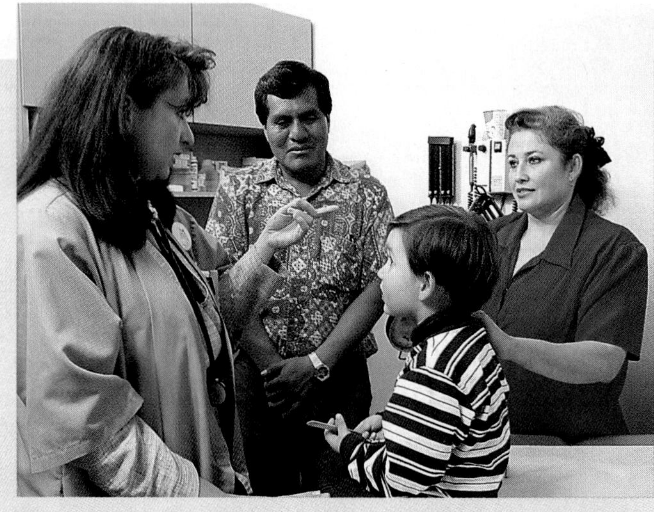

When the pediatrician explained that three-year-old Alex would have to be hospitalized for surgery, his parents chose a hospital that encouraged family support.

Ahead of time, Alex went with his parents to see the hospital and to meet several friendly nurses. Later, at home, his parents explained everything that would happen to him, using hand puppets for the doctor-patient stories.

Along with his toothbrush, robe, and pajamas, Alex was allowed to take along several favorite books, small toys, and his cuddly blanket.

After Alex's surgery, his parents took turns staying with him, so one of them was always there. His parents bathed Alex, fed him, and were present during all medical checks. His father slept by his bedside.

Back home, Alex recovered quickly. He told his brother all about his operation and how he got to ride on a bed with wheels.

THINK AND DISCUSS

1. How did Alex's parents prepare him for his experiences in the hospital? What effect do you think those preparations had?
2. What special needs do you think his brother might have had during Alex's hospitalization? How do you think their parents could have helped them?

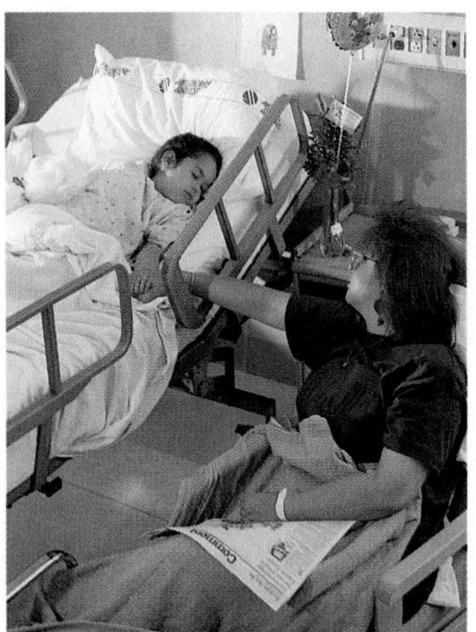

Visits from parents and other family members can help a hospitalized child keep from feeling frightened and alone.

Hospitalized youngsters often fear that their parents have abandoned them. They may be frightened that they will be hurt or mutilated, or that they will die. Some hospitalized children think they are being punished. Children have these fears because they do not understand what is happening to them.

A family who knows in advance that a child will be hospitalized can prepare the child for the event. The parents or doctor should explain to the child in simple words just what to expect. If possible, the parents should take the child to visit the hospital ahead of time. Many hospitals have special tours for children. These tours include a look in the patients' rooms and operating and recovery rooms. They may also include a puppet show or movie. Some hospitals have playrooms where children can play with stethoscopes, masks, identification bracelets, and other equipment. When the child is admitted, these things are already familiar—and less frightening.

Most hospitals realize that children recover better if a parent is allowed to stay in the hospital with them. Some hospitals move a cot into the child's room so that one parent can sleep

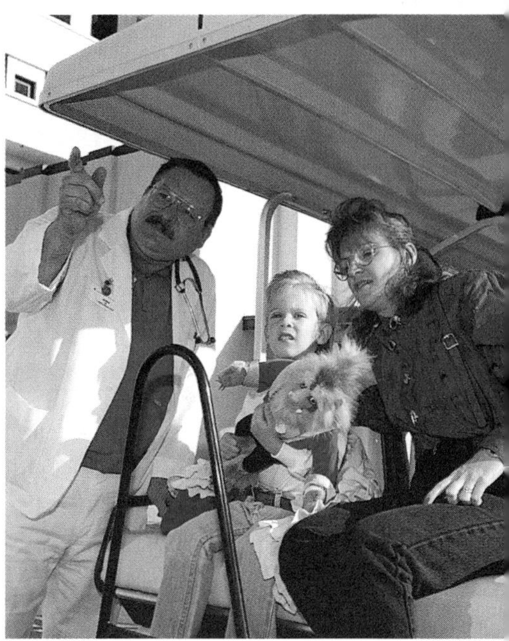

A tour of the hospital and its grounds can help eliminate fear for a child scheduled for hospitalization. Do hospitals in your area offer this service?

nearby. Other hospitals have rooms with space for both the child and a parent. Even where this arrangement is not available, visiting hours are usually quite flexible for parents. In addition, many hospitals now perform minor procedures and allow the child to go home that same day.

During hospitalization, a child often undergoes many tests and forms of treatment. When the child asks, "Will this hurt?" the parent should answer truthfully. Parents may be tempted to reassure the child by responding, "Oh, no, this won't hurt." It is actually much more helpful to the child to hear an accurate response, such as, "Yes, it will hurt for a while, but then you will feel much better. It is all right for you to cry when it hurts, if you feel like it."

If emergency hospitalization is necessary, it is important for a parent or other important caregiver to spend as much time as possible with the child. A loving adult can make a difficult situation less frightening by remaining close by, by encouraging communication between the hospital staff and the child, and by offering reassurance and attention. Although it can be agonizing to see a child sick or suffering, it is important for the parent or other caregiver to maintain a calm and encouraging attitude.

SECTION 3 REVIEW

CHECK YOUR UNDERSTANDING

1. Why is physical comforting especially important for an infant who is ill?
2. Why is it particularly difficult to keep toddlers cheerful during illness?
3. List five foods that might be included in a liquid diet.
4. What is the first symptom of chicken pox?
5. What is the recommended treatment for whooping cough?
6. List three fears common among young children who are hospitalized.

DISCUSS AND DISCOVER

1. What would you do while caring for a sick two-year-old during an entire afternoon? What quiet activities would you plan? What else would you expect to do with and for the child? Why?
2. Read about the series of DPT shots given to infants: When are they given? Why? What reactions to these shots are considered normal? What are symptoms of dangerous physical reactions to these shots? What can be done in such cases? Discuss your findings with classmates.

SUMMARY

- It is easier to prevent illnesses and accidents than to cope with their effects.
- The safety of the child is the most important responsibility of every parent and caregiver.
- Children should have regular medical checkups and should be immunized against childhood diseases.
- Emergencies must be dealt with quickly and calmly.
- Artificial respiration and CPR are rescue techniques used when breathing and heart action have stopped.
- The attitude of the caregiver toward a sick child can be as important as medical treatment to the patient's recovery.
- A hospital stay is usually an emotional crisis for a child.

REVIEWING THE FACTS

1. What is the leading cause of death among young children?
2. Why should children have regular medical checkups?
3. What are communicable diseases? How can they best be controlled?
4. What are the steps in administering the Heimlich maneuver to a child who is standing or sitting?
5. What is a convulsion? What treatment is appropriate for a person having a convulsion?
6. What are the symptoms of an allergic reaction to an insect sting? What is the appropriate response to these symptoms?
7. List four symptoms that may indicate poisoning.
8. What is shock? Why is it dangerous?
9. List three activities appropriate for four- to six-year-olds who are mildly ill.
10. How should parents respond when a child asks whether a medical treatment will hurt? Why?

EXPLORING FURTHER

1. Make up a song, a chant, or a simple game that helps reinforce a safety rule for school-aged children. Teach the song, chant, or game to a group of your classmates, and let them help you evaluate and improve your idea. Then teach your song, chant, or game to a group of five- or six-year-olds. (Section 1)
2. Using a large doll, practice the Heimlich maneuver as it is used on infants and toddlers. Then use the doll to teach the Heimlich maneuver to a friend, family member, or acquaintance who regularly cares for an infant. (Section 2)
3. Investigate the Mr. Yuk poison symbols: How are they used? Why are they effective for alerting young children to poisons? Then design and make your own stickers for labeling poisonous household materials. (Section 2)
4. Plan two days of meals for a four-year-old on a bland diet. Prepare one of your planned meals, and present it in a way that might especially appeal to a sick child. (Section 3)

THINKING CRITICALLY

1. **Analyze.** How can parents and other caregivers encourage children to take responsibility for their own health and safety habits? Who benefits as children accept this responsibility? How do they benefit?
2. **Analyze.** The Poison Prevention Council reports that one in three poisonings among children occurs when the child is visiting his or her grandparents. What do you think accounts for this high rate? What do you think parents should do to help make visits to the grandparents safer for children?
3. **Evaluate.** How do you think parents can tell that a child is too sick to attend school or a child care program? What might motivate a child to pretend to be sick? How do you think parents should respond to a child's invented illness? Why?

CROSS-CURRICULUM CONNECTIONS

1. **Management.** Plan and assemble a basic first aid kit, to be used in your home or to be taken along when you babysit. Calculate how much it costs to make your kit. How much would it cost to buy a prepackaged kit? Does your kit include anything not available in prepackaged kits? Do the prepackaged kits include any first aid supplies you left out of your kit? Could you have assembled your kit any more cheaply? If so, how?
2. **Speaking.** Gather information on Lyme disease: What causes the disease? What are its early symptoms? What other symptoms can develop? How can it be treated? Plan and deliver a short oral presentation based on your findings.

OBSERVING AND PARTICIPATING

Children's Health

Routine health care—developing health and safety habits, having regular checkups, and receiving timely immunizations—can prevent many childhood illnesses. When a child does become ill, the support and understanding of parents and other caregivers can influence the child's ability to recover.

Choose one of the following activities, and spend time observing or participating with young children. Write your observations in your journal. Then share and discuss your journal entry with other students.

- **Observing.** Visit a local elementary school, and observe a group of kindergarteners or first graders as they play outside on the school yard. What playground equipment do the children use? What are the children's other outdoor activities? Are there any apparent safety hazards on the school yard? What safety rules do the children appear to be following? Who supervises the children's play? How closely?
- **Observing.** Spend half a day shadowing a nurse in an elementary school or a teacher in a large child care center. What kinds of injuries or other health problems does the nurse or teacher deal with? What first aid techniques does he or she use? What first aid equipment appears to be available? Does the nurse or teacher deal with any injuries or illnesses that require additional medical treatment? If so, what kind of treatment?
- **Participating.** If a local hospital has a volunteer visiting program, arrange to visit at least one pediatric patient there. Before you go, ask a volunteer supervisor to advise you on appropriate activities; then spend time with a young hospital patient. How does the patient respond to your visit? What does he or she want to do? How capable is the patient?

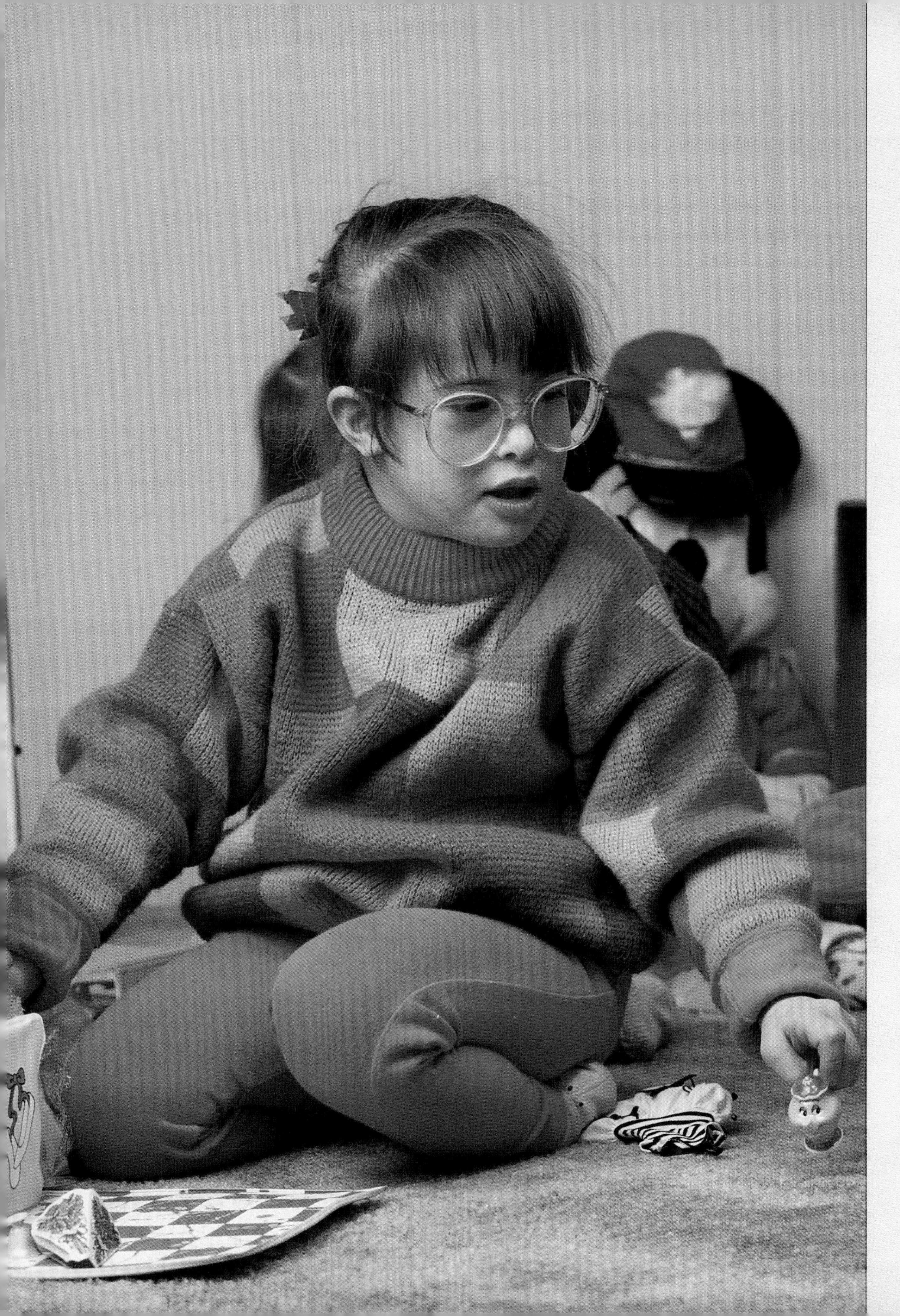

CHAPTER 18

Special Challenges for Children

Jennifer served tea to her imaginary friend, Casper. "First we put the tea leaves in the bottom of the teapot," she said. Jennifer had watched her mom make tea many times before, so now she knew how to do it herself.

"Next, we put in hot, hot water," she continued as she poured imaginary water into the miniature pot. "You have to be very careful with hot water, Casper, because it can hurt if it goes on your skin."

Turning, she picked up a saucer that held three oatmeal cookies and said, "Now we can have our cookies—one for you because you're so small and two for me." Jennifer had learned to count at the special school for children with Down syndrome. She couldn't wait until next year. Then she would be going to the same school as her sister, Sarah.

SECTION 1

Exceptional Children

OBJECTIVES

- Describe the needs of children with physical, mental, and emotional disabilities.
- Explain how parents and other caregivers can assist and encourage disabled children.

TERMS TO LEARN

empathy
therapist

Disabilities—physical, mental, emotional, or any combination of the three—present special challenges for children and their parents.

Children with Disabilities

In the past, babies with severe health or other disabling conditions often died at birth or soon after. If a child with a disability lived, he or she was often hidden away at home or sent to an institution. Fortunately, there is much more awareness of the needs and potential of disabled—also called exceptional—children today. Medical science saves the lives of many infants with physical problems. Doctors are also able to treat many disabilities to make them less severe. Children can often be taught to compensate for their disabilities. With proper care and treatment, disabled children can lead happy, productive lives.

The attitude of parents toward a child with a disability can make an important difference in the child's future. Parents can teach their child to be as independent as possible and to adapt for those limitations that cannot be overcome. Parents who pity, resent, or coddle a child with disabilities hinder the child's healthy emotional development. The child may become angry and self-pitying. Such a child will have difficulty functioning in society. A child with a positive attitude will have a happier life.

Parents of children with disabilities should contact national or community agencies that can offer information and support. Many states now require that public schools provide programs for disabled children and their parents beginning at the time of the child's birth. Many other states provide preschool experiences for children with disabilities beginning at the child's third birthday.

Special preschool programs give children with disabilities a chance to be like everyone else, enabling all the children to feel empathy.

Not all children with disabilities need to be—or even should be—in special programs. Studies have shown that many children do best when placed in regular preschool programs or mainstreamed in regular classrooms. Both the children with disabilities and those without benefit. This way of providing services, called integration or inclusion, provides an opportunity for all the children to grow intellectually, develop social skills, and learn to feel **empathy**, *a sense of understanding and sharing of another person's feelings.*

Physical Disabilities

Physical disabilities take a wide range of forms and may have widely differing impacts on the lives of children and their parents. A child who must wear leg braces and a child who is missing an arm have obvious physical disabilities, but many disabilities are not so apparent. Such conditions as a hearing loss or a heart defect can also be physical disabilities.

BUILDING SELF-ESTEEM

Meeting the Needs of Exceptional Children

Children with disabilities have the same basic needs as other children. Their most important need is to feel loved and accepted by their families and by society. Like all young children, disabled youngsters need to feel they are actively involved in their family's life. This means doing daily chores and following family rules—as well as going along on special family outings.

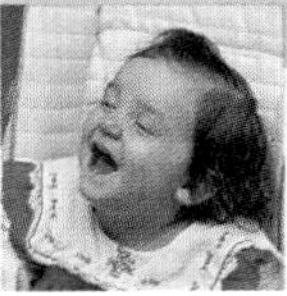

For a child with a physical handicap, exercise sessions are often part of the daily routine. Though sometimes painful, exercises are necessary to maintain and improve the child's physical abilities.

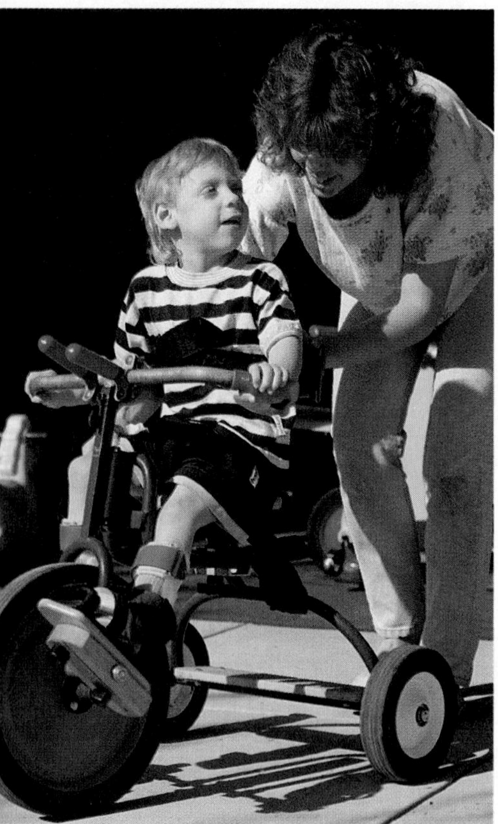

Many fun activities also help develop physical skills. Why might riding a tricycle be good for a handicapped preschooler?

Some physical disabilities are apparent at birth, but others do not become apparent for months—or even years. Parents should seek a complete diagnosis as soon as they suspect their child may have a physical disability. Then the child should begin treatment as soon as possible. Today, through early diagnosis and treatment, many children born with physical disabilities are able to lead fairly normal lives.

Each child with a physical disability has individual care needs. Routines that others take for granted can be difficult or even impossible. For example, a three-year-old with poor coordination may be unable to dress or eat without help.

Special exercises, special equipment, understanding, and patience are the keys to helping children with physical disabilities be as independent as possible. Independence is essential, not only for future living but also for the development of the child's positive self-concept. Self-care skills such as eating, dressing, bathing, and using the toilet are fundamental to this independence.

Bathing is a good example of a daily care skill in which independence can be encouraged. Many disabled children need to be lifted in and out of the tub. Others may need special assistance or supervision. Whatever the limitations a child with a disability must deal with, he or she should be encouraged to handle as much of the bathing routine as possible.

To encourage independence, the child must feel secure during the bath. This means at least a nonskid mat in the bottom of the tub. It may also mean installing rails on the sides of the tub. Some youngsters may need an inner tube or inflated cushion to keep their head above water. For those who cannot sit independently, the water level must be kept very low for safety.

Most children can perform some aspect of washing themselves. They might use a washcloth made into a mitt, which is easier to handle and less likely to be lost in the water. They can wear a bar of soap on a string around the neck, so that the soap won't slip away. They can dry off using a towel with a hole cut in the middle; this kind of towel can be slipped over the head to simplify the process of drying the whole body. Children who have less functional coordination skills might participate by splashing water on themselves.

Parents and others who care for physically disabled children may need to develop similar adaptations for eating and other routine activities. Some children may need special help with only a few tasks; others may need many adaptations because their physical abilities are limited.

Mental Disabilities

Mentally disabled children grow just as other children do. The major difference is that their mental development is slower and stops at a lower level. There are many degrees of mental retardation. Some disabled children are only a little slow. Other children have the mental ability of babies for life.

Medical professionals can usually diagnose mental retardation early and determine its cause. They can also advise parents about the child's learning potential, but this can be difficult to predict. Education and treatment must begin early to achieve the best possible results. Often doctors recommend special programs for mentally disabled children.

Mentally disabled children learn and respond best when they know what to expect. Directions for these children should be simple and direct. Example and demonstration, along with constant repetition, are usually the most effective teaching methods.

The long-range goal for children with mental disabilities is that they become as independent as possible. Many can learn living and job skills that enable them to live alone, support themselves, and perhaps marry and raise a family. Others need more care and support. Many communities have sheltered care homes that offer supervised group living for those mentally disabled adults who need it. These adults can usually work under supervision. However, some mentally disabled people remain totally dependent on others throughout their life.

Many mentally handicapped children will continue to need special supervised home and work situations as adults.

INTERNATIONAL RESEARCH BENEFITS ALL

Recently, doctors and research scientists from a variety of countries jointly studied victims of autism found in 40 countries. Because this rare disorder affects only about 1 in 3,000 children, international efforts resulted in a more comprehensive study. Then, the results could benefit more children. A similar collaborative effort is found in the study and research of AIDS. Pooling research from many nations results in added understanding and better treatment for all people.

Social acceptance is essential to people with mental retardation—just as it is to everyone else. Children with mental disabilities should be taught grooming, manners, and acceptable social behavior; these skills make social acceptance more likely.

Emotional Disabilities

How can parents know when their child is emotionally troubled and needs professional help? The child's behavior is the best indication. However, there is no clear-cut line between typical behavior and emotionally disturbed behavior. Some troublesome behavior is natural. It may result from the need for a little special attention, or it may just be part of a normal stage of development. Certainly, though, when a child's behavior prevents typical development or disturbs the lives of family members, parents should suspect and explore the possibility of a serious emotional problem.

Nervous habits, loss of appetite, sleeplessness, excessive fear, withdrawal, aggressive or violent behavior, and failing grades

Children with emotional handicaps have difficulty coping with the stresses of life.

may be signs of emotional disturbance. Keep in mind, however, that other causes for such behavior must be ruled out before emotional disabilities may be cited as their cause.

Behavior that indicates emotional disabilities usually becomes more noticeable and more disturbing over time. For example, at age two, Terry began to rock in his crib and bang his head over and over against the headboard. He resisted toilet training and had frequent toileting accidents, even when he reached school age. His speech was rapid, breathless, and hampered by stuttering. Terry's parents felt concerned, but they didn't know quite what to do. They hoped that once Terry started school, things would get easier.

In school, Terry fought with other children and disrupted classes with his outbursts. He entered the third grade still struggling to gain basic reading and writing skills. At this point, the school recommended that Terry have a psychological evaluation. The evaluation indicated that Terry needed therapy.

Even when a child's behavior shows a pattern that indicates serious emotional problems—as Terry's behavior did—parents may be reluctant to ask for help. They may be ashamed to admit they cannot handle the problem themselves. Parents cannot be expected to have all the answers, however.

When a child does need help, the parents need to find a **therapist** or a **behavior specialist,** *a professional trained in helping people work through emotional problems*. Pediatricians, school counselors, members of the clergy, or a local office of the Mental Health Association can recommend a therapist. Once they have decided to seek professional help, parents should take the time to select a therapist whom they trust and with whom they feel comfortable. Then they can expect the therapist to ask the family for background information on the problem behaviors, get to know the entire family better, observe the child in various situations, and plan treatment for the child. In some cases, the treatment may involve making a few changes in the family's pattern of interactions. For example, the therapist might suggest that the parents spend individual time with the child each day or that the child be introduced to a special activity, such as gymnastics or music, according to his or her interests.

Support groups for parents of special-needs children give parents practical guidance for everyday care. This family uses a sticker award plan for daily tasks the child completes.

Sometimes the therapist finds that a child's emotional problems have physical causes. If this is the case, the therapist may recommend medical evaluation and treatment.

Often the therapist works directly with the child—and sometimes with other family members—to improve the child's self-image. Skilled emotional therapy can change the way children view themselves and, consequently, the way they behave.

The results of therapy depend to a great extent on the child's parents. They must believe in and support the therapist's work. They must be available to listen and talk when the child is ready.

PARENTING IN ACTION

Living with Disabilities

Sylvia and Ed Sanchez hurried to the first meeting of a group of parents of infants with Down syndrome. They were scheduled to talk to the group that evening.

After they had been introduced, Sylvia said, "When I look at all of you, I see Ed and myself sitting there just a few years ago. When you have a baby with Down syndrome, it seems like your world has shattered. I remember that I cried for weeks. I want you to know, though, that your outlook will change—now I laugh much more often than I cry. Our daughter Rosa has made us a happier family."

Ed continued, "Sylvia and I have been actively involved in a local organization for mentally disabled persons. At first, we attended meetings because we needed information, and we needed to talk with other parents in the same boat. We've become more involved because we enjoy it—and because we want to help other parents."

"Rosa's been in a special preschool program since she was two," Sylvia explained. "Before that, trained parent-child educators came into our home on a regular basis. They helped assess Rosa's abilities and set up a program of learning and therapy. They taught us how to teach her most effectively. We also learned exercises to help enhance her physical skills."

"Rosa's such a lovable child! We don't know just how much independence she'll be capable of as an adult. Right now, though, each of her achievements is cause for celebration."

Sylvia paused. "I'm anxious to hear about your own situations," she went on. "Whatever your situation, remember that there are lots of other parents to help and guide you through the network of government and community programs. Give your children a chance to be the best they can be, and give them a chance to enrich your lives."

THINK AND DISCUSS

1. What kinds of disabilities does Rosa have?
2. How did her parents react initially to Rosa's disabilities? How did their reactions change? Why?
3. What are Sylvia and Ed doing to meet Rosa's special needs? What are they doing to help other families with Down's children?
4. How do you think Rosa enriches the lives of her parents?

They need to accept the changes that result from the therapy. Sharing children's personal feelings, learning to understand them, and accepting children for who and what they are—not what parents expect them to be—are actions and attitudes parents can learn to help children overcome their problems.

Raising a Disabled Child

The responsibilities and demands of raising a child with a disability can often seem overwhelming. In acknowledging their child's disabilities, parents may experience a grief process that includes guilt, sadness, anger, and frustration.

Support groups for parents of disabled children serve a valuable function. They help parents explore and accept their feelings. They also help parents meet more successfully the emotional needs of their children. Parents learn to separate the disability from the child and to appreciate the fact that they have a child who happens to have a disability. Children who receive strong emotional support are better able to develop the inner strength, patience, and courage necessary to cope with their disabilities.

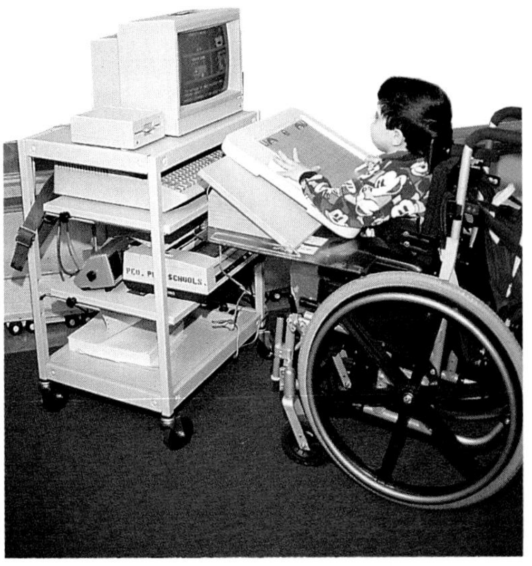

New technologies are giving children with disabilities new tools for learning.

Parents can also get together with other parents of disabled children to share comfort, advice, and solutions to everyday problems. In addition, groups can keep members up to date on research and treatment available for children with specific disabilities.

Disabled children can bring as much joy to a family as children without disabilities. Like other children, disabled children give family members a chance to love and be loved, to give, to receive, and to share.

SECTION 1 REVIEW

CHECK YOUR UNDERSTANDING

1. What is the most important need of children with disabilities?
2. Who benefits when children with disabilities are placed in regular preschool programs? How do they benefit?
3. Why is it especially important to encourage independence for children with physical disabilities?
4. Why should children with mental disabilities be trained in grooming, manners, and acceptable social behavior?
5. List five types of behavior that may be signs of emotional disturbance.
6. Who can often make recommendations about finding a therapist?

DISCUSS AND DISCOVER

1. Many children born with disabilities are so ill that they must remain in the hospital for the first weeks—or even months—of their life. How do you think this long period of separation affects the baby? The rest of the family? What do you think parents should do in trying to deal with the problems this kind of separation creates?
2. Read magazine stories, journal articles, or short books about families with at least one disabled child. Discuss your readings with classmates. How do you think siblings respond to the special needs of the disabled child in a family? How do parents deal with the needs of all their children in such families?

SECTION 2 Child Abuse and Neglect

OBJECTIVES

- Explain what child abuse is and why it happens.
- Discuss what can be done to prevent child abuse.

TERMS TO LEARN

child abuse
crisis nurseries

Child abuse is *the physical and/or emotional mistreatment of a child*. The effects of child abuse, of any type, are long-lasting. Abuse can affect the physical, emotional, mental, and social health of its victims throughout their lifetime.

What Does Abuse Involve?

Most people find it difficult to understand how anyone can abuse children. According to the National Committee for the Prevention of Child Abuse, abuse of children has reached epidemic proportions throughout the world. It is difficult to estimate the total extent because many cases go unreported, but it is believed that abused children number in the millions. Every day an average of five American children are abused so badly that they die.

Child abuse is generally considered in these four categories:

- **Nonaccidental physical injury.** Injury caused by such things as beatings, burns, bites, or scalding water.
- **Neglect.** Failing to provide a child with the basic necessities of life, such as food, clothing, shelter, and medical care.
- **Sexual molestation.** Using a child for the sexual pleasure of an adult.
- **Emotional abuse.** Placing unreasonable, unrealistic, or excessive demands on the child. Examples are constant belittling, teasing, or verbal attacks. Some children never receive the love and affection they need for normal emotional development.

A single incident does not generally indicate child abuse. Abuse involves a pattern of behavior. The longer it continues, the more serious the problem becomes for both child and parent.

Who Are Child Abusers?

Any type of abuse prevents a child from developing normally. Children who suffer continuing abuse are also more likely to become abusive parents themselves.

Contrary to what you might expect, most child abusers are not monsters. They are ordinary people, usually parents or other relatives, caught in emotional situations that they cannot handle. They are often people who feel lonely and can't cope with their own personal problems. Low self-esteem is a common trait among child abusers. In many cases, they were themselves abused as children. Because patterns involving abuse are the only kind of parenting they have known, they repeat the behavior with their own children.

Child abusers come from all income levels, ethnic groups, and religions. Often, only one parent in a family actively abuses the children. However, the other parent may participate in the abuse by refusing to recognize it, by ignoring it, or by refusing to seek help.

Parents who abuse their children are easily provoked and unable to maintain self-control. When they are irritated, they respond quickly and violently, much as a young child does. A three-year-old who is angry responds without thought. The child may kick the cat, smash a toy truck, or throw a doll across the room. An abusive adult displays the same uncontrollable emotions. An argument with a spouse, a car that won't start—almost anything—can trigger an incident of abuse. The child's words or actions are seldom the cause. The child is simply nearby, a defenseless target for violent physical or verbal abuse.

Responding to the epidemic proportion of child abuse cases, organizations are sponsoring prevention education as a method to eliminate child abuse.

Abusive parents generally believe that infants will be spoiled if they are picked up and comforted when they cry. They do not recognize this physical comforting as essential for the development of trust. Abusive parents feel that they must continually show their children "who's boss." They have unrealistic expectations of what children can do. These parents may expect their children to be perfect. For example, they may tell a toddler to "sit up and eat right." They expect the toddler to do just that—promptly—even though the nature of toddlers makes this almost impossible. Abusive parents expect young children to remember commands given only once. Of course, young children learn only after directions have been repeated many times. An abusive parent may see a child's failure to comply as stubbornness, meanness, deliberate disobedience, or revenge—behavior to be severely punished.

Are There Any Answers?

It is against the law in every state to abuse a child. All states also have laws requiring those who work with children, such as doctors, teachers, social workers, and child care workers, to report suspected cases of child abuse. However, many people, even responsible professionals, find it difficult to make such reports. It is essential for the well-being of the children involved that, in spite of personal concerns and hesitations, every case of suspected child abuse be reported to the closest social service agency or child welfare agency.

Once an agency receives a report of suspected child abuse, it begins an investigation into the case. If the child is in immediate danger, the court may place the child in a foster home. If there is a history of past abuse or the child's injuries are severe, uncooperative parents can be charged and tried.

Putting abusive people in jail does not solve the problem of the abuse. It only provides the abused children with temporary protection. In most cases, treatment and counseling are used in an attempt to correct the cause of the abuse—and so bring the abuse to an end.

Most abusive parents can learn to care for their children responsibly. To help parents achieve that goal, there are many types of government, private, and volunteer programs available. Parents Anonymous, one of the best-known groups, is made up of parents who help each other gain self-control.

Some communities have **crisis nurseries**, *child care facilities where troubled parents can leave their children for a short time*. Using a crisis nursery gives parents time to cool off and try to cope with their frustrations and anger away from their children. Volunteers or professionals associated with crisis nurseries usu-

ASK THE EXPERTS

The Cycle of Abuse

Jean Illsley Clarke is the director of J.I. Consultants in Minneapolis, Minnesota, where she designs and conducts workshops on self-esteem, parenting, and group dynamics.

I have heard that there is a cycle of child abuse, but I'm not sure what this means. What is the cycle, and how can it be broken?

Child abuse is a cycle in this sense: Once the abusive behavior is begun, a pattern of abusive behavior is established and repeated. A parent who has hit a child for "misbehaving" one day is more likely to hit the child again—probably more severely—the next day. A parent who, as a child, was abused by his or her own parent is very likely to abuse his or her own children; abuse has become part of the parenting style he or she knows best. These cycles of child abuse are understandable. They are not, however, inevitable. The cycle of abuse can—and must—be broken.

Every abuser is caught in the abuse trap, which has four distinct aspects:

- Attitudes and Beliefs
- Feelings
- Thoughts
- Actions

An abusive parent has attitudes and beliefs that reinforce the abuse. For example, an abuser may believe, "My parents hit me and I deserved it. My children deserve to be hit, too." These attitudes and beliefs lead to specific thoughts, such as, "He's been asking for it all day. I'm going to have to hit that child." These thoughts lead directly to abusive action, in this case hitting the child. In turn, the abusive action leads to feelings, such as relief of tension and anger, that then reinforce the original attitudes and beliefs.

In order to avoid getting caught in the abuse trap, an individual must be alert to all four aspects of that trap. It is essential for anyone who is a parent or who comes in contact with children to examine his or her own attitudes, thoughts, actions, and feelings, with special awareness of those that might lead to abuse.

An abuser can be freed from this trap by changing his or her attitudes, thoughts, actions, and feelings. For many people, these are deeply rooted in early experiences and are very difficult to change without help. Support groups, counselors, and social workers are good sources of help for abusers.

Since child abuse is not only a personal problem but also a societal problem, each of us can find ways to help. We can support organizations that make life better for children. We can avoid laughing at pain—our own or other people's. We can help create a community that respects all people, that honors children's needs, and that helps all children grow.

Jean Illsley Clarke

Jean Illsley Clarke

ally work with the abusive parents on a one-to-one basis. They help parents understand their frustrations and resolve their problems. They guide parents in learning how to break the cycle of child abuse.

Many family problems, including child abuse, are directly related to poor parenting skills and to a lack of knowledge about

Counselors can help abusive parents understand and change their behavior.

child development. Classes like the one you are taking help give parents—and future parents—realistic ideas about what parenting involves. You know by now that babies are not always clean and happy, and that they don't stay babies forever. You also know what normal behavior is at different ages, so you can make thoughtful decisions about discipline. Preparing people for parenthood before they become parents and providing them with help once they are parents are two basic steps society can take to help eliminate child abuse.

SECTION 2 REVIEW

CHECK YOUR UNDERSTANDING

1. What are the long-term effects of child abuse?
2. List the four general categories of child abuse, and give one example of each.
3. List three traits common among child abusers.
4. Where should child abuse be reported?
5. Who belongs to Parents Anonymous? What do members do?
6. What are two basic steps society can take to help eliminate child abuse?

DISCUSS AND DISCOVER

1. Why do people often find it very difficult to report suspected cases of child abuse? What particular problems would a person have in reporting abuse? What would you say and do to encourage a close friend to report his or her suspicions of child abuse?
2. Read about a specific case of child abuse: How was the abuse discovered and reported? What efforts were made to help the abused child? What happened to the suspected abuser? How does reading about this case make you feel? Share your reactions with your classmates.

Family Stresses

SECTION 3

OBJECTIVES

- Describe the emotional effects on children of stressful family situations, such as divorce and death.
- Explain how the emotional effects of family stresses can be minimized.

TERMS TO LEARN

joint custody

Every child is exposed to stress at one time or another. The stress may be fairly mild and short-term; for example, the child's family may move from one home to another. Sometimes, however, a child may have to face severe stress, such as when someone close to the child dies.

Children and Stress

During times of stress, everyone needs support. Children need more help and support than adults because they are less capable of understanding and dealing with the events that cause stress. Children should be encouraged to talk about their feelings, especially during periods of unusual stress. At these times, too, parents must be careful to avoid taking their own stresses out on their children. When parents feel they are faced with more stress than they can handle, they should not hesitate to ask for help. Other family members, members of the clergy, and professional counselors can help parents cope with stressful situations.

Divorce

Child and family experts generally agree that, ideally, children should have the influence of both a mother and a father while growing up. Normal development may be hindered when one parent is absent. On the other hand, experts also know that a home in which parents continually disagree or even fight can be damaging to children. Experts further acknowledge that the divorce of their parents is a fact that nearly 20 percent of children will have to deal with before they turn eighteen.

When parents divorce, a child's time is often split between two homes. Why should activities with both parents be kept as normal as possible?

If a family is about to break up, the children need to be told about the change in an honest and reassuring way. Experts advise using the following guidelines for helping children deal with separation or divorce:

- **Truth.** The children should be told the truth about the upcoming changes. If possible, both parents should sit down with the children and discuss the situation. All children, even toddlers, should be included in the discussion. Young children often understand much more than parents realize. Parents can say something like this to their children:

  "We're having a hard time right now. We are going to live apart, for a while at least. Still, no matter what happens, we will both always love you and take care of you."
- **Elimination of blame.** Parents should avoid placing blame for the divorce on one another, at least in front of the children. If the parents are not able to discuss the divorce with their children without placing blame, they can ask a counselor or a member of the clergy to help them with this discussion. Each parent should remember that the children will continue to need both their parents, even after a separation or divorce. The children should not be placed in a position where they have to take sides with one parent or the other.

Children must also be reassured that they are in no way responsible for the breakup. Parents should stress that they are separating because of their own differences, not because of anything their children have said or done—or failed to say or do. Most children feel guilty when their parents fail to get along; parents should make a special effort to be reassuring on this point.

- **Reassurance.** The children need reassurance that they will continue to be loved by both parents. After a separation or divorce, the children of a family typically live with only one parent. They need to know that the other parent is still there for emotional support and companionship. Both the parent with whom the children live and the absent parent should reassure children about this kind of continuity.
- **No false hope.** The children should not be encouraged to hope for a reconciliation if their parents are not considering the possibility. After a divorce, children usually hope that their parents will get back together again. This false hope only delays the children's adjustment to their new family situation.
- **Stability and continuity.** The children's lives should be kept as much the same as possible. Siblings should continue living together, if at all possible. Children also feel more comfortable if they do not have to change homes or schools. The absent parent should spend time with the children often and regularly. Frequent contact with relatives from both sides of the family can help retain a sense of belonging.

Emotional Effects of Divorce

Divorce requires many emotional adjustments by everyone in the family—especially children. They have a special need for security, stability, and understanding. The new lifestyle that comes with divorce or separation can cause new problems and require many adjustments.

During a divorce, decisions are made about the custody of the couple's children. Some parents agree to have **joint custody**, *an arrangement in which both parents assume responsibility for the children*. With joint custody, the children usually divide their time between their two parents' homes. More often, one parent is awarded custody of the children. In years past, that parent was almost automatically the mother. Now, most courts base the custody decision on information about which parent can better provide a loving, stable home. When sole custody is awarded, the courts encourage visitation by the other parent so that children can maintain healthy relationships with both parents.

It is not unusual for children to resent the parent they live with and idealize the absent parent. The "home" parent makes and enforces family rules, and often gets the blame for the changed lifestyle. The noncustodial parent, on the other hand, may try to make up for his or her absence by being especially lenient and by buying special gifts. This situation creates conflict for all the family members, and no one benefits.

Parents who are caught up in their own troubles can easily forget that divorce is particularly upsetting for youngsters. Many children, even very young ones, develop behavior problems in response to the family's disruption. Even children who appear to adjust well during the period of their parents' divorce may be hiding their grief and pain. If children have noticeable, continuing adjustment problems, it is wise to seek professional help.

Death

The death of someone close causes special problems for a young child. The age of the child, however, influences the youngster's reaction.

- **Under age three.** Children this young cannot understand anything more than a brief separation. A toddler will react to a parent's death in the same way as to the parent's week-long vacation.
- **Ages three to five.** Children this age think that death is like sleep—you are dead, and then you wake up and are alive again. As a result, children of this age may seem unfeeling about the death of a close relative or family friend. They are worried and concerned for a while, but they do not understand that death is permanent. Some months after her father's death, one four-year-old said, "I know Daddy's dead, but when is he coming home?"
- **Ages five to nine.** As children mature, they accept the idea that a person who has died will not come back. However, they do not view death as something that happens to everyone. They especially do not recognize that they themselves will die. To them, death happens only to other people.
- **Age nine or ten.** At this age, children finally begin to see death as inevitable for everyone. They realize that they, too, will die. This may make them afraid. At this age, children must come to terms with their fear and put it in proper perspective.

Many children first experience death when a pet dies. True understanding and acceptance may not come until much later.

By the time they are five, most children have had some contact with death and are curious about it. Perhaps a pet has died; perhaps they have seen a dead squirrel or bird. Some children will have experienced a death in the extended family. Whatever their experiences, children need an opportunity to discuss their feelings and to ask questions about death.

How Children Cope with Death

Child psychologists believe that children go through a three-step process in accepting death. Parents and other caregivers who understand this process are usually better prepared to help children cope with death and with their feelings about death. These are the three steps:

1. **Disbelief.** In this early stage, children may express anger, hostility, and defiance.
2. **Despair.** Later, children are often withdrawn and depressed. Some children revert to babyish behavior during this stage.
3. **Reorganization.** Finally, children begin to adjust to life without the person who has died.

PARENTING IN ACTION

Understanding a Child's Fears

Five-year-old Stephen was brought to a mental health clinic by his parents. They were concerned about his sudden, but continuing, bedtime problems. Until recently, they explained, Stephen had not resisted going to bed. Then he suddenly started crying at bedtime and refused to settle down. After Stephen finally fell into an exhausted sleep, he was often awakened in the night by nightmares.

Except for this one problem, Stephen's behavior and emotional adjustment seemed normal. Neither parent was able to offer an explanation.

The therapist used a play session with Stephen to try to find out the cause of his fear. During the session, Stephen told the story of a man who ". . . caught a heart attack. He fell out of bed and died." In response to the therapist's questions, Stephen revealed that he had overheard his mother talking on the telephone, telling someone about a family friend who had suffered a heart attack, fallen out of bed, and died.

Stephen had no idea what a heart attack was or where one came from, but he did understand falling out of bed. If doing that could make you have a heart attack and die, no one was going to get him into a bed again!

With this information, the therapist was able to explain to Stephen why he did not need to worry about going to bed. Then the therapist explained the problem to Stephen's parents and recommended that they try to make bedtime as happy and relaxed as possible.

THINK AND DISCUSS

1. How did Stephen's parents handle his bedtime problem? What might have happened if they had taken a different approach, such as punishing Stephen?
2. Do you think Stephen's parents could have avoided the development of his bedtime problem? If so, how? Do you think they could have solved the problem without a therapist? If so, how?
3. What questions do you think Stephen might have about death? How do you think his parents might help him understand death better?

If a loved one dies, children should be told about the death in an honest way. They may need an explanation of what death is. Children should then be encouraged to talk about their feelings. Parents, in turn, should let children know that they, too, miss the person very much. Sharing memories of the person who has died, looking at photographs, and talking about the special characteristics of the person who has died can help both parents and children deal with the death.

Children need prompt, direct answers to their questions about the death. A well-intentioned but untrue statement, such as "Grandma went on a long trip," can make the situation more difficult for children to accept. If the children believe the statement, they may be hurt that Grandma went away without saying good-bye. If the children don't believe that explanation, they may conclude that something too awful to discuss has happened to Grandma. Whatever the children think at the time, they will have to face the truth sooner or later. It is important for children to know that they can trust their parents and that their parents, even though they may be sad, are available to discuss the death.

Children who are given honest answers about the death of a loved one are more likely to be able to deal with their feelings.

Adults must be very careful about the words they use when discussing death with a child. Especially with very young children, phrases like "passed away" or "gone to sleep" only add to a child's confusion. It is best to use simple, direct references to death and dying. It is also important to remember that children understand most things in terms of themselves. For example, a child who is told that "Grandpa got very sick and died" may worry about dying the next time he or she is sick with a cold. The type of explanation an adult offers must fit the age and understanding of the child, but it should always be honest and direct, no matter how simple.

Some childhood experiences with death are more upsetting than others. A child whose parent dies needs support for an extended period. The death of a parent is the most tragic thing that can happen to a youngster. Many children react to a parent's death with guilt. The child may think, "I wasn't always good when he wanted me to be," or, "I wasn't quiet enough when she was sick." Children need the assurance that nothing they did, said, or even thought caused the death. They also need help coping with their feelings of abandonment.

In most cases, even very young children should be allowed to take part in family funerals or memorial services. Children of any age are capable of mourning. Studies have shown that even infants go through a period of excessive crying and searching for a parent who has died.

Moving

Moving is stressful for children, because their familiar settings and routines are upset. Often, children don't want to leave their present home, where they feel secure and safe.

Parents can help soothe children's fears by encouraging them to talk about their feelings. Children should also be encouraged to pack their own belongings as much as possible. This activity helps them feel more in control and more involved in the move.

If you moved as a young child, you probably still remember the fear and anxiety you felt. How can talking about these feelings help minimize them?

Parents can also stress aspects of the move that will be positive for the child, such as the opportunity to have his or her own room.

After the move is made, parents should take the time to help the child get settled. To make the adjustment easier, parents can take walks with the child around the new neighborhood, help the child meet nearby children, and take the child to visit his or her new school.

Financial Problems

When a family has financial problems, children sense the tensions even though they may not understand them. The parents may be short-tempered or less attentive then usual. In this situation, children typically believe that they themselves have done something wrong.

Even though children cannot understand complex financial situations, they should be reassured that the problems are not their fault. In addition, parents need to try not to take out their own fears and worries on their children.

Illness

When a family member is ill or hospitalized, the family's routine is disturbed. Parents can help their children cope with this kind of situation by giving a simple, clear explanation of what is happening. If the illness is minor, the child can be reassured that the person will soon be well and everything will return to normal. If the illness is serious or terminal, the child should be told the truth, but in a calm, reassuring way.

When a close relative is ill or injured, it is not unusual for children to worry that they will suffer a similar illness or injury. They may grow afraid of doctors or hospitals. Parents should take the time to explain how the relative's illness or injury differs from any the child is likely to have. As with other situations of family stress, children need their parents' patience and reassurance.

Coping Skills

Healthy families pull together for support when sickness, financial problems, death, or other stressful events occur. They accept and try to solve their problems. They also know that community social service offices offer programs to help them get through their crisis situation.

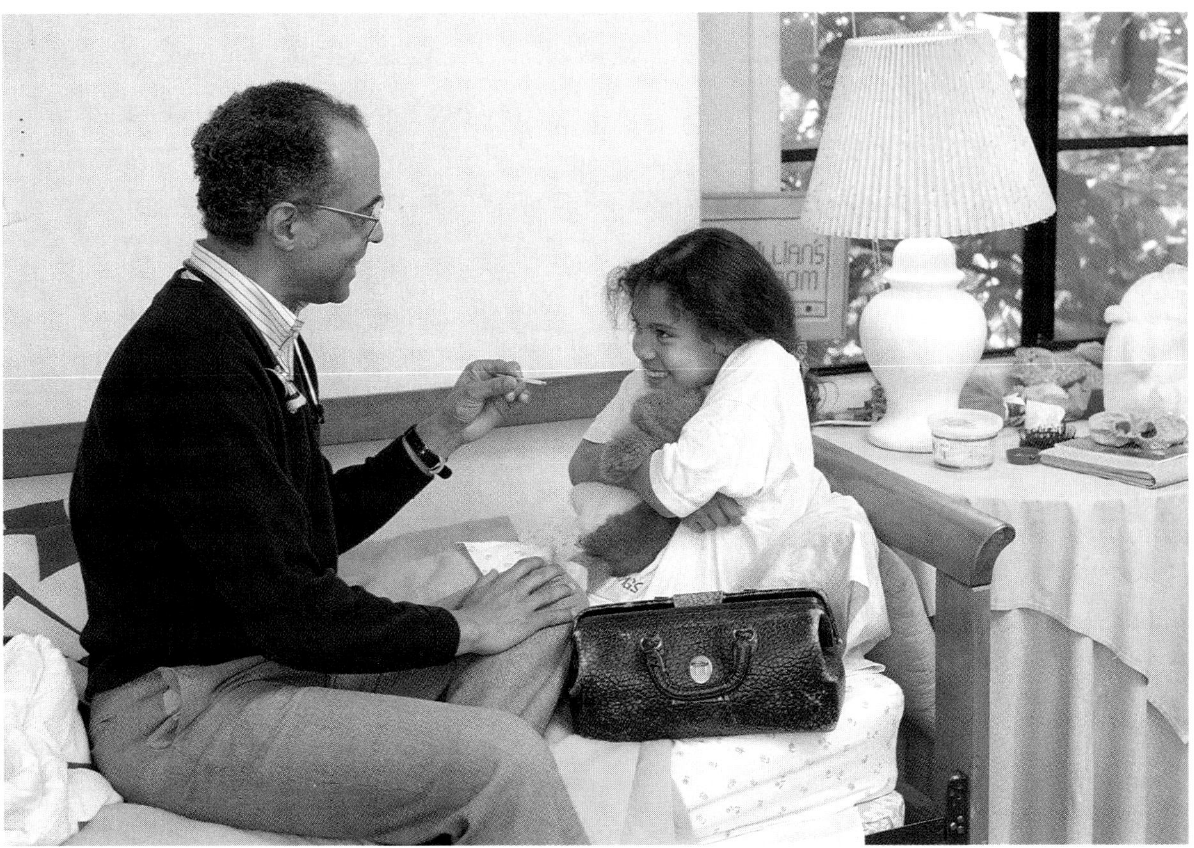

Young children who have long-term illinesses need to understand that doctors and nurses are trying to help them, not hurt them.

SECTION 3 REVIEW

CHECK YOUR UNDERSTANDING

1. List five guidelines for helping children deal with separation and divorce.
2. When sole custody is awarded after a divorce, what kind of relationship should the noncustodial parent establish with the children? Why?
3. What attitude toward death is typical of three- to five-year-olds? At what age do children usually begin to understand that death is inevitable for everyone?
4. List the three stages children often go through in accepting a death.
5. List two things parents can do to help their children feel settled after a move.

DISCUSS AND DISCOVER

1. When divorced parents agree to joint custody, what advantages does the new living arrangement have for the couple's children? For the divorced parents? What are the disadvantages of joint custody for both children and parents?
2. Read at least one article or book chapter about the long-term psychological effects of a parent's death on young children. Discuss your reading and your reactions to it with a group of classmates.

SUMMARY

- Children may have physical, mental, and/or emotional disabilities. Each child with a disability has individual care needs.
- Child abuse has severe and long-lasting effects.
- Treatment and counseling can help abusive parents learn to cope with their problems and stop the patterns of abuse.
- When a family is divided by separation or divorce, children need to be informed in an honest and reassuring way.
- Children should be told about the death of a loved one in a direct and honest way, appropriate to the child's age and ability to understand.
- Children who must cope with family stresses, including divorce, death, moving, financial problems, and illness, need special support.

REVIEWING THE FACTS

1. List two important things parents should teach their disabled children.
2. At what age should a child begin receiving treatment for a physical disability?
3. What is empathy?
4. What is the long-range goal for children with mental disabilities?
5. What is a therapist? What steps should parents expect a therapist to take in working with a child who has emotional problems?
6. List three important steps parents can take to help children overcome emotional problems.
7. What is child abuse?
8. What are crisis nurseries?
9. Who should tell children about their parents' decision to divorce? How should children be told of the decision?
10. List two things parents and children can do together that will help them deal with the death of a loved one.
11. Why do a family's financial problems create stress for children?
12. What fears are common among children who have a close relative who has been hospitalized?

EXPLORING FURTHER

1. Working with other students, compile a list of local groups for parents of children with various kinds of disabilities. When and where does each group meet? What are the specific interests of the members of each group? How can interested parents contact each group? Publish your list in a format and place that will make it readily available to new parents. (Section 1).
2. Write and illustrate a storybook for three-year-olds. Include a disabled child or animal as one of the main characters in your story. Share an early draft of your book with other students, and ask them to help you revise your work. Then make a finished copy of your book, and share it with a group of preschoolers. (Section 1)
3. Gather information about the work of organizations in your area that provide shelter for families and help with child abuse problems. How can the local office be contacted? What information and help is available through the association's office? Then make a flier or a poster presenting the information you have gathered. (Section 2)
4. Working with one or two other students, plan and present three skits about families in which a death has occurred. In your skits, show how a parent or other adult might explain the death to a three-year-old, a six-year-old, and a nine-year-old. (Section 3)

THINKING CRITICALLY

1. **Analyze.** Disabled children are more likely than nondisabled children to be abused. What factors do you think contribute to this high rate of abuse? What do you think can and should be done to help disabled victims of child abuse? To help those who abuse disabled children?
2. **Synthesize.** Which do you think is more difficult for a child—being raised by a single mother or experiencing the divorce of married parents? Why? What advantages can you identify for a child in each situation? On the basis of your opinions about a child's welfare, would you recommend that two people who are expecting a baby should get married, even if they had not considered marriage otherwise? Why or why not?
3. **Compare and contrast.** How do you think the death of a school friend would affect a seven-year-old? Why? How would the effects of the friend's death be similar to the effects of the death of an older relative? How would they be different?

CROSS-CURRICULUM CONNECTIONS

1. **Reading.** Read several current articles about mainstreaming: What attitudes are expressed toward the practice of mainstreaming disabled students in public school classes of mostly nondisabled children? What advantages of mainstreaming are identified? What disadvantages are discussed? How have attitudes toward mainstreaming changed in recent years? Why? Discuss your reading with other students.
2. **Writing.** Plan and write a short story about moving. Write the story from the point of view of a six-year-old who has had to move several times. Use this sentence beginning to start your story: "Every time my family has to move to a new town, I feel . . ."

OBSERVING AND PARTICIPATING

Children with Special Needs

Current medical practices have made it possible to prevent many disabilities and to cure others. For children whose disabilities cannot be cured, treatment and education can help a great deal. In all cases, children with disabilities have the same basic needs as nondisabled children—a safe and healthy environment and the development of a positive self-concept. In addition, special-needs children need to be encouraged to become as independent as possible.

Choose one of the following activities for observing and participating with children. After you have completed the activity, write a journal entry about your observations and responses. Then discuss your observations and responses with other students.

- **Observing.** Visit a preschool class in which some of the students are disabled and others are not. How completely do the disabled children appear to be integrated into the classroom activities? What special needs do the disabled children have? How do the other children respond to those needs? What evidence do you see that all the children are learning empathy?
- **Participating.** Volunteer to help out in a nursery or elementary classroom for disabled children. What special needs do the children in the class have? How are you advised to help the children? How are you advised to encourage their independence? How do you see teachers interacting with the children? Which part of the class program do the children seem to enjoy most? Why?
- **Observing.** Visit a sheltered workshop or school for disabled children or adults. What special skills are being taught? How are they being taught? How do the students react to the instruction? What special learning needs do the students appear to have? What special interests do they seem to have?

CHAPTER 19

Caring for Children

Three-year-old Julie skips into the preschool classroom and dashes over to the building block area. She begins stacking the triangles, squares, rectangles, and cylinders into interesting creations.

"Good morning, Julie," greets Deborah, the child care assistant. "How are you today?"

"Fine," replies Julie, "but my house keeps falling down."

"Would you like me to help you?" asks Deborah.

Julie nods her head in agreement.

"The trick of building a big house is being sure that you carefully balance each block on top of the other. You already have a good start. Now, let's take the triangle and carefully place it on top of the cylinder," explains Deborah as she guides Julie's hand. "There I think it's working better, don't you?"

Julie smiles and gives Deborah a big hug. "Thanks, Deborah. Will you help me build a city?"

SECTION 1

Being a Babysitter and Child Care Provider

OBJECTIVES

- List the personal qualities needed for being a good babysitter or child care provider.
- Describe the responsibilities of a child care provider when caring for children of various ages.
- List safety guidelines that are especially important for child care providers.

The most common first child care job is babysitting. Actually, *babysitting* is not a very accurate term. When you undertake this job, you are really providing care for children. The job allows little time for sitting—unless the children are asleep.

Responsibilities

Child care providers have a lot of responsibility. When the parents are gone, they are completely responsible for the safety and welfare of the children. Good caregivers are interested primarily in the children, not just in the money they are earning. They have patience, a sense of humor, and an understanding of children's physical, emotional, social, and intellectual needs. Good caregivers are flexible and can get along well with all types of children. They handle unexpected situations well and make sound judgments in emergencies.

Good Beginnings

When you provide child care, some families may hire you regularly. However, you will probably also receive an occasional call from families you do not know. When you receive such a call, ask how the new family learned about you. If you were recommended by a family you work for regularly, you can ask them about the new family, if necessary. You need to be aware of your own safety, as well as that of the children for whom you provide care. During this first phone call, you will also want to agree on your charges, learn how long the parents intend to be gone, and make arrangements for getting to and from their home. Before you leave for any child care job, be sure your own family knows the name, address, and phone number of the people you will be working for and the approximate time you will return.

The first time you provide child care for a family, make arrangements to arrive about 20 minutes early. This will give the children a chance to get used to you while their parents are still home. It will also allow you enough time to find out any additional information from the parents. When bedtimes are, where the parents will be, how the parents can be reached, and when they will return are obvious questions you will want to ask. Also, learning the family's rules and routines will help you do the job better. For example, knowing that two-year-old Kevin never sleeps without his special blanket might save a lot of problems at bedtime.

When you start a new child care job, the parent should give you a tour of the home and explain the children's routines.

Caring for Children of Different Ages

Children of different ages have different needs. When you watch children, you should be prepared to provide different types of care for children in each age group.

Babies

Babies need a great deal of physical care and protection. This means that when you agree to care for an infant, you should have the necessary care skills and understand the characteristics of babies. You may want to review the information on infant care in Chapter 8.

When handling a small baby, be sure to hold the infant firmly, and always support the baby's head and neck. Babies can sense whether their caregiver is confident or nervous, and they will react accordingly.

Never leave a baby on a bed, sofa, or other raised surface. Even a tiny baby can wiggle enough to fall off. Also, be sure to keep harmful objects out of the reach of crawling infants.

When a baby cries, always find out what is troubling him or her. Is the baby too cold or too warm? Perhaps hunger, sickness, or a wet diaper is the trouble. Except for very young infants, babies do cry when they are lonely. If loneliness is the problem, a few minutes of cuddling will help.

Changing diapers is a frequent duty of child care providers. Be sure to gather all the necessary supplies so that they are nearby before you start changing the diaper.

Child care providers are not usually asked to bathe the baby. However, a qualified care provider should be able to undertake this task. Before you agree to do it as part of a child care job, review what is involved and practice bathing a baby under capable supervision.

Toddlers and Preschoolers

Providing care for young children involves giving care different from that required by babies. Young children are more sensitive to their parents' leaving and may need comforting. They like being read to, played with, or talked to.

Because toddlers and preschoolers sleep less and are more adventuresome, they require more watching. Do not leave them alone—even for a minute—while they are awake.

When you are caring for young children, bedtime can be a problem. Toddlers and preschoolers usually don't want to go to bed. Try to follow the child's regular bedtime routine. Undressing, brushing teeth, and going to the bathroom prepare children physically and psychologically for bed. Ask the parents in advance about other bedtime activities the child is used to.

A young child may be awakened, frightened or crying, because of a bad dream. Cuddle and comfort the child until he or she can get back to sleep. Later, tell the parents about the bad dream—or about anything else unusual.

Older Children

When you care for older children, you may find some who try to give you a difficult time. Some may feel they are too old for a babysitter. Others are jealous of the time and attention given to younger siblings. Still others try to get away with behavior their parents wouldn't permit.

You can get the relationship off to a good start by making friends with older children. If you show a genuine interest in their possessions, games, or activities, you'll win over even the most independent youngsters.

It helps if the parents establish your authority with the children before they leave. At no time is your maturity as a care provider more important than when a child deliberately misbehaves. You will have better control of the situation if you remain calm. Be fair—but firm.

Children will be fun if you involve yourself with their interests while they are in your care.

Should you punish children? No matter how a child behaves, avoid using physical punishment, even if the parents have given you permission. Bribery and threats don't work well, either. If you feel you need to punish a child, use a reasonable punishment, such as no TV. You may want to review the information in Chapter 3 on guiding behavior.

Safety Tips for Child Care Providers

Whenever you care for children, you should keep in mind the common causes of childhood accidents, as well as basic first aid procedures. You may want to review the information in Chapter 17.

Caring for children requires your full attention. If you are alert and on the scene when something starts to happen, you can usually succeed in preventing serious problems. You should never let anything distract you from your primary job, which is watching the children

One of the most dangerous situations you might encounter as a child care provider is fire. Fire is fascinating to children, even those old enough to understand its dangers. When you begin a child care job, locate all the outside doors. Note escape routes from various parts of the home. Find out whether the house has smoke detectors and a fire extinguisher. Ask whether the parents have a family escape plan to be used in case of fire; if they do, ask them to review the plan for you.

When you are caring for children, don't let them wander off alone in the home; check on them frequently. Matches, cigarette lighters, candles, fireplaces, gas or electric heaters, and burning trash are all possible sources of fire.

If a fire does break out, remember that the children are your first responsibility. Lead or carry them to safety. Then alert anyone else who may be in danger, and call the fire department. Notify the parents at once.

How Do You Rate as a Care Provider?

As you can see, successful child care requires a careful balance and thoughtful attention to the children. You can raise your rating by learning about the toys, games, and other activities that appeal to children of different ages. Providing purchased toys is surely not the only way—or even the best way—to keep children amused and happy. More important are your interests, imagination, and enthusiasm. An attentive care provider with a headful of stories, rhymes, songs, tricks, and games is more welcome than toys. These kinds of activities can make a child care job a pleasant and worthwhile experience.

Admiring Jennifer's rock collection helped Susan start her babysitting job on a positive note.

You will rate well with parents if the children are well cared for, safe, and happy. Parents also want a care provider to arrive on time and to follow the routines or directions provided. In addition, parents appreciate a care provider who straightens up, making sure that toys, books, and games have been put away and any snacks or meals have been cleared away.

SECTION 1 REVIEW

CHECK YOUR UNDERSTANDING

1. What responsibilities does a child care provider undertake?
2. List five qualities of a good care provider.
3. List four questions a care provider who is working for a new family should ask before the parents leave.
4. How should a care provider respond to a crying infant?
5. What should a care provider do to help make bedtime easier for a toddler or preschooler?
6. Why do older children sometimes try to give a care provider a difficult time?

DISCUSS AND DISCOVER

1. Imagine that you are providing care for a family with an eight-year-old, a toddler, and an infant. The eight-year-old is clearly interested in finding out how much she can get away with. What methods would you use in encouraging appropriate behavior? Under what conditions, if any, would you punish the child? What kinds of punishment would you use?
2. Work with a group of other students. Select and teach to the rest of your group at least two songs, stories, or games appropriate for five- or six-year-olds. Gather as many ideas as possible to be used while caring for children.

SECTION 2

Observing Young Children

OBJECTIVES

- Explain the importance of observing young children.
- Discuss guidelines for observing young children.

TERMS TO LEARN

anecdotal record
baseline
confidentiality
developmental checklist
frequency count
interpret
objective
running record
subjective

Child development really comes to life when you can observe children in action. Learning how to observe young children is an important skill for parents, for teachers, and for others who take care of children.

Why Is Observing Children Important?

One of the most important reasons for observing children is to gain a better understanding of their growth and development. For instance, infants pass through a complex sequence of motor development in learning to walk. Observing infants at various stages of this development makes it easy to see how each motor skill leads to the next. When you understand this sequence, you can appreciate each achievement and provide experiences that will promote each skill as it emerges.

Observing young children also helps you learn about individual children. All children progress through similar stages, but each progresses at his or her individual rate. By observing, you can come to know the skills and needs of individual children, and thus become better able to help develop those skills and meet those needs.

Another reason for observing children is to gain feedback about your own parenting or teaching abilities. For example, you might be trying to develop the guidance technique of using positive reinforcement. By observing how children react to your positive reinforcement, you can determine how effective your methods have been.

Finally, observing children can help you identify those children who might have special needs or disabilities. Once they have been identified, the children can receive the special care and learning opportunities they need to reach their potential.

How to Observe Young Children

Observing children means more than just watching what children do and telling what you think their actions mean. Knowing what you want to observe and understanding how to observe effectively will make your observations more valuable.

Objective Versus Subjective Observations

One of the most difficult aspects of becoming a good observer of young children is learning to separate facts from opinions. Study the following two examples of observations of the same event:

- **Example 1.** Robbie is feeling selfish. He won't let anyone play with the toys in the sandbox. He gets mad at Eric a lot.
- **Example 2.** Robbie is sitting in the sandbox. He reaches out and takes a truck away from Eric. Eric grabs for the truck, but Robbie pulls it away with a jerk. "It's my turn now," says Robbie, looking Eric straight in the face.

Example 1 is a **subjective** observation, an observation *using one's personal opinions and feelings, rather than facts, to judge or describe things*. Notice that, from reading this observation, you cannot tell what really happened between Robbie and Eric. The observer in Example 1 is recording not facts, but his or her opinion about Robbie's feelings.

Example 2 is an **objective** observation, an observation *using facts, not personal feelings or prejudices, to describe things*. The observation is factual. It describes what the observer saw and heard—and nothing more.

Objective observations are much more valuable than subjective observations. One of the main problems with a subjective observation is that it is based on a false assumption—the assumption that the observer knows what is going on inside the child's mind. Because no one, even an experienced observer, can know a child's emotions or motivations, subjective observations are necessarily inaccurate.

The interpretations included in subjective observations present another problem. They add to the potential for inaccuracy. For example, in example 1, the observer interpreted Robbie's actions as signs of selfishness. A teacher who knew that Robbie was generally shy at school would not find example 1 helpful. However, that same teacher, reading example 2, might interpret Robbie's behavior as a sign of emerging self-assertion.

A third problem with subjective observations is that their use is very limited. Because they do not record facts, they are hard for others to use and may be meaningless after time has passed.

Observing children in a class activity period can help you lean how they interact with each other and with teachers.

Objective observations, on the other hand, can be studied at a later date or by another person.

It takes practice and discipline to write good objective observations. When you begin observing, you may find it helpful to imagine yourself as a video camera. You should record (in writing) only what you see and hear. With this guideline in mind, you will avoid abstract words such as *happy* or *sad*, *good* or *bad*. A video camera cannot see or hear happiness. It may see a smile or hear a laugh. The conclusion that the smiling, laughing person is happy is an interpretation of those actions, and interpretations do not belong in an objective observation. Using only concrete terms to record the actions, language, and physical surroundings you observe can help you make objective observations.

Types of Observation Records

Depending on your purpose, you can choose one of several types of observation recording methods. You will find the running record, the anecdotal record, the frequency count, and the developmental checklist most useful.

- **Running record.** The **running record** is *an observation recording method that involves recording for a set period of time everything observed about a particular child, group, or teacher.* This recording technique is useful if you are just getting to know a child or just learning about what goes on in a group child care setting. A running record can also be used for analyzing a certain area of development, such as social interaction or motor skills.
- **Anecdotal record.** The **anecdotal record** is *a method of recording observations that focus on a particular event or setting.* An anecdotal record is similar to a running record; both involve recording what you observe. However, the anecdotal record focuses on a particular event or setting. For example, you might want to see how a child is adjusting to a new child care setting. You could keep an anecdotal record, observing the child at arrival time each day for several days. If the child is adjusting well, your anecdotal record will show that the child's separation from his or her parent becomes easier during that period.
- **Frequency count.** The **frequency count** is *a tally of how often a certain behavior occurs.* To keep this kind of record, you focus on a specific child and use a tally mark on a record sheet to note how often that child takes a particular action. A frequency count is especially useful when you are trying to change a child's undesirable behavior. For example, you might notice that a particular child seems to hit other

children quite often. To be objective, you should make an actual count of how often the child hits in a given period of time. You can begin by taking a **baseline,** *a frequency count taken before efforts are made to correct a particular undesirable behavior.* As you work with the child to change this behavior, you can make periodic frequency counts. When you compare these counts with the baseline, you can see whether the child's behavior is beginning to change.

- **Developmental checklist.** The **developmental checklist** is *a list that identifies a series of specific skills or behaviors that a child of a certain age range should be mastering.* To use the developmental checklist as an observation record, you can check off the specific skills or behaviors you observe in a particular child.

  Occasionally, an observer using a developmental checklist must set up certain circumstances in the environment or must interact with the child in some way to ensure that certain behavior occurs. For example, in the sequence of motor development that leads to walking, one skill is pulling up on furniture to a standing position. This behavior could not be observed if furniture were not provided for the infant to use. Another skill is learning to walk while holding an adult's hand. In some cases, the observer may need to be available to provide this support.

One advantage of a developmental checklist is that it is easy to use while observing. Less time is needed to check off items than to write a description of what the child is doing.

Each of these methods of recording your observations of young children will give you valuable information. The method or methods you select will depend on your purpose for observing. Your purpose for observing, in turn, will depend on how you plan to use or interpret the information you gather.

Appropriate Behavior While Observing

While observing young children, you want to be as unnoticed as possible. Your very presence can affect the behavior of the children you are observing and make it difficult for you to gather objective information. There is also the possibility that you might disrupt the teacher or parent who is with the children you are observing. For these reasons, you should position yourself so that once you have responded to the children's initial interest, you can blend into the background.

To accomplish this, choose a spot outside the area in which the children are working or playing. Sit in a comfortable, adult-sized chair, or stand off to one side and use a clipboard. Have your notepad, observation assignment, and pen or pencil ready. Once you are settled, try to remain still. At first, the children may come to you to ask who you are and what you are doing. Answer their questions politely, but briefly. Avoid asking the

PARENTING IN ACTION

Observing and Helping Children

Christine was observing three active kindergartners chasing each other on the outdoor play equipment. The well-built wooden structure included two ladders, one more difficult than the other. Both ladders led to a wooden platform, from which a suspension bridge led to a tower and two slides. Christine noted that Carl easily took the more difficult route and slid down the higher slide quickly, while Troy and Sean were more cautious; they both moved slowly along the easier route. Carl repeatedly called to his friends, "Come on up here, you guys. It's more fun—don't be a sissy."

After several tries, Troy became more confident. He soon joined Carl on the higher slide, and before long, both boys were yelling at Sean, "Come on! Don't be a baby." Christine saw Carl push Sean once as he hurried past him on the bridge.

Christine felt relieved when she heard Sean say to the other two, "Leave me alone. I'm going somewhere else to play." Before he could get down, however, Carl and Troy began to urge him up to the top of the tower, pushing and pulling and taunting him, "Scaredy-cat! Scaredy-cat!"

Christine knew that the kindergarten teacher was indoors, and she saw the aide on the other side of the playground, helping another group of children. Worried about the boys' safety, she jumped up and ran to the play structure. "Troy! Carl! Sean!" she called up to them. All three boys looked down at her in surprise.

THINK AND DISCUSS

1. What made Christine decide to abandon her role as an observer? Do you agree with her decision? Why or why not?
2. What might have happened if Christine had not intervened?
3. If you had been in Christine's position, what would you have said to the three boys? What response would you have expected?
4. What do you think Christine should tell the kindergarten teacher about this incident? Why?

children any questions, which would only encourage further conversation. If the children need to be encouraged to return to their own activities, you might say, "I am writing a story about how children play. If you go back to playing, I can write about you in my story."

A time may arise, however, when you must stop being just an observer and take action. For example, you might see that a child has been hurt and that the child's teacher or parent is unaware of the problem. In this kind of situation, your concern for the safety of children should override your goal of remaining unnoticed as an observer.

Interpreting and Using Information from Observations

When you set out to observe young children, you decide on your purpose, choose the best method of gathering and recording information, and then gather that information. Once you have the information you need, the next step is to interpret and use it. To **interpret** is *to find meaning in, explain, or make sense of something*. As you gathered information, you made every effort to be objective, to avoid all interpretation. Now, however, it is time for you to express your ideas and opinions about what you observed. An hour's running record of a child's behavior is of little use until you analyze and interpret what you observed.

Objective observations, combined with thoughtful interpretations, can be used in a number of ways. Monitoring a child's pattern of growth and development is one of the most important applications of observation information. A teacher or parent who understands a particular child's stage of development can form appropriate expectations of the child. The parent or teacher can also provide an environment and activities that will help the child reach his or her potential. Children who appear to be far behind in certain areas of development can be referred to specialists, so that any special needs can be identified early.

Information from observations is also useful in solving problems related to children's behavior or to adult-child interaction. When a parent or teacher is having a problem with undesirable child behavior, close observation of the situation can often reveal the underlying cause of the problem and suggest possible solutions. For example, a preschool teacher might be having trouble keeping the noise level down in the classroom. An objective observation by another person might reveal that the teacher uses a very loud voice in speaking to children across the room. This information suggests that the solution might begin with a change in the teacher's behavior; the teacher should use a quieter voice and avoid shouting across the classroom.

Anyone who observes children and interprets information about them should remember and follow the basic rule of **confidentiality**, or *privacy*. In observing young children, confidentiality involves keeping all observations and findings about a child to yourself, sharing them only with the child's parents or with your child development teacher.

Remember that, as part of your course in child development, you will be with the children for only a brief time. What you interpret about a child's behavior during that time may not be accurate, because you may not have all the relevant facts. For this reason, it is especially important to avoid commenting to anyone that, for example, "Devon is spoiled" or "Kendra's child is a slow learner." Any such comments might lead to rumors that could hurt the child and his or her family.

You may, of course, have questions and concerns about a child you observe or about a child care facility you visit. You should discuss those questions and concerns with your teacher—and with no one else.

Becoming a good observer of young children is not easy, but it is a skill worth learning. It will help you become an effective parent or teacher—one who makes a positive difference in the life of a child.

SECTION 2 REVIEW

CHECK YOUR UNDERSTANDING

1. List four reasons for observing children.
2. What is the difference between a subjective observation and an objective observation?
3. List the four types of observation records. What determines which type of record an observer uses?
4. List three things an observer can do to avoid disrupting the children he or she is observing.
5. Which goal should an observer consider more important than the goal of remaining unnoticed?
6. What does it mean to interpret an observation?
7. What is confidentiality? What does confidentiality involve in relation to observing young children?

DISCUSS AND DISCOVER

1. Why do you think confidentiality is considered a basic rule in observing children? Who do you think should follow the rule of confidentiality? What kinds of problems might arise if those people fail to follow it? Are there ever circumstances under which people who work with children should disregard the rule of confidentiality? If so, what are those circumstances?
2. From a magazine, newspaper, or book, choose a photograph showing at least two children; other people may be included in the photo as well. Imagine that you are observing the scene in the photograph, and write two observations of it—one objective and one subjective. Then show the photograph to classmates, and read your observations aloud. Let your classmates help you evaluate and, if necessary, revise your objective observation.

Participating in Child Care and Education

SECTION 3

OBJECTIVES

- Describe effective plans for organizing early childhood classrooms.
- Discuss methods of protecting health and safety in early childhood classrooms.
- Explain how to plan daily schedules and appropriate activities for classes of young children.
- Discuss methods of promoting positive behavior.

TERMS TO LEARN

learning centers
time-out
transitions

As a part of your class in child development, you may have the opportunity to participate in setting up an early childhood classroom. The following guidelines will help you get started and suggest ways that both you and the children can learn together.

The Early Childhood Classroom

Before you can invite young children to your school, you must prepare a place that is designed especially for them. Young children have physical, social, emotional, and intellectual needs different from those of older children and adults. Their environment should be designed to meet those needs and make learning possible.

The first requirement is to make everything possible child-sized. The furniture, including chairs, tables, and shelves, should all be of a size and design that is comfortable for young children. For example, when young children sit in a chair, their feet should easily touch the floor. Shelves should be low so that children can get and return materials independently. A child-sized environment promotes independence. The better the surroundings fit the young children, the more able those children will be to work and play without having to ask adults for help.

Learning Centers

Learning centers are *areas of the classroom that are designed for certain types of play, equipment, or learning*. Learning centers vary according to the aims of the program and the space and equipment available. A well-equipped program might have the following centers.

- **Block center.** Small and large blocks, building logs, trucks and cars, people and animal figures, flat boards, shelves or bins for storage.
- **Dramatic play center.** Child-sized play kitchen, table and chairs, dishes, empty food cartons, dress-up clothes, dolls, play money, telephone, mirror.
- **Art center.** Paper, crayons, paints and brushes, markers, easels, clay, paste, yarn, felt, blunt-tip scissors, table and chairs, smocks.
- **Library center.** Books, pictures, puppets, low shelves, rug, large pillows.
- **Discovery center.** Plants, fish, other small animals (such as a hamster), magnets, magnifying glass, shells, thermometers, scale, soil, seeds, plastic tub of water, strainers.
- **Manipulative center.** Puzzles, large beads to string, string, various types of interlocking block or other building sets, board and card games, table and chairs.
- **Music center.** Record player and records or tape recorder and tapes, drums, shakers, tambourines, triangles, bells, piano, rug.

Each learning center should be marked off or distinguished in some way from other centers and from other areas of the room. Low, open shelves work well for defining centers. You might also define centers with pegboard dividers, low book cases, fabric panels suspended securely from the ceiling, different kinds or colors of floor covering, or even colored tape on the floor.

Other guidelines for setting up learning centers include the following:

- Separate noisy centers from quiet centers.
- Place the art center near a sink or other convenient source of water.

A classroom for young children must be designed for their activities and their needs. Discovery centers must have interesting objects to explore. Play equipment and storage areas should be safe, sturdy, and child-sized.

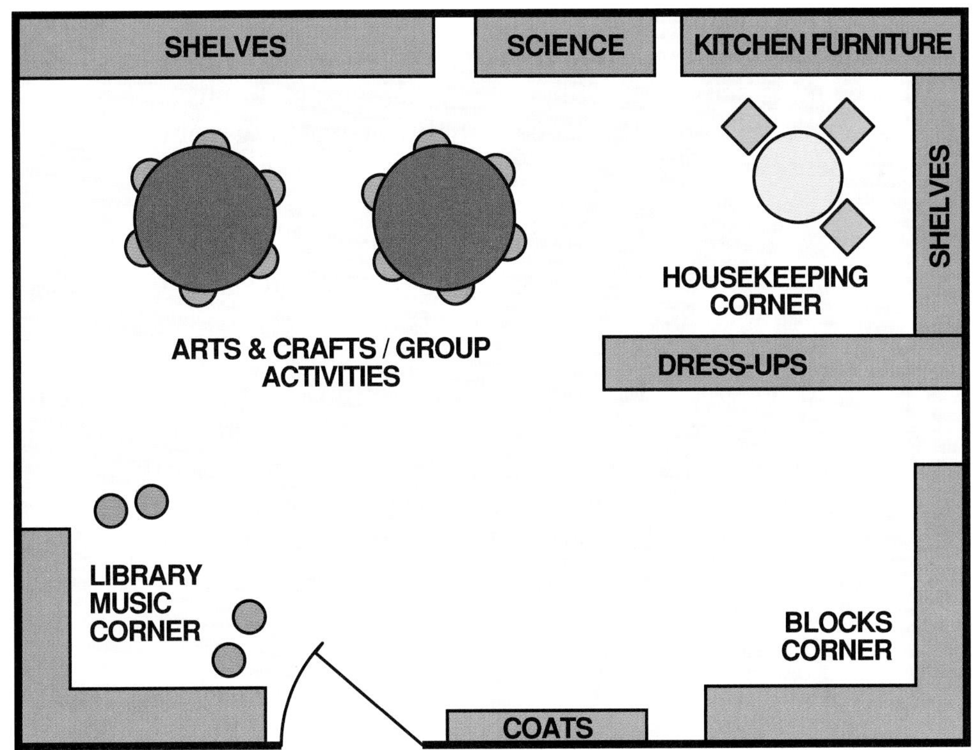

This diagram shows one possbile arangement for an early childhood classroom.

- Keep equipment and supplies neatly organized within easy reach for the children.
- Leave one large, open area for large-group activities.

Learning centers offer children learning choices. Children can select activities, explore different skills and areas of knowledge, and learn through hands-on experiences.

Health and Safety

Protecting the health and safety of the children is the first responsibility of teachers and other staff members in an early childhood classroom. While children are in your care, you must encourage health care routines that will prevent illness, make sure the environment is safe, and supervise their play.

Health Care Routines

Health care routines for young children prevent the spread of illness. They also help make sure the children are well nourished and rested.

The single most important routine for preventing illness is hand washing. The children should be taught to wash their own hands, using a brisk, scrubbing motion, with warm water and soap. They should also be taught to dry their hands completely with a clean paper towel. All the children should wash their hands after using the toilet or blowing their nose, and before cooking activities, eating, or playing with materials such as clay.

You should also make a habit of washing your hands frequently while caring for the children, both to protect everyone's health and to set a good example. Be sure to wash your hands after helping a child in the rest room or using a tissue to wipe a child's nose. Always wash your hands after you use the rest room and before you handle food.

In addition to learning the importance of hand-washing, the children should learn several other important health care habits. Teach them how to blow and wipe their nose and to dispose of the tissue. Be sure each child uses only his or her own comb, brush, or head wear—never those of another child. Teach the children not to take bites of each other's food and not to share the same cup or eating utensils. Finally, be sure family members understand that children who are sick should not be in a group child care setting.

Children need to feel healthy in order to participate in learning activities. They should be well rested, and they should have had a good breakfast before coming to your early childhood classroom. In some cases, it may be necessary to discuss these needs with family members or others who can help the children. The children will need a nutritious snack about midmorning or midafternoon, if they are staying for a half-day program. You can also help the children feel good and remain healthy by pacing their activities so that they do not become too tired. During the course of each program day, the children need time for both active play and quiet play.

Be sure there is at least one caregiver monitoring each area in which children are playing.

Safety

To keep young children safe, you must check their environment and make sure it is childproof. In addition, you need to supervise the children closely as they work and play.

Check the children's classroom and outdoor play areas for any possible safety hazards. Many of the safety guidelines discussed in Chapter 17 can be applied to child care centers.

Check the classroom thoroughly before each visit from the children. While they are there, the children must be supervised at all times. There should always be an adequate number of teens or adults present to monitor the children playing in each area of the room. If an emergency arises, there should be several teens or adults who can stay with the children in the classroom while someone goes for help. If the rest rooms are located outside the classroom, several teens or adults must accompany children to the rest room while the other children are supervised in the classroom.

SAFETY TIP

It helps to look at things from a child's point of view. Get down on your knees and look around. What do you see that a child could get into? Be sure to check for these safety precautions:

- There are no sharp edges on furniture or equipment.
- Electrical outlets are covered.
- Electrical cords are all in good condition and are secured to the walls or floor.
- Poisonous substances, such as cleaning supplies, are securely locked away.
- Traffic paths around the room are free of clutter.
- Fire exits are clearly marked, and there is a fire exit plan.
- Dangerous items such as sharp scissors or staplers are locked away.

Planning Appropriate Activities

Planning also plays an important role in providing appropriate learning experiences for the young children in your care. Much of this planning has already been done by the time you have set up the classroom and equipped the learning centers. Within the framework of this planned environment, the children will learn through play. In addition, you should provide a balanced schedule of activities for individuals and for small and large groups of children. These activities should focus on each important area of development.

Planning activities for each day will help make your experiences with children more successful. What would happen if you didn't plan ahead?

Learning Through Play

For a young child, play means having hands-on experiences that involve the senses and opportunities to talk. It does not mean doing a worksheet or coloring page, and it does not mean listening to an adult lecture. As you plan activities for young children, remember that the more involved they are and the more realistic their experiences are, the more the children learn. For example, a story about a fire truck is not nearly as effective a learning tool as a trip to the fire station and a chance to climb on a real fire truck.

Play experiences for young children can be considered in several ways. One way is to observe how the children are playing in relation to each other. Children may play alone. For example, a child may curl up in a large box with a book and a pillow for some quiet time alone. Children may also play individually but alongside one another, as when several children sit together at a table, each working his or her own puzzle. Children may play in small groups, cooperating in acting out going to the store, for instance. Children may also play in one large group under the guidance of a teacher, as during a music or movement activity.

Another way to consider children's play is by the area of development that is being stimulated. For example, children need many experiences in language. They need opportunities to listen and to speak, to become familiar with written language, and to develop their vocabulary. Learning experiences that stimulate language development include story times, open-ended questions, field trips, games, activity records, and cooking activities, to name but a few of many possibilities.

Play activities can be described according to how children play in relation to each other. Here the children are playing in one large group. Another way to describe play is the area of development being stimulated—in this case, motor skills.

ASK THE EXPERTS

Evaluating Child Care Programs

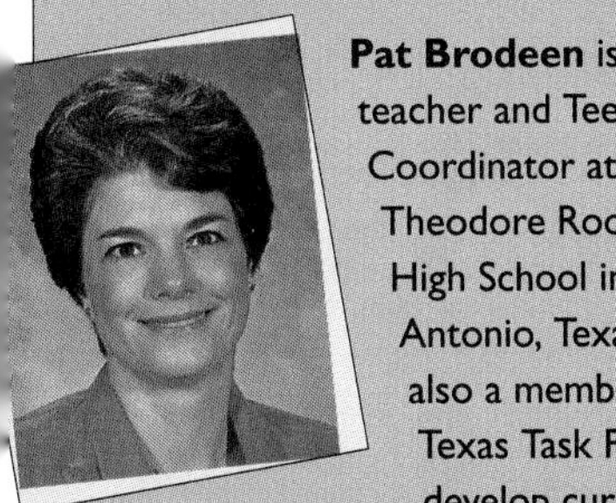

Pat Brodeen is a teacher and Teen Parent Coordinator at Theodore Roosevelt High School in San Antonio, Texas. She is also a member of the Texas Task Force to develop curriculum for School Age Parenting courses.

Choosing a child care setting is such an important decision! How can I know that I'm choosing the best program for my child?

I agree—it's a very important, and often a very difficult choice, for parents to make. Let me suggest a unique and effective approach to making this decision. Once you have found a program that is convenient and affordable and that offers the hours and services you need, approach that program from your child's point of view.

I want to spend my time with a loving person. Does the caregiver here know how to communicate with me? Will the caregiver give me gentle but firm guidelines for my behavior? Does the caregiver have a high stress tolerance for my noisy activity level? Will the caregiver interact with me beyond simply caring for my physical needs? Will he or she love and appreciate me—and all the other children here? If my caregiver's children are also here, will I get equal treatment? Has the caregiver had any educational preparation for dealing with me? Can I trust this person to care for me for an extended period of time, or is he or she likely to find other employment soon? Does he or she treat me the way my parents do, so I will have consistency in my day? Do I really like this person?

The facility where I stay is also important to me. After all, I will spend the majority of my time here during the week. Are there few enough children so that I can feel secure in getting plenty of attention? Is the food served nutritious, attractive, and tasty? Will I get regular meals and snacks, so I won't ever feel too hungry? Will I be safe here? Will I be encouraged to explore and learn, to be creative, to use all my muscles, to pretend, and to laugh—or will I be left in a playpen and expected to watch television most of the time? Is this place clean? Is it attractive, with bright colors and lots of air and light? Does it look neat but still "lived in," so I will feel comfortable about playing with my cars or building a highway out of blocks? Will I get to go outside often and play on lots of different kinds of equipment? After I have played and am really tired, will there be a special place for me to rest—a spot with soft, clean sheets that only I use?

Of course, these questions are just a start. You know your own child best, and you are the person who can most fully adopt your child's perspectives and interests in selecting a child care program.

Pat Brodeen

Pat Brodeen

In addition to language, children need play experiences that focus on these areas of development:

- Thinking and problem solving.
- Movement or motor skills for both large and small muscles.
- Creativity, including music, dance, dramatic play, and art.
- Relationships with others in the social world.

When planning experiences for young children, keep these types of play in mind. Help the children participate in individual, small-group, and large-group activities each day, and offer experiences that focus on each area of development. Children who are actively involved in the experiences you provide will learn more effectively—and be better behaved—than children who only sit by, watching and waiting.

The Daily Schedule

Planning the daily sequence of events for an early childhood classroom is just as important as planning and preparing the environment. The daily schedule is the master plan for how the children will use their time. Schedules vary greatly from program to program. Study the following schedule for a three-hour session:

8:30-8:45	Arrival and free play
8:45-9:00	Circle time
9:00-9:30	Small-group activities
9:30-9:45	Large-group music activity
9:45-10:00	Toileting and hand-washing
10:00-10:15	Snack
10:15-10:45	Outdoor play
10:45-11:15	Learning centers
11:15-11:30	Large group story time

Good schedules for young children in group settings feature a balance of active and quiet activities, small- and large-group activities, and teacher-directed and child-selected activities. Notice in the sample schedule how these elements are alternated. The small-group activities are learning activities planned and directed by the teaching staff. After these activities, the children move to the large, open area of the classroom for group music experiences. After music, snack time provides the children with an opportunity for relaxed conversations with their friends. Then the children are ready for brisk physical activity, such as outdoor play. If outdoor play is not possible, it is easy to plan an indoor group session for movement or creative dance. After this period of physical activity, the children are ready for the quieter involvement of the learning centers. Here, they can select for themselves the learning centers they want to play in. Finally, the session ends with a story or language activity. This kind of closing allows the children to put away their learning center materials, have quiet time as a group, and be ready to leave on time.

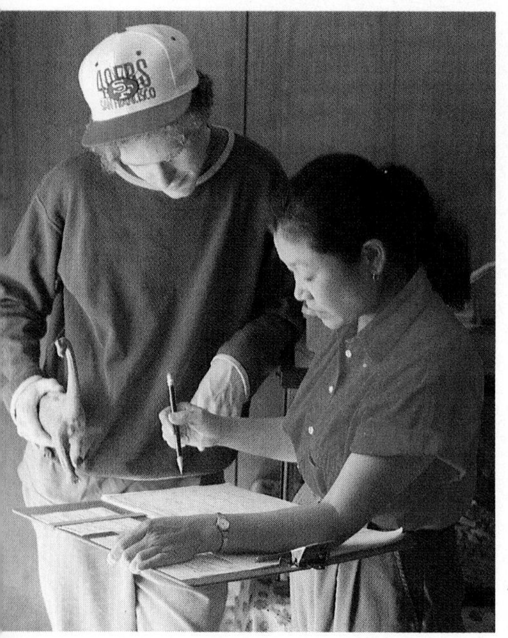

A well-planned schedule ensures that children can participate in a balanced variety of activities.

A good daily schedule allows time for **transitions**, *periods during which children move from one scheduled activity to the next.* During a transition, the children need to conclude one activity, put their materials away, and get ready for the next activity. To help the children feel more comfortable during transitions, always let them know a few minutes ahead of time that they will soon have to make a change. Whenever possible, use a song or a game to move the children from one place to another or from one activity to the next. For example, you might sing a special cleanup song as you and the children put away materials after learning centers time. When it is time for the children to go outside, you might make a game of getting ready; name one color at a time, and let all the children wearing that color move to the door.

Whether you are preparing a two-, three-, or four-hour session for the children, plan a schedule carefully to include each of these important features. A well-planned daily schedule will do much to ensure that the children feel involved and interested throughout the session.

Writing Learning Activity Plans

A daily schedule provides an outline for the children's activities each day. With that outline in mind, the coordinator plans the specific activities he or she wants to use during each period of the day.

A field trip activity to a science exhibit or a museum expands learning and promotes socialization.

There are two types of planning forms that can be used to write plans for the children's activities. The first form is based on the daily schedule and on the days or sessions that the children will attend. This planning chart or overview lists the names of the activities that will be provided in each learning center and during each period on the daily schedule. For example, if you are preparing a one-week overview based on the daily schedule shown on page 562, you will record your plans for each day. For each of the music activities, you would note the songs you plan to help the children sing; for each of the story times, you would note the books you want to share.

The second form you might use allows you to record more detailed information about each activity you have planned. On this form, you would include specific information under each of the following headings:

- Title of the activity.
- Objective, or purpose, of the activity.
- Type of activity (for a learning center, small group, or large group).
- Materials needed.
- Procedures to be followed.
- Evaluation—how did the activity go?

The type of forms you use is not as important as the fact that you do have written plans. Writing out your plans ahead of time helps you think through the appropriateness of each activity. It also provides a list of everything you need so that the materials can be set up before the children arrive. Also, if you feel nervous or rushed, your written procedures are handy for quick reference when you are presenting the activity.

Following a consistent daily schedule and having written plans for the children's activities will help each session run smoothly—which, in turn, encourages appropriate behavior from the children.

Promoting Positive Behavior

If you have carefully prepared an environment designed for young children, constructed a well-balanced daily schedule, and planned appropriate activities, you have done most of what it takes to promote positive behavior among the children. Most

Children are usually eager to earn the praise of caregivers. By establishing a way to recognize their positive efforts, you can help them behave well and feel good about themselves.

inappropriate behavior is the result of poor planning on the part of the teacher. However, even the most organized teacher has times when direct guidance of children's behavior becomes necessary. To promote positive behavior, you need to establish classroom rules, use positive reinforcement effectively, be a positive role model, and develop some strategies for dealing with unacceptable behavior.

Establishing Classroom Rules

Young children need classroom rules, but too many rules can overwhelm them. The classroom rules should be stated in positive terms. That is, each rule should instruct the children in what they should do—not what they shouldn't do.

Each classroom rule should also have a clear purpose. The most effective rules are those that deal with protecting the safety of children and property.

The following list shows one possible set of rules for an early childhood classroom:

1. Use your hands gently.
2. Walk inside the classroom.
3. Put materials away when you are finished.
4. Use an inside voice in the classroom.
5. Be a friend to other people.
6. Keep your feet away from others.

Of course, you need to provide activities that help the children understand the meaning of each rule. For example, you might have a collection of pictures showing gentle, friendly touching and aggressive, hurtful touching. Using an open-ended questioning technique, you could explore the pictures with the children and help them understand what each type of touching feels like. Make it very clear that hurtful touching is not allowed in your classroom.

Using Positive Reinforcement

Children enjoy being recognized and rewarded with attention, and they tend to repeat behaviors that are positively reinforced. To make this technique effective, however, you must be sincere in your positive response to a child's behavior. Automatic or inattentive comments and praise do not provide true positive reinforcement.

Being a Good Role Model

Your own behavior in the classroom has a very powerful influence on the children. For this reason, you must be especially careful to be a good role model. Children are more likely to do what you do—not what you say. For example, if you want the

BUILDING SELF-ESTEEM

Using Positive Reinforcement

Probably the most useful direct guidance technique is positive reinforcement. This technique involves giving children recognition or encouragement for appropriate behavior—in other words, a reward. The reward may be very simple. It might be a smile or a hug or a comment such as, "I like the way you wipe your paintbrush on the side of the jar before you paint." Occasionally, when children are just learning a new behavior, the reward might be a small treat, such as a sticker or ribbon.

PROMOTING MULTICULTURAL AWARENESS

As infants enter the world, they are alert and aware of their surroundings. As they grow, their perceptions also grow, and even as infants they begin to notice differences in people. For example, four-year-old Sara proudly announces "My new friend has chocolate skin." This awareness is common to the learning process and develops into another natural step—classification. Again, this developmental process is neutral until the child is infected with a prejudiced attitude. Then perceived differences can become an excuse for unfairness and a justification for angry behavior.

Parents, teachers, and caregivers can nurture an appreciation of the inherent values of all cultures. Think about your own attitudes. How do you communicate unbiased feelings toward others?

children to use inside voices, then you, too, must always use a quiet voice indoors. If you want the children to treat each other with kindness, you, too, must deal kindly with everyone. Through your example, the children will learn how to play and use materials properly and how to treat each other with respect.

Dealing with Misbehavior

In spite of careful planning and a clear encouragement of positive behavior, you should be prepared for the fact that children will occasionally behave in unacceptable ways in the classroom. You should know in advance how you will respond. The children should also understand what will happen if they behave in unacceptable ways.

In most cases, a simple statement of what you want the child to do is effective. If a child is using too loud a voice, for example, you might simply say, "Marlie, please use your inside voice. I can't hear well when you are shouting." In other situations, you may offer the child a choice of more acceptable activities. For instance, if a child is not playing well in the block center, you might say, "Heather, you may choose to go to the dramatic play center or the art center now. I can't let you stay in the block center because you are still trying to take Ariel's blocks away from her." Notice that each suggested statement includes an explanation of why the child's behavior was unacceptable.

Some schools provide large indoor areas that allow children to run to use up excess energy that could lead to misbehavior if it were not channeled into play.

For some types of unacceptable behavior, a stronger response is necessary. Behavior that hurts other people or property must not be permitted at any time. Children who break this type of rule should receive an immediate and consistent response. One effective approach is to give the child a **time-out**, *a short period of time spent sitting away from the main activities of the classroom.* See page 77.

Here's how one teacher, Ms. Black, used the time-out technique. After one child hit another child with a block, Ms. Black said, "Don, I can't let you hit Mark. It hurts. Go and sit in time-out for two minutes." After two minutes, Ms. Black went to Don and asked him to choose one of two centers to go to; she did not include the block center in his choices. Using this technique, Ms. Black was able to deal with Don's unacceptable behavior without becoming angry and without raising her voice.

With these basic strategies and skills, you will be able to provide a warm, supportive learning environment for young children. It takes a lot of advance planning, patience, and practice, but you will find that your efforts are worthwhile.

SECTION 3 REVIEW

CHECK YOUR UNDERSTANDING

1. What are learning centers?
2. List seven kinds of learning centers that might be part of a well-equipped preschool program.
3. List three methods that can be used to define a learning center, separating it from other parts of the classroom.
4. How and when should young children wash their hands?
5. List six safety precautions that should be checked for in an early childhood classroom.
6. What are transitions? How can teachers help young children feel comfortable during transition times?
7. What is a time-out? When should it be used?

DISCUSS AND DISCOVER

1. Why do you think it is especially important for early childhood teachers to act as good role models? During what ages are children most attentive to their teachers as role models?
2. Working with several other students, brainstorm a list of possible rules for an early childhood classroom. Then consider and discuss all the rules on your group's list. Select the four most important rules, combining several from your original list, if appropriate. Then carefully plan the most appropriate wording for your four selected rules. Share your group's rules with the rest of the class.

SUMMARY

- A child care provider must be a responsible person who can relate to children of different ages.
- Observing children can help teachers, parents, and other caregivers understand child growth and development, learn about individual children, gain feedback about their teaching or parenting methods, and identify children with special needs.
- Observations, which should be objective, can be recorded using several different recording methods.
- After they have been recorded, observations should be analyzed, interpreted, and used.
- An early childhood classroom should be organized with several different learning centers.
- Encouraging learning through play, following a consistent daily schedule, and writing learning activity plans all help create a comfortable, stimulating classroom environment.
- Early childhood teachers can promote positive behavior by establishing classroom rules, using positive reinforcement, and being good role models.

REVIEWING THE FACTS

1. Why should a child care provider arrange to arrive about 20 minutes early the first time he or she provides care for a family?
2. How should a care provider respond to a toddler who awakens, crying, in the night?
3. Who can benefit from learning how to observe young children?
4. Which is more useful, a subjective observation or an objective observation? Why?
5. What is the difference between a frequency count and a developmental checklist?
6. With whom should you discuss any questions or concerns about a child you observe?
7. List four health care habits that should become routine for children in an early childhood classroom.
8. How often should an early childhood classroom be checked for safety?
9. List the five areas of development on which children's play experiences should focus.
10. What kinds of activities should be balanced in a daily schedule?
11. List three advantages to writing out plans for specific activities in an early childhood classroom.
12. How should classroom rules be stated?

EXPLORING FURTHER

1. Make a "care provider bag" of free or found materials that you could take along on child care jobs and use to help keep the children entertained. Share and discuss your materials with other students. (Section 1)
2. Write your own checklist of behavior that is appropriate for those who are observing young children. Share and discuss your checklist with classmates, and then revise your list as necessary. Finally, observe another student who is observing young children; use your checklist to record your observations of the observer. (Section 2)
3. Make up your own song or game to use during a specific kind of transition in an early childhood classroom. Teach your song or game to a group of other students, and ask them to help you evaluate and improve your work. Make any appropriate improvements to your song or game; then share it with a group of young children in a child care setting. (Section 3)

THINKING CRITICALLY

1. **Analyze.** What factors do you think account for the different interpretations people might make from the same observation records? Is there usually one "right" interpretation of an observation? Why or why not?
2. **Synthesize.** What criteria do you think parents should use in selecting a child care setting for their children? How do you think the information in this chapter might help parents in choosing a child care center? What other factors should parents take into consideration? Why?
3. **Compare and contrast.** Compare the use of time-outs with other methods of dealing with unacceptable behavior. What problems does a time-out solve for the child? For the teacher? What problems, if any, do you think might be associated with using time-outs? How could such problems be avoided?

CROSS-CURRICULUM CONNECTIONS

1. **Writing.** Plan and write your own *Care Provider's Handbook.* Use an appealing format to present guidelines for successfully providing care for children in a particular age range: infants, toddlers and preschoolers, or school-aged children.
2. **Science.** Read about the role of observation in scientific research: How is this kind of observation similar to observations of young children? How are the two kinds of observations different? Share your findings and ideas with your classmates.

OBSERVING AND PARTICIPATING

Evaluating Child Care Programs

It takes more than one visit to evaluate a child care program. You will need to look carefully at the facility, observe how the children and adults interact, and watch how the children play with each other. Ask for printed information about the program, and phone ahead to schedule your visit.

Choose one of the following activities, and observe or participate in a group of young children. After you have completed the activity, write a journal entry about your observations. Then share and discuss your observations with other students.

- **Observing.** Observe an early childhood classroom, both before the students arrive and while the students are there. Notice what kinds and sizes of furniture are in the room. Where and how is it arranged? How comfortable do the children seem with the furniture? In your opinion, should the classroom have more or less furniture? Should the arrangement of the furniture be changed in any way? Why or why not?
- **Observing.** Spend time observing teachers and children in a group care setting. What specific actions do the teachers take to protect the health and safety of the children? How many teachers are available to supervise how many children? In your opinion, are there enough teachers for safety?
- **Participating.** Volunteer to spend half a day helping in an early childhood classroom. Before the children arrive, discuss classroom procedures with the teachers. As you work with the children, notice how they respond to the classroom rules. How often do children need to be reminded of the rules? How do the teachers use positive reinforcement? How do the children respond to your comments of praise and encouragement?

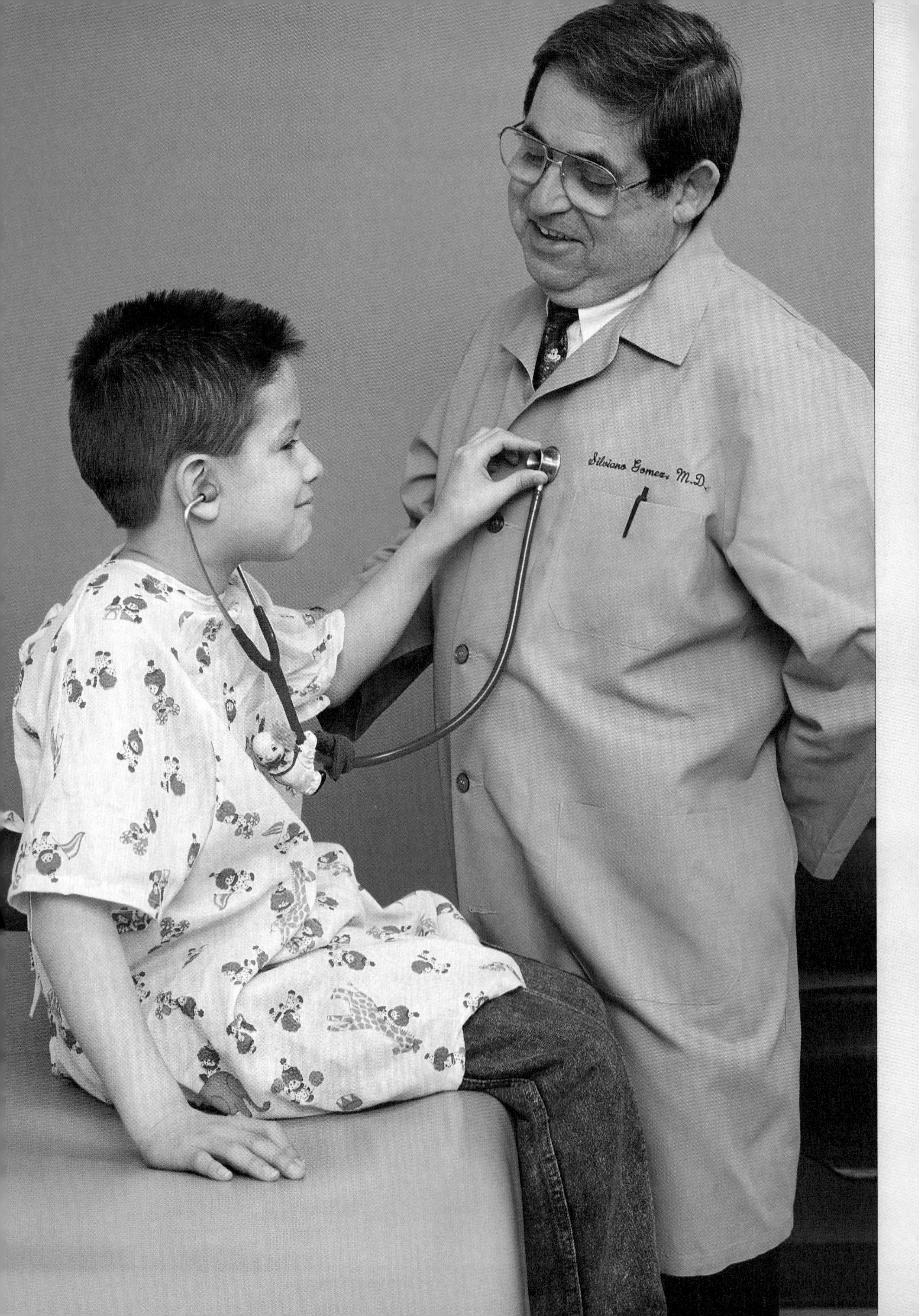
Silviano Gomez, M.D.

CHAPTER 20

Careers Relating to Children

As Victor sat on a high examination table swinging his feet back and forth, Dr. Gomez entered the small, white room. Victor stopped swinging his feet and sat very still as he watched Dr. Gomez move closer.

"How are you today, Victor?" Dr. Gomez smiled as he ruffled Victor's short, dark hair.

Victor swallowed and answered in a small voice, "I'm fine."

"Well, there's no need to be frightened, Victor. You're only here for a checkup. I'll listen to your heart and your lungs, and look in your eyes, ears, and throat."

Dr. Gomez removed his stethoscope from around his neck and put the two ear pieces in Victor's ears saying, "Victor, how would you like to listen to my heartbeat? That way you can hear what I listen for when I put this little cup against your chest."

Victor held the end of the stethoscope with the little metal cup on it against Dr. Gomez's chest and smiled for the first time as he listened to the lub-dub, lub-dub sound of Dr. Gomez's heart. Visiting the doctor didn't seem so scary anymore. Victor thought that he might like to be a doctor someday.

SECTION 1 Which Career for You?

OBJECTIVES

- Evaluate your personal interests and aptitudes in light of future career decisions.
- Explain the importance of education and experience in finding and progressing in a job.

TERMS TO LEARN

aptitude test
entry-level job
interest inventory
paraprofessional
professional
reference

Various people and experiences have influenced you toward particular careers since early childhood. At five, you may have visited a fire station and decided to become a fire fighter. In grade school, liking a certain teacher may have convinced you that you wanted to teach. Parents may also influence you by encouraging some of your interests and discouraging others.

Aptitude Tests

Unfortunately, you cannot try out every job you think might interest you. However, psychologists have developed tests that give insight into people's strengths and weaknesses. These tests, combined with some thoughtful self-appraisal, can help point you in the right direction. Similar tests are also given by employers. These tests help employers know whether prospective employees are suited to the job they are applying for.

An **aptitude test** is *a test that measures a person's abilities and probable success in various skill areas*. A person's scores on an aptitude test can help predict how successful he or she might be in jobs of a particular type. Aptitude tests are often given to students in high school and college to help them plan their careers. Nonstudents can often arrange to take the tests at local colleges or counseling agencies. The following skills are usually checked by aptitude tests:

- **Verbal reasoning.** This is the ability to understand ideas expressed in words and to use words in thinking through your own ideas. Teachers, writers, social workers, and salespeople are among those who should have good scores in verbal reasoning.

- **Abstract reasoning.** Picture in your mind a number of objects with different shapes. Now try to move the objects around to form different patterns. This is an example of thinking logically without using words or numbers—abstract reasoning. Carpenters, scientists, and computer programmers are among those who need to be good at abstract thinking.
- **Numerical ability.** If you are good at solving mathematical problems and working with figures, you may have good numerical ability. This is important in many careers, including engineering, economics, accounting, and banking.
- **Mechanical reasoning.** Those who understand the mechanical principles involved in motors and tools have high scores in this area. Mechanics obviously need these skills, but so do many other workers. They include machinists, medical technicians, technical repairpersons, and engineers.
- **Spatial relationships.** Can you look at a flat drawing of an object and picture in your mind its actual size, shape, and position in relation to other objects? If so, you have an aptitude in spatial relationships, which is important for architects, truckers, interior designers, artists, and laboratory technicians.
- **Clerical speed and accuracy.** A high score in this area indicates good hand-eye coordination, necessary for bookkeepers, bank tellers, and precision assembly workers, among others.
- **Spelling.** Secretaries, editors, writers, and word processors are among those who need to be good spellers.
- **Language usage.** Putting words together correctly and effectively is necessary for many jobs. Careers using these skills include writing, editing, law, teaching, and sales.

Your score in a single aptitude isn't as important as the pattern formed by your three or four highest scores. Most jobs demand a combination of skills. A good aptitude test can guide you in considering career possibilities based on your personal strengths.

Taking part in an actual child care situation can be a learning experience for both you and the children. It can be fun for all of you, too!

Your Interests and Values

Having the ability to master a particular skill doesn't mean that you would be happy spending your life using that skill. In other words, your interests may differ from your aptitudes. Many people aren't sure how their interests fit in with possible careers. If you are unsure what jobs might fit your personal interests, you may want to take an **interest inventory**, *a test designed to suggest jobs related to a person's interests.*

Interest inventories vary; most help you examine how you feel about different "themes" related to occupations. For example, if you score highest on the "realistic" theme, you might be interested in work as a mechanic, laboratory technician, farmer, or skilled industrial worker. Other themes suggest different jobs.

Remember, though, that tests are only part of the answer. They cannot measure such things as motivation, personality, or ambition. What's more, career decisions are often influenced by other factors, such as job security and prestige. Tests can show fairly accurately what you could do and what you might like doing, but you have to decide what's most important to you.

Be sure you consider the impact of your career choice on your long-range family values and goals. A career that requires frequent travel, for example, makes close family relationships more difficult. People in high-stress jobs may carry their tensions home with them. These are factors to consider as you evaluate possible careers.

Combining information from an aptitude test will help you make a wise career choice. What aptitudes and interest do you think are needed to work in a child care center?

Education and Experience

Having a career is much like climbing a ladder. In every career area, there are many levels of jobs. The more education and work experience you have, the higher you can climb on the career ladder. However, it is essential to remember that jobs at any level are important and worth doing well.

When you read about jobs at various levels, you will probably see words like *entry-level, paraprofessional,* and *professional.* Understanding these terms will help you know what qualifications are needed.

An **entry-level job** is *a position for beginners with limited education and training.* As the name indicates, this is the kind of job many people take when they are entering a career area. Most people, however, don't stay at this level. As they become more experienced and perhaps get more education, many people move up to more responsible and better-paying jobs.

A **paraprofessional** is *a person with education beyond high school that trains him or her for a certain field.* Many paraprofessional jobs require a related degree from a two-year college. A paraprofessional typically works in a team with more qualified professionals. For example, a paraprofessional might work in a child care center as an assistant teacher.

A **professional** is *a person employed in a position that requires at least a degree from a four-year college (a bachelor's degree) or technical school in a particular field.* Many professionals have more advanced degrees—a master's degree or a doctorate—and years of experience. Professionals may be in charge of programs or supervise paraprofessionals and entry-level workers.

Education

Have you thought about getting more education after high school? You may not feel you can afford to go on to college or to a technical school, or you may not want to continue your education. However, you should consider carefully before you make a decision.

If you feel you cannot afford to continue your education after high school, you may find that financial help is available. Government groups, schools, and other institutions offer scholarships and loans. Many schools offer part-time on-campus jobs to students who need money to pay for their education. Most areas have community colleges, where costs are reasonable. These colleges offer academic programs and a variety of training programs that take two years or less to complete. After you graduate from a two-year college, you can transfer to a four-year college or university if you want to continue your studies for a bachelor's degree. Another possibility for financing further education is to work for two or three years after high school, saving enough money to go back to school later.

If you are not interested in education after high school now, you may find that you change your mind after you've been working awhile. You may want a better-paying, more responsible job that requires additional education. You may even become so interested in your work that you want to take classes to learn more about it.

In the years ahead, you may want more education or training so that you can change careers. Experts predict that most people entering the job market now will have several different careers during their working lives. Some jobs will disappear because there will no longer be a need for them. Other jobs may be taken over by machines. Even if your job continues to be available, you may discover that your interests change over time. Perhaps you will find your job boring after several years, or perhaps you will develop an interest in a different field. Any of these developments could motivate you to continue your education in the future.

Experience

If you have ever looked for a job, you know that most employers want to know about your work experience. You may wonder how you can get that experience if you can't get a job. That is a puzzle—but the puzzle has a solution.

PARENTING IN ACTION

Discussing Career Choices

Carolyn Dunn is the successful owner of a child care center. When she was asked what led her to that profession, this is what she said:

I think I'm in this career mainly because I've always loved kids. Even when I was a kid myself, I loved playing with babies. At family picnics, I was always carrying someone's baby around.

I started babysitting when I was pretty young. I was a good babysitter, too. Babysitting wasn't work for me—it was fun! To become even better at it, I enrolled in all the free babysitting clinics I could.

When I was in high school, our home economics department had an in-school nursery as part of a child study course. We had about a dozen children at a time, from babies to preschoolers. After school and during the summer, I got a part-time job as an assistant in a real nursery school downtown. I'd dress, feed, and entertain the little ones, help the older ones with their art projects and games, and answer countless questions.

By that time, I knew I wanted to make a career of working with children. I enrolled in our local college and began working toward a degree in early childhood education.

About the time I graduated from college, a computer company in town built a child care center for employees' children. I applied for a job and was hired as assistant to the director. Within four years, I had moved up to the director's position.

During those early years, I'd often hear friends complain about the trouble they had finding good child care for their children. They'd switch from one center to another, trying to find the right one. They complained about poor food, lack of cleanliness, unhappy children, and high prices. I decided that I should start my own child care center, giving customers everything I'd want in a center if I had children of my own. I knew I'd have no trouble getting clients.

I started small, renting space in a church basement. Then we moved to larger quarters in a mall. I remodeled the space, hired the best people I could find, and here we are today—two years later and going strong. We have a waiting list of parents who have heard about us from satisfied customers.

THINK AND DISCUSS

1. How did Carolyn Dunn's love for children develop into her current business? What did she do to gain both the experience and the education she needed?
2. If you were interested in a career in a child-related field, what would you begin doing today? What goals might you set for yourself?

Too often, people think about experience only in terms of a paying job. However, there are many other ways to gain experience. One of the best is through volunteer work. Many programs and agencies depend on volunteer help. In addition to learning the job, volunteers enjoy the satisfaction and pride gained in helping others.

As a volunteer, you will have an opportunity to gain actual experience, build up a good work record, and improve your work skills and attitudes. The people you work with as a volunteer can be good references when you apply for a paying job. (A **reference** is *a person a prospective employer can contact to find out about an applicant's character and skills.*)

If you want to be a pediatric nurse, you might consider working as a nurse's aide. It can give you valuable experience and help with the cost of nursing school.

Another advantage of volunteering is that it gives you experience you can use in securing a job. As a volunteer, you can learn how important a neat, clean appearance is. You can gain practice in selling your skills and talents to others. Being able to present yourself well will be an important advantage when you interview for a job.

Another good way to get work-related experience is to create your own job. You can do this by finding a need and filling it. Mowing lawns and shoveling snow are among the more obvious types of "created" jobs. However, other students have become house-sitters, dog-walkers, and even "human alarm clocks" who call to awaken people each morning. Perhaps your area needs someone to repair bicycles—and you know how. Maybe parents in your neighborhood would pay you to entertain and supervise their children on weekend afternoons. These kinds of created jobs can provide good experience in work areas that you find especially appealing.

SECTION 1 REVIEW

CHECK YOUR UNDERSTANDING

1. How do parents influence their children's choice of career?
2. List eight types of skills usually checked by an aptitude test.
3. What is an interest inventory?
4. What is an entry-level job?
5. What is the difference between a professional and a paraprofessional?
6. List three benefits of volunteer work.

DISCUSS AND DISCOVER

1. What career choices are you currently considering? Which of the aptitudes listed on pages 572-573 do you think you have? How does your own evaluation of your aptitudes relate to your career interests?
2. Interview a local employer about entry-level jobs in his or her business: What qualifications are needed to be hired? What is the pay for entry-level jobs? What are the working conditions? What are the requirements and potential for advancement? Share your findings with classmates.

SECTION 2

Careers Related to Child Care

OBJECTIVE

- Describe a number of specific jobs in the child care field.

TERMS TO LEARN

entrepreneur
speech-language pathologist

Within the area of child care, there is an almost endless variety of careers. Some careers involve working with a single child; others, with a group. Some require extensive study beyond high school; others require only a high school education. Some jobs, such as teaching in schools or child care centers, involve working with children all day. Others, may involve less contact with children.

Child-Related Careers

Brief descriptions of a few child-related careers follow. These descriptions will give you an idea of the various kinds of jobs that are available. After reading about these careers, you may have a clearer idea of whether you are interested in a child-related career.

All jobs have pluses and minuses. You should be aware of them before you make a final career choice. The chart on page 579 summarizes the advantages and disadvantages of child care careers.

Child Care Workers

You may have noticed an increasing number of child care centers in your community. There is a growing need for child care because, in more and more families, there is no parent at home during the day to care for the children. With this increase in child care centers, there is an increasing demand for child care workers.

Many child care centers are run by government or community agencies. Some large businesses provide child care centers for their employees' children. A few child care centers are part of nationwide or regional chains. However, most centers are run by **entrepreneurs**, *people who start up and run their own businesses, or who create and market new products.*

ADVANTAGES AND DISADVANTAGES OF CHILD CARE CAREERS

ADVANTAGES	DISADVANTAGES
• Job opportunities at all levels of education, experience, and responsibility. • Work available in every area of the country. • Opportunities for both part-time and full-time work. • Flexible working hours. • Personal satisfaction for those who enjoy helping others. • Contact with all age groups, from infants to adults.	• Salaries vary, but they are often not as high as in other careers with comparable educational requirements. • Work is often emotionally draining. • May be necessary to work evenings and weekends. • Great responsibility for the health, safety, and development of children. • Requires exceptional energy and patience. • Few periods of relaxation during working hours.

Starting and owning a child care center can be an appealing way to enter the business world. In order to succeed, an entrepreneur must have good business management skills, leadership ability, and relationship skills. An entrepreneur must also recognize that there are great risks in owning a business.

Because there are so many different kinds of child care centers, there are many different educational and personal requirements for child care workers. Some states now have regulations and licensing requirements that apply to child care workers.

Jobs in child care, even babysitting, can give you knowledge and experience that will help you be a good parent.

I'M SPECIAL

Multicultural activities in the preschool or child care center raise awareness and interest. To emphasize ethnic heritage, children can bring pictures of parents and grandparents for a bulletin board display of families. Pictures of children in everyday settings around the world reinforce appreciation of different lifestyles. An assortment of ethnic foods opens discussion about the value of new and different experiences. As with all child-related efforts, activities should be suitable for the developmental stage of the group of children.

Special education teachers face extra challenges but know they make a difference in children's lives.

Teachers

Teaching is the largest profession in the industrialized world. In many parts of the country, there are more qualified teachers than positions available in elementary and secondary schools. Opportunities for teachers are usually best in preschools, in kindergartens, in grades one to three, and in classrooms for children with mental or physical disabilities.

Teachers are responsible for planning and teaching lessons. The content of those lessons must conform to the guidelines of the state and of the individual school district. In addition, teachers must take the needs and learning abilities of their individual students into consideration.

Most elementary teachers have a class of 20 to 35 students, whom they instruct in several subjects. Some elementary teachers and all secondary teachers specialize in one or two subject areas. They teach their special subjects to the students in several grades or several classes.

In most states, a full-time teacher must have at least a bachelor's degree from a four-year college, usually with an approved teacher education program. Teaching salaries vary with geographic areas, level of education, and experience. The starting salaries for teachers are typically in the low-to-medium range. A common complaint is that, compared with other professionals, teachers do not receive salaries that match the educational requirements and responsibilities of their job. Experience, advanced degrees, and administrative responsibilities can raise teachers' salaries to the middle range and above.

Special Education Teachers

Special education teachers are trained to teach those students with needs beyond the average. This includes students with learning disabilities, mental impairments, social or emotional adjustment problems, and physical disabilities. Sometimes gifted students—those with above-average potential—also receive special education.

Since students vary greatly in the type and degree of their needs, special education teachers must tailor their programs to their individual students.

Special education teachers must complete a four-year program at an approved college or university. Some school districts require special education teachers to have a master's degree, which requires an additional one or two years of study. Special education teachers must be dependable, sensible, patient, and enthusiastic. Their salaries may be somewhat higher than those of regular classroom teachers.

Speech-Language Pathologists and Audiologists

About ten percent of all Americans have some communication disorder. Children who have trouble speaking or hearing cannot participate fully with other children in play or in normal classroom activities.

A **speech-language pathologist** is *a professional specially trained to work with people who have speech, language, and voice disorders.* These disorders may be caused by deafness, brain injury, cleft palate, mental retardation, cerebral palsy, or environmental problems. A speech-language pathologist is typically responsible for both diagnosing and treating communication disorders.

An audiologist is a professional specially trained to test for, diagnose, and help treat hearing problems. Because speech and hearing are so closely related, a person trained either as a speech-language pathologist or as an audiologist must be familiar with both fields.

The duties of speech-language pathologists and audiologists vary with their education, experience, and place of employment. Speech and hearing clinics—generally held in schools—use special machines, tests, and diagnostic procedures to identify and evaluate disorders. Then, in cooperation with other health professionals, the speech-language pathologist or audiologist plans and arranges for organized programs of treatment.

A person who chooses either of these professions should approach problems objectively and should have a concern for the needs of others. Both speech-langauge pathology and audiology require patience, because progress is often slow. Speech-language pathologists and audiologists must accept responsibility, work independently, and be able to instruct others. Working with detail is also important.

Most states require a master's degree or its equivalent for both professions. Some states also require a teaching certificate if work is done in schools. Since the educational requirements for these careers are advanced, starting salaries begin in the above-average range, and later salaries tend to be high.

Social Workers

Social workers help people who have social or emotional problems. There are many different jobs within this broad field. Caseworkers help people on a one-to-one basis; community social workers are involved with groups of people.

The aim of all social service is to strengthen and improve individual and family life and to protect children. Caseworkers

Many different types of community agencies employ social workers. This agency helps young parents and their children get off to a good start.

interview individuals or families who need help. Social workers with this specialty must be skillful at gathering information, getting along with people, and gaining the confidence of their clients. They decide what type of help their clients need—from counseling to medical services—and arrange for the clients to receive that help.

Some social workers place children in foster homes or with adoptive families. School social workers help troubled students adapt to classes, receive tutoring, or benefit from special community services.

A social worker must have a bachelor's degree from a school with an officially recognized social work program. A master's degree is required for some social work jobs.

Social work graduates are qualified for jobs in many government and private agencies. Salaries are in the medium range for entry-level jobs and the high range for administrators. Many social workers find satisfaction in their work because they are helping others. Some, however, find it difficult to cope with the emotional strain of social work.

Pediatricians

A pediatrician's job is the same as your family doctor's, except that all the patients are children. Pediatricians generally examine and treat their patients in their own offices and in hospitals. Some work full-time in hospitals.

Those who want to become pediatricians must have a strong desire to serve the sick and injured. They must be willing to study and keep up with the latest advances in medical science. They will need sincerity and a pleasant personality to help gain the confidence of children. Pediatricians must be able to make quick decisions in an emergency.

All states require a license to practice medicine. To qualify, candidates must graduate from an approved medical school. Most medical schools require applicants to complete at least three years of college before entering; some require four years. Most students receive a bachelor's degree before they enter medical school. After completing medical school, pediatricians must pass a state licensing examination, serve a one- or two-year hospital internship, and usually complete a hospital residency program.

Medical training is very expensive, and it takes a long time to earn a degree. Physicians usually have a high annual income, but most work many hours a week and are often on call day and night for emergencies.

Pediatric Dentists

Dentists are responsible for the health and care of the teeth and gums. They take X rays, fill cavities, straighten teeth, and treat gum disease. Pediatric dentists specialize in the care of children's teeth.

A dentist must be a graduate of an approved dental school and must pass a state examination to receive a license. Dental colleges usually require candidates to have completed four years of college. Then dental training lasts another four years.

Dental education requires an investment of both time and money. Setting up an office and buying equipment are also expensive. However, dentists can expect high earnings after their practice is established. Dentistry, like medicine, is one of the highest paid professions.

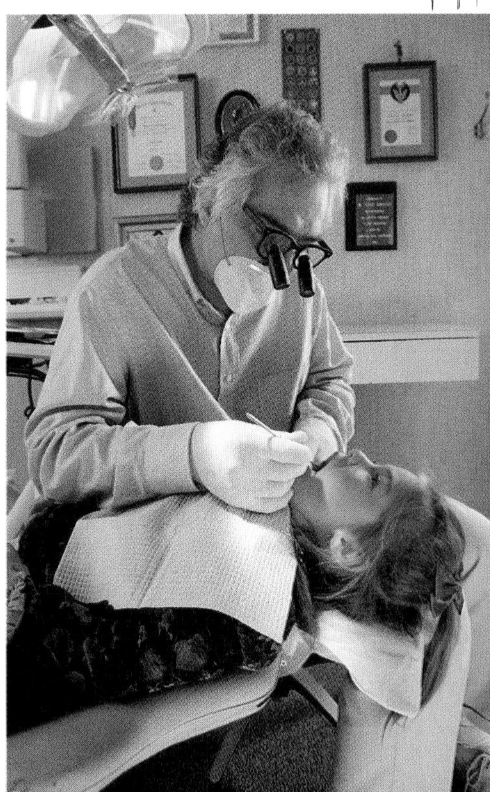

Orthodontists specialize in straightening teeth to improve both health and appearance. Many of their patients are children. The advantages and disadvantages of this career are similar to those of a pediatric dentist.

Physical Therapists

Physical therapists work with people who have muscle, nerve, joint, or bone diseases or injuries. They help patients cope with or overcome their disabilities.

Physical therapists test patients for muscle strength, motor abilities, and proper body functioning. They develop programs for treatment, and they help patients do exercises to improve their strength and coordination.

Physical therapists must have a license to practice. To earn a license, a candidate must have a degree or certificate and must pass a state examination. Most approved schools of physical therapy offer bachelor's degree programs. A person who already has a bachelor's degree in another field can enroll in a 12- to 16-month course that leads to a certificate in physical therapy.

A master's degree in physical therapy, combined with clinical experience, increases a therapist's opportunities for advancement.

ASK THE EXPERTS

Child Care Careers

Jackie Mault is Director of Special Services for the Toppenish School District where she develops special programs for children from birth through high school.

I'm planning to prepare for a child care career, but I'm concerned about opportunities in this field. What is the outlook for child care careers in the decades ahead?

Good for you! I think you—and others who choose to pursue child-care related careers—have a bright future. Opportunities in child care and education will be increasing in the coming decades. In addition, more and more disciplines are addressing children's issues.

Perhaps the greatest number of career opportunities will develop in response to the growing demand for quality child care. I anticipate an increasing need for well-trained child care providers with education beyond high school and with special licensing and certification. Nurses, educators, therapists, and other professionals will also find career opportunities in child care settings.

The need for teachers is also increasing again. Many schools are extending their services to include preschool programs, after-school programs, and transition programs for students beyond the twelfth grade.

Social service agencies, both public and private, are expanding their services to children and their families. Health-related fields continue to need individuals with the interest and ability to become pediatricians, pediatric nurses, pediatric dentists, and child psychiatrists.

Specialists who provide specific services to children are always in demand. There are now nationwide shortages of psychologists, speech- language pathologists, physical therapists, occupational therapists, recreational therapists, audiologists, and nutritionists who can address the special needs of children. Demands for specialists exist in schools, private practice, clinics, and hospitals.

In other career fields, there will continue to be an increased need for those who design, create, and produce products for children and their families. There will be special opportunities in creating and publishing children's books; designing and producing children's clothing, toys, and furniture; creating and producing quality television programs for children; writing and publishing parent-education materials; and developing and publishing textbooks and educational software.

Jacqueline L Mault

Jackie Mault

Creative Artists and Designers

Careers in publishing offer creative opportunities for people who enjoy writing or illustrating books, recording stories or music, or designing computer software.

There may be various education requirements for entering these careers. However, talent, creativity, and an understanding of what appeals to young children are essential. Those who want to become software designers should have training in computer science and experience with various microcomputer systems.

High school classes can give the basic foundations for these careers, but most people in these fields benefit from a college education. Work experience can sometimes be gained by assisting people already active in the field. The income from this kind of work often takes the form of royalties—a percentage of the profits earned by the book, tape, or software. Only rarely do people in these careers have high earnings.

The work hours can be flexible, but the work involves deadlines that must be met. Some people in these careers work part-time and combine their work with another job.

Illustrating books for children and teens is just one example of a publishing career. Advantages of working in this field include flexibility and the chance to be creative.

SECTION 2 REVIEW

CHECK YOUR UNDERSTANDING

1. List three advantages of having a child care career. Then list three disadvantages.
2. Why is there an increasing demand for child care workers?
3. Which school positions offer the most opportunities for teachers?
4. What are the unique responsibilities of special education teachers?
5. What is the difference between a speech-language pathologist and an audiologist?
6. Why do some people find social work especially rewarding? Why do others find it difficult?
7. Describe the job responsibilities of a physical therapist.

DISCUSS AND DISCOVER

1. Starting and running a child care center is just one child-related opportunity for entrepreneurs. What other kinds of business might be appropriate for people who want careers that involve working with or for children? Which of those businesses already exist in your community?
2. Choose and evaluate a software program designed for children: For what age range is the program marketed? Does it suit the needs and interests of children in that age range? What does the program teach? Is it intended to be educational? What teaching methods are used? How appealing do you think most children find the program? Why? Share your evaluation with a group of classmates.

SUMMARY

- Your aptitudes and interests, which may differ, are both important in your choice of careers. Aptitude tests and interest inventories can help you measure each.
- Every career has jobs at different levels. As you climb the career ladder, your responsibilities and salary may grow.
- Additional education and work experience help you advance in a job.
- Many career fields include jobs related to children.

REVIEWING THE FACTS

1. What is an aptitude test? Where can students usually arrange to take aptitude tests? Where can nonstudents take them?
2. List three career-related factors that tests cannot measure.
3. What kind of education does a professional usually have? What kinds of responsibilities does he or she usually have?
4. What is a reference?
5. What is an entrepreneur?
6. List three factors teachers must consider in planning and teaching lessons.
7. What are the two major goals of all social workers?
8. With what kinds of students do special education teachers work?
9. List three characteristics pediatricians should have.
10. What are the responsibilities of pediatric dentists?

EXPLORING FURTHER

1. Find out about the aptitude tests given at your school. Which tests are offered? When are they given? To whom are the tests available? What registration process, if any, is required? With a partner, plan, make, and display posters advertising the available tests. (Section 1)
2. Working with a group of classmates, compile a list of volunteer opportunities in your community. Then prepare an information sheet about those opportunities, giving pertinent information about each. Distribute copies of your information sheet to interested students. (Section 1)
3. Interview a social worker in your community. Who employs the social worker? What are the social worker's responsibilities? With whom does he or she work? What does he or she find most satisfying and most difficult about the position? With a group of other students, discuss what you learned from the interview. (Section 2)

THINKING CRITICALLY

1. **Analyze.** What are ten factors that might influence a person's career decisions? Of those factors, which three do you consider most important? Why? How strong a role do you think television and other media play in influencing career decisions? Do you believe television limits or expands people's views about careers? Why?
2. **Synthesize.** What personal characteristics do you feel are important for success in any job? Why are those characteristics important? What do you think you and other students should be doing to foster these characteristics in yourselves? Why?
3. **Compare and contrast.** Compare the salary usually earned by teachers with the salary earned by most other professionals with comparable education and responsibilities. Do you think teachers' salaries should be increased? Why or why not? What do you think the level of teachers' salaries indicates about our society's attitude toward teachers? Toward children? Toward education? What, if anything, do you believe should be done to change those attitudes?

CROSS-CURRICULUM CONNECTIONS

1. **Reading.** Read the current edition of *What Color Is Your Parachute?* by Richard Nelson Bolles. Think about the ideas in the book, and write a list of the four most important things you learned from your reading. Then share and discuss your list with your classmates.
2. **Management.** Read about liability insurance: What is this kind of insurance? Who needs it? Why? Then investigate the costs of liability insurance for a small, private child care center: How much insurance would be necessary? How much would that insurance cost per year? How would the cost of the insurance be defrayed? Share and discuss your findings with a group of classmates.

OBSERVING AND PARTICIPATING

On the Job

As you think more about child development and about your own future, you may discover that you have also taken a step toward a career in working with children.

Complete one of the observation or participation activities below. Then write about your observations in your journal, and discuss your observations with a group of classmates.

- **Observing.** Spend at least an hour observing at a child care center, paying particular attention to the employees and their responsibilities. Can you identify which employees have entry-level jobs? Which are paraprofessionals? Which are professionals? What are the indicators of each job level? How much contact do employees at each job level have with the children in the center?
- **Observing.** Spend half a day observing in an elementary school classroom. How many students are in the class? What subjects do they study while you are there? How much time does the teacher spend working with the class as a whole? With groups of students? With individual students? How do the students respond to the teacher? What indications are there that the teacher enjoys his or her job?
- **Participating.** Volunteer to help with the Special Olympics activities in your community, or volunteer with a similar local program. Ask for guidance from activity leaders, as necessary. What special needs does each participant have? What can you do to help each participant? What should you allow or encourage each participant to do independently? How do the participants regard their own achievements? Each other's achievements? What makes this volunteer work rewarding for you?

Glossary

A

abstinence. Avoiding or abstaining from sexual intercourse. (4-1)

adoption. Legal process in which people obtain the permanent right to raise a child not biologically their own as if they were the natural parents. (2-1)

aggressive. Unusually strong-willed and determined. (9-2)

allergy. An oversensitivity to one or more common substances. (17-1)

alternative birth center. A homelike facility, separate from any hospital, for giving birth. (6-3)

ambidextrous (AM-bih-DECK-struhs). Able to use both hands with equal skill. (14-1)

amniocentesis (AM-nee-oh-sen-TEE-suhs). The process of withdrawing a sample of the amniotic fluid surrounding an unborn baby with a special needle and testing that fluid for indications of specific birth defects or other health problems. (5-3)

amniotic fluid (AM-nee-AHT-ik). A special fluid that surrounds and protects the developing baby during pregnancy. (5-1)

anecdotal record (AN-ik-DOTE-uhl). A method of recording observations that focuses on a particular event or setting. (19-2)

anemia (un-NEE-me-uh). A condition caused by lack of iron, which results in poor appetite, tiredness, and weakness. (6-1)

Apgar scale. A method of evaluating a newborn's physical condition. The infant is rated on a scale from 0 to 2 on five items: pulse, breathing, muscle tone, responsiveness, and skin color. (7-2)

aptitude test. A test that measures a person's abilities and probable success in various skill areas. (20-1)

articulation. The ability to use clear, distinct speech. (13-2)

artificial respiration. A procedure for forcing air into the lungs of a person whose own breathing has stopped. (17-2)

attachment. A special strong bond between two people. (9-2)

attention deficit hyperactivity disorder (ADHD). A condition involving the inability to control one's activity or to concentrate for a normal length of time. (16-2)

attention span. The length of time a person can concentrate on a task without getting bored. (10-1)

audiologist. A professional specially trained to test for, diagnose, and help treat hearing problems. (8-1, 20-2)

B

baseline. A frequency count taken before efforts are made to correct a particular undesirable behavior. (19-2)

behavior. A way of acting or responding. (1-1)

birth defect. An abnormality, present at birth, that affects the structure or function of the body. (5-3)

blended family. A family group that consists of a married couple and at least one child from a parent's previous relationship. (2-1)

bonding. The process of forming lifelong emotional ties. (7-2)

budget. A spending plan. (6-2)

C

cardiopulmonary resuscitation (CPR). A rescue technique used to sustain life when both breathing and heart action have stopped. (17-2)

caregiver. Anyone who cares for a child, whether on a long-term or short-term basis.

cause and effect. The concept that one action results in another action or condition. (10-1)

central nervous system. The spinal cord and the brain. Sensory impulses are passed to this area and motor impulses are passed back. (10-1)

cervix. The lower part of the uterus. (7-1)

Cesarean birth. Delivery of a baby through a surgical incision in the mother's abdomen. (7-1)

child abuse. The physical and/or emotional mistreatment of a child. (18-2)

child care aide. An assistant to the person in charge of a child care program. (3-3)

child care center. A facility designed primarily to provide care for children of working parents. (3-3)

child development. The study of how children grow in different ways—physically, mentally, emotionally, and socially. (1-1)

chorionic villi sampling (CORE-ee-AHN-ik VILL-eye). The process of testing for specific birth defects by sampling small amounts of the tissue from the membrane that encases the fetus. (5-3)

chromosomes. Tiny threadlike particles in the nucleus of every cell that carry hereditary characteristics. (5-2)

circumference. Measurement around something roughly circular in shape, such as a child's head or chest. (11-1)

colostrum. The first breast milk, secreted from the mother's breasts shortly before and after birth. This fluid precedes the milk flow and provides the newborn with nourishment and antibodies to help protect against disease. (7-2)

commitment. A pledge or promise of loyalty. (2-2)

communicable diseases. Diseases that are easily passed from one person to another. (17-1)

conception. The union of an ovum and a sperm, resulting in the beginning of pregnancy. (5-1)

concepts. General categories of objects and information. (13-1)

concrete operations period. Piaget's third stage of learning, lasting usually from seven to eleven years of age, during which children are able to think logically but still learn best from direct experiences. (10-1)

confidentiality. Privacy. (19-2)

conscience. An inner sense of right and wrong that prompts good behavior and causes feelings of guilt following bad behavior. (3-2, 15-2)

consequences. The results that come from a decision. (4-1)

consistency. Repeatedly acting the same way. (9-2)

contraceptives. Devices or methods that prevent pregnancy. (4-1)

contractions. The tightening and releasing of the uterine muscle. (7-1)

convulsion. A period of unconsciousness with uncontrolled jerking or twitching of the muscles. (17-2)

cooperative play. Play among children that includes interaction and cooperation. (12-2)

coping skills. Techniques that help people solve a problem or adapt to a situation. (2-2)

cortex. The outer layer of the brain, which permits more complex learning. (10-1)

cradle cap. A skin condition in which the scalp develops patches of yellowish, crusty scales. (8-3)

creativity. The use of imagination to produce something. (13-1)

crisis nurseries. Child care facilities where troubled parents can leave their children to be cared for while they try to cope with anger and other problems. (18-2)

D

delivery. The birth itself. (6-3)

deprivation. The lack of a healthy, nurturing environment. (3-1)

depth perception. The ability to recognize that an object is three-dimensional, not flat. (8-1)

developmental checklist. A list that identifies a series of specific skills or behaviors that a child of a certain age range should be mastering. (19-2)

dexterity. The skilled use of the hands and fingers. (14-1)

diaper rash. Patches of rough, irritated skin in the diaper area. (8-3)

dilates. Widens. The cervix dilates during labor. (7-1)

directed learning. Learning from being taught, either formally or informally. (13-1)

discipline. The task of helping children learn to behave in acceptable ways. (3-2, 12-3)

dominant. Describes a gene for a particular trait (such as eye color) that is stronger and dictates the outcome of the trait when paired with a weaker, or recessive, gene. (5-2)

dramatic play. Imitating real-life situations, such as playing house or playing school. (16-1)

dyslexia (dis-LEK-see-uh). A learning disability that prevents a person from handling language in a normal way. (16-2)

E

egocentric. Thinking only about himself or herself. (10-1)

embryo (EM-bree-oh). The developing cluster of cells in the uterus during about the third through eighth weeks of pregnancy. (5-1)

emotional development. The process of learning to recognize and express one's feelings and learning to establish one's identity and individuality. (9-1)

empathy. A sense of understanding and sharing another person's feelings. (18-1)

entrepreneurs (AHN-truh-pruh-NUHRS). People who start up and run their own businesses, or who create and market new products. (20-2)

entry-level job. A position for beginners with limited education and training. (20-1)

enuresis (EN-yuh-REE-suhs). A lack of bladder control. (14-2)

environment. The people, places, and things that surround and influence an individual. (1-2)

extended family. A family group that includes relatives other than parents and children within a single household. (2-1)

F

failure to thrive. A condition in which the baby does not grow and develop properly. (9-2)

family child care. A child care arrangement in which a small number of children are cared for in the caregiver's home. (3-3)

family life cycle. A series of stages in a predictable order. (2-1)

family. A group of two or more people who care about each other and are committed to each other. (2-1)

fetal alcohol effects. A less severe condition involving some, but not all, of the symptoms of fetal alcohol syndrome. (5-4)

fetal alcohol syndrome. A condition of physical deformities and cognitive problems resulting from a mother's consumption of alcohol during pregnancy. (5-4)

fetus. The unborn baby from about the eighth or ninth week of pregnancy until birth. (5-1)

finger plays. Songs or chants with accompanying hand motions. (16-1)

fixed expenses. The costs of items that cannot be changed, such as rent, mortgage payments, taxes, insurance payments, and loan payments. (6-2)

flammable. Burns easily. (13-2)

flexible expenses. Costs for items over which people have some control and which can be cut back if necessary. (6-2)

fontanels. Open spaces where the bones of the baby's skull have not yet permanently joined. (7-1)

forceps. Specialized tongs made from bands of surgical steel that are molded to fit the shape of a baby's head. (7-1)

formal operations period. Piaget's fourth stage of learning, lasting from about age eleven through adulthood, during which children become capable of abstract thinking. (10-1)

formula. A mixture of milk or milk substitutes and added nutrients. (1-2)

foster child. Child placed in the temporary legal responsibility of an adult. (2-1)

fracture. A break or a crack in a bone. (17-2)

frequency count. A tally of how often a certain behavior occurs. (19-2)

G

genes. The parts of the chromosomes that determine inherited characteristics. (5-2)

gifted children. Children with an IQ of 130 or above. (16-2)

grasp reflex. The automatic response of a newborn's hand to close over anything that comes in contact with the baby's palm. (7-3)

group identification. The need for a feeling of belonging. (14-2)

H

hand-eye coordination. The ability to move the hands and fingers precisely in relation to what is seen. (8-1)

Head Start. A program of locally operated child care facilities designed to help lower-income and disadvantaged children function effectively at home, in school, and in the community. (3-3)

Heimlich maneuver. A technique for using pressure on the air within the body to force an object interfering with breathing from the throat. (17-2)

heredity. The passing on of characteristics that are physically inherited from previous generations. (1-2)

hormones. Body chemicals. (4-1)

I

imitation. Method of learning by watching and copying others. (13-1)

immunize. To protect a person against a particular disease, usually by giving a vaccine. (17-1)

incidental learning. Unplanned learning. (13-1)

incubator. A special enclosed crib in which the oxygen supply, temperature, and humidity can be closely controlled. Used for premature infants. (7-2)

infant mortality rate. The percentage of deaths during the first year of life. (17-1)

infertility. Inability to conceive children. (5-2)

intelligence quotient (IQ). A numerical standard that tells whether a person's intelligence is average or above or below average for his or her age. (16-1)

intelligence. The ability to interpret or understand everyday situations and to use that experience when faced with new situations or problems. (13-1)

interest inventory. A test designed to suggest jobs related to a person's interests. (20-1)

interpret. To find meaning in, explain, or make sense of something. (19-2)

J

joint custody. An arrangement in which both divorced parents assume responsibility for the children. (18-3)

K-L

labor. The process by which the baby gradually moves out of the uterus into the vagina to be born. (6-3)

large motor skills. Physical skills that depend on the use and control of the large muscles of the back, legs, shoulders, and arms. (11-1)

latchkey children. Children who are unsupervised from the time they come home from school until their parents return from work. (3-3)

lay midwife. A person who has special training in the care of pregnant women and uncomplicated deliveries but does not have a nursing degree. (6-3)

learning centers. Areas of the classroom that are designed for certain types of play, equipment, or learning. (19-3)

learning disability. A disorder in psychological processes that prevents a person from using information received through the senses in a normal way for learning. (16-2)

M

malnutrition. A health problem resulting from not getting enough food or adequate amounts of needed nutrients. (8-2)

manipulation. Skillful use of the hands and fingers. (11-1)

maternity leave. Time off from a job allowing a woman to give birth, recuperate, and care for her new baby. This time may range from several weeks to several months. (6-2)

miscarriage. The natural ending of a pregnancy before the embryo or fetus could possibly survive. (5-3)

Montessori preschool. An educational facility for three- to six-year-olds that provides special learning materials which children are free to explore on their own. (3-3)
moral development. The process of gradually learning to base one's behavior on personal beliefs of right and wrong. (15-2)
motor skills. Abilities that depend on the use and control of muscles. (8-1)

N

nanny. A specially trained person employed to provide live-in child care services. (3-3)
natural fibers. Fibers that come from plants or animals. (11-2)
negative reinforcement. A response that tends to discourage a particular behavior from being repeated. (3-2)
negative self-concept. An inclination to see oneself as bad, unimportant, and incapable. (12-2)
negativism. Doing the opposite of what others want. (12-1)
nontoxic. Not poisonous. (17-1)
nuclear family. A family group with two generations—a father and mother and at least one child—sharing the same household. (2-1)
nurse-midwife. A registered nurse with advanced training in the care of normal, uncomplicated pregnancy and birth. (6-3)
nurturing. Providing love, support, attention, and encouragement.
nutrition. A balance of all the food substances needed for health and growth. (1-2)

O

object permanence. An understanding of the fact that objects continue to exist even when they are not in sight. (10-1)
objective. Using facts, not personal feelings or prejudices, to describe things. (19-2)
obstetrician. A doctor who specializes in pregnancy and birth. (6-1)
ovum. A female cell or egg. (5-1)

P

pacifier. A nipple attached to a plastic ring. (9-1)
parallel play. Playing independently near, but not actually play with, another child. (12-2)
paraprofessional. A person with education beyond high school that trains him or her for a certain field. (20-1)
parent cooperative. A child care facility in which part of the supervision is provided by the parents of enrolled children, who take turns donating their services. (3-3)
parenthood. The state of being a parent. (3-1)
parenting. The process of caring for children and helping them grow and learn. (3-1)
paternity leave. Time off from a job allowing a father to care for his new baby. (6-2)
pediatrician. A doctor who specializes in the care of babies and young children. (6-2)
peer pressure. The influence of people one's own age. (4-1)
peers. Other people of one's own age. (15-2)
perception. Learning from the senses. (10-1)
permanent teeth. The set of 32 teeth that will not be naturally replaced. (14-1)
personality. The total of all the specific traits (such as shyness or cheerfulness) that are consistent in an individual's behavior. (9-2)
placenta. The tissue that connects the sacs around the unborn baby to the mother's uterus. (5-1)
placid. Remarkably easygoing and accepting of his or her surroundings. (9-2)
play group. A child care arrangement in which a group of parents take turns caring for each other's children in their own homes. (3-3)
poison control centers. Special hospital units that are equipped to advise and treat poison victims. (17-2)
positive reinforcement. A response that encourages a particular behavior. (3-2)
positive self-concept. An inclination to see oneself as good, worthwhile, and capable. (12-2)
postnatal. After the baby's birth. (6-2)
pregnancy test. A test to determine whether or not a woman is going to have a baby. (6-1)

premature. Born before development is complete. (5-3)
prenatal. During the period before birth. (5-1)
preoperational period. Piaget's second stage of learning, lasting typically from age two to age seven, during which children think about everything in terms of their own activities and in terms of what they can perceive at the moment. (10-1)
prepared childbirth. A method of giving birth in which pain is reduced through the elimination of fear and the use of special conditioning exercises. (6-3)
preschool. A child care center that provides educational programs, usually for children aged three to five. (3-3)
preschoolers. Children aged three, four, and five. (14-2)
primary teeth. The first set of teeth a baby gets. (8-1)
professional. A person employed in a position that requires at least a degree from a four-year college (a bachelor's degree) or technical school in a particular field. (20-1)
proportion. The size relationship of one thing to another. (8-1)

Q-R

recessive. Describes a gene which can determine a particular trait (such as eye color) only when paired with a similar gene. If paired with a stronger, or dominant, gene, the dominant gene will determine the trait, and the characteristic of the recessive gene will not be seen. (5-2)
reference. A person a prospective employer can contact to find out about an applicant's character and skills. (20-1)
reflexes. Instinctive, automatic responses, such as sneezing and yawning. (7-3)
rooming-in. An arrangement in which the baby stays in the mother's room, rather than in a hospital nursery, after birth. (7-2)
rooting reflex. A newborn's automatic response, when touched on the lips or cheek, of turning toward the touch and beginning to suck. (7-3)
running record. An observation recording method that involves recording for a set period of time everything observed about a particular child, group, or teacher. (19-2)

S

self-centered. Constantly thinking of one's own needs and wants, not those of others. (12-1)
self-concept. A person's feelings about himself or herself. (9-2)
self-discipline. The ability to control one's own behavior. (3-2, 12-3)
self-esteem. Positive sense of self-worth. (15-1)
sensitive. Unusually aware of his or her surroundings and of any changes in those surroundings. (9-2)
sensorimotor period. Piaget's first stage of learning, lasting from birth until about the age of two, during which babies learn primarily through their senses and their own actions. (10-1)
separation anxiety. A fear of being away from parents, familiar caregivers, or their normal environment. (12-1)
sequence. A step-by-step pattern. (1-2)
sexuality. A person's concept of himself or herself as a male or female. (4-1)
sibling rivalry. Competition between brothers and/or sisters for their parents' affection and attention. (12-1)
single-parent family. A family group that consists of one parent and one or more children sharing a household. (2-1)
sleeper. A one-piece stretch garment with feet. (8-3)
small motor skills. Physical skills that depend on the use and control of the finer muscles of the wrists, fingers, and ankles. (11-1)
social development. The process of learning to interact with others and to express one's self to others. (9-1)
socialization. The process of learning to get along with others. (12-2)

speech therapist. A professional trained to diagnose and help correct speech problems. (13-2)

speech-language pathologist. A professional specially trained to work with people who have speech, language, and voice disorders. (20-2)

sperm. A male cell. (5-1)

sphincter muscles (SFINK-tuhr). The muscles that control elimination. (11-2)

sprain. An injury caused by sudden, violent stretching of a joint or muscle. (17-2)

startle reflex. A newborn's automatic physical response—legs thrown up, fingers spread, legs extended and then brought rapidly back to the midline while the fingers close in a grasping action—to a loud noise or to a touch on the stomach. (7-3)

stillbirth. The natural ending of a pregnancy after 20 weeks. (5-3)

strained foods. Solids processed to make them smooth and runny. (8-2)

stranger anxiety. A fear, usually expressed by crying, of unfamiliar people. (9-2)

subjective. Using one's personal opinions and feelings, rather than facts, to judge or describe things. (19-2)

symbolic thinking. The use of words and numbers to represent ideas. (10-1)

synthetic fibers. Fibers manufactured from chemicals rather than natural sources. (11-2)

T

temper tantrums. Incidents in which children release their anger or frustration by screaming, crying, kicking, pounding, and sometimes even holding their breath. (12-1)

temperament. Style of reacting to the world and of relating to others. (7-3)

therapist. A professional trained in helping people work through emotional problems. (18-1)

time-out. A short period of time spent sitting away from the presence of others or from the center of activity. (3-2, 19-3)

toddlers. Children from the age of first walking, usually about twelve months, until the age of three years. (11-1)

training pants. Heavy, absorbent underpants. (11-2)

transitions. Periods during which children move from one scheduled activity to the next. (19-3)

trial-and-error learning. Learning in which a child tries several solutions before finding out what works. (13-1)

U

ultrasound. A technique of using sound waves to make a video image of an unborn baby to check for specific health problems. (5-3)

umbilical cord. A long tube that connects the placenta to the unborn baby, and through which nourishment and oxygen are carried to the baby. (5-1)

uterus (YOOT-uh-ruhs). The organ in a woman's body in which a baby develops during pregnancy. (5-1)

V

vaccine. A small amount of an antigen introduced to the body, usually by injection, so that the body can build resistance to the disease. (17-1)

values. The principles a person considers important, and uses to guide his or her life. (4-1)

vocabulary. The number of words a person uses. (16-2)

W-X-Y-Z

weaning. A process of changing from drinking from the bottle or breast to drinking from a cup. (8-2)

zygote. Fertilized egg. (5-1)

Credits

Interior Design: William Seabright & Associates
Cover Photography: Robert F. Kusel
American Red Cross, 148
Arnold & Brown, 39, 52, 77, 78, 108, 122, 126, 195, 363
Jim Ballard, 19, 25, 40, 41, 65, 94, 177, 194, 211, 238, 266, 292, 320, 324, 331, 352, 353, 360, 365, 390, 391, 396, 414, 415, 417, 421, 427, 436, 444, 450, 461, 462, 464, 470, 507, 517, 542, 548, 565, 572
Bassett Furniture Industries, Inc., 174
Roger B. Bean, 7, 18, 27, 33, 49, 66, 69, 87, 104, 138, 142, 144, 150, 151, 158, 167, 169, 170, 173, 177, 185, 188, 201, 206, 210, 212, 213, 217, 218, 311, 329, 370, 384, 385, 388, 460, 464, 475, 486, 516, 521
Marshal Berman Photography/Design Office, 21, 27, 29, 31, 32, 42, 46, 50, 51, 53, 61, 64, 68, 69, 70, 72, 73, 74, 75, 76, 81, 82, 84, 86, 95, 96, 98, 101, 107, 464, 487, 489, 491, 497, 498, 503, 508, 520, 525, 528, 530, 533, 536, 537, 543, 545, 547, 549, 551, 556, 558, 559, 560, 562, 564, 573, 579, 580, 585
Keith Berry, 19, 63, 143, 148, 157, 159, 162, 171, 178, 179, 183, 207, 285, 350, 355, 563
Robert Brisbane, 422
A Child's World/Roger B. Bean, 297, 401
Pete Christie, 321, 335
© Ronald H. Cohn/The Gorilla Foundation, 278
Gail Denham, 214, 399
Laima Druskis, 345
Friendship House/Roger B. Bean, 418
Tim Fuller Photography/Morgan-Cain & Associates, 39, 40, 54, 102, 103, 490, 497, 501, 510, 511, 512, 517, 518, 519, 574, 577, 582, 583
James Gaffney, 206
Bob Gangloff, 117, 118, 119, 120, 122, 137, 195, 196, 197, 198, 199
Ann Garvin, 150, 161, 280, 284, 286, 340, 343, 351, 368, 386, 387, 392, 393, 401, 426, 449, 596
Grand Illusions, 41
Greater Peoria Family YMCA- Child Care Center/Roger B. Bean, 299, 321, 553
Steve Greiner, 450, 453, 478, 479
Hasbro/Playschool, 354
Linda K. Henson, 168, 208, 218, 298, 299, 300, 326, 330, 332, 336, 339, 341, 353, 354, 356, 360, 379, 417, 423, 424, 437, 440, 446, 524
Impact Communications, 163
Johnson & Johnson, 228
Robert F. Kusel, 1, 2, 5, 6, 7, 8, 9, 14-15, 16, 36, 58, 92, 112-113, 114, 154, 192, 224-225, 226, 264, 290, 316-317, 318, 348, 382, 410-411, 412, 434, 458, 482-483, 484, 514, 540, 570
LeLeche League International/D. C. Arendt, 172
McGraw YMCA Evanston, IL?/Mishima, 29
March of Dimes, 131, 139, 578
Mead Johnson Nutritional Group, 80, 116, 124, 130, 182, 203, 216, 344
The Methodist Medical Center of Illinois, 187
Ted Mishima, 6, 8, 23, 24, 38, 47, 55, 67, 79, 83, 97, 100, 151, 156, 161, 247, 276, 356, 362, 367, 371, 372, 439, 448, 465, 473, 496, 531, 532
Murray Language Academy/Mishima, 31, 415, 439, 581
Cristen Nestor Photographers, 367
Leonard Nilsson, Time/Life, 121
PALS Preschool & Kindergarten/Roger B. Bean, 28, 30, 64, 109, 397, 447
Vicki Pedesky, 495
Pegco, 304
PhotoTake, 140
Photo Researchers, Inc.
Petit Format/Nestle/Science Source, 121
Porterfield-Chickering, 127
Will & Deni McIntyre, 159
Nancy Durrell McKenna, 205
Lawrence Migdale, 159, 204
Hank Morgan, Science Source, 208
Larry Mulvehill, 131
Post Saturday Evening/PhotoTake NYC, 199
Steven Prochnow, 11
Proctor Hospitol New Horizons Employee Child Care Center/Roger B. Bean, 175
Liz Purcell, 118, 119, 125, 253, 293
Research Plus, 88
St. Francis Medical Center, 172
Jeff Stoecker, 557
Linda Sullivan, 20, 26, 44, 71, 88, 106, 128, 145, 171, 180, 186, 200, 209, 257, 258, 270, 280, 306, 309, 322, 337, 338, 355, 368, 394, 400, 419, 428, 443, 446, 449, 467, 473, 477, 487, 488, 500, 506, 510, 520, 522, 534, 552, 566, 576, 580
Superstock, 406
Thomas Jefferson School/Roger B. Bean, 132, 523
Texas Highways, 555
Troll Associates, Inc., 137
USDA, 164
Mary Vogel, 282
WestLight, Julie Houck, 89
Dana C. White, Dana White Productions, 20, 33, 71, 72, 85, 127, 145, 166, 180, 184, 186, 209, 229, 230, 231, 233, 235, 236, 237, 239, 240, 241, 242, 244, 248, 249, 250, 251, 252, 254, 257, 258, 260, 261, 263, 267, 268, 269, 270, 273, 274, 275, 277, 278, 279, 281, 282, 283, 284, 287, 294, 301, 303, 305, 306, 307, 308, 309, 310, 312, 313, 322, 323, 324, 337, 328, 333, 334, 351, 355, 357, 358, 359, 364, 365, 366, 372, 373, 374, 376, 378, 379, 385, 389, 391, 394, 395, 403, 404, 407, 416, 419, 428, 430, 438, 442, 443, 445, 454, 455, 461, 462, 468, 469, 471, 474, 476, 477, 478, 479, 488, 510, 522, 529, 534, 535, 552, 560, 575, 576
Gloria Olsen Williams, 345, 441
Nancy Wood, 125, 220, 221, 315
Duane R. Zehr, 188, 189, 295, 296, 361, 451

Poetry Acknowledgments

"Some Things Don't Make Any Sense At All" by Judith Voirst from IF I WERE IN CHARGE OF THE WORLD AND OTHER WORRIES. Copyright © 1981 by Judith Voirst. Reprinted with permission of Atheneum Publishers, an imprint of Macmillan Publishing Company.

"Thinking About Baby" by Anonymous from A LITTLE BOOK ABOUT BABY. Copyright © 1981 by C. R. Gibson, Norwalk, CT. Used by permission. All rights reserved.

"Everybody Says" by Dorothy Aldis reprinted by permission of G. P. Putnam's Sons from EVERYTHING AND ANYTHING by Dorothy Aldis. Copyright © 1925-1927, copyright renewed 1953-1955 by Dorothy Aldis.

"The End" from NOW WE ARE SIX by A. A. Milne. Copyright 1927 by E.P. Dutton, renewed © 1955 by A. A. Milne. Used by permission of Dutton Children's Books, a division of Penguin Books USA Inc.

"The Biggest Problem" by Don Haynie, from FREE TO BE...A FAMILY by Marlo Thomas & Friends. Copyright © 1987 by Free to Be Foundation, Inc. Used by permission of Bantam Books, a division of Bantam Doubleday Dell Publishing Group, Inc.

Special thanks to the following individuals, schools, businesses, and organizations for their assistance with photographs in this book. **In Peoria, Illinois:** Friendship House, Greater Peoria Family YMCA Childcare Center, PALS Preschool & Kindergarten, Rogy's Gingerbread House, St. Andrew's Day Care Center, St. Francis Medical Center, St. Francis Woods. **In Bloomington/Normal, Illinois:** Mom & Me, Ryan Pharmacy. **In Chicago, Illinois:** Murray Language Academy. **In Oakpark, Illinois:** West Suburban Hospital. In Southern California: Lara Belmonte, The Final Frontier, Mt. Olive Pre-School, Santa Monica High School SAPID Program, Consuela Perez, Richland Avenue Children's Center, Jim & Beth Strang, Venice Family Clinic, Westside Women's Health Clinic, Windward School. **In Tuscon, Arizona:** Carondelet, Casita Maria; Carondelet St. Mary's Hospital, Pediatrics Unit; Cerebral Palsy Foundation.

Models and fictional names have been used to portray characters in stories and examples in this text.

Index

C

G

H